Put Yourself In His Place

HARPER'S LIBRARY OF SELECT NOVELS.

☞ *Mailing Notice.*—HARPER & BROTHERS *will send their Books by Mail, postage free, to any part of the United States, on receipt of the Price.*

☞ HARPER'S CATALOGUE *and* TRADE-LIST *will be sent by mail on receipt of Five Cents, or they may be obtained gratuitously on application to the Publishers personally.*

		PRICE
1.	Pelham. By Bulwer	$0 75
2.	The Disowned. By Bulwer	75
3.	Devereux. By Bulwer	50
4.	Paul Clifford. By Bulwer	50
5.	Eugene Aram. By Bulwer	50
6.	The Last Days of Pompeii. By Bulwer	50
7.	The Czarina. By Mrs. Hofland	50
8.	Rienzi. By Bulwer	75
9.	Self-Devotion. By Miss Campbell	50
10.	The Nabob at Home	50
11.	Ernest Maltravers. By Bulwer	50
12.	Alice; or, The Mysteries. By Bulwer	50
13.	The Last of the Barons. By Bulwer	1 00
14.	Forest Days. By James	50
15.	Adam Brown, the Merchant. By H. Smith	50
16.	Pilgrims of the Rhine. By Bulwer	25
17.	The Home. By Miss Bremer	50
18.	The Lost Ship. By Captain Neale	75
19.	The False Heir. By James	50
20.	The Neighbors. By Miss Bremer	50
21.	Nina. By Miss Bremer	50
22.	The President's Daughters. By Miss Bremer	25
23.	The Banker's Wife. By Mrs. Gore	50
24.	The Birthright. By Mrs. Gore	25
25.	New Sketches of Every-day Life. By Miss Bremer	50
26.	Arabella Stuart. By James	50
27.	The Grumbler. By Miss Pickering	50
28.	The Unloved One. By Mrs. Hofland	50
29.	Jack of the Mill. By William Howitt	25
30.	The Heretic. By Lajetchnikoff	50
31.	The Jew. By Spindler	75
32.	Arthur. By Sue	75
33.	Chatsworth. By Ward	50
34.	The Prairie Bird. By C. A. Murray	1 00
35.	Amy Herbert. By Miss Sewell	50
36.	Rose d'Albret. By James	50
37.	The Triumphs of Time. By Mrs. Marsh	75
38.	The H—— Family. By Miss Bremer	50
39.	The Grandfather. By Miss Pickering	50
40.	Arrah Neil. By James	50
41.	The Jilt	50
42.	Tales from the German	50
43.	Arthur Arundel. By H. Smith	50
44.	Agincourt. By James	50
45.	The Regent's Daughter	50
46.	The Maid of Honor	50
47.	Safia. By De Beauvoir	50
48.	Look to the End. By Mrs. Ellis	50
49.	The Improvisatore. By Andersen	50
50.	The Gambler's Wife. By Mrs. Grey	50
51.	Veronica. By Zschokke	50
52.	Zoe. By Miss Jewsbury	50
53.	Wyoming	50
54.	De Rohan. By Sue	50
55.	Self. By the Author of "Cecil"	75
56.	The Smuggler. By James	75
57.	The Breach of Promise	50
58.	Parsonage of Mora. By Miss Bremer	25
59.	A Chance Medley. By T. C. Grattan	50
60.	The White Slave	1 00
61.	The Bosom Friend. By Mrs. Grey	50
62.	Amaury. By Dumas	50
63.	The Author's Daughter. By Mary Howitt	25
64.	Only a Fiddler, &c. By Andersen	50
65.	The Whiteboy. By Mrs. Hall	50
66.	The Foster-Brother. Edited by Leigh Hunt	50
67.	Love and Mesmerism. By H. Smith	75
68.	Ascanio. By Dumas	75
69.	Lady of Milan. Edited by Mrs. Thomson	75
70.	The Citizen of Prague	1 00
71.	The Royal Favorite. By Mrs. Gore	50
72.	The Queen of Denmark. By Mrs. Gore	50
73.	The Elves, &c. By Tieck	50
74, 75.	The Stepmother. By James	1 25
76.	Jessie's Flirtations	50
77.	Chevalier d'Harmental. By Dumas	50
78.	Peers and Parvenus. By Mrs. Gore	50
79.	The Commander of Malta. By Sue	50
80.	The Female Minister	50
81.	Emilia Wyndham. By Mrs. Marsh	$0 75
82.	The Bush-Ranger. By Charles Rowcroft	50
83.	The Chronicles of Clovernook	25
84.	Genevieve. By Lamartine	25
85.	Livonian Tales	25
86.	Lettice Arnold. By Mrs. Marsh	25
87.	Father Darcy. By Mrs. Marsh	75
88.	Leontine. By Mrs. Maberly	50
89.	Heidelberg. By James	50
90.	Lucretia. By Bulwer	75
91.	Beauchamp. By James	75
92, 94.	Fortescue. By Knowles	1 00
93.	Daniel Dennison, &c. By Mrs. Hofland	50
95.	Cinq-Mars. By De Vigny	50
96.	Woman's Trials. By Mrs. S. C. Hall	75
97.	The Castle of Ehrenstein. By James	50
98.	Marriage. By Miss S. Ferrier	50
99.	Roland Cashel. By Lever	1 25
100.	The Martins of Cro' Martin. By Lever	1 25
101.	Russell. By James	50
102.	A Simple Story. By Mrs. Inchbald	50
103.	Norman's Bridge. By Mrs. Marsh	50
104.	Alamance	50
105.	Margaret Graham. By James	25
106.	The Wayside Cross. By E. H. Milman	25
107.	The Convict. By James	50
108.	Midsummer Eve. By Mrs. S. C. Hall	50
109.	Jane Eyre. By Currer Bell	75
110.	The Last of the Fairies. By James	25
111.	Sir Theodore Broughton. By James	50
112.	Self-Control. By Mary Brunton	75
113, 114.	Harold. By Bulwer	1 00
115.	Brothers and Sisters. By Miss Bremer	50
116.	Gowrie. By James	50
117.	A Whim and its Consequences. By James	50
118.	Three Sisters and Three Fortunes. By G. H. Lewes	75
119.	The Discipline of Life	50
120.	Thirty Years Since. By James	50
121.	Mary Barton. By Mrs. Gaskell	50
122.	The Great Hoggarty Diamond. By Thackeray	25
123.	The Forgery. By James	50
124.	The Midnight Sun. By Miss Bremer	25
125, 126.	The Caxtons. By Bulwer	75
127.	Mordaunt Hall. By Mrs. Marsh	50
128.	My Uncle the Curate	50
129.	The Woodman. By James	75
130.	The Green Hand. A "Short Yarn"	75
131.	Sidonia the Sorceress. By Meinhold	1 00
132.	Shirley. By Currer Bell	1 00
133.	The Ogilvies. By Miss Mulock	50
134.	Constance Lyndsay. By G. C. H.	50
135.	Sir Edward Graham. By Miss Sinclair	1 00
136.	Hands not Hearts. By Miss Wilkinson	50
137.	The Wilmingtons. By Mrs. Marsh	50
138.	Ned Allen. By D. Hannay	50
139.	Night and Morning. By Bulwer	75
140.	The Maid of Orleans	75
141.	Antonina. By Wilkie Collins	50
142.	Zanoni. By Bulwer	50
143.	Reginald Hastings. By Warburton	50
144.	Pride and Irresolution	50
145.	The Old Oak Chest. By James	50
146.	Julia Howard. By Mrs. Martin Bell	50
147.	Adelaide Lindsay. Edited by Mrs. Marsh	50
148.	Petticoat Government. By Mrs. Trollope	50
149.	The Luttrells. By F. Williams	50
150.	Singleton Fontenoy, R. N. By Hannay	50
151.	Olive. By Miss Mulock	50
152.	Henry Smeaton. By James	50
153.	Time, the Avenger. By Mrs. Marsh	50
154.	The Commissioner. By James	1 00
155.	The Wife's Sister. By Mrs. Hubback	50
156.	The Gold Worshipers	50
157.	The Daughter of Night. By Fullom	50
158.	Stuart of Dunleath. By Hon. Caroline Norton	50
159.	Arthur Conway. By Captain E. H. Milman	50
160.	The Fate. By James	50
161.	The Lady and the Priest. By Mrs. Maberly	50

PRICE

162. Aims and Obstacles. By James $0 50
163. The Tutor's Ward 50
164. Florence Sackville. By Mrs. Burbury 75
165. Ravenscliffe. By Mrs. Marsh.............. 50
166. Maurice Tiernay. By Lever............... 1 00
167. The Head of the Family. By Miss Mulock... 75
168. Darien. By Warburton.................... 50
169. Falkenburg 75
170. The Daltons. By Lever.................. 1 50
171. Ivar; or, The Skjuts-Boy. By Miss Carlen .. 50
172. Pequinillo. By James 50
173. Anna Hammer. By Temme 50
174. A Life of Vicissitudes. By James 50
175. Henry Esmond. By Thackeray............. 75
176. 177. My Novel. By Bulwer 1 50
178. Katie Stewart. By Mrs. Oliphant 25
179. Castle Avon. By Mrs. Marsh.............. 50
180. Agnes Sorel. By James 50
181. Agatha's Husband. By Miss Mulock 50
182. Villette. By Currer Bell.................. 75
183. Lover's Stratagem. By Miss Carlen 50
184. Clouded Happiness. By Countess D'Orsay... 50
185. Charles Auchester. A Memorial 75
186. Lady Lee's Widowhood 50
187. The Dodd Family Abroad. By Lever........ 1 25
188. Sir Jasper Carew. By Lever.............. 75
189. Quiet Heart. By Mrs. Oliphant 25
190. Aubrey. By Mrs. Marsh 75
191. Ticonderoga. By James 50
192. Hard Times. By Dickens 50
193. The Young Husband. By Mrs. Grey........ 50
194. The Mother's Recompense. By Grace Aguilar. 75
195. Avillion, and other Tales. By Miss Mulock .. 1 25
196. North and South. By Mrs. Gaskell........ 50
197. Country Neighborhood. By Miss Dupuy..... 50
198. Constance Herbert. By Miss Jewsbury 50
199. The Heiress of Haughton. By Mrs. Marsh... 50
200. The Old Dominion. By James 50
201. John Halifax. By Miss Mulock 75
202. Evelyn Marston. By Mrs. Marsh.......... 50
203. Fortunes of Glencore. By Lever.......... 50
204. Leonora d'Orco. By James 50
205. Nothing New. By Miss Mulock 50
206. The Rose of Ashurst. By Mrs. Marsh 50
207. The Athelings. By Mrs. Oliphant 75
208. Scenes of Clerical Life. By George Eliot..... 50
209. My Lady Ludlow. By Mrs. Gaskell........ 25
210, 211. Gerald Fitzgerald. By Lever........... 50
212. A Life for a Life. By Miss Mulock 50
213. Sword and Gown. By Geo. Lawrence 25
214. Misrepresentation. By Anna H. Drury 1 00
215. The Mill on the Floss. By George Eliot..... 75
216. One of Them. By Lever.................. 75
217. A Day's Ride. By Lever.................. 50
218. Notice to Quit. By Wills 50
219. A Strange Story. By Bulwer 1 00
220. The Struggles of Brown, Jones, and Robinson.
     By Trollope............................ 50
221. Abel Drake's Wife. By John Saunders 75
222. Olive Blake's Good Work. By Jeaffreson.... 75
223. The Professor's Lady.................... 25
224. Mistress and Maid. By Miss Mulock 50
225. Aurora Floyd. By M. E. Braddon 75
226. Barrington. By Lever................... 75
227. Sylvia's Lovers. By Mrs. Gaskell......... 75
228. A First Friendship...................... 50
229. A Dark Night's Work. By Mrs. Gaskell 50
230. Mrs. Lirriper's Lodgings.................. 25
231. St. Olave's 75
232. A Point of Honor....................... 50
233. Live it Down. By Jeaffreson.............. 1 00
234. Martin Pole. By Saunders................ 50
235. Mary Lyndsay. By Lady Emily Ponsonby... 50
236. Eleanor's Victory. By M. E. Braddon 75
237. Rachel Ray. By Trollope................. 50
238. John Marchmont's Legacy. By M. E. Braddon 75
239. Annis Warleigh's Fortunes. By Holme Lee.. 75
240. The Wife's Evidence. By Wills 50
241. Barbara's History. By Amelia B. Edwards... 75
242. Cousin Phillis. By Mrs. Gaskell.......... 25
243. What will he do with It? By Bulwer....... 1 50
244. The Ladder of Life. By Amelia B. Edwards.. 50
245. Denis Duval. By Thackeray.............. 50
246. Maurice Dering. By Geo. Lawrence 50
247. Margaret Denzil's History................ 75
248. Quite Alone. By George Augustus Sala.... 75
249. Mattie: a Stray........................ 50
250. My Brother's Wife. By Amelia B. Edwards.. 50
251. Uncle Silas. By J. S. Le Fanu 75
252. Lovel the Widower. By Thackeray 25
253. Miss Mackenzie. By Anthony Trollope...... 50
254. On Guard. By Annie Thomas............. 50
255. Theo Leigh. By Annie Thomas............ 50
256. Denis Donne. By Annie Thomas........... 50

PRICE

257. Belial................................$0 50
258. Carry's Confession. By the Author of "Mat-
     tie: a Stray".......................... 75
259. Miss Carew. By Amelia B. Edwards........ 50
260. Hand and Glove. By Amelia B. Edwards.... 50
261. Guy Deverell. By J. S. Le Fanu.......... 50
262. Half a Million of Money. By Amelia B. Ed-
     wards................................. 75
263. The Belton Estate. By Anthony Trollope.... 50
264. Agnes. By Mrs. Oliphant................ 75
265. Walter Goring. By Annie Thomas......... 75
266. Maxwell Drewitt. By Mrs. J. H. Riddell 75
267. The Toilers of the Sea. By Victor Hugo..... 50
268. Miss Marjoribanks. By Mrs. Oliphant 50
269. The True History of a Little Ragamuffin ... 50
270. Gilbert Rugge. By the Author of "A First
     Friendship"........................... 1 00
271. Sans Merci. By Geo. Lawrence........... 50
272. Phemie Keller. By Mrs. J. H. Riddell 50
273. Land at Last. By Edmund Yates......... 50
274. Felix Holt, the Radical. By George Eliot ... 50
275. Bound to the Wheel. By John Saunders 75
276. All in the Dark. By J. S. Le Fanu......... 50
277. Kissing the Rod. By Edmund Yates........ 75
278. The Race for Wealth. By Mrs. J. H. Riddell.. 75
279. Lizzie Lorton of Greyrigg. By Mrs. E. Lynn
     Linton................................ 50
280. The Beauclercs, Father and Son. By Clarke. 50
281. Sir Brooke Fossbrooke. By Charles Lever .. 50
282. Madonna Mary. By Mrs. Oliphant........ 50
283. Cradock Nowell. By R. D. Blackmore...... 75
284. Bernthal. From the German of L. Mühlbach. 50
285. Rachel's Secret......................... 75
286. The Claverings. By Anthony Trollope...... 50
287. The Village on the Cliff. By Miss Thackeray. 50
288. Played Out. By Annie Thomas........... 75
289. Black Sheep. By Edmund Yates.......... 50
290. Sowing the Wind. By Mrs. E. Lynn Linton.. 50
291. Nora and Archibald Lee.................. 50
292. Raymond's Heroine...................... 50
293. Mr. Wynyard's Ward. By Holme Lee....... 50
294. Alec Forbes of Howglen. By Mac Donald.... 75
295. No Man's Friend. By F. W. Robinson...... 50
296. Called to Account. By Annie Thomas....... 50
297. Caste................................. 50
298. The Curate's Discipline. By Mrs. Eiloart.... 50
299. Circe. By Babington White.............. 50
300. The Tenants of Malory. By J. S. Le Fanu.... 50
301. Carlyon's Year. By the Author of "Lost Sir
     Massingberd," &c....................... 25
302. The Waterdale Neighbors. By the Author of
     "Paul Massie".......................... 50
303. Mabel's Progress. By the Author of "The Sto-
     ry of Aunt Margaret's Trouble".......... 50
304. Guild Court. By George Mac Donald....... 50
305. The Brothers' Bet. By Emilie Flygare Carlén 25
306. Playing for High Stakes. By Annie Thomas.. 25
307. Margaret's Engagement................... 50
308. One of the Family. By the Author of "Car-
     lyon's Year".......................... 25
309. Five Hundred Pounds Reward. By a Barrister 50
310. Brownlows. By Mrs. Oliphant 37
311. Charlotte's Inheritance. By M. E. Braddon .. 50
312. Jeannie's Quiet Life. By the Author of "St.
     Olave's," &c........................... 50
313. Poor Humanity. By F. W. Robinson 50
314. Brakespeare. By Geo. Lawrence.......... 50
315. A Lost Name. By J. Sheridan Le Fanu...... 50
316. Love or Marriage? By William Black...... 50
317. Dead-Sea Fruit. By M. E. Braddon 50
318. The Dower House. By Annie Thomas....... 50
319. The Bramleighs of Bishop's Folly. By Lever. 50
320. Mildred. By Georgiana M. Craik.......... 50
321. Nature's Nobleman. By the Author of "Ra-
     chel's Secret".......................... 50
322. Kathleen. By the Author of "Raymond's He-
     roine"................................ 50
323. That Boy of Norcott's. By Charles Lever.... 25
324. In Silk Attire. By W. Black.............. 50
325. Hetty. By Henry Kingsley............... 25
326. False Colors. By Annie Thomas........... 50
327. Meta's Faith. By the Author of "St. Olave's." 50
328. Found Dead. By the Author of "Carlyon's
     Year"................................. 50
329. Wrecked in Port. By Edmund Yates....... 50
330. The Minister's Wife. By Mrs. Oliphant..... 75
331. A Beggar on Horseback. By the Author of
     "Carlyon's Year"....................... 50
332. The Vicar's Courtship. By Walter Thornbury. 75
332. Kitty. By the Author of "Doctor Jacob".... 50
333. Only Herself. By Annie Thomas.......... 50
334. Hirell. By John Saunders............... 50
335. Under Foot. By Alton Clyde............. 50
336. So Runs the World Away. By Mrs. A. C. Steele. 50

DEATH BY SUFFOCATION AT HIS BACK, AND BROKEN BONES AWAITED HIM BELOW.

PUT YOURSELF IN HIS PLACE.

A Novel.

By CHARLES READE,

AUTHOR OF

"HARD CASH," "FOUL PLAY," "GRIFFITH GAUNT," "NEVER TOO LATE TO MEND,"
"WHITE LIES," &c.

ILLUSTRATED.

"I will frame a work of fiction upon notorious fact, so that any body shall think he can do the same; shall labor and toil, attempting the same, and fail—such is the power of sequence and connection in writing."

HORACE: *Art of Poetry.*

NEW YORK:

HARPER & BROTHERS, PUBLISHERS,

FRANKLIN SQUARE.

1870.

CHARLES READE'S NOVELS.

POPULAR EDITION.

PUT YOURSELF IN HIS PLACE. Illustrated. 8vo, Paper, 75 cents.

HARD CASH. A Matter-of-Fact Romance. Illustrated. 8vo, Paper, 35 cents.

GRIFFITH GAUNT; or, Jealousy. Illustrated. 8vo, Paper, 25 cents.

NEVER TOO LATE TO MEND. 8vo, Paper, 35 cents.

LOVE ME LITTLE, LOVE ME LONG. 8vo, Paper, 35 cents.

FOUL PLAY. 8vo, Paper, 25 cents.

WHITE LIES. 8vo, Paper, 35 cents.

CLOISTER AND THE HEARTH; or, Maid, Wife, and Widow. 8vo, Paper, 50 cents.

PEG WOFFINGTON, CHRISTIE JOHNSTONE, and Other Stories. 8vo, Paper, 50 cents.

PUBLISHED BY HARPER & BROTHERS, NEW YORK.

☞ *Sent by mail, postage prepaid, to any part of the United States, on receipt of the price.*

PUT YOURSELF IN HIS PLACE.

" I will frame a work of fiction upon notorious fact, so that any body shall think he can do the same; shall labor and toil attempting the same, and fail—such is the power of sequence and connection in writing."—HORACE : *Art of Poetry.*

CHAPTER I.

HILLSBOROUGH and its outlying suburbs make bricks by the million, spin and weave both wool and cotton, forge in steel from the finest needle up to a ship's armor, and so add considerably to the kingdom's wealth.

But industry so vast, working by steam on a limited space, has been fatal to beauty : Hillsborough, though built on one of the loveliest sites in England, is perhaps the most hideous town in creation. All ups and downs and back slums. Not one of its wriggling, broken-backed streets has handsome shops in an unbroken row. Houses seem to have battled in the air, and stuck wherever they tumbled down dead out of the mêlée. But worst of all, the city is pockmarked with public-houses, and bristles with high round chimneys. These are not confined to a locality, but stuck all over the place like cloves in an orange. They defy the law, and belch forth massy vol-

umes of black smoke, that hang like acres of crape over the place, and veil the sun and the blue sky even in the brightest day. But in a fog —why, the air of Hillsborough looks a thing to plough, if you want a dirty job.

More than one crystal stream runs sparkling down the valleys, and enters the town ; but they soon get defiled, and creep through it heavily charged with dyes, clogged with putridity, and bubbling with poisonous gases, till at last they turn to mere ink, stink, and malaria, and people the churchyards as they crawl.

This infernal city, whose water is blacking, and whose air is coal, lies in a basin of delight and beauty : noble slopes, broad valleys, watered by rivers and brooks of singular beauty, and fringed by fair woods in places ; and, eastward, the hills rise into mountains, and amongst them towers Cairnhope, striped with silver rills, and violet in the setting sun.

Cairnhope is a forked mountain, with a bosom of purple heather and a craggy head. Between its forks stood, at the period of my story, a great curiosity ; which merits description on its own account, and also as the scene of curious incidents to come.

It was a deserted church. The walls were pierced with arrow-slits, through which the original worshippers had sent many a deadly shaft in defense of their women and cattle, collected within the sacred edifice at the first news of marauders coming.

Built up among the heathery hills in times of war and trouble, it had outlived its uses. Its people had long ago gone down into the fruitful valley, and raised another church in their midst, and left this old house of God alone, and silent as the tombs of their forefathers that lay around it.

It was no ruin, though on the road to decay. One of the side walls was much lower than the other, and the roof had two great waves, and was heavily clothed, in natural patterns, with velvet moss, and sprinkled all over with bright amber lichen : a few tiles had slipped off in two places, and showed the rafters brown with time and weather : but the structure was solid and sound ; the fallen tiles lay undisturbed beneath the eaves ; not a brick, not a beam, not a gravestone had been stolen, not even to build the new church : of the diamond panes full half remained ; the stone font was still in its place, with its Gothic cover, richly carved ; and four brasses reposed in the chancel, one of them loose in its bed.

What had caused the church to be deserted had kept it from being desecrated ; it was clean out of the way. No gypsy, nor vagrant, ever slept there, and even the boys of the village kept their distance. Nothing would have pleased them better than to break the sacred windows time had spared, and defile the graves of their forefathers with pitch-farthing and other arts ; but it was three miles off, and there was a lion in the way : they must pass in sight of Squire Raby's house ; and, whenever they had tried it, he and his groom had followed them on swift horses that could jump as well as gallop, had caught them in the churchyard, and lashed them heartily ; and the same night notice to quit had been given to their parents, who were all Mr. Raby's weekly tenants : and this had led to a compromise and flagellation.

Once or twice every summer a more insidious foe approached. Some little party of tourists, including a lady, who sketched in water and never finished any thing, would hear of the old church, and wander up to it. But Mr. Raby's trusty groom was sure to be after them, with orders to keep by them, under guise of friendship, and tell them outrageous figments, and see that they demolished not, stole not, sculptured not.

All this was odd enough in itself, but it astonished nobody who knew Mr. Raby. His father and predecessor had guarded the old church religiously in his day, and was buried in it, by his own orders ; and, as for Guy Raby himself, what wonder he respected it, since his own mind, like that old church, was out of date, and a relic of the past ?

An antique Tory squire, nursed in expiring Jacobitism, and cradled in the pride of race ; educated at Oxford, well read in books, versed in county business, and acquainted with trade and commerce ; yet puffed up with aristocratic notions, and hugging the very prejudices our nobility are getting rid of—as fast as the vulgar will let them.

He had a sovereign contempt for tradespeople, and especially for manufacturers. Any one of those numerous disputes between masters and mechanics, which distinguish British industry, might have been safely referred to him, for he abhorred and despised them both with strict impartiality.

The lingering beams of a bright December day still gilded the moss-clad roof of that deserted church, and flamed on its broken panes, when a young man came galloping towards it, from Hillsborough, on one of those powerful horses common in that district.

He came so swiftly and so direct, that, ere the sun had been down twenty minutes, he and his smoking horse had reached a winding gorge about three furlongs from the church. Here, however, the bridle-road, which had hitherto served his turn across the moor, turned off sharply towards the village of Cairnhope, and the horse had to pick his way over heather, and bog, and great loose stones. He lowered his nose, and hesitated more than once. But the rein was loose upon his neck, and he was left to take his time. He had also his own tracks to guide him in places, for this was by no means his first

visit ; and he managed so well, that at last he got safe to a mountain stream which gurgled past the north side of the churchyard : he went cautiously through the water, and then his rider gathered up the reins, stuck in the spurs, and put him at a part of the wall where the moonlight showed a considerable breach. The good horse rose to it, and cleared it, with a foot to spare ; and the invader landed in the sacred precincts unobserved, for the road he had come by was not visible from Raby House, nor indeed was the church itself.

He was of swarthy complexion, dressed in a plain suit of tweed, well made, and neither new nor old. His hat was of the newest fashion, and glossy. He had no gloves on.

He dismounted, and led his horse to the porch. He took from his pocket a large glittering key and unlocked the church-door ; then gave his horse a smack on the quarter. That sagacious animal walked into the church directly, and his iron hoofs rang strangely as he paced over the brick floor of the aisle, and made his way under the echoing vault, up to the very altar ; for near it was the vestry-chest, and in that chest his corn.

The young man also entered the church ; but soon came out again with a leathern bucket in his hand. He then went round the church, and was busily employed for a considerable time.

He returned to the porch, carried his bucket in, and locked the door, leaving the key inside.

That night Abel Eaves, a shepherd, was led by his dog, in search of a strayed sheep, to a place rarely trodden by the foot of man or beast, viz. the west side of Cairnhope Peak. He came home pale and disturbed, and sat by the fireside in dead silence. "What ails thee, my man ?" said Janet, his wife ; "and there's the very dog keeps a whimpering."

"What ails us, wife ? Pincher and me ? We have seen summat."

"What was it ?" inquired the woman, suddenly lowering her voice,

"Cairnhope old church all o' fire inside."

"Bless us and save us !" said Janet, in a whisper.

"And the fire it did come and go, as if hell was a blowing at it. One while the windows was a dull red like, and the next they did flare so, I thought it would all burst out in a blaze. And so 'twould, but, bless your heart, their heads ha'n't ached this hundred year and more, as lighted that there devilish fire."

He paused a moment, then said, with sudden gravity and resignation, and even a sort of half business-like air, "Wife, ye may make my shroud, and sew it and all ; but I wouldn't buy the stuff of Bess Crummles ; she is an ill-tongued woman, and came near making mischief between you and me last Lammermas as ever was."

"Shroud !" cried Mrs. Eaves, getting seriously alarmed. "Why, Abel, what is Cairnhope old church to you ? You were born in another parish."

Abel slapped his thigh. "Ay, lass, and another county, if ye go to that." And his countenance brightened suddenly.

"And as for me," continued Janet, "I'm Cairnhope ; but my mother came from Morpeth, a widdy : and she lies within a hundred yards of where I sit à talking to thee. There's none of my kin laid in old Cairnhope churchyard. Warning's not for thee, nor me, nor yet for our Jock. Eh, lad, it will be for Squire Raby. His father lies up there, and so do all his folk. Put on thy hat this minute, and I'll hood myself, and we'll go up to Raby Hall, and tell Squire."

Abel objected to that, and intimated that his own fireside was particularly inviting to a man who had seen diabolical fires that came and went, and shone through the very stones and mortar of a dead church.

"Nay, but," said Janet, "they sort o' warnings are not to be slighted neither. We must put it off on to Squire, or I shall sleep none this night."

They went up, hand in hand, and often looked askant upon the road.

When they got to the Hall, they asked to see Mr. Raby. After some demur they were admitted to his presence, and found him alone, so far as they could judge by the naked eye; but, as they arrived there charged to the muzzle with superstition, the room presented to their minds some appearances at variance with this seeming solitude. Several plates were set as if for guests, and the table groaned, and the huge sideboard blazed, with old silver. The Squire himself was in full costume, and on his bosom gleamed two orders bestowed upon his ancestors by James III. and Charles III. In other respects he was rather innocuous, being confined to his chair by an attack of gout, and in the act of sipping the superannuated compound that had given it him—port. Nevertheless, his light hair, dark eyebrows, and black eyes, awed them, and co-operated with his brilliant costume and the other signs of company, to make them wish themselves at the top of Cairnhope Peak. However, they were in for it, and told their tale, but in tremulous tones and a low deprecating voice, so that if the room *should* happen to be infested with invisible grandees from the other world, their attention might not be roused unnecessarily.

Mr. Raby listened with admirable gravity; then fixed his eyes on the pair, in silence; and then said in a tone so solemn it was almost sepulchral, "This very day, nearly a century and a half ago, Sir Richard Raby was beheaded for being true to his rightful king—"

"Eh, dear, poor gentleman! so now a walks." It was Janet who edged in this—

"And," continued the gentleman, loftily ignoring the comment, "they say that on this night such of the Rabys as died Catholics hold high mass in the church, and the ladies walk three times round the churchyard; twice with their veils down, once with bare faces, and great eyes that glitter like stars."

"I wouldn't like to see the jades," quavered Abel: "their ladyships I mean, axing their pardon."

"Nor I!" said Janet, with a great shudder.

"It would not be good for you," suggested the Squire; "for the first glance from those dead and glittering eyes strikes any person of the lower orders dumb; the second, blind; the third, dead. So I'm *informed.* Therefore—*let me advise you never to go near Cairnhope old church at night.*"

"Not I, sir," said the simple woman.

"Nor your children: unless you are very tired of them."

"Heaven forbid, sir! But oh, sir, we thought it might be a warning like."

"To whom?"

"Why, sir, th' old Squire lies there; and heaps more of your folk: and so Abel here was afear'd —but you are the best judge; we be no scholars. Th' old church warn't red-hot from eend to eend for naught; that's certain."

"Oh, it is me you came to warn?" said Raby, and his lip curled.

"Well, sir" (mellifluously), "we thought you had the best right to know."

"My good woman," said the warned, "I shall die when my time comes. But I shall not hurry myself, for all the gentlemen in Paradise, nor all the blackguards upon earth."

He spake, and sipped his port with one hand, and waved them superbly back to their village with the other.

But, when they were gone, he pondered.

And the more he pondered, the farther he got from the prosaic but singular fact.

CHAPTER II.

IN the old oak dining-room, where the above colloquy took place, hung a series of family portraits. One was of a lovely girl with oval face, olive complexion, and large dark tender eyes: and this was the gem of the whole collection; but it conferred little pleasure on the spectator, owing to a trivial circumstance—it was turned with its face to the wall; and all that met the inquiring eye was an inscription on the canvas, not intended to be laudatory.

This beauty, with her back to creation, was Edith Raby, Guy's sister.

During their father's lifetime she was petted and allowed her own way. Hillsborough, odious to her brother, was, naturally, very attractive to her, and she often rode into the town to shop and chat with her friends, and often staid a day or two in it, especially with a Mrs. Manton, wife of a wealthy manufacturer.

Guy merely sneered at her, her friends, and her tastes, till he suddenly discovered that she had formed an attachment to one of the obnoxious class, Mr. James Little, a great contract builder. He was too shocked at first to vent his anger. He turned pale, and could hardly speak; and the poor girl's bosom began to quake.

But Guy's opposition went no farther than cold aversion to the intimacy—until his father died. Then, though but a year older than Edith, he assumed authority and, as head of the house, forbade the connection. At the same time he told her he should not object, under the circumstances, to her marrying Dr. Amboyne, a rising physician, and a man of good family, who loved her sincerely, and had shown his love plainly before ever Mr. Little was heard of.

Edith tried to soften her brother; but he was resolute, and said Raby Hall should never be an appendage to a workshop. Sooner than that, he would settle it on his cousin Richard, a gentleman he abhorred, and never called, either to his face or behind his back, by any other name than "Dissolute Dick."

Then Edith became very unhappy, and temporized more or less, till her lover, who had shown considerable forbearance, lost patience at last, and said she must either have no spirit, or no true affection for him.

Then came a month or two of misery, the tender clinging nature of the girl being averse to detach itself from either of these two persons. She loved them both with an affection she could have so easily reconciled, if they would only have allowed her.

And it all ended according to Nature. She came of age, plucked up a spirit, and married Mr. James Little.

Her brother declined to be present at the wedding ; but, as soon as she returned from her tour, and settled in Hillsborough, he sent his groom with a cold, civil note, reminding her that their father had settled nineteen hundred pounds on her, for her separate use, with remainder to her children, if any ; that he and Mr. Graham were the trustees of this small fund ; that they had invested it, according to the provisions of the settlement, in a first mortgage on land ; and informing her that half a year's interest at 4½ per cent. was due, which it was his duty to pay into her own hand and no other person's ; she would therefore oblige him by receiving the enclosed check, and signing the enclosed receipt.

The receipt came back signed, and with it a few gentle lines, " hoping that, in time, he would forgive her, and bestow on her what she needed and valued more than money ; her own brother's, her only brother's affection."

On receiving this, his eyes were suddenly moist, and he actually groaned. " A lady, every inch !" he said ; " yet she has gone and married a bricklayer."

Well, blood is thicker than water, and in a few years they were pretty good friends again, though they saw but little of one another, meeting only in Hillsborough, which Guy hated, and never drove into now without what he called his antidotes : a Bible and a bottle of lavender-water. It was his humor to read the one, and sprinkle the other, as soon as ever he got within the circle of the smoky trades.

When Edith's little boy was nine years old, and much admired for his quickness and love of learning, and of making walking-stick heads and ladies' work-boxes, Mr. Little's prosperity received a severe check, and through his own fault. He speculated largely in building villas, overdid the market, and got crippled. He had contracts uncompleted, and was liable to penalties ; and at last saw himself the nominal possessor of a brick wilderness, but on the verge of ruin for want of cash.

He tried every other resource first ; but at last he came to his wife, to borrow her £1900. The security he offered was a mortgage on twelve carcasses, or houses the bare walls and roofs of which were built.

Mrs. Little wrote at once to Mr. Raby for her money.

Instead of lending the trust-money hastily, Raby submitted the proposal to his solicitor, and that gentleman soon discovered the vaunted security was a second mortgage, with interest overdue on the first ; and so he told Guy, who then merely remarked, " I expected as much. When had a tradesman any sense of honor in money matters ? This one would cheat his very wife and child."

He declined the proposal, in two words, " Rotten security !"

Then Mr. James Little found another security that looked very plausible, and primed his wife with arguments, and she implored Guy to call and talk it over with them both.

He came that very afternoon, and brought his father's will.

Then Edith offered the security, and tried to convey to the trustee her full belief that it was undeniable.

Guy picked terrible holes in it, and read their father's will, confining the funds to consols, or a first mortgage on land. " You take the money on these conditions : it is almost as improper of you to wish to evade them, as it would be of me to assist you. And then there is your child ; I am bound in honor not to risk his little fortune. See, here's my signature to that."

" My child !" cried Edith. " When he comes of age, I'll go on my knees to him and say, ' My darling, I borrowed your money to save your father's credit.' And my darling will throw his arms round me, and forgive me."

" Simpleton !" said Guy. " And how about your daughters and their husbands ? And their husbands' solicitors ? Will they throw their arms round your neck, and break forth into twaddle ? No ! I have made inquiries. Your husband's affairs are desperate. I won't throw your money into his well ; and you will both live to thank me for seeing clearer than you do, and saving this £1900 for you and yours."

James Little had writhed in his chair for some time : he now cried out wildly, " Edith, you shall demean yourself no more. He always hated me : and now let him have his will, and seal my dishonor and my ruin. Oblige me by leaving my house, Mr. Raby."

" Oh, no, James !" cried Edith, trembling, and shocked at this affront. But Guy rose like a tower. " I've noticed this trait in all tradespeople," said he grimly. " They are obsequious to a gentleman so long as they hope to get the better of him ; but, the moment they find it impossible to overreach him, they insult him." And with this he stalked out of the house.

" Oh, my poor James, how could you ?" said Edith.

" Forgive me," said he, quietly. " It is all over. That was our last chance."

Guy Raby walked down the street, stung to the quick. He went straight to his solicitor and arranged to borrow £1900 on his own property. " For," said he, " I'll show them both how little a snob can understand a gentleman. I won't tamper with her son's money, but I'll give her my own to throw into his well. Confound him ! why did she ever marry him ?"

When the business was virtually settled, he came back to the house in great haste.

Meantime Mr. James Little went up to his dressing-room, as usual, to dress for dinner ; but he remained there so long that, at last, Mrs. Little sent her maid to tell him dinner was ready.

The girl had hardly reached the top of the stairs, when she gave a terrible scream that rang through the whole house.

Mrs. Little rushed up stairs, and found her clinging to the banisters, and pointing at the floor, with eyes protruding and full of horror. Her candlestick had fallen from her benumbed hand; but the hall-lamp revealed what her finger was quivering and pointing at: a dark fluid trickling slowly out into the lobby from beneath the bed-room door.

It was blood.

The room was burst into, and the wretched tottering wife, hanging upon her sobbing servants, found her lover, her husband, her child's father, lying on the floor, dead by his own hand; stone dead. A terrible sight for strangers to see; but for her, what words can even shadow the horror of it!

I drop the veil on her wild bursts of agony, and piteous appeals to him who could not hear her cries.

The gaping wound that let out that precious life, her eye never ceased to see it, nor her own heart to bleed with it, while she lived.

She was gently dragged away, and supported down to another room. Doctor Amboyne came and did what he could for her; and that was —nothing.

At this time she seemed stupefied. But, when Guy came beaming into the room to tell her he had got her the money, a terrible scene occurred. The bereaved wife uttered a miserable scream at sight of him, and swooned away directly.

The maids gathered round her, laid her down, and cut her stays, and told Guy the terrible tidings, in broken whispers, over her insensible body.

He rose to his feet horrified. He began to gasp and sob. And he yearned to say something to comfort her. At that moment his house, his heart, and all he had, were hers.

But, as soon as she came to herself, and caught sight of him, she screamed out, "Oh, the sight of him! the sight of him!" and swooned away again.

Then the women pushed him out of the room, and he went away with uneven steps, and sick at heart.

He shut himself up in Raby Hall, and felt very sad and remorseful. He directed his solicitor to render Mrs. Little every assistance, and supply her with funds. But these good offices were respectfully declined by Mr. Joseph Little, the brother of the deceased, who had come from Birmingham to conduct the funeral and settle other matters.

Mr. Joseph Little was known to be a small master-cutler, who had risen from a workman, and even now put blades and handles together with his own hands, at odd times, though he had long ceased to forge or grind.

Mr. Raby drew in haughtily at this interference.

It soon transpired that Mr. James Little had died hopelessly insolvent, and the £1900 would really have been engulfed.

Raby waited for this fact to sink into his sister's mind; and then one day nature tugged so at his heart-strings, that he dashed off a warm letter beginning—"My poor Edith, let bygones be bygones," and inviting her and her boy to live with him at Raby Hall.

The heart-broken widow sent back a reply, in a handwriting scarcely recognizable as hers. Instead of her usual precise and delicate hand, the letters were large, tremulous, and straggling, and the lines slanted downward.

"Write to me, speak to me, no more. For pity's sake let me forget there is a man in the world who is my brother and his murderer.

"EDITH."

Guy opened this letter with a hopeful face, and turned pale as ashes at the contents.

But his conscience was clear, and his spirit high. "Unjust idiot!" he muttered, and locked her letter up in his desk.

Next morning he received a letter from Joseph Little, in a clear, stiff, perpendicular writing:

"SIR,—I find my sister-in-law wrote you, yesterday, a harsh letter, which I do not approve; and have told her as much. Deceased's affairs were irretrievable, and I blame no other man for his rash act, which may God forgive! As to your kind and generous invitation, it deserves her gratitude; but Mrs. Little and myself have mingled our tears together over my poor brother's grave, and now we do not care to part. Before your esteemed favor came to hand, it had been settled she should leave this sad neighborhood and keep my house at Birmingham, where she will meet with due respect. I am only a small tradesman; but I can pay my debts, and keep the pot boiling. Will teach the boy some good trade, and make him a useful member of society, if I am spared.

"I am, sir, yours respectfully,
"JOSEPH LITTLE."

"SIR,—I beg to acknowledge, with thanks, your respectable letter.

"As all direct communication between Mrs. James Little and myself is at an end, oblige me with your address in Birmingham, that I may remit to you, half-yearly, as her agent, the small sum that has escaped bricks and mortar.

"When her son comes of age, she will probably forgive me for declining to defraud him of his patrimony.

"But it will be too late; for I shall never forgive her, alive or dead.

"I am, sir, your obedient servant,
"GUY RABY."

When he had posted this letter he turned Edith's picture to the wall, and wrote on the canvas—

"GONE INTO TRADE."

He sent for his attorney, made a new will, and bequeathed his land, houses, goods, and chattels, to Dissolute Dick and his heirs forever.

CHAPTER III.

THE sorrowful widow was so fond of her little Henry, and the uncertainty of life was so burnt into her now, that she could hardly bear him out of her sight. Yet her love was of the true maternal stamp; not childish and self-indulgent. She kept him from school, for fear he should be brought home dead to her; but she gave her own mind with zeal to educate him. Nor was she unqualified. If she had less learning than schoolmasters, she knew better how to communicate what she did know to a budding mind. She taught him to read fluently, and to write beautifully; and she coaxed him, as only a woman can, over the dry elements of music and arithmetic. She also taught him dancing and deportment, and to sew on a button. He was a quick boy at nearly every thing, but, when he was fourteen, his true genius went ahead of his mere talents: he showed a heaven-born gift for—carving in wood. This pleased Joseph Little hugely, and he fostered it judiciously.

The boy worked, and thought, and in time arrived at such delicacies of execution, he became discontented with the humdrum tools then current. "Then learn to make your own, boy," cried Joseph Little, joyfully; and so initiated him into the whole mystery of hardening, forging, grinding, handle-making, and cutlery: and Henry, young and enthusiastic, took his turn at them all in right down earnest.

At twenty, he had sold many a piece of delicate carving, and could make graving-tools incomparably superior to any he could buy; and, for his age, was an accomplished mechanic.

Joseph Little went the way of all flesh.

They mourned and missed him; and, at Henry's earnest request, his mother disposed of the plant, and went with him to London.

Then the battle of life began. He was a long time out of employment, and they both lived on his mother's little fortune.

But Henry was never idle. He set up a little forge hard by, and worked at it by day, and at night he would often sit carving, while his mother read to him, and said he, "Mother, I'll never rest till I can carve the bloom upon a plum."

Not to dwell on the process, the final result was this. He rose at last to eminence as a carver: but as an inventor and forger of carving-tools he had no rival in England.

Having with great labor, patience, and skill, completed a master-piece of carving (there were plums with the bloom on, and other incredibles), and also a set of carving-tools equally exquisite in their way, he got a popular tradesman to exhibit both the work and the tools in his window, on a huge silver salver.

The thing made a good deal of noise in the trade, and drew many spectators to the shop window.

One day Mr. Cheetham, a master-cutler, stood in admiration before the tools, and saw his way to coin the workman.

This Cheetham was an able man, and said to himself, "I'll nail him for Hillsborough, directly. London mustn't have a hand that can beat us at any thing in our line."

He found Henry out, and offered him constant employment, as a forger and cutler of carving-tools, at £4 per week.

Henry's black eyes sparkled, but he restrained himself. "That's to be thought of. I must speak to my old lady. She is not at home just now."

He did speak to her, and she put her two hands together and said, "Hillsborough! Oh Henry!" and the tears stood in her eyes directly.

"Well, don't fret," said he: "it is only saying no."

So when Mr. Cheetham called again for the reply, Henry declined, with thanks. On this, Mr. Cheetham never moved, but smiled, and offered him £6 per week, and his journey free.

Henry went into another room, and argued the matter. "Come, mother, he is up to £6 a week now; and that is every shilling I'm worth; and, when I get an apprentice, it will be £9 clear to us."

"The sight of the place!" objected Mrs. Little, hiding her face in her hands instinctively.

He kissed her, and talked good manly sense to her, and begged her to have more courage.

She was little able to deny him, and she consented; but cried, out of his sight, a good many times about it.

As for Henry, strong in the consciousness of power and skill, he felt glad he was going to Hillsborough. "Many a workman has risen to the top of the tree in that place," said he. "Why, this very Cheetham was grinding saws in a water-wheel ten years ago, I've heard uncle Joe say. Come, mother, don't you be a baby! I'll settle you in a cottage outside the smoke; you shall make a palace of it; and we'll rise in the very town where we fell, and friends and foes shall see us."

Mr. Cheetham purchased both the carving and the tools to exhibit in Hillsborough; and the purchase-money, less a heavy commission, was paid to Henry. He showed Mrs. Little thirty pounds, and helped her pack up; and next day they reached Hillsborough by train.

Henry took a close cab, and carried his mother off to the suburbs in search of a lodging. She wore a thick veil, and laid her head on her son's shoulder, and held his brown though elegant hand with her white fingers, that quivered a little as she passed through the well-known streets.

As for Henry, he felt quite triumphant and grand, and consoled her in an off-hand, hearty way. "Come, cheer up, and face the music. They have all forgotten you by this time, and, when they do see you again, you shall be as good as the best of them. I don't drink, and I've got a trade all to myself here, and I'd rather make my fortune in this town than any other: and, mother, you have been a good friend to me; I won't ever marry till I have done you justice, and made you the queen of this very town."

And so he rattled on, in such high spirits, that the great soft thing began to smile with motherly love and pride through her tears, ere they found a lodging.

Next day to the works, and there the foreman showed him a small forge on the ground floor, and a vacant room above to make his handles in and put the tools together: the blades were to be ground, whetted, and finished by cheaper hands.

A quick-eared grinder soon came up to them, and said roughly, "Ain't we to wet new forge?"

"They want their drink out of you," said the foreman; and whispered, in great anxiety, "Don't say no, or you might as well work in a wasp's nest as here."

"All right," said Henry, cheerfully. "I'm no drinker myself, but I'll stand what is customary."

"That is right," said Foreman Bayne. "'Twill cost you fifteen shillings. But Peace is cheap at as many guineas."

The word was given, and every man who worked on the same floor with Henry turned out to drink at his expense, and left off work for a good hour. With some exceptions they were a rough lot, and showed little friendliness or good-humor over it. One even threw out a hint that no cockney forges were wanted in Hillsborough. But another took him up and said, "Maybe not; but you are not much of a man to drink his liquor and grudge him his bread."

After this waste of time and money, Henry went back to the works, and a workman told him rather sulkily, he was wanted in the foreman's office.

He went in, and there was a lovely girl of eighteen, who looked at him with undisguised curiosity, and addressed him thus: "Sir, is it you that carve wood so beautifully?"

Henry blushed, and hesitated; and that made the young lady blush herself a very little, and she said, "I wished to take lessons in carving." Then, as he did not reply, she turned to Mr. Bayne. "But perhaps he objects to teach other people?"

"*We* should object to his teaching other workmen," said the foreman; "but," turning to Henry, "there is no harm in your giving her a lesson or two, after hours. You will want a set of the tools, Miss?"

"Of course I shall. Please put them into the carriage; and—when will he come and teach me, I wonder? for I am wild to begin."

Henry said he could come Saturday afternoon, or Monday morning early.

"Whichever you please," said the lady, and put down her card on the desk; then tripped away to her carriage, leaving Henry charmed with her beauty and ease.

He went home to his mother, and told her he was to give lessons to the handsomest young lady he had ever seen. "She has bought the specimen tools too; so I must forge some more, and lose no time about it."

"Who is she, I wonder?"

"Here is her card. 'Miss Carden, Woodbine Villa, Heath Hill.'"

"Carden!" said the widow. Then, after a moment's thought, "Oh, Henry, don't go near them. Ah, I knew how it would be. Hillsborough is not like London. You can't be long hid in it."

"Why, what is the matter? Do you know the lady?"

"Oh yes. Her papa is director of an insurance company in London. I remember her being born very well. The very day she was christened—her name is Grace—you were six years old, and I took you to her christening: and oh, Harry, my brother is her godfather. Don't you go near that Grace Carden; don't visit any one that knew us in better days."

"Why, what have we to be ashamed of?" said Henry. "'Tisn't as if we sat twiddling our thumbs and howling, 'We have seen better days.' And 'tisn't as if we asked favors of any body. For my part I don't care who knows I am here, and can make three hundred a year with my own hands and wrong no man. I'd rather be a good workman in wood and steel than an arrogant old fool like your b——. No, I won't own him for yours or mine either—call him Raby. Well, I wouldn't change places with him, nor any of his sort: I'm a British workman, and worth a dozen Rabys—useless scum!"

"That you are, dear; so don't demean yourself to give any of them lessons. Her godfather would be sure to hear of it."

"Well, I won't, to please you. But you have no more pluck than a chicken—begging your pardon, mother."

"No, dear," said Mrs. Little, humbly, quite content to gain her point and lose her reputation for pluck; if any.

Henry worked regularly, and fast, and well, and in less than a fortnight a new set of his carving-tools were on view in Hillsborough, and another in London; for it was part of Mr. Cheetham's strategy to get all the London orders, and even make London believe that these superior instruments had originated in Hillsborough.

One day Miss Carden called and saw Bayne in the office. Her vivid features wore an expression of vexation, and she complained to him that the wood-carver had never been near her.

Bayne was surprised at that; but he was a man who always allayed irritation on the spot. "Rely on it, there's some reason," said he. "Perhaps he has not got settled. I'll go for him directly."

"Thank you," said the young lady. Then in the same breath, "No, take me to him, and perhaps we may catch him carving—cross thing!"

Bayne assented cheerfully, and led the way across a yard, and up a dirty stone stair, which, solid as it was, vibrated with the powerful machinery that steam was driving on every side of it. He opened a door suddenly, and Henry looked up from his work, and saw the invaders.

He stared a little at first, and then got up and looked embarrassed and confused.

"You did not keep your word, sir," said Grace, quietly.

"No," he muttered, and hung his head.

He seemed so confused and ashamed, that Bayne came to his assistance. "The fact is, no workman likes to do a hand's-turn on Saturday afternoon. I think they would rather break Sunday than Saturday."

"It is not that," said Henry, in a low voice.

Grace heard him, but answered Mr. Bayne: "Oh dear, I wish I had known. I fear I have made an unreasonable request: for, of course, after working so hard all the week—but then why did you let me purchase the tools to carve with? Papa says they are very dear, Mr. Bayne. But that is what gentlemen always say if one buys any thing that is really good. But of course they *will* be dear, if I am not to be taught how to use them." She then looked in Mr. Bayne's face with an air of infantine simplicity: "Would Mr. Cheetham take them back, I wonder, under the circumstances?"

At this sly thrust, Bayne began to look anxious; but Henry relieved him the next moment by saying, in a sort of dogged way, "There, there; I'll come." He added, after a pause, "I will give you six lessons, if you like."

"I shall be so much obliged. When will you come, sir?"

"Next Saturday, at three o'clock."

"I shall be sure to be at home, sir."

She then said something polite about not disturbing him further, and vanished with an arch smile of pleasure and victory, that disclosed a row of exquisite white teeth, and haunted Henry Little for many a day after.

He told his mother what had happened, and showed so much mortified pride that she no longer dissuaded him from keeping his word. "Only pray don't tell her your name," said she?

"Well, but what am I to do if she asks it?"

"Say Thompson, or Johnson, or any thing you like, except Little."

This request roused Henry's bile. "What, am I a criminal to deny my name? And how shall I look, if I go and give her a false name, and then she comes to Bayne and learns my right one? No, I'll keep my name back, if I can; but I'll never disown it. I'm not ashamed of it, if you are."

This reduced poor Mrs. Little to silence; followed, in due course, by a few meek, clandestine tears.

Henry put on his new tweed suit and hat, and went up to the villa. He announced himself as the workman from Cheetham's; and the footman, who had probably his orders, ushered him into the drawing-room at once. There he found Grace Carden seated, reading, and a young woman sewing at a respectful distance. This pair were types; Grace, of a young English gentlewoman, and Jael Dence of a villager by unbroken descent. Grace was tall, supple, and serpentine, yet not thin; Jael was robust and ample, without being fat; she was of the same height, though Grace looked the taller. Grace had dark brown eyes and light brown hair; and her blooming cheek and bewitching mouth shone with expression so varied, yet vivid, and always appropriate to the occasion, grave or gay, playful or dignified, that her countenance made artificial faces, and giggling-in-the-wrong-place faces, painfully ridiculous. As for such faces as Jael's, it killed them on the spot, but that was all. Jael's hair was reddish, and her full eyes were gray; she was freckled a little under the eyes, but the rest of her cheek full of rich pure color, healthy, but not the least coarse; and her neck an alabaster column. Hers was a meek, monotonous countenance; but with a certain look of concentration. Altogether, a humble beauty of the old rural type; healthy, cleanly, simple, candid, yet demure.

Henry came in, and the young lady received him with a manner very different from that she had worn down at the works. She was polite, but rather stiff and dignified.

He sat down at her request, and, wondering at himself, entered on the office of preceptor. He took up the carving-tools, and explained the use of several; then offered, by way of illustration, to work on something.

"That will be the best way, much," said Grace quietly, but her eye sparkled.

"I dare say there's some lumber to be found in a great house like this?"

"Lumber? why, there's a large garret devoted to it. Jael, please take him to the lumber-room."

Jael fixed her needle in her work, and laid it down gently on a table near her, then rose and led the way to the lumber-room.

In that invaluable repository Henry soon found two old knobs lying on the ground (a four-poster had been wrecked hard by), and a piece of deal plank jutting out of a mass of things. He pulled hard at the plank; but it was long, and so jammed in by miscellaneous articles, that he could not get it clear.

Jael looked on demurely at his efforts for some time; then she suddenly seized the plank a little higher up. "Now, pull," said she, and gave a tug like a young elephant: out came the plank directly, with a great rattle of dislocated lumber.

"Well, you are a strong one," said Henry.

"Oh, one and one makes two, sir," replied the vigorous damsel, modestly.

"That is true, but you threw your weight into it like a workman. Now hand me that rusty old saw, and I'll cut off as much as we want."

While he was sawing off a piece of the plank, Jael stood and eyed him silently a while. But presently her curiosity oozed out. "If you please, sir, be you really a working man?"

"Why what else should I be?" was the answer, given rather brusquely.

"A great many gentlefolks comes here as is no better dressed nor you be."

"Dress is no rule. Don't you go and take me for a gentleman, or we sha'n't agree. Wait till I'm as arrogant, and empty, and lazy as they are. I am a workman, and proud of it."

"It's naught to be ashamed on, that's certain," said Jael. "I've carried many a sack of grain up into our granary, and made a few hundredweight of cheese and butter, besides house-work and farm-work. Bless your heart, I bayn't idle when I be at home."

"And pray where is your home?" asked Henry, looking up a moment, not that he cared one straw.

"If you please, sir, I do come from Cairnhope village. I'm old Nat Dence's daughter. There's two of us, and I'm the youngest. Squire sent me in here, because Miss said Hillsborough girls wasn't altogether honest. She is a dear kind young lady; but I do pine for home and the farm at times; and frets about the young calves: they want so much looking after. And sister, she's a-courting, and can't give her mind to 'em as should be. I'll carry the board for you, sir."

"All right," said Henry carelessly; but, as they went along, he thought to himself, "So a skilled workman passes for a gentleman with rustics: fancy that!"

On their return to the drawing-room, Henry asked for a high wooden stool, or chair, and said it would be as well to pin some newspapers over the carpet. A high stool was soon got from the kitchen, and Jael went promptly down on her knees, and crawled about, pinning the newspapers in a large square.

Henry stood apart, superior, and thought to himself, "So much for domestic servitude. What a position for a handsome girl—creeping about on all fours!"

When all was ready, he drew some arabesque forms with his pencil on the board. He then took an exquisite little saw he had invented for this work, and fell upon the board with a rapidity that, contrasted with his previous nonchalance, looked like fury. But he was one of your fast workmen. The lithe saw seemed to twist in his hand like a serpent, and in a very short time he had turned four feet of the board into open-work. He finished the edges off with his cutting tools, and there was a transformation as complete as of linen cloth turned lace.

Grace was delighted. "Shall I ever be able to do that?"

"In half a day. That's not carving: that's trickery. The tool does it all. Before I invented this saw, a good workman would have been a day over that; but now you can do it in half an hour, when you are master of the instrument. And now I'll show you honest work." He took one of the knobs and examined it; then sawed off a piece, and worked on the rest so cunningly with his various cutters, that it grew into a human face towards their very eyes. He even indicated Jael Dence's little flat cap by a means at once simple and ingenious. All the time he was working the women's eyes literally absorbed him:

morning. He then went off with a quick independent air, as one whose every minute was gold.

"If you please, Miss," said Jael, "is he a real working man, or only a gentleman as makes it his pastime?"

"HONEST WORK."

only those of Grace flashed vivid curiosity, Jael's open orbs were fixed with admiration and awe upon his supernatural cleverness.

He now drew some more arabesques on the remaining part of the board, and told Miss Carden she must follow those outlines with the saw, and he would examine her work on Monday

"A gentleman! What an idea! Of course he is a working man. But a very superior person."

"To be sure," continued Jael, not quite convinced, "he don't come up to Squire Raby; but, dear heart, he have a grander way with him than most of the Hillsborough gentlefolks as calls here."

"Nonsense!" said Grace, authoritatively. "Look at his nails."

Henry came twice a week, and his pupil made remarkable progress. She was deferential, attentive, enthusiastic.

By degrees the work led to a little conversation; and that, in due course, expanded into a variety of subjects; and the young lady, to her surprise, found her carver well-read in History and Sciences, and severely accurate in his information, whereas her own, though abundant, was rather loose.

One day she expressed her surprise that he could have found time to be so clever with his fingers and yet cultivate his mind.

"Well," said he, "I was lucky enough to have a good mother. She taught me all she knew, and she gave me a taste for reading; and that has been the making of me; kept me out of the public-house, for one thing."

"Ah! you *were* fortunate. I lost my mother, sir, when I was but eight years old."

"Oh dear, that was a bad job," said Henry brusquely but kindly.

"A very bad job," said Grace, smiling; but the next moment she suddenly turned her fair head away and tears stole down her cheeks.

Henry looked very sorry, and Jael, without moving, looked at Grace, and opened those sluices, her eyes, and two big drops of sympathy rolled down her comely face in a moment.

That day, when young Little shut the street-door of "Woodbine Villa" and stepped into the road, a sort of dull pain seemed to traverse his chest. It made his heart ache a little, this contrast of the sweet society he had left and the smoky town towards which he now turned his face. He seemed to be ejected from Paradise for the next five days. It was Monday, yet he wished the next day was Saturday, and the intervening period could be swept away, so that he might be entering that soft Paradise instead of leaving it.

And this sentiment, once rooted, grew rapidly in an aspiring nature, and a heart that had never yet entertained a serious passion. Now the fair head that bowed over the work so near him, the lovely hand he had so often to direct, and almost to guide, and all the other perfections of mind and body this enchanting girl possessed, crept in at his admiring eyes, and began to steal into his very veins, and fill him with soft complacency. His brusque manner dissolved away, and his voice became low and soft, whenever he was in her delicious presence. He spoke softly to Jael even, if Grace was there. The sturdy workman was enthralled.

Often he wondered at himself. Sometimes he felt alarmed at the strength of his passion and the direction it had taken.

"What," said he, "have I flirted with so many girls in my own way of life, and come away heart-whole, and now to fall in love with a gentlewoman, who would bid her footman show me the door if she knew of my presumption!"

But these misgivings could neither cure him nor cow him. Let him only make money, and become a master instead of a workman, and then he would say to her, "I don't value birth myself, but if you do, why, I am not come of workpeople."

He traced a plan with workmanlike precision:—

Profound discretion and self-restraint at "Woodbine Villa:" restless industry and stern self-denial in Hillsborough.

After his day's work he used to go straight to his mother. She gave him a cup of tea, and then they had their chat; and after that the sexes were inverted, so to speak : the man carved fruit, and flowers, and dead woodcocks, the woman read the news and politics of the day, and the essays on labor and capital, and any other articles not too flimsy to bear reading aloud to a man whose time was coin. (There was a free library in Hillsborough, and a mechanic could take out standard books and reviews.) Thus they passed the evening hours agreeably, and usefully too, for Henry sucked in knowledge like a leech, and at the same time carved things that sold well in London. He had a strong inclination to open his heart about Miss Carden. Accordingly, one evening he said, "She lost her mother when she was a child."

"Who lost her mother?" asked Mrs. Little.

"Miss Carden," said Henry, very softly.

The tone was not lost on Mrs. Little's watchful ear; at least her mind seized it a few seconds afterwards.

"That is true," said she. "Poor girl! I remember hearing of it. Henry, what is that to you? Don't you trouble your head about that young lady, or she will trouble your heart. I wish you did not go near her."

And then came question upon question, and vague maternal misgivings. Henry parried them as adroitly as he could: but never mentioned Miss Carden's name again.

He thought of her all the more, and counted his gains every week, and began to inquire of experienced persons how much money was wanted to set up a wheel with steam power, and be a master instead of a man. He gathered that a stranger could hardly start fair without £500.

"That is a good lump!" thought Henry : "but I'll have it, if I work night as well as day."

Thus inspired, his life became a sweet delirium. When he walked, he seemed to tread on air : when he forged, his hammer felt a feather in his hand. The mountains in the way looked mole-hills, and the rainbow tangible, to Youth, and Health, and Hope, and mighty Love.

One afternoon, as he put on his coat and crossed the yard, after a day's work that had passed like a pleasant hour, being gilded with such delightful anticipations, the foreman of the works made him a mysterious signal. Henry saw it, and followed him into his office. Bayne looked carefully out of all the doors, then closed them softly, and his face betrayed anxiety, and even fear.

"Little," said he, almost in a whisper, "you know me : I'm a man of peace, and so for love of peace I'm going to do something that might get me into a wrangle. But you are the civilest chap ever worked under me, and the best workman, take you all together, and I can't bear to see you kept in the dark, when you are the man whose skin—only—if I act like a man to you, will you act like one to me?"

"I will," said Henry; "there's my hand on it."

Then Bayne stepped to his desk, opened it, and took out some letters.

"You must never tell a soul I showed them you, or you will get me into a row with Cheetham; and I want to be at peace in-doors as well as out."

"I give you my word."

"Then read that, to begin."

And he handed him a letter addressed to Mr. Cheetham.

"Sir,—We beg respectfully to draw your attention to a matter, which is of a nature to cause unpleasantness between you and the Trades. We allude to your bringing a workman in from another town to do work that we are informed can be done on the premises by your own hands.

"We assure you it would be more to your interest to work in harmony with the smiths and the handle-makers in your employ, and the trade generally. Yours respectfully,

"The Committee of
the Edge-Tool Forgers' Union."

Henry colored up at this, and looked grieved; but he said, "I am sorry to be the cause of any unpleasantness. But what can I do?"

"Oh," said Bayne, with a sardonic grin, "they are sure to tell you that, soon or late. Read this:"

No. 2 was dated a week later, and ran thus:

"Mr. Cheetham: Sir,—I think you do very ill to annoy a many craftsmen for one. Remember, you have suffered loss and inconvenience whenever you have gone against Trades. We had to visit you last year, and when we came your bands went and your bellows gaped. We have no wish to come again this year, if you will be reasonable. But, sir, you must part with London hand, or take consequences. Balaam."

Henry looked grave. "Can I see a copy of Mr. Cheetham's reply?"

Bayne stared at him, and then laughed in his face, but without the gayety that should accompany a laugh. "Cheetham's reply to Balaam! And where would he send it? To Mr. Beor's lodgings, No. 1, Prophet Place, Old Testament Square. My poor chap, nobody writes replies to these letters. When you get one, you go that minute to the secretary of whatever Union you are wrong with, and you don't argue, or he bids you good-morning; you give in to whatever he asks, and then you get civility; and justice too, according to Trade lights. If you don't do that, and haven't learned what a blessing Peace is, why, you make up your mind to fight the Trade; and if you do, you have to fight them all; and you are safe to get the worst of it, soon or late. Cheetham has taken no notice of these letters. All the worse for him and you too. Read that."

No. 3 ran thus:

"Dear Sir,—I take the liberty of addressing you on the subject of your keeping on this knob-stick, in defiance of them that has the power to make stones of Hillsborough too hot for you and him. Are you deaf, or blind, or a fool, Jack Cheatem? You may cheat the world, but you don't cheat the devil, nor me. Turn cockney up, with no more ado, or you'll both get kicked to hell some dark night by Balaam's Ass."

Henry was silent; quite silent. When he did speak, it was to ask why Mr. Cheetham had kept all this from him.

"Because you shouldn't take fright and leave him," was the unhesitating reply.

"For that matter they threaten him more than they do me."

"They warn the master first; but the workman's turn is sure to come, and he gets it hottest, because they have so many ways of doing him. Cheetham, he lives miles from here, and rides in across country, and out again, in daylight. But the days are drawing in, and you have got to pass through these dark streets, where the Trades have a thousand friends, and you not one. Don't you make any mistake: you are in their power; so pray don't copy any hot-headed, wrong-headed gentleman like Cheetham, but speak them fair. Come to terms—if you can—and let us be at peace; sweet, balmy peace."

"Peace is a good thing, no doubt," said Henry, "but" (rather bitterly) "I don't thank Cheetham for letting me run blindfold into trouble, and me a stranger."

"Oh," said Bayne, "he is no worse than the rest, believe me. What does any master care for a man's life? Profit and loss go down in figures; but life—that's a cipher in all their ledgers."

"Oh, come," said Henry, "it is unphilosophical and narrow-minded to fasten on a class the faults of a few individuals, that form a very moderate portion of that class."

Bayne seemed staggered by a blow so polysyllabic; and Henry, to finish him, added, "Where there's a multitude, there's a mixture." Now the first sentence he had culled from the *Edinburgh Review*, and the second he had caught from a fellow-workman's lips in a public-house; and probably this was the first time the pair of phrases had ever walked out of any man's mouth arm in arm. He went on to say, "And as for Cheetham, he is not a bad fellow, take him altogether. But you are a better for telling me the truth. Forewarned, forearmed."

He went home thoughtful, and not so triumphant and airy as yesterday; but still not dejected, for his young and manly mind summoned its energy and spirit to combat this new obstacle, and his wits went to work.

Being unable to sleep for thinking of what he should do he was the first to reach the works in the morning. He lighted his furnace, and then went and unlocked the room where he worked as a handle-maker, and also as a cutler. He entered briskly, and opened the window. The gray light of the morning came in, and showed him something on the inside of the door that was not there when he locked it overnight. It was a very long knife, broad towards the handle, but keenly pointed, and double-edged. It was fast in the door, and impaled a letter addressed, in a vile hand—

"To Jak thre trades."

Henry took hold of the handle to draw the knife out; but the formidable weapon had been driven clean through the door with a single blow.

Then Henry drew back, and, as the confusion of surprise cleared away, the whole thing began to grow on him, and reveal distinct and alarming features.

The knife was not one which the town manufactured in the way of business. It was a long,

2

glittering blade, double-edged, finely pointed, and exquisitely tempered. It was not a tool, but a weapon.

Why was it there, and, above all, how did it come there?

He distinctly remembered locking the door overnight. Indeed, he had found it locked, and the window-shutters bolted; yet there was this deadly weapon, and on its point a letter, the superscription of which looked hostile and sinister.

He drew the note gently across the edge of the keen knife, and the paper parted like a cobweb. He took it to the window and read it. It ran thus :

"This knifs wun of too made ekspres t'other is for thy hart if thou dosent harken Trade and leve Chetm. is thy skin thicks dore thinks thou if not turn up and back to Lundon or I cum again and rip thy —— carkiss with feloe blade to this thou —— cokny

                 "SLIPER JACK."

CHAPTER IV.

ANY one who reads it by the fireside may smile at the incongruous mixture of a sanguinary menace with bad spelling. But deeds of blood had often followed these scrawls in Hillsborough, and Henry knew it : and, indeed, he who can not spell his own name correctly, is the very man to take his neighbor's life without compunction ; since mercy is a fruit of knowledge, and cruelty of ignorance.

And then there was something truly chilling in the mysterious entrance of this threat on a dagger's point into a room he had locked overnight. It implied supernatural craft and power. After this, where could a man be safe from these all-penetrating and remorseless agents of a secret and irresponsible tribunal.

Henry sat down awhile, and pored over the sanguinary scrawl, and glanced from it with a shudder at the glittering knife. And, while he was in this state of temporary collapse, the works filled, the Power moved, the sonorous grindstones revolved, and every man worked at his ease, except one, the best of them all beyond comparison.

He went to his friend Bayne, and said in a broken voice, "They have put me in heart for work ; given me a morning dram. Look here." Bayne was shocked, but not surprised. "It is the regular routine," said he. "They begin civil ; but if you don't obey, they turn it over to the scum."

"Do you think my life is really in danger ?"

"No, not yet ; I never knew a man molested on one warning. This is just to frighten you. If you were to take no notice, you'd likely get another warning, or two, at most ; and then they'd do you, as sure as a gun."

"Do me ?"

"Oh, that is the Hillsborough word. It means to disable a man from work. Sometimes they lie in wait in these dark streets, and fracture his skull with life-preservers ; or break his arm, or cut the sinew of his wrist ; and that they call *doing* him. Or, if it is a grinder, they'll put powder in his trough, and then the sparks of his own making fire it, and scorch him, and perhaps blind him for life : that's *doing* him. They have gone as far as shooting men with shot, and even with a bullet, but never so as to kill the man dead on the spot. They *do* him. They are skilled workmen, you know ; well, they are skilled workmen at violence and all, and it is astonishing how they contrive to stop within an inch of murder. They'll chance it though sometimes with their favorite gunpowder. If you're very wrong with the trade, and they can't *do* you any other way, they'll blow your house up from the cellar, or let a can of powder down the chimney, with a lighted fuse, or fling a petard in at the window, and they take the chance of killing a houseful of innocent people, to get at the one that's on the black books of the trade, and has to be *done*."

"The beasts ! I'll buy a six-shooter. I'll meet craft with craft, and force with force."

"What can you do against ten thousand ? No : go you at once to the Secretary of the Edge-Tool Grinders, and get your trade into his union. You will have to pay ; but don't mind that. Cheetham will go halves."

"I'll go at dinner-time."

"And why not now ?"

"Because," said Henry, with a candor all his own, "I'm getting over my fright a bit, and my blood is beginning to boil at being threatened by a sneak, who wouldn't stand before me one moment in that yard, knife or no knife."

Bayne smiled a friendly but faint smile, and shook his head with grave disapprobation, and said, with wonder, "Fancy postponing Peace !"

Henry went to his forge, and worked till dinner-time. Nay, more, he was a beautiful whistler, and always whistled a little at his work ; so to-day he whistled a great deal : in fact, he overwhistled.

At dinner-time he washed his face and hands, and put on his coat to go out.

But he had soon some reason to regret that he had not acted on Bayne's advice to the letter.

There had been a large trade's meeting over-night, and the hostility to the London craftsman had spread more widely, in consequence of remarks that had been there made. This emboldened the lower class of workmen, who already disliked him out of pure envy, and had often scowled at him in silence: and, now, as he passed them, they spoke at him, in their peculiar language, which the great friend and supporter of mechanics in general, *The Hillsborough Liberal*, subsequently christened "THE DASH DIALECT."

"We want no —— cockneys here, to steal our work."

"Did ever a —— anvil-man handle his own blades in Hillsborough?"

"Not till this —— knobstick came," said another.

Henry turned sharp round upon them haughtily, and such was the power of his prompt defiant attitude, and his eye, which flashed black lightning, that there was a slight movement of recoil among the actual speakers. They recovered it immediately, strong in numbers; but in that same moment Little also recovered his discretion, and he had the address to step briskly towards the gate and call out the porter; he said to him in rather a loud voice, for all to hear, "If any body asks for Henry Little, say he has gone to the Secretary of the Edge-Tool Forgers' Union." He then went out of the works; but, as he went, he heard some respectable workman say to the scum, "Come, shut up now. It is in better hands than yours."

Mr. Jobson, the Secretary of the Edge-Tool Forgers, was not at home, but his servant-girl advised Little to try the "Rising Sun;" and in the parlor of that orb he found Mr. Jobson, in company with other magnates of the same class, discussing a powerful leader of the *Hillsborough Liberal*, in which was advocated the extension of the franchise, a measure calculated to throw prodigious power into the hands of Hillsborough operatives, because of their great number, and their habit of living each workman in a tenement of his own, however small.

Little waited till *The Liberal* had received its meed of approbation, and then asked respectfully if he might speak to Mr. Jobson on a trade matter. "Certainly," said Mr. Jobson. "Who are you?"

"My name is Little. I make the carving-tools at Cheetham's."

"I'll go home with you; my house is hard by."

When they got to the house, Jobson told him to sit down, and asked him, in a smooth and well-modulated voice, what was the nature of the business. This query, coming from him, who had set the stone rolling that bade fair to crush him, rather surprised Henry. He put his hand into his pocket, and produced the threatening note, but said nothing as to the time or manner of its arrival.

Mr. Jobson perused it carefully, and then returned it to Henry. "What have we to do with this?" and he looked quite puzzled.

"Why, sir, it is the act of your Union."

"You are sadly misinformed, Mr. Little. We *never threaten*. All we do is to remind the master that, if he does not do certain things, certain other things will probably be done by us; and this we wrap up in the kindest way."

"But, sir, you wrote to Cheetham against me."

"Did we? Then it will be in my letter-book." He took down a book, examined it, and said, "You are quite right. Here's a copy of the letter. Now surely, sir, comparing the language, the manners, and the spelling, with that of the ruffian whose scrawl you received this morning—"

"Then you disown the ruffian's threat, sir?"

"Most emphatically. And if you can trace it home, he shall smart for interfering in our business."

"Oh, if the trade disowns the blackguard, I can despise him. But you can't wonder at my thinking all these letters were steps of the same—yes, and Mr. Bayne thought so too; for he said this was the regular routine, and ends in *doing* a poor fellow for gaining his bread."

Mr. Jobson begged to explain.

"Many complaints are brought to us, who advise the trades. When they are frivolous, we are unwilling to disturb the harmony of employers and workmen; we reason with the complainant, and the thing dies away. When the grievance is substantial, we take it out of the individual's hands, and lay it before the working committee. A civil note is sent to the master; or a respectable member of the committee calls on him, and urges him to redress the grievance, but always in kind and civil terms. The master generally assents: experience has taught him it is his wisest course. But if he refuses, we are bound to report the refusal to a larger committee, and sometimes a letter emanates from them, reminding the master that he has been a loser before by acts of injustice, and hinting that he may be a loser again. I don't quite approve this form of communication. But certainly it has often prevented the mischief from spreading farther. Well, but perhaps he continues rebellious. What follows? We can't lock up facts that affect the trade; we are bound to report the case at the next general meeting. It excites comments, some of them perhaps a little intemperate; the lower kind of workmen get inflamed with passion, and often, I am sorry to say, write ruffianly letters, and now and then do ruffianly acts, which disgrace the town, and are strongly reprobated by us. Why, Mr. Little, it has been my lot to send a civil remonstrance, written with my own hand, in pretty fair English —for a man who plied bellows and hammer twenty years of my life—and be treated with silent contempt; and two months after to be offering a reward of twenty or thirty pounds, for the discovery of some misguided man, that had taken on himself to right this very matter with a can of gunpowder, or some such coarse expedient."

"Yes, but, sir, what hurts me is, you didn't consider me to be worth a civil note. You only remonstrated with Cheetham."

"You can't wonder at that. Our trade hasn't been together many years: and what drove us together? The tyranny of our employers. What has kept us together? The bitter experience of hard work and little pay, whenever we were out of union. Those who now direct the trades are old enough to remember when we were all ground down to the dust by the greedy masters; and therefore it is natural, when a grievance arises, we should be inclined to look to those old offenders for redress in the first instance. Sometimes the masters convince us the fault lies with workmen; and then we trouble the master no more than we are forced to do in order to act upon the offenders. But, to come to the point: what is your proposal?"

"I beg to be admitted into the union."

"What union?"

"Why, of course the one I have offended, through ignorance. The edge-tool forgers."

Jobson shook his head, and said he feared there were one or two objections.

Henry saw it was no use bidding low. "I'll pay £15 down," said he, "and I'll engage not to draw relief from your fund, unless disabled by accident or violence."

"I will submit your offer to the trade," said Jobson. He added, "Then there, I conclude, the matter rests for the present."

Henry interpreted this to mean that he had nothing to apprehend, unless his proposal should be rejected. He put the £15 down on the table, though Mr. Jobson told him that was premature, and went off as light as a feather. Being nice and clean, and his afternoon's work spoiled, he could not resist the temptation; he went to "Woodbine Villa." He found Miss Carden at home, and she looked quietly pleased at his unexpected arrival: but Jael's color came and went, and her tranquil bosom rose and fell slowly, but grandly, for a minute, as she lowered her head over her work.

This was a heavenly change to Henry Little. Away from the deafening workshop, and the mean jealousies and brutality of his inferiors, who despised him, to the presence of a beautiful and refined girl and find something to work her his superior, yet did not despise him. From sin to purity, from dirt to cleanliness, from war to peace, from vilest passions to Paradise.

Her smile had never appeared so fascinating, her manner never so polite yet placid. How softly and comfortably she and her ample dress nestled into the corner of the sofa and fitted it! How white her nimble hand! how bright her delicious face! How he longed to kiss her exquisite hand, or her little foot, or her hem, or the ground she walked on, or something she had touched, or her eye had dwelt on.

But he must not even think too much of such delights, lest he should show his heart too soon. So, after a short lesson, he proposed to go into the lumber-room and find something to work upon. "Yes, do," said Grace. "I would go too; but no; it was my palace of delights for years, and its treasures inexhaustible. I will not go to be robbed of one more illusion. It is just possible I might find it really is what the profane in this house call it—a lumber-room—and not what memory paints it, a temple of divine curiosities." And so she sent them off, and set herself to feel old—"oh, so old."

And presently Henry came back, laden with a great wooden bust of Erin, that had been the figure-head of a wrecked schooner; and set it down, and told her he should carve that into a likeness of herself, and she must do her share of the work.

Straightway she forgot she was worn out; and clapped her hands, and her eyes sparkled. And the floor was prepared, and Henry went to work like one inspired, and the chips flew in every direction, and the paint was chiselled away in no time, and the wood proved soft and kindly, and just the color of a delicate skin, and Henry said,

"The Greek Statues, begging their pardons, have all got hair like mops; but this shall have real hair, like your own: and the silk dress, with the gloss on; and the lace: but the face, the expression, how can I ever—?"

"Oh, never mind them," cried Grace. "Jael, this is too exciting. Please go and tell them 'not at home' to any body."

Then came a pretty picture: the workman, with his superb hand, brown and sinewy, yet elegant and shapely as a Duchess's, and the fingers almost as taper, and his black eye that glowed like a coal over the model, which grew under his masterly strokes, now hard, now light: the enchanting girl who sat to him, and seemed on fire with curiosity and innocent admiration: and the simple rural beauty, that plied the needle, and beamed mildly with demure happiness, and shot a shy glance upward now and then.

Yes, Love was at his old mischievous game.

Henry now lived in secret for Grace Carden, and Jael was garnering Henry into her devoted heart, unobserved by the object of her simple devotion. Yet, of the three, these two, that loved with so little encouragement, were the happiest. To them the world was Heaven this glorious afternoon. Time, strewing roses as he went, glided so sweetly and so swiftly, that they started with surprise when the horizontal beams glorified the windows, and told them the brightest day of their lives was drawing to its end.

Ah, stay a little while longer for them, Western Sun. Stand still, not as in the cruel days of old, to glare upon poor, beaten, wounded, panting warriors, and rob them of their last chance, the shelter of the night; but to prolong these holy rapturous hours of youth, and hope, and first love in bosoms unsullied by the world—the golden hours of life, that glow so warm, and shine so bright, and fleet so soon; and return in this world— Never more!

CHAPTER V.

HENRY LITTLE began this bust in a fervid hour; and made great progress the first day: but, as the work grew on him, it went slower and slower; for his ambitious love drove him to attempt beauties of execution that were without precedent in this kind of wood-carving; and, on the other hand, the fastidiousness of a true craftsman made him correct his attempts again and again. As to those mechanical parts, which he entrusted at first to his pupil, she fell so far short of his ideal even in these, that he told her bluntly she must strike work for the present; he could not have *this* spoiled.

Grace thought it hard she might not be allowed to spoil her own image; however, she submitted, and henceforth her lesson was confined to looking on. And she did look on with interest, and, at last, with profound admiration. Hitherto she had thought, with many other persons, that, if a man's hand was the stronger, a woman's was the neater: but now she saw the same hand, which had begun by hewing away the coarse outlines of the model, bestow touches of the chisel so unerring and effective, yet so exquisitely delicate, that she said to herself, "No woman's hand could be so firm, yet so feather-like, as all this."

And the result was as admirable as the process. The very texture of the ivory forehead began to come under those master-touches, executed with perfect and various instruments : and, for the first time perhaps in the history of this art, a bloom, more delicate far than that of a plum, crept over the dimpled cheek. But, indeed, when love and skill work together expect a masterpiece.

Henry worked on it four afternoons, the happiest he had ever known. There was the natural pleasure of creating, and the distinct glory and delight of reproducing features so beloved ; and to these joys were added the pleasure of larger conversation. The model gave Grace many opportunities of making remarks, or asking questions, and Henry contrived to say so many things in answer to one. Sculptor and sitter made acquaintance with each other's minds over the growing bust.

And then young ladies and gentlemen dropped in, and gazed, and said such wonderfully silly things, and thereby left their characters behind them as fruitful themes for conversation. In short, topics were never wanting now.

As for Jael, she worked, and beamed, and pondered every word her idol uttered, but seldom ventured to say any thing, till he was gone, and then she prattled fast enough about him.

The work drew near completion. The hair, not in ropes, as heretofore, but its silken threads boldly and accurately shown, yet not so as to cord the mass, and unsatin it quite. The silk dress ; the lace collar ; the blooming cheek, with its every dimple and incident ; all these were completed, and one eyebrow, a masterpiece in itself. This carved eyebrow was a revelation, and made every body who saw it wonder at the conventional substitutes they had hitherto put up with in statuary of all sorts, when the eyebrow itself was so beautiful, and might it seems have been imitated, instead of libelled, all these centuries.

But beautiful works, and pleasant habits, seem particularly liable to interruption. Just when the one eyebrow was finished, and when Jael Dence had come to look on Saturday and Monday as the only real days in the week, and when even Grace Carden was brighter on those days, and gliding into a gentle complacent custom, suddenly a Saturday came and went, but Little did not appear.

Jael was restless.

Grace was disappointed, but contented to wait till Monday.

Monday came and went, but no Henry Little.

Jael began to fret and sigh ; and, after two more blank weeks, she could bear the mystery no longer. "If you please, Miss," said she, "shall I go to that place where he works ?"

"Where who works ?" inquired Grace, rather disingenuously.

"Why, the dark young man, Miss," said Jael, blushing deeply.

Grace reflected, and curiosity struggled with discretion ; but discretion got the better, being aided by self-respect. "No, Jael," said she ; "he is charming, when he is here ; but, when he gets away, he is not always so civil as he might be. I had to go twice after him. I shall not go nor send a third time. It really is too bad of him."

"Dear heart," pleaded Jael, "mayhap he is not well."

"Then he ought to write and say so. No, no ; he is a radical, and full of conceit : and he has done this one eyebrow, and then gone off laughing and saying, 'Now let us see if the gentry can do the other amongst them.'. If he doesn't come soon, I'll do the other eyebrow myself."

"Mayhap he will never come again," said Jael.

"Oh, yes, he will," said Grace mighty cunningly ; "he is as fond of coming here as we are of having him. Not that I'm at all surprised ; for the fact is, you are very pretty, extremely pretty, abominably pretty."

"I might pass in Cairnhope town," said Jael, modestly, "but not here. The moon goes for nought when the sun is there. He don't come here for me."

This sudden elegance of language, and Jael's tone of dignified despondency, silenced Grace, somehow, and made her thoughtful. She avoided the subject for several days. Indeed, when Saturday came, not a word was said about the defaulter : it was only by her sending for Jael to sit with her, and by certain looks, and occasional restlessness, she betrayed the slightest curiosity or expectation.

Jael sat and sewed, and often looked quickly up at the window, as some footstep passed, and then looked down again and sighed.

Young Little never came. He seemed to have disappeared from both their lives ; quietly disappeared.

Next day, Sunday, Jael came to Miss Carden, after morning church, and said, meekly, "If you please, Miss, may I go home ?"

"Oh, certainly," said Grace, a little haughtily. "What for ?"

Jael hung her head, and said she was not used to be long away. Then she lifted her head, and her great candid eyes, and spoke more frankly. "I feel to be drawed home. Something have been at me all the night to that degree as I couldn't close my eyes. I could almost feel it, like a child's hand, a pulling me East. I'm afeard father's ill, or maybe the calves are bleating for me, that is better acquaint with them than sister Patty is. And Hillsborough air don't seem to 'gree with me now not altogether as it did at first. If you please, Miss, to let me go ; and then I'll come back when I'm better company than I be now. Oh dear ! oh dear !"

"Why, Jael, my poor girl, what *is* the matter ?"

"I don't know, Miss. But I feel very unked."

"Are you not happy with me ?"

"'Tis no fault of yourn, Miss," said Jael, rustic, but womanly.

"Then you are *not* happy here."

No reply, but two clear eyes began to fill to the very brim.

Grace coaxed her, and said, "Speak to me like a friend. You know, after all, you are not my servant. I can't possibly part with you altogether ; I have got to like you so : but, of course, you shall go home for a little while, if you wish it very, very much."

"Indeed I do, Miss," said Jael. "Please forgive me, but my heart feels like lead in my bosom." And, with these words, the big tears ran over, and chased one another down her cheeks.

Then Grace, who was very kind-hearted, begged her, in a very tearful voice, not to cry : she should go home for a week, a fortnight, a month even. "There, there, you shall go to-morrow, poor thing."

. Now it is a curious fact, and looks like animal magnetism or something, but the farmhouse, to which Jael had felt so mysteriously drawn all night, contained, at that moment, besides its usual inmates, one Henry Little : and how he came there is an important part of this tale, which I must deal with at once.

While Henry was still visiting Woodbine Villa, as related above, events of a very different character from those soft scenes were taking place at the works. His liberal offer to the Edge-Tool Forgers had been made about a week, when, coming back one day from dinner to his forge, he found the smoky wall written upon with chalk, in large letters, neatly executed—

"Why overlook the Handlers ?
"MARY."

. He was not alarmed this time, but vexed. He went and complained to Bayne ; and that worthy came directly and contemplated the writing, in silence, for about a minute. Then he gave a weary sigh, and said, with doleful resignation, "Take the chalk, and write. There it is."

Henry took the chalk, and prepared to write Bayne's mind underneath Mary's. Bayne dictated :

"I have offered the Handlers the same
as the Forgers."

"But that is not true," objected Henry, turning round, with the chalk in his hand.

"It will be true, in half an hour. We are going to Parkin, the Handlers' Secretary."

"What, another £15 ! This is an infernal swindle."

"What isn't ?" said Bayne, cynically.

Henry then wrote as desired ; and they went together to Mr. Parkin.

Mr. Parkin was not at home. But they hunted him from pillar to post, and caught him, at last, in the bar-parlor of "The Pack-saddle." He knew Bayne well, and received him kindly, and, on his asking for a private interview, gave a wink to two persons who were with him : they got up directly, and went out.

"What, is there any thing amiss between you and the trade ?" inquired Mr. Parkin, with an air of friendly interest.

Bayne smiled, not graciously, but sourly. "Come, come, sir, that is a farce you and I have worn out this ten years. This is the London workman himself, come to excuse himself to Mary and Co., for not applying to them before : and the long and the short is, he offers the Handlers the same as he has the Smiths, fifteen down, and to pay his natty money, but draw no scale, unless disabled. What d'ye say ? Yes, or no ?"

"I'll lay Mr. Little's proposal before the committee."

"Thank you, sir," said Little. "And, meantime, I suppose I may feel safe against violence, from the members of your union ?"

"Violence !" said Mr. Parkin, turning his eye inwards, as if he was interrogating the centuries. Then to Mr. Bayne, "Pray, sir, do you remember any deed of darkness that our union have ever committed, since we have been together ; and that is twelve years ?"

"*Well*, Mr. Parkin," said Bayne, "if you mean deeds of blood, and deeds of gunpowder, et cetera —why, no, not one: and it is greatly to your honor. But, mind you, if a master wants his tanks tapped and his hardening-liquor run into the shore, or his bellows to be ripped, his axle-nuts to vanish, his wheel-bands to go and hide in a drain or a church belfry, and his scythe-blades to dive into a wheel-dam, he has only to be wrong with your union, and he'll be accommodated as above. I speak from experience."

"Oh, rattening !" said Mr. Parkin. "That is a mighty small matter."

"It is small to you, that are not in the oven, where the bread is baked, or cooled, or burnt. But whatever parts the grindstones from the power, and the bellows from the air, and the air from the fire, makes a hole in the master's business to-day, and a hole in the workman's pocket that day six months. So, for Heaven's sake, let us be right with you. Little's is the most friendly and liberal offer that any workman ever made to any Union. Do, pray, close with it, and let us be at peace ; sweet—balmy—peace."

Parkin declared he shared that desire : but was not the committee. Then, to Henry: "I shall put your case as favorably as my conscience will let me. Meantime, of course, the matter rests as it is."

They then parted ; and Henry, as he returned home, thanked Bayne heartily. He said this second £15 had been a bitter pill at first ; but now he was glad he had offered it. "I would not leave Hillsborough for fifteen hundred pounds."

Two days after this promising interview with Mr. Parkin, Henry received a note, the envelope of which showed him it came from Mr. Jobson. He opened it eagerly, and with a good hope that its object was to tell him he was now a member of the Edge-Tool Forgers' Union.

The letter, however, ran thus :

"DEAR SIR,—I hear, with considerable surprise, that you continue to forge blades and make handles for Mr. Cheetham. On receipt of this information I went immediately to Mr. Parkin, and he assured me that he came to the same terms with you as I did. He says he intimated politely, but plainly, that he should expect you not to make any more carving-tool handles for Mr. Cheetham, till his committee had received your proposal. He now joins me in advising you to strike work for the present. Hillsborough is surrounded by beautiful scenes, which it might gratify an educated workman to inspect, during the unavoidable delay caused by the new and very important questions your case has raised.

"Yours obediently,   SAML. JOBSON.

"P.S.—A respectable workman was with me yesterday, and objected that you receive from Mr. Cheetham a higher payment than the list price. Can you furnish me with a reply to this, as it is sure to be urged at the trade meeting."

When he read this, Little's blood boiled, especially at the cool advice to lay down his livelihood, and take up scenery : and he dashed off a letter of defiance. He showed it to Bayne, and it went into the fire directly. "That is all right," said this worthy. "You have written your mind, like a man. Now sit down, and give them treacle for their honey—or you'll catch pepper."

Henry groaned, and writhed, but obeyed.

He had written his defiance in three minutes. It took him an hour to produce the following:

"DEAR SIR,—I am sorry for the misunderstanding. I did not, for a moment, attach that meaning to any thing that fell either from you or Mr. Parkin.

"I must now remind you that, were I to strike work entirely, Mr. Cheetham could discharge me, and even punish me, for breach of contract. All I can do is to work fewer hours than I have done: and I am sure you will be satisfied with that, if you consider that the delay in the settlement of this matter rests with you, and not with me.

"I am yours respectfully,
"HENRY LITTLE.

"I furnish you, as requested, with two replies to the objection of a respectable workman that I am paid above the list price.

"1.—To sell skilled labor below the statement price, is a just offense, and injury to trade. But to obtain above the statement price is to benefit trade. The high price, that stands alone to-day, will not stand alone forever. It gets quoted in bargains, and draws prices up to it. That has been proved a thousand times.

"2.—It is not under any master's skin to pay a man more than he is worth. If I get a high price, it is because I make a first-rate article. If a man has got superior knowledge, he is not going to give it away to gratify envious Ignorance."

To this, in due course, he received from Jobson the following:

"DEAR SIR,—I advised you according to my judgment and experience: but, doubtless, you are the best judge of your own affairs."

And that closed the correspondence with the Secretaries.

The gentle Jobson and the polite Parkin had retired from the correspondence with their air of mild regret and placid resignation just three days, when young Little found a dirty crumpled letter on his anvil, written in pencil. It ran thus:

"Turn up or youl wish you had droped it. Youl be made so as youl never do hands turn agin, an never know what hurt you.
(Signed) "MOONRAKER."

Henry swore.

When he had sworn, (and, as a Briton, I think he had denied himself that satisfaction long enough,) he caught up a strip of steel with his pincers, shoved it into the coals, heated it, and, in half a minute, forged two long steel nails. He then nailed this letter to his wall, and wrote under it in chalk, "I offer £10 reward to any one who will show me the coward who wrote this, but was afraid to sign it. The writing is peculiar, and can easily be identified."

He also took the knife that had been so ostentatiously fixed in his door, and carried it about him

night and day, with a firm resolve to use it in self-defense, if necessary.

And now the plot thickened: the decent workmen in Cheetham's works were passive; they said nothing offensive, but had no longer the inclination, even if they had the power, to interfere and restrain the lower workmen from venting their envy and malice. Scarcely a day passed without growls and scowls. But Little went his way haughtily, and affected not to see, nor hear them.

However, one 'day, at dinner-time, he happened, unluckily, to be detained by Bayne in the yard, when the men came out; and two or three of the roughs took this opportunity and began on him at once, in the Dash Dialect, of course; they knew no other.

A great burly forger, whose red matted hair was powdered with coal-dust, and his face bloated with habitual intemperance, planted himself insolently before Henry, and said, in a very loud voice, "How many more trade meetings are we to have for one —— knobstick?"

Henry replied, in a moment, "Is it my fault if your shilly-shallying committees can't say yes or no to £15. You'd say yes to it, wouldn't you, sooner than go to bed sober?"

This sally raised a loud laugh at the notorious drunkard's expense, and checked the storm, as a laugh generally does.

But men were gathering round, and a workman who had heard the raised voices, and divined the row, ran out of the works, with his apron full of blades, and his heart full of mischief. It was a grinder of a certain low type, peculiar to Hillsborough, but quite common there, where grinders are often the grandchildren of grinders. This degenerate face was more canine than human; sharp as a hatchet, and with forehead villainously low; hardly any chin; and—most characteristic trait of all—the eyes, pale in color, and tiny in size, appeared to have come close together, to consult, and then to have run back into the very skull, to get away from the sparks, which their owner, and his sire, and his grandsire, had been eternally creating.

This greyhound of a grinder flung down a lot of dull bluish blades, warm from the forge, upon a condemned grindstone that was lying in the yard; and they tinkled.

"—— me, if I grind cockney blades!" said he.

This challenge fired a sympathetic handlemaker. "Grinders are right," said he. "We must be a —— mean lot and all, to handle his —— work."

"He has been warned enough; but he heeds noane."

"Hustle him out o' works."

"Nay, hit him o'er th' head and fling him into shore."

With these menacing words, three or four roughs advanced on him, with wicked eyes; and the respectable workmen stood, like stone statues, in cold and terrible neutrality; and Henry, looking round, in great anxiety, found that Bayne had withdrawn.

He ground his teeth, and stepped back to the wall, to have all the assailants in the front. He was sternly resolute, though very pale, and, by a natural impulse, put his hand into his side-pocket, to feel if he had a weapon. The knife was there, the deadly blade with which his enemies themselves had armed him; and, to those who could read faces, there was death in the pale cheek and gleaming eye of this young man, so sorely tried.

At this moment, a burly gentleman walked into the midst of them, as smartly as Van Amburgh amongst his tigers, and said steadily, "What is to do now, lads?" It was Cheetham himself. Bayne knew he was in the office, and had run for him, in mortal terror, and sent him to keep the peace. "They insult me, sir," said Henry; "though I am always civil to them; and that grinder refuses to grind my blades, there."

"Is that so? Step out, my lad. Did you refuse to grind those blades?"

"Ay," said the greyhound-man, sullenly.

"Then put on your coat, and leave my premises this minute."

"He is entitled to a week's warning, Mr. Cheetham," said one of the decent workmen, respectfully, but resolutely; speaking now for the first time.

"You are mistaken, sir," replied Mr. Cheetham, in exactly the same tone. (No stranger could have divined the speakers were master and man.) "He has vitiated his contract by publicly refusing to do his work. He'll get nothing from me but his wages up to noon this day. But you can have a week's warning, if you want it."

"Nay, sir. I've nought against you, for my part. But they say it will come to that, if you don't turn Little up."

"Why, what's his fault? Come now; you are a man. Speak up."

"Nay, I've no quarrel with the man. But he isn't straight with the trade."

"That is the secretaries' fault, not mine," said Henry. "They can't see I've brought a new trade in, that hurts no old trade, and will spread, and bring money into the town."

"We are not so —— soft as swallow that," said the bloated smith. "Thou'st just come t' Hillsborough to learn forging, and when thou'st mastered that, off to London, and take thy —— trade with thee."

Henry colored to the brow at the inferior workman's vanity and its concomitant, detraction. But he governed himself, by a mighty effort, and said, "Oh, that's your grievance now, is it? Mr. Cheetham—sir—will you ask some respectable grinder to examine these blades of mine?"

"Certainly. You are right, Little. The man to judge a forger's work is a grinder, and not another forger. Reynolds, just take a look at them, will you?"

A wet grinder of a thoroughly different type and race from the greyhound, stepped forward. He was thick-set in body, fresh-colored, and of a square manly countenance. He examined the blades carefully, and with great interest.

"Well," said Henry, "were they forged by a smith, or a novice that is come here to learn anvil work?"

Reynolds did not reply to him, nor to Mr. Cheetham: he turned to the men. "Mates, I'm noane good at lying. Hand that forged these has nought to learn in Hillsbro', nor any other shop."

"Thank you, Mr. Reynolds," said Henry, in a choking voice. "That is the first gleam of justice that I—" He could say no more.

"Come, don't you turn soft for a word or two," said Cheetham. "You'll wear all this out in time. Go to the office. I have something to say to you."

The something was said. It amounted to this—"Stand by me, and I'll stand by you."

"Well, sir," said Henry, "I think I must leave you if the committees refuse my offer. It is hard for one man to fight a couple of trades in such a place as this. But I'm firm in one thing: until those that govern the unions say 'no' to my offer, I shall go on working, and the scum of the trades sha'n't frighten me away from my forge."

"That's right; let the blackguards bluster. Bayne tells me you have had another anonymous."

"Yes, sir."

"Well, look here: you must take care of yourself, outside the works; but I'll take care of you inside. Here, Bayne, write a notice that, if any man molests, intimidates, or affronts Mr. Little, in my works, I'll take him myself to the town-hall, and get him two months directly. Have somebody at the gate to put a printed copy of that into every man's hand as he leaves."

"Thank you, sir!" said Henry, warmly. "But ought not the police to afford me protection, outside?"

"The police! You might as well go to the beadle. No; change your lodging, if you think they know it. Don't let them track you home. Buy a brace of pistols, and, if they catch you in a dark place, and try to do you, give them a barrel or two before they can strike a blow. Not one of them will ever tell the police, not if you shot his own brother dead at that game. The law is a dead letter here, sir. You've nothing to expect from it, and nothing to fear."

"Good heavens! Am I in England?"

"In England? No. You are in Hillsborough."

This epigram put Cheetham in good humor with himself, and, when Henry told him he did not feel quite safe, even in his own forge, nor in his handling-room, and gave his reasons, "Oh," said cheerful Cheetham, "that is nothing. Yours is a box-lock; the blackguard will have hid in the works at night, and taken the lock off, left his writing, and then screwed the lock on again: that is nothing to any Hillsborough hand. But I'll soon stop that game. Go you to Chestnut street, and get two first-class Bramah locks. There's a pocket-knife forge up stairs, close to your handling-room. I'll send the pocket-knife hand down stairs, and you fasten the Bramah locks on both doors, and keep the keys yourself. See to that now at once: then your mind will be easy. And I shall be in the works all day now, and every day; come to me directly, if there is any thing fresh."

Henry's forge was cold, by this time; so he struck work, and spent the afternoon in securing his two rooms with the Bramah locks. He also took Cheetham's advice in another particular. Instead of walking home, he took a cab, and got the man to drive rapidly to a certain alley. There he left the cab, ran down the alley, and turned a corner, and went home round about. He doubled like a hare, and dodged like a criminal evading justice.

But the next morning he felt a pleasing sense of security when he opened his forge-room with the Bramah key, and found no letters nor threats of any kind had been able to penetrate.

Moreover, all this time you will understand he

was visiting "Woodbine Cottage" twice a week, and carving Grace Carden's bust.

Those delightful hours did much to compensate him for his troubles in the town, and were even of some service to him in training him to fence with the trades of Hillsborough: for at "Woodbine Villa" he had to keep an ardent passion within the strict bounds of reverence, and in the town he had constantly to curb another passion, wrath, and keep it within the bounds of prudence. These were kindred exercises of self-restraint, and taught him self-government beyond his years. But what he benefited most by, after all, was the direct and calming effect upon his agitated heart, and irritated nerves, that preceded, and accompanied, and followed these sweet, tranquilizing visits. They were soft, solacing, and soothing; they were periodical and certain. He could count on leaving his cares, and worries, twice every week, at the door of that dear villa; and, when he took them up again, they were no longer the same; heavenly balm had been shed over them, and over his boiling blood.

One Saturday he heard, by a side-wind, that the Unions at a general meeting had debated his case, and there had been some violent speeches, and no decision come to; but the majority adverse to him. This discouraged him sadly, and his yearning heart turned all the more towards his haven of rest, and the hours, few but blissful, that awaited him.

About 11 o'clock, that same day, the postman brought him a letter, so vilely addressed, that it had been taken to two or three places, on speculation, before it reached its destination.

Little saw at once it was another anonymous communication. But he was getting callous to these missives, and he even took it with a certain degree of satisfaction. "Well done, Bramah! Obliged to send their venom by post now." This was the feeling uppermost in his mind. In short, he opened the letter with as much contempt as anger.

But he had no sooner read the foul scrawl, than his heart died within him.

"Thou's sharp but not sharp enow. We know where thou goes courting up hill. Window is all glass and ripe for a Peter shall blow the house tatums. There's the stuff in Hillsbro and the men that have done others so, and will do her job as wells thine. Powders a good servant but a bad master.

"ONE WHO MEANS DOING WHAT HE SAYS."

At this diabolical threat, young Little leaned sick and broken over the handle of his bellows.

Then he got up, and went to Mr. Cheetham, and said, patiently, "Sir, I am sorry to say I must leave you this very day."

"Don't say that, Little, don't say that."

"Oh, it is with a heavy heart, sir; and I shall always remember your kindness. But a man knows when he is beat. And I'm beat now." He hung his head in silence awhile. Then he said, in a faint voice, "This is what has done it, sir," and handed him the letter.

Mr. Cheetham examined it, and said, "I am not surprised at your being taken aback by this. But it's nothing new to us; we have all been threatened in this form. Why, the very last time I fought the trades, my wife was threatened I should be brought home on a shutter, with my intestines sweeping the ground. That was the purport, only it was put vernacular and stronger. And they reminded me that the old gal's clothes (that is Mrs. Cheetham: she is only twenty-six, and the prettiest lass in Coventry, and has a row of ivories that would do your heart good: now these Hillsborough hags haven't got a set of front teeth among 'em, young or old). Well, they told me the old gal's clothes could easily be spoiled, and her doll's face and all, with a penn'orth of vitriol."

"The monsters!"

"But it was all brag. These things are threatened fifty times, for once they are done."

"I shall not risk it. My own skin, if you like. But not hers: never, Mr. Cheetham: oh, never; never!"

"Well, but," said Mr. Cheetham, "she is in no danger so long as you keep away from her. They might fling one of their petards in at the window, if you were there; but otherwise, never, in this world. No, no, Little, they are not so bad as that. They have blown up a whole household, to get at the obnoxious party; but they always make sure he is there first."

Bayne was appealed to, and confirmed this; and, with great difficulty, they prevailed on Little to remain with them, until the Unions should decide; and to discontinue his visits to the house on the hill in the mean time. I need hardly say they had no idea the house on the hill was "Woodbine Villa."

He left them, and, sick at heart, turned away from Heath Hill, and strolled out of the lower part of the town, and wandered almost at random, and sad as death.

He soon left the main road, and crossed a stile: it took him by the side of a babbling brook, and at the edge of a picturesque wood. Ever and anon he came to a water-wheel, and above the water-wheel a dam made originally by art, but now looking like a sweet little lake. They were beautiful places; the wheels and their attendant works were old and rugged, but picturesque and countrified; and the little lakes behind, fringed by the master-grinder's garden, were strangely peaceful and pretty. Here the vulgar labor of the grindstone was made beautiful and incredibly poetic.

"Ah!" thought poor Little, "how happy a workman must be that plies his trade here in the fresh air. And how unfortunate I am to be tied to a power-wheel, in that filthy town, instead of being here, where Nature turns the wheel, and the birds chirp at hand, and the scene and the air are all purity and peace."

One place of the kind was particularly charming. The dam was larger than most, and sloping grass on one side, cropped short by the grinder's sheep: on the other his strip of garden: and bushes and flowers hung over the edge and glassed themselves in the clear water. Below the wheel, and at one side, was the master grinder's cottage, covered with creepers.

But Henry's mind was in no state to enjoy these beauties. He envied them; and, at last, they oppressed him, and he turned his back on them, and wandered, disconsolate, home.

He sat down on a stool by his mother, and laid his beating temples on her knees.

"What is it, my darling?" said she softly.

"Well, mother, for one thing, the Unions are against me, and I see I shall have to leave Hillsborough, soon or late."

"Never mind, dear; happiness does not depend upon the place we live in: and oh, Henry, whatever you do, never quarrel with those terrible grinders and people. The world is wide. Let us go back to London; the sooner the better. I have long seen there was something worrying you. But Saturday and Monday—they used to be your bright days."

"It will come to that, I suppose," said Henry, evading her last observation. "Yes," said he, wearily, "it will come to that." And he sighed so piteously that she forbore to press him. She had not the heart to cross-examine her suffering child.

That evening, mother and son sat silent by the fire: Henry had his own sad and bitter thoughts; and Mrs. Little was now brooding over the words Henry had spoken in the afternoon; and presently her maternal anxieties found a copious vent. She related to him, one after another, all the outrages that had been perpetrated in Hillsborough, while he was a child, and had been, each in its turn, the town talk.

It was a subject on which, if her son had been older, and more experienced in her sex, he would have closed her mouth promptly, she being a woman whose own nerves had received so frightful a shock by the manner of her husband's death. But, inadvertently, he let her run on, till she told him how a poor grinder had been carried home to his wife, blinded and scorched with gunpowder, and another had been taken home, all bleeding, to his mother, so beaten and bruised with life-preservers, that he had lain between life and death for nine days, and never uttered one word all that time, in reply to all her prayers and tears.

Now Mrs. Little began these horrible narratives with a forced and unnatural calmness; but, by the time she got to the last, she had worked herself up to a paroxysm of sympathy with other wretched women in Hillsborough, and trembled all over, like one in an ague, for herself: and at last stretched out her shaking hands, and screamed to him, "Oh, Harry, Harry, have pity on your miserable mother! Think what these eyes of mine have seen—bleeding at my feet—there—there—I see it now"—(her eyes dilated terribly at the word)—"oh, promise me, for pity's sake, that these—same—eyes—shall never see *you* brought and laid down bleeding like *him!*" With this she went into violent hysterics, and frightened her son more than all the ruffians in the town had ever frightened him.

She was a long time in this pitiable condition, and he nursed her: but at last her convulsion ceased, and her head rested on her son's shoulder in a pitiable languor.

Henry was always a good son: but he never loved his mother so tenderly as he did this night. His heart yearned over this poor panting soul, so stately in form, yet so weak, so womanly, and lovable; his playmate in childhood, his sweet preceptor in boyhood; the best friend and most unselfish lover he had, or could ever hope to have, on earth; dear to him by her long life of loving sacrifice, and sacred by that their great calamity, which had fallen so much heavier on her than on him.

He soothed her, he fondled her, he kneeled at her feet, and promised her most faithfully he would never be brought home to her bruised or bleeding. No: if the Unions rejected his offer he would go back to London with her at once.

And so, thrust from Hillsborough by the trades, and by his fears for Miss Carden, and also drawn from it by his mother's terrors, he felt himself a feather on the stream of Destiny; and left off struggling: beaten, heart-sick, and benumbed, he let the current carry him like any other dead thing that drifts.

He still plied the hammer, but in a dead-alive way.

He wrote a few cold lines to Mr. Jobson, to say that he thought it was time for a plain answer to be given to a business proposal. But, as he had no great hope the reply would be favorable, he awaited it in a state bordering on apathy. And so passed a miserable week.

And all this time she, for whose sake he denied himself the joy and consolation of her company, though his heart ached and pined for it, had hard thoughts of him, and vented them too to Jael Dence.

The young are so hasty in all their judgments.

While matters were in this condition, Henry found, one morning, two fresh panes of glass broken in his window.

In these hardware works the windows seldom or never open: air is procured in all the rooms by the primitive method of breaking a pane here and a pane there; and the general effect is as unsightly as a human mouth where teeth and holes alternate. The incident therefore was nothing, if it had occurred in any other room; but it was not a thing to pass over in this room, secured by a Bramah lock, the key of which was in Henry's pocket: the panes must have been broken from the outside. It occurred to him directly that a stone had been thrown in with another threatening scrawl.

But, casting his eye all round, he saw nothing of the kind about.

. Then, for a moment, a graver suspicion crossed his mind: might not some detonating substance, of a nature to explode when trodden upon, have been flung in? Hillsborough excelled in devilries of this kind.

Henry thought of his mother, and would not treat the matter lightly or unsuspiciously. He stood still till he had lighted a lucifer match, and examined the floor of his room. Nothing.

He lighted a candle, and examined all the premises. Nothing.

But, when he brought his candle to the window, he made a discovery: the window had two vertical iron uprights, about three-quarters of an inch in circumference: and one of these revealed to his quick eye a bright horizontal line. It had been sawed with a fine saw.

Apparently an attempt had been made to enter his room from outside.

The next question was, had that attempt succeeded.

He tried the bar; it was not quite cut through.

He locked the forge up directly, and went to his handling room. There he remained till Mr. Cheetham entered the works; then he went to him, and begged him to visit his forge.

Mr. Cheetham came directly, and examined the place carefully.

He negatived, at once, the notion that any Hillsborough hand had been unable to saw through a bar of that moderate thickness. "No," said he, "they were disturbed, or else some other idea struck them all of a sudden; or else they hadn't given themselves time, and are coming again to-morrow. I hope they are. By six o'clock to-night, I'll have a common wooden shutter hung with six good hinges on each side, easy to open at the centre; only, across the centre, I'll fix a Waterloo cracker inside."

"A Waterloo cracker!"

"Ay, but such a one as you never saw. I shall make it myself. It shall be only four inches long, but as broad as my hand, and enough detonating powder in it to blow the shutter fifty feet into the air: and if there should be one of Jobson's lads behind the shutter at the time, why he'll learn flying, and nought to pay for wings."

"Why, sir, you are planning the man's death!"

"And what is *he* planning? Light your forge, and leave the job to me. I'm Hillsborough too: and they've put my blood up at last."

While Henry lighted his forge, Mr. Cheetham whipped out a rule, and measured the window exactly. This done, he went down the stairs, and crossed the yard to go to his office.

But, before he could enter it, a horrible thing occurred in the room he had just left; so horrible, it made him, brave as he was, turn and scream like a woman.

Some miscreant, by a simple but ingenious means, which afterwards transpired, had mixed a quantity of gunpowder with the smithy-slack or fine cinders of Henry's forge. The moment the forge was hot, the powder ignited with a tremendous thud, a huge mass of flame rushed out, driving the coals with it, like shot from a gun; Henry, scorched, blackened, and blinded, was swept, as by a flaming wind, against the opposite wall; then, yelling, and stark mad with fright (for nothing drives men out of their wits like an explosion in a narrow space), he sprang at the window, head foremost, and with such velocity that the sawed iron snapped like a stick of barley-sugar, and out he went head foremost; and this it was made Cheetham scream, to see him head downward, and the paving-stones below.

But the aperture was narrow: his body flew through, but his right arm went round the unbroken upright, and caught it in the bend of the elbow.

Then Cheetham roared, "Hold on, Little! Hold on, I tell you!"

The scared brain of a man accustomed to obey received the command almost without the mind; and the grinders and forgers, running wildly into the yard, saw the obnoxious workman, black as a cinder from head to foot, bleeding at the face from broken glass, hanging up there by one hand, moaning with terror, and looking down with dilating eye, while thick white smoke rushed curling out, as if his body was burning. Death by suffocation was at his back, and broken bones awaited him below.

CHAPTER VI.

At sight of this human cinder, hanging by one hand between two deaths, every sentiment but humanity vanished from the ruggedest bosom, and the skilled workmen set themselves to save their unpopular comrade with admirable quickness and judgment: two new wheel-bands, that had just come into the works, were caught up in a moment, and four workmen ran with them and got below the suspended figure: they then turned back to back, and, getting the bands over their shoulders, pulled hard against each other. This was necessary to straighten the bands: they weighed half a hundred weight each. Others stood at the centre of the bands, and directed Little where to drop, and stood ready to catch him should he be bound off them.

But now matters took an unexpected turn. Little, to all appearance, was blind and deaf. He hung there, moaning, and glaring, and his one sinewy arm supported his muscular but light frame almost incredibly. He was out of his senses, or nearly.

"Let thyself come, lad," cried a workman, "we are all right to catch thee."

He made no answer, but hung there glaring and moaning.

"The man will drop noane, till he swouns," said another, watching him keenly.

"Then get you closer to the wall, men," cried Cheetham, in great anxiety. "He'll come like a stone, when he does come." This injunction was given none too soon; the men had hardly shifted their positions, when Little's hand opened, and he came down like lead, with his hands all abroad, and his body straight; but his knees were slightly bent, and he caught the bands just below the knee, and bounded off them into the air, like a cricket-ball. But many hands grabbed at him, and the grinder Reynolds caught him by the shoulder, and they rolled on the ground together, very little the worse for that tumble. "Well done! well done!" cried Cheetham. "Let him lie, lads, he is best there for a while; and run for a doctor, one of you."

"Ay, run for Jack Doubleface," cried several voices at once.

"Now, make a circle, and give him air, men."

Then they all stood in a circle, and eyed the blackened and quivering figure with pity and sympathy, while the canopy of white smoke bellied overhead. Nor were those humane sentiments silent; and the roughs seemed to be even more overcome than the others: no brains were required to pity this poor fellow now; and so strong an appeal to their hearts, through their senses, roused their good impulses and rare sensibilities. Oh, it was strange to hear good and kindly sentiments come out in the Dash dialect.

"It's a —— shame!"

"There lies a good workman done for by some —— thief, that wasn't fit to blow his bellows, —— him!"

"Say he *was* a cockney, he was always —— civil."

"And life's as sweet to him as to any man in Hillsborough."

"Hold your —— tongue, he's coming to."

Henry did recover his wits enough to speak; and what do you think was his first word?

He clasped his hands together, and said,— "MY MOTHER! OH, DON'T LET HER KNOW!"

This simple cry went through many a rough heart; a loud gulp or two were heard soon after, and more than one hard and coaly cheek was channelled by sudden tears. But now a burly figure came rolling in; they drew back and silenced each other.—"The Doctor!" This was the remarkable person they called Jack Double-face. Nature had stuck a philosophic head, with finely-cut features, and a mouth brimful of finesse, on to a corpulent and ungraceful body, that yawed from side to side as he walked.

The man of art opened with two words. He looked up at the white cloud, which was now floating away; sniffed the air, and said, "Gunpowder!" Then he looked down at Little, and said, "Ah!" half dryly, half sadly. Indeed several sentences of meaning condensed themselves into that simple interjection. At this moment, some men, whom curiosity had drawn to Henry's forge, came back to say the forge had been blown up, and "the bellows torn limb from jacket, and the room strewed with ashes."

The doctor laid a podgy hand on the prisoner's wrist: the touch was light, though the fingers were thick and heavy. The pulse, which had been very low, was now galloping and bounding frightfully. "Fetch him a glass of brandy-and-water," said Dr. Amboyne. (There were still doctors in Hillsborough, though not in London, who would have had him bled on the spot.)

"Now, then, a surgeon! Which of you lads operates on the eye, in these works?"

A lanky file-cutter took a step forward. "I am the one that takes the motes out of their eyes."

"Then be good enough to show me his eye."

The file-cutter put out a hand with fingers prodigiously long and thin, and deftly parted both Little's eyelids with his finger and thumb, so as to show the whole eye.

"Hum!" said the Doctor, and shook his head.

He then patted the sufferer all over, and the result of that examination was satisfactory. Then came the brandy-and-water; and while Henry's teeth were clattering at the glass and he was trying to sip the liquid, Dr. Amboyne suddenly lifted his head, and took a keen survey of the countenances round him. He saw the general expression of pity on the rugged faces. He also observed one rough fellow who wore a strange wild look: the man seemed puzzled, scared, confused like one half awakened from some hideous dream. This was the grinder who had come into the works in place of the hand Cheetham had discharged for refusing to grind cockney blades.

"Hum!" said Dr. Amboyne, and appeared to be going into a brown study.

But he shook that off, and said briskly, "Now, then, what was his crime? Did he owe some mutual aid society six-and-fourpence?"

"That's right," said Reynolds, sullenly, "throw every thing on the Union. If we knew who it was, he'd lie by the side of this one in less than a minute, and, happen, not get up again so soon."

A growl of assent confirmed the speaker's words. Cheetham interposed and drew Amboyne aside, and began to tell him who the man was and what the dispute; but Amboyne cut the latter explanation short. "What," said he, "is this the carver whose work I saw up at Mr. Carden's?"

"This is the very man, no doubt."

"Why, he's a sculptor: Praxiteles in wood. A fine choice they have made for their gunpowder, a workman that did honor to the town."

A faint flush of gratified pride colored the ghastly cheek a moment.

"Doctor, shall I live to finish the bust?" said Henry, piteously.

"That and hundreds more, if you obey me. The fact is, Mr. Cheetham, this young man is not hurt, but his nerves have received a severe shock; and the sooner he is out of this place the better. Ah, there is my brougham at the gate. Come, put him into it, and I'll take him to the infirmary."

"No," said Little, "I won't go there; my mother would hear of it."

"Oh, then your mother is not to know?"

"Not for all the world! She has had trouble enough. I'll just wash my face and buy a clean shirt, and she'll never know what has happened. It would kill her. Oh, yes, it would kill her!"

The Doctor eyed him with warm approval. "You are a fine young fellow. I'll see you safe through this, and help you throw dust in your mother's eyes. If you go to her with that scratched face, we are lost. Come, get into my carriage, and home with me."

"Mayn't I wash my face first? And look at my shirt: as black as a cinder."

"Wash your face, by all means: but you can button your coat over your shirt."

The coat was soon brought, and so was a pail of water and a piece of yellow soap. Little dashed his head and face into the bucket, and soon inked all the water. The explosion had filled his hair with black dust, and grimed his face and neck like a sweep's. This ablution made him clean, but did not bring back his ruddy color. He looked pale and scratched.

The men helped him officiously into the carriage, though he could have walked very well alone.

Henry asked leave to buy a clean shirt. The Doctor said he would lend him one at home.

While Henry was putting it on Doctor Amboyne ordered his dog-cart instead of his brougham, and mixed some medicines. And soon Henry found himself seated in the dog-cart, with a warm cloak over him, and whisking over the stones of Hillsborough.

All this had been done so rapidly and unhesitatingly that Henry, injured and shaken as he was, had yielded passive obedience. But now he began to demur a little. "But where are we going, sir?" he asked.

"To change the air and the scene. I'll be frank with you—you are man enough to bear the truth —you have received a shock that will very likely bring on brain-fever, unless you get some sleep to-night. But you would not sleep in Hillsborough. You'd wake a dozen times in the night, trembling like an aspen leaf, and fancying you were blown up again."

"Yes, but my mother, sir! If I don't go home at seven o'clock, she'll find me out."

"If you went crazy wouldn't she find you out? Come, my young friend, trust to my experience, and to the interest this attempt to murder you, and your narrow escape, have inspired in me. When I have landed you in the Temple of Health, and just wasted a little advice on a pig-headed patient in the neighborhood (he is the squire of the place), I'll drive back to Hillsborough, and tell your mother some story or other: you and I will concoct that together as we go."

At this Henry was all obedience, and indeed thanked him, with the tears in his eyes, for his kindness to a poor stranger.

Dr. Amboyne smiled. "If you were not a stranger, you would know that saving cutlers' lives is my hobby, and one in which I am steadily resisted and defeated, especially by the cutlers themselves; why, I look upon you as a most considerate and obliging young man for indulging me in this way. If you had been a Hillsborough hand, you would insist upon a brain-fever, and a trip to the lunatic asylum, just to vex me, and hinder me of my hobby."

Henry stared. This was too eccentric for him to take it all in at once. "What!" said Dr. Amboyne, observing his amazement. "Did you never hear of Dr. Doubleface?"

"No, sir."

"Never hear of the corpulent lunatic, who goes about the city, chanting, like a cuckoo, 'Put yourself in his place—put yourself in her place— in their place?'"

"No, sir, I never did."

"Then such is fame. Well, never mind that just now; there's a time for every thing. Please observe that ruined house: the ancient family to whom it belongs are a remarkable example of the vicissitude of human affairs." He then told him the curious ups and downs of that family, which, at two distant periods, had held vast possessions in the county; but were now represented by the shell of one manor-house, and its dovecote, the size of a modern villa. Next he showed him an obscure battle-field, and told him that story, and who were the parties engaged; and so on. Every mile furnished its legend, and Dr. Amboyne related them all so graphically that the patient's mind was literally stolen away from himself. At last, after a rapid drive of eleven miles through the pure invigorating air, they made a sudden turn, and entered a pleasant and singularly rural village: they drew up at a rustic farmhouse, clad with ivy; and Dr. Amboyne said, "This is the temple: here you can sleep as safe from gunpowder as a field-marshal born."

The farmer's daughter came out, and beamed pleasure at sight of the doctor: he got down, and told her the case, privately, and gave her precise instructions. She often interrupted the narrative with "Lawkadaisies," and other rural interjections, and simple exclamations of pity. She promised faithful compliance with his orders.

He then beckoned Henry in, and said, "This picture of health was a patient of mine once, as you are now; there's encouragement for you. I put you under her charge. Get a letter written to your mother, and I'll come back for it in half an hour. You had a headache, and were feverish, so you consulted a doctor. He advised immediate rest and change of air, and he drove you at once to this village. Write you that, and leave the rest to me. We doctors are dissembling dogs. We have still something to learn in curing diseases; but at making light of them to the dying, and other branches of amiable mendacity, we are masters."

As soon as he was gone, the comely young hostess began on her patient. "Dear heart, sir, was it really you as was blowed up with gunpowder?"

"Indeed it was, and not many hours ago. It seems like a dream."

"Well, now, who'd think that, to look at you? Why, you are none the worse, forbye a scratch or two, and, dear heart, I've seen a young chap bring as bad home, from courting, in these parts; and wed the lass as marked him—within the year."

"Oh, it is not the scratches; but feel my hand, how it trembles. And it used to be as firm as a rock; for I never drink."

"So it do, I declare. Why, you do tremble all over; and no wonder, poor soul. Come you in this minut, and sit down a bit by the fire, while I go and make the room ready for you."

But, as soon as he was seated by the fire, the current began to flow again. "Well, I never liked Hillsborough folk much—poor, mean-visaged tykes they be—but now I do hate 'em. What, blow up a decent young man like you, and a well-favored, and hair like jet, and eyes in your head like sloes! But that's their ground of spite, I warrant me; the nasty, ugly, dirty dogs. Well, you may just snap your fingers at 'em all now. They don't come out so far as this; and, if they did, stouter men grows in this village than any in Hillsborough: and I've only to hold up my finger, for as little as I be, and they'd all be well ducked in father's horsepond, and then flogged home again with a good cart-whip well laid on. And, another thing, whatever we do, Squire, we will make it good in law: he is gentle, and we are simple; but our folk and his has stood by each other this hundred year and more. But, la, I run on so, and you was to write a letter again the doctor came back. I'll fetch you some paper this minut."

She brought him writing materials, and stood by him, with this apology, "If 'twas to your sweetheart, I'd be off. But 'tis to your mother." (With a side glance), "She have been a handsome woman in her day, I'll go bail."

"She is as beautiful as ever in my eyes," said Henry, tenderly. "And, oh, heaven! give me the sense to write to her without frightening her."

"Then I won't hinder you no more with my chat," said his hostess, with kindly good humor, and slipped away up stairs. She lighted a great wood fire in the bedroom, and laid the bed and the blankets all round it, and opened the window, and took the home-spun linen sheets out of a press, and made the room very tidy. Then she went down again, and the moment Henry saw her, he said: "I feel your kindness, Miss, but I don't know your name, nor where in the world I am." His hostess smiled. . "That is no secret. I'm Martha Dence—at your service: and this is Cairnhope town."

"Cairnhope!" cried Henry, and started back, so that his wooden chair made a loud creak upon the stones of the farmer's kitchen.

Martha Dence stared, but said nothing; for almost at that moment the Doctor returned, all in a hurry, for the letter.

Henry begged him to look at it, and see if it would do.

The Doctor read it. "Hum!" said he, "it is a very pretty, filial letter, and increases my interest in you; give me your hand: there. Well, it won't do: too shaky. If your mother once sees this, I may talk till doomsday, she'll not believe a word. You must put off writing till to-morrow night. Now give me her address, for I really must get home."

"She lives on the second floor, No. 13 Chettle Street."

"Her name?"

"Sir, if you ask for the lady that lodges on the second floor, you will be sure to see her."

Doctor Amboyne looked a little surprised, and not very well pleased, at what seemed a want of confidence. But he was a man singularly cautious and candid in forming his judgments; so he forbore all comment, and delivered his final instructions. "Here is a bottle containing only a few drops of faba Ignatii in water. It's an innocent medicine, and has sometimes a magical effect in soothing the mind and nerves. A table-spoonful three times a day. And *this* is a sedative, which you can take if you find yourself quite unable to sleep. But I wouldn't have recourse to it unnecessarily; for these sedatives are uncertain in their operation; and, when a man is turned upside down, as you have been, they sometimes excite. Have a faint light in your bedroom. Tie a cord to the bell-rope, and hold it in your hand all night. Fix your mind on that cord, and keep thinking, 'This is to remind me that I am eleven miles from Hillsborough, in a peaceful village, safe from all harm.' To-morrow, walk up to the top of Cairnhope Peak, and inhale the glorious breeze, and look over four counties. Write to your mother at night, and, meantime, I'll do my best to relieve her anxiety. Good-bye."

Memory sometimes acts like an old flint-gun: it hangs fire, yet ends by going off. While Dr. Amboyne was driving home, the swarthy, but handsome, features of the workman he had befriended seemed to enter his mind more deeply than during the hurry, and he said to himself, "Jet black hair; great black eyes; and olive skin; they are rare in these parts; and, somehow, they remind me a little of *her.*"

Then his mind went back, in a moment, over many years, to the days when he was stalwart, but not unwieldy, and loved a dark but peerless beauty, loved her deeply, and told his love, and was esteemed and pitied, but another was beloved.

And so sad, yet absorbing, was the retrospect of his love, his sorrow, and her own unhappy lot, that it blotted out of his mind, for a time, the very youth whose features and complexion had launched him into the past.

But the moment his horse's feet rang on the stones, this burly philosopher shook off the past, and set himself to recover lost time. He drove rapidly to several patients, and, at six o'clock, was at 13 Chettle Street, and asked for the lady on the second floor. "Yes, sir: she is at home," was the reply. "But I don't know; she lives very retired. She hasn't received any visits since they came. However, they rent the whole floor, and the sitting-room fronts you."

Dr. Amboyne mounted the stair and knocked at the door. A soft and mellow voice bade him enter. He went in, and a tall lady in black, with plain linen collar and wristbands, rose to receive him. They confronted each other. Time and trouble had left their trace, but there were the glorious eyes, and jet black hair, and the face, worn and pensive, but still beautiful. It was the woman he had loved, the only one.

"Mrs. Little!" said he, in an indescribable tone.

"Dr. Amboyne!"

For a few moments he forgot the task he had undertaken; and could only express his astonishment and pleasure at seeing her once more.

Then he remembered why he was there; and the office he had undertaken so lightly alarmed him now.

His first instinct was to gain time. Accordingly, he began to chide her gently for having resided in the town and concealed it from him; then, seeing her confused and uncomfortable at that reproach, and in the mood to be relieved by any change of topic, he glided off, with no little address, as follows:—"Observe the consequences: here have I been most despotically rusticating a youth who turns out to be your son."

"My son! is there any thing the matter with my son? Oh, Doctor Amboyne!"

"He must have been out of sorts, you know, or he would not have consulted me," replied the Doctor, affecting candor.

"Consult! Why, what has happened? He was quite well when he left me this morning."

"I doubt that. He complained of headache and fever. But I soon found his *mind* was worried. A misunderstanding with the trades! I was very much pleased with his face and manner; my carriage was at the door; his pulse was high, but there was nothing that country air and quiet will not restore. So I just drove him away, and landed him in a farmhouse."

Mrs. Little's brow flushed at this. She was angry. But, in a nature so gentle as hers, anger soon gave way. She turned a glance of tearful and eloquent reproach on Doctor Amboyne. "The first time we have ever been separated since he was born," said she, with a sigh.

Dr. Amboyne's preconceived plan broke down that moment. He said, hurriedly,

"Take my carriage, and drive to him. Better do that than torment yourself."

"Where is he?" asked the widow, brightening up at the proposal.

"At Cairnhope."

At this word, Mrs. Little's face betrayed a series of emotions: first confusion, then astonishment, and at last a sort of superstitious alarm. "At Cairnhope?" she faltered at last. "My son at Cairnhope?"

"Pray do not torment yourself with fancies," said the Doctor. "All this is the merest accident—the simplest thing in the world. I cured

ing who he was. Go to him, if you like. But, frankly, as his physician, I would rather you did not. Never do a wise thing by halves. He ought to be entirely separated from all his cares, even from yourself (who are doubtless one of them), for five or six days. He needs no other medicine but that, and the fine air of Cairnhope."

IT WAS THE WOMAN HE HAD LOVED, THE ONLY ONE.

Patty Dence of diphtheria, when it decimated the village. She and her family are grateful; the air of Cairnhope has a magic effect on people who live in smoke, and Martha and Jael let me send them out an invalid now and then to be reinvigorated. I took this young man there, not know-

"Then somebody must see him every day, and tell me. Oh! Doctor Amboyne, this is the beginning: what will the end be? I am miserable."

"My man shall ride there every day, and see him, and bring you back a letter from him."

"Your man!" said Mrs. Little, a little haughtily.

Doctor Amboyne met her glance. "If there was any ground for alarm, should I not go myself every day?" said he, gravely, and even-tenderly.

"Forgive me," said the widow, and gave him her hand with a sweet and womanly gesture.

The main difficulty was now got over; and Dr. Amboyne was careful not to say too much, for he knew that his tongue moved among pitfalls.

As Dr. Amboyne descended the stairs, the landlady held a door ajar, and peeped at him, according to a custom of such delicate-minded females as can neither restrain their curiosity nor indulge it openly. Dr. Amboyne beckoned to her, and asked for a private interview. This was promptly accorded.

"Would ten guineas be of any service to you, madam?"

"Eh, dear, that it would, sir. Why, my rent is just coming due."

Under these circumstances, the bargain was soon struck. Not a syllable about the explosion at Cheetham's was to reach the second-floor lodger's ears, and no Hillsborough journal was to mount the stairs until the young man's return. If inquired for, they were to be reported all sold out, and a London journal purchased instead.

Having secured a keen and watchful ally in this good woman, who, to do her justice, showed a hearty determination to earn her ten guineas, Dr. Amboyne returned home, his own philosophic pulse beating faster than it had done for some years.

He had left Mrs. Little grateful, and, apparently, in good spirits; but, ere he had been gone an hour, the bare separation from her son overpowered her, and a host of vague misgivings tortured her, and she slept but little that night. By noon next day she was thoroughly miserable; but Dr. Amboyne's man rode up to the door in the afternoon with a cheerful line from Henry.

"All right, dear mother. Better already. Letter by post.   HENRY."

She detained the man, and made up a packet of things for Cairnhope, and gave him five shillings to be sure and take them.

This was followed by a correspondence, a portion of which will suffice to eke out the narrative.

"DEAREST MOTHER,—I slept ill last night, and got up aching from head to foot, as if I had been well hided. But they sent me to the top of Cairnhope Peak, and, what with the keen air and the glorious view, I came home and ate like a hog. That pleased Martha Dence, who kept putting me slices off her own plate, till I had to cry quarter. As soon as I have addressed this letter, I'm off to bed, for it is all I can do not to fall asleep sitting.

"I am safe to be all right to-morrow, so pray don't fret. I am, dear mother," etc., etc.

"DEAREST MOTHER,—I hope you are not fretting about me. Dr. Amboyne promised to stop all that. But do write, and say you are not fretting and fancying all manner of things at my cutting away so suddenly. It was the Doctor's doing. And, mother, I shall not stay long away

from you, for I slept twelve hours at a stretch last night, and now I'm another man. But really, I think the air of that Cairnhope Peak would cure a fellow at his last gasp.

"Thank you for the linen, and the brushes, and things. But you are not the sort to forget any thing a fellow might want," etc.

"No, my darling son. Be in no hurry to leave Cairnhope. Of course, love, I was alarmed at first; for I know doctors make the best of every thing; and then the first parting!—that is always a sorrowful thing. But, now you are there, I beg you will stay till you are quite recovered. Your letters are a delight, and one I could not have, and you as well, you know.

"Since you are at Cairnhope,—how strange that seems,—pray go and see the old church, where your forefathers are buried. There are curious inscriptions, and some brasses nobody could decipher when I was a girl; but perhaps you might, you are so clever. Your grandfather's monument is in the chancel: I want you to see it. Am I getting very old, that my heart turns back to these scenes of my youth?

"P.S.—Who is this Martha Dence?"

"DEAR MOTHER,—Martha Dence is the farmer's daughter I lodge with. She is not so pretty as her sister Jael that is with Miss Carden; but she is a comely girl, and as good as gold, and bespoke by the butcher. And her putting slices from her plate to mine is a village custom, I find.

"Mother, the people here are wonderfully good and simple. First of all, there's farmer Dence, with his high bald head, like a patriarch of old; and he sits and beams with benevolence, but does not talk much. But he lets me see I can stay with him six years, if I choose. Then, there's Martha, hospitality itself, and ready to fly at my enemies like a mastiff. She is a little hot in the temper; feathers up in a moment; but, at a soft word, they go down again as quick. Then, there's the village blacksmith. I call him 'The gentle giant.' He is a tremendous fellow in height, and size, and sinew; but such a kind, sweet-tempered chap. He could knock down an ox, yet he wouldn't harm a fly. I am his idol: I sauntered in to his smithy, and forged him one or two knives; and of course he had never seen the hammer used with that nicety; but instead of hating me, as the bad forgers in Hillsborough do, he regularly worships me, and comes blushing up to the farmhouse after hours, to ask after me and get a word with me. He is the best whistler in the parish, and sometimes we march down the village at night, arm-in-arm, whistling a duet. This charms the natives so that we could take the whole village out at our heels, and put them down in another parish. But the droll thing is, they will not take me for what I am. My gentle giant would say 'Sir' till I pretended to be affronted; the women and girls will bob me courtesies, and the men and white-headed boys will take off their hats and pull their front hair to me. If a skilled workman wants to burst with vanity, let him settle in Cairnhope."

[EXTRACT.]

"Martha Dence and I have had words, and what do you think it was about? I happened to let out my opinion of Mr. Raby. Mother, it was like setting a match to a barrel of gunpowder. She turned as red as fire, and said, 'Who be you that speaks against Raby to Dence?'

"I tried to pacify her, but it was no use. 'Don't speak to me,' said she. 'I thought better of you. You and I are out.' I bowed before the storm, and, to give her time to cool, I obeyed your wishes, and walked to Cairnhope old church. What a curious place! But I could not get in; and, on my return, I found Mr. Raby keeps the key. Now, you can't do a thing here, or say a word, but what it is known all over the village. So Martha Dence meets me at the door, and says, very stiffly, she thought I might have told her I wanted to see the old church. I pulled a long, penitent face, and said, 'Yes; but, unfortunately, I was out of her good books, and had orders not to speak to her.' 'Nay,' says she, 'life is too short for long quarrels. You are a stranger, and knew no better.' Then she told me to wait five minutes while she put on her bonnet, as she calls it. Well, I waited the five-and-forty minutes, and she put on her bonnet, and so many other smart things, that we couldn't possibly walk straight up to the old church. We had to go round by the butcher's shop, and order half a pound of suet; no less. 'And bring it yourself, this evening,' said I, 'or it might get lost on the road.' Says the butcher, 'Well, sir, that is the first piece of friendly advice any good Christian has bestowed—' But I heard no more, owing to Martha chasing me out of the shop.

"To reach the old church we had to pass the old ruffian's door. Martha went in; I sauntered on, and she soon came after me, with the key in her hand. 'But,' said she, 'he told me if my name hadn't been Dence he wouldn't trust me with it, though I went on my bended knees.'

"We opened the church-door, and I spent an hour inside, examining and copying inscriptions for you. But, when I came to take up a loose brass, to try and decipher it, Martha came screaming at me, 'Oh, put it down! put it down! I pledged my word to Squire you should not touch them brasses.' What could I do, mother? The poor girl was in an agony. This old ruffian has, somehow, bewitched her, and her father too, into a sort of superstitious devotion that I can't help respecting, unreasonable as it is. So I dropped the brass, and took to reflecting. And I give you my thoughts.

"What a pity and a shame that a building of this size should lie idle! If it was mine I would carefully remove all the monuments, and the dead bones, et cetera, to the new church, and turn this old building into a factory, or a set of granaries, or something useful. It is as great a sin to waste bricks and mortar as it is bread," etc.

"MY DEAR HARRY,—Your dear sprightly letters delight me, and reconcile me to the separation; for I see that your health is improving every day, by your gayety; and this makes me happy, though I can not quite be gay.

"Your last letter was very amusing, yet, somehow, it set me thinking, long and sadly; and some gentle remarks from Dr. Amboyne (he called yesterday) have also turned my mind the same way. Time has softened the terrible blow that estranged my brother and myself, and I begin to ask myself, was my own conduct perfect? was my brother's quite without excuse? I may have seen but

one side, and been too hasty in judging him. At all events, I would have you, who are a man, think for yourself, and not rush into too harsh a view of that unhappy quarrel. Dearest, family quarrels are family misfortunes: why should they go down to another generation? You frighten me, when you wonder that Nathan and his family (I had forgotten his name was Dence) are attached to Mr. Raby. Why, with all his faults, my brother is a chivalrous, high-minded gentleman; his word is his bond, and he never deserts a friend, however humble; and I have heard our dear father say that, for many generations, uncommon acts of kindness had passed between that family of yeomen and the knights and squires of Raby.

"And now, dear, I am going to be very foolish. But, if these Dences are as great favorites with him as they were with my father, she could easily get you into the house some day, when he is out hunting; and I do want you to see one thing more before you come back from Cairnhope—your mother's picture. It hangs, or used to hang, in the great dining-room, nearly opposite the fireplace.

"I blush at my childishness, but I should like my child to see what his mother was, when she brought him into the world, that sad world in which he has been her only joy and consolation.

"P.S.—What an idea! Turn that dear old church into a factory! But you are a young man of the day. And a wonderful day it is; I can not quite keep up with it."

"DEAR MOTHER,—I have been there. Mr. Raby is a borough magistrate, as well as a county justice; and was in Hillsborough all day today. Martha Dence took me to Raby Hall, and her name was a passport. When I got to the door, I felt as if something pulled me, and said, 'It's an enemy's house; don't go in.' I wish I had obeyed the warning; but I did not.

"Well, I have seen your portrait. It is lovely. It surpasses any woman I ever saw. And it must have been your image, for it is very like you now, only in the bloom of your youth.

"And now, dear mother, having done something for you, quite against my own judgment, and my feelings too, please do something for me. Promise me never to mention Mr. Raby's name to me again, by letter, or by word of mouth either. He is not a gentleman: he is not a man; he is a mean, spiteful, cowardly cur. I'll keep out of his way, if I can; but if he gets in mine, I shall give him a devilish good hiding, then and there, and I'll tell him the reason why; and I will not tell you.

"Dear mother, I did intend to stay till Saturday, but, after this, I shall come back to you tomorrow. My own sweet dove of a mammy; who but a beast could hurt or affront you?

"So no more letters from your dutiful and affectionate son,   HARRY."

Next day young Little took leave of his friends in Cairnhope, with a promise to come over some Sunday, and see them all. He borrowed a hooked stick of his devotee, the blacksmith, and walked off with his little bundle over his shoulder, in high health and spirits, and ripe for any thing.

Some successful men are so stout-hearted, their minds seem never to flinch. Others are elastic; they give way, and appear crushed; but, let the

3

immediate pressure be removed, they fly back again, and their enemy finds he has not gained an inch. Henry's was of this sort; and, as he swung along through the clear brisk air, the world seemed his football once more.

This same morning Jael Dence was to go to Cairnhope, at her own request.

She packed her box, and corded it, and brought it down herself, and put it in the passage, and the carrier was to call for it at one. As for herself, four miles of omnibus, and the other seven on foot, was child's play to her, whose body was as lusty and active as her heart was tender and clinging.

She came in to the drawing-room, with her bonnet and shawl on, and the tear in her eye, to bid Miss Carden good-bye. Two male friends would have parted in five minutes; but this pair were a wonderful time separating, and still there was always something to say, that kept Grace detaining, or Jael lingering; and, when she had been going, going, going, for more than half an hour, all of a sudden she cried out, "Oh! There he is!" and flushed all over.

"Who?" asked Grace, eagerly.

"The dark young man. He is at the door now, Miss.—And me going away," she faltered.

"Well then, why go till he has paid his visit? Sit down. You needn't take off your bonnet."

Miss Carden then settled herself, took up her work, and prepared to receive her preceptor as he deserved, an intention she conveyed to Jael by a glance, just as Henry entered blooming with exercise and the keen air, and looking extremely handsome and happy.

His reception was a chilling bow from Miss Carden, and from Jael a cheek blushing with pleasure at the bare sight of him, but an earnest look of mild reproach. It seemed cruel of him to stay away so long, and then come just as she was going.

This reception surprised Henry, and disappointed him; however he constrained himself, and said rather coldly, that some unpleasant circumstances had kept him away; but he hoped now to keep his time better.

"Oh, pray consult your own convenience entirely," said Miss Carden. "Come, when you have nothing better to do; that is the understanding."

"I should be always coming, at that rate."

Grace took no notice. "Would you like to see how I look with my one eyebrow?" said she. "Jael, please fetch it."

While Jael was gone for the bust, Henry took a humbler tone, and in a low voice began to excuse his absence; and I think he would have told the real truth, if he had been encouraged a little; but he was met with a cold and withering assurance that it was a matter of no consequence. Henry thought this unfair, and, knowing in his own heart it was ungrateful, he rebelled. He bit his lip, sat down as gloomy as the grave, and resumed his work, silent and sullen.

As for Jael, she brought in the bust, and then sat down with her bonnet on, quaking; for she felt sure that, in such a dismal dearth of conversation, Miss Carden would be certain to turn round very soon, and say, "Well, Jael, you can go now."

But this Quaker's meeting was interrupted by a doctor looking in to prescribe for Miss Carden's

cold. The said cold was imperceptible to vulgar eyes, but Grace had detected it, and had written to her friend, Dr. Amboyne, to come and make it as imperceptible to herself as to the spectator.

In rolled the Doctor, and was not a little startled at sight of Little.

"Hallo!" cried he. "What, cured already? Cairnhope forever!" He then proceeded to feel his pulse instead of Miss Carden's, and inspect his eye, at which Grace Carden stared.

"What, is he unwell?"

"Why, a man does not get blown up with gunpowder without some little disturbance of the system."

"Blown up with gunpowder! What *do* you mean?"

"What, have you not heard about it? Don't you read the newspapers?"

"No; never."

"Merciful powers! But has he not told you?"

"No; he tells us nothing."

"Then I'll tell you. It is of no use your making faces at me. There is no earthly reason why *she* should be kept in the dark. These Hillsborough trades want to drive this young man out of the town: why—is too long and intricate for you to follow. He resists this tyranny, gently, but firmly."

"I'd resist it furiously," said Grace.

"The consequence is, they wrote him several threatening letters; and, at last, some caitiff put gunpowder into his forge; it exploded, and blew him out of a second-floor window."

"Oh! oh!" screamed Grace Carden and Jael; and by one womanly impulse they both put their hands before their faces, as if to shut out the horrible picture.

"What is that for?" said the Doctor. "You see he is all right now. But, I promise you, he cut a very different figure when I saw him directly afterwards; he was scorched as black as a coal—"

"Oh, Doctor, don't; pray don't. Oh, sir, why did you not tell me?"

"And his face bleeding," continued the merciless Doctor.

"Oh dear! oh dear!" And the sweet eyes were turned, all swimming in water, upon Henry, with a look of angelic pity.

"His nerves were terribly shaken, but there were no bones broken. I said to myself, 'He must sleep or go mad, and he will not sleep in the town that has blown him up.' I just drove the patient off to peace and pure air, and confided him to one of the best creatures in England—Martha Dence."

Jael uttered an exclamation of wonder, which drew attention to her and her glowing cheeks.

"Oh yes, Miss Jael," said Henry, "I was going to tell you. I have been a fortnight with your people, and, if I live a hundred years, I shall never forget their goodness to me. God bless them."

"'Twas the least they could do," said Jael, softly.

"What a pity you are going out. I should have liked to talk to you about your father, and Martha, and George the blacksmith. Doctor, who would live in a town after Cairnhope?"

Jael's fingers trembled at her bonnet-strings,

and, turning a look of piteous supplication on Grace, she faltered out, "If you please, Miss, might I stay over to-day?"

"Of course. And then he will tell you all about your people, and that will do just as well as you going to see them; and better."

Off came Jael's bonnet with wonderful celerity.

"Get the whole story out of him," said Dr. Amboyne. "It is well worth your attention. As for me, I must go as soon as I have prescribed for you. What is the matter?"

"The matter is that there's nothing the matter; prescribe for that. And that I'm a goose—prescribe for that—and don't read the newspapers;—prescribe for that."

"Well, then, I prescribe the *Hillsborough Liberal.* It has drawn a strong picture of this outrage, and shown its teeth to the trades. And, if I might advise a lady of your age and experience, I would say, in future always read the newspapers. They are, compared with books, what machinery is compared with hand-labor. But, in this one instance, go to the fountain-head, and ask Mr. Henry Little there, to tell you his own tragedy, with all the ins and outs."

"Ah! if he would," said Grace, turning her eyes on Henry. "But he is not so communicative to poor us. Is he, Jael?"

"No, Miss."

"He never even told us his name. Did he, Jael?"

"No, Miss. He is very close."

"Open him then," said the Doctor. "Come, come, there are a pair of you; and evidently disposed to act in concert; if you can not turn a man inside out, I disown you; you are a discredit to your sex." He then shook hands with all three of them, and rolled away.

"Jael," said Miss Carden, "oblige me by ringing the bell."

A servant entered.

"Not at home to any human creature," said the young lady.

The servant retired.

"And, if they see me at the window, all the worse—for *them.* Now, Mr. Little?"

Henry complied, and told the whole story, with the exception of the threat to his sweetheart; and passed two delightful hours. Who is so devoid of egotism as not to like to tell his own adventures to sympathizing beauty? He told it in detail, and even read them portions of the threatening letters; and, as he told it, their lovely eyes seemed on fire; and they were red, and pale, by turns. He told it, like a man, with dignity, and sobriety, and never used an epithet. It was Miss Carden who supplied the "Monsters!" "Villains!" "Cowards!" "Wretches!" at due intervals. And once she started from her seat, and said she could not bear it. "I see through it all," she cried. "That Jobson is a hypocrite; and he is at the bottom of it all. I hate him; and Parkin worse. As for the assassin. I hope God, who saw him, will punish him. What I want to do is to kill Jobson and Parkin, one after another; kill them—kill them—kill them—I'll tell papa."

As for Jael, she could not speak her mind, but she panted heavily, and her fingers worked convulsively, and clutched themselves very tight at last.

When he had done his narrative, he said sadly, "I despise these fellows as much as you do; but they are too many for me. I am obliged to leave Hillsborough."

"What, let the wretches drive you away? I would never do that—if I was a man."

"What would you do, then?" asked Henry his eye sparkling.

"Do? Why fight them; and beat them; and kill them. It is not as if they were brave men. They are only cunning cowards. I'd meet cunning with cunning. I'd outwit them somehow. I'd change my lodging every week, and live at little inns and places. I'd lock up every thing I used, as well as the rooms. I'd consult wiser heads, the editor of the *Liberal,* and the Head of the police. I'd carry fire-arms, and have a body-guard, night and day; but they should never say they had frightened me out of Hillsborough—if I was a man."

"You are right," cried Henry. "I'll do all you advise me, and I won't be driven out of this place. I love it. I'll live in it, or I'll die in it. I'll never leave it."

This was almost the last word that passed this delightful afternoon, when the sense of her own past injustice, the thrilling nature of the story told by the very sufferer, and, above all, the presence and the undisguised emotion of another sympathizing woman, thawed Grace Carden's reserve, warmed her courage, and carried her, quite unconsciously, over certain conventional bounds, which had, hitherto, been strictly observed in her intercourse with this young workman.

Henry himself felt that this day was an era in his love. When he left the door, he seemed to tread on air. He walked to the first cab-stand, took a conveyance to his mother's door, and soon he was locked in her arms.

She had been fretting for hours at his delay; but she never let him know it. The whole place was full of preparations for his comfort, and certain delicacies he liked were laid out on a little side-board, and the tea-things set, including the silver teapot, used now on high occasions only.

She had a thousand questions to ask, and he to answer. And, while he ate, the poor woman leaned back, and enjoyed seeing him eat; and, while he talked, her fine eyes beamed with maternal joy. She revelled deliciously in his health, his beauty, and his safe return to her; and thought, with gentle complacency, that they should soon return to London together.

In the morning, she got out a large light box, and said, "Harry, dear, I suppose I may as well begin to pack up. You know I take longer than you do."

Henry blushed. "Pack up?" said he, hesitatingly. "We are not going away."

"Not going away, love? Why you agreed to leave, on account of those dreadful Unions."

"Oh, I was ill, and nervous, and out of spirits; but the air of Cairnhope has made a man of me. I shall stay here, and make our fortune."

"But the air of Cairnhope has not made you friends with the Unions." She seemed to reflect a moment, then asked him at what time he had left Cairnhope.

"Eleven o'clock."

"Ah! And who did you visit before you came to me?"

"You question me like a child, mother."

"Forgive me, dear. I will answer my own question. You called on some one who gave you bad advice."

"Oh, did I ?"

"On some woman."

"Say, a lady."

"What does that matter to me ?" cried Mrs. Little, wildly. "They are all my enemies. And this one is yours. It is a woman, who is not your mother, for she thinks more of herself than of you."

CHAPTER VII.

HENRY had now to choose between his mother's advice and Miss Carden's commands; and this made him rather sullen and irritable. He was glad to get out of his mother's house, and went direct to the works. Bayne welcomed him warmly, and, after some friendly congratulations and inquiries, pulled out two files of journals, and told him he had promised to introduce him to the editor of the *Liberal*. He then begged Henry to wait in the office, and read the files—he would not be gone many minutes.

The *Constitutional* gave a dry narrative of the outrage, and mourned the frequency of such incidents.

The *Liberal* gave a dramatic narrative, and said the miscreant must have lowered himself by a rope from the parapet, and passed the powder inside without entering. "He perilled his life to perpetrate this crime; and he also risked penal servitude for ten years. That he was not deterred by the double risk, proves the influence of some powerful motive; and that motive must have been either a personal feud of a very virulent kind, or else trade fanaticism. From this alternative there is no escape."

Next day, both journals recorded a trade-meeting at "The Rising Sun." Delegates from the Edge-Tool Forgers' Union, and the Edge-Tool Handlers' Union, with some other representatives of Hillsborough Unions, were present, and passed a resolution repudiating, with disgust, the outrage that had been recently committed, and directed their secretaries to offer a reward of twenty pounds, the same to be paid to any person who would give such information as should lead to the discovery of the culprit.

On this the *Constitutional* commented as follows :—"Although we never for a moment suspected these respectable Unions of conniving at this enormity, yet it is satisfactory to find them, not merely passive spectators, but exerting their energy, and spending their money, in a praiseworthy endeavor to discover and punish the offenders."

Henry laid down the paper, and his heart felt very warm to Jobson and Parkin. "Come," said he, "I am glad of that. They are not half a bad sort, those two, after all."

Then he took up the *Liberal*, and being young and generous, felt disgusted at its comment:

"This appears very creditable to the two Unions in question. But, unfortunately, long experience proves that these small rewards never lead to any discovery. They fail so invariably, that the Unions do not risk a shilling by proffering them. In dramatic entertainments the tragedy is followed by a farce : and so it is with these sanguinary crimes in Hillsborough ; they are always followed by repudiation, and offers of a trumpery reward quite disproportionate to the offense, and the only result of the farce is to divert attention from the true line of inquiry as to who enacted the tragedy. The mind craves novelty, and perhaps these delegates will indulge that desire by informing us for once, what was the personal and Corsican feud which led—as they would have us believe—to this outrage ; and will, at the same time, explain to us why these outrages with gunpowder have never, either in this or in any preceding case, attacked any but non-union men."

When Henry had read thus far, the writer of the leader entered the room with Mr. Bayne.

A gentleman not above the middle height, but with a remarkable chest, both broad and deep ; yet he was not unwieldy, like Doctor Amboyne, but clean-built, and symmetrical. An agreeable face, with one remarkable feature, a mouth full of iron resolution, and a slight humorous dimple at the corners.

He shook hands with Henry, and said, "I wish to ask you a question or two, in the way of business : but first let me express my sympathy, as a man, and my detestation of the ruffians, that have so nearly victimized you."

This was very hearty, and Henry thanked him, with some emotion. "But, sir," said he, "if I am to reply to your questions, you must promise me you will never publish my name."

"It is on account of his mother," whispered Bayne.

"Yes, sir. It was her misfortune to lose my father by a violent death, and of course you may imagine—"

"Say no more," said Mr. Holdfast : "your name shall not appear. And—let me see—does your mother know you work here ?"

"Yes, she does."

"Then we had better keep Cheetham's name out as well."

"Oh, thank you, sir, thank you. Now I'll answer any questions you like."

"Well, then, I hear this outrage was preceded by several letters. Could I see them ?"

"Certainly. I carry mine always in my pocket, for fear my poor mother should see them : and, Mr. Bayne, you have got Cheetham's ?"

In another minute the whole correspondence was on the table, and Mr. Holdfast laid it out in order, like a map, and went through it, taking notes. "What a comedy," said he. "All but the denouement. Now, Mr. Bayne, can any other manufacturers show me a correspondence of this kind ?"

"Is there one that can't ? There isn't a power-wheel, or a water-wheel, within eight miles of Hillsborough, that can't show you just such a correspondence as this ; and rattening, or worse, at the tail of it."

Mr. Holdfast's eye sparkled like a diamond. "I'll make the round," said he. "And, Mr. Little, perhaps you will be kind enough to go with me, and let me question you, on the road. I have no sub-editor ; no staff ; I carry the whole journal on my head. Every day is a hard race between Time and me, and not a minute to spare."

Mr. Cheetham was expected at the works this afternoon : so Henry, on leaving Mr. Holdfast, returned to them, and found him there with Bayne, looking, disconsolately, over a dozen orders for carving-tools.

"Glad to see you again, my lad," said Cheetham. "Why, you look all the better."

"I'm none the worse, sir."

"Come to take your balance and leave me?" This was said half plaintively, half crossly.

"If you wish it, sir."

"Not I. How is it to be?"

"Well, sir, I say to you what you said to me the other day, Stick to me, and I'll stick to you."

"I'll stick to you."

Bayne held up his hands piteously to them both.

"What, sir?" faltered he, turning to Cheetham, "after all your experience!" then to Henry, "What, fight the trades, after the lesson they have given you?"

"I'll fight them all the more for that," said Henry, grinding his teeth; "fight them till all is blue."

"So will I. That for the trades!"

"Heaven help you both!" groaned Bayne, and looked the picture of despair.

"You promised me shutters, with a detonator, sir."

"Ay, but you objected."

"That was before they blew me up."

"Just so. Shutters shall be hung to-morrow; and the detonators I'll fix myself."

"Thank you, sir. Would you mind engaging a watchman?"

"Hum? Not—if you will share the expense."

"I'll pay one-third."

"Why should I pay two-thirds? It is not like shutters and Bramah locks: they are property. However, he'll be good against rattening; and you have lost a fortnight, and there are a good many orders. Give me a good day's work, and we won't quarrel over the watchman." He then inquired, rather nervously, whether there was any thing more.

"No, sir: we are agreed. And I'll give you good work, and full time."

The die was cast, and now he must go home and face his mother. For the first time this many years he was half afraid to go near her. He dreaded remonstrances and tears: tears that he could not dry; remonstrances that would worry him, but could not shake him.

This young man, who had just screwed his physical courage up to defy the redoubtable Unions had a fit of moral cowardice, and was so reluctant to encounter the gentlest woman in England, that he dined at a chop-house, and then sauntered into a music-hall, and did not get home till past ten, meaning to say a few kind, hurried words, then yawn, and slip to bed.

But, meantime, Mrs. Little's mind had not been idle. She had long divined a young rival in her son's heart, and many a little pang of jealousy had traversed her own. This morning, with a quickness which may seem remarkable to those who have not observed the watchful keenness of maternal love, she had seen that her rival had worked upon Henry to resign his declared intention of leaving Hillsborough. Then she had felt her way, and, in a moment, she had found the younger woman was the stronger.

She assumed, as a matter of course, that this girl was in love with Henry (who would not be in love with him?), and had hung, weeping, round his neck, when he called from Cairnhope to bid her farewell, and had made him promise to stay. This was the mother's theory; wrong, but rational.

Then came the question, What should she do? Fight against youth and nature? Fight, unlikely to succeed, sure to irritate and disturb. Risk any of that rare affection and confidence her son had always given her?

While her thoughts ran this way, seven o'clock came, and no Henry. Eight o'clock, and no Henry. "Ah!" thought the mother, "that one word of mine has had this effect already."

She prepared an exquisite little supper. She made her own toilette with particular care; and, when all was ready, she sat down and comforted herself by reading his letters, and comparing his love with the cavalier behavior of many sons in this island, the most unfilial country in Europe.

At half past ten Henry came up the stairs, not with the usual light elastic tread, but with slow, hesitating foot. Her quick ear caught that too, and her gentle bosom yearned. What, had she frightened him? He opened the door, and she rose to receive him all smiles. "You are rather late, dear," she said; "but all the better. It has given me an excuse for reading your dear letters all over again; and I have a thousand questions to ask you about Cairnhope. But sit down first, and have your supper."

Henry brightened up, and ate a good supper, and his mother plied him with questions, all about Cairnhope.

Here was an unexpected relief. Henry took a superficial view of all this. Sharp young men of twenty-four understand a great many things; but they can't quite measure their mothers yet.

Henry was selfishly pleased, but not ungrateful, and they passed a pleasant and affectionate time: and, as for leaving Hillsborough, the topic was avoided by tacit consent.

Next morning, after this easy victory, Henry took a cab and got to "Woodbine Villa" by a circuitous route. His heart beat high as he entered the room where Grace was seated. After the extraordinary warmth and familiarity she had shown him at the last interview, he took for granted he had made a lasting progress in her regard.

But she received him with a cold and distant manner, that quite benumbed him. Grace Carden's face and manner were so much more expressive than other people's, that you would never mistake or doubt the mood she was in; and this morning she was freezing.

The fact is, Miss Carden had been tormenting herself: and when beauty suffers, it is very apt to make others suffer as well.

"I am glad you are come, Mr. Little," said she, "for I have been taking myself to task ever since, and I blame myself very much for some things I said. In the first place, it was not for me" (here the fair speaker colored up to the temples) "to interfere in your affairs at all: and then, if I must take such a liberty, I ought to have advised you sensibly, and for your good. I have been asking people, and they all tell me it is madness for one person to fight against these Unions. Every body gets crushed. So now let me hope you will carry out your wise intention, and leave

Hillsborough ; and then my conscience will be at ease."

Every word fell like an icicle on her hearer's heart. To please this cold, changeful creature, he had settled to defy the unchangeable Unions, and had been ready to resist his mother, and slight her immortal and unchanging love.

"You don't answer me, sir !" said Miss Carden, with an air of lofty surprise.

"I answered you yesterday," said he sullenly. "A man can't chop and change like a weathercock."

"But it is not changing, it's only going back to your own intention. You know you were going to leave Hillsborough, before I talked all that nonsense. Your story had set me on fire, and that's my only excuse. Well, now, the same person takes the liberty to give you wise and considerate advice, instead of hot, and hasty, romantic nonsense. Which ought you to respect most—folly or reason—from the same lips ?"

Henry seemed to reflect. "That sounds reasonable," said he ; "but, when you advised me not to show the white feather, you spoke your heart ; now, you are only talking from your head. Then, your beautiful eyes flashed fire, and your soul was in your words : who could resist them ? And you spoke to me like a friend ; now you speak to me like an enemy."

"Oh, Mr. Little, that is ridiculous."

"You do, though. And I'm sure I don't know why."

"Nor I. Perhaps because I am cross with myself ; certainly not with you."

"I am glad of that. Well, then, the long and the short is, you showed me you thought it cowardly to fly from the trades. You wouldn't, said you, if you were a man. Well, I'm a man ; and I'll do as you would do in my place. I'll not throw my life away, I'll meet craft with craft, and force with force ; but fly I never will. I'll fight while I've a leg to stand on."

With these words he began to work on the bust, in a quiet dogged way that was, nevertheless, sufficiently expressive.

Grace looked at him silently for half a minute, and then rose from her chair.

"Then," said she, "I must go for somebody of more authority than I am." She sailed out of the room.

Henry asked Jael who she was gone for.

"It will be her papa," said Jael.

"As if I care what he says."

"I wouldn't show her that, if I was you," said Jael, quietly, but with a good deal of weight.

"You are right," said Henry. "You are a good girl. I don't know which is the best, you or Martha. I say, I promised to go to Cairnhope some Sunday, and see them all. Shall I drive you over ?"

"And bring me back at night ?"

"If you like. I must come back."

"I'll ask Miss Carden."

The words were quiet and composed, but the blushing face beamed with unreasonable happiness ; and Grace, who entered at that moment with her father, was quite struck with its eloquence ; she half started, but took no further notice just then. "There, papa," said she, "this is Mr. Little."

Mr. Carden was a tall gentleman, with some-

what iron features, but a fine head of gray hair : rather an imposing personage ; not the least pompous though ; quite a man of the world, and took a business view of every thing, matrimony, of course, included.

"Oh, this is Mr. Little, is it, whose work we all admire so much ?"

"Yes, Papa."

"And whose adventure has made so much noise ?"

"Yes, Papa."

"By-the-by, there is an article to-day on you : have you seen it ? No ? But you should see it ; it is very smart. My dear" (to Jael), "will you go to my study, and bring the Liberal here ?"

"Yes, but meantime, I want you to advise him not to subject himself to more gunpowder and things, but to leave the town ; that is all the wretches demand."

"And that," said Henry, with a sly, deferential tone, "is a good deal to demand in a free country, is it not, sir ?"

"Indeed it is. Ah, here comes the Liberal. Somebody read the article to us, while he works. I want to see how he does it."

Curiosity overpowered Grace's impatience, for a moment, and she read the notice out with undisguised interest.

"'THE LAST OUTRAGE.

"'In our first remarks upon this matter, we merely laid down an alternative which admits of no dispute ; and, abstaining from idle conjectures, undertook to collect evidence. We have now had an interview with the victim of that abominable outrage. Mr. —— is one of those superior workmen who embellish that class for a few years, but invariably rise above it, and leave it ' (there—Mr. Little)—' He has informed us that he is a stranger in Hillsborough, lives retired, never sits down in a public-house, and has not a single enemy in Hillsborough, great or small. He says that his life was saved by his fellow-workmen, and that as he lay scorched—' (Oh dear !")

"Well, go on, Grace."

"It is all very well to say go on, Papa— 'scorched and bleeding on the ground, and unable to distinguish faces' (poor, poor Mr. Little!) ' he heard, on all sides of him, expressions of rugged sympathy ; and sobs, and tears, from rough, but—man-ly fellows, who—' (oh ! oh ! oh !")

Grace could not go on for whimpering, and Jael cried, for company. Henry left off carving, and turned away his head, touched to the heart by this sweet and sudden sympathy.

"How badly you read," said Mr. Carden, and took the journal from her. He read in a loud business-like monotone, that, like some blessed balm, dried every tear. "'Manly fellows who never shed a tear before : this disposed of one alternative, and narrowed the inquiry. It was not a personal feud ; therefore it was a trade outrage, or it was nothing. We now took evidence bearing on the inquiry thus narrowed ; and we found the assault had been preceded by a great many letters, all of them breathing the spirit of Unionism, and none of them intimating a private wrong. These letters, taken in connection, are a literary curiosity ; and we find there is scarcely a manufacturer in the place who has not endured a similar correspondence, and violence at the end of it. This curious chapter of the human mind really deserves a separate heading, and we introduce it to our readers as

"THE LITERATURE OF OUTRAGE."

"'First of all comes a letter to the master intimating that he is doing something objectionable to some one of the many Unions that go to make a single implement of hardware. This letter has three features. It is signed with a real name. It is polite. It is grammatical.

"'If disregarded, it is speedily followed by another. No. 2 is grammatical, or thereabouts; but, under a feigned politeness, the insolence of a vulgar mind shows itself pretty plainly, and the master is reminded what he suffered on some former occasion when he rebelled against the trades. This letter is sometimes anonymous, generally pseudonymous.

"'If this reminder of the past, and intimation of the future, is disregarded, the refractory master gets a missive, which begins with an affectation of coarse familiarity, and then rises, with a ludicrous bound, into brutal and contemptuous insolence. In this letter, grammar is flung to the winds, along with good manners; but spelling survives, by a miracle. Next comes a short letter, full of sanguinary threats, and written in, what we beg leave to christen, the Dash dialect, because, though used by at least three million people in England, and three thousand in Hillsborough, it can only be printed with blanks, the reason being simply this, that every sentence is measled with oaths and indecencies. These letters are also written phonetically, and, as the pronunciation, which directs the spelling, is all wrong, the double result is prodigious. Nevertheless, many of these pronunciations are ancient, and were once universal. An antiquarian friend assures us the orthography of these blackguards, the scum of the nineteenth century, is wonderfully like that of a mediæval monk or baron.

"'When the correspondence has once descended to the Dash dialect, written phonetically, it never remounts towards grammar, spelling, or civilization; and the next step in the business is rattening, or else beating, or shooting, or blowing-up the obnoxious individual by himself, or along with a houseful of people quite strange to the quarrel. Now, it is manifest to common sense, that all this is one piece of mosaic, and that the criminal act it all ends in is no more to be disconnected from the last letter, than the last letter from its predecessor, or letter 3 from letter 2. Here is a crime first gently foreshadowed, then grimly intimated, then directly threatened, then threatened in words that smell of blood and gunpowder, and then—done. The correspondence and the act reveal—

"The various talents, but the single mind."

"'In face of this evidence, furnished by themselves, the trades' Unions, some member of which has committed this crime, will do well to drop the worn-out farce of offering a trumpery reward, and to take a direct and manly course. They ought to accept Mr. ——'s preposterously liberal offer, and admit him to the two Unions, and thereby disown the criminal act in the form most consolatory to the sufferer; or else they should face the situation, and say, "This act was done under our banner, though not by our order, and we stand by

it." The *Liberal* will continue to watch the case.'"

"This will be a pill," said Mr. Carden, laying down the paper. "Why, they call the *Liberal* the workman's advocate."

"Yes, papa," said Grace; "but how plainly he shows— But Mr. Little is a stranger, and even this terrible lesson has not— So do pray advise him."

"I should be very happy; but, when you are my age, you will know it is of little use intruding advice upon people."

"Oh, Mr. Little will treat it with proper respect, coming from one so much older than himself, and better acquainted with this wretched town. Will you not, Mr. Little?" said she, with so cunning a sweetness that the young fellow was entrapped, and assented, before he knew what he was about; then colored high at finding himself committed.

Mr. Carden reflected a moment. He then said, "I can't take upon myself to tell any man to give up his livelihood. But one piece of advice I can conscientiously give Mr. Little."

"Yes, papa."

"And that is—TO INSURE HIS LIFE."

"Oh, papa!" cried Grace.

As for Henry he was rather amused, and his lip curled satirically. But the next moment he happened to catch sight of Jael Dence's face: her gray eyes were expanded with a look of uneasiness; and, directly she caught his eye she fixed it, and made him a quick movement of the head, directing him to assent.

There was something so clear and decided in the girl's manner, that it overpowered Henry, who had no very clear idea to oppose to it, and he actually obeyed the nod of this girl, whom he had hitherto looked on as an amiable simpleton.

"I have no objection to that," said he, turning to Mr. Carden. Then, after another look at Jael, he said, demurely, "Is there any insurance office you could recommend?"

Mr. Carden smiled. "There is only one I have a right to recommend, and that is the 'Gosshawk.' I am a director. But," said he, with sudden stiffness, "I could furnish you with the names of many others."

Henry saw his way clear by this time. "No, sir, if I profit by your advice, the least I can do is to choose the one you are a director of."

Grace, who had latterly betrayed uneasiness and irritation, now rose, red as fire. "The conversation is taking a turn I did not at all intend," said she, and swept out of the room with royal disdain.

Her father apologized carelessly for her tragical exit. "That is a young lady who detests business; but she does not object to its fruits,—dresses, lace, footmen, diamonds, and a carriage to drive about in. On the contrary, she would be miserable without them."

"I should hope she never will be without them, sir."

"I'll take care of that."

Mr. Carden said this rather dryly, and then retired for a minute; and Grace, who was not far off, with an ear like a hare, came back soon after.

But in the mean time Henry left his seat and went to Jael, and, leaning over her as she worked, said, "There is more in that head of yours than I thought."

"Oh, they all talk before me," said Jael, blushing faintly, and avoiding his eye.

"Jael Dence," said the young man, warmly, "I'm truly obliged to you."

"What for?"

"For your good advice. I didn't see how good it was till after I had taken it."

"I'm afeard Miss Grace gave you better."

"She advised me against my heart. What is the use of that?"

"Ay, young men are willful."

"Come, come, don't you go back. You are my friend and counsellor."

"That is something," said Jael, in a low voice; and her hands trembled at her side.

"Why, my dear girl, what's the matter?"

"Hush! hush!"

CHAPTER VIII.

GRACE came in that moment, with a superb air. She settled herself on the sofa.

"Now, it is my turn, if you please. Pray, sir, do you think your life will be any safer for your insuring it? Insuring does not mean that you are not to be killed; but that, when you *are*, for your obstinacy, somebody else will get paid some money, to dance with over your grave."

"I beg your pardon, Grace," said Mr. Carden, entering, with some printed papers in his hand. "That is not the only use of an insurance. He may want to marry, or to borrow a sum of money to begin business; and then a policy of insurance, with two or three premiums paid, smooths the difficulty. Every body should make a will, and every body should insure his life."

"Well then, sir, I will do both."

"Stop!" said Mr. Carden, who could now afford to be candid. "First of all, you ought to satisfy yourself of the flourishing condition of the company." He handed him a prospectus. "This will show you our capital, and our disbursements last year, and the balance of profit declared. And this gives the balance-sheet of the 'Vulture' and the 'Falcon,' which have assigned their business to us, and are now incorporated in the 'Gosshawk.'"

"Oh, what a voracious bird!" observed Grace. "I hope these other chickabiddies will not prove indigestible. Were they plucked first, Papa? or did the 'Gosshawk' swallow them feathers and all?"

Little laughed heartily at this pert sally, but Mr. Carden winced under it.

"After such a meal as that, Mr. Little, you will go down like a crumb."

"Grace, that is enough," said Mr. Carden, rather severely.

Grace held her tongue directly, and the water came into her eyes. Any thing like serious remonstrance was a novelty to her.

When Henry had read the papers, Mr. Carden asked him, rather carelessly, what sum he wished to be insured for.

Now Henry had so little wish about the matter, that he had not given it a thought, and the question took him quite aback. He looked helplessly at Jael. To his surprise, she decided on the sum for him, without a moment's hesitation, and conveyed the figure with that dexterity which the simplest of her sex can command whenever telegraphy is wanted. She did it with two unbroken movements: she put up all the fingers of her right hand to her brow, and that meant five: then she turned her hand rapidly, so as to hide her mouth from the others, who were both on her right hand, and she made the word thousand clear, with her lips and tongue, especially the "th."

But the sum staggered Henry; and made him think he must be misinterpreting her.

He hesitated, to gain time. "Hum!" said he, "the sum?"

Jael repeated her pantomime as before.

Still Henry doubted, and, to feel his way, said, half interrogatively, "Five—thou—sand?"

Jael nodded.

"Five thousand pounds," said Henry, as bold as brass.

"Five thousand pounds!" cried Mr. Carden. "A workman insure his life for five thousand pounds!"

"Well, a man's life is worth five thousand pounds, or it is worth nothing. And, sir, how long do you think I shall be a workman, especially in Hillsborough, where from workman to master is no more than hopping across a gutter?"

Mr. Carden smiled approval. "But five thousand pounds! The annual premium will be considerable. May I ask about how much you make a year?"

"Oh, papa!"

"Well, sir, Mr. Cheetham pays me £300 a year, at the rate of, and I can make another £100 by carving at odd times. But, if you doubt my ability, let us stay as we are, sir. It was your proposal, not mine, you know."

"Young man," said Mr. Carden, "never be peppery in business." He said this so solemnly and paternally, it sounded like the eleventh commandment.

To conclude, it was arranged Henry should take the higher class of insurance, which provided for accidents, voyages, every thing, and should be insured for £5000, provided the physician appointed by the company should pronounce him free from disease.

Henry then rose, and said, sorrowfully, to Grace, "You will not see me here very often now; and never on Saturday afternoon or Monday morning. I am not going to have some blackguard tracking me, and flinging a can of gunpowder in at your window. When I do come, it will be in the morning, and on a working day; and I shall perhaps go ten miles round to get here. It must be diamond cut diamond, for many a month to come, between the Trades and me." He uttered these words with manly gravity, as one who did not underrate the peril he was resolved to face; and left them with a respectful bow.

"That's a rising man," said Mr. Carden; "and may draw a hundred of his class to the 'Gosshawk.' It was a good stroke of business, quite out of the common."

Grace said not a word, but she shook her head, and looked pained and ill at ease. Jael watched her fixedly.

Henry called at the works that night, and examined the new defenses, with Mr. Cheetham. He also bought a powerful magnifying-glass; and next morning he came to the factory, examined the cinders, and every thing else, with the magnifier, lighted his forge, and resumed his work.

At dinner time he went out and had his chop, and read the *Liberal*; it contained a letter from Jobson, in reply to the editor.

Jobson deplored the criminal act, admitted that the two Unions had decided no individual could be a forger, a handler, and a cutler; such an example was subversive of all the Unions in the city, based, as they were, on subdivision of crafts. "But," said Mr. Jobson, "we were dealing with the matter in a spirit quite inconsistent with outrages, and I am so anxious to convince the public of this, that I have asked a very experienced gentleman to examine our minute-books, and report accordingly."

This letter was supplemented by one from Mr. Grotait, secretary of the Saw-Grinders, which ran thus:—"Messrs. Parkin and Jobson have appealed to me to testify to certain facts. I was very reluctant to interfere, for obvious reasons; but was, at last, prevailed on to examine the minute-books of those two Unions, and they certainly do prove that on the very evening before the explosion, those trades had fully discussed Mr. ——'s case" (the real name was put, but altered by the editor), "and had disposed of it as follows: They agreed, and this is entered accordingly, to offer him his travelling expenses (first class) to London, and one pound per week, from their funds, until such time as he should obtain employment. I will only add, that both these secretaries spoke kindly to me of Mr. ——; and, believing them to be sincere, I ventured to advise them to mark their disapproval of the criminal act, by offering him two pounds per week, instead of one pound; which advice they have accepted very readily."

Henry was utterly confounded by these letters. Holdfast commented on them thus:

"Messrs. Jobson and Parkin virtually say that if A, for certain reasons, pushes a man violently out of Hillsborough, and B draws him gently out of Hillsborough for the same reasons, A and B can not possibly be co-operating. Messrs. Parkin and Jobson had so little confidence in this argument, which is equivalent to saying there is no such thing as cunning in trade, that they employed a third party to advance it with all the weight of his popularity and seeming impartiality. But who is this candid person, that objects to assume the judge, and assumes the judge? He is the treasurer and secretary of an Union that does not number three hundred persons; yet in that small Union, of which he is dictator, there has been as much rattening, and more shooting, and blowing-up wholesale and retail, with the farcical accompaniment of public repudiation, than in all the other Unions put together. We consider the entrance of this ingenious personage on the scene a bad omen, and shall watch all future proceedings with increased suspicion."

Henry had hardly done reading this, when a man came into the works, and brought him his fifteen pounds back from Mr. Jobson, and a line, offering him his expenses to London, and two pounds per week, from the Edge-Tool Forgers' box, till he should find employment. Henry took his money, and sent back word that the proposal came too late; after the dastardly attempt to assassinate him, he should defy the Unions, until they accepted his terms. Jobson made no reply. And Henry defied the Unions.

The Unions lay still, like some great fish at the bottom of a pool, and gave no sign of life or animosity. This did not lull Henry into a false security. He never relaxed a single precaution. He avoided "Woodbine Villa;" he dodged and doubled like a hare, to hide his own abode. But he forged, handled, and finished, in spite of the Unions.

The men were civil to him in the yard, and he had it all his own way, apparently.

He was examined by a surgeon, and reported healthy. He paid the insurance premium, and obtained the policy. So now he felt secure, under the ægis of the Press, and the wing of the "Gosshawk."

By-and-by, that great fish I have mentioned gave a turn of its tail, and made his placid waters bubble a little.

A woman came into the yard, with a can of tea for her husband, and a full apron. As she went out, she emptied a set of tools out of her apron on to an old grindstone, and slipped out.

The news of this soon travelled into the office, and both Cheetham and Bayne came out to look at them.

They were a set of carving-tools, well made, and highly polished; and there was a scrap of paper with this distich:

We are Hillsborough made,
Both haft and blade.

Cheetham examined them, and said, "Well, they are clever fellows. I declare these come very near Little's: call him down and let us draw him."

Bayne called to Henry, and that brought him down, and several more, who winded something.

"Just look at these," said Cheetham.

Little colored: he saw the finger of the Unions at once, and bristled all over with caution and hostility.

"I see them, sir. They are very fair specimens of cutlery; and tnere are only about twenty tools wanting to make a complete set; but there is one defect in them as carving-tools.

"What is that?"

"They are useless. You can't carve wood with them. None but a practical carver can design these tools, and then he must invent and make the steel moulds first. Try and sell them in London or Paris, you'll soon find the difference. Mr. Bayne, I wonder you should call me from my forge to examine 'prentice-work." And, with this, he walked off disdainfully, but not quite easy in his mind, for he had noticed a greedy twinkle in Cheetham's eye.

The next day all the grinders in Mr. Cheetham's employ, except the scissors-grinders, rose, all of a sudden, like a flock of partridges, and went out into the road.

"What is up now?" inquired Bayne. The answer was, their secretaries had sent for them.

They buzzed in the road, for a few minutes, and then came back to work.

At night there was a great meeting at the "Cutlers' Arms," kept by Mr. Grotait.

At noon next day, all the grinders aforesaid in Mr. Cheetham's employ walked into the office, and left, each of them, a signed paper to this effect:

"This is to give you notice that I will leave your service a week after the date thereof." (Meaning "hereof," I presume.)

Cheetham asked several of them what was up. Some replied, civilly, it was a trade matter. Others suggested Mr. Cheetham knew as much about it as they did.

Not a single hot or uncivil word was spoken on either side. The game had been played too often for that, and with results too various.

One or two even expressed a sort of dogged regret. The grinder Reynolds, a very honest fellow, admitted, to Mr. Cheetham, that he thought it a sorry trick, for a hundred men to strike against one that had had a squeak for his life. "But no matter what I think or what I say, I must do what the Union bids me, sir."

"I know that, my poor fellow," said Cheetham. "I quarrel with none of you. I fight you all. The other masters, in this town, are mice, but I'm a man."

This sentiment he repeated very often during the next six days.

The seventh came, and the grinders never entered the works.

Cheetham looked grave. However, he said to Bayne, "Go and find out where they are. Do it cleverly, now. Don't be noticed."

Bayne soon ascertained they were all in the neighboring public houses.

"I thought so," said Cheetham. "They will come in, before night. They sha'n't beat me, the vagabonds. I'm a man, I'm not a mouse."

"Orders pouring in, sir," sighed Bayne. "And the grinders are rather behind the others in their work already."

"They must have known that: or why draw out the grinders? How could they know it?"

"Sir," said Bayne, "they say old Smitem is in this one. Wherever he is, the master's business is known, or guessed, heaven knows how; and, if there is a hole in his coat, that hole is hit. Just look at the cleverness of it, sir. Here we are, wrong with the forgers and handlers. Yet

they come into the works and take their day's wages. But they draw out the grinders, and mutilate the business. They hurt you as much as if they struck, and lost their wages. But no, they want their wages to help pay the grinders on strike. Your only chance was to discharge every man in the works, the moment the grinders gave notice."

"Why didn't you tell me so, then?"

"Because I'm not old Smitem. He can see a thing beforehand. I can see it afterwards. I'm like the weatherwise man's pupil; as good as my master, give me time. The master could tell you, at sunrise, whether the day would be wet or dry, and the pupil he could tell you at sunset: and that is just the odds between old Smitem and me."

"Well, if he is old Smitem, I'm old Fightem."

At night, he told Bayne he had private information, that the grinders were grumbling at being made a catspaw of by the forgers and the handlers. "Hold on," said he; "they will break up before morning."

At ten o'clock next day he came down to the works, and some peremptory orders had poured in. "They must wait," said he, peevishly.

At twelve he said, "How queer the place seems, and not a grindstone going. It seems as still as the grave. I'm a man; I'm not a mouse."

Mr. Cheetham repeated this last fact in zoology three times, to leave no doubt of it in his own mind, I suppose.

At one, he said he would shut up the works rather than be a slave.

At 1 15 he blustered.

At 1 20 he gave in: collapsed in a moment, like a punctured bladder. "Bayne," said he, with a groan, "go to Jobson, and ask him to come and talk this foolish business over."

"Excuse me, sir," said Bayne. "Don't be offended; but you are vexed and worried, and whoever the Union sends to you will be as cool as marble. I have just heard it is Redcar carries the conditions."

"What, the foreman of my own forgers! Is he to dictate to me?" cried Cheetham, grinding his teeth with indignation.

"Well, sir, what does it matter?" said Bayne, soothingly. "He is no more than a mouth-piece."

"Go for him," said Cheetham, sullenly.

"But, sir, I can't bear that your own workman should see you so agitated."

"Oh, I shall be all right the moment I see my man before me."

Bayne went off, and soon returned with Redcar. The man had his coat on, but had not removed his leathern apron.

Cheetham received him as the representative of the Unions. "Sit down, Redcar, and let us put an end to this little bother. What do you require?"

"Mr. Little's discharge, sir."

"Are you aware he is with me on a month's notice?"

"They make a point of his leaving the works at once, sir; and I was to beg you to put other hands into his room."

"It is taking a great liberty to propose that."

"Nay. They only want to be satisfied. He has given a vast o' trouble."

"I'll give him a month's warning. If I discharge him on the spot, he can sue me."

"That has been thought on. If he sues you, you can talk to the Unions, and they will act with you. But the grinders are not to come in till Little is out."

"Well, so be it, then."

"And his rooms occupied by Union men."

"If I swallow the bolus, I may as well swallow the pills. Any thing more?"

"The grinders are not to lose their time; a day and a half."

"What! am I to pay them for not working?"

"Well, sir, if we had come to you, of course the forgers and handlers would have paid the grinders for lost time; but, as you have come to us, you will have to pay them."

Cheetham made a wry face; but acquiesced.

"And then, sir," said Redcar, "there's another little matter. The incidental expenses of the strike."

"I don't know what you mean."

"The expenses incurred by the secretaries, and a little present to another gentleman, who advised us. It comes to thirty pounds altogether."

"What!" cried Cheetham, struggling with his rising choler. "You want me to pay men thirty pounds for organizing a strike, that will cost me so dear, and rob me of a whole trade that was worth £300 a year? Why not charge me for the gunpowder you blew up Little with, and spoiled my forge? No, Bayne, no; this is too unjust and too tyrannical. Flesh and blood won't bear it. I'll shut up the works, and go back to my grindstone. Better live on bread and water than live a slave."

Redcar took a written paper out of his pocket. "There are the terms written down," said he. "If you sign them, the strike ends; if you don't, it continues—till you do."

Cheetham writhed under the pressure. Orders were pouring in; trade brisk; hands scarce. Each day would add a further loss of many pounds for wages, and doubtless raise fresh exactions. He gulped down something very like a sob, but his hand and his voice shook with strong passion as he took the pen. "I'll sign it; but if ever my turn comes, I'll remember this against you. This shows what they really are, Bayne. Oh, if ever you workmen get power, GOD HELP THE WORLD!"

These words seemed to come in a great prophetic agony out of a bursting heart.

But the representative of the Unions was neither moved by them nor irritated.

"All right," said he, phlegmatically; "the winner takes his bite; the loser gets his bark: that's reason."

Henry Little was in his handling-room, working away, with a bright perspective before him, when Bayne knocked at the door, and entered with Redcar. Bayne's face wore an expression so piteous, that Henry divined mischief at once.

"Little, my poor fellow, it is all over. We are obliged to part with you."

"Cheetham has thrown me over!"

"What could he do? I am to ask you to vacate these rooms, that we may get our half-day out of the grinders."

Henry turned pale, but there was no help for it.

He got up in a very leisurely way; and, while he was putting on his coat, he told Bayne, doggedly, he should expect his month's salary.

As he was leaving, Redcar spoke to him in rather a sheepish way. "Shake hands, old lad," said he: "thou knows one or t'other must win; and there's not a grain of spite against thee. It's just a trade matter."

Henry stood with his arms akimbo, and looked at Redcar. "I was in hopes," said he, grinding his teeth, "you were going to ask me to take a turn with you in the yard, man to man. But I can't refuse my hand to one of my own sort that asks it. There 'tis. After all, you deserve to win, for you are true to each other; but a master can't be true to a man, nor to any thing on earth, but his pocket."

He then strolled out into the yard, with his hands in his pockets, and whistled "The Harmonious Blacksmith," very sick at heart.

CHAPTER IX.

THE strike was over, the grinders poured into the works, and the grindstones revolved. Henry Little leaned against an angle of the building, and listened with aching heart to their remorseless thunder. He stood there disconsolate—the one workman out of work—and sipped the bitter cup, defeat. Then he walked out at the gates, and wandered languidly into the streets. He was miserable, and had nobody to mourn to, for the main cause of his grief lay beneath the surface of this defeat; and how could he reveal it, now that his ambitious love looked utter madness? Young as he was, he had seen there is no sympathy in the world for any man who loves out of his sphere. Indeed, whatever cures or crushes such a passion, is hailed by the by-standers as a sharp but wholesome medicine.

He sauntered about, and examined all the shops with lack-lustre eye. He looked in at every thing, but observed nothing, scarcely saw any thing. All his senses were turned inwards. It was such a pitiable and galling result of a gallant fight. Even the insurance office had got the better of him. It had taken one-third of his savings, and the very next day his trade was gone, and his life in no danger. The "Gosshawk" had plucked him, and the trade had tied his hands. Rack his invention how he would, he could see no way of becoming a master in Hillsborough, except by leaving Hillsborough and working hard and long in some other town. He felt in his own heart the love and constancy to do this; but his reason told him such constancy would be wasted; for, while he was working at a distance, the impression, if any, he had made on her would wear away, and some man born with money would step in and carry her gayly off. This thought returned to him again and again, and exasperated him so at last, that he resolved to go to "Woodbine Villa," and tell her his heart before he left the place. Then he should be rejected, no doubt, but perhaps pitied, and not so easily forgotten as if he had melted silently away.

He walked up the hill, first rapidly, then slowly. He called at "Woodbine Villa."

The answer was, "Not at home."

"Every thing is against me," said he.

He wandered wearily down again, and just at the entrance of the town he met a gentleman with a lady on each arm, and one of those ladies was

Miss Carden. The fortunate cavalier was Mr. Coventry, whom Henry would have seen long before this, but he had been in Paris for the last four months. He had come back fuller than ever of agreeable gossip, and Grace was chatting away to him, and beaming with pleasure, as innocent girls do, when out on a walk with a companion they like. She was so absorbed she did not even see Henry Little. He went off the pavement to make room for their tyrannical crinolines, and passed unnoticed.

He had flushed with joy at first sight of her, but now a deadly qualm seized him. The gentleman was handsome and commanding; Miss Carden seemed very happy, hanging on his arm; none the less bright and happy that he, her humble worshipper, was downcast and wretched.

It did not positively prove much: yet it indicated how little he must be to her: and somehow it made him realize more clearly the great disadvantage at which he lay, compared with an admirer belonging to her own class. Hitherto his senses had always been against his reason: but now for once they co-operated with his judgment, and made him feel that, were he to toil for years in London, or Birmingham, and amass a fortune, he should only be where that gentleman was already; and while the workman, far away, was slaving, that gentleman and others would be courting her. She might refuse one or two. But she would not refuse them all.

Then, in his despair, he murmured, "Would to God I had never seen her!"

He made a fierce resolve he would go home, and tell his mother she could pack up.

He quickened his steps, for fear his poor sorrowful heart should falter.

But, when he had settled on this course, lo! a fountain of universal hatred seemed to bubble in his heart. He burned to inflict some mortal injury upon Jobson, Parkin, Grotait, Cheetham, and all who had taken a part, either active or passive, in goading him to despair. Now Mr. Cheetham's works lay right in his way; and it struck him he could make Cheetham smart a little. Cheetham's god was money. Cheetham had thrown him over for money. He would go to Cheetham, and drive a dagger into his pocket.

He walked into the office. Mr. Cheetham was not there: but he found Bayne, and Dr. Amboyne.

"Mr. Bayne," said he, abruptly, "I am come for my month's wages."

The tone was so aggressive, Bayne looked alarmed. "Why, Little, poor Mr. Cheetham is gone home with a bad headache, and a sore heart."

"All the better. I don't want to tell him to his face he is a bragging cur; all I want out of him now is my money: and you can pay me that."

The pacific Bayne cast a piteous glance at Dr. Amboyne. "I have told you the whole business, sir. Oughtn't Mr. Little to wait till to-morrow, and talk it over with Mr. Cheetham? I'm only a servant: and a man of peace."

"Whether he ought or not, I think I can answer for him that he will."

"I can't, sir," said Henry, sturdily. "I leave the town to-morrow."

"Oh, that alters the case. But must you leave us so soon?"

"Yes, sir."

"I am very sorry for that. Tell me your reason. I don't ask out of mere curiosity."

Henry replied with less than his usual candor: "Is it not reason enough for leaving a place, that my life has been attempted in it, and now my livelihood is taken?"

"Those are certainly strong reasons. But, on the other hand, your life is no longer in danger: and your livelihood is not gone; for, to speak plainly, I came over here the moment I heard you were discharged, to ask you if you would enter my service on the same terms as Mr. Cheetham gave you, only guineas instead of pounds."

"What, turn doctor?"

"Oh dear, no: the doctors' Union would forbid that. No, Mr. Little, I am going to ask you to pay me a compliment; to try my service blindfold for one week. You can leave it if you don't like it; but give me one week's trial."

"How can I refuse you that?" said Henry, hanging his head. "You have been a good friend to me. But, sir, mark my words, this place will be my destruction. Well, when am I to begin work?"

"To-morrow at ten."

"So be it," said Henry, wearily, then left the works and went home; but, as he went, he said to himself, "It is not my doing." And his double-faced heart glowed and exulted secretly.

He told his mother how the Trades had beaten him, and he was out of work.

Mrs. Little consoled him hypocritically. She was delighted. Then he told her his departure had been delayed by Dr. Amboyne: that made her look a little anxious.

"One question, dear: now the Union has beaten you, they will not be so spiteful, will they?"

"Oh, no. That is all over. The conquerors can afford to be good-natured. Confound them!"

"Then that is all I care about. Then do not leave Hillsborough. Why should you? Wait here patiently. You do not know what may turn up."

"What, mother, do you want to stay here now?" said Henry, opening his eyes with astonishment.

"Wherever my son is happy and safe from harm, there I wish to stay—of course."

Next morning Henry called on Dr. Amboyne, and found him in his study, teaching what looked a boy of sixteen, but was twenty-two, to read monosyllables. On Little's entrance the pupil retired from his uphill work, and glowered with vacillating eyes. The lad had a fair feminine face, with three ill things in it: a want, a wildness, and a weakness. To be sure Henry saw it at a disadvantage: for vivid intelligence would come now and then across this mild, wild, vacant face, like the breeze that sweeps a farmyard pond.

"Good-morning, Little. This is your fellow-workman."

"He does not look up to much," said Henry, with all a workman's bluntness.

"What, you have found him out! Never mind; he can beat the town at one or two things, and it is for these we will use him. Some call him an idiot. The expression is neat and vigorous, but not precise; so I have christened him the Anomaly. Anomaly, this is Mr. Little; go and shake hands with him, and admire him."

·The Anomaly went directly, and gazed into Little's face for some time.

He then made his report. "He is beautiful and black."

"I've seen him blacker. Now leave off admiring him, and look at these pictures while I prose. Two thousand philosophers are writing us dead with 'Labor and Capital.' But I vary the bore. 'Life, Labor, and Capital,' is my chant : and, whereas Life has hitherto been banished from the discussion, I put Life in its true place, at the head of the trio. (And Life I divide into long Life, and happy Life.) The subject is too vast to be dealt with all at once ; but I'll give you a peep of it. The rustic laborer in ·the South sells his labor for too little money to support life comfortably. That is a foul wrong. The rustic laborer in the North has small wages, compared with a pitman, or a cutler ; but he has enough for health, and he lives longer and more happily than either the pitman or the cutler ; so that account is square, in my view of things. But now dive into the Hillsborough trades, and you will find this just balance of Life, Labor, and Capital regarded in some, but defied in others : a forger is paid as much or more than a drygrinder, though forging is a hard but tolerably healthy trade, and dry-grinding means an early death after fifteen years of disease and misery. The file-cutters are even more killed and less paid. What is to be done, then ? Raise the wages of the more homicidal trades ! But this could only be done by all the Unions acting in concert. Now the rival philosophers, who direct the Unions, are all against Democritus—that's myself ; they set no value on life. And indeed the most intelligent one, Grotait, smiles blandly on Death, and would grind his scythe for him— *at the statement price*—because that scythe thins the labor market, and so helps keep up prices."

"Then what can we do ? I'm a proof one can't fight the Unions."

"Do ? Why, lay hold of the stick at the other end. Let Pseudo-Philosophy set the means above the end, and fix its shortsighted eyes on Labor and Capital, omitting Life. (What does it profit a file-cutter if he gains his master's whole capital and loses his own life ?) But you and I, Mr. Little, are true philosophers, and the work we are about to enter on is—saving cutlers' lives."

"I'd rather help take them."

"Of course ; and that is why I made the pounds guineas."

"All right, sir," said Henry, coloring. "I don't expect to get six guineas a week for whistling my own tune. How are we to do the job ?"

"By putting our heads together. You have, on the side of your temple, a protuberance, which I have noticed in the crania of inventors. So I want you to go round the works, and observe for yourself how Life is thrown gayly away, in a moment, by needless accidents, and painfully gnawed away by steel-dust, stone-grit, sulphuret of lead, etc. ; and then cudgel your brain for remedies."

"Sir," said Henry, "I am afraid I shall not earn my money. My heart is not in the job."

"Revenge is what you would like to be at, not Philanthropy—eh ?"

"Ay, Doctor." And his black eye flashed fire.

"Well, well, that is natural. Humor my crotchet just now, and perhaps I may humor yours a month or two hence. I think I could lay my hand on the fellow who blew you up."

"What, sir ! Ah ! tell me that, and I'll do as much philanthropy as you like—after—"

"After you have punched your fellow-creature's head."

"But it is impossible, sir. How can you know ? These acts are kept as secret as the grave."

"And how often has the grave revealed its secrets to observant men ? Dr. Donne sauntered about among graves, and saw a sexton turn up a skull. He examined it, found a nail in it, identified the skull, and had the murderess hung. She was safe from the sexton and the rest of the parish, but not from a stray observer. Well, the day you were blown up, I observed something, and arrived at a conclusion, by my art."

"What, physic ?"

"Oh dear, no ; my other art, my art of arts, that I don't get paid for ; the art of putting myself in other people's places. I'll tell you. While you lay on the ground, in Mr. Cheetham's yard, I scanned the workmen's faces. They were full of pity and regret, and were much alike in expression—all but one. That one looked a man awakened from a dream. His face was wild, stupid, confused, astonished. 'Hallo!' said I, 'why are your looks so unlike the looks of your fellows ?' Instantly I put myself in his place. I ceased to be the Democritus, or laughing philosopher of Hillsborough, and became a low uneducated brute of a workman. Then I asked this brute, viz. myself, why I was staring and glaring in that way, stupidly astonished, at the injured man ? 'Were you concerned in the criminal act, ye blackguard ?' said I to myself. The next step was to put myself in the place of the criminal. I did so ; and I realized that I, the criminal, had done the act to please the Unions, and expecting the sympathy of all Union workmen to be with me. Also that I, being an ignorant brute, had never pictured to myself what suffering I should inflict. But what was the result ? I now saw the sufferer, and did not like my own act ; and I found all the sympathy of my fellows went with him, and that I was loathed and execrated, and should be lynched on the spot were I to own my act. I now whipped back to Dr. Amboyne with the theory thus obtained, and compared it with that face ; the two fitted each other, and I saw the criminal before me."

"Good heavens ! This is very deep."

"No slop-basin was ever deeper. So leave it for the present, and go to work. Here are cards admitting you, as my commissioner, to all the principal works. Begin with— Stop a moment, while I put myself in your place. Let me see, Cheetham's grinders think they have turned me out of Hillsborough. That mortifies a young man of merit like me. Confound 'em ! I should like to show them they have not the power to drive me out. Combine how they will, I rise superior. I forge as they could not forge : that was my real crime. Well, I'll be their superior still. I'm their inspector, and their benefactor, at higher wages than they, poor devils, will ever earn at inspecting and benefiting, or any thing else.' Ah ! your color rises. I've hit the right nail. Isn't it an excellent and most transmigratory art ? Then begin with Cheetham. By-the-by, the Anomaly has spotted a defective grindstone there. Scrutinize all his departments severely; for no man values his people's lives less than my good friend John Cheetham. Away with you both; and God speed you."

Henry walked down the street with the Anomaly, and tried to gauge his intellects.

"What's your real name, my man?"

"Silly Billy."

"Oh, then I'm afraid you can't do much to help me."

"Oh yes, I can, because—"

"Because what?"

"Because I like you."

"Well, that's lucky, any way."

"Billy can catch trout when nobody else can," said the youngster, turning his eyes proudly up to Henry's.

"Oh, indeed! But you see that is not exactly what the Doctor wants us for."

"Nay; he's wrapped up in trout. If it wasn't for Billy and the trout, he'd die right off."

Henry turned a look of silent pity on the boy, and left him in his pleasing illusion. He wondered that Dr. Amboyne should have tacked this biped on to him.

They entered Cheetham's works, and Henry marched grimly into the office, and showed Mr. Bayne his credentials.

"Why, Little, you had no need of that."

"Oh, it is as well to have no misunderstanding with your employer's masters. I visit these works for my present employer, Dr. Amboyne, with the consent of Mr. Cheetham, here written."

"Very well, sir," said Bayne, obsequiously; "and I respectfully solicit the honor of conducting our esteemed visitor."

A young man's ill-humor could not stand against this. "Come along, old fellow," said Henry. "I'm a bear, with a sore heart; but who could be such a brute as quarrel with you? Let us begin with the chaps who drove me out—the grinders. I'm hired to philanthropize 'em—d—n 'em."

They went among the dry-grinders first; and Henry made the following observations. The workmen's hair and clothes were powdered with grit and dust from the grindstones. The very air was impregnated with it, and soon irritated his own lungs perceptibly. Here was early death, by bronchitis and lung diseases, reduced to a certainty. But he also learned from the men that the quantity of metal ground off was prodigious, and entered their bodies they scarce knew how. A razor-grinder showed him his shirt: it was a deep buff-color. "There, sir," said he, "that was clean on yesterday. All the washerwomen in Hillsboro' can't make a shirt of mine any other color but that." The effect on life, health, and happiness was visible; a single glance revealed rounded shoulders and narrow chests, caused partly by the grinder's position on his horsing, a position very injurious to the organs of breathing, and partly by the two devil's dusts that filled the air; cadaverous faces, the muscles of which betrayed habitual suffering, coughs short and dry, or with a frothy expectoration peculiar to the trade.

In answer to questions, many complained of a fearful tightness across the chest, of inability to eat or to digest. One said it took him five minutes to get up the factory stairs, and he had to lean against the wall several times.

A razor-grinder of twenty-two, with death in his face, told Henry he had come into that room when he was eleven. "It soon takes hold of boys," said he. "I've got what I shall never get shut on."

Another, who looked ill, but not dying, received Henry's sympathy with a terrible apathy. "I'm twenty-eight," said he; "and a fork-grinder is an old cock at thirty. I must look to drop off my perch in a year or two, like the rest."

Only one, of all these victims, seemed to trouble his head about whether death and disease could be averted. This one complained that some employers provided fans to drive the dust from the grinder, but Cheetham would not go to the expense.

The rest that Henry spoke to accepted their fate doggedly. They were ready to complain, but not to move a finger in self-defense. Their fathers had been ground out young, and why not they?

Indifferent to life, health, and happiness, they could nevertheless be inflamed about sixpence a week. In other words, the money-price of their labor was every thing to them, the blood-price nothing.

Henry found this out, and it gave him a glimpse into the mind of Amboyne.

He felt quite confused, and began to waver between hate, contempt, and pity. Was it really these poor doomed wretches who had robbed him of his livelihood? Could men so miscalculate the size of things, as to strike because an inoffensive individual was making complete carving-tools all by himself, and yet not strike, nor even stipulate for fans, to carry disease and death away from their own vitals? Why, it seemed wasting hate, to bestow it on these blind idiots.

He went on to the wet-grinders; and he found their trade much healthier than dry-grinding: yet there were drawbacks. They suffered from the grit whenever a new stone was hung and raced. They were also subject to a canker of the hands, and to colds, coughs, and inflammations, from perspiration checked by cold draughts and drenched floors. These floors were often of mud, and so the wet stagnated and chilled their feet, while their bodies were very hot. Excellent recipe for filling graves.

Here Bayne retired to his books, and Henry proceeded to the saw-grinders, and entered their rooms with no little interest, for they were an envied trade. They had been for many years governed by Grotait, than whom no man in England saw clearer; though such men as Amboyne saw farther. Grotait, by a system of Machiavellian policy, ingeniously devised and carried out, nobly, basely, craftily, forcibly, benevolently, ruthlessly, whichever way best suited the particular occasion, had built a model Union; and still, with unremitting zeal and vigilance, contrived to keep numbers down and prices up—which is the great Union problem.

The work was hard, but it was done in a position favorable to the lungs, and the men were healthy, brawny fellows; one or two were of remarkable stature.

Up to this moment Silly Billy had fully justified that title. He had stuck to Henry's side like a dog, but with no more interest in the inquiry than a calf. Indeed, his wandering eye and vacant face had indicated that his scanty wits were wool-gathering miles from the place that contained his body.

But, as soon as he entered the saw-grinders' room, his features lighted up, and his eye kindled. He now took up a commanding position in the centre, and appeared to be listening keenly. And he had not listened many seconds before he cried out, "There's the bad music! there! there!" And he pointed to a grindstone that was turning and doing its work exactly like the others. "Oh, the bad music!" cried Billy. "It is out of tune. It says, 'Murder! murder! Out of tune!'"

Henry thought it his duty to inspect the grindstone so vigorously denounced, and, naturally enough, went in front of the grinder. But Billy pulled him violently to the side. "You mustn't stand there," said he. "That is the way they fly when they break, and kill the poor father, and then the mother lets down her hair, and the boy goes crazed."

By this time the men were attracted by the Anomaly's gestures and exclamations, and several left their work, and came round him. "What is amiss, Billy? a flawed stone, eh? which is it?"

"Here! here!" said the boy. "This is the wheel of death. Kill it, break it, smash it, before it kills another father."

Henry spoke to the grinder, and asked him if there was any thing amiss with the stone.

The man seemed singularly uneasy at being spoken to: however he made answer sullenly that he had seen better ones, and worse ones, and all.

Henry was, however, aware, that the breaking of a large grindstone, while revolving by steam-power, was a serious, and often a fatal thing; he therefore made a private mark upon the wall opposite the grindstone, and took his excited companion to Bayne. "This poor lad says he has found a defective grindstone. It is impossible for me to test it while it is running. Will you let us into the works when the saw-grinders have left?"

Bayne hem'd and haw'd a little, but consented. He would remain behind half-an-hour to oblige Little.

Henry gave the Anomaly his dinner, and then inspected the file-cutters in two great works. Here he found suicide reduced to a system. Whereof anon.

Returning, to keep his appointment with Bayne, he met a well-dressed man, who stopped Billy, and accosted him kindly.

Henry strolled on.

He heard their voices behind him all the way, and the man stopped at Cheetham's gate, which rather surprised him. "Has Billy told you what we are at?" said he.

"Yes. But the very look of him was enough. I know Billy and his ways, better than you do."

"Very likely. What, are you coming in with us?"

"If you have no objection."

The door was opened by Bayne in person. He started at the sight of the companion his friend had picked up, and asked him, with marked civility if there was any thing amiss. "Not that I know of," was the reply. "I merely thought that my experience might be of some little service to you in an inquiry of this kind."

"Not a doubt of it, sir," said Bayne, and led the way with his lantern, for it was past sunset. On the road, the visitor asked if any body had marked the accused stone. Henry said he should know it again. "That is right," said the other.

On entering the room, this personage took Billy by the arm, and held him. "Let us have no false alarms," he said, and blindfolded the boy with his handkerchief in a moment.

And now an examination commenced, which the time and the place rendered curious and striking.

It was a long, lofty room; the back part mainly occupied by the drums that were turned by the driving-power. The power was on the floor above, and acted by means of huge bands that came down through holes in the ceiling and turned the drums. From each of these drums came two leather bands, each of which turned a pulley-wheel, and each pulley-wheel a grindstone, to whose axle it was attached; but now the grindstones rested in the troughs, and the great wheel-bands hung limp, and the other bands lay along loose and serpentine. In the dim light of a single lamp, it all looked like a gigantic polypus with its limbs extended lazily, and its fingers holding semi-circular claws: for of the grindstones less than half is visible.

Billy was a timid creature, and this blindfolding business rather scared him: he had almost to be dragged within reach of these gaunt antennæ. But each time they got him to touch a grindstone, his body changed its character from shrinking and doubtful, to erect and energetic, and he applied his test. This boy carried with him, night and day, a little wooden hammer, like an auctioneer's, and with this he now tapped each stone several times, searching for the one he had denounced: and, at each experiment, he begged the others to keep away from him and leave him alone with the subject of his experiment; which they did, and held up the lamp and threw the light on him.

Six heavy grindstones he tapped, and approved; three he even praised and called "good music."

"The seventh he struck twice, first gently, then hard and drew back from it, screaming "Oh, the bad music! Oh, the wheel of death!" and tried to tear the handkerchief from his eyes.

"Be quiet, Billy," said the visitor, calmly; and, putting his arm round the boy's neck, drew him to his side, and detached the handkerchief, all in a certain paternal way that seemed to betoken a kindly disposition. But, whilst he was doing this, he said to Henry, "Now—you marked a stone in daylight; which was it?"

"No, no, I didn't mark the stone, but I wrote on the wall just opposite. Lend us the light, Bayne. By George! here is my mark right opposite this stone."

"Then Billy's right. Well done, Billy." He put his hand in his pocket and gave him a new shilling. He then inquired of Bayne, with the air of a pupil seeking advice from a master, whether this discovery ought not to be acted upon.

"What would you suggest, sir?" asked Bayne, with equal deference.

"Oh, if I was sure I should not be considered presumptuous in offering my advice, I would say, Turn the stone into the yard, and hang a new one. You have got three excellent ones outside; from Buckhurst quarry, by the look of them."

"It shall be done, sir."

This effective co-operation, on the part of a stranger, was naturally gratifying to Henry, and he said to him: "I should be glad to ask you a question. You seem to know a good deal about this trade—"

A low chuckle burst out of Bayne, but he instantly suppressed it, for fear of giving offense—

"Are serious accidents really common with these grindstones?"

"No, no," said Bayne, "not common. Heaven forbid."

"They are not common—in the newspapers,"

a twinkling. He then drew out of his waistcoat pocket a double eyeglass, gold-mounted, and examining the ceiling with it, soon directed Henry's attention to two deep dents and a brown splash. "Every one of those marks," said he, "is a history, and was written by a flying grindstone. Where you see the dents the stone struck the

THE DANGEROUS GRINDSTONE DETECTED.

replied the other. "But," (to Bayne,) "will you permit me to light these two gaslights for a moment?"

"Well, sir, it is contrary to our rules,—but—"

"All the more obliging of you," said the visitor, coolly, and lighted them, with his own match, in

ceiling;" he added, very gravely, "and, when it came down again, ask yourself, did it *always* fall right? These histories are written only on the ceiling and the walls. The floor could tell its tales too; but a crushed workman is soon swept off it, and the wheels go on again."

"That is too true," said Henry. "And it does a chap's heart good to hear a gentleman like you—"

"I'm not a gentleman. I'm an old Saw."

"Excuse me, sir, you look like a gentleman, and talk like one."

"And I try to conduct myself like one: but I *am* an old Saw."

"What! and carry a gold eyeglass?"

"The Trade gave it me. I'm an old Saw."

"Well then, all the better, for you can tell me, and please do: have you ever actually known fatal accidents from this cause?"

"I have known the light grinders very much shaken by a breaking stone, and away from work a month after it. And, working among saw-grinders, who use heavy stones, and stand over them in working, I've seen— Billy, go and look at thy shilling, in the yard, and see which is brightest, it or the moon. Is he gone? I've seen three men die within a few yards of me. One, the stone flew in two pieces: a fragment, weighing about four hundredweight I should say, struck him on the breast, and killed him on place; he never spoke. I've forgotten his very name. Another; the stone went clean out of window, but it kicked the grinder backward among the machinery, and his head was crushed like an eggshell. But the worst of all was poor Billy's father. He had been warned against his stone; but he said he would run it out. Well, his little boy, that is Billy, had just brought him in his tea, and was standing beside him, when the stone went like a pistol-shot, and snapped the horsing chains like thread: a piece struck the wall, and did no harm, only made a hole; but the bigger half went clean up to the ceiling, and then fell plump down again; the grinder he was knocked stupid like, and had fallen forward on his broken horsing: the grindstone fell right on him, and, ah,—I saw the son covered with the father's blood."

He shuddered visibly, at the recollection. "Ay," said he, "the man a corpse, and the lad an idiot. One faulty stone did that, within four yards of me, in a moment of time."

"Good heavens!"

"I was grinding at the next stone but one. He was taken, and I was left. It might just as well have been the other way. No saw-grinder can make sure, when he gets on his horsing, that he will come off it alive."

The visitor left Henry to think of this while he drew Bayne aside, and spoke on another matter.

Afterwards, all three left the works together; and Henry was so pleased with his new ally, that he told him, at the gate, he should be glad if he might be allowed to make his acquaintance.

"By all means," said the other. "I am quite at your service. You will find me at the 'Cutlers' Arms.'"

"Who shall I ask for?"

"George Grotait."

"Grotait. The devil!"

"No, no. Not quite so bad as that."

"What," said Henry, roughly, "do you mean to say you are Old Smitem?"

"That is a name *fools* give me."

Henry had no reply ready, and so the sturdy old secretary got the better of him again, and went his way unruffled.

Henry scolded Bayne for not telling him. Bayne excused himself on the ground that he thought every body knew Grotait. He added, "He knew you, and told me if he could serve you, without being unjust to the Trades, I was to tell him."

Henry replied to this only by a snort of defiance, and bade him good night.

The next day and the next were spent in other works, and then Henry, having no more facts to learn, fell into deep dejection again. He saw he must either cheat Dr. Amboyne, by shamming work, or else must leave Hillsborough.

He had the honesty to go to the Doctor and say that he had mastered the whole matter, and didn't see his way to take any more wages from a friend.

"You mean you have mastered the broad facts."

"I have, sir, and they are beyond belief; especially the file-cutters. They are the most numerous of all the Trades, and die like sheep. If your notion about Life, Labor, and Capital is right, the Trades are upside down; for the deadliest are the worst paid."

"And you are prepared with the remedies?"

"Not I."

"Yet you fancy you are at the end of your work. Why, you are only beginning. Now comes the real brain work; invention. Now are craniology and you upon your trial. But you are quite right about weekly salary. Invention must not be so degraded, but paid by the piece. Life, Labor, and Capital are upside down in this place, are they? Then you shall be the man to set them on their legs."

Henry shook his head. "Never, sir, unless I could give the masters bowels, and the men brains."

"Well, and why not? To invention all things are possible. You carry a note-book?"

"Yes, sir."

"Got it in your pocket?"

"No; on my shoulders."

"Haw! haw! haw! Then write this down in it—'THERE'S A KEY TO EVERY LOCK.'"

"It's down, sir."

"Now you must go out trout-fishing with Billy. He will take you on the hills, where the air is pure, and favorable to invention. You will divert your mind from all external subjects, especially Billy, who is a fool, and his trout-killing inhumane, and I a merciless glutton for eating them; and you will think, and think, and think, and forge the required key to this lock with three wards—Life, Labor, Capital. And, when forged, the Philanthropic Society shall pay you a good price for it. Meantime, don't dream of leaving Hillsborough, or I shall give you a stirrup-cup that will waft you much farther than London; for it shall be 'of prussic acid all composed,' or 'juice of cursed Hebenon in a phial.' Come, away with you."

"Good-bye, Doctor. God bless you. You have found 'the key to my heart' somehow. I come to you a miserable broken-hearted dog, and you put life and hope into me directly, I declare talking with you it's like drinking sunshine. I'll try all I know to please you."

He went down the street with his old elastic tread, and muttered to himself, "There's no lock without a key."

Next day he went out on the hills with Billy, and saw him tickle trout, and catch them under

3

stones, and do many strange things, and all the time he thought of Grace Carden, and bemoaned his sad fate. He could not command his mind, and direct it to philanthropy. His heart would not let him, and his personal wrongs were too recent. After a short struggle, these got so thoroughly the better, that he found himself stealing the Doctor's words for his own purposes. "No lock without a key." Then there must be some way of outwitting these cursed Trades, and so making money enough to set up as a master, and then court her, and woo her, and marry her. Heaven seemed to open on him at this prospect, and he fell into a deep reverie. By-and-by, as he pondered, it seemed to him as if the shadow of a coming idea was projected in advance of the idea itself. He knew somehow there was a way to baffle his enemies, and resume his business, and yet he could not see the way; but still he was absolutely conscious it existed.

This conviction took such hold of him, that he became restless, and asked Billy to leave off and come away. The youth consented, and they returned to the town with a basket of trout. Henry sent Billy on to the Doctor with half of them, and took the other half to his friend Bayne.

On what a trifle things turn. Bayne was very much pleased with his little attention, and asked him to take them to his lodging, and beg the landlady to cook them for dinner. "Tell her you dine with me, old fellow."

"Oh, hang it, I wasn't fishing for a dinner."

"As if I didn't know that. But you must. Then I shall enjoy your company in peace. I shall be there in an hour."

And so he was: but in that one hour events had occurred that I shall leave Mr. Bayne to relate.

During dinner neither of the friends wasted much time in talk: but after dinner, Bayne produced a bottle of port, notwithstanding Henry's remonstrances at being treated like a stranger, and it soon became apparent that the host himself was not in the habit of drinking that generous mixture every day. At the second glass he so far forgot himself as to utter the phrase "Eternal friendship," and, soon after, he began to writhe in his chair, and, at last, could no longer refrain himself, but told Henry that Miss Carden had been canvassing customers. She had just sent in six orders for sets of carving-tools, all for friends of her own.

Henry colored to the temples at this unexpected proof that she he loved thought of him too.

"Oh, Bayne," cried the poor young man, almost choking, "I little thought—God bless her!"

"Let us drink her health," said Bayne, excitedly.

"Ah, that I will!" and this was the first glass Henry drank honestly.

"Now, Little, I'm not doing quite right, you know; but I *must* tell you. When we lost you—you know that set of tools the Union dropped in our yard—well, he sent them to London for yours."

"That is just like him," said Henry, bitterly.

"And I'll tell you a good joke: they were in the place when you called, only not unpacked till just before I came away. Returned, sir! with a severe reprimand. 'Wonder you should send us such things as these for carving-tools by Little. If the error is not repaired shall consider ourselves

at liberty to communicate direct with that workman.' A regular sugar-plum."

"Oh, thank you, my kind friend, for telling me. The world isn't all bitterness, after all: a poor fellow gets a sweet drop of friendship now and then."

"Yes, and a good drop of port now and then, though I say it that shouldn't. Fill up. Well, my boy, Cheetham is in a fine way. I left him walking about the office like a hyena. So now is your time. You can't fight the Trades; but, if Cheetham will go in with you, and I know he will, for he is sorer than you are, you can trick the Trades yet."

"Ah! tell me how, that is all."

"Oh, I can't tell you exactly. I'll try, though. I say, what a glorious thing the Ruby is: it inspires us, and fires us, et cetera, and gives us ideas beyond our sphere. Did you ever see one of these new portable forges?"

"No; never heard of them."

"No wonder; they are just out. Well, buy one of them—they were invented here—and carry it to some dismal cavern, where the foot of man never treads: make Cheetham grind your blades in another county: and who will ever know? Go to him, and don't say a word, but just ask him for your month's salary. Then he will open the door of business himself—safe. I'll drink his health. He's not a bad sort, Cheetham: only he'd sell his soul for money. I hate such rubbish. Here's 'Perdition to the lot; and no heel-taps.'"

These words of fire set Henry pondering deeply; and, as he pondered, Bayne stuck to the port, and so effectually, that, at last, after an interval of silence, he came out in a new character. He disturbed his companion's reverie by informing him, in a loud aggressive tone, that it had long been his secret wish to encounter the Hillsborough Trades, in the persons of their secretaries, under the following conditions: a twenty-four feet ring, an experienced referee, and a kingdom looking on. As to the order of the pugilistic events, he was not unreasonably fastidious; must stipulate to begin with old Smitem; but, after that, they might encounter their fate in any order they chose, one down t'other come on. He let him know that this ardent desire for single combats, in an interminable series, arose from their treatment of his friend—"the best friend—the best heart—oh!—the best company—oh! oh!—the best—oh! oh! oh!" Whereupon he wept, the bellicose Bayne. And, after weeping the usual quantity, he twaddled, and, after twaddling, he became as pacific as ever, for he went to sleep in his chair.

And, while he snoozed, the words he had uttered set his friend's brain boiling and bubbling.

When the time came at which Bayne ought to return to the works, Henry called the landlady, and said, "Mr. Bayne is not very well. I am going to make his excuses. I wouldn't disturb him till five, if I was you, and then I'd give him a strong cup of tea."

Henry then went direct to the office, and found Mr. Cheetham there.

"Well?" said Mr. Cheetham, rather surlily.

"I am come to ask for my month, sir."

"So I guessed. Do you really mean to exact that?"

"Why not, sir?"

"Haven't you heard how they ground me down?"

"Yes, sir. But why did you give in? I was true to you, but you failed me. I'd have shut up the works for three months, rather than be made a slave of, and go from my word."

"Ay, ay; that's bachelor's talk. I've got a wife and children; and they make a man a mouse."

"Well, sir, I forgive you: but as to my month's wages—now all I say is—PUT YOURSELF IN MY PLACE!"

"Well?"

"You are me. You are brought from London, under an agreement, a month's notice on either side. You work, and give satisfaction. You are threatened, but you don't run from your employer. You are blown up, and nearly killed. You lose a fortnight, but you don't charge for it; 'twasn't your employer's fault. You come back to him, and face the music again. You work with the sword hanging over you. But your employer gives in, and sacks you in a minute. Oughtn't you to have your month? Come now, man to man, oughtn't you?"

"I ought, and that's the truth. I didn't look at it that way. I saw my own side. There—no more about it—I'll draw the check—with a good heart."

He drew his check-book to him, with a face as if vultures were tearing his vitals.

When Henry found him Amboynable, and saw his piteous look, he felt a little softened towards him, and he said, very impressively, "Wait one moment, sir, I've got an idea. I'm not the sort that likes to be beat. Are you?" The men looked steadily at each other.

Cheetham lowered his voice: "I've had hell inside me ever since. I thought I was a man, but they made a mouse of me. If you know any way to beat them, I'll go in with you."

"Well, sir, there is a key to every lock."

"That is well said, and I believe it; but one can't always find the key."

"I almost think I have, sir."

"See nobody is listening. Where is Bayne? He is due."

"Oh, he is not very well, sir; and I was to ask you for an hour's absence."

"Let him have the whole afternoon. I'll not have a soul in this but us two. Now come close, and tell me."

They sat opposite each other, and put their heads together over the table, and the following dialogue passed almost in a whisper. To see them, you would have thought they were conspiring against the law, instead of combining to hide a lawful act from the violaters of the law."

"I can forge the blades a dozen miles from Hillsborough."

"Not you; you will be told of. That won't do."

"I shall not be told of; for nobody will know but you. I shall only forge at night; and the building is out of the world, and wedged in, out of sight, between two bleak hills. Sir, it is a deserted church."

"What, forge blades in a church?"

"A deserted church; why not?"

"Little, you are A 1. Go on."

"I can get the blades ground by a friend at Birmingham; and my mother and I can put them together at home. The complete articles will come to you in parcels of a certain colored paper, invoiced in cipher outside, so that they need not be opened; you can trust the invoice, and dispatch them to your London agent."

"All right."

"The steel you must supply me at the current price, and charge it against me."

"Certainly. But your price per gross? For this work can't be done by time."

"Of course not." And Henry named a price per gross at which Cheetham lifted up his hands. "Why, you'll take nine pounds a week at that!"

"Ay, and more," said Henry, coolly. "But I sha'n't make it. Why, this scheme entails no end of expenses. A house, and stables with back entrance. A swift horse, to gallop to the forge at sunset, and back by noon. A cart to take the things to the railway and back, and to the parcel delivery for you. And, besides that, I must risk my neck, riding over broken ground at night: and working night and day shortens life. You can't reduce these things to Labor and Capital. It's Life, Labor, and Capital."

"Hallo! There's a new cry. I tell ye what; you know too much for me. You read the Beehive. I take you at your price."

Then he had a misgiving. "That old Smitem's as crafty as a fox. If he finds you stay here, with no visible employment, he will soon be down on us."

"Ay: but in the day-time I shall appear as a carver of wood, and also an inspector of factories for Dr. Amboyne. Who will suspect me of a night trade, as well as two day trades?"

Cheetham slapped the table triumphantly: but, recovering his caution, he whispered, "It's planned first-rate."

"And now, sir, there is one difficulty you must help me in, if you please. It is to set up the forge unobserved."

"What, am I to find the forge?"

"There's a question, sir! Of course you are. One of these new portable forges."

Cheetham reflected for some little time. He then said it was a ticklish thing, and he saw but one way. "The forge must come here, after closing hours, and you and I must fetch it away in the dead of night, and take it down to the old church, and set it up."

"Well, but, sir, we shall want assistance."

"Nay, nay. I've got the last suit of moleskin I ever worked in laid away. I'll air 'em, and put 'em on again; and, when I've got 'em on once more, I shall feel a man again. I'll have neither fool nor spy in it: the thing is too serious. I might bring some country fellow, that can't read or write; but no, these portables are small things, and I'm one of the strongest men in Hillsborough. Best keep it to ourselves. When is it to be?"

"Say next Wednesday, two hours after midnight."

"Then that is settled. And now I'll square the old account, as agreed." He drew his check-book towards him again.

But Henry stopped him. "Fair play's a jewel." said he smiling. "The moment you sacked me—"

"Say the Trades, not me."

"Dr. Amboyne hired me, at six guineas a week, to inspect the works. So you owe me nothing; but to be true to me."

This trait, though it was one of simple probity, astonished and gratified Mr. Cheetham. He looked on the young man with marked respect. "You are hard; but you are very square. I'll be true as steel to you, and we'll outwit our tyrants together, till I get a chance to put my foot on them. Yes, I'll be open with you; there are plenty of orders from London and the Continent, and one for six sets from swells in Hillsborough."

"Might I see that order?"

"Why not? There, run your eye over it. I want to go into the packing-room for a minute."

He then tossed Henry the order, as if it was nothing more than an order.

But it was a great deal more than that to Henry. It was Grace Carden's handwriting, the first specimen he had ever seen.

He took the paper in his hand, and a slight perfume came from it that went to his heart. He devoured the delicately formed letters, and they went to his heart too: he thrilled all over. And the words were as like her as the perfume. She gave the order, and the addresses of her friends, with a pretty little attempt at the business-like; but, this done, she burst out, "and we all entreat you to be good to poor Mr. Little, and protect him against the wicked, cruel, abominable Unions."

These sweet words made his heart beat violently, and brought the tears of tenderness into his eyes. He kissed the words again and again. He put them into his bosom, and took them out again, and gloated over them till they danced before his manly eyes. Then his love took another turn: he started up, and marched and strutted, like a young stag, about the room, with one hand pressing the paper to his bosom. Why had he said Wednesday? It could all have been got ready on Tuesday. No matter, he would make up for that lost day. He was on the road, once more, the road to fortune, and to her.

Cheetham came in, and found him walking excitedly, with the paper in his hand, and of course took the vulgar view of his emotion.

"Ay, lad," said he, "and they are all swells, I promise you. There's Miss Laura Craske. That's the mayor's daughter. Lady Betty Tyrone. She's a visitor. Miss Castleton! Her father is the county member."

"And who is this Mr. Coventry?" asked Henry.

"Oh, he is a landed gentleman, but spends his tin in Hillsborough; and you can't blame him. Mr. Coventry? Why, that is Miss Carden's intended."

"Her intended!" gasped Henry.

"I mean her beau. The gentleman she is going to marry, they say."

Henry Little turned cold, and a tremor ran through him; but he did not speak a word; and, with Spartan fortitude, suppressed all outward sign of emotion. He laid the paper down patiently, and went slowly away.

Loyal to his friend even in this bitter moment, he called at Bayne's place, and left word with the landlady that Mr. Bayne was not wanted at the works any more that day.

But he could not bear to talk to Bayne about his plans. They had lost their relish. He walked listlessly away, and thought it all over.

For the first time he saw his infatuation clearly. Was ever folly like his? If she had been a girl in humble life, would he not have asked whether she had a sweetheart? Yet he must go and give his heart to a lady without inquiry. There, where wisdom and prudence were most needed, he had speculated like an idiot. He saw it, and said to himself, "I have acted like a boy playing at pitch-farthing, not like a man who knew the value of his heart."

And so he passed a miserable time, bemoaning the treasure that was now quite inaccessible instead of nearly, and the treasure of his own heart he had thrown away.

He awoke with a sense of misery and deep depression, and could not eat; and that was a novelty in his young and healthy life. He drank a cup of tea, however, and then went out, to avoid his mother's tender looks of anxious inquiry. He meant to tell her all one day; but to-day he was not strong enough. He must wait till he was cured; for cured he must be, cured he would be.

He now tried to give his mind to the task Amboyne had set him; but it was too hard: he gave it up, with rage and despair.

Then he made a desperate resolve, which will not surprise those who know the human heart. He would harden himself. He would see more of Miss Carden than ever; only it should be in quite a new light. He would look at her, and keep saying to himself all the time, "You are another man's wife."

With this determination, he called at "Woodbine Villa."

Miss Carden was not at home.

"Are you sure she is not at home?"

"Not at home," replied the man stiffly.

"But you needn't to keep him at the door," said a mellow female voice.

"No, Miss," said the man, with a sudden change of manner, for he was a desperate and forlorn admirer of the last speaker. "Come in, sir." And he ushered him in to Jael Dence. She was in her bonnet, and just going out. They shook hands, and she told him Miss Carden was out walking.

"Walking with her beau?" said Henry, affecting a jaunty air, but sick within.

"That's more than I can say," replied Jael.

"You know nothing about it, of course," said Henry, roughly.

Jael looked surprised at the uncalled-for tone, and turned a mild glance of inquiry and reproach upon him.

The young man was ashamed of himself, and at that moment, too, he remembered he had already been rather ungrateful to her. So, to make amends, he said, "Didn't I promise to take you to Cairnhope?"

"Ay," said Jael; and she beamed and blushed in a moment.

"Well, I must go there, Sunday at the latest. So I will come for you, if you like. Will you be ready at ten o'clock?"

"Yes."

"I'll bring a gig, and take you like a lady."

"Any way you please. I'd as lieve walk as ride."

"I prefer riding. Ten o'clock, the day after to-morrow. Good-bye."

And he hurried away, provoked, not pleased,

at the manifest pleasure he had given. The woman he loved—inaccessible! The woman he only liked—he could spend the whole day with her. So the reasonable youth was cross with her for that, and for being so pleased, when he was wretched.

That feeling soon wore off, however, and, being a man of business, he wrote a line to Martha Dence, and told her he should visit her on Sunday. He added, with a gleam of good-humor, "and look out, for I shall bring my lass," intending to give them all an agreeable surprise; for Jael, he knew, was an immense favorite.

Next day he went on the hills with Billy, and, instead of thinking for the benefit of his enemies, as agreed with Amboyne, he set himself to hate every body, especially Miss Carden's lover, and the Hillsborough Unions. The grinders and file-cutters might die like sheep. What did he care? As much as they cared for him. Doctor Amboyne was too good for this world, and should keep his money to himself. He (Henry Little) would earn none of it, would take none of it. What invention he had should all go to outwit the Trades, and turn that old ruffian's church into his own smithy. This double master-stroke, by which he was to defeat one enemy, and secretly affront another, did make him chuckle once or twice, not with joy, but with bitterness.

He awoke in a similar mood next morning: but there was eight o'clock service near, and the silver-toned bell awakened better thoughts. He dressed hurriedly, and went to church.

He came back sadder, but rather less hot, less bitter; he had his breakfast, improved his toilette, went to the livery stable, and drove to "Woodbine Villa."

Mr. and Miss Carden had just finished breakfast, when he drove up to the door.

"Who is this?" said Mr. Carden.

"What, have you forgotten Mr. Little?"

"Indeed! Why, how he is dressed. I took him for a gentleman."

"You were not very far wrong, papa. He is a gentleman at heart."

Jael came in equipped for the ride. She was neatly dressed, and had a plain shepherd's-plaid shawl, that suited her noble bust. She looked a picture of health and happiness.

"If you please, Miss, he is come to take me to Cairnhope."

"Oh! it is for that! And I declare you expected him, too."

"Yes," said Jael, and blushed.

"You never told me," said Grace, with a slight touch of asperity.

"I didn't feel very sure he would keep his word."

"Then you don't know him as well as I do."

"I haven't the chance. He speaks a deal more to you than he do to me."

"Well, Jael, you needn't snub me, because you are going with Mr. Little."

As a bone, put between two friendly dogs, causes a growl, so when a handsome young man enters on the scene, I have seen young women lose a little of that unmitigated sweetness, which marked them a moment before.

With Grace, however, to snap and to repent generally followed in a breath. "I hope you will have a happy day, dear, as happy as you de-

serve." She then went to kiss her, but gave her cheek, instead of her lips. "There," said she, in rather a flurried way, "don't keep Mr. Little waiting."

Just as they drove off, Grace came to the window, after a slight irresolution, and kissed her hand to them enchantingly; at which a sudden flood of rapture rushed through Little's heart, and flushed his cheek, and fired his dark eye; Grace caught its flash full in hers, and instinctively retired a step. They were off.

"How bright and happy they look," said she to her father. And no wonder.

She sat down, and, somehow, she felt singularly dull and lonely.

Then she dressed for church, languidly. Then she went to church. By-and-by she came back from church.

Then she sat down, in her bonnet, and felt alone in the world, and sad; and at last she found herself quietly crying, as young ladies will sometimes, without any visible cause.

Then she asked herself what on earth she was crying about, and herself told her she was a little hysterical fool, and wanted a good beating.

Then she plucked up spirit, and dried her eyes. Then she took to yawning, and said Sunday was a dull day, and life itself rather a wearisome thing.

Then a servant came to inquire if she was at home.

"What, on Sunday? Of course not. Who is it?"

"Mr. Coventry, Miss."

"I am at home."

CHAPTER X.

PEOPLE that met Jael Dence and Henry Little driving to Cairnhope were struck with their faces; his so dark, hers so fair, and both so handsome: but the woman's lit up with lively delight, the man's clouded and sorrowful, and his brow knit with care. This very day he must take the lock off Cairnhope old Church, in spite of his uncle Raby. He had got the requisite tools with him hidden in the gig; but, even should he succeed, it was but the first step of a difficult and, perhaps, dangerous enterprise; and he was entering on it all with a heart no longer buoyed by hopeful love. But for his pledge to Mr. Cheetham, he could hardly have persisted in the struggle.

As for Jael Dence, she had no great reason to be happy either: the man she loved loved another. Still he was kind to *her*, and they belonged to the same class; she had a chance, and gleams of hope. And, after all, the future was uncertain, but the present certain: she had him to herself for the day. She was close to him—so close, that she could feel hi♦,—and he was driving her out, and to those who loved her: she basked in the present delight, and looked as if she was being taken to heaven by an angel, instead of driven to Cairnhope by a gloomy young man, whom the passers-by envied, and wondered at his good luck in having such a companion. She talked to him, and got the short answers of an absent man. But she continued to make her little remarks occasionally, and, ere they reached Cairnhope, he found himself somehow soothed by her sex, her beauty, and her mellow, kindly voice.

As they drove up to the farm-house, he told her to hide her face a moment, for they didn't know who it was.

Martha ran out. "Y'are welcome, y'are welcome; and so is your— Eh! Why it's our Jael. 'Tis no avail to hide thy face, thou jade; I know every bit o' thee." And Patty had her out of the gig in a moment, and there was a cuddling match it did one good to see.

Henry perked up for a moment and offered a suggestion. "Some of that ought to come my way, for bringing her here."

"Oh, you'll get enough o' that fun before you die," said Patty. "Now come you in; the carter's boy will take the horse."

They went in and greeted the old farmer; and soon the bell began to ring for church, and Nathan Dence told Martha to put on her bonnet.

"La, father!" said she, piteously.

"She prefers to stay at home and chat with Jael," said Henry. The fact is, he wanted to be rid of them both.

Old Dence shook his head. He was one of those simple, grand, old rustic Christians, who have somehow picked out the marrow of religion, and left the devil the bone, yclept Theology. "What?" said he, "my lasses! can't ye spare God a slice out of his own day?"

"Nay, it is not that, father."

The old man continued his remonstrance. "To be sure our Jael is a cordial. But she'll dine and sup with us. Take my word for't, all lawful pleasures are sweeter on the Lord's day after a bit o' church."

"And so they are, father; but dear heart! to think of you forgetting. Will nobody tell him? They're sworn to give me a red face, Jael and all."

This piteous appeal set Jael's wits working. "Eh, father, it will be the first of her banns!"

"Is it me you are asking such a question?" cried Patty, and turned her head away with absurd mock-modesty.

"And so 'tis," said Dence; "ah, that is a different thing."

Henry thought that was no reason for Patty's staying at home; she ought rather to go and hear the banns were cried all right.

At this proposal both sisters lifted up their hands, and he was remonstrated with, and lectured, and at last informed that, if a girl was in church when her banns were cried, her children would be all born deaf and dumb.

"Oh, indeed!" said Little, satirically. "That's a fact in natural history I was not aware of. Well, farmer, then let's you and I go by ourselves."

So Patty staid at home, in obedience to rural superstition, and Jael staid to keep her company, and Farmer Dence went to church out of piety; and as for Henry, to tell the truth, he went to church to escape the girls' tongues, and to be in a quiet, somniferous place, where he could think out his plans undisturbed.

The men were no sooner gone, than the sisters began to gossip hard.

"Eh, Jael, thou's gotten a prize."

"Not as I know of."

"I do adore a dark young man."

"So do I; but this one is not mine."

"I'll take his word before thine. Why he calls thee his lass in his very letter."

"Not he. Show me his letter."

"What will ye give me?"

"Nay, Patty, pray show it me."

"Well, and so I will."

She brought her the letter. Jael read it and changed color, and was delighted for a moment or two; but soon her good sense and humility prevailed. "'Twas to surprise you, like. I do know he looks higher than me."

"More fool he. But I don't believe it."

"You may," said Jael, and turned the conversation to Patty's approaching marriage; once launched in that direction, it flowed without intermission till the men returned, and dinner smoked upon the board.

After dinner Henry watched an opportunity, and slipped out into the yard, got the tools out, put his great-coat over them, and away to Cairnhope Church. He knew better than go past Raby Hall to it: he went back towards Hillsborough, full three miles, and then turned off the road and got on the heather. He skirted the base of a heathery mound, and at last saw the church on an elevation before him, made for it incautiously over some boggy ground, and sank in up to his waist.

He extricated himself with considerable difficulty, and cast a woeful look at his clothes.

Then he turned to, and piled up a heap of stones to mark the dangerous spot; for he foresaw he must often travel that way in all weathers. At last he reached the church, removed the lock, and fastened the door with screws. He then went back to the farm as fast as he could. But all this had taken a long time, and the sun was sinking as he got into the yard. He was in the very act of concealing the lock in the gig, when Martha Dence came out at him, as red as a turkey-cock.

"You thought but little of my sister, young man, to leave her all these hours, and you come out to spend the day with her."

"Stuff and nonsense! I came out on my own business."

"So it seems. And it have taken you into worse company. A fine figure she has made you."

"Who?"

"The hussy you have been after this while."

"That's so like you girls. You think a man has nothing to do but to run after women."

"What business can you have on the Sabbath-day, I'd like to know."

"Would you? Well, I'll tell you—when I tell the bellman."

"You are quite right, Mr. Little. Trust none but friends."

This was a bitter remark. Henry could not reply to it, and that moved his bile. Patty pursued her advantage, and let him know that, when a young man brought a young woman out for the day, he did not leave her for three hours at a stretch, unless he meant to affront her. She raised her voice in saying this, and so did he in replying, "Tell you I came out on my own business, not Jael's; but, I am a good-natured fellow, considering all I endure, so I took that opportunity to bring your sister out to see you. Could I guess you two couldn't make yourselves happy for one afternoon without flirting? So much for sisterly affection! Well, next time I'll come alone—if I come at all."

Jael came out at the raised voices, and received this last sentence full in the face. She turned pale.

"Oh, Patty, Patty, what have you been saying?"

"I've been speaking my mind, that is all."

"Ay, and you've made him say the only unkind word I ever heard from his lips."

"I'm very sorry, Jael," said the young man, penitently.

"Oh, then I'm to blame, because he is so ill-tempered." And Patty bridled.

"Partly. You should not interfere between friends." Having delivered this admonition, Jael softened it by kissing her, and whispered, "Father's asking for his tea."

Patty went in as meek as Moses.

Then Jael turned to Henry, and laid her hand on his arm, while her gray eyes searched his face.

"There's something amiss. You are never cross, except when you are unhappy. What is it?"

"Oh, Jael, my heart is broken. She is going to be married."

"Who says so?"

"Mr. Cheetham told me she was engaged to a Mr. Coventry."

"What can Mr. Cheetham know? To be sure the gentleman is a good deal with her, and I hear he has courted her this two years; and she likes his company, that's certain. But she is used to be admired, and she is very hard to please."

"What, then, you think it is not quite hopeless?"

"While there's life, there's hope."

"What had I better do?"

"Nay, you shouldn't ask me."

"Oh, yes: you advised me so wisely about the insurance."

"Ay, but then I saw it clear. He is purse-proud, and I knew he'd think a deal more of you if you insured your life for a vast o' money. But now I don't see clear; and I'm loath to advise. Happen you'd hate me afterwards if it went wrong."

"No, no, I wouldn't be so ungrateful."

Jael shook her head, doubtfully.

"Well, then," said Henry, "don't advise me; but put yourself in my place. (I'll tell you a secret I daren't trust to Patty. I have found a way to beat the Trades, and make my fortune in a year or two.) Now what would you do, if you were me?"

This question raised a tumult in Jael's heart. But her strong will, her loyalty, and, above all, her patience, conquered, though not without signs of the struggle, a bosom that heaved somewhat higher, and a low voice that trembled a little. "If I was a young man, I wouldn't shilly-shally, nor wait till I was rich, before I spoke. I'd have it out with her. I'd get her alone, and tell her all. Then, if she showed any sign of liking, I'd beg her to wait a bit, and say I'd soon be a gentleman for her sake. And if she cares nought for you, better know it, and leave her, than fare in heaven one hour and in hell the next, as I have seen thee do this while, my poor lad."

"It is wise and good advice, and I'll take it. I've kept all my courage for the Trades; I'd better have shown her a little. But there's one thing more I want to ask you."

This was too much. Jael's courage and patience failed her for once. "Keep it," she cried almost wildly. "I can't bear no more. There's not one lass in a hundred would do what I have done for you; yet you want more. D'ye think I'm not flesh and blood, as well as her?"

And she began to cry bitterly.

This took Henry quite by surprise, and grieved him. He consoled her, and coaxed her, in vague terms, that did not produce any effect. So then he kissed her cheek, and dried her eyes with his own handkerchief, and that was not quite so ineffectual. She gave a final sob, and said, with some slight remains of passion, "There, there; never heed me. It takes a deal of patience to go through the world." And so she left him.

He was not sorry to be alone a minute, and think. This short dialogue with Jael gave him some insight into female character. It made him suspect that he had been too timid with Grace Carden, and also that there were two women in the game instead of one.

When the time came to return he asked leave to borrow a horse-cloth.

He aired it by the fire, and remarked that it had turned very cold.

"Why," said Patty, "you have got your top-coat. Well, you are a soft one."

"And you are a sharp one," said Henry, ironically.

When Jael came to the gig, Henry put the cloth over her shoulders. "'Twasn't for me, ye see," said he: "'twas for my betters."

"I like you for that," said Patty.

Then there was much kissing, and shaking of hands, and promising to come again, and away they drove to Hillsborough.

On the road Henry, for the first time, was very respectful, as well as kind, to Jael. She was soft and gentle, but rather silent and reserved. They parted at the door of "Woodbine Villa."

Next day, Henry called early, and found Miss Carden alone. His heart beat tumultuously. She was very gracious, and hoped he had spent a pleasant day yesterday.

"Pretty well."

"Is that all? Why I quite envied you your ride, and your companion."

"She is a very good girl."

"She is something more than that: but one does not find her out all at once."

Now it was Henry's turn. But he was flustered, and thinking how he should begin. And, while he hesitated, the lady asked him was he come to finish the bust.

"No. I didn't come for that. I will finish it though." And thus he was diverted from his purpose, for the moment.

He took a carving tool, and eyed his model, but soon laid down the tool, and said : "I haven't thanked you yet. And I don't know how to thank you."

"What for?"

"For what you sent to Mr. Cheetham."

"Oh!" said Grace, and blushed. Then she turned it off, and said she thought if any body ought to thank her for that, it was Mr. Cheetham.

"Ay, for the order. But the sweet words that came with it? Do you think I don't prize them above all the orders in the world?"

She colored high again. "What! did he show you my note?"

"He did: and that has made me his friend. Shall I tell you the effect of those words on me?"

"No; never mind. But I'm glad I put them in, if they did you any good."

"Any good? They made me a new man. I was defeated by the Trades: I was broken-hearted: and I hated every body. Good Doctor Amboyne had set me work to do; to save the lives of my fellow-creatures. But I couldn't; I hated them so. The world had been too unjust to me, I could not return it good for evil. My heart was full of rage and bitterness."

"That's a great pity—at your age. But really it is no wonder. Yes; you have been cruelly used."

And the water stood in Grace's eyes.

"Ay, but it is all over; those sweet words of yours made a man of me again. They showed me you cared a little for me. Now I have found a way to outwit the Trades. Now I'm on the road to fortune. I won't be a workman this time next year. I'll be a master, and a thriving one."

"Ay, do, do. Beat them, defeat them ; make them scream with envy. But I am afraid you are too sanguine."

"No; I can do it, if you will only give me another word of hope to keep me going : and oh, I need it, if you knew all."

Grace began to look uneasy. "Mr. Little, can you doubt that you have my best wishes?" said she, guardedly, and much less warmly than she had spoken just before.

"No, I don't doubt that; but what I fear is, that, when I have gained the hard battle, and risen in the world, it will be too late. Too late."

Grace turned more and more uncomfortable.

"Oh, pray wait a few months, and see what I can do, before you—"

Will it be believed that Mr. Carden, who seldom came into this room at all, must walk in, just at this moment, and interrupt them? He was too occupied with his own affairs, to pay much attention to their faces, or perhaps he might have asked himself why the young man was so pale, and his daughter so red.

"I heard you were here, Little, and I want to speak to you on a matter of some importance."

Grace took this opportunity, and made her escape from the room promptly.

Henry, burning inwardly, had to listen politely to a matter he thought pitiably unimportant compared with that which had been broken off. But the "Gosshawk" had got him in its clutches; and was resolved to make him a decoy duck. He was to open a new vein of Insurances. Workmen had hitherto acted with great folly and imprudence in this respect, and he was to cure them, by precept as well as example.

Henry assented, to gratify a person whose goodwill he might require, and to get rid of a bore. But that was not so easy; the "Gosshawk" was full of this new project, and had a great deal to say, before he came to the point, and offered Henry a percentage on the yearly premium of every workman that should be insured in the "Gosshawk."

This little bargain struck, Henry was left alone; and waited for the return of Miss Carden.

He was simple enough to hope she would come back, and have it out with him.

She kept carefully out of his way, and, at last, he went sadly home.

"Ah," said he, "Jael gave me bad advice. I have been premature, and frightened her."

He would go to work his own way again.

In forty-eight hours he moved into his new house, furnished it partly : bought a quantity of mediocre wood-carving, and improved it; put specimens in his window, and painted his name over the door. This, at his mother's request and tearful entreaties, he painted out again, and substituted "Rowbotham."

Nor was Rowbotham a mere *nom de plume*. It was the real name of Silly Billy. The boy had some turn for carving, but was quite uncultivated : Henry took him into his employ, fed him, and made free with his name. With all this he found time to get a key made to fit the lock of Cairnhope old Church.

At one o'clock on Thursday morning he came to Cheetham's works, and scratched at the gate. A big workman opened it. It turned out to be Cheetham himself, in a moleskin suit, and a long beard.

The forge on wheels was all ready, also a cart containing anvil, bellows, hammers, pincers, leather buckets, and a quantity of steel laths. They attached the forge to the tail of the cart, and went on their silent expedition. Cheetham drove the cart. Henry followed afar off until they had cleared the suburbs.

They passed "Woodbine Villa." A single light was burning. Henry eyed it wistfully, and loitered long to look at it. Something told him that light was in her bedroom. He could hardly tear himself away from contemplating it: it was his pole-star.

There was only one great difficulty in their way ; a man on a horse might cross the moor, but a cart must go by "Raby Hall" to reach the church: and, before they got within a furlong of the Hall, a watch-dog began to bark.

"Stop, sir," whispered Henry. "I expected this." He then produced some pieces of thick felt, and tied them with strings round the wheels.

They then drove by the house as fast as they could. They did not deceive the dogs; but no man heard them, nor saw them.

They got to the church, opened the door, and drew the forge into the deserted building.

As soon as they got inside, Cheetham cast his eyes round and gave a shudder. "You must have a stout heart: no money should tempt me to work here by myself. Lord! What's that?"

For a low musical moan was heard.

Cheetham darted back, and got to the church-door.

Henry's heart beat faster: but he lighted his lantern, and went up the aisle. The place was solemn, grim, gaunt, and mouldering, and echoed strangely; but it was empty. He halloed to his companion that it was all right. Then they set the forge up near a pillar at the entrance into the chancel. When they had done this, and brought in the steel laths, the sacks of coals, etc., Cheetham produced a flask, and took a pull of neat brandy. This gave him courage, and he proposed to have a look round before they went. Accordingly they inspected the building.

When they came round to the chancel, suddenly there was a rattle, and a tremendous rush of some huge thing that made a cold wind, and blew out the light.

Henry was appalled, and Cheetham dropped the lantern, and ran, yelling. And soon Henry heard his voice in the churchyard calling on him to come out.

He did go out, and felt very much puzzled and alarmed. However, he got matches from Cheetham, and went back, and lighted the lantern, quaking a little, and then he found that the great mouldering picture over the altar had rotted away from some of its supports, and one half of it was now drooping, like a monstrous wing, over the altar.

He returned with the lantern, and told Cheetham what it was. Then he screwed on the lock, locked the church, and they went back to Hillsborough in good spirits.

But, as he lay in bed, Henry thought the matter over, and, for the first time in his life, felt superstitious.

"It is very odd," he said, "that old picture my forefathers have worshipped under, and prayed to, no doubt, should flap out in my face like that, the moment I offered to set up my forge among their dead bones."

Daylight dispersed these superstitious feelings, and the battle began.

As usual, the first step towards making money, was to part with it. He could do nothing without a horse and a light cart. In Hillsborough they drive magnificent horses in public cabs: Henry knew one in particular, that had often spun up the steepest hills with him; a brute of prodigious bone and spirit. He bought this animal for a moderate price, considering his value: and then the next thing was—and indeed with some of us it precedes the purchase of the animal—to learn to ride.

He had only two days to acquire this accomplishment in: so he took a compendious method. He went to the circus, at noon, and asked to see the clown. A gloomy fellow was fished out of the nearest public, and inquired what he wanted.

"The clown."

"Well, I am the clown."

"What! you the merry chap that makes the fun?" said Henry, incredulously.

"I make the fun at night," replied the man, dolefully. "If you want fun out of me, come and pay your shilling, like a man."

"But it isn't fun I'm come for. I want to learn to ride."

"Then you are too old. Why, we begin as soon as we can stand on a horse's back."

"Oh, I don't mean to ride standing. I want to sit a horse, rearing, or plunging, or blundering over rough ground."

"What will you stand?"

"A sovereign."

The clown dived into the public-house, and told a dark seedy man, with his black hair plastered and rolled effeminately, that he had got a bloke who would stand a quid for a mount. The two came out, and the plastered Italian went to the stables: the melancholy punster conducted Henry into the arena, and stood beside him, like Patience on a monument. Presently a quiet mare ran in, and stuck.

Henry was mounted, and cantered her round, the two men instinctively following in a smaller circle, with jaws as long as your arm.

"This is delightful," said Henry; "but I might as well be sitting in a chair. What I want is a Prancer."

Then they brought him another horse, just as docile as the mare. The obedient creature, at a signal, reared suddenly, and seated Mr. Little on the sawdust behind him. A similar result was attained several times, by various means. But Henry showed himself so tough, courageous, and persistent, that he made great progress, and his good-humor won his preceptors. They invited him to come to-morrow, at an earlier hour, and bring half a quid with him. He did so, and this time there was an American rider rehearsing, who showed Henry what to do, and what not to do; and gave him a most humorous and instructive lesson. Indeed, his imitations of bad riding were so truthful and funny, that even the clown was surprised into one laugh; he who rarely smiled, unless in the way of business.

"Well, sir," said Henry, "you have given me a good lesson; now take a hint from me; just you go and do all this before the public; for I never saw you do any thing half so droll."

They all three shook their heads with one accord. Go out of the beaten track, before an audience? Never. Such vagaries were only admissible in private.

After this second day the fee was reduced to a gallon of ale.

But, on the third day, the pupil combined theory with practice. He told his mother he was going to Cairnhope for the night. He then rode off to Cairnhope church. He had two large saddle-bags, containing provisions, and tools of all sorts. He got safe across the moor just before sunset. He entered the church, led the horse in with him, and put him into the Squire's pew. He then struck a light, went into the chancel, and looked at the picture. It was as he had left it; half on the wall, half drooping over the altar-place. The walls were dank, and streaked here and there with green. His footsteps echoed, and the edifice was all dark, except within the rays of his lantern; it also sang and moaned in a way to be accounted for by the action of the wind on a number of small apertures; but, nevertheless, it was a most weird and ghostly sound. He was glad of the companionship of his very horse.

He took his buckets to the mountain stream, and, in due course, filled his trough, and left one bucket full for other uses. He then prepared and lighted his forge. As he plied the bellows, and the coals gleamed brighter and brighter, monumental figures came out and glared at him; mutilated inscriptions wavered on the walls; portions of the dark walls themselves gleamed in the full light, and showed the streaks and stains of age and weather, and the shadow of a gigantic horse's head; and, as the illuminated part seemed on fire by contrast, so the dark part of the church was horribly black and mysterious, and a place out of which a ghost or phantom might be expected, at any moment, to come forth into that brilliant patch of light.

Young Little, who had entered on this business in all the skepticism of the nineteenth century, felt awed, and began to wish he had selected any other building in the world but this. He seemed to be desecrating a tomb.

However, he mustered up his manly resolution. He looked up at a small aperture in the roof and saw a star glittering above: it seemed close, and a type of that omniscient eye "from which no secrets are hid."

He clasped his hands together, and said, "I hope God, who has seen me driven from the haunts of men, will forgive me for taking refuge here; and, if he does, I don't care who else is offended, alive or dead." And, with this, he drew the white-hot strip of steel from the forge on to the anvil, and down came his hammer with a blow that sent the fiery steel flying all round, and rang and echoed through the desolate building. Instantly there was a tremendous plunge and clatter, followed by a shaking sound, and, whiz, the church was fanned by black wings going zigzag.

"Ten thousand devils!" yelled Henry, and heaved the hammer high, in his own defense.

But it was only the horse plunging and quivering with fear, and a score of bats the blow of the hammer had frightened out of the rotten pulpit.

He resumed work with a beating heart, and the building rang and echoed and re-echoed with the rapid blows; and no more interruption came. The nineteenth century conquered.

After four hours of earnest work, he fed his horse, ate a slice of bread and meat, drank water from the bucket, gave his horse some, and went to sleep in the pew beside that useful animal.

Back to Hillsborough, at peep of day, with the blades he had forged.

He now took his mother, in a great measure, into his confidence, under a strict promise to tell nobody, not even Doctor Amboyne. Mrs. Little received the communication in a way that both surprised and encouraged him. She was as willing to outwit the Unions, as she was unwilling to resist them openly; and Henry found her an admirable coadjutor.

Had she known where Henry had set up his forge, she would have been very unhappy. But he merely told her it was in a secluded place, near Cairnhope, where he could never be detected.

The carving business, being merely a blind, was not pushed. But Henry gave his apprentice, Billy, instruction, and the youth began to show an aptitude which contrasted remarkably with his general incapacity.

Mrs. Little paid one or two visits to factories, to see what women could do in this sort of work; and, one day, she told Henry she was sure she could sharpen and finish the blades.

"No, mother," said Henry. "You are a lady. I can't have you made a slave of, and your beautiful white hands spoiled."

"I shall be happier, helping you, dear; and I won't spoil my hands, since you care about them."

She insisted on a trial, and soon acquired a remarkable knack: she had a fine light hand: and it is an art easily learned by an attentive and careful woman. Indeed they can beat the men at it, if they will only make up their minds.

And so the enterprise was launched, and conducted thus: in the day time, Henry showed himself in the town, and talked big about carving; and, in the afternoon, he rode out, and did the real work of his life, over the dead bodies of his ancestors.

His saddle-bags were always full, and, gradually, he collected some comforts about him in the deserted church.

He called, more than once, at "Woodbine Villa," but Miss Carden was on a visit.

He was in the full career of fortune again, and sanguine of success, before they met. One day, having ascertained from Jael, what day she would be at home, he called, and was admitted. The room was empty, but Miss Carden soon came into it, accompanied by Jael carrying the bust.

"Ah, Mr. Little," said she, before he could possibly utter a word, "this is fortunate. There is a party here on Thursday, and I want to show the bust complete, if you don't mind."

Henry said he would finish it for her. He accordingly set to work, and waited quietly till Jael should leave the room, to have it out with Grace.

She, for her part, seemed to have forgotten his strange manner to her the other day; perhaps she chose to forget it, or overlook it. But Henry observed that Jael was not allowed to quit the room. Whatever Miss Carden wanted she fetched herself, and came back softly, and rather suddenly, as if she had a mind to surprise Jael and the other too. Female subtlety was clearly at work.

"What do you advise me?" said Henry to Jael, during one of these intervals.

Jael never lifted her eyes from her work, and spoke under her breath, "I think I'd be patient to-day. She must give you a chance to speak some day. Talk to me, when she comes back—about the Cairnhope folk, or any thing."

Henry followed this advice, and Grace, for the first time, found herself a little ignored in the conversation. She was astonished at this and I don't think she quite liked it.

Henry was still going on with warmth and volubility about the Cairnhope folk, their good hearts, and their superstitions, when a visitor was announced.

"Mr. Coventry."

Henry stopped in the middle of a sentence.

Grace brightened up, and said she was at home.

Mr. Coventry entered the room; a tall, well-made man, with an aquiline nose, and handsome face, only perhaps there were more lines in it than he was entitled to at his age, for he was barely thirty. He greeted Miss Carden with easy grace, and took no more notice of the other two, than if they were chairs and tables.

Mr. Frederick Coventry had studied the great art of pleasing, and had mastered it wonderfully;

but he was not the man to waste it indiscriminately. He was there to please a young lady, to whom he was attached, not to diffuse his sunshine indiscriminately.

He courted her openly, not indelicately, but with a happy air of respect and self-assurance.

Henry sat, sick with jealousy, and tried to work and watch; but he could only watch: his hand trembled too much to work.

What may be called oblique flattery is very pleasing to those quick-witted girls, who have had a surfeit of direct compliments: and it is oblique flattery, when a man is supercilious and distant to others, as well as tender and a little obsequious to her he would please.

Grace Carden enjoyed this oblique flattery of Mr. Coventry's all the more that it came to her just at a moment when her companions seemed disposed to ignore her. She rewarded Mr. Coventry accordingly, and made Henry Little's heart die within him. His agony became intolerable. What a position was his! Set there, with a chisel in his hand, to copy the woman he loved, while another man wooed her before his face, and she smiled at his wooing.

At last his chisel fell out of his hand, and startled every body: and then he rose up with pale cheek, and glittering eyes, and Heaven only knows what he was going to do or say. But at that moment another visitor was announced, to whom indeed the door was never closed. He entered the next moment, and Grace ran to meet him, crying, "Oh, Mr. Raby! this *is* a surprise."

Mr. Raby kissed her, and shook hands with Mr. Coventry. He then said a kind word to Jael Dence, who got up and courtesied to him. He cast a careless glance on Henry and the bust, but said nothing. He was in a hurry, and soon came to the object of his visit.

"My dear," said he, "the last time I saw you, you said you were sorry that Christmas was no longer kept in Hillsborough as it used to be."

"And so I am."

"Well, it is kept in Cairnhope, thank Heaven, pretty much as it was three centuries ago. Your father will be in London, I hear; will you honor my place and me with a visit during the Christmas holidays?"

Grace opened her eyes with astonishment. "Oh, that I will," said she, warmly.

"You will take your chance of being snowed up?"

"I am afraid I shall not be so fortunate," was the charming reply.

The Squire turned to Coventry, and said slyly, "I would ask you to join us, sir; but it is rather a dull place for a gentleman who keeps such good company."

"I never heard it spoken of as a dull place before," said the young man; "and, if it was, you have taken a sure means to make it attractive."

"That is true. Well, then, I have no scruple in asking you to join us;" and he gave Grace a look, as much as to say, "Am I not a considerate person?"

"I am infinitely obliged to you, Mr. Raby," said Coventry, seriously; "I will come."

"You will stay to luncheon, godpapa?"

"Never touch it. Good-bye. Well, then, Christmas-eve I shall expect you both. Dinner at six. But come an hour or two before, if you can: and Jael, my girl, you know you must dine at the hall on Christmas-eve, and old Christmas-eve as usual, you and your sister and the old man."

Jael courtesied, and said with homely cordiality, "We shall be there, sir, please God we are alive."

"Bring your gun, Coventry. There's a good sprinkling of pheasants left. By-the-by, what about that pedigree of yours; does it prove the point?"

"Completely. Dorothy Raby, Sir Richard's youngest sister, married Thomas Coventry, who was out in the forty-five. I'm having the pedigree copied for you, at a stationer's near."

"I should like to see it."

"I'll go with you, and show it to you, if you like."

Mr. Raby was evidently pleased at this attention, and they went off together.

Grace accompanied them to the door. On her return she was startled by the condition of young Little.

This sudden appearance of his uncle, whom he hated, had agitated him not a little, and that uncle's interference had blasted his last hope. He recognized this lover, and had sided with him: was going to shut the pair up, in a country-house, together. It was too much. He groaned, and sank back in his chair, almost fainting, and his hands began to shake in the air, as if he was in an ague.

Both the women darted simultaneously towards him. "Oh! he's fainting!" cried Grace. "Wine! wine! Fly." Jael ran out to fetch some, in spite of a despairing gesture by which the young man tried to convey to her it was no use.

"Wine can do me no good, nor death no harm. Why did I ever enter this house?"

"Oh, Mr. Little, don't look so; don't talk so," said Grace, turning pale, in her turn. "Are you ill? What is the matter?"

"Oh, nothing. What should ail me? I'm only a workman. What business have I with a heart? I loved you dearly. I was working for you, fighting for you, thinking for you, living for you. And you love that Coventry, and never showed it."

Jael came in with a glass of wine for him, but he waved her off with all the grandeur of despair.

"You tell me this to my face!" said Grace, haughtily; her bosom panted.

"Yes; I tell you so to your face. I love you, with all my soul."

"How dare you? What have I ever done, to justify— Oh, if you weren't so pale, I'd give you a lesson. What could possess you? It's not my fault, thank heaven. You have insulted me, sir. No; why should I? You must be unhappy enough. There, I'll say but one word, and that, of course, is 'good morning.'"

And she marched out of the room, trembling secretly in every limb.

Henry sat down, and hid his face, and all his frame shook.

Then Jael was all pity. She threw herself on her knees, and kissed his trembling hands with canine fidelity, and wept on his shoulder.

He took her hand, and tried hard to thank her, but the words were choked.

Grace Carden opened the door, and put her head cautiously in, for she wanted to say a word to Jael without attracting Henry's attention. But, when she saw Jael and Henry in so loving an attitude, she started, and then turned as red as fire; and presently burst out laughing.

Jael and Henry separated directly.

Grace laughed again, an unpleasant laugh. "I beg pardon, good people. I only wanted Mr. Little's address. I thought you could get it for me, Jael. And now I'm sure you can. Ha! ha! ha!"

And she was heard laughing after the door closed.

Now there was a world of contempt and insolence in this laugh. It conveyed, as plainly as words, "I was going to be so absurd as to believe in your love, and pity it, at all events, though I can't approve it: but now you have just set my mind at ease. Ha! ha! ha!"

"Let me go," cried Henry, wildly.

"Nay, tell me your address."

"What for? To tell that cruel—laughing—"

"Nay then, for myself."

"That's a different thing. I respect you. But her, I mean to hate, as much as I loved her."

He gave Jael his address, and then got out of the house as fast as he could.

That evening Grace Carden surprised her father, by coming into his study. "Papa," said she, "I am come to ask a favor. You must not refuse me. But I don't know that you ever did. Dearest, I want £50."

"Well, my child; just tell me what it is for."

"It is for Mr. Little; for his lessons."

"Well, but £50!"

"He has given me a good many. And to tell you the truth, papa, I dismissed him rather unceremoniously; and now I should be glad to soften the blow a little, if I can. Do be very good and obedient, dear papa, and write what I shall dictate. *Please!*"

"Well, spoiled child: who can resist you?"

Then Grace dictated, and Mr. Carden wrote:

"DEAR SIR,—My daughter informs me that, as yet, you have received no remuneration for the lessons you have given her. I beg your acceptance of the enclosed check and, at the same time, should be glad if you would put a price on the admirable bust you have executed of her.

"Yours obediently, WALTER CARDEN."

The reply to this letter surprised Mr. Carden, so that he brought it to Grace, and showed it her.

"DEAR SIR,—The lessons are not worth speaking of. I have learnt more in your house than I taught. I beg to return the check with thanks. Price of the bust, five hundred guineas.

"Yours obediently, HENRY LITTLE."

Grace colored up, and her eyes sparkled. "That young man wants humbling."

"I don't see that, really. He is very civil, and I presume this five hundred guineas is just a polite way of saying that he means to keep it. Wants it for an advertisement, eh?"

Grace smiled and bit her lip. "Oh, what a man of business you are!" And a little while after the tears came into her eyes. "Madman!" said she to herself. "He won't let me be his friend. Well, I can't help it."

After the brief excitement of this correspondence, Little soon relapsed into dull misery. His

mother was alarmed, and could restrain herself no longer. She implored his confidence: "Make me the partner of your grief, dear," she said; "not that you can tell me any thing I have not guessed already; but, dearest, it will do you good to open your heart; and, who knows, I may assist you. I know my sex much better than you do."

Henry kissed her sadly, and said it was too late now. "It is all over. She is going to marry another man."

"Has she told you so?"

"Not in words; but I have seen it. She has burnt it into my heart."

"I wish I knew her," said Mrs. Little, very earnestly, and almost in a whisper.

"Some day, mother, some day; but not now. Oh, the tortures one heart can suffer, and yet not break."

Mrs. Little sighed. "What, not even tell me her name?"

"I can't, I can't. Oh, mother, you mean well, but you will drive me mad."

Mrs. Little forbore to press him further just then. She sat silent at her work, and he at his, till they were aroused by a fly drawing up at the door.

A fine young woman got out, with something heavy, and holding it like a child on one arm, rapped at the door with the hand that was disengaged.

Mrs. Little opened the door to her, and she and Jael Dence surveyed each other with calm but searching eyes.

"If you please, ma'am, does Mr. Little bide here?"

Mrs. Little said yes, with a smile: for Jael's face and modesty pleased her at first sight.

"I have something for him."

"I'll give it to him."

"If you please, ma'am, I was to give it him myself."

Henry recognized the voice, opened the door, and invited her in.

Mrs. Little followed her, full of suppressed curiosity.

This put Jael out, but she was too patient to show it.

"It is the bust," said she; and put it softly down on the table with her strong arms.

Henry groaned. "She despises even that; she flings it at my head without a word."

"Nay; I have got a note for you."

"Then why didn't you give it me at once?" cried Henry impatiently.

She handed him the note without a word.

It ran thus:

"Miss Carden presents her compliments to Mr. Little, and sends him his beautiful bust. She is grieved that he will accept no remuneration for his lessons; and begs permission to offer her best wishes for his happiness and prosperity."

The gentleness of this disarmed Henry, and at the same time the firmness crushed him. "It is all over!" he cried, despairingly: "and yet I can't hate her."

He ran from the room, unable to restrain his tears, and too proud and fiery to endure two spectators of his grief.

Mrs. Little felt as mothers feel towards those who wound their young.

"Is it the woman's likeness?" said she bitterly, and then trembled with emotion.

"Ay."

"May I see it?"

"Surely, ma'am." And Jael began to undo the paper.

But Mrs. Little stopped her. "No, not yet. face: a Cairnhope face. My child, you remind me of days gone by. Come and see me again, will you? Then I shall be more able to talk to you quietly."

"Ay, that I will, ma'am." And Jael colored all over with surprise, and such undisguised pleasure that Mrs. Little kissed her at parting.

MRS. LITTLE EXAMINES THE BUST.

I couldn't bear the sight of a face that has brought misery upon him. I would rather look at yours. It is a very honest one. May I inquire your name?"

"Jael Dence—at your service."

"Dence! ah, then no wonder you have a good

She had been gone a considerable time, when Henry came back; he found his mother seated at the table, eying his masterpiece with stern and bitter scrutiny.

It was a picture, those two rare faces in such close opposition. The carved face seemed alive;

but the living face seemed inspired, and to explore the other to the bottom with merciless severity. At such work the great female eye is almost terrible in its power.

"It is lovely," said she. "It seems noble. I can not find what I know must be there. Oh, why does God give such a face as this to a fool?"

"Not a word against her," said Henry. "She is as wise, and as noble, and as good, as she is beautiful. She has but one fault; she loves another man. Put her sweet face away; hide it from me till I am an old man, and can bring it out to show young folks why I lived and die a bachelor. Good-bye, dear mother, I must saddle Black Harry, and away to my night's work."

The days were very short now, and Henry spent two-thirds of his time in Cairnhope Church. The joyous stimulus of his labor was gone, but the habit remained, and carried him on in a sort of leaden way. Sometimes he wondered at himself for the hardships he underwent merely to make money, since money had no longer the same charm for him; but a good workman is a patient, enduring creature, and self-indulgence, our habit, is after all, his exception. Henry worked heavily on, with his sore, sad heart, as many a workman had done before him. Unfortunately his sleep began to be broken a good deal. I am not quite clear whether it was the after-clap of the explosion, or the prolonged agitation of his young heart, but at this time, instead of the profound sleep that generally rewards the sons of toil, he had fitful slumbers, and used to dream strange dreams, in that old church, so full of gaunt sights and strange sounds. And, generally speaking, however these dreams began, the figure of Grace Carden would steal in ere he awoke. His senses, being only half asleep, colored his dreams; he heard her light footstep in the pattering rain, and her sweet voice in the musical moan of the desolate building; desolate as his heart when he awoke, and behold it was a dream.

The day after Christmas-day began brightly, but was dark and lowering towards afternoon. Mrs. Little advised Henry to stay at home. But he shook his head. "How could I get through the night? Work is my salvation. But for my forge, I should perhaps end like—" he was going to say "my poor father." But he had the sense to stop.

Unable to keep him at home, the tender mother got to his saddle-bags, and filled his flask with brandy, and packed up a huge piece of Yorkshire pie, and even stuffed in a plaid shawl. And she strained her anxious eyes after him as he rode off.

When he got among the hills, he found it was snowing there very hard; and then, somehow, notwithstanding all the speed he made, it was nearly dark when he got on the moor, and the tracks he used to go by, over the dangerous ground, were effaced.

He went a snail's pace, and at last dismounted, and groped his way. He got more than one fall in the snow, and thought himself very fortunate, when, at last, something black towered before him, and it was the old church.

The scene was truly dismal: the church was already overburdened with snow, and still the huge flakes fell fast and silently, and the little mountain stream, now swollen to a broad and foaming torrent, went roaring by, behind the churchyard wall.

Henry shivered, and made for the shelter.

The horse, to whom this church was merely a well-ventilated stable, went in and clattered up the aisle, saddle-bags and all.

Henry locked the door inside, and soon blew the coals to a white heat. The bellows seemed to pant unnaturally loud, all was so deadly still.

The windows were curtained with snow, that increased the general gloom, though some of the layers shone ghostly white and crystalline, in the light of the forge, and of two little grates he had set in a monument.

Two heaps of snow lay in the centre aisle, just under two open places in the 'roof, and, on these, flakes as big as a pennypiece kept falling through the air, and glittered like diamonds as they passed through the weird light of the white coals.

Oh! it was an appalling place, that night; youth and life seemed intruders. Henry found it more than he could bear. He took a couple of candles, placed them in bottles, and carried them to the western window, and there lighted them. This one window was protected by the remains of iron-work outside, and the whole figure of one female saint in colored glass survived.

This expedient broke the devilish blackness, and the saint shone out glorious.

The horrid spell thus broken in some degree, Henry plied his hammer, and made the church ring, and the flaming metal fly.

But by-and-by, as often happened to him now, a drowsiness overcame him at the wrong time. In vain he battled against it. It conquered him even as he worked; and, at last, he leaned with his arms against the handle of the bellows, and dozed as he stood.

He had a dream of that kind which we call a vision, because the dream seems to come to the dreamer where he is.

He dreamed he was there at his forge, and a soft voice called to him. He turned, and lo! between him and the western window stood six female figures, all dressed in beautiful dresses, but of another age, and of many colors, yet transparent; and their faces fair, but white as snow: and the ladies courtesied to him, with a certain respectful majesty beyond description: and, somehow, by their faces, and their way of courtesying to him, he knew they were women of his own race, and themselves aware of the relationship.

Then several more such figures came rustling softly through the wall from the churchyard, and others rose from the vaults and took their places quietly, till there was an avenue of dead beauties; and they stood in an ascending line up to the west window. Some stood on the ground, some on the air; that made no difference to them.

Another moment, and then a figure more lovely than them all shone in the window, at the end of that vista of fair white faces.

It was Grace Carden. She smiled on him and said, "I am going where I can love you. There the world can not divide us. Follow me; follow; follow!"

Then she melted away; then all melted: and he awoke with a loud cry that echoed through the edifice, now dark and cold as the grave; and a great white owl went whirling, and with his wings made the only air that stirred.

The fire was out, and the place a grave. Yet,

cold as it was, the dreamer was bathed in perspiration, so clear had been that unearthly vision, so ghostly was now that flitting owl.

Shuddering all over, he lighted his fire again, and plied his bellows with fury, till the fire glowed brighter than ever; and even then he prayed aloud that he might never see the like again, even in a dream.

He worked like mad, and his hand trembled as he struck.

Ere he had thoroughly recovered the shock, a wild cry arose outside.

He started back, awe-struck.

What with the time, the place, and that strange vision, the boundaries of the natural and the supernatural were a little confused in his mind.

"Help, help!" cried a voice; and now the familiar tone of that voice made him utter a loud cry in return.

He searched for the key, and made his way to the door; but, just as he began to insert the key, the voice was at the door outside.

"Oh, save me! A dying girl! Save me!"

The cry was now a moan, and the next moment an inert mass fell like lead against the door in a vain attempt to knock at it.

The voice was Grace Carden's, and it was Grace Carden's body that fell so inert and powerless against the church-door, within a yard of Henry Little's hand.

———

CHAPTER XI.

ON the twenty-fourth of December Miss Carden and Jael Dence drove to Cairnhope village, and stopped at the farm: but Nathan and his eldest daughter had already gone up to the Hall; so they waited there but a minute or two to light the carriage lamps, and then went on up the hill. It was pitch dark when they reached the house. Inside, one of Mr. Raby's servants was on the look-out for the sound of wheels, and the visitors

had no need to knock or ring; this was a point of honor with the master of the mansion; when he did invite people, the house opened its arms; even as they drove up, open flew the great hall-door, and an enormous fire inside blazed in their faces, and shot its flame beyond them out into the night.

Grace alighted, and was about to enter the house, when Jael stopped her, and said, "Oh, Miss, you will be going in left foot foremost. Pray don't do that: it is so unlucky."

Grace laughed, but changed her foot, and entered a lofty hall, hung with helmets, pikes, breast-plates, bows, cross-bows, antlers, etc., etc. Opposite her was the ancient chimney-piece and ingle-nook, with no grate, but two huge iron dogs, set five feet apart; and on them lay a birch log and root, the size of a man, with a dozen beech billets burning briskly and crackling underneath and aside it. This genial furnace warmed the staircase and passages, and cast a fiery glow out on the carriage, and glorified the steel helmets and breast-plates of the dead Rabies on the walls, and the sparkling eyes of the two beautiful women who now stood opposite it in the pride of their youth, and were warmed to the heart by its crackle and glow. "Oh! what a glorious fire, this bitter night. Why, I never saw such a—"

"It is the yule log, Miss. Ay, and you might go all round England, and not find its fellow, I trow. But our Squire he don't go to the chandler's shop for his yule log, but to his own woods, and fells a great tree."

A housemaid now came forward with bed-candles, to show Miss Carden to her room. Grace was going up, as a matter of course, when Jael, busy helping the footman with her boxes, called after her: "The stocking, Miss! the stocking!"

Grace looked down at her feet in surprise.

"There it is, hung up by the door. We must put our presents into it before we go up stairs."

"Must we? what on earth am I to give?"

"Oh, any thing will do. See, I shall put in this crooked sixpence."

Grace examined her purse, and complained that all her stupid sixpences were straight.

"Never mind, Miss; put in a hair-pin, sooner than pass the stocking o' Christmas Eve."

Grace had come prepared to encounter old customs. She offered her shawl-pin: and Jael, who had modestly inserted her own gift, pinned Grace's offering on the outside of the stocking with a flush of pride. Then they went up stairs with the servant, and Grace was ushered into a bedroom of vast size, with two fires burning at each end; each fireplace was flanked with a coal-scuttle full of kennel coal in large lumps, and also with an enormous basket of beech billets. She admired the old-fashioned furniture, and said, "Oh, what a palace of a bedroom! This will spoil me for my little poky room. Here one can roam about and have great thoughts. Hillsborough, good-bye! I end my days in the country."

Presently her quick ear caught the rattle of swift wheels upon the hard road: she ran to the window, and peeped behind the curtain. Two brilliant lamps were in sight, and drew nearer and dog-cart came up to the door. Before it had well nearer, like great goggling eyes, and soon a neat stopped, the hospitable door flew open, and the yule fire shone on Mr. Coventry, and his natty groom, and his dog-cart with plated axles; it illumined the silver harness, and the roan horse himself, and the breath that poured into the keen air from his nostrils red inside.

Mr. Coventry dropped from his shoulders, with easy grace, something between a coat and a cloak, lined throughout with foxes' skins; and, alighting, left his groom to do the rest. The fur was reddish, relieved with occasional white; and Grace gloated over it, as it lay glowing in the fire-light. "Ah!" said she, "I should never do for a poor man's wife: I'm so fond of soft furs and things, and I don't like poky rooms." With that she fell into a reverie, which was only interrupted by the arrival of Jael and her boxes.

Jael helped her unpack, and dress. There was no lack of conversation between these two, but most of it turned upon nothings. One topic, that might have been interesting to the readers of this tale, was avoided by them both. They had now come to have a high opinion of each other's penetration, and it made them rather timid and reserved on that subject.

Grace was dressed, and just going down, when she found she wanted a pin. She asked Jael for one.

Jael looked aghast. "Oh, Miss, I'd rather you would take one, in spite of me."

"Well, so I will. There!" And she whipped one away from the bosom of Jael's dress.

"Mind, I never gave it you."

"No. I took it by brute force."

"I like you too well to give you a pin."

"May I venture to inquire what would be the consequence?"

"I'll luck, you may be sure. Heart-trouble, they do say."

"Well, I'm glad to escape that so easily. Why, this is the temple of superstition, and you are the High-Priestess. How shall I ever get on at dinner, without you? I know I shall do something to shock Mr. Raby. Perhaps spill the very salt. I generally do."

"Ay, Miss, at home. But, dear heart, you won't see any of them nasty little salt-cellars here, that some crazy creature have invented to bring down bad luck. You won't spill the salt here, no fear: but don't ye let any body help you to it neither. If he helps you to salt, he helps you to sorrow."

"Oh, does he? Then it is fortunate nobody ever does help any body to salt. Well, yours is a nice creed. Why, we are all at the mercy of other people, according to you. Say I have a rival: she smiles in my face, and says, 'My sweet friend, accept this tribute of my esteem;' and gives me a pinch of salt, before I know where I am. I wither on the spot; and she sails off with the prize. Or, if there is no salt about, she comes behind me with a pin, and pins it to my skirt, and that pierces my heart. Don't you see what abominable nonsense it all is?"

The argument was cut short by the ringing of a tremendous bell. Grace gave the last, swift, searching, all-comprehensive look of her sex, into the glass, and went down to the drawing-room. There she found Mr. Raby, and Mr. Coventry, who both greeted her cordially; and the next moment dinner was announced.

"Raby Hall" was a square house, with two large low wings. The left wing contained the kitchen, pantry, scullery, bakehouse, brewhouse, etc.; and servants' bedrooms above. The right wing the stables, coach-houses, cattle-sheds, and several bedrooms. The main building the hall, the best bedrooms, and the double staircase, leading up to them in horse-shoe form from the hall: and, behind the hall, on the ground-floor, there was a morning-room, in which several of the Squire's small tenants were even now preparing for supper by drinking tea, and eating cakes made in rude imitation of the infant Saviour. On the right of the hall were the two drawing-rooms en suite, and on the left was the remarkable room into which the host now handed Miss Carden, and Mr. Coventry followed. This room had been, originally, the banqueting-hall. It was about twenty feet high, twenty-eight feet wide, and fifty feet long, and ended in an enormous bay window, that opened upon the lawn. It was entirely panelled with oak, carved by old Flemish workmen, and adorned here and there with bold devices. The oak, having grown old in a pure atmosphere, and in a district where wood and roots were generally burned in dining-rooms, had acquired a very rich and beautiful color, a pure and healthy reddish brown, with no tinge whatever of black: a mighty different hue from any you can find in Wardour Street. Plaster ceiling there was none, and never had been. The original joists, and beams and boards, were still there, only not quite so rudely fashioned as of old; for Mr. Raby's grandfather had caused them to be planed and varnished, and gilded a little in serpentine lines. This wood-work above gave nobility to the room, and its gilding, though worn, relieved the eye agreeably.

The farther end was used as a study, and one side of it graced with books, all handsomely bound: the other side, with a very beautiful organ that had an oval mirror in the midst of its gilt dummy-pipes. All this made a cosy nook in the grand room.

What might be called the dining-room part, though rich, was rather sombre, on ordinary occasions; but this night it was decorated gloriously. The materials were simple—wax-candles and holly; the effect was produced by a magnificent use of these materials. There were eighty candles, of the largest size sold in shops, and twelve wax pillars, five feet high, and the size of a man's calf; of these, four only were lighted at present. The holly was not in sprigs, but in enormous branches, that filled the eye with glistening green and red: and, in the embrasure of the front window stood a young holly-tree, entire, eighteen feet high, and gorgeous with five hundred branches of red berries. The tree had been dug up, and planted here in an enormous bucket, used for that purpose, and filled with mould.

Close behind this tree were placed two of the wax pillars, lighted, and their flame shone through the leaves and berries magically.

As Miss Carden entered, on Mr. Raby's arm, her eye swept the room with complacency, and settled on the holly-tree. At sight of that, she pinched Mr. Raby's arm, and cried "Oh!" three times. Then, ignoring the dinner-table altogether, she pulled her host away to the tree, and stood before it, with clasped hands. "Oh, how beautiful!"

Mr. Raby was gratified. "So then our forefathers were not quite such fools as some people say."

"They were angels, they were ducks. It is beautiful, it is divine."

Mr. Raby looked at the glowing cheek, and deep, sparkling, sapphire eye. "Come," said he; "after all, there's nothing here so beautiful as the young lady who now honors the place with her presence."

With this he handed her ceremoniously to a place at his right hand; said a short grace, and sat down between his two guests.

"But, Mr. Raby," said Grace, ruefully, "I'm with my back to the holly-tree."

"You can ask Coventry to change places."

Mr. Coventry rose, and the change was effected.

"Well, it is your doing, Coventry. Now she'll overlook *you*."

"All the better for me, perhaps. I'm content: Miss Carden will look at the holly, and I shall look at Miss Carden."

"Faute de mieux."

"C'est méchant."

"And I shall fine you both a bumper of champagne, for going out of the English language."

"I shall take my punishment like a man."

"Then take mine as well. Champagne with me means frenzy."

But, in the midst of the easy banter and jocose airy nothings of the modern dining-room, an object attracted Grace's eye. It was a picture, with its face turned to the wall, and some large letters on the back of the canvas.

This excited Grace's curiosity directly, and, whenever she could without being observed, she peeped, and tried to read the inscription; but, what with Mr. Raby's head, and a monster candle that stood before it, she could not decipher it unobserved. She was inclined to ask Mr. Raby; but she was very quick, and, observing that the other portraits were of his family, she suspected at once that the original of this picture had offended her host, and that it would be in bad taste, and might be offensive, to question him. Still the subject took possession of her.

At about eight o'clock a servant announced candles in the drawing-room.

Upon this Mr. Raby rose, and, without giving her any option on the matter, handed her to the door with obsolete deference

In the drawing-room she found a harpsichord, a spinet, and a piano, all tuned expressly for her. This amused her, as she had never seen either of the two older instruments in her life. She played on them all three.

Mr. Raby had the doors thrown open to hear her.

She played some pretty little things from Mendelssohn, Spohr, and Schubert.

The gentlemen smoked and praised.

Then she found an old music-book, and played Handel's overture to *Otho*, and the minuet.

The gentlemen left off praising directly, and came silently into the room to hear the immortal melodist. But this is the rule in music; the lips praise the delicate gelatinous, the heart beats in silence at the mighty melodious.

Tea and coffee came directly afterwards, and, ere they were disposed of, a servant announced "The Wassailers."

"Well, let them come in," said Mr. Raby.

The school-children and young people of the village trooped in, and made their obeisances, and sang the Christmas Carol—

> God rest you, merry gentlemen,
> Let nothing you dismay.

Then one of the party produced an image of the Virgin and Child, and another offered comfits in a box: a third presented the wassail-cup, into which Raby immediately poured some silver, and Coventry followed his example. Grace fumbled for her purse, and, when she had found it, began to fumble in it for her silver.

But Raby lost all patience, and said, "There. I give this for the lady, and she'll pay me *next Christmas*."

The wassailers departed, and the Squire went to say a kind word to his humbler guests.

Miss Carden took that opportunity to ask Mr. Coventry if he had noticed the picture with its face to the wall. He said he had.

"Do you know who it is?"

"No idea."

"Did you read the inscription?"

"No. But, if you are curious, I'll go back to the dining-room, and read it."

"I'm afraid he might be angry. There is no excuse for going there now."

"Send me for your pocket-handkerchief."

"Please see whether I have left my pocket-handkerchief in the dining-room, Mr. Coventry," said Grace, demurely.

Mr. Coventry smiled, and hurried away. But he soon came back to say that the candles were all out, the windows open, and the servants laying the cloth for supper.

"Oh, never mind, then," said Grace; "when we go in to supper I'll look myself."

But a considerable time elapsed before supper, and Mr. Coventry spent this time in making love rather ardently, and Grace in defending herself rather feebly.

It was nearly eleven o'clock when Mr. Raby rejoined them, and they all went into supper. There were candles lighted on the table and a few here and there upon the walls: but the room was very sombre: and Mr. Raby informed them this was to remind them of the moral darkness, in which the world lay before that great event they were about to celebrate.

He then helped each of them to a ladleful of frumety, remarking at the same time, with a grim smile, that they were not obliged to eat it; there would be a very different supper after midnight.

Then a black-letter Bible was brought him, and he read it all to himself at a side-table.

After an interval of silence so passed, there was a gentle tap at the bay window. Mr. Raby went and threw it open, and immediately a woman's voice, full, clear, and ringing, sang outside:

> The first Noel the angels did say,
> Was to three poor shepherds, in fields as they lay;
> In fields where they were keeping their sheep,
> On a cold winter's night that was so deep.
> *Chorus.* Noel, Noel, Noel, Noel,
> Born is the King of Israel.

The chorus also was sung outside.

During the chorus one of the doors opened, and Jael Dence came in by it; and the treble singer, who was the blacksmith's sister, came in at the window, and so the two women met in the room, and sang the second verse in sweetest harmony. These two did not sing like invalids, as their more refined sisters too often do; from their broad chests, and healthy lungs, and noble throats, and above all, their musical hearts, they poured out the harmony so clear and full, that every glass in the room rang like a harp, and a bolt of ice seemed to shoot down Grace Carden's backbone; and, in the chorus, gentle George's bass was like a diapason.

> They looked up and saw a star
> That shone in the East beyond them far.
> And unto the earth it gave a great light,
> And so it continued both day and night.
> *Chorus.* Noel, Noel, Noel, Noel,
> Born is the King of Israel.

As the Noel proceeded, some came in at the window, others at the doors, and the lower part of the room began to fill with singers and auditors.

The Noel ended; there was a silence, during which the organ was opened, the bellows blown, and a number of servants and others came into the room with little lighted tapers, and stood, in a long row, awaiting a signal from the Squire.

He took out his watch, and, finding it was close on twelve o'clock, directed the doors to be flung open, that he might hear the great clock in the hall strike the quarters.

There was a solemn hush of expectation, that made the sensitive heart of Grace Carden thrill with anticipation.

The clock struck the first quarter—dead silence; the second—the third—dead silence.

But, at the fourth, and with the first stroke of midnight, out burst the full organ and fifty voices, with the "Gloria in excelsis Deo:" and, as that divine hymn surged on, the lighters ran along the walls and lighted the eighty candles, and, for the first time, the twelve waxen pillars, so that, as the hymn concluded, the room was in a blaze, and it was Christmas Day.

Instantly an enormous punch-bowl was brought to the host. He put his lips to it, and said, "Friends, neighbors, I wish you all a merry Christmas." Then there was a cheer that made the whole house echo; and, by this time, the tears were running down Grace Carden's cheeks.

She turned aside, to hide her pious emotion, and found herself right opposite the picture, with this inscription, large and plain, in the blaze of light—

"Gone into trade."

If, in the middle of the pious harmony, that had stirred her soul, some blaring trumpet had played a polka, in another key, it could hardly have jarred more upon her devotional frame, than did this earthly line, that glared out between two gigantic yule candles, just lighted in honor of Him, whose mother was in trade when he was born.

She turned from it with deep repugnance, and seated herself in silence at the table.

Very early in the supper she made an excuse, and retired to her room: and, as she went out, her last glance was at the mysterious picture.

She saw it again next morning at breakfast-time; but, it must be owned, with different eyes. It was no longer contrasted with a religious ceremony, and with the sentiments of gratitude and humility proper to that great occasion, when we commemorate His birth, whose mother had gone into trade. The world, and society, whose child she was, seemed now to speak with authority

from the canvas, and to warn her how vain and hopeless were certain regrets, which lay secretly, I might say clandestinely, at her heart.

She revered her godfather, and it was no small nor irrelevant discovery to find that he had actually turned a picture in disgrace to the wall, because its owner had descended to the level, or probably not quite to the level, of Henry Little.

Jael Dence came up from the farm on Christmas afternoon, and almost the first word Grace spoke was to ask her if she knew whose picture that was in the dining-room. This vague description was enough for Jael. She said she could not tell for certain, but she had once heard her father say it was the Squire's own sister; but, when she had pressed him on the subject, the old man had rebuked her—told her not to meddle too much with other folks' business. "And to be sure, Squire has his reasons, no doubt," said Jael, rather dryly.

"The reason that is written on the back?"

"Ay: and a very poor reason too, to my mind."

"You are not the best judge of that—excuse me for saying so. Oh dear, I wish I could see it."

"Don't think of such a thing, Miss. You can't, however, for it's padlocked down that way you could never loose it without being found out. No longer agone than last Yule-time 'twas only turned, and not fastened. But they say in the kitchen, that one day last month Squire had them all up, and said the picture had been tampered with while he was at Hillsboro'; and he scolded, and had it strapped and padlocked down as 'tis."

The reader can imagine the effect of these fresh revelations. And a lover was at hand, of good birth, good manners, and approved by her godfather. That lover saw her inclining towards him, and omitted nothing to compliment and please her. To be sure, that was no uphill work, for he loved her better than he had ever loved a woman in his life, which was a good deal to say, in his case.

They spent Christmas Day very happily together. Church in the morning; then luncheon; then thick boots, a warmer shawl, and a little walk all together; for Mr. Raby took a middle course; since no positive engagement existed, he would not allow his fair guest to go about with Mr. Coventry alone, and so be compromised, even in village eyes; but, on the other hand, by stopping now and then to give an order, or exchange a word, he gave Coventry many opportunities, and that gentleman availed himself of them with his usual tact.

In the evening they sat round the great fire, and Mr. Raby mulled and spiced red wine by a family receipt, in a large silver saucepan; and they sipped the hot and generous beverage, and told stories and legends, the custom of the house on Christmas night. Mr. Raby was an inexhaustible repertory of ghost-stories and popular legends. But I select one that was told by Mr. Coventry, and told with a certain easy grace that gave it no little interest.

MR. COVENTRY'S TALE.

"When I was quite a child, there was a very old woman living in our village, that used to frighten me with her goggle eyes, and muttering. She passed for a witch, I think; and when she died—I was eight years old then—old people put their heads together, and told strange stories about her early life. It seems that this Molly Slater was away in service at Bollington, a village half way between our place and Hillsborough, and her fellow-servants used to quiz her because she had no sweetheart. At last, she told them to wait till next Hillsboro' fair, and they should see. And, just before the fair, she reminded them of their sneers, and said she would not come home without a sweetheart, though she took the Evil one himself. For all that, she did leave the fair alone. But, as she trudged home in the dark, a man overtook her, and made acquaintance with her. He was a pleasant fellow, and told her his name was William Easton. Of course she could not see his face very well, but he had a wonderfully sweet voice. After that night, he used to court her, and sing to her, but always in the dark. He never would face a candle, though he was challenged to more than once. One night there was a terrible noise heard—it is described as if a number of men were threshing out corn upon the roof—and Molly Slater was found wedged in between the bed and the wall, in a place where there was scarcely room to put your hand. Several strong men tried to extricate her by force; but both the bed and the woman's body resisted so strangely that, at last, they thought it best to send for the parson. He was a great scholar, and himself under some suspicion of knowing more than it would be good for any less pious person to know. Well, the parson came, and took a candle that was burning, and held it to the place where poor Molly was imprisoned, and moaning; and they say he turned pale, and shivered, for all his learning. I forget what he said or did next; but by-and-by there was a colloquy in a whisper between him and some person unseen; and they say that this unseen whisper was very sweet, and something like the chords of a harp, only low and very articulate. The parson whispered, 'God gives a sinner time.' The sweet voice answered, 'He can afford to; he is the stronger.' Then the parson adjured the unseen one to wait a year and a day. But he refused, still in the gentlest voice. Then the parson said these words: 'By all we hope and fear, by all you fear and hate, I adjure you to loose her, or wait till next Christmas Eve.'

"I suppose the Evil Spirit saw some trap in that proposal, for he is said to have laughed most musically. He answered, 'By all I fear and hate, I'll loose her never; but, but I'll wait for her—till the candle's burnt out;' and he chuckled most musically again.

"'Then wait to all eternity,' the parson roared; and blew the candle out directly, and held it, with his hands crossed over it."

Grace Carden's eyes sparkled in the firelight. "Go on," she cried, excitedly.

"The girl was loosed easily enough after that; but she was found to be in a swoon; and not the least bruised, though ten villagers had been pulling at her one after another."

"And what became of her afterwards?"

"She lived to be ninety-six, and died in my time. I think she had money left her. But she never married; and when she was old she wandered about the lanes, muttering, and frightening little boys, myself among the number. But now my little story follows another actor of the tale."

"Oh, I'm so glad it is not over."

"No. The parson took the candle away, and it was never seen again. But, somehow, it got wind that he had built it into the wall of the church; perhaps he didn't say so, but was only understood to say so. However, people used to look round the church for the place. And now comes the most remarkable thing of all; three years ago the present rector repaired the floor of the chancel, intending to put down encaustic tiles. Much to his surprise, the workmen found plenty of old encaustic tiles: they had been interred as rubbish at some period, when antiquity and beauty were less respected than they are now, I suppose."

Mr. Raby broke in, "The Puritans. Barbarians! beasts! It was just like them. Well, sir—?"

"When the rector found that, he excavated more than was absolutely necessary for his purpose, and the deeper he went the more encaustic tiles. In one place they got down to the foundation, and they found an oak chest fast in the rock,—a sort of channel had been cut in the rock for this chest, or rather box (for it was only about eighteen inches long), to lie in. The master mason was there luckily, and would not move it till the rector had seen it. He was sent for, but half the parish was there before him; and he tells me there were three theories firmly established, and proved, before he could finish his breakfast and get to the spot. Theory of Wilder, the village grocer: 'It is treasure hidden by them there sly old monks.' Mr. Wilder is a miser, and is known to lay up money. He is, I believe, the only man left in the North Country who can show you a hundred spade guineas."

Mr. Raby replied energetically, "I respect him. Wilder forever! What was the next theory?"

"The skeleton of a child. I forget who propounded this; but I believe it carried the majority. But the old sexton gave it a blow. 'Nay, nay,' said he; 'them's the notions of strangers. I was born here, and my father afore me. It will be Molly Slater's candle, and nought else.' Then poor Molly's whole story came up again over the suspected box. But I am very tedious."

"Tedious! You are delightful, and thrilling, and pray go on. The rector had the box opened?"

"On the spot."

"Well!"

"The box went to pieces, in spite of all their care. But there was no doubt as to its contents."

Grace exclaimed, enthusiastically, "A candle. Oh, do say a candle!"

Mr. Coventry responded, "It's awfully tempting; but I suspect the traditional part of my story is *slightly embellished*: so the historical part must be accurate. What the box did really contain, to my knowledge, was a rush-wick, much thicker than they are made nowadays; and this rushwick was impregnated with grease, and even lightly coated with a sort of brown wafer-like paste. The rector thinks it was a combination of fine dust from the box with the original grease. He shall show it you, if you are curious to see it."

"Of course we are curious. Oh, Mr. Raby, what a strange story. And how well he told it."

"Admirably. We must drink his health."

"I'll wish it him instead, because I require all my reason just now to understand his story. And I don't understand it, after all. There; you found the candle, and so it is all true. But what does the rector think?"

"Well, he says there is no connection whatever between the rush-wick and—"

"Don't tell her what *he* says," cried Raby, with a sudden fury that made Grace start and open her eyes. "I know the puppy. He is what is called a divine nowadays; but used to be called a skeptic. There never was so infidel an age. Socinus was content to prove Jesus Christ a man; but Renan has gone and proved him a Frenchman. Nothing is so gullible as an unbeliever. The right reverend father in God, Cocker, has gnawed away the Old Testament: the Oxford doctors are nibbling away the New: nothing escapes but the apocrypha: yet these same skeptics believe the impudent lies, and monstrous arithmetic, of geology, which babbles about a million years, a period actually beyond the comprehension of the human intellect; and takes up a jawbone, that some sly navvy has transplanted overnight from the churchyard into Lord knows what stratum, fees the navvy, gloats over the bone, and knocks the Bible down with it. No, Mr. Coventry, your story is a good one, and well told; don't let us defile it with the comments of a skeptical credulous pedant. Fill your glass, sir. Here's to old religion, old stories, old songs, old houses, old wine, old friends, or" (recovering himself with admirable grace) "to new friends that are to be old ones ere we die. Come, let the stronger vessel drink, and the weaker vessel sip, and all say together, after me—

> Well may we all be,
> Ill may we never see,
> That make good company
> Beneath the roof of Raby."

When this rude rhyme had been repeated in chorus, there was a little silence, and the conversation took a somewhat deeper tone. It began through Grace asking Mr. Raby, with all the simplicity of youth, whether he had ever seen any thing supernatural with his own eyes. "For instance," said she, "this deserted church of yours, that you say the shepherd said he saw on fire—did *you* see that?"

"Not I. Indeed, the church is not in sight from here. No, Grace, I never saw any thing supernatural: and I am sorry for it, for I laugh at people's notion that a dead man has any power to injure the living; how can a cold wind come from a disembodied spirit? I am all that a ghost is, and something more; and I only wish I *could* call the dead from their graves; I'd soon have a dozen gentlemen and ladies out of that old churchyard into this very room. And, if they would only come, you would see me converse with them as civilly and as calmly as I am doing with you. The fact is, I have some questions to put, which only the dead can answer—passages in the family correspondence, referring to things I can't make out for the life of me."

"Oh, Mr. Raby, pray don't talk in this dreadful way, for fear they should be angry and come." And Grace looked fearfully round over her shoulder.

Mr. Raby shook his head; and there was a dead silence.

Mr. Raby broke it rather unexpectedly. "But," said he, gravely, "if I have seen nothing, I've heard something. Whether it was supernatural, I can't say; but, at least, it was unaccountable and terrible. I have heard THE GABRIEL HOUNDS."

Mr. Coventry and Grace looked at one another, and then inquired, almost in a breath, what the Gabriel hounds were.

"A strange thing in the air that is said, in these parts, to foretell calamity."

"Oh dear!" said Grace, "this is thrilling again; pray tell us."

"Well, one night I was at Hillsborough on business, and, as I walked by the old parish church, a great pack of beagles, in full cry, passed close over my head."

"Yes; they startled me, as I never was startled in my life before. I had never heard of the Gabriel hounds then, and I was stupefied. I think I leaned against the wall there full five minutes, before I recovered myself, and went on."

"Oh dear! But did any thing come of it?"

"You shall judge for yourself. I had left a certain house about an hour and a half: there was trouble in that house, but only of a pecuniary kind. To tell the truth, I came back with some money for them, or rather, I should say, with the promise of it. I found the wife in a swoon: and, up stairs, her husband lay dead by his own hand."

"Oh, my poor godpapa!" cried Grace, flinging her arm tenderly round his neck.

"Ay, my child, and the trouble did not end there. Insult followed; ingratitude; and a family feud, which is not healed yet, and never will be —till she and her brat come on their knees to me."

Mr. Raby had no sooner uttered these last words with great heat, than he was angry with himself. "Ah!" said he, "the older a man gets, the weaker. To think of my mentioning that to you young people!" And he rose and walked about the room in considerable agitation and vexation. "Curse the Gabriel hounds! It is the first time I have spoken of them since that awful night; it is the last time I ever will speak of them. What they are, God, who made them, knows. Only I pray I may never hear them again, nor any friend of mine."

Next morning Jael Dence came up to the Hall, and almost the first question Grace asked her was, whether she had ever heard of the Gabriel hounds. Jael looked rather puzzled. Grace described them after Mr. Raby.

"Why, that will be Gabble Retchet," said Jael. "I wouldn't talk much about the like, if I was you, Miss."

But Grace persisted, and, at last, extracted from her that sounds had repeatedly been heard in the air at night, as of a pack of hounds in full cry, and that these hounds ran before Trouble.

"But," said Jael, solemnly, "they are not hounds at all; they are the souls of unbaptized children, wandering in the air till the day of judgment."

This description, however probable, had the effect of making Grace disbelieve the phenomenon altogether, and she showed her incredulity by humming a little air.

But Jael soon stopped that. "Oh, Miss, pray

don't do so. If you sing before breakfast, you'll cry before supper."

At breakfast, Mr. Coventry invited Miss Carden to go to the top of Cairnhope Peak, and look over four counties. He also told her she could see Bollinghope House, his own place, very well from the Peak.

Grace assented : and, immediately after breakfast, begged Jael to be in the way to accompany her. She divined, with feminine quickness, that Mr. Coventry would be very apt, if he pointed out Bollinghope House to her from the top of a mountain, to say, "Will you be its mistress ?" but, possibly, she did not wish to be hurried, or it may have been only a mere instinct, an irrational impulse of self-defense, with which the judgment had nothing to do ; or perhaps it was simple modesty. Any way, she engaged Jael to be of the party.

It was talked of again at luncheon, and then Mr. Raby put in a word. "I have one stipulation to make, young people, and that is that you go up the east side, and down the same way. It is all safe walking on that side. I shall send you in my four-wheel to the foot of the hill, and George will wait for you there at the 'Colley Dog' public-house, and bring you home again."

This was, of course, accepted with thanks, and the four-wheel came round at two o'clock. Jael was seated in front by the side of George, who drove ; Mr. Coventry and Grace, behind. He had his fur-cloak to keep his companion warm on returning from the hill ; but Mr. Raby, who did nothing by halves, threw in some more wraps, and gave a warm one to Jael ; she was a favorite with him, as indeed were all the Dences.

They started gayly, and rattled off at a good pace. Before they had got many yards on the high-road, they passed a fir-plantation, belonging to Mr. Raby, and a magpie fluttered out of this, and flew across the road before them.

Jael seized the reins, and pulled them so powerfully, she stopped the pony directly. "Oh, the foul bird !" she cried, "turn back ! turn back !"

"What for?" inquired Mr. Coventry.

"We shall meet with trouble else. One magpie ! and right athwart us too."

"What nonsense !" said Grace.

"Nay, nay, it is not ; Squire knows better. Wait just one minute, till I speak to Squire." She sprang from the carriage with one bound, and, holding up her dress with one hand, ran into the house like a lapwing.

"The good, kind, silly thing !" said Grace Carden.

Jael soon found Mr. Raby, and told him about the magpie, and begged him to come out and order them back.

But Mr. Raby smiled, and shook his head. "That won't do. Young ladies and gentlemen of the present day don't believe in omens."

"But you do know better, sir. I have heard father say you were going into Hillsborough with him one day, and a magpie flew across, and father persuaded you to turn back."

"That is true ; he was going in to buy some merino sheep, and I to deposit my rents in Carrington's bank. Next day the bank broke. And the merino sheep all died within the year. But how many thousand times does a magpie cross us and nothing come of it ? Come, run away, my good girl, and don't keep them waiting."

Jael obeyed, with a sigh. She went back to her party—they were gone. The carriage was just disappearing round a turn in the road. She looked at it with amazement, and even with anger. It seemed to her a brazen act of bad faith.

"I wouldn't have believed it of her," said she, and went back to the house, mortified and grieved. She did not go to Mr. Raby again ; but he happened to catch sight of her about an hour afterwards, and called to her—"How is this, Jael ? Have you let them go alone, because of a magpie ?" And he looked displeased.

"Nay, sir : she gave me the slip, while I went to speak to you for her good ; and I call it a dirty trick, saving your presence. I told her I'd be back in a moment."

"Oh, it is not her doing, you may be sure ; it is the young gentleman. He saw a chance to get her alone, and of course he took it. I am not very well pleased ; but I suppose she knows her own mind. It is to be a marriage, no doubt." He smoothed it over, but was a little put out, and stalked away without another word : he had said enough to put Jael's bosom in a flutter, and open a bright prospect to her heart ; Miss Carden once disposed of in marriage, what might she not hope ? She now reflected, with honest pride, that she had merited Henry's love by rare unselfishness. She had advised him loyally, had even co-operated with him as far as any poor girl, with her feelings for him, could do ; and now Mr. Coventry was going to propose marriage to her rival, and she believed Miss Carden would say "yes," though she could not in her heart believe that even Miss Carden did not prefer the other. "Ay, lad," said she, "if I am to win thee, I'll be able to say I won thee fair."

These sweet thoughts and hopes soon removed her temporary anger, and nothing remained to dash the hopeful joy that warmed that large and loyal heart this afternoon, except a gentle misgiving that Mr. Coventry might make Grace a worse husband than she deserved. It was thus she read the magpie, from three o'clock till six that afternoon.

When a man and a woman do any thing wrong, it is amusing to hear the judgments of other men and women thereupon. The men all blame the man, and the women all the woman. That is judgment, is it not ?

But in some cases our pitchfarthing judgments must be either heads or tails ; so Mr. Raby, who had cried heads, when a Mrs. Raby would have cried 'woman,' was right ; it was Mr. Coventry, and not Miss Carden, who leaned over to George, and whispered, "A sovereign, to drive on without her ! Make some excuse."

The cunning Yorkshire groom's eye twinkled at this, and he remained passive a minute or two : then, said suddenly, with well-acted fervor, "I can't keep the pony waiting in the cold, like this ;" applied the whip, and rattled off with such decision, that Grace did not like to interfere, especially as George was known to be one of those hard masters, an old servant.

So, by this little ruse, Mr. Coventry had got her all to himself for the afternoon. And now she felt sure he would propose that very day. She made no movement whatever either to advance or to avoid the declaration.

It is five miles from Raby Hall, through Cairnhope village, to the eastern foot of Cairnhope; and while George rattles them over the hard and frosty road, I will tell the reader something about this young gentleman, who holds the winning cards.

Mr. Frederick Coventry was a man of the world. He began life with a good estate, and a large fund accumulated during his minority.

He spent all the money in learning the world at home and abroad; and, when it was all gone, he opened one eye.

But, as a man can not see very clear with a single orb, he exchanged rouge-et-noir, etc., for the share-market, and, in other respects, lived as fast as ever, till he had mortgaged his estate rather heavily. Then he began to open both eyes.

Next, he fell in love with Grace Carden; and upon that he opened both eyes very wide, and wished very much he had his time to live over again.

Nevertheless, he was not much to be pitied. He had still an estate, which, with due care, could pay off its encumbrances; and he had gathered some valuable knowledge. He knew women better than most men, and he knew whist profoundly. Above all, he had acquired what Voltaire justly calls "le grand art de plaire;" he had studied this art, as many women study it, and few men. Why, he even watched the countenance, and smoothed the rising bristles of those he wished to please, or did not wish to displease. This was the easier to him that he had no strong convictions on any great topic. It is your plaguy convictions that make men stubborn and disagreeable.

A character of this kind is very susceptible, either of good or evil influences; and his attachment to Grace Carden was turning him the right way.

Add to this a good figure and a distinguished air, and you have some superficial idea of the gentleman towards whom Grace Carden found herself drawn by circumstances, and not unwillingly, though not with that sacred joy and thrill which marks a genuine passion.

They left George and the trap at the "Colley Dog," and ascended the mountain. There were no serious difficulties on this side; but still there were little occasional asperities, that gave the lover an opportunity to offer his arm; and Mr. Coventry threw a graceful devotion even into this slight act of homage. He wooed her with perfect moderation at first; it was not his business to alarm her at starting; he proceeded gradually; and, by the time they had reached the summit, he had felt his way, and had every reason to hope she would accept him.

At the summit the remarkable beauty of the view threw her into raptures, and interrupted the more interesting topic on which he was bent.

But the man of the world showed no impatience (I don't say he felt none); he answered all Grace's questions, and told her what all the places were.

But, by-and-by, the atmosphere thickened suddenly in that quarter, and he then told her gently he had something to show her on the other side the knob.

He conducted her to a shed the shepherds had erected, and seated her on a rude bench. "You must be a little tired," he said.

Then he showed her, in the valley, one of those delightful old red brick houses, with white stone facings. "That is Bollinghope."

She looked at it with polite interest.

"Do you like it?"

"Very much. It warms the landscape so."

He expected a more prosaic answer; but he took her cue. "I wish it was a great deal prettier than it is, and its owner a much better man; richer—wiser—"

"You are hard to please, Mr. Coventry."

"Miss Carden—Grace—may I call you Grace?"

"It seems to me you have done it."

"But I had no right."

"Then, of course, you will never do it again."

"I should be very unhappy if I thought that. Miss Carden, I think you know how dear you are to me, and have been ever since I first met you. I wish I had ten times more to offer you than I have. But I am only a poor gentleman, of good descent, but moderate means, as you see." Comedie! (Bollinghope was the sort of house that generally goes with £5000 a year at least.)

"I don't care about your means, Mr. Coventry," said Grace, with a lofty smile. "It is your amiable character that I esteem."

"You forgive me for loving you; for hoping that you will let me lead you to my poor house there, as my adored wife?"

It had come; and, although she knew it was coming, yet her face was dyed with blushes.

"I esteem you very much," she faltered. "I thank you for the honor you do me; but I—oh, pray, let me think what I am doing." She covered her face with her hands, and her bosom panted visibly.

Mr. Coventry loved her sincerely, and his own heart beat high at this moment. He augured well from her agitation; but presently he saw something that puzzled him, and gave a man of his experience a qualm.

A tear forced its way between her fingers; another, and another, soon followed.

Coventry said to himself, "There's some other man." And he sighed heavily; but even in this moment of true and strong feeling he was on his guard, and said nothing.

It was his wisest course. She was left to herself, and an amazing piece of female logic came to Mr. Coventry's aid. She found herself crying, and got frightened at herself. That, which would have made a man pause, had just the opposite effect on her. She felt that no good could come to any body of those wild and weak regrets that made her weep. She saw she had a weakness and a folly to cure herself of; and the cure was at hand. There was a magic in marriage; a gentleman could, somehow, *make* a girl love him when once she had married him. Mr. Coventry should be enabled to make her love him; he should cure her of this trick of crying; it would be the best thing for every body—for *him*, for Jael, for Mr. Coventry, and even for herself.

She dried her eyes, and said, in a low, tremulous voice: "Have you spoken to papa of—of this?"

"No. I waited to be authorized by you. May I speak to him?"

"Yes."

"May I tell him—?"

"Oh, I can't tell you what to tell him. How dark it is getting. Please take me home." Another tear or two.

Then, if Coventry had not loved her sincerely, and also been a man of the world, he would have lost his temper; and if he had lost his temper, he would have lost the lady, for she would have seized the first fair opportunity to quarrel. But no, he took her hand gently, and set himself to comfort her. He poured out his love to her, and promised her a life of wedded happiness. He drew so delightful a picture of their wedded life, and in a voice so winning, that she began to be consoled, and her tears ceased.

"I believe you love me," she murmured; "and I esteem you sincerely."

Mr. Coventry drew a family ring from his pocket. It was a sapphire of uncommon beauty.

"This was my mother's," said he. "Will you do me the honor to wear it, as a pledge?"

But the actual fetter startled her, I think. She started up, and said, "Oh, please take me home first! *It is going to snow.*"

Call her slippery, if you don't like her; call her unhappy and wavering, if you do like her.

Mr. Coventry smiled now at this attempt to put off the inevitable, and complied at once.

But, before they had gone a hundred yards, the snow did really fall, and so heavily that the air was darkened.

"We had better go back to the shed till it is over," said Mr. Coventry.

"Do you think so?" said Grace, doubtfully. "Well."

And they went back.

But the snow did not abate, and the air got darker. So, by-and-by, Grace suggested that Mr. Coventry should run down the hill, and send George up to her with an umbrella.

"What, and leave you alone?" said he.

"Well, then, we had better go together."

They started together.

By this time the whole ground was covered about three inches deep; not enough to impede their progress; but it had the unfortunate effect of effacing the distinct features of the ground; and, as the declining sun could no longer struggle successfully through the atmosphere, which was half air, half snow, they were almost in darkness, and soon lost their way. They kept slanting unconsciously to the left, till they got over one of the forks of the mountain and into a ravine: they managed to get out of that, and continued to descend; for the great thing they had to do was to reach the valley, no matter where.

But, after a long, laborious, and even dangerous descent, they found themselves beginning to ascend. Another mountain or hill barred their progress. Then they knew they must be all wrong, and began to feel rather anxious. They wished they had staid up on the hill.

They consulted together, and agreed to go on for the present; it might be only a small rise in the ground.

And so it proved. After a while they found themselves descending again.

But now the path was full of pitfalls, hidden by the snow and the darkness.

Mr. Coventry insisted on going first.

In this order they moved cautiously on, often stumbling.

Suddenly Mr. Coventry disappeared with a sudden plunge, and rolled down a ravine, with a loud cry.

Grace stood transfixed with terror.

Then she called to him.

There was no answer.

She called again.

A faint voice replied that he was not much hurt, and would try to get back to her.

This, however, was impossible, and all he could do was to scramble along the bottom of the ravine.

Grace kept on the high ground, and they called to each other every moment. They seemed to be a long way from each other: yet they were never sixty yards apart. At last the descent moderated, and Grace rejoined him.

Then they kept in the hollow for some time, but at last found another acclivity to mount: they toiled up it, laden with snow, yet perspiring profusely with the exertion of toiling uphill through heather clogged with heavy snow.

They reached the summit, and began to descend again. But now their hearts began to quake. Men had been lost on Cairnhope before to-day, and never found alive: and they were lost on Cairnhope; buried in the sinuosities of the mountain, and in a tremendous snow-storm.

They wandered and staggered, sick at heart; since each step might be for the worse.

They wandered and staggered, miserably; and the man began to sigh, and the woman to cry.

At last they were so exhausted, they sat down in despair: and, in a few minutes, they were a couple of snow-heaps.

Mr. Coventry was the first to see all the danger they ran by this course.

"For God's sake, let us go on!" he said; "if we once get benumbed, we are lost. We *must* keep moving, till help comes to us."

Then they staggered, and stumbled on again, till they both sank into a deep snow-drift.

They extricated themselves, but, oh, when they felt that deep cold snow all round them, it was a foretaste of the grave.

The sun had set, it was bitterly cold, and still the enormous flakes fell, and doubled the darkness of the night.

They staggered and stumbled on. not now with any hope of extricating themselves from the fatal mountain, but merely to keep the blood alive in their veins. And, when they were exhausted, they sat down, and soon were heaps of snow.

While they sat thus, side by side, thinking no more of love, or any other thing but this: should they ever see the sun rise, or sit by a fireside again? suddenly they heard a sound in the air behind them, and, in a moment, what seemed a pack of hounds in full cry passed close over their heads.

They uttered a loud cry.

"We are saved!" cried Grace. "Mr. Raby is hunting us with his dogs. That was the echo."

Coventry groaned. "What scent would lie?" said he. "Those hounds were in the air; a hundred strong."

Neither spoke for a moment, and then it was Grace who broke the terrible silence.

"THE GABRIEL HOUNDS!"

"The Gabriel hounds; that run before calamity! Mr. Coventry, there's nothing to be done now, but to make our peace with God. For you are a dead man, and I'm a dead woman. My poor papa! poor Mr. Little!"

She kneeled down on the snow, and prayed patiently, and prepared to deliver up her innocent soul to Him who gave it.

Not so her companion. He writhed away from death. He groaned, he sighed, he cursed, he complained. What was Raby thinking of, to let them perish?

furlong and more, and fell into a mountain-stream, swollen by floods, which whirled him along with it, like a feather. It was not deep enough to drown him by submersion, but it rolled him over and over again, and knocked him against rocks and stones, and would ipfallibly have destroyed him, but that a sudden sharp turn in the

HE THEN DARTED BACK TO HER, AND KISSED HER COLD HANDS WITH PRETTY MOANS OF LOVE.

Presently he shouted out,—"I'll not die this dog's death. I will not. I'll save myself, and come back for you."

The girl prayed on, and never heeded him.

But he was already on his feet, and set off to run; and he actually did go blundering on, for a current drove him, at last, against a projecting tree, which he clutched, and drew himself out with infinite difficulty. But, when he tried to walk, his limbs gave way; and he sank, fainting on the ground, and the remorseless snow soon covered his prostrate body.

All this time, Grace Carden was kneeling on the snow, and was, literally a heap of snow. She was patient and composed now, and felt a gentle sleep stealing over.

That sleep would have been her death.

But, all of a sudden something heavy touched her clothes, and startled her, and two dark objects passed her.

They were animals.

In a moment it darted through her mind that animals are wiser than man in some things. She got up with difficulty, for her limbs were stiffened, and followed them.

The dark forms struggled on before. They knew the ground, and soon took her to the edge of that very stream into which Coventry had fallen.

They all three went within a yard of Mr. Coventry, and still they pursued their way ; and Grace hoped they were making for some shelter. She now called aloud to Mr. Coventry, thinking he must be on before her. But he had not recovered his senses.

Unfortunately, the cry startled the sheep, and they made a rush, and she could not keep up with them :. she toiled, she called, she prayed for strength ; but they left her behind, and she could see their very forms no more. Then she cried out in agony, and still with that power of self-excitement, which her sex possess in an eminent degree, she struggled on and on, beyond her strength, till, at last, she fell down from sheer exhaustion, and the snow fell fast upon her body.

But, even as she lay, she heard a tinkling. She took it for sheep-bells, and started up once more, and once more cried to Mr. Coventry ; and this time he heard her, and shook off his deadly lethargy, and tried to hobble towards her voice.

Meantime, Grace struggled towards the sound, and lo, a light was before her, a light gleaming red and dullish in the laden atmosphere. With her remnant of life and strength, she dashed at it, and found a wall in her way. She got over it somehow, and saw the light quite close, and heard the ringing of steel on steel.

She cried out for help, for she felt herself failing. She tottered along the wall of the building, searching for a door. She found the porch. She found the church door. But by this time she was quite spent ; her senses reeled ; her cry was a moan.

She knocked once with her hands. She tried to knock again ; but the door flew suddenly open, and, in the vain endeavor to knock again, her helpless body, like a pillar of snow, fell forward ; but Henry Little caught her directly, and then she clutched him feebly, by mere instinct.

He uttered a cry of love and alarm. She opened her filmy eyes, and stared at him. Her cold neck and white cheek rested on his bare and glowing arm.

The moment he saw it was really Grace Carden that had fallen inanimate into his arms, Henry Little uttered a loud cry of love and terror, and, putting his other sinewy arm under her, carried her swiftly off to his fires, uttering little moans of fear and pity as he went ; he laid her down by the fire, and darted to the forge, and blew it to a white heat ; and then darted back to her, and kissed her cold hands with pretty moans of love ; and then blew up the other fires ; and then back

to her, and patted her hands, and kissed them with all his soul, and drew them to his bosom to warm them ; and drew her head to his heart to warm her ; and all with pretty moans of love, and fear, and pity ; and the tears rained out of his eyes at sight of her helpless condition, and the tears fell upon her brow and her hands : and all this vitality and love soon electrified her ; she opened her eyes, and smiled faintly, but such a smile, and murmured, "It's you," and closed her eyes again.

Then he panted out, "Yes, it is I,—a friend. I won't hurt you,—I won't tell you how I love you any more,—only live! Don't give way. You shall marry who you like. You shall never be thwarted, nor worried, nor made love to again ; only be brave and live ; don't rob the world of the only angel that is in it. Have mercy, and live! I'll never ask more of you than that. Oh, how pale! I am frightened. Cursed fires, have you no warmth in you ?" And he was at the bellows again. And the next moment back to her, imploring her, and sighing over her, and saying the wildest, sweetest, drollest things, such as only those who love can say, in moments when hearts are bursting.

How now ? Her cheek that was so white is pink—pinker—red—scarlet. She is blushing.

She had closed her eyes at Love's cries. Perhaps she was not altogether unwilling to hear that divine music of the heart, so long as she was not bound to reply and remonstrate,—being insensible.

But now she speaks, faintly, but clearly, "Don't be frightened. I promise not to die. Pray don't cry so." Then she put out her hand to him, and turned her head away, and cried herself, gently, but plenteously.

Henry, kneeling by her, clasped the hand she lent him with both his, and drew it to his panting heart in ecstasy.

Grace's cheeks were rosy red.

They remained so a little while in silence.

Henry's heart was too full of beatitude to speak. He drew her a little nearer to the glowing fires, to revive her quite ; but still kneeled by her, and clasped her hand to his heart. She felt it beat, and turned her blushing brow away, but made no resistance : she was too weak.

"Hallo!" cried a new voice, that jarred with the whole scene ; and Mr. Coventry hobbled in sight. He gazed in utter amazement on the picture before him.

CHAPTER XII.

GRACE snatched her hand from Henry, and raised herself with a vigor that contrasted with her late weakness. "Oh, it is Mr. Coventry. How wicked of me to forget him for a moment! Thank Heaven you are alive. Where have you been ?"

"I fell into the mountain stream, and it rolled me down, nearly to here. I think I must have fainted on the bank. I found myself lying covered with snow ; it was your beloved voice that recalled me to life."

Henry turned yellow, and rose to his feet.

Grace observed him, and replied, "Oh, Mr. Coventry, this is too high-flown. Let us both re-

turn thanks to the Almighty, who has preserved
us, and, in the next place, to Mr. Little : we
should both be dead but for him." Then, before
he could reply, she turned to Little, and said, be-
seechingly, " Mr. Coventry has been the companion of my danger."

" Oh, I'll do the best I can for him," said Henry, doggedly. " Draw nearer the fire, sir." He
then put some coal on the forge, and blew up an
amazing fire : he also gave the hand-bellows to
Mr. Coventry, and set him to blow at the small
grates in the mausoleum. He then produced a
pair of woollen stockings. " Now, Miss Carden,"
said he, " just step into that pew, if you please,
and make a dressing-room of it."

She demurred, faintly, but he insisted, and put
her into the great pew, and shut her in.

" And now, please take off your shoes and
stockings, and hand them over the pew to me."

" Oh, Mr. Little ; you are giving yourself so
much trouble."

" Nonsense. Do what you are bid." He said
this a little roughly.

" I'll do whatever you bid me," said she, meekly : and instantly took off her dripping shoes, and
stockings, and handed them over the pew. She
received, in return, a nice warm pair of worsted
stockings.

" Put on these directly," said he, " while I warm
your shoes."

He dashed all the wet he could out of the shoes,
and, taking them to the forge, put hot cinders in :
he shook the cinders up and down the shoes so
quickly, they had not time to burn, but only to
warm and dry them. He advised Coventry to
do the same, and said he was sorry he had only
one pair of stockings to lend. And that was a
lie : for he was glad he had only one pair to lend.
When he had quite dried the shoes, he turned
round, and found Grace was peeping over the
pew, and looking intolerably lovely in the fire-
light. He kissed the shoes furtively, and gave
them to her. She shook her head in a remon-
strating way, but her eyes filled.

He turned away, and, rousing all his generous
manhood, said, " Now you must both eat something, before you go." He produced a Yorkshire
pie, and some bread, and a bottle of wine. He
gave Mr. Coventry a saucepan, and set him to
heat the wine ; then turned up his sleeves to the
shoulder, blew his bellows, and, with his pincers,
took a lath of steel and placed it in the white
embers. " I have only got one knife, and you
won't like to eat with that. I must forge you
one apiece."

Then Grace came out, and stood looking on,
while he forged knives, like magic, before the
eyes of his astonished guests. Her feet were
now as warm as a toast, and her healthy young
body could resist all the rest. She stood, with
her back to the nearest pew, and her hands against
the pew too, and looked with amazement, and
dreamy complacency, at the strange scene before
her : a scene well worthy of Salvator Rosa :
though, in fact, that painter never had the luck
to hit on so variegated a subject.

Three broad bands of light shot from the fires,
expanding in size, but weakening in intensity.
These lights, and the candles at the west end,
revealed in a strange combination the middle
ages, the nineteenth century, and eternal nature.

Nature first. Snow gleaming on the windows.
Oh, it was cosy to see it gleam and sparkle, and
to think " Aha ! you all but killed me ; now King
Fire warms both thee and me." Snow-flakes, of
enormous size, softly descending, and each appearing a diamond brooch, as it passed through the
channels of fiery light.

The middle ages.—Massive old arches, chipped,
and stained ; a mouldering altar-piece, dog's-eared
(Henry had nailed it up again all but the top corner, and in it still faintly gleamed the Virgin's
golden crown). Pulpit, richly carved, but mouldering : gaunt walls, streaked and stained by time.
At the west end, one saint—the last of many—
lit by two candles, and glowing ruby red across
the intervening gulf of blackness : on the nearest
wall an inscription, that still told, in rusty letters,
how Giles de la Beche had charged his lands
with six merks a year forever, to buy bread and
white watered herrings, the same to be brought
into Cairnhope Church every Sunday in Lent,
and given to two poor men and four women ;
and the same on Good Friday with a penny dole,
and, on that day, the clerk to toll the bell at three
of the clock after noon, and read the lamentation
of a sinner, and receive one groat.

Ancient monuments, sculptures with here an
arm gone, and here a head, that yet looked half
alive in the weird and partial light.

And between one of those mediæval sculptures,
and that mouldering picture of the Virgin, stood
a living horse, munching his corn ; and in the
foreground was a portable forge, a mausoleum
turned into fires and hot plate, and a young man,
type of his century, forging table-knives amidst
the wrecks of another age.

When Grace had taken in the whole scene with
wonder, her eye was absorbed by this one figure,
a model of manly strength, and skill, and grace.
How lightly he stepped : how easily his left arm
blew the coals to a white heat, with blue flames
rising from them. How deftly he drew out the
white steel. With what tremendous force his first
blows fell, and scattered hot steel around. Yet
all that force was regulated to a hair—he beat,

he moulded, he never broke. Then came the lighter blows; and not one left the steel as it found it. In less than a minute the bar was a blade. It was work incredibly unlike his method in carving; yet, at a glance, Grace saw it was also perfection, but in an opposite style. In carving, the hand of a countess; in forging, a blacksmith's arm.

She gazed with secret wonder and admiration; and the comparison was to the disadvantage of Mr. Coventry; for he sat shivering, and the other seemed all power. And women adore power.

When Little had forged the knives and forks, and two deep saucers, with magical celerity, he plunged them into water a minute, and they hissed; he sawed off the rim of a pew, and fitted handles.

Then he washed his face and hands, and made himself dry and glowing; let down his sleeves, and served them some Yorkshire pie, and bread, and salt, and stirred a little sugar into the wine, and poured it into the saucers.

"Now eat a bit, both of you, before you go."

Mr. Coventry responded at once to the invitation.

But Grace said, timidly, "Yes, if you will eat with us."

"No, no," said he. "I've not been perished with snow, nor rolled in a river."

Grace hesitated still; but Coventry attacked the pie directly. It was delicious. "By Jove, sir," said he, "you are the prince of blacksmiths."

"Blacksmiths!" said Grace, coloring high. But Little only smiled satirically.

Grace, who was really faint with hunger, now ate a little; and then the host made her sip some wine.

The food and wine did Mr. Coventry so much good, that he began to recover his superiority, and expressed his obligations to Henry in a tone which was natural, and not meant to be offensive; but yet it was so, under all the circumstances: there was an underlying tone of condescension. It made Grace fear he would offer Henry his purse at leaving.

Henry himself writhed under it; but said nothing. Grace, however, saw his ire, his mortification, and his jealousy, in his face, and that irritated her; but she did not choose to show either of the men how much it angered her.

She was in a most trying situation, and all the woman's wit and tact were keenly on their guard.

What she did was this; she did not utter one word of remonstrance, but she addressed most of her remarks to Mr. Little; and, though the remarks were nothing in themselves, she contrived to throw profound respect into them. Indeed, she went beyond respect. She took the tone of an inferior addressing a superior.

This was nicely calculated to soothe Henry, and also to make Coventry, who was a man of tact, change his own manner.

Nor was it altogether without that effect. But then it annoyed Coventry, and made him wish to end it.

After a while he said, "My dear Grace, it can't be far from Raby Hall. I think you had better let me take you home at once."

Grace colored high, and bit her lip.

Henry was green with jealous anguish.

"Are you quite recovered, yourself?" said Grace, demurely, to Mr. Coventry.

"Quite; thanks to this good fellow's hospitality."

"Then *would* you mind going to Raby, and sending some people for me? I really feel hardly equal to fresh exertion just yet."

This proposal brought a flush of pleasure to Henry's cheek, and mortified Mr. Coventry cruelly in his turn.

"What, go and leave you here? Surely you can not be serious."

"Oh, *I* don't wish you to leave me. Only you seemed in a hurry."

Henry was miserable again.

Coventry did not let well alone. He alluded delicately but tenderly to what had passed between them, and said he could not bear her out of his sight until she was safe at Raby. The words and the tone were those of a lover, and Henry was in agony: thereupon Grace laughed it off "Not bear me out of your sight!" said she. "Why, you ran away from me, and tumbled into the river. Ha! ha! ha! And" (very seriously) "we should both be in another world but for Mr. Little."

"You are very cruel," said Mr. Coventry. "When you gave up in despair, I ran for help. You punish me for failure; punish me savagely."

"Yes, I was ungenerous," said Grace. "Forgive me." But she said it rather coolly, and not with a very penitent air.

She added an explanation more calculated to please Henry than him. "Your gallantry is always graceful; and it is charming, in a drawing-room; but in this wild place, and just after escaping the grave, let us talk like sensible people. If you and I set out for Raby Hall alone, we shall lose our way again, and perish, to a certainty. But I think Mr. Little must know the way to Raby Hall."

"Oh, then," said Coventry, catching at her idea, "perhaps Mr. Little would add to the great obligation, under which he has laid us both, by going to Raby Hall and sending assistance hither."

"I can't do that," said Henry, roughly.

"And that is not at all what I was going to propose," said Grace, quietly. "But perhaps you would be so good as to go with us to Raby Hall? Then I should feel safe; and I want Mr. Raby to thank you, for I feel how cold and unmeaning all I have said to you is; I seem to have no words." Her voice faltered, and her sweet eyes filled.

"Miss Carden," said the young man, gravely, "I can't do that. Mr. Raby is no friend of mine, and he is a bigoted old man, who would turn me out of this place if he knew. Come, now, when you talk about gratitude to me for not letting you be starved to death, you make me blush. Is there a man in the world that wouldn't? —But this I do say; it would be rather hard if you two were to go away, and cut my throat in return; and, if you open your mouths ever so little, either of you, you *will* cut my throat. Why, ask yourselves, have I set up my workshop in such a place as this,—by choice? It takes a stout heart to work here, I can tell you, and a stout heart to sleep here over dead bones."

"I see it all. The Trades Unions!"

"That is it. So, now, there are only two ways. You must promise me never to breathe a word to any living soul, or I must give up my livelihood, and leave the country."

"What, can not you trust me? Oh, Mr. Little!"

"No, no; it's this gentleman. He is a stranger to me, you know; and, you see, my life may be at stake, as well as my means."

"Mr. Coventry is a gentleman, and a man of honor. He is incapable of betraying you."

"I should hope so," said Coventry. "I pledge you the word of a gentleman I will never let any human creature know that you are working here."

"Give me your hand on that, if you please."

Coventry gave him his hand with warmth and evident sincerity.

Young Little was reassured. "Come," said he, "I feel I can trust you both. And, sir, Miss Carden will tell you what happened to me in Cheetham's works; and then you will understand what I risk upon your honor."

"I accept the responsibility; and I thank you for giving me this opportunity to show you how deeply I feel indebted to you."

"That is square enough. Well, now my mind is at ease about that, I'll tell you what I'll do; I won't take you quite to Raby Hall; but I'll take you so near to it you can't miss it: and then I'll go back to my work."

He sighed deeply at the lonely prospect, and Grace heard him.

"Come," said he, almost violently, and led the way out of the church. But he staid behind to lock the door, and then joined them.

They all three went together, Grace in the middle.

There was now but little snow falling, and the air was not so thick; but it was most laborious walking, and soon Mr. Coventry, who was stiff and in pain, fell a little behind, and groaned as he hobbled on.

Grace whispered to Henry: "Be generous. He has hurt himself so."

This made Henry groan in return. But he said nothing. He just turned back to Coventry, —"You can't get on without help, sir; lean on me."

The act was friendly, the tone surly. Coventry accepted the act, and noted the tone in his memory.

When Grace had done this, she saw Henry misunderstood it, and she was sorry, and waited an opportunity to restore the balance: but, ere one came, a bell was heard in the air; the great alarmbell of Raby Hall.

Then faint voices were heard of people calling to each other here and there in the distance.

"What is it?" asked Grace.

Henry replied, —"What should it be? The whole country is out after you. Mr. Raby has sense enough for that."

"Oh, I hope they will not see the light in the church, and find you out."

"You are very good to think of that. Ah! There's a bonfire: and here comes a torch. I must go and quench my fires. Good-bye, Miss Carden. Good-evening, sir."

With this, he retired; but, as he went, he sighed.

Grace said to Coventry, —"Oh, I forgot to ask him a question:" and ran after him. "Mr. Little!"

He heard and came back to her.

She was violently agitated. "I can't leave you so," she said. "Give me your hand."

He gave it to her.

"I mortified you: and you have saved me." She took his hand, and, holding it gently in both her little palms, sobbed out, —"Oh, think of something I can do, to show my gratitude, my esteem. Pray, pray, pray."

"Wait two years for me."

"Oh, not that. I don't mean that."

"That or nothing. In two years, I'll be as good a gentleman as he is. I'm not risking my life in that church, for nothing. If you have one grain of pity or esteem for me, wait two years."

"Incurable!" she murmured: but he was gone.

Coventry heard the prayer. That was loud and earnest enough. Her reply he could not hear.

She rejoined him, and the torch came rapidly forward.

It was carried by a lass, with her gown pinned nearly to her knees, and displaying grand and powerful limbs: she was crying, like the tenderest woman, and striding through the snow, like a young giant.

When the snow first came down, Mr. Raby merely ordered large fires to be lighted and fed in his guests' bed-rooms; he feared nothing worse for them than a good wetting.

When dinner-time came, without them, he began to be anxious, and sent a servant to the little public-house, to inquire if they were there.

The servant had to walk through the snow, and had been gone about an hour, and Mr. Raby was walking nervously up and down the hall, when Jael Dence burst in at the front door, as white as a sheet, and gasped out in his face: "THE GABRIEL HOUNDS!!"

Raby ran out directly, and sure enough, that strange pack were passing in full cry over the very house. It was appalling. He was dumb with awe for a moment. Then he darted into the kitchen and ordered them to ring the great alarmbell incessantly: then into the yard, and sent messengers to the village, and to all his tenants, and in about an hour there were fifty torches, and as many sheep-bells, directed upon Cairnhope hill; and, as men and boys came in from every quarter, to know why Raby's great alarm-bell was ringing, they were armed with torches and sent up Cairnhope.

At last the servant returned from "The Colley Dog," with the alarming tidings that Miss Carden and Mr. Coventry had gone up the hill, and never returned. This, however, was hardly news. The Gabriel hounds always ran before calamity.

At about eleven o'clock, there being still no news of them, Jael Dence came to Mr. Raby wringing her hands. "Why do all the men go east for them?"

"Because they are on the east side."

"How can ye tell that? They have lost their way."

"I am afraid so," groaned Raby.

"Then why do you send all the men as if they hadn't lost their way? East side of Cairnhope! why that is where they ought to be, but it is not where they are, man."

"You are a good girl, and I'm a fool," cried Raby. "Whoever comes in after this, I'll send them up by the old church."

"Give me a torch, and I'll run myself."

"Ay, do, and I'll put on my boots, and after you."

Then Jael got a torch, and kilted her gown to her knees, and went striding through the snow with desperate vigor, crying as she went, for her fear was great and her hope was small, from the moment she heard the Gabriel hounds.

Owing to the torch, Grace saw her first, and uttered a little scream: a loud scream of rapture replied: the torch went anywhere, and gentle and simple were locked in each other's arms, Jael sobbing for very joy after terror, and Grace for sympathy, and also because she wanted to cry, on more accounts than one.

Another torch came on, and Jael cried triumphantly, "This way, Squire! She is here!" and kissed her violently again.

Mr. Raby came up, and took her in his arms, without a word, being broken with emotion: and, after he had shaken Coventry by both hands, they all turned homewards, and went so fast that Coventry gave in with a groan.

Then Grace told Jael what had befallen him, and just then another torch came in, held by George the blacksmith, who, at sight of the party, uttered a stentorian cheer, and danced upon the snow.

"Behave, now," said Jael, "and here's the gentleman sore hurt in the river; Geordie, come and make a chair with me."

George obeyed, and put out his hands, with the fingers upwards; Jael did the same, with the fingers downwards: they took hands, and, putting their stalwart arms under Coventry, told him to fling an arm round each of their necks: he did so, and up he went; he was no more than a feather to this pair, the strongest man and woman in Cairnhope.

. As they went along, he told them his adventure in the stream, and, when they heard it, they ejaculated to each other, and condoled with him kindly, and assured him he was alive by a miracle.

They reached Raby, and, in the great hall, the Squire collected his people and gave his orders. "Stop the bell. Broach a barrel of ale, and keep open house, so long as malt, and bacon, and cheese last. Turn neither body nor beast from my door this night, or may God shut His gate in your faces. Here are two guineas, George, to ring the church bells, you and your fellows; but sup here first. Cans of hot water up stairs, for *us*. Lay supper, instead of dinner; brew a bowl of punch. Light all the Yule candles, as if it was Christmas eve. But first down on your knees, all of ye, whilst I thank God, who has baffled those Gabriel Hellhounds for once, and saved a good man and a bonny lass from a dog's death."

They all went down on their knees, on the marble floor, directly, and the Squire uttered a few words of hearty thanksgiving, and there was scarcely a dry eye.

Then the guests went up stairs, and had their hot baths, and changed their clothes, and came down to supper in the blazing room.

Whilst they were at supper, the old servant who waited on them said something in a low voice to his master. He replied that he would speak to the man in the hall.

As soon as he was gone, Miss Carden said in French, "Did you hear that?"

"No."

"Well, I did. Now, mind your promise. We shall have to fib. You had better say noth-

ing. Let me speak for you; ladies fib so much better than gentlemen."

Mr. Raby came back, and Grace waited to see if he would tell her. I don't think he intended to, at first; but he observed her eyes inquiring, and said, "One of the men, who was out after you to-night, has brought in word there is a light in Cairnhope old church."

"Do you believe it?"

"No. But it is a curious thing; a fortnight ago (I think I told you) a shepherd brought me the same story. He had seen the church on fire; at least he said so. But mark the paralyzing effect of superstition. My present informant no sooner saw this light,—probably a reflection from one of the distant torches—then he coolly gave up searching for you. 'They are dead,' says he, 'and the spirits in the old church are saying mass for their souls. I'll go to supper.' So he came here to drink my ale, and tell his cock-and-bull story."

Grace put in a word with a sweet, candid face. "Sir, if there had been a light in that church, should we not have seen it?"

"Why, of course you would: you must have been within a hundred yards of it in your wanderings. I never thought of that."

Grace breathed again.

"However, we shall soon know. I have sent George and another man right up to the church to look. It is quite clear now."

Grace felt very anxious, but she forced on a careless air. "And suppose, after all, there should be a light?"

"Then George has his orders to come back and tell me; if there *is* a light, it is no ghost nor spirit, but some smuggler, or poacher, or vagrant, who is desecrating that sacred place; and I shall turn out with fifty men, and surround the church, and capture the scoundrel, and make an example of him."

Grace turned cold and looked at Mr. Coventry. She surprised a twinkle of satisfaction in his eye. She never forgot it.

She sat on thorns, and was so distraite she could hardly answer the simplest question.

At last, after an hour of cruel suspense, the servant came in, and said, "George is come back, sir."

"Oh, please let him come in here, and tell us."

"By all means. Send him in."

George appeared, the next moment, in the doorway. "Well?" said Mr. Raby.

"Well?" said Grace, pale, but self-possessed.

"Well," said George, sulkily, "it is all a lie. Th' old church is as black as my hat."

"I thought as much," said Mr. Raby. "There, go and get your supper."

Soon after this Grace went up to bed, and Jael came to her, and they talked by the fire while she was curling her hair. She was in high spirits, and Jael eyed her with wonder and curiosity.

"But, Miss," said Jael, "the magpie was right. Oh, the foul bird! That's the only bird that wouldn't go into the ark with Noah and his folk."

"Indeed! I was not aware of the circumstance."

"'Twas so, Miss; and I know the reason. A very old woman told me."

"She must have been very old indeed, to be

an authority on that subject. Well what was the reason?"

"She liked better to perch on the roof of th' ark, and jabber over the drowning world; that was why. So, ever after that, when a magpie flies across, turn back, or look to meet ill-luck."

"That is to say the worst creatures are stronger than their Creator, and can bring us bad luck against His will. And you call yourself a Christian? Why this is Paganism. They were frightened at ravens, and you at magpies. A fig for your magpies! and another for your Gabriel hounds! God is high above them all."

"Ay, sure; but these are signs of His will. Trouble and all comes from God. And so, whenever you see a magpie, or hear those terrible hounds—"

"Then tremble! for it is all to end in a bowl of punch, and a roaring fire; and Mr. Raby, that passes for a Tartar, being so kind to me; and me being in better spirits than I have been for ever so long."

"Oh, Miss!"

"And Oh, Miss, to you. Why, what is the matter? I have been in danger! Very well; am I the first? I have had an adventure! All the better. Besides it has shown me what good hearts there are in the world, yours amongst the rest." (Kissing her.) "Now don't interrupt, but listen to the words of the wise and their dark sayings. Excitement is a blessing. Young ladies need it more than any body. Half the foolish things we do, it is because the old people are so stupid and don't provide us enough innocent excitement. Dancing till five is a good thing now and then; only that is too bodily, and ends in a headache, and feeling stupider than before. But to-night, what glorious excitement! Too late for dinner—drenched with snow—lost on a mountain —anxiety—fear—the Gabriel hounds—terror— despair—resignation—sudden relief—warm stockings—delightful sympathy—petted on every side —hungry—happy—fires—punch! I never lived till to-night—I never relished life till now. How could I? I never saw Death nor Danger near enough to be worth a straw."

Jael made no attempt to arrest this flow of spirits. She waited quietly for a single pause, and then she laid her hand on the young lady's, and, fastening her eyes on her, she said quietly,—

"You have seen *him.*"

Grace Carden's face was scarlet in a moment, and she looked with a rueful imploring glance, into those great gray searching eyes of Jael Dence.

Her fine silvery tones of eloquence went off into a little piteous whine. "You are very cunning—to believe in a magpie." And she hid her blushing face in her hands. She took an early opportunity of sending this too sagacious rustic to bed.

Next day Mr. Coventry was so stiff and sore he did not come down to breakfast. But Grace Carden, though very sleepy, made her appearance, and had a most affectionate conversation with Mr. Raby. She asked leave to christen him again. "I must call you something, you know, after all this. Mr. Raby is cold. Godpapa is childish. What do you say to—'Uncle?'"

He said he should be delighted. Then she dip-

ped her forefinger in water. He drew back with horror.

"Come, young lady," said he, "I know it is an age of burlesque. But let us spare the sacraments, and the altar, and such trifles."

"I'm not half so wicked as you think," said Grace. Then she wrote "Uncle" on his brow, and so settled that matter.

Mr. Coventry came down about noon, and resumed his courtship. He was very tender, spoke of the perils they had endured together as an additional tie, and pressed his suit with ardor.

But he found a great change in the lady.

Yesterday, on Cairnhope Peak, she was passive, but soft and complying. To-day she was polite, but cool, and as slippery as an eel. There was no pinning her.

And, at last, she said, "The fact is, I'm thinking of our great preservation, and more inclined to pray than flirt, for once."

"And so am I," said the man of tact; "but what I offer is a sacred and life-long affection."

"Oh, of course."

"A few hours ago you did me the honor to listen to me. You even hinted I might speak to your father."

"No, no. I only asked if you *had* spoken to him."

"I will not contradict you. I will trust to your own candor. Dear Grace, tell me, have I been so unfortunate as to offend you since then?"

"No."

"Have I lost your respect?"

"Oh, no."

"Have I forfeited your good opinion?"

"Dear me, no." (A little pettishly.)

"Then how is it that I love you better, if possible, than yesterday; and you seem not to like me so well as yesterday?"

"One is not always in the same humor."

"Then you don't like me do-day?"

"Oh yes, but I do. And I shall always like you: if you don't tease me, and urge me too much. It is hardly fair to hurry me so; I am only a girl, and girls make such mistakes sometimes."

"That is true; they marry on too short an acquaintance. But you have known me more than two years, and, in all that time, have I once given you reason to think that you had a rival in my admiration, my love?"

"I never watched you to see. But all that time you have certainly honored me with your attention, and I do believe you love me, more than I deserve. Please do not be angry: do not be mortified. There is no occasion; I am resolved not to marry until I am of age; that is all: and where's the harm of that?"

"I will wait your pleasure; all I ask you, at present, is to relieve me of my fears, by engaging yourself to me."

"Ah; but I have always been warned against long engagements."

"Long engagements! Why, how old are you, may I ask?"

"Only nineteen. Give me a little time to think."

"If I wait till you are of age, *that will be two years.*"

"Just about. I was nineteen on the 12th of December. What is the matter?"

"Oh, nothing. A sudden twinge. A man

does not get rolled over sharp rocks, by a mountain torrent, for nothing."

"No, indeed."

"Never mind that, if I'm not to be punished in my heart as well. This resolution, not to marry for two years, is it your own idea? or has somebody put it into your head since we stood on Cairnhope, and looked at Bollinghope?"

"Please give me credit for it," said Grace, turning very red: "it is the only sensible one I have had for a long time."

Mr. Coventry groaned aloud, and turned very pale.

Grace said she wanted to go up stairs for her work, and so got away from him.

She turned at the door, and saw him sink into a chair, with an agony in his face that was quite new to him.

She fled to her own room, to think it all over, and she entered it so rapidly that she caught Jael crying, and rocking herself before the fire.

The moment she came in Jael got up, and affected to be very busy, arranging things; but always kept her back turned to Grace.

The young lady sat down, and leaned her cheek on her hand, and reflected very sadly and seriously on the misery she had left in the drawing-room, and the tears she had found here.

Accustomed to make others bright and happy by her bare presence, this beautiful and unselfish young creature was shocked at the misery she was sowing around her, and all for something her judgment told her would prove a chimera. And again she asked herself was she brave enough, and selfish enough, to defy her father and her godfather, whose mind was written so clearly in that terrible inscription.

She sat there, cold at heart, a long time, and at last came to a desperate resolution.

"Give me my writing-desk."

Jael brought it her.

"Sit down there where I can see you; and don't hide your tears from me. I want to see you cry. I want every help. I wasn't born to make every body miserable: I am going to end it."

She wrote a little, and then she stopped, and sighed; then she wrote a little more, and stopped, and sighed. Then she burned the letter, and began again; and as she wrote, she sighed; and as she wrote on, she moaned.

And, as she wrote on, the tears began to fall upon the paper.

It was piteous to see the struggle of this lovely girl, and the patient fortitude that could sigh, and moan, and weep, yet go on doing the brave act that made her sigh, and moan, and weep.

At last, the letter was finished, and directed; and Grace put it in her bosom, and dismissed Jael abruptly, almost harshly, and sat down, cold and miserable, before the fire.

At dinner-time her eyes were so red she would not appear. She pleaded headache, and dined in her own room.

Meantime Mr. Coventry passed a bitter time.

He had heard young Little say, "Wait two years." And now Grace was evading and procrastinating, and so, literally, obeying that young man, with all manner of false pretenses. This was a revelation, and cast back a bright light on many suspicious things he had observed in the church.

He was tortured with jealous agony. And it added to his misery that he could not see his way to any hostilities.

Little could easily be driven out of the country, for that matter: he had himself told them both how certainly that would befall him if he was betrayed to the Unions. But honor and gratitude forbade this line; and Coventry, in the midst of his jealous agony, resisted that temptation fiercely, would not allow his mind even to dwell upon it for a moment.

He recalled all his experiences; and, after a sore struggle of passion, he came to some such conclusion as this; That Grace would have married him if she had not unexpectedly fallen in with Little, under very peculiar and moving circumstances: that an accident of this kind would never occur again, and he must patiently wear out the effect of it.

He had observed that in playing an uphill game of love the lover must constantly ask himself, "What should I do, were I to listen to my heart?" and having ascertained that, must do the opposite. So now Mr. Coventry grimly resolved to control his wishes for a time, to hide his jealousy, to hide his knowledge of her deceit, to hide his own anger. He would wait some months before he again asked her to marry him, unless he saw a change in her; and, meantime, he would lay himself out to please her, trusting to this, that there could be no intercourse by letter between her and a workman, and they were not likely to meet again in a hurry.

It required considerable fortitude to curb his love and jealousy, and settle on this course. But he did conquer after a hard struggle, and prepared to meet Miss Carden at dinner with artificial gayety.

But she did not appear; and that set Mr. Coventry thinking again. Why should she have a headache? He had a rooted disbelief in woman's headaches. His own head had far more reason to ache, and his heart too. He puzzled himself all dinner-time about this headache, and was very bad company.

Soon after dinner he took a leaf out of her book, pretended headache, and said he should like to take a turn by himself in the air.

What he really wanted to do was to watch Miss Carden's windows, for he had all manner of ugly suspicions.

There seemed to be a strong light in the room. He could see no more.

He walked moodily up and down, very little satisfied with himself, and at last he got ashamed of his own thoughts.

"Oh, no!" he said, "she is in her room, sure enough."

He turned his back, and strolled out into the road.

Presently he heard the rustle of a woman's dress. He stepped into the shade of the firs directly, and his heart began to beat hard.

But it was only Jael Dence. She came out within a few yards of him. She had something white in her hand, which, however, she instinctively conveyed into her bosom the moment she found herself in the moonlight. Coventry saw her do it though.

She turned to the left, and walked swiftly up the road.

Now Coventry knew nothing about this girl,

except that she belonged to a class with whom money generally goes a long way. And he now asked himself whether it might not be well worth his while to enlist her sympathies on his side.

While he was coming to this conclusion, Jael, who was gliding along at a great pace, reached a turn in the road, and Mr. Coventry had to run after her to catch her.

When he got to the turn in the road, she was just going round another turn, having quickened her pace.

Coventry followed more leisurely. She might be going to meet her sweetheart; and, if so, he had better talk to her on her return.

He walked on till he saw at some distance a building, with a light shining through it in a peculiar way: and now the path became very rugged and difficult. He came to a standstill, and eyed the place where his rival was working at that moment. He eyed it with a strange mixture of feelings. It had saved his life and hers, after all. He fell into another mood, and began to laugh at himself for allowing himself to be disturbed by such a rival.

But what is this? Jael Dence comes in sight again: she is making for the old church.

Coventry watched her unseen. She went to the porch, and, after she had been there some time, the door was opened just a little, then wide, and she entered the building. He saw it all in a moment: the girl was already bought by the other side, and had carried his rival a letter before his eyes.

A clandestine correspondence!

All his plans and his resolutions melted away before this discovery. There was nothing to be done but to save the poor girl from this miserable and degrading attachment, and its inevitable consequences.

He went home, pale with fury, and never once closed his eyes all night.

Next day he ordered his dog-cart early; and told Mr. Raby and Grace he was going to Hillsborough for medical advice: had a pain in his back he could not get rid of.

He called on the chief constable of Hillsborough, and asked him, confidentially, if he knew any thing about a workman called Little.

"What; a Londoner, sir? the young man that is at odds with the Trades?"

"I shouldn't wonder. Yes; I think he is. A friend of mine takes an interest in him."

"And so do I. His case was a disgrace to the country, and to the constabulary of the place. It occurred just ten days before I came here, and it seems to me that nothing was done which ought to have been done."

Mr. Coventry put in a question or two, which elicited from Mr. Ransome all he knew about the matter.

"Where does this Little live?" was the next inquiry.

"I don't know; but I think you could learn at Mr. Cheetham's. The only time I ever saw Little, he was walking with the foreman of those works. He was pointed out to me. A dark young man; carries himself remarkably well—doesn't look like a workman. If they don't know at Cheetham's, I'll find him out for you in twenty-four hours."

"But this Grotait. Do you know him?"

"Oh, he is a public character. Keeps 'The Cutlers' Arms,' in Black Street."

"I understand he repudiates all these outrages."

"He does. But the workmen themselves are behind the scenes; and what do they call him? Why, 'Old Smitem.'"

"Ah! You are one of those who look below the surface," said the courtier.

He then turned the conversation, and, soon after, went away. He had been adroit enough to put his questions in the languid way of a man who had no personal curiosity, and was merely discharging a commission.

Mr. Ransome, as a matter of form, took a short note of the conversation; but attached no importance to it. However, he used the means at his command to find out Little's abode. Not that Mr. Coventry had positively asked him to do it; but, his attention being thus unexpectedly called to the subject, he felt desirous to talk to Little on his own account.

Mr. Coventry went straight to "The Cutlers' Arms," but he went slowly. A powerful contest was now going on within him; jealousy and rage urged him onward, honor and gratitude held him back. Then came his self-deceiving heart, and suggested that Miss Carden had been the first to break her promise (she had let Jael Dence into Little's secret), and that he himself was being undermined by cunning and deceit; strict notions of honor would be out of place in such a combat. Lastly, he felt it his *duty* to save Miss Carden from a degrading connection.

All these considerations, taken together, proved too strong for his good faith; and so stifled the voice of conscience, that it could only keep whispering against the deed, but not prevent it.

He went direct to "The Cutlers' Arms." He walked into the parlor and ordered a glass of brandy-and-water, and asked if he could see Mr. Grotait, privately. Mr. Grotait came in.

"Sit down, Mr. Grotait. Will you have any thing?"

"A glass of ale, sir, if you please."

When this had been brought, and left, and the parties were alone, Coventry asked him whether he could receive a communication under a strict promise of secrecy.

"If it is a trade matter, sir, you can trust me. A good many have."

"Well then, I can tell you something about a workman called Little. But, before I say a word, I must make two express conditions. One is, that no violence shall be used towards him; the other, that you never reveal to any human creature, it was I who told you."

"What, is he working still?"

"My conditions, Mr. Grotait?"

"I promise you absolute secrecy, sir, as far as you are concerned. As to your other condition, the matter will work thus: if your communication should be as important as you think, I can do nothing—the man is not in the saw-trade—I shall carry the information to two other secretaries, and shall not tell them I had it from Mr. Coventry, of Bollinghope." (Mr. Coventry started at finding himself known.) "Those gentlemen will be sure to advise with me, and I shall suggest to them to take effectual measures, but to keep it, if possible, from the knowledge of all those persons who discredit us by their violent acts."

"Well then, on that understanding,—the man works all night in a deserted church at Cairnhope; it is all up among the hills."

Grotait turned red. "Are you sure of this?"

"Quite sure?"

"You have seen him?"

"Yes."

"Has he a forge?"

"Yes; and bellows, and quantities of moulds, and strips of steel. He is working on a large scale."

"It shall be looked into, sir, by the proper persons. Indeed the sooner they are informed, the better."

"Yes, but mind, no violence. You are strong enough to drive him out of the country without that."

"I should hope so."

Coventry then rose, and left the place; but he had no sooner got into the street, than a sort of horror fell on him; horror of himself, distrust and dread of the consequences, to his rival but benefactor.

Almost at the door, he was met by Mr. Ransome, who stopped him and gave him Little's address; he had obtained it without difficulty from Bayne.

"I am glad you reminded me, sir," said he; "I shall call on him myself, one of these days."

These words rang in Coventry's ears, and put him in a cold perspiration. "Fool!" thought he, "to go and ask a public officer, a man who hears every body in turn."

What he had done disinclined him to return to Cairnhope. He made a call or two first, and loitered about, and then at last back to Raby, gnawed with misgivings and incipient remorse.

Mr. Grotait sent immediately for Mr. Parkin, Mr. Jobson, and Mr. Potter, and told them the secret information he had just received.

They could hardly believe it at first; Jobson, especially, was incredulous. He said he had kept his eye on Little, and assured them the man had gone into wood-carving, and was to be seen in the town all day.

"Ay," said Parkin, "but this is at night; and, now I think of it, I met him t'other day, about dusk, galloping east, as hard as he could go."

"My information is from a sure source," said Grotait, stiffly.

Parkin.—"What is to be done?"

Jobson.—"Is he worth another strike?"

Potter.—"The time is unfavorable: here's a slap of dull trade."

The three then put their heads together, and various plans were suggested and disscussed, and, as the parties were not now before the public, that horror of gunpowder, vitriol, and life-preservers, which figured in their notices and resolutions, did not appear in their conversation. Grotait alone was silent and doubtful. This Grotait was the greatest fanatic of the four, and, like all fanatics, capable of vast cruelty: but his cruelty lay in his head, rather than in his heart. Out of Trade questions, the man, though vain and arrogant, was of a genial and rather a kindly nature; and, even in Trade questions, being more intelligent than his fellows, he was sometimes infested with a gleam of humanity.

His bigotry was, at this moment, disturbed by a visitation of that kind. "I'm perplexed," said he: "I don't often hesitate on a Trade question

6

neither. But the men we have done were always low-lived blackguards, who would have destroyed us, if we had not disabled them. Now this Little is a decent young chap. He struck at the root of our Trades, so long as he wrought openly. But on the sly, and nobody knowing but ourselves, mightn't it be as well to shut our eyes a bit? My informant is not in trade."

The other three took a more personal view of the matter. Little was outwitting, and resisting them. They saw nothing for it but to stop him, by hook or by crook.

While they sat debating his case in whispers, and with their heads so close you might have covered them all with a tea-tray, a clear musical voice was heard to speak to the barmaid, and, by her direction, in walked into the council-chamber—Mr. Henry Little.

This visit greatly surprised Messrs. Parkin, Jobson, and Potter, and made them stare, and look at one another uneasily. But it did not surprise Grotait so much, and it came about in the simplest way. That morning, at about eleven o'clock, Dr. Amboyne had called on Mrs. Little, and had asked Henry, rather stiffly, whether he was quite forgetting Life, Labor, and Capital. Now the young man could not but feel that, for some time past, he had used the good Doctor ill; had neglected and almost forgotten his benevolent hobby; so the Doctor's gentle reproach went to his heart, and he said, "Give me a day or two, sir, and I'll show you how ashamed I am of my selfish behavior." True to this pledge, he collected all his notes together, and prepared a report, to be illustrated with drawings. He then went to Cheetham's, more as a matter of form than any thing, to see if the condemned grindstone had been changed. To his infinite surprise he found it had not, and Bayne told him the reason. Henry was angry, and went direct to Grotait about it.

But as soon as he saw Jobson, and Parkin, and Potter, he started, and they started. "Oh!" said he, "I didn't expect to find so much good company. Why, here's the whole quorum."

"We will retire, sir, if you wish it."

"Not at all. My orders are to convert you all to Life, Labor, and Capital (Grotait pricked up his ears directly); and, if I succeed, the Devil will be the next to come round, no doubt. Well, Mr. Grotait, Simmons is on that same grindstone you and I condemned. And all for a matter of four shillings. I find that, in your trade, the master provides the stone, but the grinder hangs and races it, which, in one sense, is time lost. Well, Simmons declines the new stone, unless Cheetham will pay him by time for hanging and racing it; Cheetham refuses; and so, between them, that idiot works on a faulty stone. Will you use your influence with the grinder?"

"Well, Mr. Little, now, between ourselves, don't you think it rather hard that the poor workman should have to hang and race the master's grindstone for nothing?"

"Why, they share the loss between them. The stone costs the master three pounds; and hanging it costs the workman only four or five shillings. Where's the grievance?"

"Hanging and racing a stone shortens the grinder's life; fills his lungs with grit. Is the workman to give Life and Labor for a forenoon; and is Capital to contribute nothing? Is that your view of Life, Labor, and Capital, young man?"

Henry was staggered a moment. "That is smart," said he. "But a rule of trade is a rule, till it is altered by consent of the parties that made it. Now, right or wrong, it is the rule of trade here that the small grinders find their own stones, and pay for power; but the saw-grinders are better off, for they have not to find stones, nor power, and their only drawback is that they must hang and race a new stone, which costs the master sixty shillings. Cheetham is smarting under your rules, and you can't expect him to go against any rule, that saves him a shilling."

"What does the grinder think?"

"You might as well ask what the grindstone thinks."

"Well, what does the grinder say, then?"

"Says he'd rather run the stone out, than lose a forenoon."

"Well, sir, it is his business."

"It may be a man's business to hang himself; but it is the bystanders' to hinder him."

"You mistake me. I mean that the grinder is the only man who knows whether a stone is safe."

"Well, but this grinder does not pretend his stone is safe. All he says is, safe or not, he'll run it out. So now the question is, will you pay four shillings from your box, for this blockhead's loss of time in hanging and racing a new stone?"

All the four secretaries opened their eyes with surprise at this. But Grotait merely said he had no authority to do that; the funds of the Union were set apart for specified purposes.

"Very likely," said Henry, getting warm: "but, when there's life to be *taken*, your Union can find money irregularly; so why grudge it, when there's life to be saved perhaps, and ten times cheaper than you pay for blood."

"Young man," said Grotait, severely, "did you come here to insult us with these worn-out slanders?"

"No, but I came to see whether you secretaries, who can find pounds to assassinate men, and blow up women and children with gunpowder, can find shillings to secure the life of one of your own members; he risks it every time he mounts his horsing."

"Well, sir, the application is without precedent, and I must decline it; but this I beg to do as courteously, as the application has been made uncourteously."

"Oh, it is easy to be polite, when you've got no heart."

"You are the first ever brought that charge against me."

"You ought to be ashamed of yourself," said Potter, warmly. "No heart! Mr. Grotait is known for a good husband, a tender father, and the truest friend in Hillsborough."

The others echoed these sentiments warmly and sincerely; for, strange as it may appear to those who have not studied human nature at first hand, every word of this eulogy was strictly true.

"Thank you, gentlemen," said Grotait. "But we must make allowances. Mr. Little is smarting under a gross and dastardly outrage, and also under a fair defeat; and thinks his opponents must be monsters. Now I should like to show him the contrary. Let Simmons take care of himself. You have given him good advice, and

much to your credit: now have you nothing to say to us, on your own account?"

"Not a word," said Henry, steadily.

"But suppose I could suggest a way by which you could carry on your trade in Hillsborough, and offend nobody?"

"I should decline to hear it even. You and I are at war on that. You have done your worst, and I shall do my best to make you all smart for it, the moment I get a chance."

Grotait's cheek reddened with anger at this rebuff, and it cost him an effort to retain his friendly intentions. "Come, come," said he, rather surlily, "don't be in a hurry till you have heard the nature of my proposal. Here, Jess, a quart of the best ale. Now, to begin, let us drink and be comfortable together."

He passed the glass to Little, first. But the young man's blood was boiling with his wrongs, and this patronizing air irritated him to boot. He took the glass in his hand, "Here's quick exposure—sudden death—and sure damnation—to all hypocrites and assassins!" He drained the glass to this toast, flung sixpence on the table, and strode out, white with passion himself, and leaving startled faces behind.

"So be it," said Grotait; and his wicked little eye glittered dangerously.

That same evening, a signal, well known to certain workmen in Hillsborough, peeped in the window of "The Cutlers' Arms." And, in consequence, six or seven ill-conditioned fellows gathered about the doors and waited patiently for further information.

Amongst these was a sturdy fellow of about nine-and-twenty, whose existence was a puzzle to his neighbors. During the last seven years he had worked only eighteen months all together. The rest of the time he had been on the Saw-Grinders' box, receiving relief, viz.: seven shillings and sixpence weekly for himself, and two-and-sixpence for his wife, and two shillings for each child; and every now and then he would be seen with three or four sovereigns in his possession.

The name of this masterful beggar, of this invalid in theory, who, in fact, could eat three pounds of steak at a sitting, was Biggs; but it is a peculiarity of Hillsborough to defy baptismal names, and substitute others deemed spicier. Out of the parish register and the records of the police courts, the scamp was only known as Dan Tucker.

This Dan stood, with others, loitering about "The Cutlers' Arms."

Presently out came Grotait, and surveyed the rascally lot. He beckoned Dan, and retired. Dan went in after him.

"Drat his luck!" said one of the rejected candidates, "he always gets the job." The rest then dispersed.

Tucker was shown into a pitch-dark room, and there a bargain was struck between him and men unseen. He and two more were to go to Cairnhope, and *do* Little. He was to avoid all those men who had lately stood at the door with him, and was to choose for his companions Simmons the grinder, and one Sam Cole, a smooth, plausible fellow, that had been in many a dark job, unsuspected even by his wife and family, who were respectable.

Thus instructed, Tucker went to the other men,

and soon reported to Grotait that he had got Cole all right, but that Simmons looked coldly on the job. He was in full work, for one thing, and said Little had had his squeak already, and he didn't see following him eleven miles off; he had, however, asked him whether Little had a wife and children, which question he, Tucker, could not answer.

"But I can," said Grotait. "He is a bachelor. You can tell Simmons so. There are reasons why Ned Simmons must be in this. Try him to-morrow at dinner-time. Bid two pounds more; and—his wife is near her time—tell him this job will help him buy her wine and things," said the kind, parental, diabolical Grotait.

Next morning Henry worked with the pen for Doctor Amboyne till twelve o'clock. He then, still carrying out his friend's views, went down to Mr. Cheetham's works to talk to Simmons.

But he found an ill-looking fellow standing by the man's side, and close at his ear. This was no other than Dan Tucker, who by a neat coincidence was tempting him to *do* Little.

Yesterday's conversation had unsettled Simmons, and he did not come to work till twelve o'clock. He then fixed a small pulley-wheel to his grindstone, to make up for lost time.

He was still resisting the tempter, but more faintly than yesterday, when Little came in, and spoke to him. Both he and Dan were amazed at his appearance on the scene at that particular moment. They glared stupidly, but said nothing.

"Look here, Simmons," said Little. "I have been to your friend Grotait, and asked him to pay you for what you call time lost in hanging and racing a new stone. He won't do it. That is your *friend*. Now I'm your *enemy*; so the Union says. Well, enemy or not, I'll do what Grotait won't. I'll pay you the four shillings for lost time, if you will stop that stone at once, and hang another."

"Why, what's wrong with stone?"

"The best judge in Hillsborough condemned it; and now, if you are not running it with an undersized pulley-wheel, to try it worse!"

Simmons got stupid and irritated between the two. His bit of manhood revolted against Little's offer, made whilst he was half lending his ear to Tucker's proposal; and, on the other hand, that very offer irritated him with Tucker, for coming and tempting him to *do* this very Little, who was a good sort.

" —— you both!" said the rough fellow. "I wish you'd let me alone. Here I've lost my morning's work already." Then to Little, "Mind thyself, old lad. Happen thou's in more danger than I am."

"What d'ye mean by that?" said Little, very sharply.

But Simmons saw that he had gone too far, and now maintained a sullen silence.

Henry turned to Tucker. "I don't know who you are, but I call you to witness that I have done all I can for this idiot. Now, if he comes to harm, his blood be upon his own head."

Then Henry went off in dudgeon, and, meeting Bayne in the yard, had a long discussion with him on the subject.

The tempter took advantage of Little's angry departure, and steadily resumed his temptation.

But he was interrupted in his turn.

The defect in this grindstone was not so serious but that the stone might perhaps have been ground out with fair treatment: but, by fixing a small pulley-wheel, Simmons had caused it to rotate at furious speed. This tried it too hard, and it flew in two pieces, just as the grinder was pressing down a heavy saw on it with all his force.

One piece, weighing about five hundredweight, tore the horsing chains out of the floor, and went clean through the window (smashing the woodwork), out into the yard, and was descending on Little's head; but he heard the crash and saw it coming; he ran yelling out of the way, and dragged Bayne with him. The other fragment went straight up to the ceiling, and broke a heavy joist as if it had been a cane; then fell down again plump, and would have destroyed the grinder on the spot, had he been there: but the tremendous shock had sent him flying clean over the squatter-board, and he fell on his stomach on the wheel-band of the next grindstone, and so close to the drum, that, before any one could recover the shock and seize him, the band drew him on to the drum, and the drum, which was drawing away from the window, pounded him against the wall, with cruel thuds.

One ran and screamed to stop the power, another to cut the big wheel-bands. All this took several seconds; and here seconds were torn flesh and broken bones. Just as Little darted into the room, pale with his own narrow escape, and awe-stricken at the cries of horror within, the other grinders succeeded in dragging out, from between the wall and the drum, a bag of broken bones and blood and grease, which a minute before was Ned Simmons, and was talking over a deed of violence to be done.

The others carried him and laid him on a horsing; and there they still supported his head and his broken limbs, sick with horror.

The man's face was white, and his eyes stared, and his body quivered. They sprinkled him with water.

Then he muttered, "All right. I am not much hurt.—Ay, but I am though. I'm done for."

After the first terror of the scene had passed, the men were for taking him to the infirmary. But Little interposed, eagerly, "No, no. I'll pay the doctor myself sooner. He shall be nursed at home, and have all that skill can do to save him. Oh, why, why would he not listen to me?"

A stretcher was got, and a mattress put on it, and they carried him through the streets, while one ran before to tell the unhappy wife, and Little took her address, and ran to Doctor Amboyne. The Doctor went instantly to the sufferer.

Tucker assisted to carry the victim home. He then returned to Grotait, and told him the news. Dan was not so hardened but what he blubbered in telling it, and Grotait's eyes were moist with sympathy.

They neither of them spoke out, and said, "This upsets our design on Little." Each waited to see whether that job was to go on. Each was ashamed to mention it now. So it came to a stand-still.

As for Little, he was so shocked by this tragedy, and so anxious about its victim, that he would not go out to Cairnhope. He came, in the evening, to Doctor Amboyne, to inquire, "Can he live?"

"I can't say yet. He will never work again."

Then, after a silence, he fixed his eyes on young Little, and said, "I am going to make a trial of your disposition. This is the man I suspected of blowing you up; and I'm of the same opinion still."

"No. I might try and put it out of my head; but that is all I could do."

"Is it true that you are the cause of his not being taken to the infirmary?"

"Yes, I said I'd pay out of my own pocket sooner; and I'm not the sort to go from my word.

"MIND THYSELF, OLD LAD. HAPPENS THOU'S IN MORE DANGER THAN I AM."

"Then he has got his deserts," were Henry's first words, after a pause of astonishment.

"Does that mean you forgive him, or you don't forgive him?"

"I dare say I should forgive the poor wretch, if he was to ask me."

"And not without?"

The man shall want for nothing, sir. But please don't ask me to love my enemies, and all that Rot. I scorn hypocrisy. Every man hates his enemies: he may hate 'em out like a man, or palaver 'em, and beg God to forgive 'em (and that means damn 'em), and hate 'em like a sneak; but he always hates 'em."

The Doctor laughed heartily. "Oh, how refreshing a thing it is to fall in with a fellow who speaks his real mind. However, I am not your enemy, am I?"

"No. You are the best friend I ever had—except my mother."

"I am glad you think so; because I have a favor to ask you."

"Granted, before ever you speak."

"I want to know, for certain, whether Simmons was the man who blew you up: and I see but one way of learning it. You must visit him and be kind to him; and then, my art tells me, he won't leave the world without telling you. Oblige me by taking him this bottle of wine, at once, and also this sedative, which you can administer if he is in violent pain, but not otherwise."

"Doctor," said the young man, "you always get your own way with me. And so you ought."

Little stood by Simmons's bedside.

The man's eye was set, his cheek streaked with red, and his head was bandaged. He labored in breathing.

Young Little looked at him gravely, and wondered whether this battered figure was really the man who had so nearly destroyed him.

After some minutes of this contemplation, he said gravely, "Simmons, I have brought you some wine."

The man stared at him, and seemed confused. He made no reply.

"Give me a spoon," said Henry.

Mrs. Simmons sat by the bedside rocking herself; she was stupefied with grief: but her sister, a handy girl, had come to her in her trouble: she brought Henry a spoon directly.

He poured out a little wine, and put it to the sufferer's lips. He drank it, and said it was rare good stuff. Henry gave him a little more.

Simmons then looked at him more intelligently and attentively, and gave a sort of shiver. "Who be you?"

"Henry Little; who advised you not to run that stone."

"Ah!" said Simmons, "I thought it was you." He seemed puzzled. But, after a while, he said, "I wish I had hearkened thee, lad. Give me some more of yonder stuff. What is it?"

"Port wine." Then he turned to the girl, and gave her a sovereign, and sent her out for some mutton-chops. "Meat and wine are all the physic you are to have, my poor fellow."

"It won't be for long, lad. And a good job too. For I'm a bad 'un. I'm a bad 'un."

Henry then turned to the poor woman, and tried to say something to console her, but the words stuck in his throat. She was evidently near her confinement; and there lay her husband, worse than in his grave. Little broke down himself, while trying to comfort her.

The sufferer heard him, and said, all of a sudden, "Hold a light here."

Henry took the candle, and held it over him.

"Nay, nay, it is thy face I want to see."

Henry was puzzled at the request, but did as he was asked.

Simmons gave a groan. "Ay," said he, "thou's all right. And I lie here. That seems queer."

The sister now returned, and Henry wrote her his address, and conversed with her, and told her the whole story of the grindstone, and said that,

as he had hindered Simmons from being taken to the infirmary, he felt bound to see he did not suffer by that interference. He gave her his address, and said, if any thing was wanted, she must come to him, or to his mother if he should be out.

No doubt the women talked of his kindness by the sick bed, and Simmons heard it.

Early in the morning Eliza Watney called at Little's house, with her eyes very red, and said her brother-in-law wanted to speak to him.

He went with her directly; and, on the road, asked her what it was about.

"I'm ashamed to tell you," said she, and burst out crying. "But I hope God will reward you; and forgive him: he is a very ignorant man."

"Here I am, Simmons."

"So I see."

"Any thing I can do for you?"

"No."

"You sent for me."

"Did I? Well, I dare say I did. But gi' me time. Gi' me time. It's noane so easy to look a man in the face, and tell him what I'm to tell thee. But I can't die with it on me. It chokes me, ever since you brought me yonder stuff, and the women set a talking. I say—old lad—'twas I did thee yon little job at Cheetham's. But I knew no better."

There was a dead silence. And then Henry spoke.

"Who set you on?"

"Nay, that's their business."

"How did you do it?"

At this question—will it be believed?—the penitent's eye twinkled with momentary vanity. "I fastened a teacup to an iron rake, and filled the cup with powder; then I passed it in, and spilt the powder out of cup, and raked it in to the smithy slack, and so on, filling and raking in. But I did thee one good turn, lad; I put powder as far from bellows as I could. Eh, but I was a bad 'un to do the like to thee: and thou's a good 'un to come here. When I saw thee lie there, all scorched and shaking, I didn't like my work; and now I hate it. But I knew no better at the time. And, you see, I've got it worse myself. And cheap served too."

"Oh, Mr. Little," said Eliza Watney; "try and forgive him."

"My girl," said Henry, solemnly, "I thought I never could forgive the man who did that cruel deed to me, and I had never injured any one. But it is hard to know one's own mind, let alone another man's. Now I look at him lying pale and battered there, it seems all wiped out. I forgive you, my poor fellow, and I hope God will forgive you too."

"Nay. He is not so soft as thou. This is how He forgives me. But I knew no better. Old gal, learn the young 'un to read, that's coming just as I'm going; it is sore against a chap if he can't read. Right and wrong, d—n 'em, they are locked up in books, I think; locked away from a chap like me. I know a little better now. But, eh dear, dear, it is come too late." And now the poor wretch began to cry at a gleam of knowledge of right and wrong having come to him only just when he could no longer profit by it.

Henry left him at last, with the tears in his eyes. He promised them all to come every day.

He called on Dr. Amboyne, and said, "You are always right, Doctor. Simmons was the man. He has owned it, and I forgave him."

He then went and told Mr. Holdfast. That gentleman was much pleased at the discovery, and said, "Ah, but who employed him? That is what you must discover."

"I will try," said Henry. "The poor fellow had half a mind to make a clean breast; but I didn't like to worry him over it."

Returning home he fell in with Grotait and Parkin. They were talking earnestly at the door of a public-house, and the question they were discussing was whether or not Little's affair should be revived.

They were both a good deal staggered by the fate of Simmons, Parkin especially, who was rather superstitious. He had changed sides, and was now inclined to connive, or, at all events, to temporize; to abandon the matter till a more convenient time. Grotait, on the other hand, whose vanity the young man had irritated, was bent on dismounting his forge. But even he had cooled a little, and was now disinclined to violence. He suggested that it must be easy to drive a smith out of a church, by going to the parochial authorities; and they could also send Little an anonymous letter, to tell him the Trades had their eyes on him; by this double stroke, they would probably bring him to some reasonable terms.

It certainly was a most unfortunate thing that Little passed that way just then; unfortunate that Youth is so impetuous.

He crossed the street to speak to these two potentates, whom it was his interest to let alone —if he could only have known it.

"Well, gentlemen, have you seen Simmons?"

"No," said Mr. Parkin.

"What, not been to see the poor fellow, who owes his death to you?"

"He is not dead yet."

"No, thank Heaven! He has got a good work to do first; some hypocrites, assassins, and cowards to expose."

Parkin turned pale; Grotait's eye glistened like a snake's: he made Parkin a rapid signal to say nothing, but only listen.

"He has begun by telling me who it was that put gunpowder into my forge, and how it was done. I have forgiven him. He was only the tool of much worse villains; base, cowardly, sneaking villains. Those I shall not forgive. Oh, I shall know all about it before long. Good-morning."

This information and threat, and the vindictive bitterness and resolution with which the young man had delivered it, struck terror into the gentle Parkin, and shook even Grotait. The latter, however, soon recovered himself, and it became a battle for life or death between him and Little.

He invited Parkin to his own place, and there the pair sat closeted.

Dan Tucker and Sam Cole were sent for.

Tucker came first. He was instantly dispatched to Simmons, with money from the Saw-Grinders' box. He was to ascertain how much Simmons had let out, and to adjure him to be true to the Trade, and split on no man but himself. When he had been gone about twenty minutes, Sam Cole came in, and was instructed to get two other men in place of Simmons, and be in readiness to do Little.

By-and-by Tucker returned with news. Simmons had at present split only on himself; but the women were evidently in love with Little; said he was their only friend; and he, Tucker, foresaw that, with their co-operation, Simmons would be turned inside out by Little before he died.

Grotait struck his hand on the table. "The Unions are in danger," said he. "There is but one way; Little must be made so that he can't leave Cairnhope while Simmons is alive."

So important did the crisis appear to him, that he insisted on Parkin going with him at once to Cairnhope, to reconnoitre the ground.

Parkin had a gig and a fast horse; so, in ten minutes more, they were on the road.

They reached Cairnhope, put up at the village inn, and soon extracted some particulars about the church. They went up to it, and examined it, and Grotait gave Parkin a leg up, to peer through the window.

In this position they were nailed by old George.

"What be you at?"

"What is that to you?" said Grotait.

"It is plenty. You mustn't come trespassing here. Squire won't have it."

"Trespassing in a churchyard! Why it belongs to all the world."

"Nay, this one belongs to the Lord o' the manor."

"Well, we won't hurt your church. Who keeps the key?"

"Squire Raby."

Old George from this moment followed them about everywhere, grumbling at their heels, like a mastiff.

Grotait, however, treated him with cool contempt, and proceeded to make a sketch of the door, and a little map showing how the church could be approached from Hillsborough on foot without passing through Cairnhope village. This done, he went back with Parkin to the inn, and thence to Hillsborough.

It was old Christmas Eve. Henry was working at his forge, little dreaming of danger. Yet it was close at hand, and from two distinct quarters.

Four men, with crape masks, and provided with all manner of tools, and armed with bludgeons, were creeping about the churchyard, examining and listening. Their orders were to make Little so that he should not leave Cairnhope for a month. And that, in plain English, meant to beat him within an inch of his life, if not kill him.

At the same time, a body of nine men were stealing up the road, with designs scarcely less hostile to Little.

These assailants were as yet at a considerable distance; but more formidable in appearance than the others, being most of them armed with swords, and led by a man with a double-barrelled gun.

Grotait's men, having well surveyed the ground, now crept softly up to the porch, and examined the lock.

The key was inside, and they saw no means of forcing the lock without making a noise, and putting their victim on his guard.

After a long whispered consultation, they resolved to unscrew the hinges.

These hinges were of great length, and were nailed upon the door, but screwed into the doorpost with four screws each.

Two men, with excellent tools, and masters of the business, went softly to work. One stood, and worked on the upper screws; the other kneeled, and unfastened the lower screws.

They made no more noise than a rat gnawing; yet, such was their caution, and determination to surprise their victim, that they timed all their work by Little's. Whenever the blows of his hammer intermitted, they left off; and began again when he did.

When all the screws were out but two, one above, one below, they beckoned the other two men, and these two drove large gimlets into the door, and so held it that it might not fall forward when the last screw should come out.

"Are all screws out?" whispered Cole, who was the leader.

"Ay," was the whispered reply.

"Then put in two more gimlets."

That was done.

"Now, men," whispered Cole. "Lay the door softly down outside; then, up sticks—into church —and *do him!*"

CHAPTER XIII.

IF Mr. Coventry, before he set all this mischief moving, could have seen the *inside* of Grace Carden's letter to Henry Little!

"DEAR MR. LITTLE,—I do not know whether I ought to write to you at all, nor whether it is delicate of me to say what I am going; but you have saved my life, and I do so want to do all I can to atone for the pain I have given you, who have been so good to me. I am afraid you will never know happiness, if you waste your invaluable life longing after what is impossible. There is an impassable barrier between you and me.

But you might be happy if you would condescend to take my advice, and let yourself see the beauty and the goodness of another. The person who bears this letter comes nearer to perfection than any other woman I ever saw. If you would trust my judgment (and, believe me, I am not to be mistaken in one of my own sex), if you could turn your heart towards her, she would make you very happy. I am sure she could love you devotedly, if she only heard those words from your lips, which every woman requires to hear before she surrenders her affections. Pray do not be angry with me; pray do not think it cost me little to give this strange but honest advice to one I admire so. But I feel it would be so weak and selfish in me to cling to that, which, sooner or later, I must resign, and to make so many persons unhappy, when all might be happy, except perhaps myself.

"Once more, forgive me. Do not think me blind; do not think me heartless; but say, this is a poor girl, who is sadly perplexed, and is trying very hard to be good and wise, and not selfish.

"One line, to say you will consider my advice, and never hate nor despise your grateful and unhappy friend, GRACE CARDEN."

When she had dispatched this letter, she felt heroic.

The next day, she wished she had not written it, and awaited the reply with anxiety.

The next day, she began to wonder at Little's silence: and by-and-by she was offended at it. Surely what she had written with so great an effort was worth a reply.

Finally, she got it into her head that Little despised her. Upon this she was angry with him for not seeing what a sacrifice she had made, and for despising her, instead of admiring her a little, and pitying her ever so much. The old story in short —a girl vexed with a man for letting her throw dust in his eyes.

And, if she was vexed with Little for not appreciating her sacrifice, she was quite as angry with Coventry and Jael for being the causes of that unappreciated sacrifice. So then she was irritable and cross. But she could not be that long: so she fell into a languid, listless state: and then she let herself drift. She never sent Jael to the church again.

Mr. Coventry watched all her moods; and when she reached the listless stage, he came softly on again, and began to recover his lost ground.

On the fifth of January occurred a rather curious coincidence. In Hillsborough Dr. Amboyne offered his services to Mrs. Little to reconcile her and her brother. Mrs. Little feared the proposal came too late; but showed an inclination to be reconciled for Henry's sake. But Henry said he would never be reconciled to a man who had insulted his mother. He then reminded her she had sent him clandestinely into Raby Hall to see her picture. "And what did I see? Your picture was turned with its face to the wall, and insulting words written on the back,—'Gone into trade.' I didn't mean to tell you, mother; but you see I have. And, after that, you may be reconciled to the old scoundrel if you like: but don't ask me." Mrs. Little was deeply wounded by this revelation. She tried to make light of it, but failed. She had been a beauty, and the affront was too bitter. Said she, "You mustn't judge him like other people: he was always so very eccentric. Turn my picture to the wall! My poor picture! Oh, Guy, Guy, could one mother have borne you and me?" Amboyne had not a word more to say; he was indignant himself.

Now that very afternoon, as if by the influence of what they call a brain-wave, Grace Carden, who felt herself much stronger with Mr. Raby than when she first came, was moved to ask him, with many apologies, and no little inward tremor, whether she might see the other side of that very picture before she went.

"What for?"

"Don't be angry, uncle dear. Curiosity."

"I do not like to refuse you any thing, Grace. But— Well, if I lend you the key, will you satisfy your curiosity, and then replace the picture as it is?"

"Yes, I will."

"And you shall do it when I am not in the room. It would only open wounds that time has skinned. I'll bring you down the key at dinner-time." Then, assuming a lighter tone, "Your curiosity will be punished; you will see your rival in beauty. That will be new to you."

Grace was half frightened at her own success, and I doubt whether she would ever have asked for the key again; but Raby's word was his bond; he handed her the key at dinner-time.

Her eyes sparkled when she got it; but she was not to open it before him; so she fell thinking: and she determined to get the gentlemen into the drawing-room as soon as she could, and then slip back and see this famous picture.

Accordingly she left the table rather earlier than usual, and sat down to her piano in the drawing-room.

But alas, her little manœuvre was defeated. Instead of the gentlemen leaving the dining-room, a servant was sent to recall her.

It was old Christmas Eve, and the Mummers were come.

Now, of all the old customs Mr. Raby had promised her, this was the pearl.

Accordingly, her curiosity took for the time another turn, and she was soon seated in the dining-room, with Mr. Raby and Mr. Coventry, awaiting the Mummers.

The servants then came in, and, when all were ready, the sound of a fiddle was heard, and a fiddler, grotesquely dressed, entered along with two clowns, one called the Tommy, dressed in chintz and a fox's skin over his shoulders and a fox's head for a cap; and one, called the Bessy, in a woman's gown and beaver hat.

This pair introduced the true *dramatis personæ*, to the drollest violin accompaniment, consisting of chords till the end of each verse, and then a few notes of melody.

Now the first that I call on
Is George our noble king,
Long time he has been at war,
Good tidings back he'll bring.
Too-ral-loo.

Thereupon in came a man, with black breeches and red stripes at the side, a white shirt decked with ribbons over his waistcoat, and a little hat with streamers, and a sword.

The clown walked round in a ring, and King George followed him, holding his sword upright. Meantime the female clown chanted,—

The next that we call on,
He is a squire's son,
He's like to lose his love,
Because he is so young.
Too-ral-loo.

The Squire's Son followed King George round the ring; and the clowns, marching and singing at the head, introduced another, and then another sword-dancer, all attired like the first, until there were five marching round and round, each with his sword upright.

Then Foxey sang, to a violin accompaniment,

Now, fiddler, then, take up thy fiddle,
Play the lads their hearts' desire,
Or else we'll break thy fiddle,
And fling thee a back o' the fire.

On this the fiddler instantly played a dance-tune peculiar to this occasion, and the five sword-dancers danced by themselves in a ring, holding their swords out so as to form a cone.

Then a knot, prepared beforehand, was slipped over the swords, and all the swords so knotted were held aloft by the first dancer; he danced in the centre awhile, under the connected swords, then deftly drew his own sword out and handed it to the second dancer; the second gave the third dancer his sword, and so on, in rotation, till all the swords were resumed.

Raby's eyes sparkled with delight at all this, and he whispered his comments on the verses and the dance.

"King George!" said he. "Bosh! This is the old story of St. George and the Dragon, over-burdened with modern additions." As to the dance, he assured her that, though danced in honor of old Christmas, it was older than Christianity, and came from the ancient Goths and Swedes.

These comments were interrupted by a man, with a white face, who burst into the assembly crying, "Will ye believe me now? Cairnhope old church is all afire!"

CHAPTER XIV.

"Ay, Squire," said Abel Eaves, for he was the bearer of this strange news, "ye wouldn't believe *me:* now come and see for yourself."

This announcement set all staring; and George the blacksmith did but utter the general sentiment when, suddenly dropping his assumed character of King George, he said, "Bless us and save us! True Christmas Eve; and Cairnhope old church alight!"

Then there was a furious buzz of tongues, and, in the midst of it Mr. Raby disappeared, and the sword-dancers returned to the kitchen, talking over this strange matter as they went.

Grace retired to the drawing-room followed by Coventry.

She sat silent some time, and he watched her keenly.

"I wonder what has become of Mr. Raby?"

Mr. Coventry did not know.

"I hope he is not going out."

"I should think not. It is a very cold night; clear, but frosty."

"Surely he would never go to see."

"Shall I inquire?"

"No; that might put it into his head. But I wish I knew where he was."

Presently a servant brought the tea in.

Miss Carden inquired after Mr. Raby.

"He is gone out, Miss; but he won't be long, I was to tell you."

Grace felt terribly uneasy and restless! rang the bell and asked for Jael Dence. The reply was that she had not been to the hall that day.

But, soon afterwards, Jael came up from the village, and went into the kitchen of Raby. There she heard news, which soon took her into the drawing-room.

"Oh, Miss," said she, "do you know where the Squire is?"

"Gone to the church?" asked Grace, trembling.

"Ay, and all the sword-dancers at his back." And she stood there and wrung her hands with dismay.

The ancients had a proverb, "Better is an army of stags with a lion for their leader, than an army of lions with a stag for their leader." The Cairnhope sword-dancers, though stout fellows and strong against a mortal foe, were but stags against the supernatural; yet, led by Guy Raby, they advanced upon the old church with a pretty bold front, only they kept twenty yards in their leader's rear. The order was to march in dead silence.

At the last turn in the road their leader suddenly halted, and, kneeling on one knee, waved to his men to keep quiet: he had seen several dark figures busy about the porch.

After many minutes of thrilling, yet chilling, expectation, he rose and told his men, in a whisper, to follow him again.

The pace was now expedited greatly, and still Mr. Raby, with his double-barrelled gun in his hand, maintained a lead of some yards, and his men followed as noiselessly as they could, and made for the church: sure enough it was lighted inside.

The young man who was thus beset by two distinct bands of enemies, deserved a very different fate at the hands of his fellow-creatures.

For, at this moment, though any thing but happy himself, he was working some hours every day for the good of mankind; and was every day visiting as a friend the battered saw-grinder who had once put his own life in mortal peril.

He had not fathomed the letter Grace had sent him. He was a young man and a straightforward; he did not understand the amiable defects of the female character. He studied every line of this letter, and it angered and almost disgusted him. It was the letter of a lady; but beneath the surface of gentleness and politeness lay a proposal which he considered mean and cold-blooded. It lowered his esteem for her.

His pride and indignation were roused, and battled with his love, and they were aided by the healthy invigorating habits into which Dr. Amboyne had at last inveigled him, and so he resisted: he wrote more than one letter in reply to Grace Carden; but, when he came to read them over and compare them with her gentle effusion, he was ashamed of his harshness, and would not send the letter.

He fought on; philanthropy in Hillsborough, forging in Cairnhope Church; and still he dreamed strange dreams now and then: for who can work, both night and day, as this man did—with impunity?

One night he dreamed that he was working at his forge, when suddenly the floor of the aisle burst, and a dead knight sprang from the grave with a single bound, and stood erect before him, in rusty armor: out of his helmet looked two eyes like black diamonds, and a nose like a falcon's. Yet, by one of the droll contradictions of a dream, this impetuous, warlike form no sooner opened its lips, than out issued a lackadaisical whine. "See my breastplate, good sir," said he. "It was bright as silver when I made it—I was like you, I forged my own weapons, forged them with these hands.—But now the damps of the grave have rusted it. Odsbodikins! is this a thing for a good knight to appear in before his judge? And to-morrow is Doomsday, so they all say."

Then Henry pitied the poor simple knight (in his dream), and offered his services to polish the corslet up a bit against that great occasion. He pointed towards his forge, and the knight marched to it, in three wide steps that savored strongly of theatrical burlesque. But the moment he saw the specimens of Henry's work lying about, he drew back, and wheeled upon the man of the day with huge disdain. "What," said he, "do you forge toys! Learn that a gentleman can only forge those weapons of war that gentlemen do use. And I took you for a Raby!"

With these bitter words he vanished, with flashing eyes and a look of magnificent scorn, and left his fiery, haughty features imprinted clearly on Henry's memory.

One evening, as he plied his hammer, he heard a light sound at a window, in an interval of his own noise. He looked hastily up, and caught a momentary sight of a face disappearing from the window. It was gone like a flash even as he caught sight of it.

Transient as the glance was, it shook him greatly. He heated a bar of iron white hot at one end, and sallied out into the night. But there was not a creature to be seen.

Then he called aloud, "Who's there?" No reply. "Jael, was it you?" Dead silence. He returned to his work, and set the appearance down to an ocular illusion. But his dreams had been so vivid, that this really seemed only one step more into the realms of hallucination.

This was an unfortunate view of the matter.

On old Christmas Eve he lighted the fires in his mausoleum first, and at last succeeded in writing a letter to Grace Carden. He got out of the difficulty in the best way, by making it very short. He put it in an envelope, and addressed it, intending to give it to Jael Dence, from whom he was always expecting a second visit.

He then lighted his forge, and soon the old walls were ringing again with the blows of his hammer.

It was ten o'clock at night; a clear frosty night: but he was heated and perspiring with his ardent work, when, all of a sudden, a cold air seemed to come in upon him from a new quarter—the door. He left his forge, and took a few steps to where he could see the door. Instead of the door, he saw the blue sky.

He uttered an exclamation, and rubbed his eyes.

It was no hallucination. The door lay flat on

the ground, and the stars glittered in the horizon.

Young Little ran towards the door; but, when he got near it, he paused, and a dire misgiving quelled him. A workman soon recognizes a workman's hand; and he saw Hillsborough cunning and skill in this feat, and Hillsborough cunning and cruelty lurking in ambush at the door.

He went back to his forge, and, the truth must be told, his knees felt weak under him with fears of what was to come.

He searched about for weapons, and could find nothing to protect him against numbers. Pistols he had; but, from a wretched over-security, he had never brought them to Cairnhope Church.

Oh, it was an era of agony that minute, in which, after avoiding the ambuscade that he felt sure awaited him at the door, he had nothing on earth he could do but wait and see what was to come next.

He knew that however small his chance of escape by fighting, it was his only one; and he resolved to receive the attack where he was. He blew his bellows and, cold at heart, affected to forge.

Dusky forms stole into the old church.

CHAPTER XV.

LITTLE blew his coals to a white heat: then took his hammer into his left hand, and his little iron shovel, a weapon about two feet long, into his right.

Three assailants crept towards him, and his position was such that two at least could assail him front and rear. He counted on that, and measured their approach with pale cheek but glittering eye, and thrust his shovel deep into the white coals.

They crept nearer and nearer, and, at last, made an almost simultaneous rush on him back and front.

The man in his rear was a shade in advance of the other. Little, whose whole soul was in arms, had calculated on this, and turning as they came at him, sent a shovelful of fiery coals into that nearest assailant's face, then stepped swiftly out of the way of the other, who struck at him too immediately for him to parry; ere he could recover the wasted blow, Little's hot shovel came down on his head with tremendous force, and laid him senseless and bleeding on the earth, with blood running from his ears.

Little ladled the coals right and left on the other two assailants, one of whom was already yelling with the pain of the first shovelful; then, vaulting suddenly over a pew, he ran for the door.

There he was encountered by Sam Cole, an accomplished cudgel-player, who parried his blows coolly, and gave him a severe rap on the head that dazzled him. But he fought on, till he heard footsteps coming behind him, and then rage and despair seized him, he drew back, shifted his hammer into his right hand and hurled it with all his force at Cole's breast, for he feared to miss his head. Had it struck him on the breast, delivered as it was, it would probably have smashed his breastbone, and killed him; but it struck him on his throat, which was, in some degree, protected by a muffler: it struck him and sent him flying like a feather: he fell on his back in the porch, yards from where he received that prodigious blow.

Henry was bounding out after him, when he was seized from behind, and the next moment another seized him too, and his right hand was now disarmed by throwing away the hammer.

He struggled furiously with them, and twice he shook them off, and struck them with his fist, and jobbed them with his shovel quick and short, as a horse kicking.

But one was cunning enough to make a feint at his face, and then fall down and lay hold of his knees: he was about to pulverize this fellow with one blow of his shovel, when the other flung his arms round him. It became a mere struggle. Such was his fury and his vigor, however, that they could not master him. He played his head like a snake, so that they could not seize him disadvantageously; and at last he dropped his shovel and got them both by the throat, and grasped them so fiercely that their faces were purple, and their eyes beginning to fix, when to his dismay, he received a violent blow on the right arm that nearly broke it: he let go, with a cry of pain, and with his left hand twisted the other man round so quickly, that he received the next blow of Cole's cudgel. Then he dashed his left fist into Cole's eye, who staggered, but still barred the way; so Little rushed upon him, and got him by the throat, and would soon have settled him: but the others recovered themselves ere he could squeeze all the wind out of Cole, and it became a struggle of three to one.

He dragged them all three about with him; he kicked, he hit, he did every thing that a man with one hand, and a lion's heart, could do.

But gradually they got the better of him; and at last it came to this, that two were struggling on the ground with him, and Cole standing over them all three, ready to strike.

"Now, hold him so, while I settle him," cried Cole, and raised his murderous cudgel.

It came down on Little's shoulder, and only just missed his head.

Again it came down, and with terrible force.

Up to this time he had fought as mute as a fox. But now that it had come to mere butchery, he cried out, in his agony, "They'll kill me.—My mother!—Help! Murder! Help!"

"Ay! thou'lt never forge no more!" roared Cole, and thwack came down the crushing bludgeon.

"Help! Murder! Help!" screamed the victim, more faintly; and at the next blow more faintly still.

But again the murderous cudgel was lifted high, to descend upon his young head.

As the confederates held the now breathless and despairing victim to receive the blow, and the butcher, with one eye closed by Henry's fist, but the other gleaming savagely, raised the cudgel to finish him, Henry saw a huge tongue of flame pour out at them all, from outside the church, and a report, that sounded like a cannon, was accompanied by the vicious ping of shot. Cole screamed and yelled, and dropped his cudgel, and his face was covered with blood in a moment; he yelled, and covered his face with his hands; and instantly came another flash, another report, another cruel ping of shot, and this time his hands were covered with blood.

The others rolled yelling out of the line of fire, and ran up to the aisle for their lives.

Cole, yelling, tried to follow; but Henry, though sick and weak with the blows, caught him, and clung to his knees, and the next moment the place was filled with men carrying torches and gleaming swords, and led by a gentleman, who stood over Henry, in evening dress, but with the haughty expanded nostrils, the brilliant black eyes, and all the features of that knight in rusty armor who had come to him in his dream and left him with scorn.

At this moment a crash was heard : two of the culprits, with desperate agility, had leaped on to the vestry chest, and from that on to the horse, and from him headlong out of the window.

Mr. Raby dispatched all his men but one in pursuit, with this brief order,—"Take them, alive or dead,—doesn't matter which,—they are only cutlers ; and cowards."

His next word was to Cole. "What, three blackguards to one!—that's how Hillsborough fights, eh?"

"I'm not a blackguard," said Henry, faintly.

"That remains to be proved, sir," said Raby, grimly.

Henry made answer by fainting away.

CHAPTER XVI.

WHEN Henry Little came to himself, he was seated on men's hands, and being carried through the keen refreshing air. Mr. Raby was striding on in front; the horse's hoofs were clamping along on the hard road behind ; and he himself was surrounded by swordsmen in fantastic dresses.

He opened his eyes, and thought, of course, it was another vision. But no, the man, with whose blows his body was sore, and his right arm utterly numbed, walked close to him between two sword-dancers, with Raby-marks and Little-marks upon him, viz., a face spotted with blood, and a black eye.

Little sighed.

"Eh, that's music to me," said a friendly voice close to him. It was the King George of the lyrical drama, and, out of poetry, George the blacksmith.

"What, it is you, is it?" said Little.

"Ay, sir, and a joyful man to hear you speak again. The cowardly varmint ! And to think they have all got clear but this one ! Are ye sore hurt, sir ?"

"I'm in awful pain, but no bones broken." Then, in a whisper,—"Where are you taking me, George ?"

"To Raby Hall," was the whispered reply.

"Not for all the world ! If you are my friend, put me down, and let me slip away."

"Don't ask me, don't ask me," said George, in great distress. "How could I look Squire in the face? He did put you in my charge."

"Then I'm a prisoner !" said Henry, sternly.

George hung his head, but made no reply.

Henry also maintained a sullen silence after that.

The lights of Raby came in sight.

That house contained two women, who awaited the result of the nocturnal expedition with terrible anxiety.

Its fate, they both felt, had been determined before they even knew that the expedition had started.

They had nothing to do but to wait, and pray that Henry had made his escape, or else had not been so mad as to attempt resistance.

In this view of things, the number and even the arms of his assailants were some comfort to them, as rendering resistance impossible.

As for Mr. Coventry, he was secretly delighted. His conscience was relieved. Raby would now drive his rival out of the church and out of the county without the help of the Trades, and his act of treachery and bad faith would be harmless. Things had taken the happiest possible turn for him.

For all that, this courtier affected sympathy, and even some anxiety, to please Miss Carden, and divert all suspicion from himself. But the true ring was wanting to his words, and both the women felt them jar, and got away from him, and laid their heads together, in agitated whispers. And the result was, they put shawls over their heads, and went together out into the night.

They ran up the road, sighing and clasping their hands, but no longer speaking.

At the first turn they saw the whole body coming towards them.

"I'll soon know," said Jael, struggling with her agitation. "Don't you be seen, Miss ; that might anger the Squire ; and, oh, he will be a wrathful man this night, if he caught him working in yonder church."

Grace then slipped back, and Jael ran on. But no sooner did she come up with the party, than Raby ordered her back, in a tone she dared not resist.

She ran back, and told Grace they were carrying him in, hurt, and the Squire's eyes were like hot coals.

Grace slipped into the drawing-room, and kept the door ajar.

Soon afterwards, Raby, his men, and his prisoners, entered the hall, and Grace heard Raby say, "Bring the prisoners into the dining-room."

Grace Carden sat down, and leaned her head upon her hand, and her little foot beat the ground, all in a flutter.

But this ended in a spirited resolve. She rose, pale, but firm, and said, "Come with me, Jael ;" and she walked straight into the dining-room. Coventry strolled in after her.

The room was still brilliantly lighted. Mr. Raby was seated at his writing table at the far end, and the prisoners, well guarded, stood ready to be examined.

"You can't come in here," was Mr. Raby's first word to Grace.

But she was prepared for this, and stood her ground. "Excuse me, dear uncle, but I wish to see you administer justice ; and, besides, I believe I can tell you something about one of the prisoners."

"Indeed! that alters the case. Somebody give Miss Carden a chair."

She sat down, and fixed her eyes upon Henry Little,—eyes that said plainly, "I shall defend you, if necessary:" his pale cheek was flushing at sight of her.

Mr. Raby arranged his papers to make notes, and turned to Cole. "The charge against you is, that you were seen this night by several persons engaged in an assault of a cruel and aggravated character. You, and two other men, attacked and overpowered an individual here present; and, while he was helpless, and on the ground, you were seen to raise a heavy cudgel—(Got the cudgel, George?)"

"Ay, your worship, here 'tis."

"—And to strike him several times on the head and limbs, with all your force."

"Oh, cruel! cruel!"

"This won't do, Miss Carden; no observations, please. In consequence of which blows he soon after swooned away, and was for some time unconscious, and—"

"Oh!"

"—For aught I know, may have received some permanent injury."

"Not he," said Cole; "he's all right. I'm the only man that is hurt; and I've got it hot; he hit me with his hammer, and knocked me down like a bullock. He's given me this black eye too."

"In self-defense, apparently. Which party attacked the other first?"

"Why they attacked me, of course," said Henry. "Four of them."

"Four! I saw but three."

"Oh, I settled one at starting, up near the forge. Didn't you find him?" (This to George.)

"Nay, we found none of the trash but this," indicating Cole, with a contemptuous jerk of the thumb.

"Now, don't all speak at once," said Mr. Raby. "My advice to you is to say nothing, or you'll probably make bad worse. But if you choose to say any thing, I'm bound to hear it."

"Well, sir," said Cole, in a carneying voice, "what I say is this : what need we go to law over this? If you go against me for hitting him with a stick, after he had hit me with a blacksmith's hammer, I shall have to go against you for shooting me with a gun."

"That is between you and me, sir. You will find a bystander may shoot a malefactor to save the life of a citizen. Confine your defense, at present, to the point at issue. Have you any excuse, as against this young man?" (To Henry.) "—You look pale. You can sit down till your turn comes."

"Not in this house."

"And why not in this house, pray? Is your own house a better?"

No answer from Henry. A look of amazement and alarm from Grace. But she was afraid to utter a word, after the admonition she had received.

"Well, sir," said Cole, "he was desecrating a church."

"So he was, and I shall talk to him in his turn. But you desecrated it worse. He turned it into a blacksmith shop; you turned it into a shambles. I shall commit you. You will be taken to Hillsborough to-morrow; to-night you will remain in my strong-room. Fling him down a mattress and some blankets, and give him plenty to eat and drink; I wouldn't starve the devil on old Christmas Eve. There, take him away.

Stop; search his pockets before you leave him alone."

Cole was taken away, and Henry's turn came.

Just before this examination commenced, Grace clasped her hands, and cast a deprecating look on Henry, as much as to say, "Be moderate." And then her eyes roved to and fro, and the whole woman was in arms, and on the watch.

Mr. Raby began on him. "As for you, your offense is not so criminal in the eye of the law : but it is bad enough; you have broken into a church by unlawful means; you have turned it into a smithy, defiled the graves of the dead, and turned the tomb of a good knight into an oven, to the scandal of men and the dishonor of God. Have you any excuse to offer?"

"Plenty. I was plying an honest trade, in a country where freedom is the law. The Hillsborough Unions combined against me, and restrained my freedom, and threatened my life, ay, and attempted my life too, before to-day : and so the injustice and cruelty of men drove me to a sanctuary, me and my livelihood. Blame the Trades, blame the public laws, blame the useless police : but you can't blame me; a man must live."

"Why not set up your shop in the village? Why wantonly desecrate a church?"

"The church was more secret, and more safe : and nobody worships in it. The wind and the weather are allowed to destroy it; you care so little for it you let it moulder; then why howl if a fellow uses it and keeps it warm?"

At this sally there was a broad rustic laugh, which, however, Mr. Raby quelled with one glance of his eye.

"Come, don't be impertinent," said he to Little.

"Then don't you provoke a fellow," cried Henry, raising his voice.

Grace clasped her hands in dismay.

Jael Dence said, in her gravest and most mellow voice, "You do forget the good Squire saved your life this very night."

This was like oil on all the waters.

"Well, certainly I oughtn't to forget that," said Henry, apologetically. Then he appealed piteously to Jael, whose power over him struck every body directly, including Grace Carden. "Look here, you mustn't think, because I don't keep howling, I'm all right. My arm is disabled : my back is almost broken : my thigh is cut. I'm in sharp pain, all this time : and that makes a fellow impatient of being lectured on the back of it all. Why doesn't he let me go? I don't want to affront him now. All I want is to go and get nursed a bit somewhere."

"Now that is the first word of reason and common sense you have uttered, young man. It decides me not to detain you. All I shall do, under the circumstances, is to clear your rubbish out of that holy building, and watch it by night as well as day. Your property, however, shall be collected, and delivered to you uninjured : so oblige me with your name and address."

Henry made no reply.

Raby turned his eye full upon him.

"Surely you do not object to tell me your name."

"I do."

"Why?"

"Excuse me."

"What are you afraid of? Do you doubt my word, when I tell you I shall not proceed against you?"

"No: it is not that at all. But this is no place for me to utter my father's name. We all have our secrets, sir. You have got yours. There's a picture, with its face to the wall. Suppose I was to ask you to tell all the world whose face it is you insult and hide from the world?"

Raby turned red with wrath and surprise, at this sudden thrust. "You insolent young scoundrel!" he cried. "What is that to you, and what connection can there be between that portrait and a man in your way of life?"

"There's a close connection," said Henry, trembling with anger, in his turn: "and the proof is that, when that picture is turned to the light, I'll tell you my name: and, till that picture is turned to the light, I'll not tell you my name; and if any body here knows my name, and tells it you, may that person's tongue be blistered at the root!"

"Oh, how fearful!" cried Grace, turning very pale. "But I'll put an end to it all. I've got the key, and I've his permission, and I'll—oh, Mr. Raby, there's something more in this than we know." She darted to the picture, and unlocked the padlock, and, with Jael's assistance, began to turn the picture. Then Mr. Raby rose and seemed to bend his mind inwards, but he neither forbade, nor encouraged, this impulsive act of Grace Carden's.

Now there was not a man, nor a woman, in the room whose curiosity had not been more or less excited about this picture; so there was a general movement towards it, of all but Mr. Raby, who stood quite still, turning his eye inwards, and evidently much moved, though passive.

There happened to be a strong light upon the picture, and the lovely olive face, the vivid features, and glorious black eyes and eyebrows, seemed to flash out of the canvas into life.

Even the living faces, being blondes, paled before it, in the one particular of color. They seemed fair glittering moons, and this a glowing sun.

Grace's first feelings were those of simple surprise and admiration. But, as she gazed, Henry's words returned to her, and all manner of ideas struck her pell-mell. "Oh, beautiful! beautiful!" she cried. Then, turning to Henry, "You are right; it was not a face to hide from the world—oh! the likeness! just look at *him*, and then at her! can I be mistaken?"

This appeal was made to the company, and roused curiosity to a high pitch; every eye began to compare the dark-skinned beauty on the wall with the swarthy young man, now who stood there, and submitted in haughty silence to the comparison.

The words caught Mr. Raby's attention. He made a start, and elbowing them all out of his way, strode up to the picture.

"What do you say, Miss Carden? What likeness can there be between my sister and a smith?" and he turned and frowned haughtily on Henry Little.

Henry returned his look of defiance directly.

But that very exchange of defiance brought out another likeness, which Grace's quick eye seized directly.

"Why, he is still liker you," she cried. "Look,

good people! Look at all three. Look at their great black eyes, and their brown hair. Look at their dark skins, and their haughty noses. Oh, you needn't blow your nostrils out at me, gentlemen; I am not a bit afraid of either of you.— And then look at this lovely creature. She is a Raby too, only softened down by her sweet womanliness. Look at them all three. If they are not one flesh and blood, I have no eyes."

"Oh yes, Miss; and this lady is his mother. For I have *seen* her: and she is a sweet lady; and she told me I had a Cairnhope face, and kissed me for it."

Upon this from Jael, the general conviction rose into a hum that buzzed round the room.

Mr. Raby was struck with amazement. At last he turned slowly upon Henry, and said, with stiff politeness, "Is your name Little, sir?"

"Little is my name, and I'm proud of it."

"Your name may be Little, but your face is Raby. All the better for you, sir."

He then turned his back to the young man, and walked right in front of the picture, and looked at it steadily and sadly.

It was a simple and natural action, yet somehow done in so imposing a way, that the bystanders held their breath, to see what would follow.

He gazed long and steadily on the picture, and his features worked visibly.

"Ay!" he said. "Nature makes no such faces nowadays. Poor unfortunate girl!" And his voice faltered a moment.

He then began to utter, in a low grave voice, some things that took every body by surprise, by the manner as well as the matter; for, with his never once taking his eyes off the picture, and speaking in a voice softened by the sudden presence of that womanly beauty, the companion of his youth, it was just like a man speaking softly in a dream.

"Thomas, this picture will remain as it is while I live."

"Yes, sir."

"I find I can bear the sight of you. As we get older we get tougher. You look as if you didn't want me to quarrel with your son? Well, I will not: there has been quarreling enough. Any of the loyal Dences here?" But he never even turned his head from the picture to look for them.

"Only me, sir; Jael Dence, at your service. Father's not very well."

"Nathan, or Jael, it is all one, so that it is Dence. You'll take that young gentleman home with you, and send him to bed. He'll want nursing: for he got some ugly blows, and took them like a gentleman. The young gentleman has a fancy for forging things—the Lord knows what. He shall not forge things in a church, and defile the tombs of his own forefathers; but" (with a groan) "he can forge in your yard. All the snobs in Hillsborough shan't hinder him, if that is his cursed hobby. Gentlemen are not to be dictated to by snobs. Arm three men every night with guns; load the guns with ball, not small shot, as I did; and if those ruffians molest him again, kill them, and then come to me and complain of them. But, mind you kill them first—complain afterwards. And now take half-a-dozen of these men with you, to carry him to the farm, if he needs it. THERE, EDITH!"

And still he never moved his eyes from the

picture, and the words seemed to drop out of him.

Henry stood bewildered, and, ere he could say any thing that might revive the dormant irritation of Mr. Raby against him, female tact interposed. Grace clasped her hands to him, with tears in her eyes; and as for Jael Dence, she assumed the authority with which she had been invested, and hurried him bodily away; and the sword-dancers all gathered round him, and they carried him in triumphant procession, with the fiddler playing, and George whistling, the favorite tune of "Raby come home again," while every sturdy foot beat the hard and ringing road in admirable keeping with that spirit-stirring march.

When he was gone, Grace crept up to Mr. Raby, who still stood before the picture, and eyed it and thought of his youth. She took his arm wondrous softly with her two hands, rested her sweet head against his shoulder, and gazed at it along with him.

When she had nestled to him some time in this delicate attitude, she turned her eyes up to him, and murmured, "How good, how noble you are: and how I love you." Then, all in a moment, she curled round his neck, and kissed him with a tender violence, that took him quite by surprise.

As for Mr. Coventry, he had been reduced to a nullity, and escaped attention all this time: he sat in gloomy silence, and watched with chilled and foreboding heart the strange turn events had taken, and were taking; events which he, and no other man, had set rolling.

CHAPTER XVII.

FREDERICK COVENTRY, being still unacquaint-ed with the contents of Grace's letter, was now al-most desperate. Grace Carden, inaccessible to an unknown workman, would she be inaccessible to a workman whom Mr. Raby, proud as he was, had publicly recognized as his nephew? This was not to be expected. But something was to be ex-pected, viz., that in a few days the door would be closed with scorn in the face of Frederick Coven-try, the miserable traitor, who had broken his solemn pledge, and betrayed his benefactor to those who had all but assassinated him. Little would be sure to suspect him, and the prisoner, when he came to be examined, would furnish some clue.

A cold perspiration bedewed his very back, when he recollected that the chief constable would be present at Cole's examination, and supply the link, even if there should be one missing. He had serious thoughts of leaving the country at once.

Finding himself unobserved, he walked out of the room, and paced up and down the hall.

His thoughts now took a practical form. He must bribe the prisoner to hold his tongue.

But how? and when? and where?

After to-night there might be no opportunity of saying a word to him.

While he was debating this in his mind, Knight the butler crossed the hall.

Coventry stopped him, and asked where the prisoner was.

"Where Squire told us to put him, sir."

"No chance of his escaping—I hope?"

"Not he, sir."

"I should like to take a look at him."

Knight demurred. "Well, sir, you see the or-ders are—but, of course, Master won't mind you. I'll speak to him."

"No, it is not worth while. I am only anxious the villain should be secure." This of course was a feeler.

"Oh, there's no fear of that. Why, he is in the strong room. It's right above yours. If you'll come with me, sir, I'll show you the door." Cov-entry accompanied him, and Thomas Knight showed him a strong door with two enormous bolts outside, both shot.

Coventry felt despair, and affected satisfaction. Then, after a pause, he said, "But is the win-dow equally secure?"

"Two iron bars, almost as thick as these bolts: and, if it stood open, what could he do but break his neck, and cheat the gallows? He is all right, sir; never you fear. We sarched him, from head to foot, and found no eend o' tools in his pockets. He is a deep 'un. But we are York-shire too, as the saying is. He goes to Hills-bro' town-hall to-morrow; and glad to be shut on him."

Coventry complimented him, and agreed with him that escape was impossible.

He then got a light, and went to his own bed-room, and sat down, cold at heart, before the fire.

He sat in that state, till two o'clock in the morning, distracting his brain with schemes, that were invented only to be dismissed as idle.

At last an idea came to him. He took his fish-ing-rod, and put the thinner joints together, and laid them on the bed. He then opened his win-dow very cautiously. But as that made some noise, he remained quite quiet for full ten min-utes. Then he got upon the window-seat, and passed the fishing-rod out. After one or two at-tempts he struck the window above, with the fine end.

Instantly he heard a movement above, and a window cautiously opened.

He gave a low "Hem!"

"Who's that?" whispered the prisoner, from above.

"A man who wants you to escape."

"Nay; but I have no tools."

"What do you require?"

"I think I could do summut with a screw-driver."

"I'll send you one up."

The next minute a couple of small screw-dri-vers were passed up—part of the furniture of his gun.

Cole worked hard, but silently, for about an hour, and then he whispered down that he should be able to get a bar out. But how high was it from the ground?

"About forty feet."

Coventry heard the man actually groan at the intelligence.

"Let yourself down on my window-sill. I can find you rope enough for that."

"What, d'ye take me for a bird, that can light of a gate?"

"But the sill is solid stone, and full a foot wide."

"Say ye so, lad? Then luck is o' my side. Send up rope."

The rope was sent up, and presently was fast

to something above, and dangled down a little past the window-sill.

"Put out a light on sill," whispered the voice above.

"I will."

Then there was a long silence, during which Coventry's blood ran cold.

here. Come,—think! It will be five years' penal servitude if you don't."

"Is the rope long enough?"

"Plenty for that."

Then there was another awful silence.

By-and-by a man's legs came dangling down,

"HOW GOOD, HOW NOBLE, YOU ARE," SHE MURMURED.

As nothing further occurred, he whispered, "What is the matter?"

"My stomach fails me. Send me up a drop brandy, will ye? Eh, man, but this is queer work."

"I can't get it up to you; you must drink it

and Cole landed on the sill, still holding tight by the rope. He swung down on the sill, and slid into the room, perspiring and white with fear.

Coventry gave him some brandy directly,—Cole's trembling hand sent it flying down his throat, and the two men stared at each other.

"Why, it is a gentleman!"

"Yes."

"And do you really mean to see me clear?"

"Drink a little more brandy, and recover yourself, and then I'll tell you."

When the man was fortified and ready for fresh exertions, Coventry told him he must try and slip out of the house at the front door: he would lend him a feather and some oil to apply to the bolts if necessary.

When the plan of operation was settled, Coventry asked him how long it would take him to get to Hillsborough.

"I can run it in two hours."

"Then if I give the alarm in an hour and a half, it won't hurt."

"Give me that start and you may send bloodhounds on my heels, they'll never catch me."

"Now take off your shoes."

While he was taking them off, Cole eyed his unexpected friend very keenly, and took stock of all his features.

When he was ready, Coventry opened his door very carefully, and placed a light so as to be of some use to the fugitive. Cole descended the stairs like a cat, and soon found the heavy bolts and drew them; then slipped out into the night, and away, with fleet foot and wondering heart, to Hillsborough.

Coventry put out his light and slipped into bed.

About four o'clock in the morning the whole house was alarmed with loud cries, followed by two pistol-shots: and all those who ran out of their bed-rooms at all promptly, found Coventry in his night-gown and trowsers, with a smoking pistol in his hand, which he said he had discharged at a robber. The account he gave was, that he had been suddenly awakened by hearing his door shut, and had found his window open; had slipped on his trowsers, got to his pistols, and run out just in time to see a man opening the great front door: had fired twice at him, and thought he must have hit him the second time.

On examining the window the rope was found dangling.

Instantly there was a rush to the strong room. The bird was flown.

"Ah!" said Coventry. "I felt there ought to be some one with him, but I didn't like to interfere."

George the groom and another were mounted on swift horses, and took the road to Hillsborough.

But Cole, with his start of a hundred minutes, was safe in a back slum before they got half way.

What puzzled the servants most was how Cole could have unscrewed the bar, and where he could have obtained the cord. And while they were twisting this matter every way, in hot discussion, Coventry quaked, for he feared his little gun-screws would be discovered. But no, they were not in the room.

It was a great mystery; but Raby said they ought to have searched the man's body as well as his pockets.

He locked the cord up, however, and remarked it was a new one, and had probably been bought in Hillsborough. He would try and learn where.

At breakfast-time a bullet was found in the door. Coventry apologized.

"Your mistake was missing the man, not hitting the door," said Raby. "One comfort, I tickled the fellow with small shot. It shall be slugs next time. All we can do now is to lay the matter before the police. I must go into Hillsborough, I suppose."

He went into Hillsborough accordingly, and told the chief constable the whole story, and deposited the piece of cord with him. He found that zealous officer already acquainted with the outline of the business, and on his mettle to discover the authors and agents of the outrage, if possible. And it occurred to his sagacity that there was at this moment a workman in Hillsborough, who must know many secrets of the Trades, and had now nothing to gain by concealing them.

CHAPTER XVIII.

THUS the attempt to do Little was more successful than it looks. Its object was to keep Little and Simmons apart, and sure enough those two men never met again in life.

But, on the other hand, this new crime embittered two able men against the Union, and put Grotait in immediate peril. Mr. Ransome conferred with Mr. Holdfast, and they both visited Simmons, and urged him to make a clean breast before he left the world.

Simmons hesitated. He said repeatedly, "Gi' me time! gi' me time!"

Grotait heard of these visits, and was greatly alarmed. He set Dan Tucker and another to watch by turns and report.

Messrs. Holdfast and Ransome had an ally inside the house. Eliza Watney had come in from another town, and had no Hillsborough prejudices. She was furious at this new outrage on Little, who had won her regard, and she hoped her brother-in-law would reveal all he knew. Such a confession, she thought, might remove the stigma from himself to those better-educated persons, who had made a tool of her poor ignorant relative.

Accordingly, no sooner did the nurse Little had provided inform her, in a low voice, that there was *a change*, than she put on her bonnet, and went in all haste to Mr. Holdfast, and also to the chief constable, as she had promised them to do.

But of course she could not go without talking. She met an acquaintance not far from the door, and told her Ned was near his end, and she was going to tell the gentlemen.

Dan Tucker stepped up to this woman, and she was as open-mouthed to him as Eliza had been to her. Dan went directly with the news to Grotait.

Grotait came all in a hurry, but Holdfast was there before him, and was actually exhorting Simmons to do a good action in his last moments, and reveal those greater culprits who had employed him, when Grotait, ill at ease walked in, sat down at the foot of the bed, and fixed his eye on Simmons.

Simmons caught sight of him and stared, but said nothing to him. Yet, when Holdfast had done, Simmons was observed to look at Grotait, though he replied to the other. "If you was a Hillsbro' man, you'd know we tell on dead folk, but not on quick. I told on Ned Simmons, becanse he was as good as dead; but to tell on Trade, that's different."

"And I think, my poor fellow," suggested Grotait, smoothly, "you might spend your last moments better in telling *us* what you would wish the Trade to do for your wife, and the child, if it lives."

"Well, I think ye might make the old gal an allowance till she marries again."

"Oh, Ned, Ned!" cried the poor woman. "I'll have no man after thee." And a violent burst of grief followed.

"Thou'll do like the rest," said the dying man. "Hold thy bellering, and let me speak, that's got no time to lose. How much will ye allow her, old lad ?"

"Six shillings a week, Ned."

"And what is to come of young 'un ?"

"We'll apprentice him."

"To my trade ?"

"You know better than that, Ned. You are a freeman; but he won't be a freeman's son by our law, thou know'st. But there's plenty of outside trades in Hillsbro'. We'll bind him to one of those, and keep an eye on him, for thy sake."

"Well, I must take what I can get."

"And little enough too," said Eliza Watney. "Now do you know that they have set upon Mr. Little and beaten him within an inch of his life? Oh, Ned, you can't approve that, and him our best friend."

"Who says I approve it, thou fool ?"

"Then tell the gentleman who the villain was; for I believe you know."

"I'll tell 'em summut about it."

Grotait turned pale; but still kept his glittering eye fixed on the sick man.

"The job was offered to me; but I wouldn't be in it. I know that much. Says I, 'He has had his squeak.'"

"Who offered you the job ?" asked Mr. Holdfast. And at this moment Ransome came in.

"What, another black coat!" said Simmons. "——, if you are not like so many crows over a dead horse." He then began to wander, and Holdfast's question remained unanswered.

This aberration continued so long, and accompanied with such interruptions of the breathing, that both Holdfast and Ransome despaired of ever hearing another rational word from the man's lips.

They lingered on, however, and still Grotait sat at the foot of the bed, with his glittering eye fixed on the dying man.

Presently Simmons became silent, and reflected. "Who offered me the job to do Little?" said he, in a clear rational voice.

"Yes," said Mr. Holdfast. "And who paid you to blow up the forge?"

Simmons made no reply. His fast fleeting powers appeared unable now to hold an idea for above a second or two.

Yet, after another short interval, he seemed to go back a second time to the subject as intelligibly as ever.

"Master Editor!" said he, with a sort of start.

"Yes." And Holdfast stepped close to his bedside.

"Can you keep a secret?"

Grotait started up.

"Yes!" said Holdfast, eagerly.

7

"THEN SO CAN I."

These were the last words of Ned Simmons. He died, false to himself, but true to his fellows, and faithful to a terrible confederacy, which, in England and the nineteenth century, was Venice and the middle ages over again.

CHAPTER XIX.

MR. COVENTRY, relieved of a great and immediate anxiety, could now turn his whole attention to Grace Carden; and she puzzled him. He expected to see her come down beaming with satisfaction at the great event of last night. Instead of that she appeared late, with cheeks rather pale, and signs of trouble under her fair eyes.

As the day wore on, she showed positive distress of mind; irritable and dejected by turns, and quite unable to settle to any thing.

Mr. Coventry, with all his skill, was quite at fault. He could understand her being in anxiety for news about Little; but why not relieve her anxiety by sending a servant to inquire? Above all, why this irritation? this positive suffering?

A mystery to him, there is no reason why it should be one to my readers. Grace Carden, for the first time in her life, was in the clutches of a fiend, a torturing fiend, called jealousy.

The thought that another woman was nursing Henry Little all this time distracted her. It would have been such heaven to her to tend him, after those cruel men had hurt him so; but that pure joy was given to another, and that other loved him, and could now indulge and show her love. Show it? Why, she had herself opened his eyes to Jael's love, and advised him to reward it.

And now she could do nothing to defend herself. The very improvement in Henry's circumstances held her back. She could not write to him and say, "Now I know you are Mr. Raby's nephew, that makes all the difference." That would only give him fresh offense, and misrepresent herself; for in truth she had repented her letter long before the relationship was discovered.

No; all she could do was to wait till Jael Dence came up, and then charge her with some subtle message, that might make Henry Little pause if he still loved her.

She detected Coventry watching her. She fled directly to her own room, and there sat on thorns, waiting for her rival to come and give her an opportunity.

But afternoon came, and no Jael; evening came, and no Jael.

"Ah!" thought Grace, bitterly, "she is better employed than to come near me. She is not a self-sacrificing fool like me. When I had the advantage, I gave it up; now she has got it, she uses it without mercy, decency, or gratitude. And that is the way to love. Oh! if my turn could but come again! But it never will."

Having arrived at this conclusion, she lay on the couch in her own room, and was thoroughly miserable.

She came down to dinner, and managed to take a share in the conversation, but was very languid; and Coventry detected that she had been crying.

After dinner, Knight brought in a verbal message from Jael to Mr. Raby, to the effect that the young gentleman was stiff and sore, and she had sent into Hillsborough for Doctor Amboyne.

"Quite right of her," said the Squire. "You needn't look so alarmed, Grace; there are no bones broken: and he is in capital hands: he couldn't have a tenderer nurse than that great strapping lass, nor a better doctor than my friend and maniac Amboyne."

Next morning, soon after breakfast, Raby addressed his guests as follows:—"I was obliged to go into Hillsborough yesterday, and postpone the purification of that sacred building. But I set a watch on it; and this day I devote to a pious purpose; I'm going to un-Little the church of my forefathers; and you can come with me, if you choose." This invitation, however, was given in a tone so gloomy, and so little cordial, that Coventry, courtier-like, said in reply, he felt it would be a painful sight to his host, and the fewer witnesses the better. Raby nodded assent, and seemed pleased. Not so Miss Carden. She said: "If that is your feeling, you had better stay at home. *I* shall go. I have something to tell Mr. Raby when we get there; and I'm vain enough to think it will make him not quite so angry about the poor dear old church."

"Then come, by all means," said Raby: "for I'm angry enough at present."

Before they got half way to the church, they were hailed from behind; and turning round, saw the burly figure of Dr. Amboyne coming after them.

They waited for him, and, he came up with them. He had heard the whole business from Little, and was warm in the praises of his patient.

To a dry inquiry from Raby, whether he approved of his patient desecrating a church, he said, with delicious coolness, he thought there was not much harm in that, the church not being used for divine service.

At this, Raby uttered an inarticulate but savage growl; and Grace, to avert a hot discussion, begged the Doctor not to go into that question, but to tell her how Mr. Little was.

"Oh, he has received some severe contusions, but there is nothing serious. He is in good hands, I assure you. I met him out walking with his nurse; and I must say I never saw a handsomer couple. He is dark; she is fair. She is like the ancient statues of Venus, massive and grand, but not clumsy; he is lean and sinewy, as a man ought to be."

"Oh, Doctor, this from you?" said Grace, with undisguised spite.

"Well, it *was* a concession. He was leaning on her shoulder, and her face and downcast eyes were turned towards him so sweetly—said I to myself—Hum!"

"What!" said Raby. "Would you marry him to a farmer's daughter?"

"No; I'd let him marry who he likes: only, having seen him and his nurse together, it struck me that, between two such fine creatures of the same age, the tender relation of patient and nurse, sanctioned, as I hear it is, by a benevolent uncle—"

"Confound your impudence!"

"—Would hardly stop there. What do you think, Miss Carden?"

"I'll tell you, if you will promise, on your honor, never to repeat what I say." And she

slackened her pace, and lingered behind Mr. Raby.

He promised her.

"Then," she whispered in his ear, "I HATE YOU!"

And her eyes flashed blue fire at him, and startled him.

Then she darted forward, and took Mr. Raby's arm, with a scarlet face, and a piteous deprecating glance shot back at the sagacious personage she had defied.

Dr. Amboyne proceeded instantly to put himself in this young lady's place, and so divine what was the matter. The familiar process soon brought a knowing smile to his sly lip.

They entered the church, and went straight to the forge.

Raby stood with folded arms, and contemplated the various acts of sacrilege with a silent distress that was really touching.

Amboyne took more interest in the traces of the combat. "Ah!" said he, "this is where he threw the hot coals in their faces—he has told me all about it. And look at this pool of blood on the floor! Here he felled one of them with his shovel. What is this?—traces of blood leading up to this chest!"

He opened the chest, and found plain proofs inside that the wounded man had hid himself in it for some time. He pointed this out to Raby; and gave it as his opinion that the man's confederates had come back for him, and carried him away. "These fellows are very true to one another. I have often admired them for that."

Raby examined the blood-stained interior of the chest, and could not help agreeing with the sagacious doctor.

"Yes," said he, sadly; "if we had been sharp, we might have caught the blackguard. But I was in a hurry to leave the scene of sacrilege. Look here; the tomb of a good knight defiled into an oven, and the pews mutilated—and all for the base uses of trade." And in this strain he continued for a long time so eloquently that, at last, he roused Grace Carden's ire.

"Mr. Raby," said she, firmly, "please add to those base uses one more. One dismal night, two poor creatures, a man and a woman, lost their way in the snow; and, after many a hard struggle, the cold and the snow overpowered them, and death was upon them. But, just at her last gasp, the girl saw a light, and heard the tinkling of a hammer. She tottered towards it; and it was a church. She just managed to strike the door with her benumbed hands, and then fell insensible. When she came to herself, gentle hands had laid her before two glorious fires in that cold tomb there. Then the same gentle hands gave her food and wine, and words of comfort, and did every thing for her that brave men do for poor weak suffering women. Yes, sir, it was my life he saved, and Mr. Coventry's too; and I can't bear to hear a word against him, especially while I stand looking at his poor forge, and his grates, that you abuse; but I adore them, and bless them; and so would you, if they had saved your life, as they did mine. You don't love me one bit: and it is very cruel."

Raby stood astonished and silent. At last he said, in a very altered tone, quite mild and deprecating, "Why did you not tell me this before?"

"Because he made us promise not. Would you have had me betray my benefactor?"

"No. You are a brave girl, an honest girl. I love you more than a bit, and, for your sake, I forgive him the whole thing. I will never call it sacrilege again, since its effect was to save an angel's life. Come, now, you have shown a proper spirit, and stood up for the absent, and brought me to submission by your impetuosity, so don't spoil it all by crying."

"No, I won't," said Grace, with a gulp. But her tears would not cease all in a moment. She had evoked that tender scene, in which words and tears of true and passionate love had rained upon her. They were an era in her life; had swept forever out of her heart all the puny voices that had prattled what they called love to her; and that divine music, should she ever hear it again? She had resigned it, had bidden it shine upon another. For this, in reality, her tears were trickling.

Mr. Raby took a much lighter view of it, and, to divert attention from her, he said, "Hallo! why this inscription has become legible. It used to be only legible in parts. Is that his doing?"

"Not a doubt of it," said Amboyne. "Set that against his sacrilege."

"Miss Carden and I are both agreed it was not sacrilege. What is here in this pew? A brass! Why this is the brass we could none of us decipher. Hang me, if he has not read it, and restored it!"

"So he has. And where's the wonder? We live in a glorious age" (Raby smiled) "that has read the written mountains of the East, and the Abyssinian monuments: and he is a man of the age, and your mediæval brasses are no more to him than cuneiform letters to Rawlinson. Let me read this resuscitated record. 'Edith Little, daughter of Robert Raby, by Leah Dence his wife:' why here's a hodge-podge! What! have the noble Rabys intermarried with the humble Dences?"

"So it seems. A younger son."

"And a Raby, daughter of Dence, married a Little three hundred years ago?"

"So it seems."

"Then what a pity this brass was not deciphered thirty years ago. But never mind that. All I demand is tardy justice to my protégé. Is not this a remarkable man? By day he carves wood, and carries out a philanthropic scheme (which I mean to communicate to you this very day, together with this young man's report); at night he forges tools that all Hillsborough can't rival; in an interval of his work he saves a valuable life or two; in another odd moment he fights like a lion, one to four; even in his moments of downright leisure, when he is neither saving life nor taking it, he practises honorable arts, restores the fading letters of a charitable bequest, and deciphers brasses, and vastly improves his uncle's genealogical knowledge, who, nevertheless, passed for an authority, till my Crichton stepped upon the scene."

Raby bore all this admirably. "You may add," said he, "that he nevertheless finds time to correspond with his friends. Here is a letter, addressed to Miss Carden, I declare!"

"A letter to me!" said Grace, faintly.

Raby handed it over the pew to her, and turned the address, so that she could judge for herself.

She took it very slowly and feebly, and her color came and went.

"You seemed surprised; and so am I. It must have been written two days ago."

"Yes."

"Why, what on earth could he have to say to you?"

"I suppose it is the reply to mine," stammered Grace.

Mr. Raby looked amazement, and something more.

Grace faltered out an explanation. "When he had saved my life, I was so grateful I wanted to make him a return. I believed Jael Dence and he—I have so high an opinion of her—I ventured to give him a hint that he might find happiness there."

Raby bit his lip. "A most singular interference on the part of a young lady," said he, stiffly. "You are right, Doctor; this age resembles no other. I suppose you meant it kindly: but I am very sorry you felt called upon, at your age, to put any such idea into the young man's head."

"So am I," said poor Grace. "Oh, pray forgive me. I am so unhappy." And she hid her face in her hands.

"Of course I forgive you," said Raby. "But, unfortunately, I knew nothing of all this, and went and put him under her charge; and here he has found a precedent for marrying a Dence—found it on this confounded brass! Well, no matter. Life is one long disappointment. What does he say? Where is the letter gone to? It has vanished."

"I have got it safe," said Grace, deprecatingly.

"Then please let me know what he says."

"What, read his letter to you?"

"Why not, pray? I'm his uncle. He is my heir-at-law. I agree with Amboyne, he has some fine qualities. It is foolish of me, no doubt, but I am very anxious to know what he says about marrying my tenant's daughter." Then, with amazing dignity, "Can I be mistaken in thinking I have a right to know who my nephew intends to marry?" And he began to get very red.

Grace hung her head, and, trembling a little, drew the letter very slowly out of her bosom.

It just flashed through her mind how cruel it was to make her read out the death-warrant of her heart before two men; but she summoned all a woman's fortitude and self-defense, prepared to hide her anguish under a marble demeanor, and quietly opened the letter.

CHAPTER XX.

"You advise me to marry one, when I love another: and this, you think, is the way to be happy. It has seldom proved so, and I should despise happiness, if I could only get it in that way.

"Yours, sadly but devotedly, H. LITTLE.

"Will you wait two years?"

Grace, being on her defense, read this letter very slowly, and as if she had to decipher it. That gave her time to say, "Yours, et cetera," instead of "sadly and devotedly." (Why be needlessly precise?) As for the postscript, she didn't trouble them with that at all.

She then hurried the letter into her pocket, that it might not be asked for, and said, with all the nonchalance she could manage to assume, "Oh, if he loves somebody else!"

"No; that is worse still," said Mr. Raby. "In his own rank of life, it is ten to one if he finds any thing as modest, as good, and as loyal as Dence's daughter. It's some factory-girl, I suppose."

"Let us hope not," said Grace, demurely; but Amboyne noticed that her cheek was now flushed, and her eyes sparkling like diamonds. Soon afterwards she strolled apart, and took a wonderful interest in the monuments and things, until she found an opportunity to slip out into the churchyard. There she took the letter out, and kissed it again and again, as if she would devour it; and all the way home she was as gay as a lark. Amboyne put himself in her place.

When they got home, he said to her, "My dear Miss Carden, I have a favor to ask you. I want an hour's conversation with Mr. Raby. Will you be so very kind as to see that I am not interrupted?"

"Oh yes. No; you must tell me, first, what you are going to talk about. I can't have gentlemen talking nonsense, together, uninterrupted-ly."

"You ladies claim to monopolize nonsense, eh? Well, I am going to talk about my friend, Mr. Little. Is he nonsense?"

"That depends. What are you going to say about him?"

"Going to advance his interests—and my own hobby. Such is man."

"Never mind what is man; what is your hobby?"

"Saving idiotic ruffians' lives."

"Well, that is a hobby. But, if Mr. Little is to profit by it, never mind; you shall not be interrupted, if I can keep 'les fâcheux' away."

Accordingly she got her work, and sat in the hall. Here, as she expected, she was soon joined by Mr. Coventry, and he found her in a gracious mood, and in excellent spirits.

After some very pleasant conversation, she told him she was keeping sentinel over Dr. Amboyne and his hobby.

"What is that?"

"Saving idiotic ruffians' lives. Ha! ha! ha!" Her merry laugh rang through the hall like a peal of bells.

Coventry stared, and then gave up trying to understand her and her eternal changes. He just set himself to please her, and he never found it easier than that afternoon.

Meantime Dr. Amboyne got Raby alone, and begged leave, in the first place, to premise that his (Raby's) nephew was a remarkable man. To prove it, he related Little's whole battle with the Hillsborough Trades; and then produced a Report the young man had handed him that very day. It was actually in his pocket during the fight, mute protest against that barbarous act.

The Report was entitled—"LIFE, LABOR, AND CAPITAL IN HILLSBOROUGH," and was divided into two parts.

Part 1 was entitled—"PECULIARITIES OF CUTLERY HURTFUL TO LIFE AND HEALTH."

And part 2 was entitled—"THE REMEDIES TO THE ABOVE."

Part 2 was divided thus:—

A. What the masters could do.

B. What the workmen could do.

C. What the Legislature could do.

Part 1 dealt first with the diseases of the grinders; but instead of quoting it, I ask leave to refer to Chapter VIII., where the main facts lie recorded.

Having thus curtailed the Report, I print the remainder in an Appendix, for the use of those few readers who can endure useful knowledge in works of this class.

Raby read the Report without moving a muscle.

"Well, what do you think of him?" asked Amboyne.

"I think he is a fool to trouble his head whether these animals live or die."

"Oh, that is my folly; not his. At bottom, he cares no more than you do."

"Then I retract my observation."

"As to its being folly, or as to Little being the fool?"

"Whichever you like best."

"Thank you. Well, but to be serious, this young man is very anxious to be a master, instead of a man. What do you say? Will you help his ambition, and my sacred hobby?"

"What, plunge you deeper in folly, and him in trade? Not I. I don't approve folly: I hate trade. But I tell you what I'll do. If he and his mother can see my conduct in its proper light, and say so, they can come to Raby, and he can turn gentleman, take the name of Raby, as he has got the face, and be my heir."

"Are you serious, Raby?"

"Perfectly."

"Then you had better write it, and I'll take it to him."

"Certainly." He sat down and wrote as follows:—

"SIR,—What has recently occurred appears calculated to soften one of those animosities which, between persons allied in blood, are always to be regretted. I take the opportunity to say, that if your mother, under your advice, will now reconsider the duties of a trustee, and my conduct in that character, and her remarks on that conduct, I think she will do me justice, and honor me once more with her esteem. Should this be the result, I further hope that she and yourself will come to Raby, and that you will change that way of life which you have found so full of thorns, and prepare yourself to succeed to my name and place. ,I am, your obedient servant,

"GUY RABY."

"There, read that."

Amboyne read it, and approved it. Then he gave a sigh, and said, "And so down goes my poor hobby."

"Oh, never mind," said Raby; "you've got one or two left in your stable."

Doctor Amboyne went out, and passed through the hall. There he found Mr. Coventry and Miss Carden: the latter asked him, rather keenly, if the conference was over.

"Yes, and not without a result: I'll read it to you." He did so, and Grace's cheek was dyed with blushes, and her eyes beamed with joy.

"Oh, how noble he is, and how good you are. Run! Fly!"

"Such movements are undignified, and unsuited to my figure. Shall I roll down the hill? That would be my quickest way."

This discussion was cut short by a servant, who came to tell the Doctor that a carriage was ordered for him, and would be round in a minute.

Doctor Amboyne drove off, and Miss Carden now avoided Coventry: she retired to her room. But, it seems, she was on the watch; for, on the Doctor's return, she was the person who met him in the hall.

"Well?" said she, eagerly.

"Well, would you believe it? he declines. He objects to leave his way of life, and to wait for dead men's shoes."

"Oh, Doctor Amboyne! And you were there to advise him!"

"I did not venture to advise him. There was so much to be said on both sides." Then he went off to Raby, with the note; but, as he went, he heard Grace say, in a low voice, "Ah, you never thought of me."

Little's note ran thus:—

"SIR,—I thank you for your proposal, and as to the first part of it, I quite agree, and should be glad to see my mother and you friends again. But, as to my way of life, I have chosen my path, and mean to stick to it. I hope soon to be a master, instead of a workman; and I shall try and behave like a gentleman, so that you may not have to blush for me.. Should blush for myself if I were to give up industry, and independence, and take to waiting for dead men's shoes; that is a baser occupation than any trade in Hillsborough, I think. This is not as politely written as I could wish; but I am a blunt fellow, and I hope you will excuse it. I am not ungrateful to you for shooting those vermin, nor for your offer, though I can not accept it. Yours respectfully,
          . "HENRY LITTLE."

Raby read this, and turned white with rage.

He locked the letter up along with poor Mrs. Little's letters, and merely said, "I have only one request to make. Never mention the name of Little to me again."

Doctor Amboyne went home very thoughtful.

That same day Mr. Carden wrote from London to his daughter, informing her he should be at Hillsborough next day to dinner. She got the letter next morning, and showed it to Mr. Raby. He ordered his carriage after breakfast for Hillsborough.

This was a blow to Grace. She had been hoping all this time a fair opportunity might occur for saying something to young Little.

She longed to write to him, and set his heart, and her own, at rest. But a great shyness and timidity paralyzed her, and she gave up the idea of writing, and had hitherto been hoping they might meet, and she might reinstate herself by some one cunning word. And now the end of it all was, that she was driven away from Raby Hall without doing any thing but wish, and sigh, and resolve, and give up her resolutions with a blush.

The carriage passed the farm on its way to Hillsborough. This was Grace's last chance.

Little was standing at the porch.

. A thrill of delight traversed Grace's bosom.

It was followed, however, by a keen pang. Jael Dence sat beside him, sewing: and Grace saw, in a moment, she was sewing complacently. It was more than Grace could bear. She pulled the check-string, and the carriage stopped.

CHAPTER XXI.

HENRY LITTLE, at this moment was in very low spirits. His forge was in the yard, and a faithful body-guard at his service: but his right arm was in a sling, and so he was brought to a stand-still; and Coventry was with Grace at the house; and he, like her, was tortured with jealousies; and neither knew what the other suffered.

But every thing vanished in a flood of joy when the carriage stopped and that enchanting face looked out at him, covered with blushes, that told him he could not be indifferent to her.

"Oh, Mr. Little, are you better?"

"I'm all right. But, you see, I can't work."

"Ah, poor arm! But why should you work? Why not accept Mr. Raby's offer? How proud you are!"

"Should you have thought any better of me, if I had?"

"No. I don't want you altered. It would spoil you. You will come and see us at Woodbine Villa! Only think how many things we have to talk of now."

"May I?"

"Why of course."

"And will you wait two years for me?"

"Two years!" (blushing like a rose.) "Why I hope it will not be two days, before you come and see us."

"Ah, you mock me."

"No; no. But suppose you should take the advice I gave you in my mad letter?"

"There's no fear of that."

"Are you sure?" (with a glance at Jael.)

"Quite sure."

"Then—Good-bye. Please drive on."

She wouldn't answer his question; but her blushes and her radiant satisfaction, and her modest but eloquent looks of love, fully compensated her silence on that head, and the carriage left him standing there, a figure of rapture.

Next day Doctor Amboyne rode up to the farm with a long envelope, and waved it over his head in triumph. It contained a communication from the Secretary of the Philanthropic Society. The committee were much struck with Mr. Little's report, but feared that no manufacturer would act on his suggestions. They were willing to advance £500 towards setting Mr. Little himself up as a manufacturer, if he would bind himself to adopt and carry out the improvements suggested in his report. The loan to bear no interest, and the return of the capital to depend upon the success of the scheme. Dr. Amboyne, for the society, to have the right of inspecting Mr. Little's books, if any doubt should arise on that head. An agreement was enclosed, and this was more full, particular, and stringent in form than the above, but the purport substantially the same.

Little could not believe his good fortune at first. But there was no disbelieving it; the terms were so cold, precise, and business-like.

"Ah, Doctor," said he, "you have made a man of me; for this is your doing, I know."

"Of course I used my influence. I was stimulated by two spurs, friendship and my hobby. Now shake hands over it, and no fine speeches, but tell me when you can begin. 'My soul's in arms, and eager for the fray.'"

"Begin? Why as soon as I get the money."

"That will come down directly, if I telegraph that you accept the terms. Call in a witness, and sign the agreement."

Jael Dence was called in, and the agreement signed and witnessed, and away went the Doctor in high spirits, after making an appointment with Henry in Hillsborough for the next day.

Henry and Jael Dence talked eagerly over his new prospects. But though they were great friends, there was nothing to excite Grace's jealousy. No sooner was Little proved to be Raby's nephew than Jael Dence, in her humility, shrank back, and was inwardly ashamed of herself. She became respectful as well as kind; called him "the young master" behind his back, and tried to call him "Sir" to his face, only he would not let her.

Next day Little went to his mother and told her all. She was deeply interested, but bitterly disappointed at Henry's refusal of Raby's offer. "He will never forgive us now," she said. "And oh, Henry, if you love Grace Carden, that was the way to marry her." This staggered him; but he said he had every reason to hope she would marry him without his sacrificing his independence, and waiting with his hands in his pockets for dead men's shoes.

Then he went to Doctor Amboyne, and there were the five hundred pounds waiting for him; but, never having possessed such a sum before, he begged the Doctor to give him only £100 at a time. To finish for the present with this branch of the story, he was lucky enough to make an excellent bargain, bought the plant and stock of a small master-grinder recently deceased. He then confined the grinding to saws and razors; and this enabled him to set up his own forge on the premises, and to employ a few file-cutters. It was all he could do at starting. Then came the important question, What would the Trades say? He was not long in suspense; Grotait called on him, expressed his regret at the attack that had been made on him, and his satisfaction that now the matter could be happily arranged. "This," said he, "is the very proposal I was going to make to you (but you wouldn't hear me), to set up as a small master, and sell your carving-tools to London instead of to Hillsbro'."

"What? will that make me right with the Trade?"

"Pretty near. We protect the workmen from unfair competition, not the masters. However, if you wish to cure the sore altogether, let your own hands grind the tools, and send them out to be handled by Parkin: he has got men on the Box; trade is dull."

"Well, I don't object to that."

"Then, I say, let by-gones be gone-byes."

They shook hands over this, and in a very few hours it was known that Mr. Little was right with the Trade.

His early experiences as a philanthropic master were rather curious; but I shall ask leave to relate them in a series of their own, and to deal at present with matters of more common interest.

He called twice on Grace Carden; but she was out. The third time he found her at home; but there was a lady with her, talking about the ball Mr. and Miss Carden were about to give. It was a subject calculated to excite volubility, and Henry could not get in a word edgeways. But he received some kind glances that made his heart beat.

The young lady sat there and gabbled; for she felt sure that no topic imported by a male creature could complete in interest with "the ball." So, at last, Henry rose in despair. But Grace, to whom her own ball had been a bore for the last half hour, went with him to the door; and he seized the opportunity to tell her he was a workman no longer, but a master, having workmen under him.

Grace saw he was jubilant, so she was glad directly, and said so.

But then she shook her pretty head, and hoped he would not have to regret Mr. Raby's offer.

"Never," said he, firmly; "unless I lose you. Now I'm a master, instead of a man, won't you wait two years for me?"

"No," said Grace, archly. Then, with a look that sent him to heaven, "Not two, but twenty, sooner than you should be unhappy, after all you and I—"

The sentence was never completed. She clapped one hand swiftly before her scarlet face, and ran away to hide, and think of what she had done. It was full five minutes before she would bring her face under the eye of that young gossip in the drawing-room.

As for Henry, he received the blow full in his heart, and it quite staggered him. He couldn't believe it at first; but when he realized it, waves and waves of joy seemed to rise inside him, and he went off in such a rapture he hardly trod the earth.

He went home, and kissed his mother, and told her, and she sympathized with him perforce, though she was jealous at bottom, poor thing.

The next day Grace received an unexpected visitor—Jael Dence.

Grace stared at sight of her, and received her very coldly.

"Oh, Miss," said Jael, "don't look so at me that love you dearly;" and with this threw her arms round her neck, and kissed her.

Grace was moved by this; but felt uncomfortable, and even struggled a little, but in vain. Jael was gentle, but mighty. "It's about your letter, Miss."

"Then let me go," cried Grace. "I wish I had never written it."

"Nay; don't say so. I should never have known how good you are."

"What a fool I am, you mean. How dare you read my letter? Oh! did he show it you? That was very cruel, if he did."

"No, Miss, he never showed it me; and I never read it. I call it mean to read another body's letter. But, you know, 'tisn't every woman thinks so; and a poor lass that is very fond of me—and I scolded her bitterly—she took the letter out of his pocket, and told me what was in it."

"Very well, then," said Grace, coldly, "it is right you should also read his answer. I'll bring it you."

"Not to-day, Miss, if you please. There is no need. I know him: he is too much of a man to marry one girl when he loves another; and 'tis you he loves, and I hope you will be happy together."

A few quiet tears followed these brave words, and Grace looked at her askant, and began to do her justice.

"Ah!" said she, with a twinge of jealousy, "you know him better than I. You have answered for him, in his very words. Yet you can't love him as I do. I hope you are not come to ask me to give him up again, for I can't." Then she said, with quick defiance, "Take him from me if you can." Then, piteously, "And if you do, you will kill me."

"Dear heart, I came of no such errand. I came to tell you I know how generous you have been to me, and made me your friend till death; and, when a Dence says that, she means it. I have been a little imprudent: but not so very. First word I said to him, in this very house, was, 'Are you really a workman?' I had the sense to put that question; for, the first moment I clapped eyes on him, I saw my danger like. Well, he might have answered me true: but you see he didn't. I think I am not so much to blame. Well, he is the young Squire now, and no mate for me; and he loves you, that are of his own sort. That is sure to cure me—after a while. Simple folk like me aren't used to get their way, like the gentry. It takes a deal of patience to go through the world. If you think I'll let my heart cling to another woman's sweetheart—nay, but I'd tear it out of my breast first. Yes, I dare say it will be a year or two before I can listen to another man's voice without hating him for wooing of me; but Time cures all that don't fight against the cure. And you'll love me a little, Miss, now, won't you? You used to do, before I deserved it half as well as I do to-day."

"Of course I shall love you, my poor Jael. But what is my love, compared with that you are now giving up so nobly?"

"It is not much," said Jael, frankly; "but 'a little breaks a high fall.' And I'm one that can only enjoy my own. Better a penny roll with a clear conscience, than my neighbor's loaf. I'd liever take your love, and deserve it, than try to steal his."

All this time Grace was silently watching her, to see if there was any deceit, or self-deceit, in all this: and, had there been, it could not have escaped so keen and jealous an eye. But no, the limpid eye, the modest, sober voice, that trembled now and then, but always recovered its resolution, repelled doubt or suspicion.

Grace started to her feet, and said, with great enthusiasm, "I give you the love and respect you deserve so well; and I thank God for creating such a character now and then—to embellish this vile world."

Then she flung herself upon Jael, with wonderful abandon and grace, and kissed her so eagerly that she made poor Jael's tears flow very fast indeed.

She would not let her go back to Cairnhope.

Henry remembered about the ball, and made up his mind to go and stand in the road: he might catch a glimpse of her somehow. He told his mother he should not be home to supper; and, to get rid of the time before the ball, he went to the theatre: thence, at ten o'clock, to "Woodbine Villa," and soon found himself one of a motley group. Men, women, and children were there to see the company arrive; and, as, amongst working-people, the idle and the curious are seldom well-to-do, they were rather a scurvy lot, and each satin or muslin belle, brave with flowers and sparkling with gems, had to pass through a little avenue of human beings in soiled fustian, dislocated bonnets, rags, and unwashed faces.

Henry got away from this class of spectators, and took up his station right across the road. He leaned against the lamp-post, and watched the drawing-room windows for Grace.

The windows were large, and, being French, came down to the balcony. Little saw many a lady's head and white shoulders, but not the one he sought.

Presently a bed-room window was opened, and a fair face looked out into the night for a moment. It was Jael Dence.

She had assisted Miss Carden to dress, and had then, at her request, prepared the room, and decked it with flowers, to receive a few of the young lady's more favored friends. This done, she opened the window, and Henry Little saw her.

Nor was it long before she saw him; for the light of the lamp was full on him.

But he was now looking intently in at the drawing-room windows, and with a ghastly expression.

The fact is, that in the short interval between his seeing Jael and her seeing him, the quadrilles had been succeeded by a waltz, and Grace Carden's head and shoulders were now flitting, at intervals, past the window in close proximity to the head of her partner. What with her snowy, glossy shoulders, her lovely face, and her exquisite head and brow encircled with a coronet of pearls, her beauty seemed half regal, half angelic; yet that very beauty, after the first thrill of joy which the sudden appearance of a beloved one always causes, was now passing cold iron through her lover's heart. For why? A man's arm was round that supple waist, a man's hand held that delicate palm, a man's head seemed wedded to that lovely head, so close were the two together. And the encircling arm, the pressing hand, the head that came and went, and rose and sank, with hers, like twin cherries on a stalk, were the arm, the hand, and the head of Mr. Frederick Coventry.

Every time those two heads flitted past the window together, they inflicted a spasm of agony on Henry Little, and, between the spasms, his thoughts were bitter beyond expression. An icy barrier still between them, and none between his rival and her! Coventry could dance voluptuously with her before all the world; but he could only stand at the door of that Paradise, and groan and sicken with jealous anguish at the sight.

Now and then he looked up, and saw Jael Dence. She was alone. Like him, she was excluded from that brilliant crowd. He and she were born to work; these butterflies on the first floor, to enjoy.

Their eyes met; he saw soft pity in hers. He cast a mute, but touching appeal. She nodded, and withdrew from the window. Then he knew the faithful girl would try and do something or other for him.

But he never moved from his pillar of torture. Jealous agony is the one torment men can not fly from; it fascinates, it holds, it maddens.

Jael came to the drawing-room door just as the waltz ended, and tried to get to Miss Carden; but there were too many ladies and gentlemen, especially about the door.

At last she caught Grace's eye, but only for a moment; and the young lady was in the very act of going out on the balcony for air, with her partner.

She did go out, accompanied by Mr. Coventry, and took two or three turns. Her cheek was flushed, her eye kindled, and the poor jealous wretch over the way saw it, and ascribed all that to the company of his rival.

While she walked to and fro with fawn-like grace, conversing with Mr. Coventry, yet secretly wondering what that strange look Jael had given her could mean, Henry leaned, sick at heart, against the lamp-post over the way; and, at last, a groan forced its way out of him.

Faint as the sound was, Grace's quick ear caught it, and she turned her head. She saw him directly, and blushed high, and turned pale, all in a moment; for, in that single moment, her swift woman's heart told her why he was so ghastly, and why that sigh of distress.

She stopped short in her walk, and began to quiver from head to foot.

But, after a few moments of alarm, distress, and perplexity, love and high spirit supplied the place of tact, and she did the best and most characteristic thing she could. Just as Mr. Coventry, who had observed her shiver, was asking her if she found it too cold, she drew herself up to her full height, and turning round, kissed her hand over the balcony to Henry Little, with a sort of princely grandeur, and an ardor of recognition and esteem that set his heart leaping, and his pale cheek blushing, and made Coventry jealous in his turn. Yes, one eloquent gesture did that in a moment.

But the brave girl was too sensitive to prolong such a situation: the music recommenced at that moment, and she seized the opportunity, and retired to the room; she courtesied to Little at the window, and this time he had the sense to lift his hat to her.

The moment she entered the room, Grace Carden slipped away from Mr. Coventry, and winded her way like a serpent through the crowd, and found Jael Dence at the door. She caught her by the arm, and pinched her. She was all trembling. Jael drew her up the stairs a little way.

"You have seen him out there?"

"Yes: and I—oh!"

"There! there! Think of the folk. Fight it down."

"I will. Go to him, and say I can't bear it. Him to stand there—while those I don't care a pin for—oh, Jael, for pity's sake get him home to his mother."

"There, don't you fret. I know what to say."

Jael went down; borrowed the first shawl she could lay her hand on; hooded herself with it, and was across the road in a moment.

"You are to go home directly."

"Who says so?"

"She does."

"What, does she tell me to go away, and leave her to him?"

"What does that matter? her heart goes with you."

"No, no."

"Won't you take my word for it? I'm not given to lying."

"I know that. Oh, Jael, sweet, pretty, good-hearted Jael, have pity on me, and tell me the truth: is it me she loves, or that Coventry?"

"It is you."

"Oh, bless you! bless you! Ah, if I could only be sure of that, what wouldn't I do for her? But, if she loves me, why, why send me away? It is very cruel that so many should be in the same room with her, and he should dance with her, and I must not even look on, and catch a glimpse of her now and then. I won't go home."

"Ah!" said Jael, "you are like all the young men: you think only of yourself. And you call yourself a scholar of the good Doctor's."

"And so I am."

"Then why don't you go by his rule, and put yourself in a body's place? Suppose you was in her place, master of this house like, and dancing with a pack of girls you didn't care for, and she stood out here, pale, and sighing; and suppose things were so that you couldn't come out to her, nor she come in to you, wouldn't it cut you to the heart to see her stand in the street and look so unhappy—poor lad? Be good, now, and go home to thy mother. Why stand here and poison the poor young lady's pleasure — such as 'tis—and torment thyself." Jael's own eyes filled, and that proof of sympathy inclined Henry all the more to listen to her reason. "You are wise, and good, and kind," he said. "But oh, Jael, I adore her so, I'd rather be in hell with her than in heaven without her. Half a loaf is better than no bread. I can't go home and turn my back on the place where she is. Yes, I'm in torments; but I see her. They can't rob my *eyes* of her."

"To oblige *her!*"

"Yes; I'll do any thing to oblige *her.* If I could only believe she loves me."

"Put it to the proof, if you don't believe me."

"I will. Tell her I'd much rather stay all night, and catch a glimpse of her now and then; but yet, tell her I'll go home, if she will promise me not to dance with that Coventry again."

"There is a condition!" said Jael.

"It is a fair one," said Henry, doggedly, "and I won't go from it."

Jael looked at him, and saw it was no use arguing the matter. So she went in to the house with this ultimatum.

She soon returned, and told him that Miss Grace, instead of being angry, as she expected, had smiled and looked pleased, and promised not to dance with Mr. Coventry nor any body else any more that night, "if he would go straight home and consult his beautiful mother." "Those were her words," said the loyal Dence. "She did say them twice over to make sure."

"God bless her!" cried Henry, warmly; "and bless you too, my best friend. I'll go this moment."

He cast a long, lingering look at the window, and went slowly down the street.

When he got home, his mother was still up and secretly anxious.

He sat down beside her, and told her where he had been and how it had all ended. "I'm to consult my beautiful mother," said he, kissing her.

"What, does she think I am like my picture now?"

"I suppose so. And you are as beautiful as ever in my eyes, mother. And I do consult you."

Mrs. Little's black eyes flashed; but she said, calmly,

"What about, dearest?"

"I really don't know. I suppose it was about what happened to-night. Perhaps about it all."

Mrs. Little leaned her head upon her hand and thought.

After a moment's reflection, she said to Henry, rather coldly, "If she is not a very good girl, she must be a very clever one."

"She is both," said Henry, warmly.

"Of that I shall be the best judge," said Mrs. Little, very coldly indeed.

Poor Henry felt quite chilled. He said no more; nor did his mother return to the subject till they parted for the night, and then it was only to ask him what church Miss Carden went to—a question that seemed to be rather frivolous, but he said he thought St. Margaret's.

Next Sunday evening, Mrs. Little and he being at tea together, she said to him quietly,—"Well, Harry, I have seen her."

"Oh, mother! where?"

"At St. Margaret's Church."

"But how did you know her? By her beauty?"

Mrs. Little smiled, and took a roll of paper out of her muff, that lay on the sofa. She unfolded it, and displayed a drawing. It represented Grace Carden in her bonnet, and was a very good likeness.

The lover pounced on it, and devoured it with astonishment and delight.

"Taken from the bust, and retouched from nature," said Mrs. Little. "Yes, dear, I went to St. Margaret's, and asked a pew-opener where she sat. I placed myself where I could command her features; and, you may be sure, I read her very closely. Well, dear, she bears examination. It is a bright face, a handsome face, and a good face : and almost as much in love as you are."

"What makes you fancy that? Oh, you spoke to her?"

"Certainly not. But I observed her. Restless and listless by turns—her body in one place, her mind in another. She was so taken up with her own thoughts she could not follow the service. I saw the poor girl try very hard several times, but at last she gave it up in despair. Sometimes she knitted her brow; and a young girl seldom does that unless she is thwarted in her love. And I'll tell you a surer sign still: sometimes tears came for no visible reason, and stood in her eyes. She is in love; and it can not be with Mr. Coventry of Bollinghope; for, if she loved him, she would have nothing to brood on but her wedding-dress; and they never knit their brows, nor bedew their eyes, thinking of that; that's a smiling subject. No, it is true love on both sides, I do believe; and that makes my woman's heart yearn. Harry, dear, I'll make you a confession. You have heard that a mother's love is purer and more unselfish than any other love : and so it is. But even mothers are not quite angels always. Sometimes they are just a little jealous : not, I think, where they are blessed with many children; but you are my one child, my playmate, my companion, my friend, my only love. That sweet girl has come, and I must be dethroned. I felt this, and—no, nothing could ever make me downright thwart your happiness; but a mother's jealousy made me passive, where I might have assisted you if I had been all a mother should be."

"No, no, mother; I am the one to blame. You see, it looked so hopeless at first, I used to be ashamed to talk freely to you. It's only of late I have opened my heart to you as I ought."

"Well, dear, I am glad you think the blame is not all with me. But what I see is my own fault, and mean to correct it. She gave you good advice, dear—to consult your mother. But you shall have my assistance as well; and I shall begin at once, like a zealous ally. When I say at once—this is Sunday—I shall begin to-morrow, at one o'clock."

Then Henry sat down at her knee, and took her white hand in his brown ones.

"And what shall you do at one o'clock, my beautiful mother?"

"I shall return to society."

CHAPTER XXII.

NEXT morning Mrs. Little gave her son the benefit of her night's reflections.

"You must let me have some money—all you can spare from your business; and whilst I am doing something with it for you, you must go to London, and do exactly what I tell you to do."

"Exactly? Then please write it down."

"A very good plan. Can you go by the express this morning?"

"Why, yes, I could; only then I must run down to the works this minute, and speak to the foreman."

"Well, dear, when you come back, your instructions shall be written, and your bag packed."

"I say, mother, you are going into it in earnest. All the better for me."

At twelve he started for London, with a beautiful set of carving-tools in his bag, and his mother's instructions in his pocket: those instructions sent him to a fashionable tailor that very afternoon. With some difficulty he prevailed on this worthy to make him a dress-suit in twenty-four hours. Next day he introduced himself to the London trade, showed his carving-tools, and, after a hard day's work, succeeded in obtaining several orders. Then he bought some white ties and gloves and an opera hat, and had his hair cut in Bond Street.

At seven he got his clothes at the tailor's, and at eight he was in the stalls of the opera. His mother had sent him there, to note the dress and public deportment of gentlemen and ladies, and use his own judgment. He found his attention terribly distracted by the music and the raptures it caused him; but still he made some observations; and, consequently, next day he bought some fashionable shirts and sleeve-studs and ribbon ties; ordered a morning suit of the same tailor, to be sent to him at Hillsborough; and after canvassing for customers all day, telegraphed his mother, and reached Hillsborough at eleven P.M.

At first sight of him Mrs. Little exclaimed:

"Oh! What have you done with your beautiful hair?"

He laughed, and said this was the fashion.

"But it is like a private soldier."

"Exactly. Part of the Volunteer movement, perhaps."

"Are you sure it is the fashion, dear?"

"Quite sure. All the swells in the opera were bullet-headed just like this."

"Oh, if it is the fashion!" said Mrs. Little; and her mind succumbed under that potent word.

She asked him about the dresses of the ladies in the opera.

His description was very lame. He said he didn't know he was expected to make notes of them.

"Well, but you might be sure I should like to know. Were there no ladies dressed as you would like to see your mother dressed?"

"Good heavens, no! I couldn't fancy you in a lot of colors: and your beautiful head deformed into the shape of a gourd, with a beast of a chignon stuck out behind, made of dead hair."

"No matter, Mr. Henry; I wish I had been with you at the opera. I should have seen something or other, that would have become me." She gave a little sigh.

He was not to come home to dinner that day, but stay at the works, till she sent for him.

At six o'clock, Jael Dence came for him in a fly, and told him he was to go home with her.

"All right," said he; "but how did you come there?"

"She bade me come and see her again—that day I brought the bust. So I went to see her, and I found her so busy, and doing more than she was fit, poor thing, so I made bold to give her a hand. That was yesterday: and I shall come every day—if 'tis only for an hour—till the curtains are all up."

"The curtains! what curtains?"

"Ask no questions, and you will hear no lies."

Henry remonstrated; Jael recommended patience: and, at last, they reached a little villa,

half way up Heath Hill. "You are at home now," said Jael, dryly. The new villa looked very gay that evening, for gas and fires were burning in every room.

The dining-room and drawing-room were both on the ground-floor, and each one enormous window with plate glass, and were rooms of very fair size, divided by large folding-doors. These were now open, and Henry found his mother seated in the dining-room, with two workwomen, making curtains, and in the drawing-room were two more, sewing a carpet.

The carpet was down in the dining-room. The tea-table was set, and gave an air of comfort and housewifely foresight, in the midst of all the surrounding confusion.

Young Little stared. Mrs. Little smiled.

"Sit down, and never mind us: give him his tea, my good Jael."

Henry sat down, and while Jael was making the tea, ventured on a feeble expostulation. "It's all very fine, mother, but I don't like to see you make a slave of yourself."

"Slaving!" said Jael, with a lofty air of pity. "Why, she is working for her own." Rural logic!

"Oh," said Mrs. Little to her, "these clever creatures we look up to so are rather stupid in some things. Slave! Why, I am a General leading my Amazons to victory." And she waved her needle gracefully in the air.

"Well, but why not let the shop do them, where you bought the curtains?"

"Because, my dear, the shop would do them very badly, very dearly, and very slowly. Do you remember reading to me about Cæsar, and what he said?—'that a General should not say to his troops "go and attack the enemy, but come and attack the enemy."' Well, that applies to needlework. I say to these ladies, 'come sew these curtains, with me; and the consequence is, we have done in three days what no shop in Hillsborough would have done for us in a fortnight; but, as for slaves, the only one has been my good Jael there. She insisted on moving all the heavy boxes herself. She dismissed the porter; she said he had no pith in his arms—that was your expression, I think?"

"Ay, ma'am; that was my word: and I never spoke a truer; the useless body. Why, ma'am, the girls in Cairnhope are most of them well-grown hussies, and used to work in the fields, and carry full sacks of grain up steps. Many's the time I have run with a sack of barley on my back: so let us hear no more about your bits of boxes. I wish my mind was as strong."

"Heaven forbid!" said Mrs. Little, with comic fervor. Henry laughed. But Jael only stared, rather stupidly. By-and-by she said she must go now.

"Henry shall take you home, dear."

"Nay, I can go by myself."

"It is raining a little. He will take you home in the cab."

"Nay, I've got legs of my own," said the rustic.

"Henry, dear," said the lady, quietly, "take her home in the cab, and then come back to me."

At the gate of Woodbine Villa, Jael said "it was not good-night this time; it was good-bye: she was going home for Patty's marriage."

"But you will come back again?" said Henry.

"Nay, father would be all alone. You'll not see me here again, unless you were in sorrow or sickness."

"Ah, that's like you, Jael. Good-bye then, and God bless you wherever you go."

Jael summoned all her fortitude, and shook hands with him in silence. They parted, and

of manufactures and things, you could not be persuaded to sit down as a country gentleman. 'Indeed,' I said, 'his love of the thing is so great that, in order to master it in all its branches, nothing less would serve him than disguising himself, and going as a workman. But now,' I said, 'he has had enough of that, so he has set up a

"I AM A GENERAL LEADING MY ARMY," AND SHE WAVED HER NEEDLE IN THE AIR.

she fought down her tears, and he went gayly home to his mother. She told him she had made several visits, and been cordially received. "And this is how I paved the way for you. So, mind! I said my brother Raby wished you to take his name, and be his heir; but you had such a love

small factory, and will, no doubt, soon achieve a success.' Then I told them about you and Doctor Amboyne. Your philanthropic views did not interest them for a single moment; but I could see the poor dear Doctor's friendship was a letter of introduction. There will be no difficulty, dear.

There shall be none. What society Hillsborough boasts, shall open its arms to you."

"But I'm afraid I shall make mistakes."

"Our first little parties shall be given in this house. Your free and easy way will be excused in a host; the master of the house has a latitude; and, besides, you and I will rehearse. By the way, please be more careful about your nails; and you must always wear gloves when you are not working; and every afternoon you will take a lesson in dancing with me."

"I say, mother, do you remember teaching me to dance a minuet, when I was little?"

"Perfectly. We took great pains; and, at last, you danced it like an angel. And, shall I tell you, you carry yourself very gracefully?—well, that is partly owing to the minuet. But a more learned professor will now take you in hand. He will be here to-morrow at five o'clock."

Mrs. Little's room being nearly square, she set up a round table, at which eight could dine. But she began with five or six.

Henry used to commit a solecism or two. Mrs. Little always noticed them, and told him. He never wanted telling twice. He was a genial young fellow, well read in the topics of the day, and had a natural wit; Mrs. Little was one of those women who can fascinate when they choose; and she chose now; her little parties rose to eight; and as, at her table, every body could speak without rudeness to every body else, this round table soon began to eclipse the long tables of Hillsborough in attraction.

She and Henry went out a good deal; and, at last, that which Mrs. Little's good sense had told her must happen, sooner or later, took place. They met.

He was standing talking with one of the male guests, when the servant announced Miss Carden; and, whilst his heart was beating high, she glided into the room, and was received by the mistress of the house with all that superabundant warmth which ladies put on and men don't: guess why?

When she turned round from this exuberant affection, she encountered Henry's black eye full of love and delight, and his tongue tied, and his swarthy cheek glowing red. She half started, and blushed in turn; and with one glance drank in every article of dress he had on. Her eyes beamed pleasure and admiration for a moment, then she made a little courtesy, then she took a step towards him, and held out her hand a little coyly.

Their hands and eyes encountered; and, after that delightful collision, they were both as demure as cats approaching cream.

Before they could say a word of any consequence, a cruel servant announced dinner, to the great satisfaction of every other soul in the room.

Of course they were parted at dinner-time; but they sat exactly opposite each other, and Henry gazed at her so, instead of minding his business, that she was troubled a little, and fain to look another way. For all that, she found opportunity once or twice to exchange thoughts with him. Indeed, in the course of the two hours, she gave him quite a lesson how to speak with the eye—an art in which he was a mere child compared with her.

She conveyed to him that she saw his mother, and recognized her; and also she hoped to know her.

But some of her telegrams puzzled him.

When the gentlemen came up after dinner, she asked him if he would not present her to his mother.

"Oh, thank you!" said he, naïvely; and introduced them to each other.

The ladies courtesied with grace, but a certain formality, for they both felt the importance of the proceeding, and were a little on their guard.

But they had too many safe, yet interesting topics, to be very long at a loss.

"I should have known you by your picture, Mrs. Little."

"Ah, then I fear it must be faded since I saw it last."

"I think not. But I hope you will soon judge for yourself."

Mrs. Little shook her head. Then she said, graciously, "I hear it is to you I am indebted that people can see I was once—what I am not now."

Grace smiled, well pleased. "Ah," said she, "I wish you could have seen that extraordinary scene, and heard dear Mr. Raby—Oh, madam, let nothing make you believe you have no place in his great heart!"

"Pray, pray do not speak of that. This is no place. How could I bear it?" and Mrs. Little began to tremble.

Grace apologized. "How indiscreet I am; I blurt out every thing that is in my heart."

"And so do I," said Henry, coming to her aid.

"Ah, you!" said Grace, a little saucily.

"We do not accept you for our pattern, you see. Pray excuse our bad taste, Harry."

"Oh, excuse me, Mrs. Little. In some things I should indeed be proud if I could imitate him; but in others—of course—you know."

"Yes, I know. My dear, there is your friend Mr. Applethwaite."

"I see him," said Henry, carelessly.

"Yes; but you don't see every thing," said Grace, slyly.

"Not all at once, like you ladies. Bother my friend Applethwaite. Well, if I must, I must. Here goes—from Paradise to Applethwaite."

He went off, and both ladies smiled, and one blushed; and, to cover her blush, said, "It is not every son that has the grace to appreciate his mother so."

Mrs. Little opened her eyes at first, and then made her nearest approach to a laugh, which was a very broad smile, displaying all her white teeth. "That is a turn I was very far from expecting," said she.

The ice was now broken, and, when Henry returned, he found them conversing so rapidly and so charmingly, that he could do little more than listen.

At last Mr. Carden came in from some other party, and carried his daughter off, and the bright evening came too soon to a close; but a great point had been gained; Mrs. Little and Grace Carden were acquaintances now, and cordially disposed to be friends.

The next time these lovers met, matters did not go quite so smoothly. It was a large party, and Mr. Coventry was there. The lady of the house was a friend of his, and assigned Miss Carden to him. He took her down to dinner, and Henry sat a long way off, but on the opposite side of the table.

He was once more doomed to look on at the assiduities of his rival, and it spoiled his dinner for him.

But he was beginning to learn that these things must be in society; and his mother, on the other side of the table, shrugged her shoulders to him, and conveyed by that and a look that it was a thing to make light of.

In the evening the rivals came into contact.

Little, being now near her he loved, was in high spirits, and talked freely and agreeably. He made quite a little circle round him; and as Grace was one of the party, and cast bright and approving eyes on him, it stimulated him still more, and he became quite brilliant.

Then Coventry, who was smarting with jealousy, set himself to cool all this down by a subtle cold sort of jocoseness, which, without being downright rude, operates on conversation of the higher kind like frost on expanding buds. It had its effect, and Grace chafed secretly, but could not interfere. It was done very cleverly. Henry was bitterly annoyed; but his mother, who saw his rising ire in his eye, carried him off to see a flowering cactus in a hot-house that was accessible from the drawing-room. When she had got him there, she soothed him and lectured him. "You are not a match for that man in these petty acts of annoyance, to which a true gentleman and a noble rival would hardly descend, I think; at all events, a wise one would not; for, believe me, Mr. Coventry will gain nothing by this."

"Isn't driving us off the field something? Oh, for the good old days when men settled these things in five minutes, like men; the girl to one, and the grave to t'other."

"Heaven forbid those savage days should ever return. We will defeat this gentleman quietly, if you please."

"How?"

"Well, whenever he does this sort of thing, hide your anger; be polite and dignified; but gradually drop the conversation, and manage to convey to the rest that it is useless contending against a wet blanket. Why, you foolish boy, do you think Grace Carden likes him any the better? Whilst you and I talk, she is snubbing him finely. So you must stay here with me, and give them time to quarrel. There, to lessen the penance, we will talk about her. Last time we met her, she told me you were the best-dressed gentleman in the room."

"And did she like me any better for that?"

"Don't you be ungracious, dear. She was proud of you. It gratified her that you should look well in every way. Oh, if you think that we are going to change our very natures for you, and make light of dress—why did I send you to a London tailor? and why am I always at you about your gloves?"

"Mother, I am on thorns."

"Well, we will go back. Stop; let me take a peep first."

She took a peep, and reported,

"The little circle is broken up. Mr. Coventry could not amuse them as you did. Ah! she is in the sulks, and he is mortified. I know there's a French proverb 'Les absens ont toujours tort.' But it is quite untrue; judicious absence is a weapon, and I must show you how and when to use it."

"Mother, you are my best friend. What shall we do next?"

"Why, go back to the room with me, and put on imperturbable good-humor, and ignore him; only mind you do that politely, or you will give him an advantage he is too wise to give you."

Henry was about to obey these orders, but Miss Carden took the word out of his mouth.

"Well! the cactus?"

Then, as it is not easy to reply to a question so vague, Henry hesitated.

"There, I thought so," said Grace.

"What did you think?" inquired Mrs. Little.

"Oh, people don't go into hot-houses to see cactus; they go to flirt, or else gossip. I'll tell Mrs. White to set a short-hand writer in the great aloe, next party she gives. Confess, Mrs. Little, you went to criticise poor us, and there is no cactus at all."

"Miss Carden, I'm affronted. You shall smart for this. Henry, take her directly and show her the cactus, and clear your mother's character."

Henry offered his arm directly, and they went gayly off.

"Is she gone to flirt, or to gossip?" asked a young lady.

"Our watches must tell us that," said Mrs. Little. "If they stay five minutes—gossip."

"And how many—flirtation?"

"Ah, my dear, you know better than I do. What do you say? Five-and-twenty?"

The young ladies giggled.

Then Mr. Coventry came out strong. He was mortified, he was jealous; he saw a formidable enemy had entered the field, and had just outwitted and out-manœuvred him. So what does he do but step up to her, and say to her, with the most respectful grace, "May I be permitted to welcome you back to this part of the world? I am afraid I can not exactly claim your acquaintance; but I have often heard my father speak of you with the highest admiration. My name is Coventry."

"Mr. Coventry, of Bollinghope?" (He bowed.) "Yes; I had the pleasure of knowing your mother in former days."

"You have deserted us too long."

"I do not flatter myself I have been missed."

"Is any body ever missed, Mrs. Little? Believe me, few persons are welcomed so cordially as you are."

"That is very flattering, Mr. Coventry. It is for my son's sake I have returned to society."

"No doubt; but you will remain there for your own. Society is your place. You are at home in it, and were born to shine in it."

"What makes you think that, pray?" and the widow's cheek flushed a little.

"Oh, Mrs. Little, I have seen something of the world. Count me amongst your most respectful admirers. It is a sentiment I have a right to, since I inherit it."

"Well, Mr. Coventry, then I give you leave to admire me—if you can. Ah, here they come. Two minutes! I am afraid it was neither gossip nor flirtation, but only botany."

Grace and Henry came back, looking very radiant.

"What do you think?" said Grace, "I never was more surprised in my life; there really is a cactus, and a night ceres into the bargain. Mrs. Little, behold a penitent. I bring you my apology, and a jardenia."

"Oh, how sweet! Never mind the apology. Quarrel with me often, and bring me a jardenia. I'll always make it up on those terms."

"Miss White," said Grace, pompously, "I shall require a few dozen cuttings from your tree, please tell the gardener. Arrangements are such, I shall have to grow jardenias on a scale hitherto unprecedented."

There was a laugh, and, in the middle of it, a servant announced Miss Carden's carriage.

"What attentive servants you have, Miss White. I requested that man to be on the watch, and, if I said a good thing, to announce my carriage directly; and he did it pat. Now see what an effective exit that gives me. Good-bye, Miss White, good-bye, Mrs. Little; may you all disappear as neatly."

Mr. Coventry stepped smartly forward, and offered her his arm with courteous deference; she took it, and went down with him, but shot over his shoulder a side-glance of reproach at Little, for not being so prompt as his rival.

"What spirits!" said a young lady.

"Yes," said another; "but she was as dull as the grave last time I met her."

So ended that evening, with its little ups and downs.

Soon after this, Henry called on Miss Carden, and spent a heavenly hour with her. He told her his plans for getting on in the world, and she listened with a demure complacency, that seemed to imply she acknowledged a personal interest in his success. She told him she had always *admired* his independence in declining his uncle's offer, and now she was beginning to *approve* it: "It becomes a man," said she.

From the future they went to the past, and she reminded him of the snow-storm and the scene in the church; and, in speaking of it, her eye deepened in color, her voice was low and soft, and she was all tenderness.

If love was not directly spoken, it was constantly implied, and, in fact, that is how true love generally speaks. The eternal "*Je vous aime*" of the French novelist is false to nature, let me tell you.

"And, when I come back from London, I hope your dear mother will give me opportunities of knowing her better."

"She will be delighted: but, going to London!"

"Oh, we spend six weeks in London every year; and this is our time. I was always glad to go, before—London is very gay now, you know—but I am not glad now."

"No more am I, I can assure you. I am very sorry."

"Six weeks will soon pass."

"Six weeks of pain is a good long time. You are the sunshine of my life. And you are going to shine on others, and leave me dark and solitary."

"But how do you know I shall shine on others? Perhaps I shall be duller than you will, and think all the more of Hillsborough, for being in London."

The melting tone in which this was said, and the coy and tender side-glance that accompanied it, were balm of Gilead to the lover.

He took comfort, and asked her, cheerfully, if he might write to her.

She hesitated a single moment, and then said "Yes."

She added, however, after a pause, "But you can't; for you don't know my address."

"But you will tell me."

"Never! never! Fifty-eight Clarges Street."

"When do you go?"

"The day after to-morrow: at 12 o'clock."

"May I see you off at the train?"

She hesitated. "If—you—like," said she, slowly: "but I think you had better not."

"Oh, let me see the last of you."

"Use your own judgment, dear."

The monosyllable slipped out, unintentionally: she was thinking of something else. Yet, as soon as she had uttered it, she said "Oh!" and blushed all over. "I forgot I was not speaking to a lady," said she, innocently: then, right archly, "please forgive me."

He caught her hand, and kissed it devotedly. Then she quivered all over. "You mustn't," said she with the gentlest possible tone of reproach. "Oh dear, I am so sorry I am going." And she turned her sweet eyes on him, with tears in them.

Then a visitor was announced, and they parted.

He was deep in love. He was also, by nature, rather obstinate. Although she had said she thought it would be better for him not to see her off, yet he would go to the station, and see the last of her.

He came straight from the station, to his mother. She was up stairs. He threw himself into a chair, and there she found him, looking ghastly.

"Oh, mother! what shall I do?"

"What is the matter, love?"

"She is false; she is false. She has gone up to London with that Coventry."

APPENDIX.

Extract from Henry Little's Report.

The File-cutters.

"This is the largest trade, containing about three thousand men and several hundred women and boys. Their diseases and deaths arise from poisoning by lead. The file rests on a bed of lead during the process of cutting, which might more correctly be called stamping; and, as the stamping-chisel can only be guided to the required nicety by the finger-nail, the lead is constantly handled and fingered, and enters the system through the pores.

"Besides this, fine dust of lead is set in motion by the blows that drive the cutting-chisel, and the insidious poison settles on the hair and the face, and is believed to go direct to the lungs, some of it.

"The file-cutter never lives the span of life allotted to man. After many small warnings his thumb weakens. He neglects that; and he gets touched of paralysis in the thumb, the arm, and the nerves of the stomach: can't digest: can't sweat; at last, can't work; goes to the hospital: there they galvanize him, which does him no harm; and boil him, which does him a deal of good. He comes back to work, resumes his dirty habits, takes in fresh doses of lead, turns dirty white or sallow, gets a blue line round his teeth, a dropped wrist, and to the hospital again or on to the file-cutters' box; and so he goes miserably on and off, till he drops into a premature grave, with as much lead in his body as would lap a hundredweight of tea."

THE REMEDIES.

"A. *What the masters might do.*

"1. Provide every forge with two small fires, eighteen inches from the ground. This would warm the lower limbs of the smiths. At present their bodies suffer by uneven temperature; they perspire down to the waist, and then freeze to the toe.

"2. For the wet grinders they might supply fires in every wheel, abolish mud floors, and pave with a proper fall and drain.

"To prevent the breaking of heavy grindstones, fit them

with the large strong circular steel plate—of which I subjoin a drawing—instead of with wedges or insufficient plates. They might have an eye to life, as well as capital, in buying heavy grindstones. I have traced the death of one grinder to the master's avarice: he went to the quarry and bought a stone for thirty-five shillings the quarry-master had set aside as imperfect; its price would have been sixty shillings if it had been fit to trust a man's life to. This master goes to church twice a Sunday, and is much respected by his own sort: yet he committed a murder for twenty-five shillings. Being Hillsborough, let us hope it was a murderer he murdered.

"For the dry-grinders they might all supply fans and boxes. Some do, and the good effect is very remarkable. Moreover the present fans and boxes could be much improved.

"One trade—the steel-fork grinders—is considerably worse than the rest; and although the fan does much for it, I'm told it must still remain an unhealthy trade. If so, and Dr. Amboyne is right about Life, Labor, and Capital, let the masters co-operate with the Legislature, and extinguish the handicraft.

"For the file-cutters, the masters might—

"1st. Try a substitute for lead. It is all very well to say a file must rest on lead to be cut. Who has ever employed brains on that question? Who has tried iron, wood, and gutta-percha, in layers? Who has ever tried any thing, least of all the thing called Thought?

"2d. If lead is the only bed—which I doubt, and the lead must be bare—which I dispute, then the master ought to supply every gang of file-cutters with hooks, taps, and basins and soap, in some place adjoining their work-rooms. Lead is a subtle, but not a swift, poison; and soap and water every two hours is an antidote.

"3d. They ought to forbid the introduction of food into file-cutting rooms. Workmen are a reckless set, and a dirty set; food has no business in any place of theirs, where poison is going.

"*B. What the workmen might do.*

"1st. Demand from the masters these improvements I have suggested, and, if the demand came through the secretaries of their Unions, the masters would comply.

"2d. They might drink less and wash their bodies with a small part of the money so saved: the price of a gill of gin and a hot bath are exactly the same; only the bath is health to a dry-grinder, or file-cutter; the gin is worse poison to him than to healthy men.

"3d. The small wet-grinders, who have to buy their grindstones, might buy sound ones, instead of making bargains at the quarry, which prove double bad bargains when the stone breaks, since then a new stone is required, and sometimes a new man, too.

"4th. They might be more careful not to leave the grindstone in water. I have traced three broken stones in one wheel to that abominable piece of carelessness.

"5th. They ought never to fix an under-sized pulley-wheel. Simmons killed himself by that, and by grudging the few hours of labor required to hang and race a sound stone.

"6th. If files can only be cut on lead, the file-cutters might anoint the lead over night with a hard-drying ointment, soluble in turps, and this ointment might even be medicated with an antidote to the salt of lead.

"7th. If files can only be cut on *bare* lead, the men ought to cut their hair close, and wear a light cap at work. They ought to have a canvas suit in the adjoining place (see above); don it when they come, and doff it when they go. They ought to leave off their insane habit of licking the thumb and finger of the left hand—which is the leaded hand—with their tongues. This beastly trick takes the poison direct to the stomach. They might surely leave it to get there through the pores; it is slow, but sure. I have also repeatedly seen a file-cutter eat his dinner with his filthy poisoned fingers, and so send the poison home by way of salt to a fool's bacon. Finally, they ought to wash off the poison every two hours at the taps.

"8th. Since they abuse the masters, and justly, for their greediness, they ought not to imitate that greediness by driving their poor little children into unhealthy trades, and so destroying them body and soul. This practice robs the children of education at the very seed-time of life, and literally murders many of them; for their soft and porous skins, and growing organs, take in all poisons and disorders quicker than an adult."

"*C. What the Legislature might do.*

"It might issue a commission to examine the Hillsborough trades, and, when accurately informed, might put some practical restraints both on the murder and the suicide that are going on at present. A few of the suggestions I have thrown out might, I think, be made law.

"For instance, the master who should set a dry-grinder to a trough without a fan, or put his wet-grinders on a mud floor and no fire, or his file-cutters in a room without taps and basins, or who should be convicted of willfully buying a faulty grindstone, might be made subject to a severe penalty; and the municipal authorities invested with rights of inspection, and encouraged to report.

"In restraint of the workmen, the Legislature ought to extend the Factory Acts to Hillsborough trades, and so check the heartless avarice of the parents. At present, no class of her Majesty's subjects cries so loud, and so vainly, to her motherly bosom, and the humanity of Parliament, as these poor little children; their parents, the lowest and most degraded set of brutes in England, teach them swearing and indecency at home, and rob them of all decent education, and drive them to their death, in order to squeeze a few shillings out of their young lives; for what?—to waste in drink and debauchery. Count the public houses in this town.

"As to the fork-grinding trade, the Legislature might assist the masters to extinguish it. It numbers only about one hundred and fifty persons, all much poisoned, and little paid. The work could all be done by fifteen machines and thirty hands, and, in my opinion, without the expense of grindstones. The thirty men would get double wages: the odd hundred and twenty would, of course, be driven into other trades, after suffering much distress. And, on this account, I would call in Parliament, because then there would be a temporary compensation offered to the temporary sufferers by a far-sighted and beneficent measure. Besides, without Parliament, I am afraid the masters could not do it. The fork-grinders would blow up the machines, and the men who worked them, and their wives and their children, and their lodgers, and their lodgers' visitors.

"For all that, if your theory of Life, Labor, and Capital is true, all incurably destructive handicrafts ought to give way to machinery, and will, as Man advances."

CHAPTER XXIII.

"WHAT! eloped?"

"Heaven forbid! Why, mother, I didn't say she was alone with him; her father was of the party."

"Then surely you are distressing yourself more than you need. She goes to London with her papa, and Mr. Coventry happens to go up the same day; that is really all."

"Oh, but, mother, it was no accident. I watched his face, and there was no surprise when he came up with his luggage and saw her."

Mrs. Little pondered for a minute, and then said, "I dare say all her friends knew she was going up to London to-day; and Mr. Coventry determined to go up the same day. Why, he is courting her: my dear Henry, you knew before to-day that you had a rival, and a determined one. If you go and blame her for his acts, it will be apt to end in his defeating you."

"Will it? Then I won't blame her at all."

"You had better not till you are quite sure: it is one way of losing a high-spirited girl."

"I tell you I won't. Mother!"

"Well, dear?"

"When I asked leave to come to the station and see her off, she seemed put out."

"Did she forbid you?"

"No; but she did not like it somehow. Ah, she knew beforehand that Coventry would be there."

"Gently, gently! She might think it possible, and yet not know it. More likely it was on account of her father. You have never told him that you love his daughter?"

"No."

"And he is rather mercenary: perhaps that is too strong a word; but, in short, a mere man of the world. Might it not be that Grace Carden would wish him to learn your attachment either from your lips, or from her own, and not detect it in an impetuous young man's conduct on the platform of a railway, at the tender hour of parting?"

"Oh, how wise you are, and what an insight you have got! Your words are balm. But, there—he is with her for ever so long, and I am here all alone."

"Not quite alone, love; your counsellor is by your side, and may, perhaps, show you how to turn this to your advantage. You write to her every day, and then the postman will be a powerful rival to Mr. Coventry, perhaps a more powerful one than Mr. Coventry to you."

Acting on this advice, Henry wrote every day to Grace Carden. She was not so constant in her replies; but she did write to him now and then, and her letters breathed a gentle affection that allayed his jealousy, and made this period of separation the happiest six weeks he had ever known. As for Grace, about three o'clock she used to look out for the postman, and be uneasy and restless if he was late, and, when his knock came, her heart would bound, and she generally flew up stairs with the prize, to devour it in secret. She fed her heart full with these letters, and loved the writer better and better. For once the present suitor lost ground, and the absent suitor gained it. Mrs. Little divined as much from Grace's letters and messages to herself; and she said, with a smile, "You see 'Les absents n'ont pas toujours tort.'"

CHAPTER XXIV.

I MUST now deal briefly with a distinct vein of incidents, that occurred between young Little's first becoming a master and the return of the Cardens from London.

Little, as a master, acted up to the philanthropic theories he had put forth when a workman.

The wet-grinders in his employ submitted to his improved plates, his paved and drained floor, and cosy fires, without a murmur or a word of thanks. By degrees they even found out they were more comfortable than other persons in their condition, and congratulated themselves upon it.

The dry-grinders consented, some of them, to profit by his improved fans. Others would not take the trouble to put the fans in gear, and would rather go on inhaling metal-dust and stone-grit.

Henry reasoned, but in vain; remonstrated, but with little success. Then he discharged a couple: they retired with mien of martyrs; and their successors were admitted on a written agreement that left them no option. The fan triumphed.

The file-cutters were more troublesome; they clung to death and disease, like limpets to established rocks; they would not try any other bed than bare lead, and they would not wash at the taps Little had provided; and they would smuggle in dinners and eat with poisoned hands.

Little reasoned, and remonstrated, but with such very trifling success, that, at last, he had to put down the iron heel; he gave the file-cutters a printed card, with warning to leave on one side, and his reasons on the other.

In twenty-four hours he received a polite remonstrance from the secretary of the File-cutters' Union.

He replied that the men could remain, if they would sign an agreement to forego certain suicidal practices, and to pay fines in case of disobedience; said fines to be deducted from their earnings.

Then the secretary suggested a conference at the "Cutler's Arms." Little assented; and there was a hot argument. The father of all file-cutters objected to tyranny and innovation: Little maintained that Innovation was nearly always Improvement,—the world being silly,—and was manifestly improvement in the case under consideration. He said also he was merely doing what the Union itself ought to do: protecting the life of Union men who were too childish and wrong-headed to protect it themselves."

"We prefer a short life, and a merry one, Mr. Little," said the father of all file-cutters.

"A life of disease is not a merry one: slow poisoning is not a pleasant way of living, but a miserable way of dying. None but the healthy are happy. Many a Crœsus would give half his fortune for a poor man's stomach; yet you want your cutlers to be sick men all their days, and not gain a shilling by it. Man alive, I am not trying to lower their wages."

"Ay, but you are going the way to do it."

"How do you make that out?"

"The trade is full already; and, if you force the men to live to three score and ten, you will overcrowd it so, they will come to starvation wages."

Little was staggered at this thunderbolt of logic, and digested the matter in silence for a moment. Then he remembered something that had fallen from Dr. Amboyne; and he turned to Grotait. "What do you say to that, sir? would you grind Death's scythe for him (at the list price) to thin the labor-market?"

Grotait hesitated for once. In his heart he went with the file-cutter: but his understanding encumbered him.

"Starvation," said he, "is as miserable a death as poisoning. But why make a large question out of a small one, with rushing into generalities? I really think you might let Mr. Little settle this matter with the individual workmen. He has got a little factory, and a little crotchet; he chooses to lengthen the lives of six file-cutters. He says to them, 'My money is my own, and I'll give you so much of it, in return for so much work plus so much washing and other novelties.' The question is, does his pay cover the new labor of washing, etc., as well as the old?"

"Mr. Grotait, I pay the highest price that is going."

"In that case, I think the Unions are not bound to recognize the discussion. Mr. Little, I have some other reasons to lay before my good friend here, and I hope to convince him. Now, there's a little party of us going to dine to-morrow at 'Savage's Hotel,' up by the new reservoir; give us the pleasure of your company, will you? and, by that time, perhaps I may have smoothed this little matter for you." Little thanked him, accepted the invitation, and left the pair of secretaries together.

When he was gone, Grotait represented that public opinion would go with Little on this question; and the outrages he had sustained would be all ripped up by the *Hillsborough Liberal*, and the two topics combined in an ugly way; and all for what?—to thwart a good-hearted young fellow in a philanthropical crotchet, which, after all, did him honor, and would never be imitated by any other master in Hillsborough. And so, for once, this Machiavel sided with Henry, not from the purest motives, yet, mind you, not without a certain mixture of right feeling and humanity.

On the Sunday Henry dined with him and his party, at "Savage's Hotel," and the said dinner rather surprised Henry; the meats were simple, but of good quality, and the wines, which were all brought out by Grotait, were excellent. That Old Saw, who retailed ale and spirits to his customers, would serve nothing less to his guests than champagne and burgundy. And, if the cheer was generous, the host was admirable; he showed, at the head of his genial board, those qualities which, coupled with his fanaticism, had made him the Doge of the Hillsborough trades. He was primed on every subject that could interest his guests, and knew something about nearly every thing else. He kept the ball always going, but did not monologuize, except when he was appealed to as a judge, and then did it with a mellow grace that no man can learn without Nature's aid. There is no society, however distinguished, in which Grotait would not have been accepted as a polished and admirable converser.

Add to this that he had an art, which was never quite common, but is now becoming rare, of making his guests feel his friends—for the time, at all events.

Young Little sat amazed, and drank in his words with delight, and could not realize that this genial philosopher was the person who had launched a band of ruffians at him. Yet, in his secret heart, he could not doubt it: and so he looked and listened with a marvellous mixture of feelings, on which one could easily write pages of analysis, very curious, and equally tedious.

They dined at three; and, at five, they got up, as agreed beforehand, and went to inspect the reservoir in course of construction. A more compendious work of art was never projected: the contractors had taken for their basis a mountain gorge, with a stream flowing through it down towards Hillsborough; all they had to do was to throw an embankment across the lower end of the gorge, and turn it to a mighty basin open to receive the stream, and the drainage from four thousand acres of hill. From this lake a sixty-foot weir was to deal out the water-supply to the mill-owners below, and the surplus to the people of Hillsborough, distant about eight miles on an easy decline.

Now, as the reservoir must be full at starting, and would then be eighty feet deep in the centre, and a mile long, and a quarter of a mile broad, on the average, an embankment of uncommon strength was required to restrain so great a mass of water; and this was what the Hillsborough worthies were curious about. They strolled out to the works, and then tea was to come out after them, the weather being warm and fine. Close to the works they found a foreman of engineers smoking his pipe, and interrogated him. He showed them a rising wall, five hundred feet wide at the base, and told them it was to be ninety feet high, narrowing, gradually, to a summit twelve feet broad. As the whole embankment was to be twelve hundred feet long at the top, this gave some idea of the bulk of the materials to be used: those materials were clay, shale, mill-stone, and sandstone of looser texture. The engineer knew Grotait, and brought him a drawing of the mighty cone to be erected. "Why, it will be a mountain!" said Little.

"No far from that, sir: and yet you'll never see half the work. Why, we had an army of navvies on it last autumn, and laid a foundation sixty feet deep; and these first courses are all bonded in to the foundation, and bonded together, as you see. We are down to solid rock, and no water can get to undermine us. The puddle wall is sixteen feet wide at starting, and diminishes to four feet at the top: so no water can creep in through our jacket."

"But what are these apertures?" inquired Grotait.

"Oh, those are the waste-pipes. They pass through the embankment obliquely, to the weir-dam: they can be opened, or shut, by valves, and run off ten thousand cubic feet of water a minute."

"But won't that prove a hole in your armor? Why, these pipes must be in twenty joints, at least."

"Say fifty-five; you'll be nearer the mark."

"And suppose one or two of these fifty-five joints should leak? You'll have an everlasting solvent in the heart of your pile, and you can't get at them, you know, to mend them."

"Of course not; but they are double as thick as ever were used before; and have been severely tested before laying 'em down: besides, don't you see each of them has got his great-coat on? eighteen inches of puddle all the way."

"Ah," said Grotait, "all the better. But it is astonishing what big embankments will sometimes burst if a leaky pipe runs through them. I don't think it is the water, altogether; the water seems to make air inside them, and that proves as bad for them as wind in a man's stomach."

"Governor," said the engineer, "don't you

let bees swarm in your bonnet. Ousely reservoir will last as long as them hills there."

"No doubt, lad, since thou's had a hand in making it."

The laugh this dry rejoinder caused was interrupted by the waitress bringing out tea; and these Hillsborough worthies felt bound to chaff her; but she, being Yorkshire too, gave them as good as they brought, and a trifle to spare.

Tea was followed by brandy-and-water and pipes: and these came out in such rapid succession, that when Grotait drove Little and two others home, his utterance was thick, and his speech sententious.

Little found Bayne waiting for him, with the news that he had left Mr. Cheetham.

"How was that?"

"Oh, fell between two stools. Tried to smooth matters between Cheetham and the hands: but Cheetham, he wants a manager to side with him through thick and thin; and the men want one to side with them. He has sacked me, and the men are glad I'm going: and this comes of loving peace, when the world hates it."

"And I am glad of it, for now you are my foreman. I know what you are worth, if those fools don't."

"Are you in earnest, Little?"

"Why not?"

"I hear you have been dining with Grotait, and he always makes the liquor fly. Wait till to-morrow. Talk it over with Mrs. Little here. I'm afraid I'm not the right sort for a servant. Too fond of 'the balmy,' and averse to the whole hog." (The poor fellow was quite discouraged.)

"The very man I want to soothe me at odd times: they rile me so with their suicidal folly. Now, look here, old fellow, if you don't come to me, I'll give you a good hiding."

"Oh! well, sooner than you should break the peace—. Mrs. Little, I'd rather be with him at two guineas a week, than with any other master at three."

When he had got this honest fellow to look after his interests, young Little gave more way than ever to his natural bent for invention, and he was often locked up for twelve hours at a stretch, in a room he called his studio. Indeed, such was his ardor, that he sometimes left home after dinner, and came back to the works, and then the fitful fire of his forge might be seen, and the blows of his hammer heard, long after midnight.

Dr. Amboyne encouraged him in this, and was, indeed, the only person admitted to his said studio. There the Democritus of Hillsborough often sat and smoked his cigar, and watched the progress towards perfection of projected inventions great and small.

One day the Doctor called and asked Bayne whether Henry was in his studio. Bayne said no; he thought he had seen him in the saw-grinder's hull. "And that struck me; for it is not often his lordship condescends to go there now."

"Let us see what 'his lordship' is at."

They approached stealthily, and, looking through a window, saw the inventor standing with his arms folded, and his eyes bent on a grinder at his work: the man was pressing down a six-feet saw on a grindstone with all his might; and Little was looking on, with a face compounded of pity, contempt, and lofty contemplation.

"That is the game now, sir," whispered Bayne: "always in the clouds, or else above 'em. A penny for your thoughts, sir!"

Henry started, as men do who are roused from deep contemplation; however, he soon recovered himself, and, with a sort of rude wit of his own, he held out his hand for the penny.

Amboyne fumbled in his pocket, and gave him a stamp.

Little seized it, and delivered himself as follows: "My thoughts, gentlemen, were general and particular. I was making a reflection how contented people are to go bungling on, doing a thing the wrong way, when the right way is obvious: and my particular observation was—that these long saws are ground in a way which offends the grammar of mechanics. Here's a piece of steel six feet long, but not so wide as the grindstone: what can be plainer than that such a strip ought to be ground lengthwise? then the whole saw would receive the grindstone in a few seconds. Instead of that, on they go, year after year, grinding them obliquely, and with a violent exertion that horrifies a fellow like me, who goes in for economy of labor, and have done all my life. Look at that fellow working. What a waste of muscle! Now, if you will come to my studio, I think I can show you how long saws *will* be ground in the days of civilization."

His eye, which had been turned inward during his reverie, dullish and somewhat fish-like, now sparkled like a hot-coal, and he led the way eagerly.

"Pray humor him, sir," said Bayne, compassionately.

They followed him up a horrid stair, and entered his studio; and a marvellous place it was: a forge on one side, a carpenter's bench and turning-lathe on the other; and the floor so crowded with models, castings, and that profusion of new ideas in material form which housewives call litter, that the artist had been obliged to cut three little ramified paths, a foot wide, and so meander about the room, as struggles a wasp over spilt glue.

He gave the Doctor the one chair, and wriggled down a path after pencil and paper: he jumped with them, like a cat with a mouse, on to the carpenter's bench, and was soon absorbed in drawing.

When he had drawn a bit, he tore up the paper, and said, "Let me think."

"The request is unusual," said Dr. Amboyne; "however, if you will let us smoke, we will let you think."

No reply from the inventor, whose eye was already turned inward, and fish-like again.

Dr. Amboyne and Bayne smoked peaceably awhile. But presently the inventor uttered a kind of shout.

"Eureka," said the Doctor calmly, and emitted a curly cloud.

Little dashed at the paper, and soon produced a drawing. It represented two grindstones set apparently to grind each other, a large one below, a small one above.

"There—the large stone shall revolve rapidly, say from north to south; the small one from south to north: that is the idea which has just struck me, and completes the invention. It is to be worked, not by one grinder, but two. A stands south, and passes the saw northward between the two grindstones to B. The stones must be hung, so as just to allow the passage of the saw. B draws it out, and reverses it, and passes it back to A. Those two journeys of the saw will grind the whole length of it for a breadth of two or three inches, and all in forty seconds. Now do you see what I meant by the grammar of mechanics? It was the false grammar of those duffers, grinding a long thing sideways instead of lengthways, that struck my mind first. And now see what one gets to at last if one starts from grammar. By this machine two men can easily grind as many big saws as twenty men could grind on single stones: and instead of all that heavy, coarse labor, and dirt, and splashing, my two men shall do the work as quietly and as easily as two printers, one feeding a machine with paper, and his mate drawing out the printed sheet at the other end."

"By Jove," said Dr. Amboyne, "I believe this is a great idea. What do you say, Mr. Bayne?"

"Well, sir, a servant mustn't always say his mind."

"Servant be hanged!" said Little. "That for a friend who does not speak his mind."

"Well, then, gentlemen, it is the most simple and beautiful contrivance I ever saw. And there's only one thing to be done with it."

"Patent it?"

"No; hide it; lock it up in your own breast, and try and forget it. Your life won't be worth a week's purchase, if you set up that machine in Hillsborough."

"Hillsborough is not all the world. I can take it to some free country—America or—Russia; there's a fortune in it. Stop; suppose I was to patent it at home and abroad, and then work it in the United States and the Canadas. That would force the invention upon this country, by degrees."

"Yes, and then, if you sell the English patent and insure the purchaser's life, you may turn a few thousands, and keep a whole skin yourself."

Little assured Bayne he had no intention of running his head against the Saw-grinders' Union. "We are very comfortable as it is, and I value my life more than I used to do."

"I think I know why," said Doctor Amboyne. "But, whatever you do, patent your invention. Patent them all."

Henry promised he would; but soon forgot his promise, and, having tasted blood, so to speak, was soon deep in a far more intricate puzzle, viz., how to grind large circular saws by machinery. This problem, and his steel railway clip, which was to displace the present system of fastening down the rails, absorbed him so, that he became abstracted in the very streets, and did not see his friends when they passed.

One day, when he was deeply engaged in his studio, Bayne tapped at the door, and asked to speak to him.

"Well, what is it?" said the inventor, rather peevishly.

"Oh, nothing," said Bayne, with a bitter air of mock resignation. "Only a cloud on the peaceful horizon; that is all. A letter from Mary Anne."

"Sir,—Four of your saws are behindhand with their contributions, and, being deaf to remonstrance, I am obliged to apply to you, to use your influence. MARY ANNE."

"Well," said Henry, "Mary Anne is in the right. Confound their dishonesty: they take the immense advantages the Saw-grinders' Union gives them, yet they won't pay the weekly contribution, without which the Union can't exist. Go and find out who they are, and blow them up."

"What! me disturb the balmy?"

"Bother the balmy! I can't be worried with such trifles. I'm inventing."

"But, Mr. Little, would not the best way be for you just to stop it quietly and peaceably out of their pay, and send it to Grotait?"

Little, after a moment's reflection, said he had no legal right to do that. Besides, it was not his business to work the Saw-grinders' Union for Grotait. "Who is this Mary Anne?"

"The saw-grinders, to be sure."

"What, all of them? Poor Mary Anne!"

He then inquired how he was to write back to her.

"Oh, write under cover to Grotait. He is Mary Anne, to all intents and purposes."

"Well, write the jade a curt note, in both our names, and say we disapprove the conduct of the defaulters, and will signify our disapproval to them; but that is all we can do."

This letter was written, and Bayne made it as oleaginous as language permits; and there the matter rested apparently.

But, as usual, after the polite came the phonetic. Next week Henry got a letter thus worded:—

"MISTER LITL,—If them grinders of yores dosent send their money i shall com an' fech strings if the devil stans i t' road.
"MOONRAKER."

Mr. Little tossed this epistle contemptuously into the fire, and invented on.

Two days after that he came to the works, and found the saw-grinders standing in a group, with their hands in their pockets.

"Well, lads, what's up?"

"Mary Anne has been here."

"And two pair of wheel-bands gone."

"Well, men, you know whose fault it is."

"Nay, but it is —— hard my work should be stopped because another man is in arrears with trade. What d'ye think to do, Governor? buy some more bands?"

"Certainly not. I won't pay for your fault. It is a just claim, you know. Settle it among yourselves."

With this, he retired to his studio.

When the men saw he did not care a button whether his grindstones revolved or not, they soon brought the defaulters to book. Bayne was sent up stairs, to beg Mr. Little to advance the trade contributions, and stop the amount from the defaulters' wages.

This being settled, Little and Bayne went to the "Cutlers' Arms," and Bayne addressed the barmaid thus, "Can we see Mary Anne?"

"He is shaving."

"Well, when she is shaved, we shall be in the parlor, tell her."

In a moment or two Grotait bustled in, wiping his face with a towel as he came, and welcomed his visitors cordially. "Fine weather, gentlemen."

Bayne cut that short. "Mr. Grotait, we have lost our bands."

"You surprise me."

"And perhaps you can tell us how to get them back."

"Experience teaches that they always come back when the men pay their arrears."

"Well, it is agreed to stop the sum due, out of wages."

"A very proper course."

"What is it we have got to pay?"

"How can I tell without book? Pray, Mr. Little, don't imagine that I set these matters agate. All I do is to mediate afterwards. I'll go and look at the contribution-book."

He went out, and soon returned, and told them it was one sovereign contribution for each man, and five shillings each for Mary Anne.

"What, for her services in rattening us?" said Little, dryly.

"And her risk," suggested Grotait, in dulcet tones.

Little paid the five pounds, and then asked Grotait for the bands.

"Good heavens, Mr. Little, do you think I have got your bands?"

"You must excuse Mr. Little, sir," said Bayne. "He is a stranger, and doesn't know the comedy. Perhaps you will oblige us with a note where we can find them."

"Hum!" said Grotait, with the air of one suddenly illuminated. "What did I hear somebody say about these bands? Hum! Give me an hour or two to make inquiries."

"Don't say an hour or two, sir, when the men have got to make up lost time. We will give you a little grace; we will take a walk down street, and perhaps it will come to your recollection."

"Hum!" said Grotait; and as that was clearly all they were to get out of him just then, they left and took a walk.

In half an hour they came back again, and sat down in the parlor.

Grotait soon joined them. "I've been thinking," said he, "what a pity it is we can't come to some friendly arrangement with intelligent masters, like Mr. Little, to deduct the natty money every week from the men's wages."

"Excuse me," said Bayne, "we are not here for discussion. We want our bands."

"Do you doubt that you will get them, sir? Did ever I break faith with master or man?"

"No, no," said the pacific Bayne, alarmed at the sudden sternness of his tone. "You are as square as a die—when you get it all your own way. Why, Mr. Little, Cheetham's bands were taken one day, and, when he had made the men pay their arrears, he was directed where to find the bands; but, meantime, somebody out of trade had found them, and stolen them. Down came bran-new bands to the wheel directly, and better than we had lost. And my cousin Godby, that has a water-wheel, was rattened, by his scythe-blades being flung in the dam. He squared with Mary Anne, and then he got a letter to say where the blades were. But one was missing. He complained to Mr. Grotait here, and Mr. Grotait put his hand in his pocket directly, and paid the trade-price of the blade—three shillings, I think it was."

"Yes," said Grotait; "'but,' I remember I said at the time, 'you must not construe this that I was any way connected with the rattening.' But some are deaf to reason. Hallo!"

"What is the matter, sir?"

"Why, what is that in the fender? Your eyes are younger than mine."

And Mr. Grotait put up his gold double eye-glass, and looked, with marked surprise and curiosity, at a note that lay in the fender.

Mr. Bayne had been present at similar comedies, and was not polite enough to endorse Mr. Grotait's surprise. He said, coolly, "It will be the identical note we are waiting for." He stooped down and took it out of the fender, and read it.

"'*To* MR. LITTLE, *or* MR. BAYNE.

"'GENTLEMEN,—In the bottom hull turn up the horsing, and in the trough all the missing bands will be found. Apologizing for the little interruption, it is satisfactory things are all arranged without damage, and hope all will go agreeably when the rough edge is worn off. Trusting these nocturnal visits will be no longer necessary, I remain,   'THE SHY MAIDEN.'"

As soon as he had obtained this information, Bayne bustled off; but Mary Anne detained Henry Little, to moralize.

Said she, "This rattening for trade contributions is the result of bad and partial laws. If A contracts with B, and breaks his contract, B has no need to ratten A: he can sue him. But if A, being a workman, contracts with B and all the other letters, and breaks his contract, B and all the other letters have no legal remedy. This bad and partial law, occurring in a country that has tasted impartial laws, revolts common sense and the consciences of men. Whenever this sort of thing occurs in any civilized country, up starts that pioneer judge we call Judge Lynch; in other words, private men combine, and make their own laws, to cure the folly of legislatures. And, mark me, if these irregular laws are unjust, they fail; if they are just, they stand. Rattening could never have stood its ground so many years in Hillsborough, if it had not been just, and necessary to the place, under the partial and iniquitous laws of Great Britain."

"And pray," inquired Little, "where is the justice of taking a master's gear because his paid workman is in your debt?"

"And where is the justice of taking a lodger's goods in execution for the house-tenant's debt, which debt the said lodger is helping the said tenant to pay? We must do the best we can. No master is rattened for a workman's fault without several warnings. But the masters will never co-operate with justice till their bands and screws go. That wakes them up directly."

"Well, Mr. Grotait, I never knew you worsted in an argument: and this nut is too hard for my teeth, so I'm off to my work. Ratten me now and then for your own people's fault, if you are *quite* sure justice and public opinion demand it; but no more gunpowder, please."

"Heaven forbid, Mr. Little. Gunpowder! I abhor it."

CHAPTER XXV.

THERE came a delightful letter from Grace Carden, announcing her return on a certain evening, and hoping to see Henry next morning.

He called accordingly, and was received with outstretched hands, and sparkling eyes, and words that repaid him for her absence.

After the first joyful burst, she inquired tenderly why he was so pale: had he been ill?

"No."

"No trouble nor anxiety, dear?"

"A little, at first, till your sweet letters made me happy. No; I did not even know that I was pale. Overstudy, I suppose. Inventing is hard work."

"What are you inventing?"

"All manner of things. Machine to forge large axes; another to grind circular saws; a railway clip: but you don't care about such things."

"I beg your pardon, sir. I care about whatever interests you."

"Well, these inventions interest me very much. One way or other, they are roads to fortune; and you know why I desire fortune."

"Ah, that I do. But excuse me, you value independence more. Oh, I respect you for it. Only don't make yourself pale, or you will make me unhappy, and a foe to invention."

On this Mr. Little made himself red instead of pale, and beamed with happiness.

They spent a delightful hour together, and, even when they parted, their eyes lingered on each other.

Soon after this the Cardens gave a dinner-party, and Grace asked if she might invite Mrs. Little and Mr. Little.

"What, is he presentable?"

"More than that," said Grace, coloring. "They are both very superior to most of our Hillsborough friends."

"Well, but did you not tell me he had quarrelled with Mr. Raby?"

"No, not quarrelled. Mr. Raby offered to make him his heir: but he chooses to be independent, and make his own fortune, that's all."

"Well, if you think our old friend would not take it amiss, invite them by all means. I remember her a lovely woman."

So the Littles were invited; and the young ladies admired Mr. Little on the whole, but sneered at him a little for gazing on Miss Carden, as if she was a divinity: the secret, which escaped the father, girls of seventeen detected in a minute, and sat whispering over it in the drawing-room.

After this invitation, Henry and his mother called, and then Grace called on Mrs. Little; and this was a great step for Henry, the more so as the ladies really took to each other.

The course of true love was beginning to run smooth, when it was disturbed by Mr. Coventry. That gentleman's hopes had revived in London; Grace Carden had been very kind and friendly to him, and always in such good spirits, that he thought absence had cured her of Little, and his turn was come again. The most experienced men sometimes mistake a woman in this way. The real fact was that Grace, being happy herself, thanks to a daily letter from the man she adored, had not the heart to be unkind to another, whose only fault was loving her, and to whom she feared she had not behaved very well. However, Mr. Coventry did mistake her. He was detained in town, by business: but he wrote Mr. Carden a charming letter, and proposed formally for his daughter's hand.

Mr. Carden had seen the proposal coming this year and more; so he was not surprised; but he was gratified. The letter was put into his hand while he was dressing for dinner. Of course he did not open the subject before the servants: but, as soon as they had retired, he said, "Grace, I want your attention on a matter of importance."

Grace stared a little, but said faintly, "Yes, papa," and all manner of vague maidenly misgivings crowded through her brain.

"My child, you are my only one, and the joy of the house; and need I say I shall feel your loss bitterly whenever your time comes to leave me?"

"Then I never will leave you," cried Grace, and came and wreathed her arms round his neck.

He kissed her, and parting her hair, looked with parental fondness at her white brow, and her deep clear eyes.

"You shall never leave me, for the worse," said he: "but you are sure to marry some day, and therefore it is my duty to look favorably on a downright good match. Well, my dear, such a match offers itself. I have a proposal for you."

"I am sorry to hear it."

"Wait till you hear who it is. It is Mr. Coventry, of Bollinghope."

Grace sighed, and looked very uncomfortable.

"Why, what is the matter? you always used to like him."

"So I do now; but not for a husband."

"I see no one to whom I could resign you so willingly. He is well born and connected, has a good estate, not too far from your poor father."

"Dear papa!"

"He speaks pure English: now these Hillsborough manufacturers, with their provincial twang, are hardly presentable in London society."

"Dear papa, Mr. Coventry is an accomplished gentleman, who has done me the highest honor he can. You must decline him very politely: but, between ourselves, I am a little angry with him, because he knows I do not love him; and I am afraid he has made this offer to you, thinking you might be tempted to constrain my affections: but you won't do that, my own papa, will you? you will not make your child unhappy, who loves you?"

"No, no. I will never let you make an imprudent match; but I won't force you into a good one."

"And you know I shall never marry without your consent, papa. But I'm only nineteen, and I don't want to be driven away to Bollinghope."

"And I'm sure I don't want to drive you away anywhere. Mine will be a dull, miserable home without you. Only please tell me what to say to him."

"Oh, I leave that to you. I have often admired the way you soften your refusals. 'Le seigneur Jupiter sait dorer la pillule'—there, that's Molière."

"Well, I suppose I must say—"

"Let me see what he says first."

She scanned the letter closely, to see whether there was any thing that could point to Henry Little. But there was not a word to indicate he feared a rival, though the letter was any thing but presumptuous.

Then Grace coaxed her father, and told him she feared her inexperience had made her indiscreet. She had liked Mr. Coventry's conversation, and perhaps had, inadvertently, given him more encouragement than she intended : would he be a good, kind papa, and get her out of the scrape, as creditably as he could ? She relied on his superior wisdom. So then he kissed her, and said he would do his best.

He wrote a kind, smooth letter, gilding and double-gilding the pill. He said, amongst the rest, that there appeared to be no ground of refusal, except a strong disinclination to enter the wedded state. "I believe there is no one she likes as well as you; and, as for myself, I know no gentleman to whom I would so gladly confide my daughter's happiness," etc., etc.

He handed this letter to his daughter to read, but she refused. "I have implicit confidence in you," said she.

Mr. Coventry acknowledged receipt of the letter, thanked Mr. Carden for the kind and feeling way in which he had inflicted the wound, and said that he had a verbal communication to make before he could quite drop the matter; would be down in about a fortnight.

Soon after this Grace dined with Mrs. Little : and, the week after that, Henry contrived to meet her at a ball, and, after waiting patiently some time, he waltzed with her.

This waltz was another era in their love. It was an inspired whirl of two lovers, whose feet hardly felt the ground, and whose hearts bounded and thrilled, and their cheeks glowed, and their eyes shot fire ; and when Grace was obliged to stop, because the others stopped, her elastic and tense frame turned supple and soft directly, and she still let her eyes linger on his, and her hand nestle in his a moment : this, and a faint sigh of pleasure and tenderness, revealed how sweet her partner was to her.

Need I say the first waltz was not the last ? and that evening they were more in love than ever, if possible.

Mr. Coventry came down from London, and, late that evening, he and Mr. Carden met at the Club.

Mr. Carden found him in an arm-chair, looking careworn and unhappy, and felt quite sorry for him. He hardly knew what to say to him ; but Coventry with his usual grace relieved him ; he rose, and shook hands, and even pressed Mr. Carden's hand, and held it.

Mr. Carden was so touched, that he pressed his hand in return, and said, "Courage! my poor fellow ; the case is not desperate, you know."

Mr. Coventry shook his head, and sat down. Mr. Carden sat down beside him.

"Why, Coventry, it is not as if there was another attachment."

"There is another attachment; at least I have too much reason to fear so. But you shall judge for yourself. I have long paid my respectful addresses to Miss Carden, and I may say without vanity that she used to distinguish me beyond her other admirers ; I was not the only one who thought so ; Mr. Raby has seen us together, and he asked me to meet her at Raby Hall. There I became more particular in my attentions, and those attentions, sir, were well received."

"But were they *understood* ? that is the question."

"Understood and received, upon my honor."

"Then she will marry you, soon or late : for I'm sure there is no other man. Grace was never deceitful."

"All women are deceitful."

"Oh, come !"

"Let me explain : all women, worthy of the name, are cowards ; and cowardice drives them to deceit, even against their will. Pray hear me to an end. On the fifth of last December, I took Miss Carden to the top of Cairnhope hill. I showed her Bollinghope in the valley, and asked her to be its mistress."

"And what did she say ? Yes, or no ?"

"She made certain faint objections, such as a sweet, modest girl like her makes as a matter of course, and then she yielded."

"What ! consented to be your wife ?"

"Not in those very words ; but she said she esteemed me, and she knew I loved her ; and, when I asked her whether I might speak to you, she said ' Yes.' "

"But that was as good as accepting you."

"I am glad you agree with me. You know, Mr. Carden, thousands have been accepted in that very form. Well, sir, the next thing was we were caught in that cursed snow-storm."

"Yes, she has told me all about that."

"Not all, I suspect. We got separated for a few minutes, and I found her in an old ruined church, where a sort of blacksmith was working at his forge. I found her, sir, I might say almost in the blacksmith's arms. I thought little of that at first : any man has a right to succor any woman in distress : but, sir, I discovered that Miss Carden and this man were acquaintances : and, by degrees, I found, to my horror, that he had a terrible power over her."

"What do you mean, sir ? Do you intend to affront us ?"

"No. And, if the truth gives you pain, pray remember it gives me agony. However, I must tell you the man was not what he looked, a mere blacksmith ; he is a sort of Proteus, who can take all manner of shapes : at the time I'm speaking of, he was a maker of carving-tools. Well, sir, you could hardly believe the effect of this accidental interview with that man : the next day, when I renewed my addresses, Miss Carden evaded me, and was as cold as she had been kind : she insisted on it she was not engaged to me, and said she would not marry any body for two years ; and this, I am sorry to say, was not her own idea, but this Little's ; for I overheard him ask her to wait two years for him."

"Little ! What, Raby's new nephew ?"

"That is the man."

Mr. Carden was visibly discomposed by this communication. He did not choose to tell Coventry how shocked he was at his own daughter's conduct ; but, after a considerable pause, he said, "If what you have told me is the exact truth, I shall interpose parental authority, and she shall keep her engagement with you, in spite of all the Littles in the world."

"Pray do not be harsh," said Coventry.

"No, but I shall be firm."

"Insanity in his family, for one thing," suggested Coventry, scarcely above a whisper.

"That is true ; his father committed suicide. But really that consideration is not needed. My daughter must keep her engagements, as I keep mine."

With this understanding the friends parted.

CHAPTER XXVI.

GRACE happened to have a headache next morning, and did not come down to breakfast: but it was Saturday, and Mr. Carden always lunched at home on that day. So did Grace, because it was one of Little's days. This gave Mr. Carden the opportunity he wanted. When they were alone he fixed his eyes on his daughter, and said quietly, "What is your opinion of—a jilt ?"

"A heartless, abominable creature," replied Grace, as glibly as if she was repeating some familiar catechism.

"Would you like to be called one ?"

"Oh, papa!"

"Is there nobody who has the right to apply the term to you ?"

"I hope not." (Red.)

"You encouraged Mr. Coventry's addresses ?"

"I am afraid I did not discourage them, as I wish I had. It is so hard to foresee every thing."

"Pray do you remember the fifth day of last December ?"

"Can I ever forget it ?" (Redder.)

"Is it true that Mr. Coventry proposed for you, that day ?"

"Yes."

"And you accepted him."

"No; no. Then he has told you so ? How ungenerous! All I did was, I hesitated, and cried, and didn't say ' no,' downright,—like a fool. Oh, papa, have pity on me, and save me." And now she was pale.

Mr. Carden's paternal heart was touched by this appeal, but he was determined to know the whole truth. "You could love him, in time, I suppose ?"

"Never."

"Why ?"

"Because—"

"Now tell me the truth. Have you another attachment ?"

"Yes, dear papa." (In a whisper and as red as fire.)

"Somebody of whom you are not proud."

"I *am* proud of him. He is Mr. Coventry's superior. He is every body's superior in every thing in the world."

"No, Grace, you can hardly be proud of your attachment ; if you had been, you would not have hidden it all this time from your father." And Mr. Carden sighed.

Grace burst out crying, and flung herself on her knees and clung, sobbing, to him.

"There, there," said he, "I don't want to reproach you ; but to advise you."

"Oh, papa! Take and kill me. Do: I want to die."

"Foolish child! Be calm now; and let us talk sense."

At this moment there was a peculiar ring at the door, a ring not violent, but vigorous.

Grace started and looked terrified : "Papa!" said she, "say what you like to me, but do not affront *him ;* for you might just as well take that knife and stab your daughter to the heart. I love him so. Have pity on me."

The servant announced "Mr. Little!"

Grace started up, and stood with her hand gripping the chair; her cheek was pale, and her eyes glittered; she looked wild, and evidently strained up to defend her lover.

All this did not escape Mr. Carden. He said gently, "Show him into the library." Then to Grace, as soon as the servant had retired, "Come here, my child."

She knelt at his knees again, and turned her imploring, streaming eyes up to him.

"Is it really so serious as all this ?"

"Papa, words can not tell you how I love. But if you affront him, and he leaves me, you will *see* how I love him ; you will know, by my grave-side, how I love him."

"Then I suppose I must swallow my disappointment how I can."

"It shall be no disappointment : he will do you honor and me too."

"But he can't make a settlement on his wife, and no man shall marry my daughter till he can do that."

"We can wait," said Grace, humbly.

"Yes, wait—till you and your love are both worn out."

"I shall wear out before my love."

Mr. Carden looked at her, as she knelt before him, and his heart was very much softened. "Will you listen to reason at all ?" said he.

"From you, I will, dear papa." She added, swiftly, "and then you will listen to affection, will you not ?"

"Yes. Promise me there shall be no formal engagement, and I will let him come now and then."

This proposal, though not very pleasant, relieved Grace of such terrible fears, that she consented eagerly.

Mr. Carden then kissed her, and rose, to go to young Little ; but, before he had taken three steps, she caught him by the arm, and said, imploringly, "Pray remember while you are speaking to him that you would not have me to bestow on any man but for him; for he saved my life, and Mr. Coventry's too. Mr. Coventry forgets that: but don't you : and, if you wound him, you wound me; he carries my heart in his bosom."

Mr. Carden promised he would do his duty as kindly as possible ; and with that Grace was obliged to content herself.

When he opened the library door, young Little started up, his face irradiated with joy. Mr. Carden smiled a little satirically ; but he was not altogether untouched by the eloquent love for his daughter, thus showing itself in a very handsome and amiable face. He said, "It is not the daughter this time, sir, it is only the father."

Little colored up and looked very uneasy.

"Mr. Little, I am told you pay your addresses to Miss Carden. Is that so ?"

"Yes, sir."

"You have never given me any intimation."

Little colored still more. He replied, with some hesitation, "Why, sir, you see I was brought up amongst workmen, and they court the girl first, and make sure of her, before they trouble the parents ; and, besides, it was not ripe for your eye yet."

"Why not ?"

"Because I'm no match for Miss Carden. But I hope to be, some day."

"And she is to wait for you till then ?"

"She says she will."

"Well, Mr. Little, this is a delicate matter ; but you are a straightforward man, I see, and it is the best way. Now I must do my duty as a parent, and I am afraid I shall not be able to do that without mortifying you a little; but believe me, it is not from any dislike or disrespect to you, but only because it *is* my duty."

"I'm much obliged to you, sir; and I'll bear more from you than I would from any other I am disappointed. But, although I am disappointed, I will not be harsh nor unreasonable to you. All I say is this: my daughter shall never marry any man, nor engage herself to any man, who can not make a proper settlement on her. Can *you* make a proper settlement on her?"

"IS IT REALLY SO SERIOUS AS ALL THIS?"

man. You are her father, and I hope you'll be mine one day."

"Well then, Mr. Little, I always thought my daughter would marry a gentleman in this neighborhood, who has paid her great attention for years, and is a very suitable match for her. You are the cause of that match being broken off, and

"Not at present," said Little, with a sigh.

"Then I put it to you, as a man, is it fair of you to pay her open attentions, and compromise her? You must not think me very mercenary; I am not the man to give my daughter to the highest bidder. But there is a medium."

"I understand you, sir, so far. But what am

I to do? Am I to leave off loving, and hoping, and working, and inventing? You might as well tell me to leave off living."

"No, my poor boy; I don't say that, neither. If it is really for her you work, and invent, and struggle with fortune so nobly as I know you do, persevere, and may God speed you. But, meantime, be generous, and don't throw yourself in her way to compromise her."

The young man was overpowered by the kindness and firmness of his senior, who was also Grace's father. He said, in a choking voice, there was no self-denial he would not submit to, if it was understood that he might still love Grace, and might marry her as soon as he could make a proper settlement on her.

Then Mr. Carden, on his part, went farther than he had intended, and assented distinctly to all this, provided the delay was not unreasonable in point of time. "I can't have her whole life wasted."

"Give me two years: I'll win her or lose her in that time." He then asked, piteously, if he might see her.

"I am sorry to say No to that," was the reply; "but she has been already very much agitated, and I should be glad to spare her further emotion. You need not doubt her attachment to you, nor my esteem. You are a very worthy, honest young man, and your conduct does much to reconcile me to what I own is a disappointment."

Having thus gilded the pill, Mr. Carden shook hands with Henry Little, and conducted him politely to the street door.

The young man went away slowly; for he was disconsolate at not seeing Grace.

But, when he got home, his stout Anglo-Saxon heart reacted, and he faced the situation.

He went to his mother and told her what had passed. She colored with indignation, but said nothing.

"Well, mother, of course it might be better; but then it might be worse. It's my own fault now if I lose her. Cutlery won't do it in the time, but Invention will: so, from this hour, I'm a practical inventor, and nothing but death shall stop me."

CHAPTER XXVII.

GRACE CARDEN ran to the window, and saw Henry Little go away slowly, and hanging his head. This visible dejection in her manly lover made her heart rise to her throat, and she burst out sobbing and weeping with alarming violence.

Mr. Carden found her in this state, and set himself to soothe her. He told her the understanding he had come to with Mr. Little, and begged her to be as reasonable and as patient as her lover was. But the appeal was not successful. "He came to see me," she cried, "and he has gone away without seeing me. You have begun to break both our hearts, with your reason and your prudence. One comfort, mine will break first; I have not his fortitude. Oh, my poor Henry! He has gone away, hanging his head, broken-hearted: that is what you have done for me. After that, what are words? Air—air: and you can't feed hungry hearts with air."

"Well, my child, I am sorry now I did not

bring him in here. But I really did it for the best. I wished to spare you further agitation."

"Agitation!" And she opened her eyes with astonishment. "Why, it is you who agitate me. He would have soothed me in a moment. One kind and hopeful word from him, one tender glance of his dear eye, one pressure of his dear hard hand, and I could have borne any thing; but that drop of comfort you denied us both. Oh, cruel! cruel!"

"Calm yourself, Grace, and remember whom you are speaking to. It was an error in judgment, perhaps—nothing more."

"But, then, if you know nothing about love, and its soothing power, why meddle with it at all?"

"Grace," said Mr. Carden, sadly, but firmly, "we poor parents are all prepared for this. After many years of love and tenderness bestowed on our offspring, the day is sure to come when the young thing we have reared with so much care and tenderness will meet a person of her own age, a *stranger;* and, in a month or two, all our love, our care, our anxiety, our hopes, will be nothing in the balance. This wound is in store for us all. We foresee it; we receive it; we groan under it; we forgive it. We go patiently on, and still give our ungrateful children the benefit of our love and our experience. I have seen in my own family that horrible mixture, Gentility and Poverty. In our class of life, poverty is not only poverty, it is misery, and meanness as well. My income dies with me. My daughter and her children shall not go back to the misery and meanness out of which I have struggled. They shall be secured against it by law, before she marries, or she shall marry under her father's curse."

Then Grace was frightened, and said she should never marry under her father's curse; but (with a fresh burst of weeping) what need was there to send Henry away without seeing her, and letting them comfort each other under this sudden affliction. "Ah, I was too happy this morning," said the poor girl. "I was singing before breakfast. Jael always told me not to do that. Oh! oh! oh!"

Mr. Carden kept silence; but his fortitude was sorely tried.

That day Grace pleaded headache, and did not appear to dinner. Mr. Carden dined alone, and missed her bright face sadly. He sent his love to her, and went off to the club, not very happy. At the club he met Mr. Coventry, and told him frankly what he had done. Mr. Coventry, to his surprise, thanked him warmly. "She will be mine in two years," said he. "Little will never be able to make a settlement on her." This remark set Mr. Carden thinking.

Grace watched the window day after day, but Henry never came nor passed. She went a great deal more than usual into the town, in hopes of meeting him by the purest accident. She longed to call on Mrs. Little, but feminine instinct withheld her; she divined that Mrs. Little must be deeply offended.

She fretted for a sight of Henry, and for an explanation, in which she might clear herself, and show her love, without being in the least disobedient to her father. Now all this was too subtile to be written. So she fretted and pined for a meeting.

While she was in this condition, and losing

color every day, who should call one day—to re-connoitre, I suppose—but Mr. Coventry."

Grace was lying on the sofa, languid and distraite, when he was announced. She sat up directly, and her eye kindled.

Mr. Coventry came in with his usual grace and cat-like step. "Ah; Miss Carden!"

Miss Carden rose majestically to her feet, made him a formal courtesy, and swept out of the room, without deigning him a word. She went to the study, and said, "Papa, here's a friend of yours —Mr. Coventry."

"Dear me, I am very busy. I wish you would amuse him for a few minutes till I have finished this letter."

"Excuse me, papa; I can not stay in the same room with Mr. Coventry."

"Why not, pray?"

"He is a dangerous man: he compromises one. He offered me an engagement-ring, and I refused it; yet he made you believe we were engaged. You have taken care I shall not be compromised with the man I love; and shall I be compromised with the man I don't care for? No, thank you."

"Very well, Grace," said Mr. Carden, coldly.

Shortly after this Mr. Carden requested Dr. Amboyne to call; he received the Doctor in his study, and told him that he was beginning to be uneasy about Grace; she was losing her appetite, her color, and her spirits. Should he send her to the sea-side?

"The sea-side! I distrust conventional remedies. Let me see the patient."

He entered the room and found her coloring a figure she had drawn: it was a beautiful woman, with an anchor at her feet. The door was open, and the Doctor, entering softly, saw a tear fall on the work from a face so pale and worn with pining, that he could hardly repress a start: he did repress it though, for starts are unprofessional; he shook hands with her in his usual way. "Sorry to hear you are indisposed, my dear Miss Grace." He then examined her tongue, and felt her pulse: and then he sat down, right before her, and fixed his eyes on her. "How long have you been unwell?"

"I am not unwell that I know of," said Grace, a little sullenly.

"One reason I ask, I have another patient, who has been attacked somewhat in the same way."

Grace colored, and fixed a searching eye on the Doctor. "Do I know the lady?"

"No. For it happens to be a male patient."

"Perhaps it is going about."

"Possibly; this is the age of competition. Still it is hard you can't have a little malady of this kind all to yourself; don't you think so?"

At this Grace laughed hysterically.

"Come, none of that before me," said the Doctor sternly.

She stopped directly, frightened. The Doctor smiled.

Mr. Carden peeped in from his study. "When you have done with her, come and prescribe for me. I am a little out of sorts too." With this, he retired. "That means you are to go and tell him what is the matter with me," said Grace bitterly.

"Is his curiosity unjustifiable?"

"Oh no. Poor papa!" Then she asked him dryly if he knew what was the matter with her.

"I think I do."

"Then cure me." This with haughty incredulity.

"I'll try; and a man can but do his best. I'll tell you one thing; if I can't cure you, no doctor in the world can: see how modest I am. Now for papa."

She let him go to the very door: and then a meek little timid voice said, in a scarce audible murmur, "Doctor!"

Now when this meek murmur issued from a young lady who had, up to this period of the interview, been rather cold and cutting, the sagacious Doctor smiled. "My dear?" said he, in a very gentle voice.

"Doctor! about your other patient!"

"Well?"

"Is he as bad as I am? For indeed, my dear friend, I feel—my food has no taste—life itself no savor. I used to go singing, now I sit sighing. Is he as bad as I am?"

"I'll tell you the truth: his malady is as strong as yours; but he has the great advantage of being a man; and, again, of being a man of brains. He is a worker, and an inventor; and now, instead of succumbing tamely to his disorder, he is working double tides, and inventing with all his might, in order to remove an obstacle between him and one he loves with all his manly soul. A contest so noble and so perpetual sustains and fortifies the mind. He is indomitable; only, at times, his heart of steel will soften, and then he has fits of deep dejection and depression, which I mourn to see; for his manly virtues, and his likeness to one I loved deeply in my youth, have made him dear to me."

During this Grace turned her head away, and, ere the Doctor ended, her tears were flowing freely; for to her, being a woman, this portrait of a male struggle with sorrow was far more touching than any description of feminine and unresisted grief could be: and, when the Doctor said he loved his patient, she stole her little hand into his in a way to melt Old Nick, if he is a male. Ladies, forgive the unchivalrous doubt.

"Doctor," said she, affecting all of a sudden a little air of small sprightliness, very small, "now, do —you—think—it would do your patient—the least good in the world—if you were to take him this?"

She handed him her work, and then she blushed divinely.

"Why, it is a figure of Hope."

"Yes."

"I think it might do him a great deal of good."

"You could say I painted it for him."

"So I will. That will do him no harm neither. Shall I say I found you crying over it?"

"Oh, no! no! That would make him cry too, perhaps."

"Ah, I forgot that. Grace, you are an angel."

"Ah, no. But you can tell him I am—if you think so. That will do him no great harm,—will it?"

"Not an atom to him; but it will subject me to a pinch for stale news. There, give me my patient's picture, and let me go."

She kissed the little picture half-furtively, and gave it him, and let him go; only, as he went out at the door, she murmured, "Come often."

Now, when this artful doctor got outside the door, his face became grave all of a sudden, for he had seen enough to give him a degree of anxiety he had not betrayed to his interesting patient herself.

"Well, Doctor?" said Mr. Carden, affecting more cheerfulness than he felt. "Nothing there beyond your skill, I suppose?"

"Her health is declining rapidly. Pale, hollow-eyed, listless, languid—not the same girl."

"Is it bodily do you think, or only mental?"

"Mental as to its cause; but bodily in the result. The two things are connected in all of us, and very closely in Miss Carden. Her organization is fine, and therefore, subtle. She is tuned in a high key. Her sensibility is great; and tough folk, like you and me, must begin by putting ourselves in her place before we prescribe for her, otherwise our harsh hands may crush a beautiful, but too tender, flower."

"Good heavens!" said Carden, beginning to be seriously alarmed, "do you mean to say you think, if this goes on, she will be in any danger?"

"Why, if it were to go on at the same rate, it would be very serious. She must have lost a stone in weight already."

"What, my child! my sweet Grace! Is it possible her life—"

"And do you think your daughter is not mortal like other people? The young girls that are carried past your door to the churchyard one after another, had they no fathers?"

At this blunt speech the father trembled from head to foot.

———

CHAPTER XXVIII.

"Doctor," said Mr. Carden, "you are an old friend, and a discreet man; I will confide the truth to you."

"You may save yourself the trouble. I have watched the whole progress of this amour up to the moment when you gave them the advantage of your paternal wisdom, and made them both miserable."

"It is very unreasonable of them, to be miserable."

"Oh, lovers parted could never yet make themselves happy with reason."

"But why do you say parted? All I said was, 'No engagement till you can make a settlement: and don't compromise her in the meanwhile.' I did not mean to interdict occasional visits."

"Then why not say so? That is so like people. You made your unfavorable stipulation plain enough; but the little bit of comfort, you left that in doubt. This comes of not putting yourself in his place. I have had a talk with him about it, and he thinks he is not to show his face here till he is rich enough to purchase your daughter of you."

"But I tell you he has misunderstood me."

"Then write to him and say so."

"No, no; you take an opportunity to let him know he has really rather overrated my severity, and that I trust to his honor, and do not object to a visit—say once a week."

"It is a commission I will undertake with pleasure."

"And do you really think that will do her bodily health any good?"

Before Doctor Amboyne could reply, the piano was suddenly touched in the next room, and a sweet voice began to sing a cheerful melody. "Hush!" said Doctor Amboyne. "Surely I know that tune. Yes, I have heard *the other* whistle it."

"She has not sung for ever so long," remarked Mr. Carden.

"And I think I can tell you why she is singing now: look at this picture of Hope; I just told her I had a male patient afflicted with her complaint, and the quick-witted creature asked me directly if I thought this picture would do him any good. I said yes, and I'd take it to him."

"Come, Doctor, that couldn't make her *sing*."

"Why not? Heart can speak to heart, even by a flower or a picture. The separation was complete; sending this symbol has broken it a little, and so she is singing. This is a lesson for us ruder and less subtle spirits. Now mind, thwarted love seldom kills a busy man; but it often kills an idle woman, and your daughter is an idle woman. He is an iron pot, she is a china vase. Please don't hit them too hard with the hammer of paternal wisdom, or you will dent my iron pot, and break your china vase to atoms."

Having administered this warning, Doctor Amboyne went straight from Woodbine Villa to Little's factory; but Little was still in London; he had gone there to take out patents. Bayne promised to send the Doctor a line immediately on his return. Nevertheless, a fortnight elapsed, and then Doctor Amboyne received a short, mysterious line to tell him Mr. Little had come home, and would be all the better of a visit. On receipt of this the Doctor went at once to the works, and found young Little lying on his carpenter's bench in a sort of gloomy apathy. "Hallo!" said the Doctor, in his cheerful way, "why what's the matter now?"

"I'm fairly crushed," groaned the inventor.

"And what has crushed you?"

"The roundabout swindle."

"There, now, he invents words as well as

things. Come, tell me all about the roundabout swindle."

"No, no; I haven't the heart left to go through it all again, even in words. One would think an inventor was the enemy of the human race. Yes, I will tell you the sight of you has revived me a bit; it always does. Well, then, you know I am driven to invention now; it is my only chance: and, ever since Mr. Carden spoke to me, I have given my whole soul to the best way of saw-grinding by machinery. The circular saws beat me for a while, but I mastered them: see, there's the model. I'm going to burn it this very afternoon. Well, a month ago, I took the other model—the long-saw grinder—up to London, to patent the invention, as you advised me. I thought I'd just have to exhibit the model, and lodge the description in some Government office, and pay a fee, of course, to some swell, and so be quit of it. Lord bless you—first I had to lay the specification before the Court of Chancery, and write a petition to the Queen, and pay, and, what is worse, wait. When I had paid and waited, I got my petition signed, not by the Queen, but by some go-between, and then I must take it to the Attorney-general. He made me pay—and wait. When I had waited ever so long, I was sent back to where I had come from—the Home Office. But even then I could not get to the Queen. Another of her go-betweens nailed me, and made me pay, and wait: these locusts steal your time as well as your money. At last, a copy of a copy of a copy of my patent got to the Queen, and she signed it like a lady at once, and I got it back. Then I thought I was all right. Not a bit of it: the Queen's signature wasn't good till another of her go-betweens had signed it. I think it was the Home Secretary this time. This go-between bled me again, and sent me with my hard-earned signatures to the Patent Office. There they drafted, and copied, and docketed, and robbed me of more time and money. And, when all was done, I had to take the document back to one of the old go-betweens that I hoped I had worn out, the Attorney-General. He signed, and bled me out of some more money. From him to the other go-betweens at Whitehall. From them to the Stamp Office, if I remember right, and, oh Lord, didn't I fall among leeches there? They drafted, they copied, they engrossed, they juggled me out of time and money without end. The first leech was called the Lord Keeper of the Seal; the second leech was called the Lord Chancellor; it was some go-between that acted in his name; the third leech was the Clerk of the Patents. They demanded more copies, and then employed more go-betweens to charge ten times the value of a copy, and nailed the balance, no doubt. 'Stand and deliver thirty pounds for this stamp.' 'Stand and deliver to me that call myself the Chancellor's purse-bearer—and there's no such creature—two guineas.' 'Stand and deliver seven, thirteen, to the clerk of the Hanaper'—and there's no such thing as a Hanaper. 'Stand and deliver three, five,' to a go-between that calls himself the Lord Chancellor again, and isn't. 'Stand and deliver six, nought, to a go-between that acts for the deputy, that ought to put a bit of sealing-wax on the patent, but hasn't the brains to do it himself, so you must pay *me* a fancy price for doing it, and then I won't do it; it will be done by a clerk at twenty-five shillings a week.' And,

all this time, mind you, no disposition to soften all this official peculation by civility; no misgiving that the next wave of civilization may sweep all these go-betweens and leeches out of the path of progress; no, the deputy-vice-go-betweens all scowled, as well as swindled: they broke my heart so, often I sat down in their antechambers, and the scalding tears ran down my cheeks, at being pillaged of my time as well as my money, and treated like a criminal—for what? For being, in my small way, a national benefactor."

"Ay," said the Doctor, "you had committed the crime of Brains; and the worse crime of declining to be starved in return for them. I don't rebel against the fees so much: their only fault is that they are too heavy, since the monopoly they profess to secure is short-lived, and yet not very secure; the Lord Chancellor, as a judge, has often to upset the patent which he has sold in another character. But that system of go-betweens, and deputy-go-betweens, and deputy-lieutenant-go-betweens, and of nobody doing his own business in matters of State, it really is a national curse, and a great blot upon the national intellect. It is a disease; so let us name it. We doctors are great at naming diseases; greater than at curing them.

"'Let us call it VICARIA,
This English malaria.'

Of this Vicaria, the loss of time and money you have suffered is only one of the fruits, I think."

"All I know is, they made my life hell for more than a month; and if I have ever the misfortune to invent any thing more, I'll keep it to myself. I'll hide it, like any other crime. But no; I never will invent another thing: never, never."

"Stuff! Methinks I hear a duck abjure natation. You can't help inventing."

"I will help it? What, do you think I'll be such an ass as to have Brains in a country where Brains are a crime? Doctor, I'm in despair."

"Then it is time to cast your eyes over this little picture."

The inventor turned the little picture listlessly about. "It is a woman, with an anchor. It's a figure of Hope."

"Beautifully painted, is it not?"

"The tints are well laid on: but, if you'll excuse me, its rather flat." He laid the picture down, and turned away from it. "Ah, Hope, my lass, you've come to the wrong shop."

"Not she. She was painted expressly for you, and by a very beautiful girl."

"Oh, Doctor, not by—"

"Yes; she sends it you."

"Ah!" And he caught Hope up, and began to devour her with kisses, and his eyes sparkled finely.

"I have some good news, too, for you. Mr. Carden tells me he never intended to separate you entirely from his daughter. If you can be moderate, discreet, old before your time, etc., and come only about once a week, and not compromise her publicly, you will be as welcome as ever."

"That *is* good news, indeed. I'll go there this very day; and I'll patent the circular saw."

"There's a non-sequitur for you!"

"Nothing of the kind, sir. Why, even the Queen's go-betweens will never daunt me, now I can go and drink love and courage direct from *her* eyes; nothing can chill nor discourage me now. I'll light my forge again and go to work, and make a few sets of carving-tools, and that will pay the go-betweens for patenting my circular-saw grinder. But first I'll put on my coat and go to heaven."

"Had you not better postpone that till the end of your brilliant career as an inventor and a lover?"

"No; I thirst for heaven, and I'll drink it." So he made his toilette, thanked and blessed the good Doctor, and off to Woodbine Villa.

Grace Carden saw him coming, and opened the door to him herself, red as scarlet, and her eyes swimming. She scarcely made an effort to contain herself this time, and when she got him into the drawing-room all to herself, she cried, for joy and tenderness, on his shoulder; and it cost him a gulp or two, I can tell you: and they sat hand in hand, and were never tired of gazing at each other: and the hours flew by unheeded. All their trouble was as though it had never been. Love brightened the present, the future, and even the past. He did not tell Grace one word of what he had suffered from Vicaria—I thank thee, Doctor, for teaching me that word—it had lost all interest to him. Love and happiness had annihilated its true character—like the afternoon sun gilding a far-off pig-sty.

He did mention the subject, however, but it was in these terms: "And, dearest, I'm hard at work inventing, and I patent all my inventions; so I hope to satisfy your father before two years."

And Grace said, "Yes; but don't overwork your poor brain and worry yourself. I am yours in heart, and that is something, I hope. I know it is to me; I wouldn't change with any wife in Christendom."

CHAPTER XXIX.

At the end of two months the situation of affairs was as follows:

Grace Carden received a visit every week from Henry, and met him now and then at other houses: she recovered her health and spirits, and, being of a patient sex, was quite contented, and even happy. Frederick Coventry visited her often, and she received his visits quite graciously, now that the man she loved was no longer driven from her. She even pitied him, and was kind to him, and had misgivings that she had used him ill. This feeling he fostered, by a tender, dejected, and inoffensive manner. Boiling with rage inside, this consummate actor had the art to feign resignation; whereas, in reality, he was secretly watching for an opportunity to injure his rival. But no such opportunity came.

Little, in humble imitation of his sovereign, had employed a go-between to employ a go-between, to deal with the State go-betweens and deputy go-betweens, that hampered the purchase —the word "grant" is out of place, bleeding is no boon—of a patent from the crown, and by this means, he had done, in sixty days, what a true inventor will do in twenty-four hours, whenever the various metallic ages shall be succeeded by the age of reason; he had secured his two saw-grinding inventions, by patent, in Great Britain, the Canadas, and the United States of America. He had another invention perfected: it was for forging axes and hatchets by machinery: but this

he did not patent: he hoped to find his remuneration in the prior use of it for a few months. Mere priority is sometimes a great advantage in this class of invention, and there are no fees to pay for it, nor deputy-lieutenant-vice-go-betweens' antechambers for genius to cool its heels and heart in.

But one thing soon became evident. He could not work his inventions without a much larger capital.

Dr. Amboyne and he put their heads together over this difficulty, and the Doctor advised him in a more erudite style than usual.

"True invention," said he, "whether literary or mechanical, is the highest and hardest effort of the mind. It is an operation so absorbing that it often weakens those pettier talents which make what we call the clever man. Therefore the inventor should ally himself with some person of talent and energy, but no invention. Thus supported, he can have his fits of abstraction, his headaches, his heart-aches, his exultations, his depressions, and no harm done; his dogged associate will plough steadily on all the time. So, after all, your requiring capital is no great misfortune; you must look out for a working capitalist. No sleeping partner will serve your turn; what you want is a good, rich, vulgar, energetic man, the pachydermatouser the better."

Henry acted on this advice, and went to London in search of a moneyed partner. Oh, then, it was he learned—

"The hell it is in suing long to bide."

He found capitalists particularly averse to speculate in a patent. It took him many days to find out what moneyed men were open to that sort of thing at all; and, when he got to them, they were cold. They had all been recently bitten by harebrained inventors.

Then he represented that it was a matter of judgment, and offered to prove by figures that his saw-grinding machines must return three hundred per cent. Those he applied to would not take the trouble to study his figures. In other words, he came at the wrong time. And the wrong time is as bad as the wrong thing, or worse. Take a note of that, please: and then forget it.

At last he gave up London in despair, and started for Birmingham.

The train stopped at Tring, and, as it was going on again, a man ran towards the third-class carriage Little was seated in. One of the servants of the company tried to stop him, very properly. He struggled with that official, and eventually shook him off. Meantime the train was accelerating its pace. In spite of that, this personage made a run and a bound, and, half leaping, half scrambling, got his head and shoulders over the door, and there oscillated, till Little grabbed him with both hands, and drew him powerfully in, and admonished him. "That is a foolhardy trick, sir, begging your pardon."

"Young man," panted the invader, "do you know who you're a speaking to?"

"No. The Emperor of China?"

"No such trash; it's Ben Bolt, a man that's bad to beat."

"Well, you'll get beat some day, if you go jumping in and out of trains in motion."

"A many have been killed that way," suggested a huge woman in the corner with the meekest and most timid voice imaginable.

Mr. Bolt eyed the speaker with a humorous glance. "Well, if I'm ever killed that way, I'll send you a letter by the post. Got a sweetheart, ma'am?"

"I've got a good husband, sir," said she, with mild dignity, and pointed to a thin, sour personage opposite, with his nose in a newspaper. Deep in some public question, he ignored this little private inquiry.

"That's unlucky," said Bolt, "for here am I, just landed from Victoria, and money in both pockets. And where do you think I am going now? to Chester, to see my father and mother, and show them I was right after all. They wanted me to go to school: I wouldn't. Leathered me; I howled, but wouldn't spell; I was always bad to beat. Next thing was, they wanted to make a tanner of me. I wouldn't. 'Give me fifty pounds and let me try the world,' says I. *They* wouldn't. We quarrelled. My uncle interfered one day, and gave me fifty pounds. 'Go to the devil,' said he, 'if you like; so as you don't come back.' I went to Sydney, and doubled my fifty; got a sheep-run, and turned my hundred into a thousand. Then they found gold, and that brought up a dozen ways of making money, all of 'em better than digging. Why, ma'am, I made ten thousand pounds by selling the beastliest lemonade you ever tasted for gold-dust at the mines. That was a good swop, wasn't it? So now I'm come home to see if I can stand the Old Country and its ways; and I'm going to see the old folk. I haven't heard a word about them this twenty years."

"Oh, dear, sir," said the meek woman, "twenty years is a long time. I hope you won't find them dead an' buried."

"Don't say that; don't say that!" And the tough, rough man showed a grain of feeling. He soon recovered himself, though, and said more obstreperously than ever, "If they are, I disown 'em. None of your faint-hearted people for me. I despise a chap that gives in before eighty. I'm Ben Bolt, that is bad to beat. Death himself isn't going to bowl me out till I've had my innings."

"La, sir; pray don't talk so, or you'll anger them above, and, ten to one, upset the train."

"That's one for me, and two for yourself, ma'am."

"Yes, sir," said the mild soul. "I have got my husband with me, and you are only a bachelor, sir."

"How d'ye know that?".

"I think you'd ha' been softened down a bit, if you'd ever had a good wife."

"Oh, it is because I speak loud. That is with bawling to my shepherds half a mile off. Why, if I'm loud, I'm civil. Now, young man, what is *your* trouble?"

Henry started from his reverie, and looked astonished.

"Out with it," shouted Mr. Bolt; "don't sit grizzling there. What with this lady's husband, dead and buried in that there newspaper, and you, that sets brooding like a hen over one egg, it's a Quaker's meeting, or nearly. If you've been and murdered any body, tell us all about it. Once off your mind, you'll be more sociable."

"A man's thoughts are his own, Mr. Bolt. I'm not so fond of talking about myself as you seem to be."

"Oh, I can talk, or I can listen. But you won't do neither. Pretty company *you* are, a hatching of your egg."

"Well, sir," said the meek woman to Henry, "the rough gentleman he is right. If you are in trouble, the best way is to let your tongue put it off your heart."

"I'm sure you are very kind," said Henry, "but really my trouble is one of those out-of-the-way things that do not interest people. However, the long and the short is, I'm an inventor. I have invented several things, and kept them dark, and they have paid me. I live at Hillsborough. But now I have found a way of grinding long saws and circular saws by machinery, at a saving of five hundred per cent. labor. That saving of labor represents an enormous profit—a large fortune; so I have patented the invention at my own expense. But I can't work it without a capitalist. Well, I have ransacked London, and all the moneyed men shy me. The fools will go into railways, and bubbles, and a lot of things that are blind chance, but they won't even study my drawings and figures, and I've made it clear enough too."

"I'm not of their mind, then," said Bolt. "My rule is never to let another man work my money. No railway shares nor gold mines for Ben Bolt. My money goes with me, and I goes with my money."

"Then you are a man of sense; and I only wish you had money enough to go into this with me."

"How do you know how much money I've got? You show me how to turn twenty thousand into forty thousand, or forty thousand into eighty thousand, and I'll soon find the money."

"Oh, I could show you how to turn fifteen thousand into fifty thousand." He then unlocked his black bag, and showed Bolt some drawings that represented the grinders by hand at work on long saws and circular saws. "This," said he, "is the present system." He then pointed out its defects. "And this," said he, "is what I propose to substitute." Then he showed him drawings of his machines at work. "And these figures represent the saving in labor. Now, in this branch of cutlery, the labor is the manufacturer's main expense. Make ten men grind what fifty used, you put forty workmen's wages in your pocket."

"That's tall talk."

"Not an inch taller than the truth."

Mr. Bolt studied the drawings, and, from obstreperous, became quite quiet and absorbed. Presently he asked Henry to change places with him; and, on this being complied with, he asked the meek woman to read him Henry's figures, slowly. She stared, but complied. Mr. Bolt pondered the figures, and examined the drawings again. He then put a number of questions to Henry, some of them very shrewd; and, at last, got so interested in the affair that he would talk of nothing else.

As the train slackened for Birmingham, he said to Henry, "I'm no great scholar; I like to see things in the body. On we go to Hillsborough."

"But I want to talk to a capitalist or two at Birmingham."

"That is not fair; I've got the refusal."

"The deuce you have!"

"Yes, I've gone into it with you; and the others wouldn't listen. Said so yourself."

"Well, but, Mr. Bolt, are you really in earnest? Surely this is quite out of your line?"

"How can it be out of my line if it pays? I've bought and sold sheep, and wool, and land, and water, and houses, and tents, and old bad to beat. Here goes—high, low, Jack, and the game."

"Did you ever deal in small beer?" asked Henry, satirically.

"No," said Bolt, innocently. "But I would in a minute if I saw clear to the nimble shilling. Well, will you come on to Hillsborough and set-

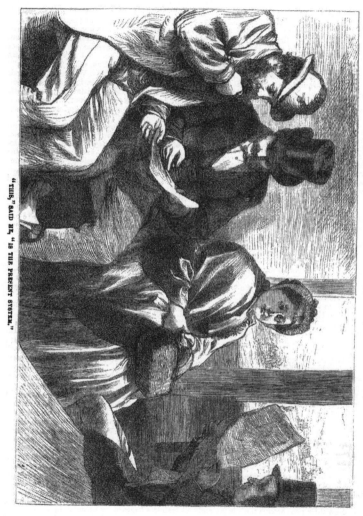

"THIS," SAID HE, "IS THE PRESENT SYSTEM."

clothes, and coffee, and tobacco, and cabs. And swopped—my eye, how I have swopped! I've swopped a housemaid under articles for a pew in the church, and a milch cow for a whale that wasn't even killed yet; I paid for the chance. I'm at all in the ring, and devilish tle this? I've got the refusal for twenty-four hours, I consider."

"Oh, if you think so, I will go on to Hillsborough. But you said you were going to see your parents, after twenty years' absence and silence."

"So I am; but they can keep: what signifies

a day or two more after twenty years ?" He added, rather severely, as one whose superior age entitled him to play the monitor, " Young man, I never make a toil of a pleasure."

" No more do I. But how does that apply to visiting your parents ?"

" If I was to neglect business to gratify my feelings, I should be grizzling all the time ; and wouldn't that be making a toil of a pleasure ?"

Henry could only grin in reply to this beautiful piece of reasoning ; and that same afternoon the pair were in Hillsborough, and Mr. Bolt, under Henry's guidance, inspected the grinding of heavy saws, both long and circular. He noted, at Henry's request, the heavy, dirty labor. He then mounted to the studio, and there Henry lectured on his models, and showed them working. Bolt took it all in, his eye flashed, and then he put on, for the first time, the coldness of the practised dealer. "It would take a good deal of money to work this properly," said he, shaking his head.

" It has taken a good deal of brains to invent it."

" No doubt, no doubt. Well, if you want me to join you, it must be on suitable terms. Money is tight."

" Well, propose your own terms."

" That's not my way. I'll think it over before I put my hand to paper. Give me till to-morrow."

" Certainly."

On this Mr. Bolt went off as if he had been shot.

He returned next day, and laid before Henry an agreement drawn by the sharpest attorney in Hillsborough, and written in a clerk's hand. "There," said he, briskly, " you sign that, and I'll make my mark, and at it we go."

" Stop a bit," said Henry. " You've been to a lawyer, have you ? Then I must go to one too ; fair play's a jewel."

Bolt looked disappointed; but the next moment he affected cheerfulness, and said, " That is fair. Take it to your lawyer directly."

" I will," said Henry ; but, instead of a lawyer, he took it to his friend Doctor Amboyne, told him all about Ben Bolt, and begged his advice on the agreement. " Ought he to have the lion's share like this ?"

" The moneyed man generally takes that. No commodity is sold so far beyond its value as money. Let me read it."

The purport of the agreement was as follows : —New premises to be built by Bolt, a portion of the building to be constructed so that it could be easily watched night and day, and in that part the patent saw-grinding machines to be worked. The expenses of this building to be paid off by degrees out of the gross receipts, and meanwhile Mr. Bolt was to receive five per cent. interest for his outlay and two-thirds of the profits, if any. Mr. Little to dispose of his present factory, and confine his patents to the joint operation.

Doctor Amboyne, on mature consideration, advised Little to submit to all the conditions, except the clause confining his operations and his patents. They just drew their pen through that clause, and sent the amended agreement to Bolt's hotel. He demurred to the amendment ; but Henry stood firm, and proposed a conference of four. This took place at Doctor Amboyne's house, and at last the agreement was thus modified : the use of the patents in Hillsborough to be confined to the firm of Bolt and Little ; but Little to be free to sell them, or work them in any other town, and also free, in Hillsborough, to grind saws by hand, or do any other established operation of cutlery.

The parties signed ; and Bolt went to work in earnest. With all his resolution, he did not lack prudence. He went into the suburbs for his site and bought a large piece of ground. He advertised for contracts and plans, and brought them all to Henry, and profited by his practical remarks.

He warned the builders it must be a fortress, as well as a factory ; but, at Henry's particular request, he withheld the precise reason. " I'm not to be rattened," said he. " I mean to stop that little game. I'm Ben Bolt, that's bad to beat."

At last the tender of Mr. White was accepted, and as Mr. Bolt, experienced in the delays of builders, tied him tight as to time, he, on his part, made a prompt and stringent contract with Messrs. Whitbread, the brickmakers, and began to dig the foundations.

All this Henry communicated to Grace, and was in high spirits over it, and then so was she. He had a beautiful frame made for the little picture she had given him, and hung it up in his studio. It became the presiding genius, and indeed the animating spirit, of his life.

Both to him and Grace the bright and hopeful period of their love had come at last. Even Bolt contributed something to Little's happiness. The man, hard as he was in business, was not without a certain rough geniality ; and then he was so brisk and bustling. His exuberant energy pleased the inventor, and formed an agreeable relief to his reveries and deep fits of study.

The prospect was bright, and the air sunny. In the midst of all which there rose in the horizon a cloud, like that seen by Elijah's servant, a cloud no bigger than a man's hand.

Bolt burst into the studio one day, like a shell, and, like a shell, exploded.

" Here's a pretty go ! We are all at a standstill. The brickmakers have struck."

" Why, what is the matter ?"

" Fourpence. Young Whitbread, our brickmaker's son, is like you—a bit of an inventor ; he altered the shape of the bricks, to fit a small hand-machine, and Whitbreads reckoned to save tenpence a thousand. The brickmakers objected directly. Whitbreads didn't want a row, so they offered to share the profit. The men sent two of their orators to parley : I was standing by Whitbread when they came up ; you should have heard 'em ; any body would have sworn the servants were masters, and the masters negro slaves. When the servants had hectored a bit, the masters, meek and mild, said they would give them sixpence out of the tenpence sooner than they should feel dissatisfied. No ; that wouldn't do. 'Well, then,' says young Whitbread, 'are you agreed what will do ?' 'Well,' said one of the servants, 'we *will allow you to make the bricks,* if you give us the tenpence.'"

" That was cool," said Henry. " To be sure, all brainless beggars try to starve invention."

" Yes, my man : and you grumbled at my taking two-thirds. Labor is harder on you inventors than capital is, you see. Well, I told 'em I wondered at their cheek ; but the old man stopped me, and spoke quite mild : says he, 'You are too hard on us; we ought to gain a trifle by our own improvement; if it had come from you, we should pay you for it;' and he should stand by his offer of sixpence. So then the men told them it would be the worse for them, and the old gentleman gave a bit of sigh, and said he couldn't help that, he must live in the trade, or leave it, he didn't much care which. Next morning they all struck work; and there we are—stopped."

"Welh," said Henry, "it is provoking: but you mustn't ask me to meddle. It's your business."

"It is, and I'll show you I'm bad to beat." With this doughty resolve he went off and drove the contractors; they drove the brickmakers, and the brickmakers got fresh hands from a distance, and the promise of some more.

Bolt rubbed his hands, and kept popping into the yard to see how they got on. By this means he witnessed an incident familiar to brickmakers in that district, but new to him. Suddenly loud cries of pain were heard, and two of the brickmakers held up hands covered with blood, and transfixed by needles. Some ruffian had filled the clay with needles. The sufferers were both disabled, and one went to the hospital. Tempered clay enough to make two hundred thousand bricks had been needled, and had to be cleared away at a loss of time and material.

Bolt went and told Henry, and it only worried him; he could do nothing. Bolt went and hired a watchman and a dog, at his own expense. The dog was shot dead one dark night, and the watchman's box turned over and sat upon, watchman included, while the confederates trampled fifty thousand raw bricks into a shapeless mass.

The brickmasters, however, stood firm, and at last four of the old hands returned to him, and accepted the sixpence profit due to the master's invention. These four were contribution-men, that is to say, they paid the Union a shilling per week for permission to make bricks; but this weekly payment was merely a sort of black-mail, it entitled them to no relief from the Union when out of work: so a three-weeks' strike brought them to starvation, and they could co-operate no longer with the genuine Union men, who were relieved from the box all this time. Nevertheless, though their poverty, and not their will, brought them back to work, they were all threatened, and found themselves in a position that merits the sympathy of all men, especially of the very poor. Starvation on one side, sanguinary threats on the other, from an Union which abandoned them in their need, yet expected them to stick by it and starve. In short, the said Union was no pupil of Amboyne; could not put itself in the place of these hungry men, and realize their dilemma; it could only see the situation from its own point of view. From that intellectual defect sprang a crime. On a certain dark night, Thomas Wilde, one of these contribution-men, was burning bricks all by himself, when a body of seven men came crawling up to within a little distance. These men were what they call "victims," i.e., men on strike, and receiving pay from the box.

Now, when a man stands against the fire of a kiln, he can not see many yards from him; so five of the "victims" stood waiting, and sent two forward. These two came up to Wilde, and asked him a favor. "Eh, mister, can you let me

and my mate lie down for an hour by your fire?"

"You are welcome," said honest Wilde. He then turned to break a piece of coal, and instantly one of those who had accepted his hospitality struck him on the back of the head, and the other five rushed in, and they all set on him, and hit him with cartlegs, and kicked him with their heavy shoes. Overpowered as he was, he struggled away from them, groaning and bleeding, and got to a shed about thirty yards off. But these relentless men, after a moment's hesitation, followed him, and rained blows and kicks on him again, till he gave himself up for dead. He cried out, in his despair, "Lord, have mercy on me; they have finished me!" and fainted away in a pool of his own blood. But, just before he became insensible, he heard a voice say, "Thou'll burn no more bricks." Then the "victims" retired, leaving this great criminal for dead.

After a long while he came to himself, and found his arm was broken, and his body covered with cuts and bruises. His house was scarcely a furlong distant, yet he was an hour crawling to it. His room was up a short stair of ten steps. The steps beat him; he leaned on the rail at the bottom, and called out piteously, "My wife! my wife! my wife!" three times.

Mrs. Wilde ran down to him, and caught hold of his hand, and said, "Whatever is to do?"

When she took his hand the pain made him groan, and she felt something drip on to her hand. It was blood from his wounded arm. Then she was terrified, and, strong with excitement, she managed to get him into the house and lay him on the floor. She asked him, had he fallen off the kiln? He tried to reply, but could not, and fainted again. This time he was insensible for several hours. In the morning he came to, and told his cruel story to Whitbread, Bolt, and others. Bolt and Whitbread took it most to heart. Bolt went to Mr. Ransome, and put the case in his hands.

Ransome made this remark:—"Ah, you are a stranger, sir. The folk hereabouts never come to us in these Union cases. I'll attend to it, trust me."

Bolt went with this tragedy to Henry, and it worried him; but he could do nothing. "Mr. Bolt," said he, "I think you are making your own difficulties. Why quarrel with the Brickmakers' Union? Surely that is superfluous."

"Why, it is them that quarrelled with me; and I'm Ben Bolt, that is bad to beat." He armed himself with gun and revolver, and watched the Whitbreads' yard himself at night.

Two days after this, young Whitbread's wife received an anonymous letter, advising her, as a friend, to avert the impending fate of her husband, by persuading him to dismiss the police and take back his Hands. The letter concluded with this sentence, "He is generally respected; but we have come to a determination to shoot him."

Young Whitbread took no apparent notice of this, and soon afterwards the secretary of the Union proposed a conference. Bolt got wind of this, and was there when the orators came. The deputation arrived, and, after a very short preamble, offered to take the sixpence.

"Why," said Bolt, "you must be joking. Those are the terms poor Wilde came back on, and you have hashed him for it."

9

Old Whitbread looked the men in the face, and said, gravely, "You are too late. You have shed that poor man's blood, and you have sent an anonymous letter to my son's wife. That lady has gone on her knees to us to leave the trade, and we have consented. Fifteen years ago, your Union wrote letters of this kind to my wife (she was pregnant at the time), and drove her into her grave, with fright and anxiety for her husband. You shall not kill Tom's wife as well. The trade is a poor one at best, thanks to the way you have ground your employers down, and, when you add to that needling our clay, and burning our gear, and beating our servants to death's door, and driving our wives into the grave, we bid you good-bye. Mr. Bolt, I'm the sixth brickmaster this Union has driven out of the trade by outrages during the last ten years."

"Thou's a wrong-headed old chap," said the Brickmakers' spokesman: "but thou casn't run away with place. Them as takes to it will have to take us on."

"Not so. We have sold our plant to the Barton Machine Brickmaking Company; and you maltreated them so at starting that now they won't let a single Union man set his foot on their premises."

The company in question made bricks better and cheaper than any other brickmaster; but, making them by machinery, were *always* at war with the Brickmakers' Union, and, whenever a good chance occurred for destroying their property, it was done. They, on their part, diminished those chances greatly by setting up their works five miles from the town, and by keeping armed watchmen and police. Only these ran away with their profits.

Now, when this company came so near the town, and proceeded to work up Whitbread's clay, in execution of the contract with which their purchase saddled them, the Brickmakers' Union held a great meeting, in which full a hundred brickmakers took part, and passed extraordinary resolutions, and voted extraordinary sums of money, and recorded both in their books. These books were subsequently destroyed, for a reason the reader can easily divine who has read this narrative with his understanding.

Soon after that meeting, one Kay, a brickmaker who was never seen to make a brick—for the best of all reasons, he lived by blood alone—was observed reconnoitring the premises, and that very night a quantity of barrows, utensils, and tools were heaped together, naphtha poured over them, and the whole set on fire.

Another dark night, twenty thousand bricks were trampled so noiselessly that the perpetrators were neither seen nor heard.

But Bolt hired more men, put up a notice he would shoot any intruder dead, and so frightened them by his blustering that they kept away, being cowards at bottom, and the bricks were rapidly made, and burnt, and some were even delivered; these bricks were carted from the yard to the building-site by one Harris, who had nothing to do with the quarrel; he was a carter by profession, and wheeled bricks for all the world.

One night this poor man's haystack and stable were all in flames in a moment, and unearthly screams issued from the latter.

The man ran out, half-naked, and his first thought was to save his good gray mare from

the fire. But this act of humanity had been foreseen and provided against. The miscreants had crept into the stable, and tied the poor docile beast fast by the head to the rack; then fired the straw. Her screams were such as no man knew a horse could utter. They pierced all hearts, however hard, till her burnt body burst the burnt cords, and all fell together. Man could not aid her. But God can avenge her.

As if the poor thing could tell whether she was drawing machine-made bricks, or hand-made bricks!

The incident is painful to relate; but it would be unjust to omit it. It was characteristic of that particular Union; and, indeed, without it my reader could not possibly appreciate the brickmaking mind.

Bolt went off with this to Little; but Amboyne was there, and cut his tales short. "I hope," said he, "that the common Creator of the four-legged animal and the two-legged beasts, will see justice done between them; but you must not come here tormenting my inventor with these horrors. Your business is to relieve him of all such worries, and let him invent in peace."

"Yes," said Little, "and I have told Mr. Bolt we can't avoid a difficulty with the cutlers. But the brickmakers—what madness to go and quarrel with them! I will have nothing to do with it, Mr. Bolt."

"The cutlers! Oh, I don't mind them," said Bolt. "They are angels compared with the brickmakers. The cutlers don't poison cows, and hamstring horses, and tie them to fire; the cutlers don't fling little boys into water-pits, and knock down little girls with their fists, just because their fathers are non-Union men; the cutlers don't strew poisoned apples and oranges about, to destroy whole families like rats. Why, sir, I have talked with a man the brickmakers tried to throw into boiling lime; and another they tried to poison with beer, and, when he wouldn't drink it, threw vitriol in his eyes, and he's blind of an eye to this day. There's full half-a-dozen have had bottles of gunpowder and old nails flung into their rooms, with lighted fusees, where they were sleeping with their families; they call that 'bottling a man;' it's a familiar phrase. I've seen three cripples crawling about that have been set on by numbers and spoiled for life, and as many fired at in the dark; one has got a slug in his head to this day. And, with all that, the greatest cowards in the world,—daren't face a man in daylight, any two of them; but I've seen the woman they knocked down with their fists, and her daughter too, a mere child at the time. No, the cutlers are men, but the brickmakers are beasts."

"All the more reason for avoiding silly quarrels with the brickmakers," said Little.

Thus snubbed, Mr. Bolt retired, muttering something about "bad to beat." He found Harris crying over the ashes of his mare, and the man refused to wheel any more machine-made bricks. Other carters being applied to, refused also. They had received written warning, and dared not wheel one of those bricks for their lives.

The invincible Bolt bought a cart and a horse, hired two strangers, armed them and himself with revolvers, and carted the bricks himself. Five brickmakers waylaid him in a narrow lane; he took out his revolver, and told them he'd send them all to hell if one laid a finger on him; at this rude observation they fled like sheep.

The invincible carted his bricks by day, and at night rode the horse away to an obscure inn, and slept beside him, armed to the teeth.

The result of all which was that one day he burst into Little's studio shouting "Victory!" and told him two hundred thousand bricks were on the premises, and twenty bricklayers would be at work on the foundations that afternoon.

Henry Little was much pleased at that, and when Bolt told him how he had carted the bricks in person, said, "You are the man for me; you really are bad to beat."

While they were congratulating each other on this hard-earned victory, Mr. Bayne entered softly, and said, "Mr. White—to speak to Mr. Bolt."

"That is the builder," said Bolt. "Show him up."

Mr. White came in with a long face.

"Bad news, gentlemen; the Machine Brickmaking Company retires from business, driven out of trade by their repeated losses from violence."

"All the worse for the nation," said Bolt; "houses are a fancy article—got to be. But it doesn't matter to us. We have got bricks enough to go on with."

"Plenty, sir: but that is not where the shoe pinches now. The Brickmakers' Union has made it right with the Bricklayers' Union, and the Bricklayers' Union orders us to cart back every one of those machine-made bricks to the yard."

"See them —— first," said Bolt.

"Well, sir, have you considered the alternative?"

"Not I. What is it?"

"Not a bricklayer in Hillsboro', or for fifty miles round, will set a brick for us; and if we get men from a distance they will be talked away, or driven away, directly. The place is picketed on every side at this moment."

Even Bolt was staggered now. "What is to be done, I wonder?"

"There's nothing to be done, but submit. When two such powerful Unions amalgamate, resistance is useless, and the law of the land a dead letter. Mr. Bolt, I'm not a rich man; I've got a large family; let me beg of you to release me from the contract."

"White, you are a cur. Release you? never!"

"Then, sir, I'll go through the court, and release myself."

Henry Little was much dejected by this monstrous and unforeseen obstacle arising at the very threshold of his hopes. He felt so sad, that he determined to revive himself with a sight of Grace Carden. He pined for her face and voice. So he went up to Woodbine Villa, though it was not his day. As he drew near that Paradise, the door opened, and Mr. Frederick Coventry came out. The two men nearly met at the gate. The rejected lover came out looking bright and happy, and saw the accepted lover arrive, looking depressed and careworn: he saw in a moment something was going wrong, and turned on his heel with a glance of triumph.

Henry Little caught that glance, and stood at the gate black with rage. He stood there about a minute, and then walked slowly home again:

he felt he should quarrel with Grace if he went in, and, by a violent effort of self-restraint, he retraced his steps; but he went home sick at heart.

The mother's eye read his worn face in a moment, and soon she had it all out of him. It cost her a struggle not to vent her maternal spleen on Grace; but she knew that would only make her son more unhappy. She advised him minutely what to say to the young lady about Mr. Coventry: and, as to the other matters, she said, "You have found Mr. Bolt not so bad to beat as he tells you: for he is beaten, and there's an end of him. Now let *me* try."

"Why what on earth can you do in a case of this kind?"

"Have I ever failed, when you have accepted my assistance?"

"No: that's true. Well, I shall be glad of your assistance now, heaven knows; only I can't imagine—"

"Never mind: will you take Grace Carden if I throw her into your arms?"

"Oh, mother, can you ask me?"

Mrs. Little rang the bell, and ordered a fly. Henry offered to accompany her. She declined. "Go to bed early," said she, "and trust to your mother. We are harder to beat sometimes than a good many Mr. Bolts."

She drove to Dr. Amboyne's house, and sent in her name. She was ushered into the doctor's study, and found him shivering over an enormous fire. "Influenza."

"Oh dear," said she, "I'm afraid you are very ill."

"Never mind that. Sit down. You will not make me any worse, you may be sure of that." And he smiled affectionately on her.

"But I came to intrude my own troubles on you."

"All the better. That will help me forget mine."

Mrs. Little seated herself, and, after a slight hesitation, opened her battery thus:—"Well, my good friend, I am come to ask you a favor. It is to try and reconcile my brother and me. If any one can do it, you can."

"Praise the method, not the man. If one could only persuade you to put yourself in his place, and him to put himself in yours, you would be both reconciled in five minutes."

"You forget we have been estranged this five-and-twenty years."

"No, I don't. The only question is, whether you can and will deviate from the practice of the world into an obese lunatic's system, both of you."

"Try *me*, to begin."

The doctor's eyes sparkled with satisfaction. "Well, then," said he, "first you must recollect all the differences you have seen between the male and female mind, and imagine yourself a man."

"Oh, dear! that is so hard. But I have studied Henry. Well, there—I have unsexed myself—in imagination."

"You are not only a man but a single-minded man, with a high and clear sense of obligation. You are a trustee, bound by honor to protect the interests of a certain woman and a certain child. The lady, under influence, wishes to borrow her son's money, and risk it on rotten security. You decline, and the lady's husband affronts you. In spite of that affront, being a high-minded man, not to be warped by petty irritation, you hurry to your lawyers to get two thousand pounds of your own, for the man who had affronted you."

"Is that so?" said Mrs. Little. "I was not aware of that."

"I have just learned it, accidentally, from the son of the solicitor Raby went to that fatal night."

A tear stole down Mrs. Little's cheek.

"Now, remember, you are not a woman, but a brave, high-minded man. In that character you pity poor Mr. Little, but you blame him a little because he fled from trouble, and left his wife and child in it. To you, who are Guy Raby—mind that, please—it seems egotistical and weak to desert your wife and child even for the grave." (The widow buried her face and wept. Twenty-five years do something to withdraw the veil the heart has cast over the judgment.) "But, whatever you feel, you utter only regret, and open your arms to your sister. She writes back in an agony, for which, being a man, you can not make all the allowance you would if you were a woman, and denounces you as her husband's murderer, and bids you speak to her and write to her no more, and with that she goes to the Littles. Can you blame yourself that, after all this, you wait for her to review your conduct more soberly, and to invite a reconciliation."

Mrs. Little gave Dr. Amboyne her hand. "Bitter, but wholesome medicine!" she murmured, and then was too overcome to speak for a little while.

"Ah, my good, wise friend!" said she at last, "thick clouds seem clearing from my mind; I begin to see I was the one to blame."

"Yes; and if Raby will be as docile as you, and put himself in your place, he will tell me he was the one to blame. There's no such thing as 'the one to blame;' there very seldom is. You judged him as if he was a woman, he judged you as if you were a man. Enter an obese maniac, and applies the art of arts; the misunderstanding dissolves under it, and you are in each other's arms. But, stop,"—and his countenance fell again a little: "I am afraid there is a new difficulty. Henry's refusal to take the name of Raby and be his heir. Raby was bitterly mortified, and I fear he blames me and my crotchets; for he has never been near me since. To be sure you are not responsible for Henry's act."

"No, indeed; for, between you and me, it mortified me cruelly. And now things have taken a turn,—in short, what with his love, and his jealousy, and this hopeless failure to make a fortune by inventing, I feel I can bring him to his senses. I am not pleased with Grace Carden about something; but no matter, I shall call on her and show her she must side with me in earnest. You will let my brother know I was always on his side in that matter, whatever other offense I may have given him years ago."

"And I am on your side, too. Your son has achieved a small independence. Bayne can carry on the little factory, and Henry can sell or lease his patents; he can never sink to a mere dependent. There, I throw my crotchets to the wind, and we will Raby your son, and marry him to Grace Carden."

"God bless you, my good and true friend! How can I ever thank you?" Her cheek flushed, and her great maternal eye sparkled, and half the beauty of her youth came back. Her gratitude gave a turn to the conversation which she neither expected nor desired.

"Mrs. Little," said Doctor Amboyne, "this is the first time you have entered my den, and the place seems transformed by your presence. My youth comes back to me with the feelings I thought time had blunted; but no, I feel that, when you leave my den again, it will be darker than ever, if you do not leave me a hope that you will one day enter it for good."

"For shame!—At our age!" said the widow.

But she spoilt the remonstrance by blushing like a girl of eighteen.

"You are not old in my eyes; and, as for me, let my years plead for me, since all those years I have lived single for your sake."

This last appeal shook Mrs. Little. She said she could not entertain any such thoughts whilst her son was unhappy. "But marry him to his Grace, and then—I don't know what folly I might not be persuaded into."

The Doctor was quite content with that. He said he would go to Raby, as soon as he could make the journey with safety, and her troubles and her son's should end.

Mrs. Little drove home, a happy mother. As for the promise she had made her old friend, it vexed her a little, she was so used to look at him in another light; but she shrugged her maternal shoulders, as much as to to say, "When once my Henry leaves me—why not?"

She knew she must play the politician a little with Henry, so she opened the battery cautiously.

"My dear," said she, at breakfast, "good news! Doctor Amboyne undertakes to reconcile us both to your uncle."

"All the better. Mr. Raby is a wrong-headed man, but he is a noble-minded one, that is certain."

"Yes, and I have done him injustice. Doctor Amboyne has shown me that."

She said no more. One step at a time.

Harry went up to Woodbine Villa, and Grace received him a little coldly. He asked what was the matter. She said, "They tell me you were at the very door the other day, and did not come in."

"It is true," said he. "Another had just come out—Mr. Coventry."

"And you punished me because that poor man had called on me. Have you not faith in me? or what is it? I shall be angry one of these days."

"No, you will not, if I can make you understand my feelings. Put yourself in my place, dearest. Here am I, fighting the good fight for you, against long odds; and, at last, the brickmakers and bricklayers have beat us. Now you know that is a bitter cup for me to drink. Well, I come up here for my one drop of comfort; and out walks my declared rival, looks into my face, sees my trouble there, and turns off with a glance of insolent triumph." (Grace flushed.) "And then consider: I am your choice, yet I am only allowed to visit you once a week."

"That is papa's doing."

"No matter; so it is. Yet my rival can come when he pleases: and no doubt he does come every other day."

"You fancy that."

"It is not all fancy; for—by heaven! there he

is at the gate. Two visits to my one; there. Well, all the better, I'll talk to *him*."

He rose from his seat black with wrath.

Grace turned pale, and rang the bell in a moment.

The servant entered the room, just as Mr. Coventry knocked at the door.

"Not at home to any body," said she.

Mr. Coventry's voice was heard to say incredulously, "Not at home?" Then he retired slowly, and did not leave the neighborhood. He had called at an hour when Grace was always at home.

Henry sat down, and said, "Thank you, Grace." But he looked very gloomy and disturbed.

She sat down too, and then they looked at each other.

Henry was the first to speak. "We are both pupils of the good Doctor. Put yourself in my place. That man troubles our love, and makes my heavy heart a sore heart."

The tears were in Grace's eyes. "Dearest," said she, "I will not put myself in your place; you would lose by that, for I love you better than myself. Yes, it is unjust that you should be allowed to visit me but once a week, and he should visit me when he chooses. I assure you I have permitted his visits out of pure good-nature; and now I will put an end to them."

She drew her desk towards her, and wrote to Mr. Coventry. It took her some little time. She handed Henry the letter to read. He took it in his hand; but hesitated. He inquired what would be the effect of it?

"That he will never visit me again till you and I are married, or engaged, and that is the same thing. Why don't you read it?"

"I don't know: it goes against me, somehow. Seems unmanly. I'll take your word for it."

This charmed Grace. "Ah," said she, "I have chosen right."

Then he kissed her hands, and blessed her: and then she told him it was nothing; he was a goose, and had no idea what she would do for him; "more than you would do for me, I know," said she.

That he denied, and then she said she might perhaps put him to the proof some day.

They were so happy together, time slipped away unheeded. It was full three hours before Henry could tear himself away, though he knew he was wanted at the works; and he went out at the gate, glowing with happiness: and Coventry, who was ready to drop with the fatigue of walking and watching just above, saw him come out triumphant.

Then it was his turn to feel a deadly qualm. However, he waited a little longer, and then made his call.

"Not at home."

Henry, on his way to the works, looked in on his mother, and told her how nobly Grace had behaved.

Mrs. Little was pleased, and it smoothed down her maternal bristles, and made it much easier for her to carry out her design. For the first time since Mr. Carden had offended her by his cold-blooded treatment of her son, she called at Woodbine Villa.

Grace was at home to see her, and met her with

a blushing timidity, and piteous, wistful looks, not easy to misunderstand nor to resist.

They soon came to an understanding, and Mrs. Little told Grace what Doctor Amboyne had promised to do, and represented to her how much better it would be for Henry to fall into his uncle Raby's views, than to engage in hopeless struggles like that in which Mr. Bolt and he had just been so signally defeated. "And then, you know, my dear, you could marry next month—you two; that is to say, if *you* felt disposed: I will answer for Henry."

Grace's red face and swimming eyes told how this shaft went home. In short, she made a coy promise that she would co-operate with Mrs. Little: "and," said she, "how lucky! I am almost promised to grant me the first favor I ask him. Well, I shall entreat him to be a good nephew, and do whatever dear Mr. Raby asks him. But of course I shall not say, and then if you do, you and I "—here the young lady cut her sentence very short.

"Of course not," said Mrs. Little. "*That* will follow as a matter of course. Now, my dear, you and I are conspirators—for his good: and we must write often and let each other know all we do."

With this understanding, and a good many pretty speeches and kisses, they parted.

Doctor Amboyne did not recover so quickly as they could have wished; but they employed the interval. Feelers were adroitly applied to Henry by both ladies, and they were pleased to find that he rather admired his wrong-headed uncle, and had been deeply touched by the old gentleman's address to his mother's picture.

Bolt never came near him, and the grass was beginning to grow on the condemned bricks. In short, every thing seemed to incline in one direction.

There was, however, something very serious going on out of their sight.

"Not at home!" That white lie made Mr. Coventry feel sick at heart. He went home disconsolate. The same evening he received Miss Carden's letter.

The writer treated him like a gentleman, said a few words about her own peculiar position, and begged him to consider that position, and to be very generous; to cease his visits entirely for the present, and so give him one more title to her esteem, which was all she had to give him. This was the purport, and the manner was simply perfect, so gentle yet firm; and then she flattered his *amour propre* by asking that from his generosity which she could have taken as a right: she did all she could to soften the blow. But she failed. The letter was posted too soon after Henry's visit. Behind the velvet paw that struck him, Coventry saw the claws of the jealous lover. He boiled with rage and agony, and cursed them both in his fury.

After an hour or two of phrensy, he sat down and wrote back a letter full of bitter reproaches and sneers. He reflected. He lighted a cigar and smoked it, biting it almost through, now and then. He burned his letter. He lay awake all night, raging and reflecting alternately, as passion or judgment got the upper hand.

In the morning he saw clearer. "Don't quarrel with *her*. Destroy *him*." He saw this as plainly as if it was written.

He wrote Grace a few sad lines, to say that of course he submitted to her will. The letter ended thus : " Since I can do nothing to please you, let me suffer to please you : even that is something." (This letter brought the tears to Grace's eyes, and she pitied and esteemed the writer.)

He put on a plain suit, and drove into Hillsborough, burning with wild ideas of vengeance. He had no idea what he should do ; but he was resolved to do something. He felt capable of assassinating Little with his own hand.

I should be sorry to gain any sympathy for him ; but it is only fair the reader should understand that he felt deeply aggrieved, and that we should all feel aggrieved under similar circumstances. Priority is a title, all the world over ; and he had been the lady's lover first, had been encouraged, and supplanted.

Longing to wound, but not knowing how to strike, he wandered about the town, and went into several factories, and talked to some of the men, and contrived to bring the conversation round to Little, and learn what he was doing. But he gathered no information of any use to him. Then he went to Grotait's place, and tried to pump him. That sagacious man thought this odd, and immediately coupled this with his previous denunciation of Little, and drew him on.

Coventry was too much under the influence of passion to be quite master of himself that day ; and he betrayed to this other Machiavel that he wished ill to Henry Little. As soon as he had thoroughly ascertained this, Grotait turned coolly on him, and said, " I am sorry Mr. Little has got enemies ; for he and his partner talk of building a new factory, and that will be a good thing for us : take a score of saw-grinders off the box." Then Coventry saw he had made a mistake, and left " The Cutlers' Arms " abruptly.

Next day he took a lodging in the town, and went about groping for information, and hunting for a man, whose face he knew, but not his name. He learned all about Bolt and Little's vain endeavor to build, and went and saw the place, and the condemned bricks. The sight gratified him. He visited every saw-grinder's place he could hear of ; and, at last, he fell in with Sam Cole, and recognized him at once. That worthy affected not to know him, and went on grinding a big saw. Coventry stepped up to him, and said in his ear, " I want to speak with you. Make an appointment."

Cole looked rather sulky and reluctant at being drawn from his obscurity. However, he named a low public-house in a back slum, and there these two met that night, and for greater privacy were soon seated in a place bigger than a box and smaller than a room, with discolored walls, and a rough wooden table before them, splashed with beer. It looked the very den to hatch villainy in, and drink poison to its success.

Coventry, pale and red alternately, as fear and shame predominated, began to beat about the bush.

" You and I have reason to hate the same man. You know who I mean."

" I can guess. Begins with a Hel."

" He has wronged me deeply ; and he hurt you."

" That is true, sir. I think he broke my windpipe, for I'm as hoarse as a raven ever since : and I've got one or two of the shot in my cheek still."

" Well, then, now is your time to be revenged."

" Well, I don't know about that. What he done was in self-defense ; and if I play bowls I must look for rubs."

Coventry bit his lip with impatience.

After a pause, he said, " What were you paid for that job ?"

" Not half enough."

" Twenty pounds ?"

" Nor nothing like it."

" I'll give you a hundred to do it again, only more effectually." He turned very pale when he had made this offer.

" Ah," said Cole, " any body could tell you was a gentleman."

" You accept my offer, then ?"

" Nay, I mean it is easy to see you don't know trades. I mustn't meddle with Mr. Little now ; he is right with the Trade."

" What, not if I pay you five times as much ? say ten times then ; two hundred pounds."

" Nay, we Union chaps are not malefactors. You can't buy us to injure an unoffending man. We have got our laws, and they are just ones, and, if a man will break them, after due warning, the order is given to ' do ' him, and the men are named for the job ; and get paid a trifle for their risk ; and the risk is not much, the Trade stand by one another too true, and in so many ways. But if a man is right with the Trade, it is treason to harm him. No, I mustn't move a finger against Little."

" You have set up a conscience !" said Coventry bitterly.

" You dropped yours, and I picked it up," was the Yorkshireman's ready reply. He was nettled now.

At this moment the door was opened and shut very swiftly, and a whisper came in through the momentary aperture, " Mind your eye, Sam Cole."

Coventry rushed to the door and looked out ; there was nobody to be seen.

" You needn't trouble yourself," said Cole. " You might as well run after the wind. That was a friendly warning. I know the voice, and Grotait must be on to us. Now, sir, if you offered me a thousand pounds, I wouldn't touch a hair of Mr. Little : he is right with the Trade, and we should have Grotait and all the Trade as bitter as death against us. I'll tell you a secret, sir, that I've kept from my wife "—(he lowered his voice to a whisper)—" Grotait could hang me any day he chose. You must chink your brass in some other ear, as the saying is : only mind, you did me a good turn once, and I'll do you one now ; you have been talking to somebody else besides me, and blown yourself : so now drop your little game, and let Little alone, or the Trade will make it their job to lay you."

Coventry's face betrayed so much alarm, that the man added, " And penal servitude wouldn't suit the likes of you. Keep out of it."

With this rough advice the conference ended, and Mr. Coventry went home thoroughly shaken in his purpose, and indeed not a little anxious on his own account. Suppose he had been overheard ! his offer to Cole was an offense within reach of the criminal law. What a mysterious labyrinth was this Trade confederacy, into which he had put his foot so rashly, and shown his game, like a novice, to the subtle and crafty Grotait.

He now collected all his powers, not to injure Little, but to slip out of his own blunder.

He seized this opportunity to carry out a coup he had long meditated : he went round to a dozen timber-merchants, and contracted with them for the sale of every tree, old or young, on his estate ; and, while the trees were falling like grain, and the agents on both sides measuring the fallen, he vanished entirely from Hillsborough and Bollinghope.

Doctor Amboyne's influenza was obstinate, and it was nearly a fortnight before he was strong enough to go to Cairnhope ; but at last Mrs. Little received a line from him, to say he was just starting, and would come straight to her on his return ; perhaps she would give him a cup of tea.

This letter came very opportunely. Bolt had never shown his face again ; and Henry had given up all hopes of working his patents, and had said more than once he should have to cross the water and sell them.

As for Mrs. Little, she had for some time maintained a politic silence. But now she prepared for the Doctor's visit as follows: "So, then, you have no more hopes from the invincible Mr. Bolt ?"

"None whatever. He must have left the town in disgust."

"He is a wise man. I want you to imitate his example. Henry, my dear, what is the great object of your life at present ? Is it not to marry Grace Carden ?"

"You know it is."

"Then take her from my hands. Why do you look so astonished ? Have you forgotten my little boast ?" Then, in a very different tone, "You will love your poor mother still, when you are married ? You will say, 'I owe her my wife,' will you not ?"

Henry was so puzzled he could not reply even to this touching appeal, made with eyes full of tears at the thought of parting with him.

Mrs. Little proceeded to explain : "Let me begin at the beginning. Dr. Amboyne has shown me I was more to blame than your uncle was. Would you believe it ? although he refused your poor father the trust-money, he went that moment to get £2000 of his own, and lend it to us. Oh, Henry, when Dr. Amboyne told me that, and opened my eyes, I could have thrown myself at poor Guy's feet. I have been the most to blame in our unhappy quarrel ; and I have sent Dr. Amboyne to say so. Now, Henry, my brother will forgive me, the Doctor says ; and, oh, my heart yearns to be reconciled. You will not stand in my way, dearest ?"

"Not likely. Why, I am under obligations to him, for my part."

"Yes, but Doctor Amboyne says dear Guy is deeply mortified by your refusal to be his heir. For my sake, for your own sake, and for Grace Carden's sake, change your mind now."

"What, go into his house, and wait for dead men's shoes ! Find myself some day wishing in my heart that noble old fellow would die ! Such a life turns a man's stomach even to think of it."

"No, no. Doctor Amboyne says that Mr. Bayne can conduct your business here, and hand you a little income, without your meddling."

"That is true."

"And, as for your patents, gentlemen can sell them to traders, or lease them out. My brother would make a settlement on Grace and you—she is his god-daughter—now that is all Mr. Carden demands. Then you could marry, and, on your small present income, make a little tour together : and dispose of your patents in other places."

"I could do great things with them in the United States."

"That is a long way."

"Why, it is only twelve days."

"Well, marry first," said the politic mother.

Henry flushed all over. "Ah !" said he, "you tempt me. Heaven seems to open its gates as you speak. But you can not be in earnest ; he made it an express condition I should drop my father's name, and take his. Disown my poor dead father ? No, no, no !"

Now in reality this condition was wormwood to Mrs. Little ; but she knew that if she let her son see her feeling, all was over. She was all the mother now, and fighting for her son's happiness : so she sacrificed truth to love with an effort, but without a scruple. "It is not as if it was a strange name. Henry, you compel me to say things that tear my heart to say, but—which has been your best friend, your mother, or your poor dear father ?"

Henry was grieved at the question : but he was a man who turned his back on nothing. "My father loved me," said he: "I can remember that ; but he deserted me, and you, in trouble ; but you—you have been friend, parent, lover, and guardian angel to me. And, oh, how little I have done to deserve it all !"

"Well, dear, the mother you value so highly, her name was Raby. Yes, love ; and, forgive me, I honor and love my mother's name even more than I do the name of Little "—(the tears ran out of her eyes at this falsehood)—"pray take it, to oblige me, and reconcile me to my dear brother, and end our troubles forever." Then she wept on his neck, and he cried with her.

After a while, he said, "I feel my manhood all melting away together. I am quite confused. It is hard to give up a noble game. It is hard to refuse such a mother as you. Don't cry any more, for mercy's sake ! I'm like to choke. Mind, crying is work I'm not used to. What does she say. I am afraid I shall win her, but lose her respect."

"She says she admires your pride ; but you have shown enough. If you refuse any longer, she will begin to fear you don't love her as well as she loves you."

This master-stroke virtually ended the battle. Henry said nothing but the signs of giving way were manifest in him, so manifest that Mrs. Little became quite impatient for the Doctor's arrival to crown all.

He drove up to the door at last, and Henry ran out and brought him in. He looked pale, and sat down exhausted.

Mrs. Little restrained her impatience, and said, "We are selfish creatures to send you on our business before you are half well."

"I am well enough in health," said he, "but I am quite upset."

"What is the matter ? Surely you have not failed ? Guy does not refuse his forgiveness ?"

"No, it is not that. Perhaps, if I had been in time—but the fact is, Guy Raby has left England."

"What, for good? Impossible!"

"Who can tell? All I know is that he has sold his horses, discharged his servants all but one, and gone abroad without a word. I was the friend of his youth—his college chum; he must be bitterly wounded to go away like that, and not even let me know."

Mrs. Little lifted up her hands. "What have we done? what have we done? Wounded! no wonder. Oh, my poor, wronged, insulted brother!"

She wept bitterly, and took it to heart so, it preyed on her health and spirits. She was never the same woman from that hour.

While her son and her friend were saying all they could to console her, there appeared at the gate the last man any of them ever expected to see—Mr. Bolt.

Henry saw him first, and said so.

"Keep him out," cried the Doctor, directly. "Don't let that bragging fool in to disturb our sorrow." He opened the door and told the servant-girl to say "Not at home."

"Not at home," said the girl.

"That's a lie!" shouted Bolt, and shoved her aside and burst into the room. "None of your tricks on travellers," said he, in his obstreperous way. "I saw your heads through the window. Good news, my boy! I've done the trick. I wouldn't say a word till it was all settled, for Brag's a good dog, but Holdfast's a better. I've sold my building-site to some gents that want to speculate in a church, and I've made five hundred pounds profit by the sale. I'm always right, soon or late. And I've bought a factory ready made—the Star Works; bought 'em, sir, with all the gear and plant, and working hands."

"The Star Works? The largest but one in Hillsborough!"

"Ay, lad. Money and pluck together, they'll beat the world. We have got a noble place, with every convenience. All we have got to do now is to go in and win."

Young Little's eyes sparkled. "All right," said he, "I like this way the best."

Mrs. Little sighed.

CHAPTER XXX.

In that part of London called "the City" are shady little streets, that look like pleasant retreats from the busy, noisy world; yet are strongholds of business.

One of these contained, and perhaps still contains, a public office full of secrets, some droll, some sad, some terrible. The building had a narrow, insignificant front, but was of great depth, and its south side lighted by large bay windows all stone and plate-glass; and these were open to the sun and air, thanks to a singular neighbor. Here, in the heart of the City, was wedged a little rustic church, with its church-yard, whose bright-green grass first startled, then soothed and refreshed the eye, in that wilderness of stone—an emerald set in granite. The grass flowed up to the south wall of the "office;" those massive stone windows hung over the graves; the plumed clerks could not look out of window and doubt that all men are mortal: and the article the office sold was Immortality.

It was the Gosshawk Life Insurance.

On a certain afternoon anterior to the Hillsborough scenes last presented, the plumed clerks were all at the south windows, looking at a funeral in the little church-yard, and passing some curious remarks; for know that the deceased was insured in the Gosshawk for nine hundred pounds, and had paid but one premium.

The facts, as far as known, were these. Mr. Richard Martin, a Londoner by birth, but residing in Wales, went up to London to visit his brother. Towards the end of the visit the two Martins went up the river in a boat, with three more friends, and dined at Richmond. They rowed back in the cool of the evening. At starting they were merely jovial; but they stopped at nearly all the public-houses by the water-side, and, by visible gradations, became jolly—uproarious—sang songs—caught crabs. At Vauxhall they got a friendly warning, and laughed at it: under Southwark bridge they ran against an abutment, and were upset in a moment: it was now dusk, and, according to their own account, they all lost sight of each other in the water. One swam ashore in Middlesex, another in Surrey, a third got to the chains of a barge, and was taken up much exhausted, and Robert Martin laid hold of the buttress itself, and cried loudly for assistance. They asked anxiously after each other, but their anxiety appeared to subside in an hour or two, when they found there was nobody missing but Richard Martin. Robert told the police it was all right, Dick could swim like a cork. However, next morning he came with a sorrowful face to say his brother had not reappeared, and begged them to drag the river. This was done, and a body found, which the survivors and Mrs. Richard Martin disowned.

The insurance office was informed, and looked into the matter; and Mrs. Martin told their agent, with a flood of tears, she believed her husband had taken that opportunity to desert her, and was not drowned at all. Of course this went to the office directly.

But a fortnight afterwards a body was found in the water down at Woolwich, entangled in some rushes by the water-side.

Notice was given to all the survivors.

The friends of Robert Martin came, and said the clothes resembled those worn by Richard Martin; but beyond that they could not be positive.

But, when the wife came, she recognized the body at once.

The brother agreed with her, but, on account of the bloated and discolored condition of the face, asked to have the teeth examined: his poor brother, he said, had a front tooth broken short in two. This broken tooth was soon found; also a pencil-case, and a key, in the pocket of the deceased. These completed the identification.

Up to this moment the conduct of Richard Martin's relatives and friends had been singularly apathetic; but now all was changed: they broke into loud lamentations, and he became the best of husbands, best of men: his lightest words were sacred. Robert Martin now remembered that "poor Dick" had stood and looked into that little church-yard and said, "If you outlive me, Bob, bury me in this spot; father lies here." So Robert Martin went to the church-warden for leave to do this last sad office. The church-warden refused, very properly, but the brother's entreaties, the widow's tears, the tragedy itself, and other influences, extorted at last a reluctant consent, coupled with certain sanatory conditions.

The funeral was conducted unobtrusively, and the grave dug out of sight of Gosshawk. But of course it could not long escape observation; that is to say, it was seen by the clerks; but the directors and manager were all seated round a great table up stairs absorbed in a vital question, viz., whether or not the Gosshawk should imitate some other companies, and insure against fire as well as death. It was the third and last discussion; the minority against this new operation was small, but obstinate and warm, and the majority so absorbed in bringing them to reason, that nobody went to the window until the vote had passed, and the Gosshawk was a Life and Fire Insurance. Then some of the gentlemen rose and stretched their legs, and detected the lugubrious enormity. "Hallo!" cried Mr. Carden, and rang a bell. Edwards, an old clerk, appeared, and, in reply to Mr. Carden, told him it was one of their losses being buried—Richard Martin.

Mr. Carden said this was an insult to the office, and sent Edwards out to remonstrate.

Edwards soon reappeared with Robert Martin, who represented, with the utmost humility, that it was the wish of the deceased, and they had buried him, as ordered, in three feet of charcoal.

"What, is the ceremony performed?"

"Yes, sir, all but filling in the grave. Come and see the charcoal."

"Hang the charcoal!"

"Well," said the humane but somewhat pompous director, "if the ceremony has gone so far—but, Mr. Martin, this must never recur, charcoal or no charcoal."

Mr. Martin promised it never should: and was soon after observed in the church-yard urging expedition.

The sad company speedily dispersed, and left nothing to offend nor disgust the Life and Fire Insurance, except a new grave, and a debt of nine hundred pounds to the heirs or assigns of Richard Martin.

Not very far from this church-yard was a public-house; and in that public-house a small parlor up stairs, and in that parlor a man, who watched the funeral rites with great interest, but not in a becoming spirit; for his eyes twinkled with the intensest merriment all the time, and at each fresh stage of the mournful business he burst into peals of laughter. Never was any man so thoroughly amused in the City before, at all events in business hours.

Richard Martin's executor waited a decent time, and then presented his claim to the Gosshawk. His brother proved a lien on it for £300, and the rest went by will to his wife. The Gosshawk paid the money, after the delay accorded by law.

CHAPTER XXXI.

MESSRS. BOLT AND LITTLE put their heads together, and played a prudent game. They kept the works going for a month, without doing any thing novel, except what tended to the health and comfort of their workmen.

But, meantime, they cleared out two adjacent rooms: one was called the studio, the other the experiment-room.

In due course they hired a couple of single men from Birmingham to work the machine under lock and key.

Little, with his own hands, effected an aperture in the party-wall, and thus conveyed long saws from his studio to the machine, and received them back ground.

The men were lodged three miles off, were always kept at work half an hour later than the others, and received six pounds per week apiece, on pain of instant dismissal should they breathe a syllable. They did the work of twenty-four men; so, even at that high rate of wages, the profit was surprising. It actually went beyond the inventor's calculation, and he saw himself at last on the road to rapid fortune, and, above all, to Grace Carden.

This success excited Bolt's cupidity, and he refused to contract the operation any longer.

Then the partners had a quarrel, and nearly dissolved. However, it ended in Little dismissing his Birmingham hands and locking up his "experiment-room," and in Bolt openly devoting another room to the machines: two long, two circular.

These machines coined money, and Bolt chuckled and laughed at his partner's apprehensions for the space of twenty-one days.

On the twenty-second day, the Saw-grinders' Union, which had been stupefied at first, but had now realized the situation, sent Messrs. Bolt and Little a letter, civil and even humble: it spoke of the new invention as one that, if adopted, would destroy their handicraft, and starve the craftsmen and their families, and expressed an earnest hope that a firm which had shown so much regard for the health and comfort of the workmen would not persist in a fatal course, on which they had entered innocently and for want of practical advice.

The partners read this note differently. Bolt saw timidity in it. Little saw a conviction, and a quiet resolution, that foreboded a stern contest.

No reply was sent, and the machines went on coining.

Then came a warning to Little, not violent, but short, and rather grim. Little took it to Bolt, and he treated it with contempt.

Two days afterwards the wheel-bands vanished, and the obnoxious machines stood still.

Little was for going to Grotait, to try and come to terms. Bolt declined. He bought new bands, and next day the machines went on again.

This pertinacity soon elicited a curious epistle:

"MESSRS. BOLT AND LITTLE,—When the blood is in an impure state, brimstone and treacle is applied as a mild purgative; our taking the bands was the mild remedy; but, should the seat of disease not be reached, we shall take away the treacle, and add to the brimstone a necessary quantity of saltpetre and charcoal.
"TANTIA TOPEE."

On receipt of this, Little, who had tasted the last-mentioned drugs, showed such undisguised anxiety that Bolt sent for Ransome. He came directly, and was closeted with the firm. Bolt handed him the letters, told him the case, and begged leave to put him a question. "Is the police worth any thing, or nothing, in this here town?"

"It is worth something, I hope, gentlemen."

"How much, I wonder? Of all the bands that have been stolen, and all the people that have been blown up, and scorched, and vitrioled, and shot at, and shot, by Union men, did ever you and your bobbies nail a single malefactor?"

Now Mr. Ransome was a very tall man, with a handsome, dignified head, a long black beard, and pleasant, dignified manners. When short, round, vulgar Mr. Bolt addressed him thus, it really was like a terrier snapping at a Newfoundland dog. Little felt ashamed, and said Mr. Ransome had been only a few months in office in the place. "Thank you, Mr. Little," said the chief constable. "Mr. Bolt, I'll ask you a favor. Meet me at a certain place this evening, and let me reply to your question then and there."

This singular proposal excited some curiosity, and the partners accepted a rendezvous. Ransome came to the minute, and took the partners into the most squalid part of this foul city. At the corner of a narrow street he stopped and gave a low whistle. A policeman in plain clothes came to him directly.

"They are both in the 'Spotted Dog,' sir, with half a dozen more."

"Follow me, and guard the door. Will you come, too, gentlemen?"

The "Spotted Dog" was a low public, with one large room and a sanded floor. Mr. Ransome walked in and left the door open, so that his three companions heard and saw all that passed.

"Holland and Cheetham, you are wanted."

"What for?"

"Wilde's affair. He has come to himself, and given us your names."

On this the two men started up and were making for the door. Ransome whipped before it. "That won't do."

Then there was a loud clatter of rising feet, oaths, threats, and even a knife or two drawn; and, in the midst of it all, the ominous click of a

pistol, and then dead silence; for it was Ransome who had produced that weapon. "Come, no nonsense," said he. "Door's guarded, street's guarded, and I'm not to be trifled with."

He then handed his pistol to the officer outside with an order, and, stepping back suddenly, collared Messrs. Holland and Cheetham with one movement, and, with a powerful rush, carried them out of the house in his clutches. Meantime the policeman had whistled, there was a conflux of bobbies, and the culprits were handcuffed and marched off to the Town Hall.

"Five years' penal servitude for that little lot," said Ransome. "And now, Mr. Bolt, I have answered your question to the best of my ability."

"You have answered it like a man. Will you do as much for us?"

"I'll do my best. Let me examine the place, now that none of them are about."

Bolt and Ransome went together, but Little went home; he had an anxiety even more pressing, his mother's declining health. She had taken to pining and fretting ever since Doctor Amboyne brought the bad news from Cairnhope; and now, instead of soothing and consoling her son, she needed those kind offices from him; and, I am happy to say, she received them. He never spent an evening away from her. Unfortunately he did not succeed in keeping up her spirits, and the sight of her lowered his own.

At this period Grace Carden was unmixed comfort to him: she encouraged him to encroach a little, and visit her twice a week instead of once, and she coaxed him to confide all his troubles to her. He did so; he concealed from his mother that he was at war with the trade again, but he told Grace every thing, and her tender sympathy was the balm of his life. She used to put on cheerfulness for his sake, even when she felt it least.

One day, however, he found her less bright than usual, and she showed him an advertisement—Bollinghope house and park for sale; and she was not old enough nor wise enough to disguise from him that this pained her. Some expressions of regret and pity fell from her; that annoyed Henry, and he said, "What is that to us?"

"Nothing to you: but I feel I am the cause. I have not used him well, that's certain."

Henry said, rather cavalierly, that Mr. Coventry was probably selling his house for money, not for love, and (getting angry) that he hoped never to hear the man's name mentioned again.

Grace Carden was a little mortified by his tone, but she governed herself and said sadly, "My idea of love was to be able to tell you every thought of my heart, even where my conscience reproaches me a little. But if you prefer to exclude one topic—and have no fear that it may lead to the exclusion of others—"

They were on the borders of a tiff; but Henry recovered himself and said firmly, "I hope we shall not have a thought unshared one day: but, just for the present, it will be kinder to spare me that one topic."

"Very well, dearest," said Grace. "And, if it had not been for the advertisement—" she said no more, and the thing passed like a dark cloud between the lovers.

Bollinghope house and park were actually sold that very week; they were purchased, at more than their value, by a wealthy manufacturer: and the proceeds of this sale and the timber sale cleared off all Coventry's mortgages, and left him with a few hundred pounds in cash, and an estate which had not a tree on it, but also had not a debt upon it.

Of course he forfeited, by this stroke, his position as a country gentleman; but that he did not care about, since it was all done with one view, to live comfortably in Paris, far from the intolerable sight of his rival's happiness with the lady he loved.

He bought in at the sale a few heirlooms and articles of furniture—who does not cling, at the last moment, to something of this kind?—and rented a couple of unfurnished rooms in Hillsborough to keep them in. He fixed the day of his departure, arranged his goods, and packed his clothes. Then he got a letter of credit on Paris, and went about the town buying numerous articles of cutlery.

But this last simple act led to strange consequences. He was seen and followed; and in the dead of the evening, as he was cording with his own hands a box containing a few valuables, a heavy step mounted the stair, and there was a rude knock at the door.

Mr. Coventry felt rather uncomfortable, but he said, "Come in."

The door was opened, and there stood Sam Cole.

Coventry received him ill. He looked up from his packing and said, "What on earth do you want, sir?"

But it was not Cole's business to be offended. "Well, sir," said he, "I've been looking out for you some time, and I saw you at our place; so I thought I'd come and tell you a bit o' news."

"What is that?"

"It is about him you know of; begins with a hel."

"Curse him! I don't want to hear about him. I'm leaving the country. Well, what is it?"

"He is wrong with the trade again."

"What is that to me?—Ah! sit down, Cole, and tell me."

Cole let him know the case, and assured him that, sooner or later, if threats did not prevail, the Union would go any length.

"Should you be employed?"

"If it was a dangerous job, they'd prefer me."

Mr. Coventry looked at his trunks, and then at Sam Cole. A small voice whispered "Fly." He stifled that warning voice, and told Cole he would stay and watch this affair, and Cole was to report to him whenever any thing fresh occurred. From that hour this gentleman led the life of a malefactor, dressed like a workman, and never went out except at night.

Messrs. Bolt and Little were rattened again, and never knew it till morning. This time it was not the bands, but certain axle-nuts and screws that vanished. The obnoxious machines came to a stand-still, and Bolt fumed and cursed. However, at ten o'clock, he and the foreman were invited to the Town Hall, and there they found the missing gear, and the culprit, one of the very workmen employed at high wages on the obnoxious machines.

Ransome had bored a small hole in the ceiling, by means of which this room was watched from above; the man was observed, followed, and

nabbed. The property found on him was identified, and the magistrate offered the prisoner a jury, which he declined; then the magistrate dealt with the case summarily, refused to recognize rattening, called the offense "petty larceny," and gave the man six months' prison.

Now as Ransome, for obvious reasons, concealed the means by which this man had been detected, a conviction so mysterious shook that sense of security which ratteners had enjoyed for many years, and the trades began to find that craft had entered the lists with craft.

Unfortunately, those who directed the Sawgrinders' Union thought the existence of the trade at stake, and this minor defeat merely exasperated them.

Little received a letter telling him he was acting worse than Brinsley, who had been shot dead in the Briggate; and asking him, as a practical man, which he thought was likely to die first, he or the Union? "'You won't let us live; why should we let you?"

Bolt was threatened in similar style, but he merely handed the missives to Ransome; he never flinched.

Not so Little. He got nervous; and, in a weak moment, let his mother worm out of him that he was at war with the trades again.

This added anxiety to her grief, and she became worse every day.

Then Dr. Amboyne interfered, and, after a certain degree of fencing—which seems inseparable from the practice of medicine—told Henry plainly he feared the very worst if this went on; Mrs. Little was on the brink of jaundice. By his advice Henry took her to Aberystwith in Wales, and, when he had settled her there, went back to his troubles.

To those was now added a desolate home; gone was the noble face, the maternal eye, the soothing voice, the unfathomable love. He never knew all her value till now.

One night, as he sat by himself sad and disconsolate, his servant came to tell him there was a young woman inquiring for Mrs. Little. Henry went out to her, and it was Jael Dence. He invited her in, and told her what had happened. Jael saw his distress, and gave him her womanly sympathy. "And I came to tell her my own trouble," said she; "fie on me!"

"Then tell it me, Jael. There, take off your shawl and sit down. They shall make you a cup of tea."

Jael complied, with a slight blush; but as to her trouble, she said it was not worth speaking of in that house.

Henry insisted, however, and she said, "Mine all comes of my sister marrying that Phil Davis. To tell you the truth, I went to church with a heavy heart on account of their both beginning with a D—Dence and Davis; for 'tis an old saying—

"'If you change the name, and not the letter,
You change for the worse, and not for the better.'

Well, sir, it all went wrong somehow. Parson, he was South country; and, when his time came to kiss the bride, he stood and looked ever so helpless, and I had to tell him he must kiss her; and even then he stared foolish-like a bit before he kissed her, and the poor lass's face getting up and the tear in her eye at being slighted. And that put Patty out for one thing: and then she wouldn't give away the ribbon to the fastest runner—the lads run a hundred yards to the bride, for ribbon and kiss, you know;—wasn't the ribbon she grudged, poor wench; but the fastest runner in Cairnhope town is that Will Gibbon, a nasty, ugly, slobbering chap, that was always after her, and Philip jealous of him: so she did for the best, and Will Gibbon safe to win it. But the village lads they didn't see the reason, and took it all to themselves. Was she better than her granddam? and were they worse than their grandsires? They ran on before, and fired the anvil when she passed: just fancy! an affront close to her own door: and, sir, she walked in a doors crying. There was a wedding for you! George the blacksmith was that hurt at their making free with his smithy to affront her, he lifted his arm for the first time, and pretty near killed a couple of them, poor thoughtless bodies. Well, sir, Phil Davis always took a drop, you know, and, instead of mending, he got worse; they live with father, and of course he has only to go to the barrel: old-fashioned farmers like us don't think to spy on the ale. He was so often in liquor, I checked him; but Patty indulged him in every thing. By-and-by my lord gets ever so civil to me: 'What next?' said I to myself. One fine evening we are set up stairs at our tea; in he comes drunk, and says many things we had to look at one another and excuse. Presently he tells us all that he has made a mistake: he has wedded Patty, and I'm the one he likes the best. I thought the fool was in jest; but Patty she gave a cry as if a knife had gone through her heart. Then my blood got up in a moment. 'That's an affront to all three,' said I: 'and take your answer, ye drunken sow,' said I. I took him by the scruff of the neck and just turned him out of the room and sent him to the bottom of the stairs headforemost. Then Patty she quarrelled with me, and father he sided with her. And so I gave them my blessing, and told them to send for me in trouble; and I left the house I was born in. It all comes of her changing her name, and not her letter." Here a few tears interrupted further comment.

Henry consoled her, and asked her what she was going to do.

She said she did not know; but she had a good bit of money put by, and was not afraid of work, and, in truth, she had come there to ask Mrs. Little's advice, "poor lady. Now don't you mind me, Mr. Henry, your trouble is a deal worse than mine."

"Jael," said he, "you must come here and keep my house till my poor mother is better."

Jael colored and said, "Nay, that will not do. But if you could find me something to do in your great factory—and I hear you have enemies there; you might as well have a friend right in the middle of them. Eh, but I'd keep my eyes and ears open for you."

Henry appreciated this proposal, and said there were plenty of things she could do; she could hone, she could pack, she could superintend, and keep the girls from gabbling; "That," said he, "is the real thing that keeps them behind the men at work."

So Jael Dence lodged with a female cousin in Hillsborough, and filled a position of trust in the factory of Bolt and Little: she packed, and super-

intended, and the foreman paid her thirty shillings a week. The first time this was tendered her she said severely, "Is this right, young man?" meaning, "Is it not too much?"

"Oh, you will be raised if you stay with us three months."

"Raised?" said the virtuous rustic! Then, looking loftily round on the other women, "What ever do these factory folk find to grumble at?"

Henry told Grace all about this, and she said, rather eagerly, "Ah, I am glad of that. You'll have a good watch-dog."

It was a shrewd speech. The young woman soon found out that Little was really in danger, and she was all eyes, and ears, and no tongue.

Yet neither her watchfulness, nor Ransome's, prevailed entirely against the deviltries of the offended Union. Machinery was always breaking down by pure accident; so every body swore, and nobody believed: the water was all let out of a boiler, and the boiler burst. Bands were no longer taken, but they were cut. And, in short, the works seemed to be under a curse.

And, lest the true origin of all these mishaps should be doubted, each annoyance was followed by an anonymous letter. These were generally sent to Little. A single sentence will indicate the general tone of each.

1. "All these are but friendly warnings, to save your life if possible."

2. "I never give in. I fight to death, and with more craft and duplicity than Bolt and Ransome. They will never save you from me, if you persist. Ask others whether I ever failed to keep my word."

3. "If I but move my finger, you are sent into eternity."

Henry Little's nerve began to give way more and more.

Meantime Cole met Mr. Coventry, and told him what was going on beneath the surface: at the same time he expressed his surprise at the extraordinary forbearance shown by the Union. "Grotait is turning soft, I think. He will not give the word to burn Sebastopol."

"Then do it without him."

Cole shook his head, and said he daren't. But, after some reflection, he said there was a mate of his, who was not so dependent on Grotait: he might be tempted perhaps to do something on his own hook, Little being wrong with the trade, and threatened. "How much would you stand?"

"How far would your friend go?"

"I'll ask him."

Next day Cole walked coolly into the factory at dinner-time and had a conversation with Hill, one of the workmen, who he knew was acting for the Union, and a traitor in his employers' camp. He made Hill a proposal. Hill said it was a very serious thing; he would think of it, and meet him at a certain safe place and tell him.

Cole strolled out of the works, but not unobserved. Jael Dence had made it her business to know every man in the factory by sight, and observing, from a window, a stranger in conversation with Hill, she came down and met Cole at the gate. She started at sight of him: he did not exactly recognize her; but, seeing danger in her eye, took to his heels, and ran for it like a deer: Jael called to some of the men to follow him, but nobody moved. They guessed it was a Union matter. Jael ran to Little, and told him that villain, who had escaped from Raby Hall, had been in the works colloguing with one of the men.

Ransome was sent for, and Cole described to him.

As for Hill, Jael watched him like a cat from that hour, since a man is known by his friends. She went so far as to follow him home every evening.

Cole got fifty pounds out of Coventry for Hill, and promised him twenty. For this sum Hill agreed to do Little. But he demanded some little time to become proficient in the weapon he meant to use.

During the interval events were not idle. A policeman saw a cutler and a disguised gentleman talking together, and told Ransome. He set spies to discover, if possible, what that might mean.

One day the obnoxious machines were stopped by an *accident* to the machinery, and Little told Jael this, and said, "Have you a mind to earn five pound a week?"

"Ay, if I could do it honestly."

"Let us see the arm that flung Phil Davis down stairs."

Jael colored a little, but bared her left arm at command.

"Good heavens!" cried Little. "What a limb! Why mine is a shrimp compared with it."

"Ay, mine has the bulk, but yours the pith."

"Oh, come; if your left arm did that, what must your right be?"

"Oh," said Jael, "you men do every thing with your right hand; but we lasses know no odds. My left is as strong as my right, and both at your service."

"Then come along with me."

He took her into the "Experiment Room," explained the machine to her, gave her a lesson or two; and so simple was the business that she soon mastered her part of it; and Little, with his coat off, and Jael, with her noble arms bare, ground long saws together secretly; and Little, with Bolt's consent, charged the firm by the gross. He received twenty-four pounds per week, out of which he paid Jael six, in spite of her "How can a lass's work be worth all that?" and similar remonstrances.

Being now once more a workman, and working with this loyal lass so many hours a day, his spirits rose a little, and his nerves began to recover their tone.

But meantime Hill was maturing his dark design.

In going home, Little passed through one place he never much liked. It was a longish close, with two sharp rectangular turns.

Since he was threatened by the trade, he never entered this close without looking behind him. He did not much fear an attack in front, being always armed with pistols now.

On a certain night he came to this place as usual, went as far as the first turn, then looked sharply round to see if he was followed; but there was nobody behind except a woman, who was just entering the court. So he went on.

But a little way down this close was a small public-house, and the passage-door was ajar, and a man watching. No sooner was Little out of sight than he emerged, and followed him swiftly on tiptoe.

The man had in his hand a weapon that none but a Hillsborough cutler would have thought of; yet, as usual, it was very fit for the purpose, being noiseless and dangerous, though old-fashioned. It was a long strong bow, all made of yew-tree. The man fitted an arrow to this, and running lightly to the first turn, obtained a full view of Little's retiring figure, not fifteen yards distant.

So well was the place chosen, that he had only to discharge his weapon and then run back. His victim could never see him.

He took a deliberate aim at Little's back, drew the arrow to the head, and was about to loose it, when a woman's arm was flung round his neck.

CHAPTER XXXII.

COVENTRY and Cole met that night near a little church.

Hill was to join them, and tell them the result.

Now, as it happens, Little went home rather late that night; so these confederates waited, alternately hoping and fearing, a considerable time.

Presently, something mysterious occurred that gave them a chill. An arrow descended, as if from the clouds, and stuck quivering on a grave not ten yards from them. The black and white feathers shone clear in the moonlight.

To Coventry it seemed as if Heaven was retaliating on him.

The more prosaic but quick-witted cutler, after the first stupefaction, suspected it was the very arrow destined for Little, and said so.

"And Heaven flings it back to us," said Coventry, and trembled in every limb.

"Heaven has nought to do in it. The fool has got drunk, and shot it in the air. Anyway, it mustn't stick there to tell tales."

Cole vaulted over the church-yard, drew it out of the grave, and told Coventry to hide it.

"Go you home," said he. "I'll find out what this means."

Hill's unexpected assailant dragged him back so suddenly and violently that the arrow went up at an angle of forty-five, and, as the man loosed the string to defend himself, flew up into the sky, and came down full a hundred yards from the place.

Hill twisted violently round and, dropping the bow, struck the woman in the face with his fist: he had not room to use all his force; yet the blow covered her face with blood. She cried out, but gripped him so tight by both shoulders that he could not strike again, but he kicked her savagely. She screamed, but slipped her arms down and got him tight round the waist. Then he was done for: with one mighty whirl she tore him off his feet in a moment, then dashed herself and him under her to the ground with such ponderous violence that his head rang loud on the pavement and he was stunned for a few seconds. Ere he quite recovered she had him turned on his face, and her weighty knee grinding down his shoulders, while her nimble hands whipped off her kerchief and tied his hands behind him in a twinkling.

So quickly was it all done, that by the time Little heard the scrimmage, ascertained it was behind him, and came back to see, she was seated on her prisoner, trembling and crying after her athletic feat, and very little fit to cope with the man if he had not been tied.

Little took her by the hands. "Oh, my poor Jael! What is the matter? Has the blackguard been insulting you?" And, not waiting for an answer, gave him a kick that made him howl again.

They took Jael Dence to a chemist's shop, and gave her cold water and salts: the first thing she did, when she was quite herself, was to seize Henry Little's hand and kiss it with such a look of joy as brought tears into his eyes.

Then she told her story, and was taken in a cab to the police-office, and repeated her story there.

THE ARROW WENT UP AT AN ANGLE OF FORTY-FIVE.

"Yes, kill him, the villain! he wanted to murder you. Oh, oh, oh!"

She could say no more, but became hysterical.

Henry supported her tenderly, and wiped the blood from her face; and, as several people came up, and a policeman, he gave the man in charge, on Jael's authority, and he was conveyed to the station accordingly, he and his bow.

Then Henry took her to Woodbine Villa, and Grace Carden turned very pale at Henry's danger, though passed: she wept over Jael, and kissed her; and nobody could make enough of her.

Grace Carden looked wistfully at Henry and said, "Oh that I had a strong arm to defend you!"

"Oh, Miss Grace," said Jael, " don't you envy

me. Go away with him from this wicked, mur-
dering place. That will be a deal better than any
thing I can do for him."

"Ah, would to Heaven I could this minute!"
said Grace, clinging tenderly to his shoulder.
She insisted on going home with him and shar-
ing his peril for once.

Hill was locked up for the night.

In the morning a paper was slipped into his
hand. "Say there was no arrow."

He took this hint, and said that he was innocent as a babe of any harm. He had got a bow
to repair for a friend, and he went home twang-
ing it, was attacked by a woman, and, in his confusion, struck her once, but did not repeat the
blow.

Per contra, Jael Dence distinctly swore there
was an arrow, with two white feathers and one
black one, and that the prisoner was shooting at
Mr. Little. She also swore that she had seen
him colloguing with another man, who had been
concerned in a former attempt on Mr. Little, and
captured, but had escaped from Raby Hall.

On this the magistrate declined to discharge
the prisoner; but, as no arrow could be found at
present, admitted him to bail, two securities fifty
pounds each, which was an indirect way of im-
prisoning him until the Assizes.

This attempt, though unsuccessful in one way,
was very effective in another. It shook Henry
Little terribly; and the effect was enhanced by
an anonymous letter he received, reminding him
there were plenty of noiseless weapons. Brinsley had been shot twice, and no sound heard.
"When your time comes, you'll never know what
hurt you." The sense of a noiseless assassin
eternally dogging him preyed on Little's mind and
spirits, and at last this life on the brink of the
grave became so intolerable that he resolved to
leave Hillsborough, but not alone.

He called on Grace Carden, pale and agitated.

"Grace," said he, "do you really love me?"

"Oh, Henry! Do I love you?"

"Then save me from this horrible existence.
Oh, my love, if you knew what it is to have been
a brave man, and to find your courage all oozing
away under freezing threats, that you know, by
experience, will be followed by some dark, subtle,
bloody deed or other. There, they have brought
me down to this, that I never go ten steps without
looking behind me, and, when I go round a corner, I turn short and run back, and wait at the
corner to see if an assassin is following me. I
tremble at the wind. I start at my own shadow."

Grace threw her arms round his neck, and
stopped him with tears and kisses.

"Ah, bless you, my love!" he cried, and kissed
her fondly. "You pity me—you will save me
from this miserable, degrading life?"

"Ah, that I will, if I can, my own."

"You can."

"Then tell me how."

"Be my wife—let us go to the United States
together. Dearest, my patents are a great success. We are making our fortune, though we
risk our lives. In America I could sell these inventions for a large sum, or work them myself at
an enormous profit. Be my wife, and let us fly
this hellish place together."

"And so I would in a moment; but"(with a
deep sigh) "papa would never consent to that."

"Dispense with his consent."

"Oh, Henry; and marry under my father's
curse!"

"He would not curse you, if he loves you half
as well as I do; and if he does not, why sacrifice
me, and perhaps my life, to him?"

"Henry, for pity's sake, think of some other
way. Why this violent haste to get rich? Have
a little patience. Mr. Raby will not always be
abroad. Oh, pray give up Mr. Bolt, and go quietly on, at peace with these dreadful Trades. You
know I'll wait all my life for you. I will implore
papa to let you visit me oftener. I will do all a
faithful, loving girl can do to comfort you."

"Ay," said Henry, bitterly, "you will do any
thing but the one thing I ask."

"Yes, any thing but defy my father. He is
father and mother both to me. How unfortunate
we both are! If you knew what it costs me to
deny you any thing, if you knew how I long to
follow you round the world—"

She choked with emotion, and seemed on the
point of yielding, after all.

But he said, bitterly, "You long to follow me
round the world, and you won't go a twelve-
days' voyage with me to save my life. Ah, it is
always so. You don't love me as poor Jael
Dence loves me. She saved my life without my
asking her; but you won't do it when I implore
you."

"Henry, my own darling, if any woman on
earth loves you better than I do, for God's sake
marry her, and let me die to prove I loved you a
little."

"Very well," said he, grinding his teeth. "Next
week I leave this place with a wife. I give you
the first offer, because I love you. I shall give
Jael the second, because she loves me."

So then he flung out of the room, and left
Grace Carden half fainting on the sofa, and drowned in tears.

But before he got back to the works he repented his violence, and his heart yearned for her
more than ever.

With that fine sense of justice which belongs
to love, he spoke roughly to Jael Dence.

She stared, and said nothing, but watched him
furtively, and saw his eyes fill with tears at the
picture memory recalled of Grace's pale face and
streaming eyes.

She put a few shrewd questions, and his heart
was so full he could not conceal the main facts,
though he suppressed all that bore reference to
Jael herself. She took Grace's part, and told him
he was all in the wrong; why could not he go to
America alone, and sell his patents, and then come
back and marry Grace with the money? "Why
drag her across the water, to make her quarrel
with her father?"

"Why, indeed?" said Henry: "because I'm
not the man I was. I have no manhood left. I
have not the courage to fight the Trades, nor yet
the courage to leave the girl I love so dearly."

"Eh, poor lad," said Jael, "thou hast courage
enough; but it has been too sore tried, first and
last. You have gone through enough to break a
man of steel."

She advised him to go and make his submission
at once.

He told her she was his guardian angel, and
kissed her, in the warmth of his gratitude; and
he went back to Woodbine Villa, and asked
Grace's forgiveness, and said he would go alone

to the States, and come back with plenty of money to satisfy Mr. Carden's prudence, and—

Grace clutched him gently with both hands, as if to hinder him from leaving her. She turned very pale, and said, "Oh my heart!"

Then she laid her head on his shoulder, and wept piteously.

He comforted her, and said, "What is it? a voyage of twelve days! And yet I shall never have the courage to bid you good-bye."

"Nor I you, my own darling."

Having come to this resolution, he was now seized with a fear that he would be assassinated before he could carry it out: to diminish the chances, he took up his quarters at the factory, and never went out at night. Attached to the works was a small building near the water-side. Jael Dence occupied the second floor of it. He had a camp-bed set up on the first floor, and established a wire communication with the police-office. At the slightest alarm he could ring a bell in Ransome's ear. He also clandestinely unscrewed a little postern door that his predecessors had closed, and made a key to the lock, so that if he should ever be compelled to go out at night he might baffle his foes, who would naturally watch the great gate for his exit.

With all this he became very depressed and moody, and alarmed Doctor Amboyne, who remembered his father's end.

The Doctor advised him to go and see his mother for a day or two; but he shook his head, and declined.

A prisoner detained for want of bail is allowed to communicate with his friends, and Grotait soon let Hill know he was very angry with him for undertaking to do Little without orders. Hill said that the job was given him by Cole, who was Grotait's right-hand man, and Grotait had better bail him, otherwise he might be induced to tell tales.

Grotait let him stay in prison three days, and then sent two householders with the bail.

Hill was discharged, and went home. At dusk he turned out to find Cole, and tracing him from one public-house to another, at last lighted on him in company with Mr. Coventry.

This set him thinking; however, he held aloof till they parted; and then following Cole, dunned him for his twenty pounds.

Cole gave him five pounds on account. Hill grumbled, and threatened.

Grotait sent for both men, and went into a passion, and threatened to hang them both if they presumed to attack Little's person again in any way. "It is the place I mean to destroy," said Grotait, "not the man."

Cole conveyed this to Coventry, and it discouraged him mightily, and he told Cole he should give it up and go abroad.

But soon after this some pressure or other was brought to bear on Grotait, and Cole, knowing this, went to him, and asked him whether Bolt and Little were to be done or not.

"It is a painful subject," said Grotait.

"It is a matter of life and death to us," said Cole.

"That is true. But mind—the place, and not the man."

Cole assented, and then Grotait took him on to a certain bridge, and pointed out the one weak side of Bolt and Little's fortress, and showed him how the engine-chimney could be got at and blown down, and so the works stopped entirely: "And I'll tell you something," said he; "that chimney is built on a bad foundation, and was never very safe; so you have every chance."

Then they chaffered about the price, and at last Grotait agreed to give him £20.

Cole went to Coventry, and told him how far Grotait would allow him to go: "But," said he, "£20 is not enough. I run an even chance of being hung or lagged."

"Go a step beyond your instructions, and I'll give you a hundred pounds."

"I daren't," said Cole: "unless there was a chance to blow up the place with the man in it." Then, after a moment's reflection, he said: "I hear he sleeps in the works. I must find out where."

Accordingly, he talked over one of the women in the factory, and gained the following information, which he imparted to Mr. Coventry:

Little lived and slept in a detached building recently erected, and the young woman who had overpowered Hill slept in a room above him. She passed in the works for his sweetheart, and the pair were often locked up together for hours at a time in a room called the "Experiment Room."

This information took Coventry quite by surprise, and embittered his hatred of Little. While Cole was felicitating him on the situation of the building, he was meditating how to deal his hated rival a stab of another kind.

Cole, however, was single-minded in the matter; and the next day he took a boat and drifted slowly down the river, and scanned the place very carefully.

He came at night to Coventry, and told him he thought he might perhaps be able to do the trick without seeming to defy Grotait's instructions. "But," said he, "it is a very dangerous job. Premises are watched: and, what do you think? they have got wires up now that run over the street to the police-office, and Little can ring a bell in Ransome's room, and bring the bobbies across with a rush in a moment. It isn't as it was under the old chief constable; this one's not to be bought nor blinded. I must risk a halter."

"You shall have fifty pounds more."

"You are a gentleman, sir. I should like to have it in hard sovereigns. I'm afraid of notes. They get traced somehow."

"You shall have it all in sovereigns."

"I want a little in advance, to buy the materials. They are costly, especially the fulminating silver."

Coventry gave him ten sovereigns, and they parted with the understanding that Cole should endeavor to blow up the premises on some night when Little was in them, and special arrangements were made to secure this.

Henry Little and Grace Carden received, each of them, an anonymous letter, on the same day. Grace Carden's ran thus:—

"I can't abide to see a young lady made a fool of by a villain. Mr. Little have got his miss here: they dote on each other. She lives in the works, and so do he, ever since she came, which he usen't afore. They are in one room, as many as eight hours at a stretch, and that room always locked.

It is the talk of all the girls. It is nought to me, but I thought it right you should know, for it is quite a scandal. She is a strapping country lass, with a queerish name. This comes from a stranger, but a well-wisher. **FAIR PLAY."**

The letter to Henry Little was as follows:—

"The reason of so many warnings, and ne'er a blow, you had friends in the trade. But you have worn them out. You are a doomed man. Prepare to meet your God.

This was the last straw on the camel's back, as the saying is.

He just ground it in his hand, and then he began to act.

He set to work, packed up models, and dispatched them by train: clothes ditto, and wrote a long letter to his mother.

Next day he was busy writing and arranging papers till the afternoon. Then he called on Grace, as related, and returned to the works about six o'clock: he ordered a cup of tea at seven, which Jael brought him. She found him busy writing letters, and one of these was addressed to Grace Carden.

That was all she saw of him that night; for she went to bed early, and she was a sound sleeper.

It was nine o'clock of this same evening.

Mr. Coventry, disguised in a beard, was walking up and down a certain street opposite the great door of the works.

He had already walked and lounged about two hours. At last Cole joined him for a moment and whispered in a tone full of meaning, "Will it do now?"

Coventry's teeth chattered together as he replied, "Yes; now is the time."

"Got the money ready?"

"Yes."

"Let us see it."

"When you have done what you promised me."

"That very moment?"

"That very moment."

"Then I'll tell you what you must do. In about an hour go on the new bridge, and I'll come to you; and, before I've come to you many minutes, you'll see summut and hear summut that will make a noise in Hillsbro', and, perhaps, get us both into trouble."

"Not if you are as dexterous as others have been."

"Others! I was in all those jobs. But this is the queerest. I go to it as if I was going to a halter. No matter, a man can but die once."

And, with these words, he left him and went softly down to the water-side. There, in the shadow of the new bridge, lay a little boat, and in it a light-jointed ladder, a small hamper, and a basket of tools. The rowlocks were covered with tow, and the oars made no noise whatever, except the scarce audible dip in the dark stream. It soon emerged below the bridge like a black spider crawling down the stream, and melted out of sight the more rapidly that a slight fog was rising.

Cole rowed softly past the works, and observed a very faint light in Little's room. He thought it prudent to wait till this should be extinguished, but it was not extinguished. Here was an unexpected delay.

However, the fog thickened a little, and this encouraged him to venture; he beached the boat very gently on the muddy shore, and began his work, looking up every now and then at that pale light, and ready to fly at the first alarm.

He took out of the boat a large varnish-can, which he had filled with gunpowder, and wrapped tightly round with wire, and also with a sash-line; this can was perforated at the side, and a strong tube screwed tightly into it; the tube protruded twelve inches from the can in shape of an 8: by means of this a slow-burning fuse was connected with the powder; some yards of this fuse were wrapt loosely round the can.

Cole crept softly to the engine-chimney, and, groping about for the right place, laid the can in the engine bottom and uncoiled the fuse. He took out of his pocket some small pieces of tile, and laid the fuse dry on these.

Then he gave a sigh of relief, and crept back to the boat.

Horrible as the action was, he had done all this without much fear, and with no remorse, for he was used to this sort of work; but now he had to commit a new crime, and with new and terrible materials, which he had never handled in the way of crime before.

He had in his boat a substance so dangerous that he had made a nest of soft cotton for the receptacle which held it; and when the boat touched the shore, light as the contact was, he quaked lest his imprisoned giant-devil should go off and blow him to atoms.

He put off touching it till the last moment. He got his jointed ladder, set it very softly underneath the window where the feeble gas-light was, and felt about with his hands for the grating he had observed when he first reconnoitred the premises from the river. He found it, but it was so high that he had to reach a little, and the position was awkward for working.

The problem was how to remove one of those bars, and so admit his infernal machine; it was about the shape and size of an ostrich's egg.

It must be done without noise, for the room above him was Little's, and Little, he knew, had a wire by means of which he could summon Ransome and the police in the turn of a hand.

The cold of the night, and the now present danger, made Cole shiver all over, and he paused.

But he began again, and, taking out a fine steel saw highly tempered, proceeded to saw the iron slowly and gently, ready at the first alarm to spring from his ladder and run away.

With all his caution, steel grated against steel, and made too much noise in the stilly night. He desisted. He felt about, and found the grating was let into wood, not stone; he oiled the saw, and it cut the wood like butter; he made two cuts like a capital V, and a bar of the grating came loose; he did the same thing above, and the bar came out.

Cole now descended the ladder, and prepared for the greatest danger of all. He took from its receptacle the little metal box lined with glazed paper, which contained the fulminating silver and its fuse; and, holding it as gently as possible, went and mounted the ladder again, putting his foot down as softly as a cat.

But he was getting colder and colder, and at this unfortunate moment he remembered that, when he was a lad, a man had been destroyed by fulminating silver—quite a small quantity—in a plate over which he was leaning; yet the poor wretch's limbs had been found in different places, and he himself had seen the head; it had been torn from the trunk and hurled to an incredible distance.

That trunkless head he now fancied he saw, in the middle of the fog; and his body began to sweat cold, and his hands to shake so that he could hardly hold the box. But if he let it fall—

He came hastily down the ladder and sat down on the dirty ground, with the infernal engine beside him.

By-and-by he got up and tried to warm his hands and feet by motion, and at last he recovered his fortitude, and went softly and cat-like up the steps again, in spite of the various dangers he incurred.

Of what was this man's mind composed, whom neither a mere bribe could buy to do this deed, nor pure fanaticism without a bribe; but, where both inducements met, neither the risk of immediate death, nor of imprisonment for life, nor both dangers united, could divert him from his deadly purpose, though his limbs shook, and his body was bedewed with a cold perspiration?

He reached the top of the ladder, he put his hand inside the grate; there was an aperture, but he could not find the bottom. He hesitated.

Here was a fresh danger: if he let the box fall it might explode at once and send him to eternity.

Once more he came softly down, and collected all the tow and wool he could find. He went up the ladder and put these things through the grating; they formed a bed.

Then he went back for the fatal box, took it up the ladder and put these things, laid it softly in its bed, uncoiled the fuse and let it hang down.

So now these two fiendish things were placed, and their devilish tails hanging out behind them. The fuses had been cut with the utmost nicety to burn the same length of time—twelve minutes.

But Cole was too thoughtful and wary to light the fuses until every thing was prepared for his escape. He put the ladder on board the boat, disposed the oars so that he could use them at once; then crept to the engine-chimney, kneeled down beside the fuse, looked anxiously up at the faint light glimmering above, and took off his hat.

With singular cunning and forethought he had pasted a piece of sand-paper into his hat. By this means he lighted a lucifer at once, and kept it out of sight from the windows, and also safe from the weather; he drew the end of the fuse into the hat, applied the match to it out of sight, then blew the match out and darted to his other infernal machine. In less than ten seconds he lighted that fuse too; then stepped into the boat, and left those two devilish sparks creeping each on its fatal errand. He pulled away with exulting bosom, beating heart, and creeping flesh. He pulled swiftly up stream, landed at the bridge, staggered up the steps, and found Coventry at his post, but almost frozen, and sick of waiting.

He staggered up to him and gasped out, "I've done the trick, give me the brass, and let me go. I see a halter in the air." His teeth chattered.

But Coventry, after hoping and fearing for two hours and a half, had lost all confidence in his associate, and he said, "How am I to know you've done any thing?"

"You'll see and you'll hear," said Cole. "Give me the brass."

"Wait till I see and hear," was the reply.

"What, wait to be nabbed? Another minute, and all the town will be out after me. Give it me, or I'll take it."

"Will you?" And Coventry took out a pistol and cocked it. Cole recoiled.

"Look here," said Coventry; "there are one hundred and fifty sovereigns in this bag. The moment I receive proof you have not deceived me, I give you the bag."

"Here, where we stand?"

"Here, on this spot."

"Hush! not so loud. Didn't I hear a step?" They both listened keenly. The fog was thick by this time.

Cole whispered, "Look down the river. I wonder which will go off first? It is very cold; very." And he shook like a man in an ague.

Both men listened, numbed with cold, and quivering with the expectation of crime.

A clock struck twelve.

At the first stroke the confederates started and uttered a cry. They were in that state when every thing sudden shakes men like thunder.

All still again, and they listened and shook again with fog and crime.

Sudden a lurid flash, and a report, dull and heavy, and something tall seemed to lean towards them from the sky, and there was a mighty rushing sound, and a cold wind in their faces, and an awful fall of masonry on the water, and the water spurted under the stroke. The great chimney had fallen in the river. At this very moment came a sharp, tremendous report like a clap of thunder close at hand. It was so awful, that both bag and pistol fell out of Coventry's hand and rang upon the pavement, and he fled, terror-stricken.

Cole, though frightened, went down on his knees, and got the bag, and started to run the other way.

But almost at the first step he ran against a man, who was running towards him.

Both were staggered by the shock, and almost knocked down.

But the man recovered himself first, and seized Cole with a grip of iron.

When Coventry had run a few steps he recovered his judgment so far as to recollect that this would lay him open to suspicion. He left off running, and walked briskly instead.

Presently the great door of the works was opened, and the porter appeared crying wildly for help, and that the place was on fire.

The few people that were about made a rush, and Coventry, driven by an awful curiosity, went in with them; for why should he be suspected any more than they?

He had not gone in half a minute when Mr. Ransome arrived with several policemen, and closed the doors at once against all comers.

Strange to say, the last explosion had rung the bell in the police-office; hence this prompt appearance of the police.

The five or six persons who got in with Covent·y knew nothing, and ran hither and thither. Coventry, better informed, darted at once to Little's quarters, and there beheld an awful sight; the roof presented the appearance of a sieve: of the second floor little remained but a few of the joists, and these were most of them broken and stood on end and across each other, like a hedgehog's bristles.

In Little's room, a single beam in the centre, with a fragment of board, kept its place, but the joists were all dislocated or broken in two, and sticking up here and there in all directions: huge holes had been blown in the walls of both rooms, and much of the contents of the rooms blown out by them: so vast were these apertures, that it seemed wonderful how the structure hung together; the fog was as thick in the dismembered and torn building as outside, but a large gas-pipe in Little's room was wrenched into the form of a snake and broken, and the gas set on fire and flaring, so that the devastation was visible; the fire-place also hung on, heaven knows how.

Coventry cast his eyes round, and recoiled with horror at what he had done: his foot struck something; it was the letter-box, full of letters, still attached to the broken door. By some instinct of curiosity he stooped and peered. There was one letter addressed "Grace Carden."

He tried to open the box; he could not: he gave it a wrench, it was a latticed box, and came to pieces. He went down the stairs with the fragments and the letters in his hand; feet approached, and he heard a voice close to him say, "This way, Mr. Ransome, for God's sake!" A sort of panic seized him; he ran back, and in his desperation jumped on to the one beam that was standing, and from that through the open wall, and fell on the soft mud by the river bank. Though the ground was soft, the descent shook him and embedded him so deeply he could not extricate himself for some time. But terror lends energy, and he was now thoroughly terrified: he thrust the letters in his pocket, and, being an excellent swimmer, dashed at once into the river; but he soon found it choked up with masonry and débris of every kind: he coasted this, got into the stream, and swam across to the other side. Then taking the lowest and darkest streets, contrived at last to get home, wet and filthy, and quaking.

Ransome and his men examined the shattered building within and without; but no trace could be found of any human being, alive or dead.

Then they got to the river-side with lights, and here they found foot-marks. Ransome set men to guard these from being walked over.

Attention was soon diverted from these. Several yards from the torn building, a woman was found lying all huddled together on a heap of broken masonry. She was in her night-dress, and a counterpane half over her. Her forehead and head were bleeding, and she was quite insensible. The police recognized her directly. It was Jael Dence.

She was alive, though insensible, and Ransome had her conveyed at once to the infirmary.

"Bring more lights to the water-side," said he; "the explosion has acted in that direction."

Many torches were brought. Keen eyes scanned the water. One or two policemen got out upon the ruins of the chimney, and went ankle-deep in water. But what they sought could not be found.

Ransome said he was glad of it. Every body knew what he meant.

He went back to Little's room, and examined it minutely. In the passage he found a card-case. It was lying on the door. Ransome took it up mechanically, and put it in his pocket. He did not examine it at this time: he took for granted it was Little's. He asked one of his men whether a man had not been seen in that room. The officer said "Yes."

"Did he come down?"

"No; and I can't think how he got out."

"It is plain how he got out; and that accounts for something I observed in the mud. Now, Williams, you go to my place for that stuff I use to take the mould of foot-prints. Bring plenty. Four of you scour the town, and try and find out who has gone home with river-mud on his shoes or trowsers. Send me the porter."

When the porter came, he asked him whether Mr. Little had slept in the works.

The porter could not say for certain.

"Well, but what was his habit?"

"He always slept here of late."

"When did you see him last?"

"I let him into the works."

"When?"

"I should think about seven o'clock."

"Did you let him out again?"

"No, Mr. Ransome."

"Perhaps you might, and not recollect. Pray think."

The porter shook his head.

"Are you sure you did not let him out?"

"I am quite sure of that."

"Then the Lord have mercy on his soul!"

CHAPTER XXXIII.

THAT was Grace Carden's first anonymous letter. Its contents curdled her veins with poison. The poor girl sat pale and benumbed, turning the letter in her hand, and reading the fatal words over and over again.

There was a time when she would have entirely disbelieved this slander; but now she remembered, with dismay, how many things had combined to attach Henry to Jael Dence. And then the letter stated such hard facts; facts unknown to her, but advanced positively.

But what terrified her most was that Henry had so lately told her Jael Dence loved him best.

Yet her tossed and tortured mind laid hold of this comfort, that not the man only, but the woman too, were loyal, faithful spirits. Could they both have changed? Appearances are deceitful, and might have deceived this anonymous writer.

After hours of mere suffering, she began to ask herself what she should do?

Her first feminine impulse was to try and find out the truth without Henry's aid.

But no; on second thoughts she would be open and loyal, show Henry the letter, and ask him to tell her how much truth, if any, there was in it.

The agony she endured was a lesson to her. Now she knew what jealousy was; and saw at once she could not endure its torments. She thought to herself he was quite right to make her dismiss Mr. Coventry, and he must dismiss Jael; she should insist on it.

This resolution formed, she lived on thorns, awaiting Henry Little's next visit.

He came next day, but she was out.

She asked the servant if he had said any thing.

The servant said, " He seemed a good deal put out at first, Miss, but afterwards he said, 'No, it was all for the best.'"

This was another blow. Grace connected these words of Henry in some mysterious way with the anonymous letter, and spent the night crying : but in the morning, being a brave, high-spirited girl, she resolved to take a direct course ; she would go down to the works, and request an explanation on the premises. She would see the room where Henry was said to pass so many hours with Jael, and she would show him that the man she loved, and lived for, must place himself above suspicion, or lose her forever. "And if he quarrels with me for that," she thought, "why, I can die." She actually carried out her resolution, and went early next morning to the works to demand an explanation. She took the letter with her. As she went along she discussed in her own mind how she should proceed, and at last she resolved to just hand him the letter and fix her eye on him. His face would tell her the truth.

She drove up to the great gate ; there were a good many people about, talking, in excited groups.

The porter came out to her. She said she wished to see Mr. Little.

The porter stared ; the people within hearing left off talking, and stared too, at her, and then at one another.

At last the porter found his voice. "Mr. Little ! why, we can't find him anywhere, dead or alive."

Just then Ransome came out, and, seeing Miss Carden, gave a start, and looked much concerned. Grace noticed this look, and her own face began to fill with surprise, and then with alarm. " Not to be found !" she faltered.

She did not know Mr. Ransome, but he knew her ; and he came to the carriage-window, and said, in a low voice, "Miss Carden, I am the chief-constable. I would advise you to return home. The fact is, there has been an explosion here, and a young woman nearly killed."

"Poor creature ! But Mr. Little ! Oh, sir ! Oh, sir !"

"We can't find him," said Ransome, solemnly : "and we fear—we sadly fear—"

Grace uttered a low cry, and then sat trembling.

Ransome tried to console her ; said it was just possible he might have not slept in the works.

The porter shook his head.

Grace sprang from the carriage. "Show me the place," said she, hoarsely.

Ransome demurred. "It is an ugly sight for any one to see."

"Who has a better right to see it than I ? I shall find him if he is there. Give me your arm : I have heard him speak of you."

Then Ransome yielded reluctantly, and took her to the place.

He showed her Henry's room, all rent and mutilated.

She shuddered, and, covering her face with her hands, leaned half fainting against her conductor ; but soon she shook this off, and became inspired with strange energy, though her face was like marble.

She drew him, indeed almost dragged him, hither and thither, questioning him, and listening to every body's conjectures ; for there were loud groups here of work-people and townspeople.

Some thought he was buried under the great chimney in the river, others intimated plainly their fear that he was blown to atoms.

At each suggestion Grace Carden's whole body winced and quivered as if the words were sword-cuts, but she would not be persuaded to retire. "No, no," she cried, "amongst so many, some one will guess right. I'll hear all they think, if I die on the spot : die! What is life to me now ? Ah ! what is that woman saying ?" And she hurried Ransome towards a work-woman who was haranguing several of her comrades.

The woman saw Ransome coming towards her with a strange lady. "Ah !" said she, "here's the constable. Mr. Ransome, will ye tell me where you found the lass, yesternight ?"

"She was lying on that heap of bricks : I marked the place with two pieces of chalk ; ay, here they are ; her head lay here, and her feet here."

"Well then," said the woman, "he will not be far from that place. You clear away those bricks and rubbish, and you will find him underneath. She was his sweetheart, that is well known here ; and he was safe to be beside her when the place was blown up."

"No such thing," said Ransome, angrily, and casting a side-look at Grace. "She lay on the second floor, and Mr. Little on the first floor."

"Thou simple body," said the woman. "What's a stair to a young man when a bonny lass lies awaiting him, and not a soul about ? They were a deal too close together all day, to be distant at night."

A murmur of assent burst at once from all the women.

Grace's body winced and quivered, but her marble face never stirred, nor did her lips utter a sound.

"Come away from their scandalous tongues," said Ransome, eagerly.

"No," said Grace; and such a "No." It was like a statue uttering a chip of its own marble.

Then she stood quivering a moment; then, leaving Ransome's arm, she darted up to the place where Jael Dence had been found.

She stood like a bird on the broken masonry, and opened her beautiful eyes in a strange way, and demanded of all her senses whether the body of him she loved lay beneath her feet.

After a minute, during which every eye was riveted on her, she said, "I don't believe it; I don't feel him near me. But I will know."

She took out her purse, full of gold, and held it up to the women. "This for you, if you will help me." Then, kneeling down, she began to tear up the bricks and throw them, one after another, as far as her strength permitted. The effect on the work-women was electrical: they swarmed on the broken masonry, and began to clear it away brick by brick. They worked with sympathetic fury, led by this fair creature, whose white hands were soon soiled and bloody, but never tired. In less than an hour they had cleared away several wagon-loads of débris.

The body of Henry Little was not there.

Grace gave her purse to the women, and leaned heavily on Mr. Ransome's arm again. He supported her out of the works.

As soon as they were alone, she said, "Is Jael Dence alive or dead?"

"She was alive half an hour ago."

"Where is she?"

"At the hospital."

"Take me to the hospital."

He took her to the hospital, and soon they stood beside a clean little bed, in which lay the white but still comely face of Jael Dence: her luxuriant hair was cut close, and her head bandaged; but for her majestic form, she looked a fair, dying boy.

"Stand back," said Grace, "and let me speak to her." Then she leaned over Jael, where she lay.

Gentle women are not all gentleness. Watch them, especially in contact with their own sex, and you shall see now and then a trait of the wild animal. Grace Carden at this moment was any thing but dove-like: it was more like a falcon the way she clutched the bedclothes, and towered over that prostrate figure, and then, descending slowly nearer and nearer, plunged her eyes into those fixed and staring orbs of Jael Dence.

So she remained riveted. Had Jael been conscious, and culpable, nothing could have escaped a scrutiny so penetrating.

Even unconscious as she was, Jael's brain and body began to show some signs they were not quite impervious to the strange magnetic power which besieged them so closely. When Grace's eyes had been close to hers about a minute, Jael Dence moved her head slightly to the left, as if those eyes scorched her.

But Grace moved her own head to the right, rapid as a snake, and fixed her again directly.

Jael Dence's bosom gave a heave.

"Where—is—Henry Little?" said Grace, still holding her tight by the eye, and speaking very slowly, and in such a tone, low, but solemn and commanding; a tone that compelled reply.

"Where—is—Henry Little?"

When this was so repeated, Jael moved a little, and her lips began to quiver.

"Where—is—Henry Little?"

Jael's lips opened feebly, and some inarticulate sounds issued from them.

"Where—is—Henry Little?"

Jael Dence, though unconscious, writhed and moaned so that the head nurse interfered, and said she could not have the patient tormented.

Ransome waved her aside, but taking Grace Carden's hand drew her gently away.

She made no positive resistance; but, while her body yielded and retired, her eye remained riveted on Jael Dence, and her hand clutched the air like a hawk's talons, unwilling to lose her prey, and then she turned so weak, Ransome had to support her to her carriage.

As Grace's head sunk on Ransome's shoulder, Jael Dence's eyes closed for the first time.

As Ransome was lifting Grace Carden into the carriage, she said, in a sort of sleepy voice, "Is there no way out of these works but one?"

"Not that I know of; but I will go at once and see. Shall he drive you home?"

"Yes. No—to Doctor Amboyne."

Doctor Amboyne was gone to Woodbine Villa. She waited in his study, moving about the room all the time, with her face of marble, and her poor restless hands.

At last the Doctor returned: they told him at the door Miss Carden was there: he came in to her with both hands extended, and his face working with emotion.

She fell sobbing into his arms; sobbing, but not a tear.

"Is there any hope?"

"I have one. May he not have left the country in a fit of despair? He often threatened. He talked of going to the United States."

"So he did. Ah, he called on me yesterday afternoon. Might not that have been to bid me good-bye?"

She looked so imploringly in Doctor Amboyne's face that he assented, though full of doubt.

And now there was a ring at the bell, and Mr. Ransome came to say there was a little postern gate by which Mr. Little might possibly have gone out, and the porter not seen him; and, what was more, this gate, by all accounts, had been recently opened: it was closed before Bolt and Little took the premises.

Mr. Ransome added that he should now make it his business to learn, if possible, whether it had been opened by Mr. Little's orders.

Grace thanked him earnestly, and looked hopeful; so did Doctor Amboyne.

"But, Doctor!" said Grace, "if he has gone away at all, he must have told somebody. Even if there was nobody he loved, he would tell—ah! Mr. Bolt!!"

"You are right. Let us go to him at once."

They found Mr. Bolt in quite a different frame of mind from their own; he was breathing vengeance. However, he showed some feeling for Grace, and told the Doctor plainly he feared the worst. Little had been down-hearted for some time, and at last he (Bolt) had lost patience with him, and had proposed to him to take an annual payment of nine hundred pounds instead of a share, and leave the concern. Little had asked two days to consider this proposal. "Now," argued Bolt, "if he meant to leave England, he could not do better than take my offer : and he would have taken it before he left. He would have called, or else sent me a letter. But no ; not a word! It's a bad job: I'm fond of money, but I'd give a few thousands to see him alive again. But I don't think I ever shall. There are five hundred thousand bricks of ours in that river, and a foot and a half of mud."

While they were both shuddering at this dark allusion, he went off into idle threats, and Grace left him, sick and cold, and clinging to Doctor Amboyne like a drowning woman.

"Have courage," said Doctor Amboyne. "There is one chance left us. His mother! I will telegraph to Aberystwith."

They drove together to the telegraph-office, and sent a telegram. The Doctor would not consent to frighten Mrs. Little to death. He simply asked whether her son had just visited or written to her. The answer was paid for ; but four hours elapsed, and no answer came.

Then Grace implored the Doctor to go with her to Aberystwith. He looked grave, and said she was undertaking too much. She replied, almost fiercely, that she must do all that could be done, or she should go mad.

"But your father, my dear!"

"He is in London. I will tell him all when he returns. He would let me go anywhere with you. I must go ; I will!"

At four o'clock they were in the train. They spoke to each other but little on the way ; their hearts were too full of dire forebodings to talk about nothings. But, when they were in the fly at Aberystwith, going from the station to Mrs. Little's lodgings, Grace laid her head on her friend's shoulder and said, "Oh, Doctor, it has come to this ; I hope he loved his mother better than me." Then came a flood of tears—the first.

They went to Mrs. Little's lodgings. The landlady had retired to bed, and, on hearing their errand, told them, out of the second-floor window, that Mrs. Little had left her some days ago, and gone to a neighboring village for change of air.

Grace and Doctor Amboyne drove next morning to that village, and soon learned where Mrs. Little was. Doctor Amboyne left Grace at the inn, for he knew the sight of her would at once alarm Mrs. Little ; and in a matter so uncertain as this, he thought the greatest caution necessary. Grace waited for him at the inn in an agony of suspense. She watched at the window for him, and at last she saw him coming towards her. His head was down, and she could not read his face, or she could have told in a moment whether he brought good news or bad.

She waited for him, erect but trembling. He opened the door, and stood before her, pale and agitated ; so pale and agitated she had never seen him before.

He faltered out, "She knows nothing. She must know nothing. She is too ill and weak, and, indeed, in such a condition that to tell her the fatal news would probably have killed her on the spot. All I dared do was to ask her with assumed indifference if she had heard from Henry lately. No, Grace, not for these three days."

He sat down and groaned aloud.

"You love the son," said he, "but I love the mother: loved her years before you were born."

At this unexpected revelation Grace Carden kissed him, and wept on his shoulder. Then they went sadly home again.

Doctor Amboyne now gave up all hopes of Henry, and his anxiety was concentrated on Mrs. Little. How on earth was he to save her from a shock likely to prove fatal in her weak condition? To bring her to Hillsborough in her present state would be fatal. He was compelled to leave her in Wales, and that looked so like abandoning her. He suffered torture, the torture that only noble minds can know. At midnight, as he lay in bed, and revolved in his mind all the difficulties and perils of this pitiable situation, an idea struck him. He would try and persuade Mrs. Little to marry him. Should she consent, he could then take her on a wedding-tour, and that tour he could easily extend from place to place, putting off the evil time until, strong in health and conjugal affection, she might be able to endure the terrible, the inevitable blow. The very next morning he wrote her an eloquent letter ; he told her that Henry had gone suddenly off to Australia to sell his patents ; that almost his last word had been, "My mother! I leave her to you." This, said the Doctor, is a sacred commission ; and how can I execute it? I can not invite you to Hillsborough, for the air is fatal to you. Think of your half-promise, and my many years of devotion, and give me the right to carry out your son's wishes to the full.

Mrs. Little replied to this letter, and the result of the correspondence was this: she said she would marry him if she could recover her health, but that she feared she never should until she was reconciled to her brother.

Meantime Grace Carden fell into a strange state: fits of feverish energy ; fits of death-like stupor. She could do nothing, yet it maddened her to be idle. With Bolt's permission, she set workmen to remove all the remains of the chimney that could be got at—the water was high just then: she had a barge and workmen, and often watched them, and urged them by her presence. Not that she ever spoke ; but she hovered about with her marble face and staring eyes, and the sight of her touched their hearts and spurred them to exertion.

Sometimes she used to stand on a heap of bricks hard by, and peer, with dilated eyes, into the dark stream, and watch each bucket, or basket, as it came up with bricks, and rubbish, and mud, from the bottom.

At other times she would stand on the bridge and lean over the battlements so far as if she would fly down and search for her dead lover.

One day as she hung thus, glaring into the water, she heard a deep sigh. She looked up, and there was a face almost as pale as her own, and even more haggard, looking at her with a strange mixture of pain and pity. This ghastly spectator of her agony was himself a miserable man. It was Frederick Coventry. His crime had brought him no happiness, no hope of happiness.

At sight of him Grace Carden groaned, and covered her face with her hands.

Coventry drew back dismayed. His guilty conscience misinterpreted this.

"You can forgive us now," said Grace, with a deep sob: then turned away with sullen listlessness, and continued her sad scrutiny.

Coventry loved her, after his fashion, and her mute but eloquent misery moved him.

He drew nearer to her, and said softly, "Do not look so; I can't bear it. He is not there."

"Ah! How do you know?"

Coventry was silent for a moment, and seemed uneasy; but at last he replied thus: "There were two explosions. The chimney fell into the river a moment before the explosion that blew up the works. So how can he be buried under the ruins of the chimney? I know this from a workman who was standing on the bridge when the explosions took place."

"Bless the tongue that tells me that! Oh, how much wiser you are than the rest of us! Mr. Coventry, pity and forgive a poor girl who has used you ill. Tell me—tell me—what can have become of him?"

Coventry was much agitated, and could not speak for some time, and when he did, it was in a faint voice as of one exhausted by a mental struggle. "Would you rather he was—dead—or—false?"

"Oh, false—a thousand times! Prove to me he is not dead, but only false to his poor Grace, and I will bless you on my knees."

Coventry's eye flashed. "Well, then, he was the lover of Jael Dence, the girl who fought for him, and shed her blood for him, and saved his life. The connection was open and notorious."

Grace was silent.

"Many a man has fled from two women, who could have been happy with either of them. I believe that this man found himself unable to play the double game any longer, and that he has fled the country—"

"I pray God it may be so," sobbed Grace.

"—Through remorse, or from dread of exposure. Have patience. Do not kill yourself, and break all our hearts. Take my word for it, you will hear from him in a few days, and he will give you reasons for his strange disappearance—excellent, business-like reasons, but not the true ones: there will not be a word about Jael Dence." This last with a sneer.

Grace turned on him with eyes that literally gleamed: "You hated him living, you slander him dead. Falsehood was not in him: his affection for Jael Dence was no secret. I knew it, and approved it. It was as pure as heaven. His poor mutilated body will soon contradict these vile calumnies. I hate you! I hate you!"

Coventry drew back at first from this burst of ire, but soon he met her glance with one of fiendish bitterness. "You hate me for pitying you, and saying that man is not dead. Well, have your own way, then; he is not false, but dead."

He turned on his heel, and went away.

As for Mr. Carden, he declined to admit that Little was dead, and said his conduct was unpardonable, and, indeed, so nearly resembled madness, that, considering the young man's father had committed suicide, he was determined never to admit him into his house again—at all events as a suitor to Grace.

Mr. Coventry had now taken spacious apartments, and furnished them. He resumed his visits to the club. Mr. Carden met him there, and spoke more confidentially to him than he did to his daughter, and admitted he had grave doubts, but said he was a director of the Gosshawk, and would never, either in public or private, allow that Little was dead unless his body should be found and properly identified.

All this time there was a hot discussion in the journals, and the Saw-grinders' Union repudiated the outrage with horror, and offered a considerable reward.

Outsiders were taken in by this, but not a single manufacturer or workman.

Mr. Holdfast denounced it as a Trade outrage, and Ransome groped the town for evidence.

The latter, however, was rather puzzled one day by an anonymous letter telling him he was all on the wrong tack; it was not a Trade job, but contrived by a gentleman for his private ends. Advantage had been taken of Little being wrong with the Trade: "but," said the letter, "you should look to the head for the motive, not to the hands. One or two saw them together a good many times before the deed was done, and the Swell was seen on the very bridge when the explosion took place."

This set Ransome thinking very seriously and comparing notes.

Week after week went by and left the mystery unsolved.

Mr. Coventry saw Mr. Carden nearly every day, and asked him was there no news of Little? The answer was always in the negative, and this surprised Coventry more and more.

When a whole month had elapsed, even he began to fancy strange things, and to nurse wild projects that had never entered his head before. He studied books of medical jurisprudence, and made all manner of experiments. He resumed his intimacy with Cole, and they were often closeted together.

Five weeks had elapsed, and Grace Carden had lost all her feverish energy, and remained passive, lethargic, fearing every thing, hoping nothing, but quivering all day with expectation of the next blow; for what had she left to expect now but sorrow in some form or other?

She often wished to visit Jael Dence again at the hospital; but for some time an invincible repugnance withheld her.

She asked Doctor Amboyne to go instead, and question the unhappy girl.

Doctor Amboyne did so; but Jael was now in a half-stupid condition, and her poor brain not clear enough to remember what she was wanted to remember. Her memory was full of gaps, and, unluckily, one of these gaps embraced the whole period between her battle with Hill and the present time.

At last Grace was irritated, and blamed the Doctor for his failure. She reminded him she had herself magnetized Jael, and had almost made her speak. She resolved to go to the hospital herself. "I'll make her tell me one thing," said she, "though I tear her heart out, and my own too."

She dressed plainly, and walked rapidly down

towards the hospital. There were two ways to it, but she chose the one that was sure to give her pain. She could not help it; her very feet dragged her to that fatal spot.

When she drew near the fatal bridge, she observed a number of persons collected on it, looking down in the river at some distance.

At the same time people began to hurry past her, making for the bridge.

She asked one of them what it was.

"Summut in the river," was the reply, but in a tone so full of meaning, that at these simple words she ran forward, though her knees almost gave way under her.

The bridge was not so crowded yet, but that she contrived to push in between two women, and look.

All the people were speaking in low murmurs. The hot weather had dried the river up to a stream in the middle, and, in mid-stream, about fifty yards from the foot of the bridge, was a pile of broken masonry, which had once been the upper part of Bolt and Little's chimney. It had fallen into water twelve feet deep; but now the water was not above five feet, and a portion of the broken bricks and tiles were visible, some just above, some just under the water.

At one side of this wreck jutted out the object on which all eyes were now fastened. At first sight it looked a crooked log of wood sticking out from among the bricks. Thousands, indeed, had passed the bridge, and noticed nothing particular about it; but one, more observant or less hurried, had peered, and then pointed, and collected the crowd.

It needed but a second look to show that this was not a log of wood, but the sleeve of a man's coat. A closer inspection revealed that the sleeve was not empty.

There was an arm inside that sleeve, and a little more under the water one could see distinctly a hand white and sodden by the water.

The dark stream just rippled over this hand, half veiling it at times, though never hiding it.

"The body will be jammed among the bricks," said a by-stander; and all assented with awe.

"Eh! to think of its sticking out an arm like that!" said a young girl.

"Dead folk have done more than that, sooner than want Christian burial," replied an old woman.

"I warrant ye they have. I can't look at it."

"Is it cloth, or what?" inquired another.

"It's a kind of tweed, I think."

"What's that glittering on its finger?"

"It's a ring—a gold ring."

At this last revelation there was a fearful scream, and Grace Carden fell senseless on the pavement.

A gentleman who had been hanging about and listening to the comments now darted forward, with a face almost as white as her own, and raised her up, and implored the people to get her a carriage.

It was Mr. Coventry. Little had he counted on this meeting. Horror-stricken, he conveyed the insensible girl to her father's house.

He handed her over to the women, and fled, and the women brought her round; but she had scarcely recovered her senses, when she uttered another piercing scream, and swooned again.

CHAPTER XXXIV.

COVENTRY passed a night of agony and remorse. He got up broken and despondent, and went straight to Woodbine Villa to do a good action.

He inquired for Miss Carden. They told him she was very ill. He expressed an earnest wish to see her. The servants told him that was impossible. Nobody was allowed to see her but Doctor Amboyne. He went next day to Doctor Amboyne, and the Doctor told him that Miss Carden was dangerously ill. Brain fever appeared inevitable.

"But, sir," said Coventry, eagerly, "if one could prove to her that those were not the remains of Henry Little?"

"How could you prove that? Besides, it would be no use now. She is delirious. Even should she live, I should forbid the subject for many a day. Indeed, none but the man himself could make her believe those remains are not his; and even he could not save her now. If he stood by her bedside, she would not know him."

The doctor's lip trembled a little, and his words were so grave and solemn that they struck to the miserable man's marrow. He staggered away, like a drunken man, to his lodgings, and there flung himself on the floor, and grovelled in an agony of terror and remorse.

CHAPTER XXXV.

ONE day it occurred to Raby he could play the misanthrope just as well at home as abroad, so he returned home.

He found old Dence dead and buried, and Patty Dence gone to Australia with her husband.

He heard Jael was in the hospital. He called at Woodbine Villa, and they told him Grace was lying between life and death.

He called on Doctor Amboyne, and found him as sad as he used to be gay. The Doctor told him all, and even took him to the town hall, and showed him an arm and part of the trunk of a man preserved in spirits, and a piece of tweed cloth, and a plain gold ring.

"There," said he, "is all that remains to us of your nephew, and my friend. Genius, beauty, courage—all come to this!" He could say no more.

The tears filled Raby's eyes, and all his bitterness melted away. With respect to his sister, he said he was quite willing to be reconciled, and even to own himself in the wrong, if Dr. Amboyne, on reading the correspondence, should think so. Dr. Amboyne said he would come to Raby Hall for that purpose. He communicated this at once to Mrs. Little.

Grace had a favorable crisis, and in a few days more she was out of danger, but in a deplorable state of weakness. Doctor Amboyne ordered her to the sea-side. A carriage was prepared expressly for her, and her father took her there.

Woodbine Villa was put up to let furnished, and it was taken by—Mr. Coventry.

Jael Dence began to recover strength rapidly, but she wore at times a confused look. The very day Grace left for Eastbank she was discharged as cured, and left the hospital. This was in the morning.

In the afternoon Dr. Amboyne, being now relieved of his anxiety as to Grace, remembered he had not been to see this poor girl for some time ; so he went to the hospital.

When he heard she was discharged, he felt annoyed with himself for not having paid her closer attention. And besides, Grace had repeatedly told him Jael Dence could make a revelation if she chose. And now, occupied with Grace herself, he had neglected her wishes.

"Where is she gone ? do you know ?"

One of the nurses said she was gone home.

Another said the patient had told her she should go down to the work first.

"And that is the very last place you should have let her go to," said the Doctor. "A fine shock the poor creature will get there. You want her back here again, I suppose !" He felt uneasy, and drove down to the works. There he made some inquiries among the women, and elicited that Jael Dence had turned faint at sight of the place, and they had shown her, at her request, where she had been picked up, and had told her about the discovery of Little's remains, and she had persuaded a little girl to go to the town hall with her.

"Oh, the tongue ! the tongue !" groaned Amboyne.

He asked to see the little girl, and she came forward of her own accord, and told him she had gone to the town hall with the lass, but " (regretfully) "that the man would not show them it without an order from the Mayor." "It !"

Doctor Amboyne said he was very glad that common sense had not quite deserted the earth. "And where did you go next ?"

"I came back here."

"So I see ; but the lass ?"

"She said she should go home. 'My dear,' says she, 'there's nobody left me here ; I'll go and die among my own folk.' That was her word."

"Poor thing ! poor thing ! Why—"

He stopped short, for that moment he remembered Raby had said old Dence was dead, and Patty gone to Australia. If so, here was another blow in store for poor Jael, and she weakened by a long illness.

He instantly resolved to drive after her, and see whether she was really in a fit state to encounter so many terrible shocks. If not, he should take her back to the infirmary, or into his own house ; for he had a great respect for her, and indeed for all her family.

He drove fast, but he could see nothing of her on the road. So then he went on to Cairnhope.

He stopped at the farm-house. It was sadly deteriorated in appearance. Inside he found only an old carter and his daughter. The place was in their charge.

The old man told him apathetically Jael had come home two hours ago and asked for her father and Patty, and they had told her the old farmer was dead and buried, and Patty gone to foreign parts.

"What, you blurted it out like that ! You couldn't put yourself in that poor creature's place, and think what a blow it would be ? How, in Heaven's name, did she take it ?"

"Well, sir, she stared a bit, and looked stupid-like ; and then she sat down. She sat crowded all together like in yon corner best part of an hour, and then she got up and said she must go and see his grave."

"You hadn't the sense to make her eat, of course ?"

"My girl here set meat afore her, but she couldn't taste it."

Dr. Amboyne drove to Raby Hall and told Raby. Raby said he would have Jael up to the hall. It would be a better place for her now than the farm. He ordered a room to be got ready for her, and a large fire lighted, and at the same time ordered the best bedroom for Doctor Amboyne. "You must dine and sleep here," said he, " and talk of old times."

Doctor Amboyne thanked him—it was dusk by this time—and was soon seated at that hospitable table, with a huge wood fire blazing genially.

Meantime Jael Dence sat crouched upon her father's grave, stupefied with grief. When she had crouched there a long time she got up, and muttered, "Dead and gone ! dead and gone!" Then she crept up to the old church, and sat down in the porch, benumbed with grief, and still a little confused in her poor head.

She sat there for nearly two hours, and then she got up, and muttered, "Dead and gone—he is dead and gone !" and wandered on the hill desolate.

Her feet wandered, her brain wandered. She found herself at last in a place she recognized. It was Squire Raby's lawn. The moon had just risen, and shone on the turf, and on the little river that went curling round with here and there a deep pool.

She crept nearer, and saw the great bay-window, and a blaze of light behind it.

There she had sung the great Noel with her father ; and now he was dead and gone.

There she had been with Henry Little, and seen him recognize his mother's picture ; and now he was dead and gone. She had saved his life in vain ; he was dead and gone. Everybody was dead and gone.

She looked up at the glowing window. She looked down at the pool, with the moon kissing it.

She flung her arms up with a scream of agony, and sank into the deep pool, where the moon seemed most to smile on it.

Directly after dinner Amboyne asked to see the unhappy correspondence of which he was to be the judge.

Raby went for the letters, and laid them before him. He took up the fatal letter. "Why, this is not written by Mrs. Little. I know her neat Italian hand too well. See how the letters slant and straggle."

"Oh ! but you must allow for the writer's agitation."

"Why should I allow for it ? You didn't. Who can look at this scrawl, and not see that the poor heart-broken creature was not herself when she wrote it ? This is not a letter, it is a mere scream of agony. Put yourself in her place. Imagine yourself a woman—a creature in whom the feelings overpower the judgment. Consider the shock, the wound, the frenzy ; and, besides, she had no idea that you left this house to get her husband the money from your own funds."

"She never shall know it either."

"She does know it. I have told her. And, poor thing, she thinks she was the only one to blame. She seeks your forgiveness. She pines for it. This is the true cause of her illness; and I believe, if you could forgive her and love her, it might yet save her life."

"Then tell her I blame myself as much as her. Tell her my house, my arms, and my heart are open to her. Amboyne, you are a true friend, and a worthy man. God bless you. How shall we get her here, poor soul? Will you go for her, or shall I?"

"Let me sleep on that," said Doctor Amboyne.

In the course of the evening, Doctor Amboyne told Raby all the reports about Jael Dence and Henry Little.

"What does that matter now?" said Raby, with a sigh.

Whenever a servant came into the room, Amboyne asked him if Jael had arrived.

Raby shared his curiosity, but not his anxiety. "The girl knows her friends," said he. "She will have her cry out, you may depend; but after that she will find her way here, and, when she has got over it a little, I shall be sure to learn from her whether he was her lover, and where he was when the place was blown up. A Dence never lies to a Raby."

But when nine o'clock struck and there were no tidings of her, Raby began to share the Doctor's uneasiness, and also to be rather angry and impatient.

"Confound the girl!" said he. "Her grandfathers have stood by mine, in their danger and trouble, for two hundred years; and now, in her trouble, she slinks away from me."

"Put yourself in her place," said Amboyne. "Ten to one she thinks you are offended about her and Henry. She is afraid to come near you."

"What, when I ask her?"

"Through your stupid lazy servants, who, to save themselves trouble, have very likely told somebody else to tell her; and we know what comes of that process. Ten to one the invitation has either missed her altogether, or come to her divested of all that is kind and soothing. And remember, she is not a man. She is a poor girl, full of shame and apprehension, and needs a gentle encouraging hand to draw her here. Do, for once, put yourself in a woman's place—you were born of a woman."

"You are right," said Raby. "I will send down a carriage for her, with a line in my own hand."

He did so.

At eleven the servant came back with the news that Jael Dence was not at home. She had been seen wandering about the country, and was believed to be wrong in her head. George, the blacksmith, and others, were gone up to the old church after her.

"Turn out with torches, every man Jack of you, and find her," said Raby.

As for Raby and Amboyne, they sat by the fireside and conversed together—principally about poor Mrs. Little; but the conversation was languid.

A few minutes after midnight a terrible scream was heard. It was uttered out of doors, yet it seemed to penetrate the very room where Raby and Amboyne were seated. Both men started to their feet. The scream was not repeated. They looked at each other.

"It was in my garden," said Raby; and, with some little difficulty, he opened the window and ran out, followed by Amboyne.

They looked, but could see nothing.

But, with that death-shriek ringing in their ears, they wasted no time. Raby waved Amboyne to the left, and himself dashed off to the right, and they scoured the lawn in less than a minute.

A cry of horror from Raby! He had found the body of a woman floating in a pool of the river, head downward.

He dashed into the water directly and drew it to the bank: Doctor Amboyne helped him, and they got it out on dry land. The face was ghastly, the body still.

"Turn her face downward," said Amboyne, "give her every chance. Carry her gently."

One took the shoulders, the other the feet; they carried her slowly in and laid her gently down before the fire.

She lay like dripping marble.

Her clothes clinging tightly round her, revealed her marvellous form and limbs of antique mould —but all so deadly still.

Amboyne kneeled over her, searching, in vain, for some sign of life. He groaned.

"Oh!" said he, "is it possible that such a creature as this can be cut off in its prime?"

"Dead!" cried Raby, trembling all over. "Oh, God forbid! One of her ancestors saved a Raby's life in battle, another saved a Raby in a foaming flood; and I couldn't save her in a dead pool! She is the last of that loyal race, and I'm the last Raby. Farewell, Dence! Farewell, Raby!"

Whilst he bemoaned her thus, and his tears actually dripped upon her pale face, Amboyne detected a slight quivering in the drowned woman's throat.

"Hush!" said he to Raby.

There was a pair of old-fashioned bellows by the side of the fire; Amboyne seized them, and opened Jael's mouth with more ease than he expected. "That is a good sign," said he.

He inflated the bellows, and inserted the tube very carefully; then he discharged the air, then gently sucked it back again. When he had done this several times something like a sigh escaped from Jael's breast. The Doctor removed the bellows, and felt her heart and examined her eyes. "Curious!" said he. "Give me some brandy. It is more like syncope than drowning."

Acting on this notion, he laid her flat on her back, and applied neat brandy to her nostrils and ears.

After a while she moved her whole body like a wounded snake, and moaned feebly.

Raby uttered a loud shout of joy. "She is saved!" he cried. "She is saved!" He jumped about the room like a boy, and, anxious to do something or other, was for ringing up the female servants. But Amboyne would not hear of it. "On the contrary," said he, "lock the door, and let only you and I see the poor girl's distress when she comes back to this bitter world. Raby, don't you shut your eyes to the truth. This was no accident."

"I am afraid not," said Raby. "She knows the water as well as I do, and she picked out the deepest hole: poor girl! poor girl!"

He then asked Amboyne in a whisper what he thought she would do when she came to her senses.

"Impossible to say. She may be violent, and if so we shall have enough to do to hold her. They tell me she threw that workman like a sack."

At this moment Jael stretched her great arms and sighed. The movement, though gentle and feminine, had a grandeur and freedom that only goes with power.

The Doctor lowered his voice to a whisper. "She is a good Christian, and most likely she will be penitent, and then she will cry her heart out. Any way, she is pretty sure to be hysterical, so mind and be firm as well as kind. There, her color is coming back. Now put yourself in her place. You and I must call this an accident. Stick to that through thick and thin. Ah, she is coming round fast. She shall see you first. You take her right hand, and look at her with all the pity and kindness I am sure you feel."

Mr. Raby took Jael's hand in both his, and fixed his eyes on her with pity and anxiety.

She came to her senses, and stared at him a long time.

Then she looked down at her wet clothes. Then she snatched her hand away, and covered her face with both hands, and began to rock and moan, and finally turned round and hid her face against the very floor as if she would grovel and burrow into it.

"Are you better, my dear?" said the Doctor, quietly.

No reply. And the face still crushed against the floor.

"The next time you faint away, don't let it be on the banks of a river. You have been going too long without food; and you fainted away and fell into the river. Luckily it was not very deep or it might have been serious. You have given us a fine fright, I can tell you."

While these words were being uttered, Jael, who did not miss a syllable, began to look very, very slowly round with scared and troubled eyes, and to defend herself. "I remember nought," said she, doggedly. "Who took me out?"

"Mr. Raby."

She looked timidly at him, and saw his wet clothes.

"Oh, Squire, why did you spoil your clothes for me?" and she laid her head on his knee and began to cry.

"My clothes!" said Raby. "The girl wants to break my heart."

"Eh, dear! and I've spoiled the beautiful carpet," said Jael, piteously.

"D—n the carpet!" said Raby, nearly blubbering.

All this time Amboyne was putting himself in Jael's Dence's place.

"Is there a good fire in her room?" asked he, with a significant look.

Raby took the hint, and said he would go and see.

As soon as he was out of the room, the transmigrator began to talk very fast to Jael. "Now look here, Jael, that poor man is alone in the world now, and very sad; he wants you to keep his house for him. He has been sending messages all day after you, and your room has been ready ever so long."

"My room in this house!"

"Yes. But we could not find you. However, here you are. Now you must not go back to the farm. The poor Squire won't be quite so sad if he sees you about him. You know he was always fond of you Dences. You should have seen him cry over you just now when he thought you were dead."

"I am more cared for than I thought," said Jael, softly.

"Yes, but not more than you deserve, my dear." He dipped a sponge-cake in wine. "Oblige me by eating that."

She took it submissively.

"Now another."

She ate another, and a third.

"It's a very wicked lass you are so good to," said she, softly, and some gentle tears began to flow.

"Stuff and nonsense!" said the Doctor. "What do you know about wickedness? I'm a better judge of that than you, and I say you are the best girl and the most unselfish girl in the world; and the proof is that, instead of sitting down and nursing your own griefs, you are going to pluck up courage, and be a comfort to poor Mr. Raby in his lonely condition."

These words appeared to sink into Jael's mind: she put her hands to her head, and pondered them. Perhaps she might have replied to them, but Raby came down, and ordered her to her apartment.

She took a step or two in that direction, but presently drew back and would not move. "The women-folk! They'll see me on the stair, this figure."

"Not they. They are all in bed."

"Are they so? Then please let me go to the kitchen for a dry cloth or two."

"What to do?"

"To dry the rug a bit. Just look—what a mess I've made!"

"I'll say it was the dog."

"Will you, though? Oh, but you are a good friend to me this night. Then I'll go. Let me wring my gown a bit, not to mess the stairs as well."

"No, no; I'll take all the blame. Will you go, or must the Doctor and I carry you?"

"Nay, nay, there's no need. Your will is my pleasure, sir."

So Mr. Raby showed Jael to her room, and opened a great wardrobe, and took out several armfuls of antique female habiliments, and flung them on the floor: rich velvets, more or less faded, old brocades, lace scarves, chemises with lace borders; in short, an accumulation of centuries. He soon erected a mound of these things in the middle of the floor, and told her to wear what she liked, but to be sure and air the things well first; "for," said he, "it is a hundred years or so since they went on any woman's back. Now, say your prayers like a good girl, and go to bed."

"Ay," said Jael, solemnly, "I shall say my prayers, you may be sure."

As he left the room she said, in a sort of patient way, "Good Squire, I am willing to live, since you are so lonely."

CHAPTER XXXVI.

EARLY next morning Mr. Raby was disturbed by female voices in a high key. He opened his window quietly, intending to throw in his bass with startling effect, when, to his surprise, he found the disputants were his dairymaid and Jael Dence.

"And who are you that interferes with me in my work? Where do you come from? Did ye get in over the wall? for ye never came in at no door. Who are you?"

"I am one who won't see the good Squire wronged. Aren't ye ashamed? What, eat his bread, and take his wage, and then steal his butter!"

"If ye call me a thief, I'll law ye. Thief yourself! you don't belong to the house; whose gown have you got on your back? Here, James! Tom! here's a strange woman making off with the Squire's lady's clothes, and two pounds of butter to boot."

Jael was taken aback for a moment by this audacious attack, and surveyed her borrowed habiliments with a blush of confusion. Several servants came about at the noise, and her situation bade fair to be a very unpleasant one: but Mr. Raby put in his word; "Hold your tongues, all of ye. Now, Jael Dence, what is the matter?"

Instantly all eyes were turned up to the window with a start, and Jael told her tale: "Sir," said she, "I did see this young woman take out something from under her apron and give it to a little girl. I thought there was something amiss, and I stopped the girl at the gate, and questioned her what she was carrying off so sly. She gives a squeak and drops it directly, and takes to her heels. I took it up and brought it in, and here it is, two beautiful pounds of butter, fresh churned; look else!"—here she undid a linen wrap, and displayed the butter—"so I challenged the dairymaid here. She says I'm a thief—and that I leave to you, Squire; you know whether I come of thieves or honest folk; but what I want to know from her is, why her lass dropped the butter and took to her heels at a word?"

"Now, my good Jael," said the Squire, "if you are going to interfere every time you catch my servants pilfering, you will have a hard time of it. However, zeal is too rare a thing for me to discourage it. I must make an example. Hy, you young woman: I dare say you are no worse than the rest, but you are the one that is found out; so you must pack up your clothes and begone."

"Not without a month's warning, or a month's wage, sir, if you please," said the dairy-maid, pertly.

"If I catch you in the house when I come down, I'll send you to prison on my own warrant, with the butter tied round your neck."

At this direful threat the offender began to blubber, and speedily disappeared to pack her box.

Mr. Raby then told the other servants that Jael Dence was the new housekeeper, and that a person of her character was evidently required in the house; they must all treat her with respect, or leave his service. Thereupon two gave warning, and Mr. Raby, who never kept a servant a day after that servant had given him warning, had them up to his room, and paid them a month's wages. "And now," said he, "for the honor of the house, don't leave us fasting, but eat a good breakfast, and then go to the devil."

At his own breakfast he related the incident to Doctor Amboyne, with a characteristic comment: "And the fools say there is nothing in race. So likely, that of all animals man alone should be exempt from the law of nature! Take a drowning watch-dog out of the water and put him in a strange house, he is scarcely dry before he sets to work to protect it. Take a drowning Dence into your house, and she is up with the lark to look after your interests. That girl connive and let the man be robbed whose roof shelters her? She *couldn't*; it is not in her blood. I'm afraid there's to be a crusade against petty larceny in this house, and more row about it than it is worth. No matter; I shall support the crusader, on principle. It is not for me to check honest impulses, nor to fight against nature in almost the only thing where she commands my respect."

"Very well," said the Doctor, "that is settled: so now let us talk of something more important. How are we to get your sister, in her delicate state, from Wales to this place?"

"Why, I will go for her myself, to be sure."

"Raby, your heart is in the right place, after all. But when she is here, how are we to conceal her unhappy son's fate from her? It will be more difficult than ever, now Jael Dence is in the house."

"Why so? We must take the girl into our confidence—that is all."

"The sooner the better then. Let us have her in here."

Jael was sent for, and Mr. Raby requested her to take a seat, and give all her attention to something Doctor Amboyne had to say.

Doctor Amboyne then told her, with quiet earnestness, that Mrs. Little was at present so ill and weak he felt sure the news of Henry's death would kill her.

"Ay, poor soul!" said Jael, and began to cry bitterly.

The Doctor held his peace, and cast a disconsolate look on Raby, as much as to say, "We shall get no efficient aid in this quarter."

After a little while Jael dried her eyes, and said, "Go on, sir. I must needs cry before you now and then: 'tisn't to say I shall ever cry before *her*."

"Well, then, if we *can* get her safe to this place, and keep her in the dark for a few months, I think we may save her life. Every thing else will be in her favor here: her native air, cherished memories, her brother's love—and, after all, it was fretting about her quarrel with him that first undermined her health and spirits. Well, we shall remove the cause, and then perhaps the effect may go. But how are we to keep the sad truth from her?"

"Let me think," said Jael Dence. "My head is a deal clearer since last night."

She leaned her chin upon her hand, and her face and brow showed signs of intellectual power no one had ever observed in them before.

"Who is to go for her?" said she at last.

"I am going myself."

"That is a mistake at starting, begging your worship's pardon. Why, the very sight of you might startle her into her grave. Nay, you'll give me the money—for mine is all in the Savings Bank—and I shall go for her myself. I shall tell her Squire is longing for her, and that I'm to be here for fear she might feel strange. She always liked me, poor soul. I shall get her safe here, you needn't fear for that. But when she is here"—the chin rested on the hand again— "well, the Doctor must forbid visitors. Miss Grace must be told not to write. Every newspaper must be read before she is allowed to see it. And, Squire, you will be very kind to her when you are in her company; but we must manage, somehow or other, so that you can keep out of her way."

"What for, in Heaven's name?"

"Sir, we shall have to lie from morn to night; and you will be a bungler at that, saving your presence. If there's a servant left in the house who knows, I'd give that servant a present, and part with her before Mrs. Little sets her foot in the house."

"This sounds very sensible," said Raby. "I am a novice at lying. But I shall cultivate the art for poor Edith's sake. I'm not a fanatic: there is justifiable homicide, so why not justifiable facticide?"

"Raby," said the Doctor, "this young woman has said enough to show me that she is more fit to conduct this delicate undertaking than either you or I. Let us profit by the discovery, put our vanity in our pocket, and give her the command. My dear, you see the importance, you see the difficulty; now will you undertake it?"

"I will, sir," said Jael, firmly; "and I look to succeed, God willing. I shall be in Wales this afternoon."

"Well, but would you not be the better yourself for one day's rest?"

"No, sir. I've learned, with a sad heart, what one day may bring forth. After that, I'm sworn never to throw away a day. And, as for sitting down and thinking, 'tis the worst thing I can do. I do thank God that in this, my own heavy trouble, I'm not tied to my sad thoughts, but can get about, and do a little bit of good for Raby House. Do what I will, 'tis but giving them back one pig out of their own farrow; for we owe all we have to them."

With this she retired to prepare for her journey, leaving both the gentlemen lost in admiration of her simple virtues, and the clear intelligence she had shown them in few words.

She travelled into Wales that very day, and many a burst of bitter grief she had all by herself, in the train.

At six P.M. she stood before Mrs. Little with a smiling countenance. Mrs. Little welcomed her with some little pleasure and much surprise.

"Good news, madam," said Jael. "Squire Raby has sent me to bring you to Raby Hall. He wanted to come himself, but I would not let him."

"That is good news," said Mrs. Little languidly. "Now I shall die at peace with my brother —at peace with all mankind, I hope."

"You'll die when your time comes," said Jael. "But you have got a shorter journey before you at present, and that is to Raby Hall."

"Raby Hall! I shall never see it again. I have no strength to move. I am worn out with the battle of life. Stay with me here, and close my eyes."

"Of course I shall stay with you," said Jael, and began to gossip with every appearance of carelessness.

Next morning, with infinite difficulty, she persuaded the poor jaundiced lady to show her Aberystwith. She took the tickets herself, and got her patient half-way to Hillsborough; next day, with less difficulty, to Raby Hall. All had been settled before. Edith Little was shown into her old bedroom, adorned with pyramids of flowers in her honor; and there she found a loving line from Guy, begging her pardon for his past harshness, and telling her she was to send for him as soon as she felt strong enough to meet.

That evening brother and sister were clasped in each other's arms, and wept tears of affection and regret over each other.

Jael Dence slept on a camp-bed in Mrs. Little's room, which was very spacious, and watched her, and was always about her. Under private advice from Doctor Amboyne, she superintended her patient's diet, and, by soft, indomitable perseverance, compelled her to walk every day, and fight against her fatal lassitude.

Heaven rewarded her by giving her a warm and tender affection for her poor patient that did something to fill her own yearning and desolate heart.

Here I must leave them both for the present, and show how these events affected the main characters of my story.

CHAPTER XXXVII.

JUST outside the little sea-side town of Eastbank is a house which, being very old, contrasts agreeably with the pretentious villas fashion has raised. It is roomy inside, yet outside it looks like a cottage: low, rambling, gabled, and picturesque. It stands on a slope just above the sea, and its front garden runs down almost to the sea-shore. The aspect is southerly. The placid sea looks like a beautiful lake; for, about two miles out, a great tongue of land runs across, and keeps the tempests out.

The cottage itself was now clothed deep with green creepers, and its verandah with jessamine; and the low white walls of the garden were beautiful with vine-leaves and huge fig-leaves, that ran up them and about them, and waved over them in tropical luxuriance. In short, the house was a very bower, and looked the abode of bliss; and this time last year a young couple had spent their honeymoon there, and left it with a sigh. But one place sees many minds; and now this sweet place was the bed on which drooped the broken lily of this tale, Grace Carden.

She lay in the warm air of the verandah, and turned her hollow eyes upon the sea; and every day life crept slowly back to her young body, but not to her desolate heart.

A brain fever either kills or blunts, and Grace's agony was blunted. Her mind was in a strange state. She was beginning to look two things in the face: that the man she loved was dead; that the man she loved, and had nearly died for, had loved another as well as herself: and this last grief, strange to say, was the saving of her. She forgave him with all her heart, for he was dead; she made excuses for him, for she loved him; but, since his whole heart had not been hers, her pride and modesty rebelled against dying for him, and she resolved to live; she fought hard to live and get well. Finally, being a very woman, though a noble one, she hated Jael Dence.

She was not alone in the world. Her danger, her illness, and her misery had shown her the treasure of a father's love. He had found this sweet bower for her; and here he sat for hours by her side, with his hand in hers, gazing on her with touching anxiety and affection. Business compelled him to run into Hillsborough now and then, but he dispatched it with feverish haste, and came back to her: it drove him to London; but he telegraphed to her twice a day, and was miserable till he got back. She saw the man of business turned into a man of love for her, and she felt it. "Ah, papa," she said one day, "I little thought you loved your poor Grace so much. You don't love any other child but me, do you, papa?" and with this question she clung weeping round his neck.

"My darling child, there's nothing on earth I love but you. When shall I see you smile again?".

"In a few years, perhaps. God knows."

One evening—he had been in Hillsborough that day—he said, "My dear, I have seen an old friend of yours to-day, Mr. Coventry. He asked very kindly after you."

Grace made no reply.

"He is almost as pale as you are. He has been very ill, he tells me. And really, I believe it was your illness upset him."

"Poor Mr. Coventry!" said Grace, but with a leaden air of indifference.

"I hope I didn't do wrong, but when he asked after you so anxiously, I said, 'Come, and see for yourself.' Oh, you need not look frightened; he is not coming. He says you are offended with him."

"Not I.. What is Mr. Coventry to me?"

"Well, he thinks so. He says he was betrayed into speaking ill to you of some one who, he thought, was living; and now that weighs upon his conscience."

"I can understand that. I am miserable, but let me try and be just. Papa, Mr. Coventry was trying to comfort me, in his clumsy way; and what he said he did not invent—he heard it; and so many people say so that I—I—oh, papa! papa!"

Mr. Carden dropped the whole subject directly. However, she returned to it herself, and said, listlessly, that Mr. Coventry, in her opinion, had shown more generosity than most people would in his case. She had no feeling against him; he was of no more importance in her eyes than that stool, and he might visit her if he pleased, but on one condition—that he should forget all the past, and never presume to speak to her of love. "Love! Men are all incapable of it." She was thinking of Henry, even while she was speaking of his rival.

The permission, thus limited, was conveyed to Mr. Coventry by his friend Carden; but he showed no hurry to take advantage of it; and, as for Grace, she forgot she had given it.

But this coolness of Coventry's was merely apparent. He was only waiting the arrival of Patrick Lally from Ireland. This Lally was an old and confidential servant, who had served him formerly in many intrigues, and with whom he had parted reluctantly some months ago, and allowed him a small pension for past services. He dared not leave the villa in charge of any person less devoted to him than this Lally.

The man arrived at last, received minute instructions, and then Mr. Coventry went to Eastbank.

He found what seemed the ghost of Grace Carden lying on the sofa, looking on the sea.

At the sight of her he started back in dismay.

"What have I done?"

Those strange words fell from him before he knew what he was saying.

Grace heard them but did not take the trouble to inquire into their meaning. She said, doggedly, "I am alive, you see. Nothing kills. It is wonderful: we die of a fall, of a blow, of swallowing a pin; yet I am alive. But never mind me; you look unwell yourself. What is the matter?"

"Can you ask me?"

At this, which implied that her illness was the cause of his, she turned her head away from him with weariness and disgust, and looked at the sea, and thought of the dead.

Coventry sat speechless, and eyed her silent figure with miserable devotion. He was by her side once more, and no rival near. He set himself to study all her moods, and begin by being inoffensive to her; in time he might be something more.

He spent four days in Eastbank, and never uttered a word of love; but his soft soothing voice was ever in her ear, and won her attention now and then; not often.

When he left her, she did not ask him to come again.

Her father did, though, and told him to be patient; better days were in store. "Give her time," said he, "and, a month or two hence, if you have the same feeling for her you used to have—"

"I love her more than ever. I worship her—"

"Then you will have me on your side, stronger than ever. But you must give her time."

And now Coventry had an ally far more powerful than himself—an ally at once zealous and judicious. Mr. Carden contented himself at first with praising him in general terms; next he affected to laugh at him for renting the villa, merely to be in the place which Grace had occupied. Then Grace defended him. "Don't laugh at an honest love. Pity it. It is all we can do, and the least we can do."

But when he advanced farther, and began to remind his daughter she had once given this gentleman hopes, and all but engaged herself to him, she drew back with fear and repugnance, and said, "If he can not forget that, pray let him never come near me again."

"Oh," said Mr. Carden, "I believe he has no hopes of the kind; it is of you I am thinking, not of him. It has got about that poor Little had a connection with some girl in humble life, and that he was in love with her, and you in love with him. That wounds a father's pride, and makes me grateful to Coventry for his unshaken devotion, whilst others are sneering at my poor child for her innocent love."

Grace writhed, and the tears ran down her cheeks at this. "Oh, spare the dead!" she faltered.

Then her father kissed her, and begged her to forgive him; he would avoid all these topics in future: and so he did, for some time; but what he had said rankled.

A few days after this, Coventry came again, and did nothing but soothe Grace with words; only he managed so that Grace should detect him looking very sad when he was not actually employed in cheering her.

She began to pity him a little, and wonder at his devotion.

He had not been gone many hours when another visitor arrived quite unexpectedly — Mr. Raby. He came to tell her his own news, and warn her of the difficult game they were now playing at Raby Hall, that she might not thwart it inadvertently.

Grace was much agitated, and shed tears of sympathy. She promised, with a sigh, to hold no communication with Mrs. Little. She thought it very hard, but she promised.

In the course of his narrative Mr. Raby spoke very highly of Jael Dence, and of her conduct in the matter.

To this Grace did not respond. She waited her opportunity, and said, keenly and coldly, "How did she come to be in your house?"

"Well, that is a secret."

"Can you not trust me with a secret?"

"Oh yes," said Raby, "provided you will promise faithfully to tell no one."

Grace promised, and he then told her that Jael Dence, in a moment of desperation, had thrown herself into the river at the back of his house. "Poor girl!" said he, "her brain was not right at the time. Heaven keep us all from those moments of despair. She has got over it now, and nurses and watches my poor sister more like a mother watching her child than a young woman taking care of an old one. She is the mainspring of the house."

At all this Grace turned from pale to white, but said nothing; and Raby ran on in praise of Jael, little dreaming what pain his words inflicted.

When he left her, she rose and walked down to the sea: for her tortured spirit gave her body energy. Hitherto she found she had only suspected; now she was sure. Hitherto she had feared Henry Little had loved Jael Dence a little; now she was sure he had loved her best. Jael Dence would not have attempted self-destruction for any man unless he loved her. The very act proved her claim to him more eloquently than words could do. Now she believed all—the anonymous letter—Mr. Coventry's report—the woman's words who worked in the same factory, and could not be deceived. And her very godfather accepted Jael Dence and her claim to sympathy: she was taken into his house, and set to nurse Henry Little's mother: poor Grace was slighted on all sides; she must not even write to Mrs. Little, nor take part in the pious falsehood they were concocting together, Raby and his Jael Dence, whom every body loved best—every body except this poor faithful ill-used wretch, Frederick Coventry; and him she hated for loving her better than the man she loved had loved her.

Tender, but very proud, this sensitive creature saw herself dethroned from her love. Jael Dence had eclipsed her in every way; had saved his life with her strong arm, had almost perished with

him; and had tried to kill herself when he was dead. She was far behind this rival in every thing. She had only loved, and suffered, and nearly died. "No, no," she said to herself, "she could not love him better than I did: but he loved her best; and she knew it, and that made her arm strong to fight, and her heart strong to die for him. I am nobody—nothing." Then the scalding tears ran down her cheeks.

But soon her pride got the upper hand, and dried her cheeks, and nearly maddened her.

She began to blush for her love, to blush for her illness. She rose into that state of exasperation in which persons of her sex do things they look back upon with wonder, and, strange to say, all this without one unkind thought of him whose faults she saw, but excused—he was dead.

She now began to struggle visibly, and violently, against her deadly sorrow. She forced herself to take walks and rides, and to talk, with nothing to say. She even tried to laugh now and then. She made violent efforts to be gracious and pitiful to Mr. Coventry, and the next minute made him suffer for it by treating him like a troublesome hound.

He loved her madly, yet sometimes he felt tempted to kill her, and end both her torture and his own.

Such was the inner life of Grace Carden for many days; devoid of striking incident, yet well worthy of study by those who care to pierce below the surface, and see what passes in the hearts of the unhappy, and to learn how things come gradually about that sound incredible when not so traced, yet are natural and almost inevitable results of certain conflicting passions in a virgin heart.

One day Mr. Carden telegraphed from London to Mr. Coventry at Hillsborough that he was coming down to Eastbank by the midday express, and would be glad to meet him there at four o'clock. He also telegraphed to Grace, and said, "Dinner at five."

Both gentlemen arrived about the same time, a little before dinner.

Soon after dinner was over, Grace observed a restlessness in her father's manner, which convinced her he had something private to say to Mr. Coventry. Her suspicions were aroused: she fancied he was going to encourage Mr. Coventry to court her. Instantly the whole woman was in arms, and her love for the deceased came rushing back tenfold: She rose, soon after dinner, and retired to the drawing-room; but, as soon as she got there, she slipped quietly into the verandah, and lay softly down upon her couch. The dining-room window was open, and, with her quick ears, she could hear nearly every word.

She soon found that all her bitterness and her preparation for hostilities were wasted. Her father was telling Mr. Coventry the story of Richard Martin; only he carried it a step farther than I have done.

"Well, sir," said he, "the money had not been paid more than a month, when an insurance office down at Liverpool communicated with us. The same game had been played with them; but, somehow, their suspicions were excited. We compared notes with them, and set detectives to work. They traced Martin's confederates, and found one of them was in prison awaiting his trial for some minor offense. They worked on him to tell the truth (I am afraid they compounded), and he let out the whole truth. Every one of those villains could swim like ducks, and Richard Martin like a fish. Drowned ? not he : he had floated down to Greenwich or somewhere—the blackguard ! and hid himself. And what do you think

mouth ; and they kept toasting this ghastly corpse as the thing that was to make all their fortunes." —At this grotesque and horrible picture, a sigh of horror was uttered in the verandah. Mr. Carden, occupied with his narrative, did not hear it, but Coventry did.—" Then, when it was pitch dark, they staggered down to the water with it,

"A SIGH OF HORROR WAS UTTERED IN THE VERANDAH."

the miscreants did next ? Bought a dead marine ; and took him down in a box to some low public-house by the waterside. They had a supper, and dressed their marine in Richard Martin's clothes, and shaved its whiskers, and broke its tooth, and set it up in a chair, table beetrofw his it, and a pot of ale, and fastened a pipe in its

and planted it in the weeds. And, mark the cunning ! when they had gone through their farce of recognizing it publicly for Richard Martin, they bribed a churchwarden and buried it under our very noses : it was all done in a way to take in the very devil. There's no Richard Martin ; there never was a Richard Martin ; there never will be : all this was contrived and executed by a swindler well known to the police, only they can't catch him ; he is here, and there, and everywhere ; they call him 'Shifty Dick.' He and his myrmidons have bled the 'Gosshawk' to the tune of nine hundred pounds."

He drew his breath and proceeded more calmly. "However, a lesson of this kind is never thrown away upon a public man, and it has given me some very curious ideas about another matter. You know what I mean."

Coventry stared, and looked quite taken aback by this sudden turn.

However he stammered out, "I suppose you mean—but, really, I can't imagine what similarity—" he paused, and, inadvertently, his eye glanced uneasily towards the verandah.

"Oh," said Mr. Carden, "these diabolical frauds are not done upon one pattern, or, of course, there would soon be an end of their success. But come now, what proof have we got that what they found in the river at Hillsborough was the remains of Henry Little ?"

"I don't know, I am sure. But nobody seems to doubt it. The situation, the clothes, the ring—so many coincidences."

"That is all very well, if there were no rogues in the world. But there are ; and I know it, to my cost. The 'Gosshawk' has just lost nine hundred pounds by not suspecting. It shall not lose five thousand by the same weakness ; I'll take care of that."

He paused a moment, and then proceeded to argue the matter :

"The very idea of an imposture has never occured to any body ; in Little's case, it did not occur to me until this business of Shifty Dick enlightened me. But, come now, just admit the idea of imposture into that honest, unsuspicious mind of yours, and you'll find the whole thing wears a very doubtful appearance directly. A common workman— he was no more at the time—insures his life, for how much ? three hundred pounds ? no ; five thousand. Within one year after that he disappears, under cover of an explosion. Some weeks afterwards—about as many as the Martin swindle—there is found in the river a fragment of humanity ; an arm, and a hand, and a piece of a human trunk ; but no face, mind you : arms are pretty much alike, faces differ. The fragment is clad in brown tweed, and Little wore brown tweed : that is all very well ; but the marine was found dressed from head to foot in Shifty Dick's very clothes. But let us go on. There was a plain gold ring found on the hand in Hillsborough river, and my poor daughter had given Little a plain gold ring. But what was there to hinder an impostor from buying some pauper's body, and putting a plain gold ring on the hand ? Why, paupers' bodies are constantly sold, and the funeral service gabbled over a coffin full of stones. If I had paper and ink here, and could put Little's case and Martin's in two columns, I should soon show you that Martin and his gang faced and overcame more and greater difficulties in the way of imposture than any that have been overcome in Little's case. The Martin gang dealt with the face ; here, that is shirked. The Martin gang planted a body, not a fragment. Does it not strike you as very odd that the rest of Henry Little is not to be found ? It may be all right ; but, of the two, I incline to think it is a plant, and that

11

some person, calling himself the heir or assign of Little, will soon apply to the 'Gosshawk' for five thousand pounds. Well, let him. I shall look on that person as the agent of a living man, not the heir of a dead one ; and I shall tell him I don't believe in arms, and shoulders, and tweed suits, and plain gold rings—(why, wedding-rings are the very things conjurors take from the public at random to play hanky-panky with ; they are so like one another). I shall demand to see the man's face ; and the mother who bore him must identify that face before I will pay one shilling to his heirs or assigns. I am waiting to see who will come forward and claim. Nobody moves ; and that is curious. Well, when they do, I shall be ready for them. You look pale ! But no wonder : it is really no subject for an after-dinner conversation."

Coventry was pale indeed, and his mind all in a whirl as to what he should say ; for Mr. Carden's sagacity terrified him, and the worst of it was, he felt sure that Grace Carden heard every word.

At last, however, his natural cunning came to his aid, and he made a very artful speech, directed principally to his unseen hearer.

"Mr. Carden," said he, "this seems to me very shrewd ; but surely it fails in one respect : you leave the man's character out of the account. Mr. Little came between me and one I love, and inflicted great misery on me ; but I will try and be just to him. I don't believe he was an impostor of that kind. He was false in love ; he had been reared amongst workmen, and every body says he loved a working-girl more than he did your daughter ; but as for his cheating you or any other person out of five thousand pounds, I can't believe it. They all say he was as honest a man in money matters as ever breathed."

"You judge him by yourself. Besides, men begin by deceiving women, but they go on to— Why, Grace, my poor child— Good heavens ! have you— ?"

Grace was leaning against the open window, ghastly and terrible.

"Yes," said she haughtily, "I have been guilty of the meanness of listening, and I suffer for it. It is but one pang more to a broken heart. Mr. Coventry, you are just, you are generous ; and I will try and reward you for those words. No, papa, no impostor, but a man sore tried, sore tempted. If he is alive, we shall soon know."

"How ?"

"He will write—to Jael Dence."

Having uttered this strange speech, she rushed away with a wild cry of agony, and nobody saw her face again that night.

She did not come down stairs next day. Mr. Carden went up to her. He staid with her an hour, and came down looking much dejected ; he asked Mr. Coventry to take a turn in the garden with him. When they were alone, he said gravely, "Mr. Coventry, that unfortunate conversation of ours has quite upset my poor girl. She tells me now she will not believe he is dead until months and months have passed without his writing to Jael Dence."

"Well but, sir," said Coventry, "could you not convince her ?"

"How can I, when I am myself convinced he is alive, and will give us a great deal of trouble yet ; for it is clear to me the poor girl loves him more than she knows? Look here, Coventry, there's no man I so desire for a son-in-law as yourself; you have shown a patience, a fidelity! —but as a just man, and a man of honor, I must now advise you to give up all thoughts of her. You are not doing yourself justice; she will never marry you while that man is alive and unmarried. I am provoked with her: she will not leave her room while you are in the house. Shall I tell you what she said? 'I respect him, I admire him, but I can't bear the sight of him now.' That is all because I let out last night that I thought Little was alive. I told her, alive or not, he was dead to her."

"And what did she say to that?"

"Not a word. She wrung her hands, and burst out crying terribly. Ah! my friend, may you never know what it is to be a father, and see your child wring her hands, and cry her heart out, as I have seen mine."

His own tears flowed, and his voice was choked. He faltered out, "We are two miserable creatures; forgive us, and leave us to our fate."

Coventry rose, sick at heart, and said, "Tell her I will not intrude upon her."

He telegraphed to Lally, and went back to Hillsborough as miserable as those he left behind; but with this difference, he deserved his misery, deserved it richly.

Ere he had been two days in Hillsborough a telegram came from him to Mr. Carden—

"_Re Little. Important discovery. Pray come here at once._"

Mr. Carden had the prudence to withhold from Grace the nature of this communication. He merely told her business called him suddenly to Hillsborough. He started by the next train, and found Mr. Coventry awaiting him at "Woodbine Villa" with strange news: it was not conjecture, nor a matter of deduction, but a piece of undeniable evidence; and it knocked both Mr. Carden's theory and his daughter's to atoms at one blow.

———

CHAPTER XXXVIII.

MEANTIME the history of Raby House was the history of what French dramatists call "a pious lie."

Its indirect effect in keeping Grace Carden apart both from Mrs. Little and Jael Dence was unforeseen and disastrous; its immediate and direct effect on Mrs. Little was encouraging to those concerned: what with the reconciliation to her brother, the return to native air and beloved scenes, the tenderness and firmness of Jael Dence, and the conviction that her son was safe out of the clutches of the dreaded Unions, she picked up flesh and color and spirit weekly.

By-and-by she turned round upon Jael Dence, and the nurse became the pupil. Mrs. Little taught her grammar, pronunciation, dancing, carriage, and deportment. Jael could already sing from notes; Mrs. Little taught her to accompany herself on the pianoforte. The teacher was so vigilant, and the pupil so apt and attentive, that surprising progress was made. To be sure, they were together night and day.

This labor of love occupied Mrs. Little's mind agreeably, and, as the pupil was equally resolute

in making the teacher walk or ride on horseback with her every day, the hours glided swiftly, and, to Mrs. Little, pleasantly.

Her brother rather avoided her, by order of Jael Dence; but so many probable reasons were given for his absences that she suspected nothing. Only she said one day, "What a gad-about he is now. This comes of not marrying. We must find him a wife."

When he was at home they breakfasted together, all three, and then Mrs. Little sometimes spoke of Henry, and so hopefully and cheerfully, that a great qualm ran through her hearers, and Raby, who could not command his features so well as Jael could, looked gloomy, and sometimes retired behind his newspaper.

Mrs. Little observed this one day, and pointed it out to Jael. "Oh," said Jael, "take no notice. You know he wanted Mr. Henry to stay quietly here and be his heir."

"And so did I. But his very name seems to—"

"He likes him well, for all that, ma'am; only he won't own it yet. You know what Squire is."

"_The_ Squire you should say, dear. But 'Mr. Raby' is better still. As a rule, avoid all small titles: the Doctor, the Squire, the Baronet, the Mayor."

Jael seized this handle, and, by putting questions to her teacher, got her away from the dangerous topic.

Ever on the watch, and occupied in many ways with Mrs. Little, Jael began to recover resignation; but this could not be without an occasional paroxysm of grief.

These she managed to hide from Mrs. Little.

But one day that lady surprised her crying. She stood and looked at her a moment, then sat down quietly beside her and took her hand. Jael started, and feared discovery.

"My child," said Mrs. Little, "if you have lost a father, you have gained a mother; and then, as to your sister, why my Henry is gone to the very same country; yet, you see, I do not give way to sorrow. As soon as he writes, I will beg him to make inquiries for Patty, and send them home if they are not doing well." Then Mrs. Little kissed Jael, and coaxed her and rocked with her, and Jael's tears began to flow, no longer for her own great grief, but for this mother, who was innocently consoling her, unconscious of the blow that must one day fall upon herself.

So matters went on pretty smoothly; only one morning, speaking of Henry, Mrs. Little surprised a look of secret intelligence between her brother and Jael Dence. She made no remark at the time, but she puzzled in secret over it, and began at last to watch the pair.

She asked Raby at dinner, one day, when she might hope to hear from Henry.

"I don't know," said he, and looked at Jael Dence like a person watching for orders.

Mrs. Little observed this, and turned keenly round to Jael.

"Oh," said Jael, "the Doctor—I beg pardon, Doctor Amboyne—can tell you that better than I can. It is a long way to Australia."

"How you send me from one to another," said Mrs. Little, speaking very slowly.

They made no reply to that, and Mrs. Little said no more. But she pondered all this. She wrote to Dr. Amboyne, and asked him why no letter had come from Henry.

Doctor Amboyne wrote back that, even if he had gone in a steamboat, there was hardly time for a letter to come back: but he had gone in a sailing-vessel. "Give him three months and a half to get there, and two months for his letters to come back."

In this same letter he told her he was glad to hear she was renewing her youth like an eagle, but reminded her it would entail some consequences more agreeable to him than to her.

She laid down the letter with a blush and fell into a reverie.

Doctor Amboyne followed up this letter with a visit or two, and urged her to keep her promise and marry him.

She had no excuse for declining, but she procrastinated; she did not like to marry without consulting Henry, or, at least, telling him by letter.

And whilst she was thus temporizing, events took place at Eastbank which ended by rudely disturbing the pious falsehood at Raby Hall.

That sequence of events began with the interview between Mr. Carden and Mr. Coventry at Woodbine Villa.

"Little had made a will. My own solicitor drew it, and holds it at this moment." This was the intelligence Coventry had to communicate.

"Very well; then now I shall know who is coming to the 'Gosshawk' for the five thousand pounds. That will be the next act of the comedy, you will see."

"Wait a moment. He leaves to Mrs. Little his own reversion to a sum of nineteen hundred pounds, in which she has already the life interest; he gives a hundred pounds to his sweetheart Dence: all the rest of his estate, in possession or expectation, he bequeaths to—Miss Carden."

"Good heavens!—Why then—" Mr. Carden could say no more, for astonishment.

"So," said Coventry, "if he is alive, she is the confederate who is to profit by the fraud; those

five thousand pounds belong to her at this moment."

"Are you sure? Who is your authority?"

"A communicative clerk, who happens to be the son of a tenant of mine. The solicitor himself, I believe, chooses to doubt his client's decease. It is at his private request that horrible object is refused Christian burial."

"On what grounds, pray?"

"Legal grounds, I suppose; the man did not die regularly, and according to precedent. He omitted to provide himself with two witnesses previously to being blown up. In a case of this kind we may safely put an old-fashioned attorney's opinion out of the question. What do you think? That is all I care to know."

"I don't know what to think now. But I foresee one thing; I shall be placed in rather an awkward position. I ought to defend the 'Gosshawk;' but I am not going to rob my own daughter of five thousand pounds, if it belongs to her honestly."

"Will you permit me to advise you?"

"Certainly, I shall be very much obliged: for really I don't see my way."

"Well, then, I think you ought to look into the matter carefully, but without prejudice. I have made some inquiries myself: I went down to the works, and begged the workmen, who knew Little, to examine the remains, and then come here and tell us their real opinion."

"Oh, to my mind, it all depends on the will. If that answers the description you give—hum!"

Next morning they breakfasted together, and during breakfast two workmen called, and, at Coventry's request, were ushered into the room. They came to say they knew Mr. Little well, and felt sure that was his dead hand they had seen at the Town Hall. Coventry cross-examined them severely, but they stuck to their conviction; and this will hardly surprise the reader when I tell him the workmen in question were Cole and another, suborned by Coventry himself to go through this performance.

Mr. Carden received the testimony readily, for the best of all reasons—he wanted to believe it.

But, when they were gone, he recurred to the difficulty of his position. Director of the "Gosshawk," and father to a young lady who had a claim of five thousand pounds on it, and that claim debatable, though, to his own mind, no longer doubtful.

Now Mr. Coventry had a great advantage over Mr. Carden here: he had studied this very situation profoundly for several hours, and at last had seen how much might be done with it.

He began by artfully complimenting Mr. Carden on his delicacy, but said Miss Carden must not be a loser by it. "Convince her, on other grounds, that the man is dead; encourage her to reward my devotion with her hand, and I will relieve you of every thing disagreeable. Let us settle on Miss Carden, for her separate use, the five thousand pounds, and any thing else derivable from Mr. Little's estate; but we must also settle my farm of Hindhope: for it shall never be said she took as much from that man as she did from me. Well, in due course I apply to the 'Gosshawk' for my wife's money. I am not bound to tell your Company it is not mine but hers; that is between you and me. But you really ought to write to London at once and withdraw the charge of fraud; you owe that piece of justice to Miss Carden, and to the memory of the deceased."

"That is true; and it will pave the way for the demand you propose to make on Mrs. Coventry's behalf. Well, you really are a true friend, as well as a true lover."

In short, he went back to Hillsborough resolved to marry his daughter to Coventry as soon as possible. Still, following that gentleman's instructions, he withheld from Grace that Little had made a will in her favor. He knew her to be quite capable of refusing to touch a farthing of it, or to act as executrix. But he told her the workmen had identified the remains, and that other circumstances had also convinced him he had been unjust to a deceased person, which he regretted.

When her father thus retracted his own words, away went Grace's last faint hope that Henry lived; and now she must die for him, or live for others.

She thought of Jael Dence, and chose the latter.

Another burst or two of agony, and then her great aim and study appeared to be to forget herself altogether. She was full of attention for her father, and, whenever Mr. Coventry came, she labored to reward him with kind words, and even with smiles; but they were sad ones.

As for Coventry, he saw, with secret exultation, that she was now too languid and hopeless to resist the joint efforts of her father and himself, and that, some day or other, she must fall lifeless into his arms.

He said to himself, "It is only a question of time."

He was now oftener at the villa than at Hillsborough, and, with remarkable self-denial, adhered steadily to the line of soothing and unobtrusive devotion.

One morning at breakfast the post brought him a large envelope from Hillsborough. He examined it, and found a capital "L" in the corner of the envelope, which "L" was written by his man Lally, in compliance with secret instructions from his master.

Coventry instantly put the envelope into his pocket, and his hand began to shake so that he could hardly hold his cup to his lips. His agitation, however, was not noticed.

Directly after breakfast he strolled, with affected composure, into the garden, and sat down in a bower where he was safe from surprise, as the tangled leaves were not so thick but he could peep through them.

He undid his inclosure, and found three letters; two were of no importance; the third bore a foreign post-mark, and was addressed to Miss Carden in a handwriting which he recognized at a glance as Henry Little's.

But as this was not the first letter from Henry to Grace which he had intercepted and read, perhaps I had better begin by saying a few words about the first.

Well, then, the letters with which Coventry swam the river on the night of the explosion were six, viz., to Mr. Bolt, to Doctor Amboyne, to Mr. Baynes, to Jael Dence, to Mrs. Little, and to Grace Carden. The letter to Grace Carden was short but touching, full of devotion, hope, resolution, and grief at parting. He told her he had come to take leave that afternoon, but she had

been out, luckily; for he felt he ought to go, and must go, but how could he look at her and then leave her? This was the general purport, and expressed with such anguish and fortitude as might have melted a heart of marble.

The reader may have observed that, upon his rival's disappearance, Coventry was no happier. This letter was the secret cause. First, it showed him his rival was alive, and he had wasted a crime; secondly, it struck him with remorse, yet not with penitence; and to be full of remorse, yet empty of that true penitence which confesses or undoes the wrong, this is to be miserable.

But, as time rolled on, bringing the various events I have related, but no news of Little, Coventry began to think that young man must really have come to some untimely end.

From this pleasant dream he was now awakened by the second intercepted letter. It ran thus:

"Boston, U. S., June 20th.

"MY OWN DEAR LOVE,—It is now nine weeks since I left England, and this will be a fortnight more getting to you; that is a long time for you to be without news from me, and I sadly fear I have caused you great anxiety. Dearest, it all happened thus: Our train was delayed by an accident, and I reached Liverpool just in time to see the steam-packet move down the Mersey. My first impulse, of course, was to go back to Hillsborough; but a seaman, who saw my vexation, told me a fast schooner was on the point of sailing for Boston, U. S. My heart told me if I went back to Hillsborough, I should never make the start again. I summoned all my manhood to do the right thing for us both; and I got into the schooner, heaven knows how; and, when I got there, I hid my face for ever so many hours, till, by the pitching and tossing, I knew that I was at sea. Then I began to cry and blubber. I couldn't hold it any longer.

"At such a time a kind word keeps the heart from breaking altogether; and I got some comfort from an old gentleman, a native of Boston: a grave old man he was, and pretty reserved with all the rest; but seeing me in the depths of misery, he talked to me like a father, and I told him all my own history, and a little about you too—at least, how I loved you, and why I had left England with a heavy heart.

"We had a very long passage, not downright tempestuous, but contrary winds, and a stiff gale or two. Instead of twenty days, as they promised, we were six weeks at sea, and what with all the fighting and the threats—I had another letter signed with a coffin just before I left that beautiful town—and the irritation at losing so much time on the ocean, it all brought on a fever, and I have no recollection of leaving the boat. When I came to myself, I was in a house near Boston, belonging to the old gentleman I spoke of. He and his nieces nursed me, and now I am as well as ever, only rather weak.

"Mr. Ironside, that is his name, but it should be Mr. Goldheart, if I had the christening of him—he has been my good Samaritan. Dear Grace, please pray for him and his family every night. He tells me he comes of the pilgrim fathers, so he is bound to feel for pilgrims and wanderers from home. Well, he has been in patents a little, and, before I lost my little wits with the fever, he and I had many a talk. So now he is sketching out a plan of operation for me, and I shall have to travel many a hundred miles in this vast country. But they won't let me move till I am a little stronger, he and his nieces. If he is gold, they are pearls.

"Dearest, it has taken me two days to write this; but I am very happy and hopeful, and do not regret coming. I am sure it was the right thing for us both.

"Please say something kind for me to the good doctor, and tell him I have got over this one trouble already.

"Dearest, I agreed to take so much a year from Bolt, and he must fight the trades alone. Such a life is not worth having. Bayne won't wrong me of a shilling. Whatever he makes, over his salary and the men's wages, there it will be for me when I come home; so I write to no one at Hillsborough but you. Indeed, you are my all in this world. I travel, and fight, and work, and breathe, and live for you, my own beloved; and if any harm came to you, I wouldn't care to live another moment."

At this point in the letter the reader stopped, and something cold seemed to pass all through his frame. It struck him that all good men would pity the writer of this letter, and abhor him who kept it from that pale, heart-broken girl inside the cottage.

He sat freezing, with the letter in his hand, and began to doubt whether he could wade any deeper in crime.

After a minute or two he raised his head, and was about to finish reading the letter.

But, in the mean time, Grace Carden had resumed her accustomed place in the verandah. She lay upon the couch, and her pale face, and hollow, but still beautiful eyes, were turned seaward. Out of those great sad eyes the sad soul looked across the waste of waters—gazed, and searched, and pined in vain. Oh, it was a look to make angels weep, and hover close over her head with restless, loving pinions, longing to shadow, caress, and heal her!

Coventry, with Henry Little's letter in his hand, peered through the leaves, and saw the woman he loved fix this look of despair upon the sea—despair of which he was the sole cause, and could dispel it with a gesture.

"And this brings me back to what is my only great trouble now. I told you, in the letter I left behind me, you would hear from me in a month at farthest. It will be not a month, but eleven weeks. Good heavens! when I think what anxiety you may have suffered on my account! You know I am a pupil of the good Doctor, and so I put myself in your place, and I say to myself, 'If my Grace had promised to write in a month, and eleven weeks had passed without a word, what would my feelings be?' Why, I think I should go mad; I should make sure you were ill; I should fear you were dead; I should fancy every terrible thing on earth, except that you were false to your poor Henry. That I should never fear: I judge you by myself. Fly, steamboat, with this letter to my love, and set her mind at ease. Fly back with a precious word from her dear hand, and with that in my bosom, nothing will ever daunt me.

"God bless you! angel of my life, darling of my heart, star on which all my hopes are fixed! Oh, what miserable bad tools words are! When

I look at them, and compare them with how I love you, I seem to be writing that I love you no more than other people love. What I feel is so much greater than words.

"Must I say farewell? Even on paper, it is like tearing myself away from heaven again. But that was to be: and now this is to be. Good-bye, my own beloved. Yours till death,

"HENRY."

Coventry read this sentence by sentence, still looking up, nearly every sentence, at her to whom it was addressed.

The letter pleaded on his knee, the pale face pleaded a few yards off; he sat between the two bleeding lovers, their sole barrier and bane.

His heart began to fail him. The mountain of crime looked high. Now remorse stung him deeper than ever; jealousy spurred him harder than ever; a storm arose within his breast, a tempest of conflicting passion, as grand and wild as ever distracted the heart; as grand and wild as any poet has ever tried to describe, and, half succeeding, won immortal fame.

"See what I can do!" whispered conscience. "With one bound I can give her the letter, and bring the color back to that cheek and joy to that heart. She will adore me for it, she will be my true and tender friend till death. She will weep upon my neck and bless me."

"Ay," whispered jealousy, "and then she will marry Henry Little."

"And am I sure to succeed if I persist in crime? Deserve her hatred and contempt, and is it certain they will not both fall on me?"

"The fault began with them. He supplanted me—she jilted me. I hate him—I love her. I can't give her up now; I have gone too far. What is intercepting a letter? I have been too near murder to stop at that."

"But her pale face! her pale face!"

"Once married, supplant him as he has supplanted you. Away to Italy with her. Fresh scenes—constant love—the joys of wedlock! What will this Henry Little be to her then?—a dream."

"Eternal punishment! if it is not a fable, who has ever earned it better than I am earning it if I go on?"

"It is a fable; it must be. Philosophers always said so, and now even divines have given it up."

"Her pale face! her pale face! Never mind him, look at her. What sort of love is this that shows no pity? Oh, my poor girl, don't look so sad—so pale! What shall I do? Would to God I had never been born, to torture myself and her!"

His good angel fought hard for him that day; fought and struggled and hoped, until the miserable man, torn this way and that, ended the struggle with a blasphemous yell by tearing the letter to atoms.

That fatal act turned the scale.

The next moment he wished he had not done it.

But it was too late. He could not go to her with the fragments. She would see he had intercepted it purposely.

Well, all the better. It was decided. He would not look at her face any more. He could not bear it.

He rushed away from the bower and made for the sea-side; but he soon returned another way, gained his own room, and there burnt the fragments of the letter to ashes.

But, though he was impenitent, remorse was not subdued. He could not look Grace Carden in the face now. So he sent word he must go back to Hillsborough directly.

He packed his bag and went down stairs with it. On the last landing he met Grace Carden. She started a little.

"What! going away?"

"Yes, Miss Carden."

"No bad news, I hope?" said she, kindly.

The kindly tone coming from her, to whom he had shown no mercy, went through that obdurate heart.

"No — no," he faltered; "but the sight of your unhappiness— Let me go. I am a miserable man!"

And with this he actually burst out crying and ran past her.

Grace told her father, and asked him to find out what was the matter with Mr. Coventry.

Mr. Carden followed Coventry to the station, and Coventry, who had now recovered his self-possession and his cunning, told him that for some time Miss Carden had worn a cheerful air, which had given him hopes; but this morning, watching her from a bower in the garden, he had seen such misery in her face that it had quite upset him; and he was going away to try and recover that composure, without which he felt he would be no use to her in any way.

This tale Carden brought back to his daughter, and she was touched by it. "Poor Mr. Coventry!" said she. "Why does he waste so much love on me?"

Her father, finding her thus softened, pleaded hard for his friend, and reminded Grace that she had not used him well. She admitted that at once, and went so far as to say that she felt bound never to marry any one but Mr. Coventry, unless time should cure him, as she hoped it would, of his unfortunate attachment.

From this concession Mr. Carden urged her daily to another, viz., that Mr. Coventry might be permitted to try and win her affection.

Her answer was, "He had much better content himself with what I can and do give him—my esteem and gratitude and sincere pity."

Mr. Carden, however, persisted, and the deep affection he had shown his daughter gave him great power. It was two against one; and the two prevailed.

Mr. Coventry began to spend his whole time at Eastbank Cottage.

He followed Grace about with a devotion to which no female heart could be entirely insensible; and, at last, she got used to him, and rather liked to have him about her. He broke her solitude as a dog does, and he fetched and carried for her, and talked when she was inclined to listen, and was silent when he saw his voice jarred upon her bereaved heart.

Without her father, matters might have gone on so for years; but Mr. Carden had now so many motives for marrying his daughter to Coventry, that he used all his judgment and all his influence. He worked on his daughter's pride, her affection, her sense of honor, and her sense of duty.

She struggled, she sighed, she wept; but, by little and little, she submitted. And, since three months more passed with no striking event, I will deviate from my usual custom and speak a little of what passed in her mind.

First of all, then, she was so completely deceived by appearances, that she believed the exact opposite of the truth in each particular. To her not only did black seem white, but white black. Her dead lover had given her but half his heart. Her living lover was the soul of honor and true devotion. It was her duty, though not her pleasure, to try and love him; to marry him would be a good and self-denying action.

And what could she lose by it? Her own chance of happiness was gone. All she could hope for hereafter was the gentle satisfaction that arises from making others happy. She had but a choice of evils: never to marry at all, or to marry Frederick Coventry.

Thus far she was conscious of her own feelings, and could, perhaps, have put them into words; but here she drifted out of her depth.

Nature implants in women a genuine love of offspring that governs them unconsciously. It governs the unconscious child; it governs the half-conscious mother who comes home from the toyshop with a waxen child for her girl, and a drum for her boy.

Men desire offspring—when they desire it at all—from vanity alone. Women desire it from pure love of it.

This instinct had probably its share in withholding Grace from making up her mind never to marry; and so operated negatively, though not positively, in Coventry's favor.

And so, by degrees and in course of time, after saying "no" a dozen times, she said "yes" once in a moment of utter lassitude, and afterwards she cried and wished to withdraw her consent, but they were two to one, and had right on their side, she thought.

They got her to say she would marry him some day or other.

Coventry intercepted several letters, but he took care not to read them with Grace's sad face in sight. He would not give conscience such a power to torment him. The earlier letters gave him a cruel satisfaction. They were written each from a different city in the United States, and all tended to show that the writer had a year or two to travel yet, before he could hope to return home in triumph and marry his Grace.

In all these letters she was requested to send her answers to New York (and, now I think of it, there was a postscript to that effect in the very letter I have given in extenso).

But at last came a letter that disturbed this delightful dream. It was written from the western extremity of the States, but the writer was in high spirits; he had sold his patents in two great cities, and had established them in two more on a royalty; he had also met with an unexpected piece of good-fortune: his railway clip had been appreciated, a man of large capital and enterprise had taken it up with spirit, and was about to purchase the American and Canadian right for a large sum down and a percentage. As soon as this contract should be signed he should come home and claim Mr. Carden's promise. He complained a little that he got no letters, but concluded the post-office authorities were in fault, for he had written to New York to have them forwarded. However, he soon should be in that city and revel in them.

This troubled Coventry, and drove him to extremities. He went on his knees to Grace, and implored her to name the day.

She drew back with horror and repugnance; said, with a burst of tears, she was a widow, and would not marry till a decent time had elapsed since—; then, with sudden doggedness, "I will never marry at all."

And so she left him to repent his precipitation.

He was at his wits' end, and could do nothing but look unhappy, and temporize, and hope the wind might change.

The wind did not change, and he passed a week or two of outward sorrow, but inward rage.

He fell ill, and Mr. Carden pitied him openly. Grace maintained a sullen silence.

One day, as he was in bed, an envelope was brought him, with a large "L." He opened it slowly, fearing the worst.

The letter was full of love, and joy, and triumph that made the reader's heart faint within him till he came to this sentence:

"The gentleman who treats with me for the railway clip makes it an express stipulation that I shall spend a month in his works at Chicago, superintending the forging and perfecting of the clip. As he intends to be there himself, and to buy it out-and-out if it answers his expectations, I shall certainly go, and wear a smith's apron once more for your sake. He is even half inclined to go into another of my projects—the forging of large axes by machinery. It was tried at Hillsborough two years ago, but the Union sent a bullet through the manufacturer's hat, and he dropped it."

The letter from which I give this extract was a reprieve. He had five or six weeks before him still.

Soon after this, his faithful ally, Mr. Carden, worked on Grace's pity; and as Coventry never complained, nor irritated her in any way, she softened to him. Then all the battery of imploring looks was brought to bear on her by Coventry, and of kind admonition and entreaty by her father; and so, between them, they gently thrust her down the slope.

"Stop all their tongues," said Mr. Carden. "Come back to Hillsborough a wife. I gave up my choice to yours once. Now give me my way. I am touched to the heart by this young man's devotion: he invites me to live with him when you are married. What other young fellow would show me so much mercy?"

"Does he?" said Grace. "I will try and reward him for that, and for speaking well of one who could not defend himself. But give me a little time."

Mr. Carden conveyed this to Coventry with delight, and told him he should only have another month or so to wait. Coventry received this at first with unmixed exultation, but by-and-by he began to feel superstitious. Matters were now drawing to such a point that Little might very well arrive before the wedding-day, and just before it. Perhaps Heaven had that punishment in store for him; the cup was to be in his very grasp, and then struck out of it.

Only a question of time! But what is every race? The space between winner and loser strikes the senses more obviously; but the race is just as much a question of time as of space. Buridan runs second for the Derby, defeated by a length. But give Buridan a start of one second, and he shall beat the winner—by two lengths.

Little now wrote from Chicago that every thing was going on favorably, and he believed it would end in a sale of the patent clip in the United States and Canada for fifty thousand dollars, but no royalty.

This letter was much shorter than any of the others; and, from that alone, his guilty reader could see that the writer intended to follow it in person almost immediately.

Coventry began almost to watch the sun in his course. When it was morning he wished it was evening, and when it was evening he wished it was morning.

Sometimes he half wondered to see how calmly the sun rose and set, and Nature pursued her course, whilst he writhed in the agony of suspense, and would gladly have given a year out of his life for a day.

At last, by Mr. Carden's influence, the wedding-day was fixed. But soon after this great triumph came another intercepted letter. He went to his room, and his hands trembled violently as he opened it.

His eye soon fixed on this passage:

"I thought to be in New York by this time, and looking homeward; but I am detained by another piece of good-fortune, if any thing can be called good-fortune that keeps me a day from you. Oh, my dear Grace, I am dying to see your handwriting at New York, and then fly home and see your dear self, and never, never quit you more. I have been wonderfully lucky; I have made my fortune, our fortune. But it hardly pays me for losing the sight of you so many months. But what I was going to tell you is, that my method of forging large axes by machinery is wonderfully praised, and a great firm takes it up on fair terms. This firm has branches in various parts of the world, and, once my machines are in full work, Hillsborough will never forge another axe. Man can not suppress machinery; the world is too big. That bullet sent through Mr. Tyler's hat loses Great Britain a whole trade. I profit in money by their short-sighted violence, but I must pay the price; for this will keep me another week at Chicago, perhaps ten days. Then home I come, with lots of money to please your father, and an ocean of love for you, who don't care about the filthy dross; no more do I, except as the paving-stones on the road to you and heaven, my adored one."

The effect of this letter was prodigious. So fearful had been the suspense, so great was now the relief, that Coventry felt exultant, buoyant. He went down to the sea-side, and walked, light as air, by the sands, and his brain teemed with delightful schemes. Little would come to Hillsborough soon after the marriage, but what of that? On the wedding-night he would be at Dover. Next day at Paris, on his way to Rome, Athens, Constantinople. The inevitable exposure should never reach his wife until he had so won her, soul and body, that she should adore him for the crimes he had committed to win her—he knew the female heart to be capable of that.

He came back from his walk another man, color in his cheek and fire in his eye.

He walked into the drawing-room, and found Mr. Raby, with his hat on, just leaving Grace, whose eyes showed signs of weeping.

"I wish you joy, sir," said Raby. "I am to have the honor of being at your wedding."

"It will add to my happiness, if possible," said Coventry.

To be as polite in deed as in word, he saw Mr. Raby into the fly.

"Curious creatures, these girls," said Raby, shrugging his shoulders.

"She was engaged to me long ago," said Coventry, parrying the blow.

"Ah! I forgot that. Still—well, well; I wish you joy."

He went off, and Coventry returned to Grace. She was seated by the window, looking at the sea.

"What did godpapa say to you?"

"Oh, he congratulated me. He reminded me you and I were first engaged at his house."

"Did he tell you it is to be at Woodbine Villa?"

"What?"

"The wedding." And Grace blushed to the forehead at having to mention it.

"No, indeed, he did not mention any such thing, or I should have shown him how unadvisable—"

"You mistake me. It is *I* who wish to be married from my father's house by good old Doctor Fynes. He married my parents, and he christened me, and now he shall marry me."

"I approve that, of course, since you wish it; but, my own dearest Grace, Woodbine Villa is associated with so many painful memories—let me advise, let me earnestly entreat you, not to select it as the place to be married from. Dr. Fynes can be invited here."

"I have set my heart on it," said Grace. "Pray do not thwart me in it."

"I should be very sorry to thwart you in any thing. But, before you finally decide, pray let me try and convince your better judgment."

"I *have* decided; and I have written to Doctor Fynes, and to the few persons I mean to invite. They can't all come here; and I have asked Mr. Raby; and it is my own desire; and it is one of those things that the lady and her family always decide. I have no wish to be married at all. I only marry to please my father and you. There, let us say no more about it, please. I will not be married at Woodbine Villa, nor anywhere else. I wish papa and you would show your love by burying me instead."

These words, and the wild and panting way they were uttered in, brought Coventry to his knees in a moment. He promised her, with abject submission, that she should have her own way in this and every thing. He petted her, and soothed her, and she forgave him, but so little graciously, that he saw she would fly out in a moment again, if the least attempt were made to shake her resolution.

Grace talked the matter over with Mr. Carden, and that same evening he begged Coventry to leave the Villa as soon as he conveniently could, for he and his daughter must be there a week before the wedding, and invite some relations, whom it was his interest to treat with respect.

"You will spare me a corner," said Coventry, in his most insinuating tone. "Dear Woodbine! I could not bear to leave it."

"Oh, of course you can stay there till we actually come; but we can't have the bride and bridegroom under one roof. Why, my dear fellow, you know better than that."

There was no help for it. It sickened him with fears of what might happen in those few fatal days, during which Mr. Carden, Grace herself, and a household over which he had no control, would occupy the house, and would receive the postman, whose very face showed him incorruptible.

He staid till the last moment; stopped a letter of five lines from Little, in which he said he should be in New York very soon, en route for England; and the very next day he received the Cardens, with a smiling countenance and a fainting heart, and then vacated the premises. He ordered Lally to hang about the Villa at certain hours when the post came in, and do his best. But this was catching at a straw. His real hope was that neither Little himself, nor a letter in his handwriting, might come in that short interval.

It wanted but five days to the wedding.

Hitherto, it had been a game of skill, now it was a game of chance; and every morning he wished it was evening, every evening he wished it was morning.

The day Raby came back from Eastbank he dined at home, and, in an unguarded moment, said something or other, on which Mrs. Little cross-examined him so swiftly and so keenly that he stammered, and let out Grace Carden was on the point of marriage.

"Marriage, while my son is alive!" said Mrs. Little, and looked from him to Jael Dence, at first with amazement, and afterwards with a strange expression that showed her mind was working.

A sort of vague alarm fell upon the other two, and they waited, in utter confusion, for what might follow.

But the mother was not ready to suspect so horrible a thing as her son's death. She took a more obvious view, and inveighed bitterly against Grace Carden.

She questioned Raby as to the cause, but it was Jael who answered her. "I believe nobody knows the rights of it but Miss Carden herself."

"The cause is her utter fickleness; but she never really loved him. My poor Henry!"

"Oh yes, she did," said Raby. "She was at death's door a few months ago."

"At death's door for one man, and now going to marry another!"

"Why not?" said Raby, hard pushed; "she is a woman."

"And why did you not tell me till now?" asked Mrs. Little, loftily ignoring her brother's pitiable attempt at a sneer.

Raby's reply to this was happier.

"Why, what the better are you for knowing it now? We had orders not to worry you unnecessarily. Had we not, Jael?"

"That is all very well, in some things. But, where my son is concerned, pray never keep the truth from me again. When did she break off with Henry—or did he quarrel with her?"

"I have no idea. I was not in the country."

"Do *you* know, dear?"

"No, Mrs. Little. But I am of your mind. I think she could not have loved Mr. Henry as she ought."

"When did you see her last?"

"I could not say justly, but it was a long while ago."

Mrs. Little interpreted this that Jael had quarrelled with Grace for her fickleness, and gave her a look of beaming affection; then fell into a dead silence, and soon tears were seen stealing down her cheek.

"But I shall write to her," said she, after a long and painful silence.

Mr. Raby hoped she would do nothing of the kind.

"Oh, I shall not say much. I shall put her one question. Of course *she* knows why they part."

Next morning Jael Dence asked Mr. Raby whether the threatened letter must be allowed to go.

"Of course it must," said Raby. "I have gone as far off the straight path as a gentleman can. And I wish we may not repent our ingenuity. Deceive a mother about her son! what can justify it, after all?"

Mrs. Little wrote her letter, and showed it to Jael:

"DEAR MISS CARDEN, — They tell me you are about to be married. Can this be true, and Henry Little alive?"

An answer came back, in due course.

"DEAR MRS. LITTLE,—It is true, and I am miserable. Forgive me, and forget me."

Mrs. Little discovered the marks of tears upon the paper, and was sorely puzzled.

She sat silent a long time: then, looking up, she saw Jael Dence gazing at her with moist eyes, and an angelic look of anxiety and affection.

She caught her round the neck, and kissed her, almost passionately.

"All the better," she cried, struggling with a sob. "I shall have my own way for once. You shall be my daughter instead."

Jael returned her embrace with ardor, but in silence, and with averted head.

When Jael Dence heard that Grace Carden was in Hillsborough, she felt very much drawn to go and see her: but she knew the meeting must be a sad one to them both; and that made her put it off till the very day before the wedding. Then, thinking it would be too unkind if she held entirely aloof, and being, in truth, rather curious to know whether Grace had really been able to transfer her affections in so short a time, she asked Mr. Raby's leave, and drove one of the ponies in to Woodbine Villa.

CHAPTER XXXIX.

THE short interval previous to the wedding-day passed, to all appearance, as that period generally does. Settlements were drawn, and only awaited signature. The bride seemed occupied with dress, and receiving visits and presents, and reading and writing letters of that sort which ought to be done by machinery.

The bridegroom hovered about the house, running in and out on this or that pretext.

She received his presence graciously, read him the letters of her female friends, and forced herself to wear a look of languid complacency, especially before others.

Under all this routine she had paroxysms of secret misery, and he was in tortures.

These continued until the eve of the wedding, and then he breathed freely. No letter had come from the United States, and to-morrow was the wedding day. The chances were six to one no letter came that day, and, even if one should, he had now an excuse ready for keeping Lally on the premises that particular morning. At one o'clock he would be flying south with his bride.

He left the villa to dress for dinner. During this interval Jael Dence called.

The housemaid knocked at Grace's door—she was dressing—and told her Jael wished to see her.

Grace was surprised, and much disturbed. It flashed on her in a moment that this true and constant lover of Henry Little had come to enjoy her superiority. She herself had greatly desired this meeting once, but now it could only serve to mortify her. The very thought that this young woman was near her set her trembling; but she forced herself to appear calm, and, turning to her maid, said, "Tell her I can see no one to-day."

The lady's maid gave this message to the other servant, and she went down stairs with it.

The message, however, had not been gone long when the desire to put a question to Jael Dence returned strongly upon Grace Carden.

She yielded to an uncontrollable impulse, and sent her maid down to say that she would speak to Jael Dence, in her bedroom, the last thing at night.

"The last thing at night!" said Jael, coloring with indignation; "and where am I to find a bed after that?"

"Oh," said the late footman, now butler, "you shall not leave the house. I'll manage that for you with the housekeeper."

At half past eleven o'clock that night Grace dismissed her maid, and told her to bring Jael Dence to her.

Jael came, and they confronted each other once more.

"You can go," said Grace to the maid.

They were alone, and eyed each other strangely.

"Sit down," said Grace, coldly.

"No, thank you," said Jael, firmly. "I shall not stay long after the way I have been received."

"And how did you expect to be received?"

"As I used to be. As a poor girl who once saved *his* life, and nearly lost her own, through being his true and faithful servant."

"Faithful to him, but not to me."

Jael's face showed she did not understand this.

"Yes," said Grace, bitterly, "you are the real cause of my marrying Mr. Coventry, whom I don't love, and never can love. There, read that. I can't speak to you. You look all candor and truth, but I know what you are; all the women in that factory knew about you and him—read that." She handed her the anonymous letter, and watched her like an eagle.

Jael read the poison, and colored a little, but was not confounded.

"Do you believe this, Miss Carden?"

"I did not believe it at first, but too many people have confirmed it. Your own conduct has confirmed it, my poor girl. This is cruel of me."

"Never mind," said Jael, resolutely. "We have gone too far to stop. My conduct! What conduct, if you please?"

"They all say that, when you found he was no more, you attempted self-destruction."

"Ah," cried Jael, like a wounded hare; "they must tell you that!" and she buried her face in her hands.

Now this was a young woman endowed by nature with great composure, and a certain sobriety and weight; so, when she gave way like that, it produced a great effect on those who knew her.

Grace sighed, and was distressed. But there was no help for it now. She awaited Jael's reply, and Jael could not speak for some time. She conquered her agitation, however, at last, and said, in a low voice, "Suppose you had a sister, whom you loved dearly—and then you had a quarrel with her, and neither of you much to blame, the fault lay with a third person; and suppose you came home suddenly, and found that sister had left England in trouble, and gone to the other end of the world—would not that cut you to the heart?"

"Indeed it would. How correctly you speak. Now who has been teaching you?"

"Mrs. Little."

"Ah!"

"You have a father. Suppose you left him for a month, and then came back and found him dead and buried—think of that—buried!"

"Poor girl!"

"And all this to fall on a poor creature just off a sick-bed, and scarcely right in her head. When I found poor Mr. Henry was dead, and you at death's door, I crawled home for comfort, and there I found desolation: my sister gone across the sea, my father in the church-yard. I wandered about all night, with my heavy heart and distraught brain, and at last they found me in the river. They may say I threw myself in, but it is my belief I swooned away and fell in. I wouldn't swear, though, for I remember nothing of it. What does it prove against me?"

"Not much, indeed, by itself. But they all say you were shut up with him for hours."

"And that is true; ten hours, every day. He was at war with these trades, and his own workman had betrayed him. He knew I was as strong as a man at some kinds of work—of course I can't strike blows, and hurt people like a man—so he asked me, would I help him grind saws with his machine on the sly—clandestinely, I mean. Well, I did, and very easy work it was—child's play to me that had wrought on a farm. He gave me six pounds a week for it. That's all the harm we did together; and, as for what we said, let me tell you a first-rate workman, like poor Mr. Henry, works very silently; that is where they beat us women. I am sure we often ground a dozen saws, and not a word, except upon the business. When we did talk, it was sure to be about you. Poor lad, the very last time we wrought together, I mind he said, 'Well done, Jael, that's good work; it brings me an inch nearer her.' And I said, All the better, and I'd

give him another hour or two every day if he liked. That very evening I took him his tea at seven o'clock. He was writing letters; one was to you. He was just addressing it. 'Good-night, Jael,' said he. 'You have been a good friend to her and me.'"

"Oh! did he say that? What became of that letter?"

"Upon my soul he did: ay, and it was his last word to me in this world. But you are not of his mind, it seems. The people in the factory! I know they used to say we were sweethearts. You can't wonder at that; they didn't know about you, nor any of our secrets; and, of course, vulgar folk like them could not guess the sort of affection I had for poor Mr. Henry; but a lady like you should not go by their lights. Besides, I was always open with you. Once I had a different feeling for him: did I hide it from you? When I found he loved you, I set to work to cure myself. I did cure myself before your very eyes; and, after that, you ought to be ashamed of yourself to go and doubt me. There, now, I have made her cry."

Her own voice faltered a moment, and she said, with gentle dignity, "Well, I forgive you, for old kindness past; but I shall not sleep under this roof now. God bless you, and give you many happy days yet with this gentleman you are going to marry. Farewell."

She was actually going; but Grace caught her by the arm. "No, no, you shall not leave me so."

"Ay, but I will." And Jael's eyes, so mild in general, began to sparkle with anger, at being detained against her will; but, generous to the last, she made no use of her great strength to get clear from Grace.

"You will not go, if you are the woman you were. I believe your words, I believe your honest face, I implore your forgiveness. I am the most miserable creature in this world. Pray do not abandon me."

This appeal, made with piteous gestures and streaming eyes, overpowered Jael Dence, and soon they were seated, rocking together, and Grace pouring out her heart.

Jael then learned, to her dismay, that Grace's belief in Henry's falsehood was a main cause of this sudden marriage. Had she believed her Henry true, she would have mourned him, as a widow, two years at least.

The unhappy young lady lamented her precipitation, and the idea of marrying Mr. Coventry to-morrow became odious to her. She asked Jael wildly whether she should not be justified in putting an end to her life.

Jael consoled her all she could; and, at her request, slept in the same bed with her. Indeed she was afraid to leave her; for she was wild at times, and said she would prefer to be married to that dead hand people said was at the Town Hall, and then thrown into one grave with it. "That's the bridal I long for," said she.

In the morning she was calmer, and told Jael she thought she was doing right.

"I shall be neither more nor less wretched for marrying this poor man," said she: "and I shall make two people happy; two people that deserve the sacrifice I make."

So, after all, the victim went calmly.

Early in the morning came a letter from Doctor Fynes. He was confined by gout, and sorry to say the ceremony he had hoped to perform must be done by his curate.

Now this curate was quite a stranger to Grace, and indeed to most people in Hillsborough. Doctor Fynes himself knew nothing about him except that he had come in answer to his inquiry for a curate, had brought good letters of recommendation, and had shown himself acquainted with the learned doctor's notes to *Apollonius Rhodius*; on which several grounds the doctor, who was himself a better scholar than a priest, had made him his curate, and had heard no complaints, except from a few puritanical souls. These he looked on as barbarians, and had calmly ignored them and their prejudices ever since he transferred his library from St. John's College, Cambridge, to St. Peter's Rectory, and that was thirty years ago.

This sudden substitute of an utter stranger for Doctor Fynes afflicted Grace Carden not a little, and her wedding-day began with a tear or two on that account. But, strange as it may appear, she lived to alter her mind, and to thank and bless Mr. Beresford for taking her old friend's place on that great occasion.

But while the bride dressed for church, and her bridesmaids and friends drove up, events were taking place, to deal with which I must retrograde a step.

Jael Dence having gone to Woodbine Villa, Mrs. Little and her brother dined tête-à-tête; and the first question she asked was, "Why, where is Jael?"

"Don't you know? gone to Woodbine Villa. The wedding is to-morrow."

"What, my Jael gone to that girl's wedding!" And her eyes flashed with ire.

"Why not? I am going to it myself."

"I am sorry to hear you say so—very sorry."

"Why, she is my godchild. Would you have me affront her?"

"If she is your godchild, Henry is your nephew."

"Of course, and I did all I could to marry him to Grace; but, you see, he would be wiser than me."

"Dear Guy, my poor Henry was to blame for not accepting your generous offer; but that does not excuse this heartless, fickle girl."

Raby's sense of justice began to revolt. "My dear Edith, I can't bear to hear you speak so contemptuously of this poor girl, who has so nearly died for love of your son. She is one of the noblest, purest, most unselfish creatures I ever knew. Why judge so hastily? But that is the way with you ladies: it must be the woman who is in the wrong. Men are gods, and women devils; that is your creed."

"Is *Henry* going to marry another?"

"Not that I know of."

"Then what excuse can there be for her conduct? Does wrong become right, when this young lady does it? It is you who are prejudiced, not I. Her conduct is without excuse. I have written to her: she has replied, and has offered me no excuse. 'Forgive me,' she says, 'and forget me.' I shall never forgive her; and you must permit me to despise her for a few years before I forget her."

"Well, don't excite yourself so. My poor Edith, some day or other you will be sorry you

ever said a word against that amiable and most unfortunate girl."

He said this so sadly and solemnly that Mrs. Little's anger fell directly, and they both sat silent a long time.

"Guy," said Mrs. Little, "tell me the truth. Has my son done any thing wrong—any thing rash? It was strange he should leave England without telling me. He told Doctor Amboyne. Oh, there is some mystery here. If I did not know you so well, I should say there is some deceit going on in this house. There *is*— You hang your head. I can not bear to give you pain, so I will ask you no more questions. But—"

There was a world of determination in that "but."

She retired early to bed; to bed, but not to rest.

In the silence of the night she recalled every thing, every look, every word that had seemed a little strange to her, and put them all together. She could not sleep; vague misgivings crawled over her agitated mind. At length she slumbered from sheer exhaustion. She rose early; yet, when she came down stairs, Raby was just starting for Woodbine Villa.

Mrs. Little asked him to take her into Hillsborough. He looked uneasy, but complied, and, at her desire, set her down in the market-place of Hillsborough. As soon as he was out of sight she took a fly, and directed the driver to take her to Mr. Little's works. "I mean," said she, "the works where Mr. Bayne is."

She found Mr. Bayne in his counting-house, dressed in deep mourning.

He started at sight of her, and then she saw his eye fall with surprise on her gray dress.

"Mr. Bayne," said she, "I am come to ask you a question or two."

"Be seated, madam," said Bayne, reverently. "I expected a visit from you or from your agent, and the accounts are all ready for your inspection. I keep them as clear as possible."

"I do not come here about accounts. My son has perfect confidence in you, and so have I."

"Thank you, madam; thank you kindly. He did indeed honor me with his confidence, and with his friendship. I am sure he was more like a brother to me than an employer. Ah, madam! I shall never, never, see his fellow again." And honest Bayne turned away with his hand to his eyes.

This seemed to Mrs. Little to be more than the occasion required, and did not tend to lessen her misgivings. However, she said gravely, "Mr. Bayne, I suppose you have heard there is to be a wedding in the town to-day—Miss Carden?"

"That is sudden! No, madame, I didn't know it. I can hardly believe it."

"It is so. She marries a Mr. Coventry. Now I think you were in my son's confidence; can you tell me whether there was any quarrel between him and Miss Carden before he left us?"

"Well, madam, I didn't see so much of him lately, he was always at the other works. Would to heaven he had never seen them. But I don't believe he ever gave that lady an unkind word. He was not that sort. He was ready of his hand against a man, but a very lamb with women he was. And so she is going to marry? Well, well; the world, it must go round. She loved him dearly, too. She was down at Bolt and Little's works day after day searching for him. She spent money like water, poor thing! I have seen her with her white face and great eyes watching the men drag the river for him; and, when that horrible thing was found at last, they say she was on the bridge and swooned dead away, and lay at death's door. But you will know all this, madam; and it is sad for me to speak of, let alone you that are his mother."

The color died out of Mrs. Little's cheek as he spoke; but, catching now a glimpse of the truth, she drew Bayne on with terrible cunning, and so learned that there had been a tremendous explosion, and Jael Dence taken up for dead; and that, some time after, an arm and a hand had been found in the river and recognized for the remains of Henry Little.

When she had got this out of the unwary Bayne she uttered a piercing scream, and her head hung over the chair, and her limbs writhed, and the whole creature seemed to wither up.

Then Bayne saw with dismay what he had done, and began to falter out expressions of regret. She paid no attention.

He begged her to let him fetch her some salts or a cordial.

She shook her head, and lay weak as water and white as a sheet.

At last she rose, and, supporting herself for a moment by the back of the chair, she said, "You will take me to see my son's remains."

"Oh, for heaven's sake don't think of it!"

"I must; I can not keep away from them an instant. And how else can I know they are his? Do you think I will believe any eye but my own? Come."

He had no power to disobey her. He trembled in every limb at what was coming, but he handed her into her carriage, and went with her to the Town Hall.

When they brought her the tweed sleeves, she trembled like an aspen leaf. When they brought her the glass receptacle, she seized Bayne by the shoulder and turned her head away. By degrees she looked round, and seemed to stiffen all of a sudden. "It is not my son," said she.

She rushed out of the place, bade Mr. Bayne good-morning, and drove directly to Doctor Amboyne. She attacked him at once. "You have been deceiving me all this time about my son; and what am I the better? what is any body the better? Now tell me the truth. You think him dead?"

(Doctor Amboyne hung his head in alarm and confusion.)

"Why do you think so? Do you go by those remains? I have seen them. My child was vaccinated on the left arm, and carried the mark. He had specks on two of his finger-nails; he had a small wart on his little finger; and his fingers were not blunt and uncouth, like that; they were as taper as any lady's in England; that hand is nothing like my son's; you are all blind; yet you must go and blind the only one who had eyes, the only one who really loved him, and whose opinion is worth a straw."

Doctor Amboyne was too delighted at the news to feel these reproaches very deeply. "Thank God!" said he. "Scold me, for I deserve it. But I did for the best; but, unfortunately, we

have still to account for his writing to no one all this time. No matter. I begin to hope. *That* was the worst evidence. Edith, I must go to Woodbine Villa. That poor girl must not marry in ignorance of this. Believe me, she will never marry Coventry, if *he* is alive. Excuse my leaving you at such a time, but there is not a moment to be lost."

He placed her on a sofa, and opened the window; for, by a natural reaction, she was beginning to feel rather faint. He gave his housekeeper strict orders to take care of her, then, snatching his hat, went hastily out.

At the door he met the footman with several letters (he had a large correspondence), shoved them pell-mell into his breast-pocket, shouted to a cabman stationed near, and drove off to Woodbine Villa.

It was rather up-hill, but he put his head out of the window and offered the driver a sovereign to go fast. The man lashed his horse up the hill, and did go very fast, though it seemed slow to Doctor Amboyne, because his wishes flew so much faster.

At last he got to the villa, and rang furiously.

After a delay that set the Doctor stamping, Lally appeared.

"I must see Miss Carden directly."

"Step in, sir; she won't be long now."

Doctor Amboyne walked into the dining-room, and saw it adorned with a wealth of flowers, and the wedding-breakfast set out with the usual splendor; but there was nobody there; and immediately an uneasy suspicion crossed his mind.

He came out into the passage, and found Lally there.

"Are they gone to the church?"

"They are," said Lally, with consummate coolness.

"You Irish idiot!" roared the Doctor; "why couldn't you tell me that before?" And, notwithstanding his ungainly figure, he ran down the road, shouting, like a Stentor, to his receding cabman.

"Bekase I saw that every minute was goold," said Lally, as soon as he was out of hearing.

The cabman, like most of his race, was rather deaf and a little blind, and Doctor Amboyne was much heated and out of breath before he captured him. He gasped out, "To St. Peter's Church, for your life!"

It was rather down-hill this time, and about a mile off.

In little more than five minutes the cab rattled up to the church door.

Doctor Amboyne got out, told the man to wait, and entered the church with a rapid step.

Before he had gone far up the centre aisle, he stopped.

Mr. Coventry and Grace Carden were coming down the aisle together in wedding costume, the lady in her bridal veil.

They were followed by the bridesmaids.

Doctor Amboyne stared, and stepped aside into an open pew to let them pass.

They swept by; he looked after them, and remained glued to his seat till the church was clear of the procession.

He went into the vestry, and found the curate there.

"Are that couple really married, sir?" said he.

The curate looked amazed. "As fast as I can make them," said he, rather flippantly.

"Excuse me," said the Doctor, faintly. "It was a foolish question to ask."

"I think I have the honor of speaking to Doctor Amboyne?"

Doctor Amboyne bowed, mechanically.

"You will be at the wedding-breakfast, of course?"

"Humph!"

"Why, surely you are invited."

"Yes" (with an equally absent air).

Finding him thus confused, the sprightly curate laughed and bade him good-morning, jumped into a hansom, and away to Woodbine Villa.

Doctor Amboyne followed him slowly.

"Drive me to Woodbine Villa. There's no hurry now."

On the way, he turned the matter calmly over, and put this question to himself: Suppose he had reached the villa in time to tell Grace Carden the news! Certainly he would have disturbed the wedding; but would it have been put off any the more? The bride's friends and advisers would have replied, "But that is no positive proof that he is alive; and, if he is alive, he has clearly abandoned her. Not a line for all these months."

This view of the matter appeared to him unanswerable, and reconciled him, in a great degree, to what seemed inevitable.

He uttered one deep sigh of regret, and proceeded now to read his letters; for he was not likely to have another opportunity for an hour or two at least, since he must be at the wedding-breakfast. His absence would afflict the bride.

The third letter he took out of his breast-pocket bore an American postmark. At the first word of it he uttered an ejaculation, and his eye darted to the signature.

Then he gave a roar of delight. It was signed "Henry Little," and the date only twelve days old.

His first thought was the poor lady who, at this moment, lay on a sofa in his house, a prey to doubts and fears he could now cure in a moment.

But no sooner had he cast his eyes over the contents, than his very flesh began to creep with dire misgivings and suspicions.

To these succeeded the gravest doubts as to the course he ought to pursue at Woodbine Villa.

He felt pretty sure that Grace Carden had been entrapped into marrying a villain, and his first impulse was to denounce the bridegroom before the assembled guests.

But his cooler judgment warned him against acting in hot blood, and suggested it would be better to try and tell her privately.

And then he asked himself what would be the consequence of telling her.

She was a lady of great spirit, fire, and nobility. She would never live with this husband of hers.

And then came the question, what would be her life?

She might be maid, wife, and widow all her days.

Horrible as it was, he began almost to fear her one miserable chance of happiness might lie in ignorance.

But then how long could she be in ignorance? Little was coming home; he would certainly speak out.

Dr. Amboyne was more tormented with doubts than a man of inferior intellect would have been. His was an academic mind, accustomed to look at every side of a question: and, when he reached Woodbine Villa, he was almost distracted with doubt and perplexity. However, there was one person from whom the news must not be kept a moment. He took an envelope out of his pocket-book, and sent the cabman to Mrs. Little with this line:

"Thank God, I have a letter from Henry Little by this day's post. He is well. Wait an hour or two for me. I can not leave Woodbine Villa at present."

He sent this off by his cabman, and went into the breakfast-room in a state of mind easier to imagine than to describe.

The party were all seated, and his the only vacant place.

It was like a hundred other weddings at which he had been; and, seeing the bride and bridegroom seated together as usual, and the pretty bridesmaids tittering, as usual, and the gentle dullness lighted up with here and there a feeble jest, as usual, he could hardly realize that horrible things lay beneath the surface of all this snowy bride-cake, and flowers, and white veils, and weak jocoseness.

He stared, bowed, and sank into his place like a man in a dream.

Bridesmaids became magnetically conscious that an incongruous element had entered; so they tittered. At what does sweet silly seventeen not titter?

Knives and forks clattered, champagne popped, and Doctor Amboyne was more perplexed and miserable than he had ever been. He had never encountered a more hopeless situation.

Presently Lally came and touched the bridegroom. He apologized, and left the room a moment.

Lally then told him to be on his guard, for the fat doctor knew something. He had come tearing up in a fly, and had been dreadfully put out when he found Miss Carden was gone to the church.

"Well, but he might merely wish to accompany her to the church: he is an old friend."

Lally shook his head and said there was much more in it than that; he could tell by the man's eye, and his uneasy way. "Master, dear, get out of this, for heaven's sake, as fast as ye can."

"You are right; go and order the carriage round, as soon as the horses can be put to."

Coventry then went hastily back to the bridal guests, and Lally ran to the neighboring inn which furnished the four post-horses.

Coventry had hardly settled down in his chair before he cast a keen but furtive glance at Doctor Amboyne's face.

Then he saw directly that the Doctor's mind was working, and that he was secretly and profoundly agitated.

But, after all, he thought, what could the man know? And if he had known any thing, would he have kept it to himself?

Still he judged it prudent to propitiate Doctor Amboyne; so, when the time came for the usual folly of drinking healths, he leaned over to him, and, in the sweetest possible voice, asked him if he would do them both the honor to propose the bride's health.

At this unexpected call from Mr. Coventry, Doctor Amboyne stared in the bridegroom's face. He stared at him so that other people began to stare. Recovering himself a little, he rose mechanically, and surprised every body who knew him.

Instead of the easy gayety natural to himself and proper to the occasion, he delivered a few faltering words of affection for the bride; then suddenly stopped, and, after a pause, said, "But some younger man must foretell her the bright career she deserves. I am unfit. We don't know what an hour may bring forth." With this he sank into his chair.

An uneasy grin, and then a gloom, fell on the bright company at these strange words, and all looked at one another uncomfortably.

But this situation was unexpectedly relieved. The young curate rose, and said, "I accept the honor Doctor Amboyne is generous enough to transfer to the younger gentlemen of the party—accept it with pride."

Starting from this exordium, he pronounced, with easy volubility, a charming panegyric on the bride, congratulated her friends, and then congratulated himself on being the instrument to unite her in holy wedlock with a gentleman worthy of her affection. Then, assuming for one moment the pastor, he pronounced a blessing on the pair, and sat down, casting glances all round out of a pair of singularly restless eyes.

The loud applause that followed left him in no doubt as to the favorable effect he had produced. Coventry, in particular, looked most expressively grateful.

The bridegroom's health followed, and Coventry returned thanks in a speech so neat and well delivered that Grace felt proud of his performance.

Then the carriage and four came round, and Coventry gave Grace an imploring glance on which she acted at once, being herself anxious to escape from so much publicity. She made her courtesies, and retired to put on her travelling-dress.

Then Doctor Amboyne cursed his own indecision, but still could not make up his mind, except to tell Raby, and make him the judge what course was best.

The gayety, never very boisterous, began to flag altogether; when suddenly a noise was heard outside, and one or two young people, who darted unceremoniously to the window, were rewarded by the sight of a man and a woman struggling and quarrelling at the gate. The disturbance in question arose thus: Jael Dence, looking out of Grace's window, saw the postman coming, and ran to get Grace her letters (if any) before she went.

The postman, knowing her well, gave her the one letter there was.

Lally, returning from the inn, where he had stopped one unlucky minute to drain a glass, saw this, and ran after Jael and caught her just inside the gate.

"That is for me," said he, rudely.

"Nay, it's for thy betters, young man; 'tis for Miss Grace Carden."

"She is Mrs. Coventry now, so give it me."

"I'll take her orders first."

On this Lally grabbed at it and caught Jael's right hand, which closed directly on the letter like a vice.

"Are these your manners?" said she. "Give over now."

"I tell you I will have it!" said he, fiercely, for he had caught sight of the handwriting.

He seized her hand and applied his knuckles to the back of it with all his force. That hurt her, and she gave a cry, and twisted away from him and drew back; then, putting her left hand to his breast, she gave a great yaw, and then a forward rush with her mighty loins, and a contemporaneous shove with her amazing left arm, that would have pushed down some brick walls, and the weight and strength so suddenly applied sent Lally flying like a feather. His head struck the stone gate-post, and he measured his length under it.

Jael did not know how completely she had conquered him, and she ran in with a face as red as fire, and took the letter up to Grace, and was telling her, all in a heat, about the insolence of her new husband's Irish servant, when suddenly she half recognized the handwriting, and stood staring at it, and began to tremble.

"Why, what is the matter?" said Grace.

"Oh, nothing, Miss. I'm foolish. The writing seems to me like a writing we shall never see again." And she stood and trembled still more, for the handwriting struck her more and more.

Grace ran to her, and at the very first glance uttered a shriek of recognition. She caught it from Jael, tore it open, saw the signature, and sank into a chair, half fainting, with the letter pressed convulsively to her breast.

Jael, trembling, but comparatively self-possessed, ran to the door directly and locked it.

"My darling! my darling! he is alive! The dear words, they swim before my eyes. Read! read! tell me what he says. Why has he abandoned me? He has not abandoned me! O God! what have I done? what have I done?"

Before that letter was half read, or rather sobbed, out to her, Grace tore off all her bridal ornaments and trampled them under her feet, and moaned, and twisted, and writhed as if her body was being tortured as well as her heart; for Henry was true as ever, and she had married a villain.

She took the letter from Jael, and devoured every word; though she was groaning and sobbing with the wildest agony all the time.

"New York, July 18th.

"MY OWN DEAREST GRACE,—I write you these few lines in wonder and pain. I have sent you at least fifteen letters, and in most of them I have begged you to write to me at the Post-office, New York; yet not one line is here to greet me in your dear handwriting. Yet my letters must have all reached Woodbine Villa, or why are they not sent back? Of three letters I sent to my mother, two have been returned from Aberystwith, marked, 'Gone away, and not left her address.'

"I have turned this horrible thing every way in my mind, and even prayed God to assist my understanding; and I come back always to the same idea that some scoundrel has intercepted my letters.

"The first of these I wrote at the works on the evening I left Hillsborough; the next I wrote from Boston, after my long illness, in great distress of mind on your account; for I put myself in your place, and thought what agony it would be to me if nine weeks passed, and no word from you. The rest were written from various cities, telling you I was making our fortune, and should soon be home. Oh, I can not write of such trifles now!

"My own darling, let me find you alive; that is all I ask. I know I shall find you true to me, if you are alive.

"Perhaps it would have been better if my heart had not been so entirely filled by you. God has tried me hard in some things, but He has blessed me with true friends. It was ungrateful of me not to write to such true friends as Doctor Amboyne and Jael Dence. But, whenever I thought of England, I saw only you.

"By this post I write to Doctor Amboyne, Mr. Bolt, Mr. Bayne, and Jael Dence.

"This will surely baffle the enemy who has stopped all my letters to you, and will stop this one, I dare say.

"I say no more, beloved one. What is the use? You will perhaps never see this letter, and you know more than I can say, for you know how I love you: and that is a great deal more than ever I can put on paper.

"I sail for England in four days. God help me to get over the interval.

"I forget whether I told you I had made my fortune. Your devoted and most unhappy lover,
"HENRY."

Grace managed to read this, in spite of the sobs and moans that shook her, and the film that half blinded her; and, when she had read it, sank heavily down, and sat all crushed together, with hands working like frenzy.

Jael kneeled beside her, and kissed and wept over her, unheeded.

Then Jael prayed aloud beside her, unheeded.

At last she spoke, looking straight before her, as if she was speaking to the wall.

"Bring my godfather here."

"Won't you see your father first?" said Jael, timidly.

"I have no father. I want something I can lean on over the gulf—a man of honor. Fetch Mr. Raby to me."

Jael kissed her tenderly, and wept over her once more a minute, then went softly down stairs and straight into the breakfast-room.

Here, in the mean time, considerable amusement had been created by the contest between Lally and Jael Dence, the more so on account of the triumph achieved by the weaker vessel.

When Lally got up, and looked about him ruefully, great was the delight of the younger gentlemen.

When he walked in-doors, they chaffed him through the open window, and none of them noticed that the man was paler than even the rough usage he had received could account for.

This jocund spirit, however, was doomed to be short-lived.

Lally came into the room, looking pale and troubled, and whispered a word in his master's ear; then retired, but left his master as pale as himself.

Coventry, seated at a distance from the window, had not seen the scrimmage outside, and Lally's whispered information fell on him like a thunderbolt.

Mr. Beresford saw at once that something was wrong, and hinted as much to his neighbor. It went like magic round the table, and there was an uneasy silence.

In the midst of this silence, mysterious sounds began to be heard in the bride's chamber: a faint scream; feet rushing across the floor; a sound as of some one sinking heavily on to a chair or couch.

Presently came a swift stamping that told a tale of female passion; and after that confused sounds that could not be interpreted through the ceiling, yet somehow the listeners felt they were unusual. One or two attempted conversation, out of politeness; but it died away—curiosity and uneasiness prevailed.

Lally put his head in at the door, and asked if the carriage was to be packed.

"Of course," said Coventry; "and soon the servants, male and female, were seen taking boxes out from the hall to the carriage.

Jael Dence walked into the room, and went to Mr. Raby.

"The bride desires to see you immediately, sir."

Raby rose, and followed Jael out.

The next minute a lady's maid came, with a similar message to Doctor Amboyne.

He rose with great alacrity, and followed her.

There was nothing remarkable in the bride's taking private leave of these two valued friends. But somehow the mysterious things that had preceded made the guests look with half-suspicious eyes into every thing; and Coventry's manifest discomfiture, when Doctor Amboyne was sent for, justified this vague sense that there was something strange going on beneath the surface.

Neither Raby nor Amboyne came down again, and Mr. Beresford remarked aloud that the bride's room was like the lion's den in the fable, "'Vestigia nulla retrorsum.'"

At last the situation became intolerable to Coventry. He rose, in desperation, and said, with a ghastly attempt at a smile, that he must, nevertheless, face the dangers of the place himself, as the carriage was now packed, and Mrs. Coventry and he, though loath to leave their kind friends, had a longish journey before them. "Do not move, I pray; I shall be back directly."

As soon as he had got out of the room, he held a whispered consultation with Lally, and then, collecting all his courage, and summoning all his presence of mind, he went slowly up the stairs, determined to disown Lally's acts (Lally himself had suggested this), and pacify Grace's friends, if he could; but, failing that, to turn round, and stand haughtily on his legal rights, ay, and enforce them too.

But, meantime, what had passed in the bride's chamber?

Raby found Grace Carden, with her head buried on her toilet-table, and her hair all streaming down her back.

The floor was strewn with pearls and broken ornaments, and fragments of the bridal veil. On the table lay Henry Little's letter.

Jael took it, without a word, and gave it to Raby.

He took it, and, after a loud ejaculation of surprise, began to read it.

He had not quite finished it when Doctor Amboyne tapped at the door, and Jael let him in. The crushed figure with dishevelled hair, and Raby's eye gleaming over the letter in his hand, told him at once what was going on.

He ceased to doubt, or vacillate, directly: he a low voice to Mr. Raby; but it afterwards appeared the bride heard every word.

"MY BEST FRIEND,—Forgive me for neglecting you so long, and writing only to her I love with all my soul. Forgive me, for I smart for it.

RABY FOUND GRACE CARDEN WITH HER HEAD BURIED ON HER TOILET-TABLE.

whispered Jael Dence to stand near Grace, and watch her closely.

He had seen a woman start up and throw herself, in one moment, out of a window for less than this—a woman crushed apparently, and more dead than alive, as Grace Carden was.

Then he took out his own letter, and read it in

I have written fifteen letters to my darling Grace, and received no reply. I wrote her one yesterday, but have now no hope she will ever get it. This is terrible, but there is worse behind. This very day I have learned that my premises were blown up within a few hours of my leaving, and poor, faithful Jael Dence nearly killed; and then a report of my own death was raised, and some remains found in the ruins that fools said were mine. I suppose the letters I left in the box were all destroyed by the fire.

"Now, mark my words, one and the same villain has put that dead man's hand and arm in the river, and has stopped my letters to Grace; I am sure of it. So what I want you to do is, first of all, to see my darling, and tell her I am alive and well, and then put her on her guard against deceivers.

"I suspect the postman has been tampered with. I write to Mr. Ransome to look into that. But what you might learn for me is, whether any body lately has had any opportunity to stop letters addressed to 'Woodbine Villa.' That seems to point to Mr. Carden, and he was never a friend of mine. But, somehow, I don't think he would do it.

"You see, I ask myself two questions. Is there any man in the world who has a motive strong enough to set him tampering with my letters? and, again, is there any man base enough to do such an act? And the answer to both questions is the same. I have a rival, and he is base enough for any thing. Judge for yourself. I as good as saved that Coventry's life one snowy night, and all I asked in return was that he wouldn't blow me to the Trades, and so put my life in jeopardy. He gave his word of honor he wouldn't. But he broke his word. One day, when Grotait and I were fast friends, and never thought to differ again, Grotait told me this Coventry was the very man that came to him and told him where I was working. Such a lump of human dirt as that—for you can't call him a man—must be capable of any thing."

Here the reading of the letter was interrupted by an incident.

There was on the toilet-table a stiletto, with a pearl handle. It was a small thing, but the steel rather long, and very bright and pointed.

The unfortunate bride, without lifting her head from the table, had reached out her hand, and was fingering this stiletto. Jael Dence went and took it gently away, and put it out of reach. The bride went on fingering, as if she had still got hold of it.

Amboyne exchanged an approving glance with Jael, and Raby concluded the letter.

"I shall be home in a few days after this; and, if I find my darling well and happy, there's no great harm done. I don't mind my own trouble and anxiety, great as they are, but if any scoundrel has made her unhappy, or made her believe I am dead, or false to my darling, by God, I'll kill him, though I hang for it next day!"

Crushed, benumbed, and broken as Grace Coventry was, this sentence seemed to act on her like an electric shock.

She started wildly up. "What! my Henry die like a felon—for a villain like him, and an idiot like me! You won't allow that; nor you—nor I."

A soft step came to the door, and a gentle tap.

"Who is that?" said Dr. Amboyne.

"The bridegroom," replied a soft voice.

"You can't come in here," said Raby, roughly.

"Open the door," said the bride.

12

Jael went to the door, but looked uncertain.

"Don't keep the bridegroom out," said Grace, reproachfully. Then, in a voice as sweet as his own, "I want to see him; I want to speak to him."

Jael opened the door slowly, for she felt uneasy. Raby shrugged his shoulders contemptuously at Grace's condescending to speak to the man, and in so amiable a tone.

Coventry entered, and began, "My dear Grace, the carriage is ready—"

No sooner had she got him fairly into the room, than the bride snatched up the stiletto, and flew at the bridegroom with gleaming eyes, uplifted weapon, the yell of a furious wild beast, and hair flying out behind her head like a lion's mane.

CHAPTER XL.

DOCTOR AMBOYNE and Raby cried out, and tried to interfere; but Grace's movement was too swift, furious, and sudden; she was upon the man, with her stiletto high in the air, before they could get to her, and indeed the blow descended, and, inspired as it was by love, and hate, and fury, would doubtless have buried the weapon in a rascal's body; but Jael Dence caught Grace's arm: that weakened, and also diverted the blow; yet the slight, keen weapon pierced Coventry's cheek, and even inflicted a slight wound upon the tongue. That very moment Jael Dence dragged her away, and held her round the waist, writhing and striking the air; her white hand and bridal sleeve sprinkled with her bridegroom's blood.

As for him, his love, criminal as it was, supplied the place of heroism: he never put up a finger in defense. "No," said he, despairingly, "let me die by her hand; it is all I hope for now." He even drew near her to enable her to carry out her wish: but, on that, Jael Dence wrenched her round directly, and Doctor Amboyne disarmed her, and Raby marched between the bride and the bridegroom, and kept them apart: then they all drew their breath, for the first time, and looked aghast at each other.

Not a face in that room had an atom of color left in it; yet it was not until the worst was over that they realized the savage scene.

The bridegroom leaned against the wardrobe, a picture of despair, with blood trickling from his cheek, and channelling his white waistcoat and linen; the bride, her white and bridal sleeve spotted with blood, writhed feebly in Jael Dence's arms, and her teeth clicked together, and her eyes shone wildly. At that moment she was on the brink of frenzy.

Raby, a man by nature, and equal to great situations, was the first to recover self-possession and see his way. "Silence!" said he, sternly. "Amboyne, here's a wounded man; attend to him."

He had no need to say that twice: the doctor examined his patient zealously, and found him bleeding from the tongue as well as the cheek; he made him fill his mouth with a constant supply of cold water, and applied cold water to the nape of his neck.

And now there was a knock at the door, and a voice inquired, rather impatiently, what they were about all this time. It was Mr. Carden's voice.

They let him in, but instantly closed the door. "Now, hush!" said Raby, "and let me tell him." He then, in a very few hurried words, told him the matter. Coventry hung his head lower and lower.

Mr. Carden was terribly shaken. He could hardly speak for some time. When he did, it was in the way of feeble expostulation. "Oh, my child! my child! what, would you commit murder?"

"Don't you see I would?" cried she, contemptuously, "sooner than *he* should do it, and suffer for it like a felon. You are all blind, and no friends of mine. I should have rid the earth of a monster, and they would never have hanged *me*. I hate you all, you worst of all, that call yourself my father, and drove me to marry this villain. One thing—you won't be always at hand to protect him."

"I'll give you every opportunity," said Coventry, doggedly. "You shall kill me for loving you so madly."

"She shall do no such thing," said Mr. Carden. "Opportunity? do you know her so little as to think she will ever live with you? Get out of my house, and never presume to set foot in it again. My good friends, have pity on a miserable father, and help me to hide this monstrous thing from the world."

This appeal was not lost: the gentlemen put their heads together, and led Coventry into another room. There Doctor Amboyne attended to him, while Mr. Carden went down and told his guests the bridegroom had been taken ill, so seriously indeed that anxiety and alarm had taken the place of joy.

The guests took the hint and dispersed, wondering and curious.

Meantime, on one side of a plaster wall Amboyne was attending the bridegroom, and stanching the effusion of blood; on the other, Raby and Jael Dence were bringing the bride to reason.

She listened to nothing they could say until they promised her most solemnly that she should never be compelled to pass a night under the same roof as Frederick Coventry. That pacified her not a little.

Doctor Amboyne had also great trouble with his patient: the wound in the cheek was not serious; but, by a sort of physical retribution—of which, by-the-by, I have encountered many curious examples—the tongue, that guilty part of Frederick Coventry, though slightly punctured, bled so persistently that Amboyne was obliged to fill his mouth with ice, and at last support him with stimulants. He peremptorily refused to let him be moved from Woodbine Villa.

When this was communicated to Grace, she instantly exacted Raby's promise; and, as he was a man who never went from his word, he drove her and Jael to Raby Hall that very night, and they left Coventry in the villa, attended by a surgeon, under whose care Amboyne had left him with strict injunctions. Mr. Carden was secretly mortified at his daughter's retreat, but raised no objection.

Next morning, however, he told Coventry; and then Coventry insisted on leaving the house. "I am unfortunate enough," said he: "do not let me separate my only friend from his daughter."

Mr. Carden sent a carriage off to Raby Hall, with a note, telling Grace Mr. Coventry was gone of his own accord, and appeared truly penitent, and much shocked at having inadvertently driven her out of the house. He promised also to protect her, should Coventry break his word and attempt to assume marital rights without her concurrence.

This letter found Grace in a most uncomfortable position. Mrs. Little had returned late to Raby Hall; but in the morning she heard from Jael Dence that Grace was in the house, and why.

The mother's feathers were up, and she could neither pity nor excuse. She would not give the unhappy girl a word of comfort. Indeed, she sternly refused to see her. "No," said she: "Mrs. Coventry is unhappy; so this is no time to show her how thoroughly Henry Little's mother despises her."

These bitter words never reached poor Grace, but the bare fact of Mrs. Little not coming down stairs by one o'clock, nor sending a civil message, spoke volumes, and Grace was sighing over it when her father's letter came. She went home directly, and so heart-broken, that Jael Dence pitied her deeply, and went with her, intending to stay a day or two only.

But every day something or other occurred, which combined with Grace's prayers to keep her at Woodbine Villa.

Mr. Coventry remained quiet for some days, by which means he pacified Grace's terrors.

On the fourth day Mr. Beresford called at Woodbine Villa, and Grace received him, he being the curate of the parish.

He spoke to her in a sympathetic tone, which let her know at once he was partly in the secret. He said he had just visited a very guilty, but penitent man; that we all need forgiveness, and that a woman, once married, has no chance of happiness but with her husband.

Grace maintained a dead silence, only her eye began to glitter.

Mr. Beresford, who had learned to watch the

countenance of all those he spoke to, changed his tone immediately, from a spiritual to a secular adviser.

"If I were you," said he, in rather an off-hand way, "I would either forgive this man the sin into which his love has betrayed him, or I would try to get a divorce. This would cost money : but, if you don't mind expense, I think I could suggest a way—"

Grace interrupted him. "From whom did you learn my misery, and his villainy? 'I let you in, because I thought you came from God ; but you come from a villain. Go back, sir, and say that an angel, sent by him, becomes a devil in my eyes." And she rang the bell with a look that spoke volumes.

Mr. Beresford bowed, smiled bitterly, and went back to Coventry, with whom he had a curious interview, that ended in Coventry lending him two hundred pounds on his personal security. To dispose of Mr. Beresford for the present, I will add that, soon after this, his zeal for the poor subjected him to an affront. He was a man of soup-kitchens and subscriptions. One of the old fogies, who disliked him, wrote letters to *The Liberal*, and demanded an account of his receipts and expenditure in these worthy objects, and repeated the demand with a pertinacity that implied suspicion. Then Mr. Beresford called upon Doctor Fynes, and showed him the letters, and confessed to him that he never kept any accounts, either of public or private expenditure. "I can construe *Apollonius Rhodius* — with your assistance, sir," said he, "but I never could add up pounds, shillings, and pence ; far less divide them except amongst the afflicted." "Take no notice of the cads," said Doctor Fynes. But Beresford represented meekly that a clergyman's value and usefulness were gone when once a slur was thrown upon him. Then Doctor Fynes gave him high testimonials, and they parted with mutual regret.

It took Grace a day to get over her interview with Mr. Beresford ; and when with Jael's help she was calm again, she received a letter from Coventry, indited in tones of the deepest penitence, but reminding her that he had offered her his life, had made no resistance when she offered to take it, and never would.

There was nothing in the letter that irritated her, but she saw in it an attempt to open a correspondence. She wrote back :

"If you really repent your crimes, and have any true pity for the poor creature whose happiness you have wrecked, show it by leaving this place, and ceasing all communication with her."

This galled Coventry, and he wrote back :

"What! leave the coast clear to Mr. Little? No, Mrs. Coventry ; no."

Grace made no reply, but a great terror seized her, and from that hour preyed constantly on her mind—the fear that Coventry and Little would meet, and the man she loved would do some rash act, and perhaps perish on the scaffold for it.

This was the dominant sentiment of her distracted heart, when one day, at eleven A.M., came a telegram from Liverpool :

"Just landed. Will be with you by four.
"HENRY LITTLE."

Jael found her shaking all over, with this telegram in her hand.

"Thank God you are with me!" she gasped. "Let me see him once more, and die.

This was her first thought ; but all that day she was never in the same mind for long together. She would burst out into joy that he was really alive, and she should see his face once more. Then she would cower with terror, and say she dared not look him in the face ; she was not worthy. Then she would ask wildly, who was to tell him? What would become of him?

"It would break his heart, or destroy his reason.

"After all he had done and suffered for her!" Oh! why could she not die before he came? Seeing her dead body, he would forgive her. She should tell him she loved him still, should always love him. She would withhold no comfort. Perhaps he would kill her. If so, Jael must manage so that he should not be taken up or tormented any more, for such a wretch as she was.

But I might as well try to dissect a storm, and write the gusts of a tempest, as to describe all the waves of passion in that fluctuating and agonized heart : the feelings and the agitation of a life were crowded into those few hours, during which she awaited the lover she had lost.

At last, Jael Dence, though she was also much agitated and perplexed, decided on a course of action. Just before four o'clock she took Grace up stairs and told her she might see him arrive, but she must not come down until she was sent for. "I shall see him first, and tell him all ; and, when he is fit to see you, I will let you know."

Grace submitted, and even consented to lie down for half an hour. She was now, in truth, scarcely able to stand, being worn out with the mental struggle. She lay passive, with Jael Dence's hand in hers.

When she had lain so about an hour, she started up suddenly, and the next moment a fly stopped at the door. Henry Little got out at the gate, and walked up the gravel to the house.

Grace looked at him from behind the curtain, gazed at him till he disappeared, and then turned round, with seraphic joy on her countenance. "My darling!" she murmured ; "more beautiful than ever! Oh misery! misery!"

One moment her heart was warm with rapture, the next it was cold with despair. But the joy was blind love ; the despair was reason.

She waited, and waited, but no summons came. She could not deny herself the sound of his voice. She crept down the stairs, and into her father's library, separated only by thin folding-doors from the room where Henry Little was with Jael Dence.

Meantime Jael Dence opened the door to Henry Little, and, putting her finger to her lips, led him into the dining-room and shut the door.

Now, as his suspicions were already excited, this reception alarmed him seriously. As soon as ever they were alone, he seized both Jael's hands, and, looking her full in the face, said :

"One word—is she alive?"

"She is."

"Thank God! Bless the tongue that tells me that. My good Jael! my best friend!" And, with that, kissed her heartily on both cheeks.

She received this embrace like a woman of wood; a faint color rose, but retired directly, and left her cheek as pale as before.

He noticed her strange coldness, and his heart began to quake.

"There is something the matter?" he whispered.

"There is."

"Something you don't like to tell me?"

"Like to tell you! I need all my courage, and you yours."

"Say she is alive, once more."

"She is alive, and not likely to die; but she does not care to live now. They told her you were dead; they told her you were false; appearances were such she had no chance not to be deceived. She held out for a long time; but they got the better of her—her father is much to blame—she is—married."

"Married!"

"Yes!"

"Married!" He leaned, sick as death, against the mantel-piece, and gasped so terribly that Jael's fortitude gave way, and she began to cry.

After a long time he got a word or two out in a broken voice.

"The false—inconstant—wretch! Oh Heaven! what I have done and suffered for her—and now married!—married! And the earth doesn't swallow her, nor the thunder strike her! Curse her, curse her husband, curse her children! may her name be a by-word for shame and misery—"

"Hush! hush! or you will curse your own mad tongue. Hear all, before you judge her."

"I have heard all; she is a wife; she shall soon be a widow. Thought I was false! What business had she to think I was false? It is only false hearts that suspect true ones. She thought me dead? Why? Because I was out of sight. She heard there was a dead hand found in the river. Why didn't she go and see it? Could all creation pass another hand off on me for hers? No; for I loved her. She never loved me."

"She loved you, and loves you still. When that dead hand was found, she fell swooning, and lay at death's door for you, and now she has stained her hands with blood for you. She tried to kill her husband, the moment she found you were alive and true, and he had made a fool of her."

"Tried to kill him! Why didn't she do it? I should not have failed at such work. I love her."

"Blame me for that; I stopped her arm, and I am stronger than she is. I say she is no more to blame than you. You have acted like a madman, and she suffers for it. Why did you slip away at night like that, and not tell me?"

"I left letters to you and her, and other people besides."

"Yes, left them, and hadn't the sense to post them. Why didn't you tell me? Had ever any young man as faithful and true a friend in any young woman as you had in me? Many a man has saved a woman's life, but it isn't often that a woman fights for a man, and gets the upper hand: yet you gave me nothing in return; not even your confidence. Look the truth in the face, my lad; all your trouble, and all hers, comes of your sneaking out of Hillsborough in that daft way, without a word to me, the true friend, that was next door to you; which I nearly lost my life by

your fault; for, if you had told me, I should have seen you off, and so escaped a month's hospital, and other troubles that almost drove me crazy. Don't you abuse that poor young lady before me, or I shan't spare you. She is more to be pitied than you are. Folk should look at home for the cause of their troubles; her misery, and yours, it is all owing to your own folly and ingratitude; ay, you may look; I mean what I say—ingratitude."

The attack was so sudden and powerful that Henry Little was staggered and silenced; but an unexpected defender appeared on the scene; one of the folding-doors was torn open, and Grace darted in.

"How dare you say it is his fault, poor ill-used angel! No, no, no, no; I am the only one to blame. I didn't love you as you deserved. I tried to die for you, and *failed*. I tried to kill that monster for you, and *failed*. I am too weak and silly; I shall only make you more unhappy. Give me one kiss, my own darling, and then kill me out of the way." With this she was over his knees and round his neck in a moment, weeping, and clutching him with a passionate despair that melted all his anger away, and soon his own tears fell on her like rain.

"Ah, Grace! Grace!" he sobbed, "how could you? how could you?"

"Don't speak unkindly to her," cried Jael, "or she won't be alive a day. She is worse off than you are; and so is he too."

"You mock me; he is her husband. He can make her live with him. He can—" Here he broke out cursing and blaspheming, and called Grace a viper, and half thrust her away from him with horror, and his face filled with jealous anguish: he looked like a man dying of poison.

Then he rose to his feet, and said, with a sort of deadly calm, "Where can I find the man?"

"Not in this house, you may be sure," said Jael; "nor in any house where she is."

Henry sank into his seat again, and looked amazed.

"Tell him all," said Grace. "Don't let him think I do not love him at all."

"I will," said Jael. "Well, the wedding was at eleven; your letter came at half-past twelve, and I took it her. Soon after that the villain came to her, and she stabbed him directly with this stiletto. Look at it; there's his blood upon it; I kept it to show you. I caught her arm, or she would have killed him, I believe. He lost so much blood, the doctor would not let him be moved. Then she thought of you still, and would not pass a night under the same roof with him; at two o'clock she was on the way to Raby; but Mr. Coventry was too much of a man to stay in the house and drive her out; so he went off next morning, and, as soon as she heard that, she came home. She is wife and no wife, as the saying is, and how it is all to end Heaven only knows."

"It will end the moment I meet the man; and that won't be long."

"There! there!" cried Grace, "that is what I feared. Ah, Jael! Jael! why did you hold my hand? They would not have hung *me*. I told you so at the time: I knew what I was about."

"Jael," said the young man, "of all the kind things you have done for me, that was the kindest. You saved my poor girl from worse trouble than she is now in. No, Grace; you shall not dirty your hand with such scum as that: it is my business, and mine only."

In vain did Jael expostulate, and Grace implore. In vain did Jael assure him that Coventry was in a worse position than himself, and try to make him see that any rash act of his would make Grace even more miserable than she was at present. He replied that he had no intention of running his neck into a halter; he should act warily, like the Hillsborough Trades, and strike his blow so cunningly that the criminal should never know whence it came. "I've been in a good school for homicide," said he; "and I am an inventor. No man has ever played the executioner so ingeniously as I will play it. Think of all this scoundrel has done to me: he owes me a dozen lives, and I'll take one. Man shall never detect me: God knows all, and will forgive me, I hope. If He doesn't, I can't help it."

He kissed Grace again and again, and comforted her; said she was not to blame; honest people were no match for villains : if she had been twice as simple, he would have forgiven her at sight of the stiletto; that cleared her, in his mind, better than words.

He was now soft and gentle as a lamb. He begged Jael's pardon humbly for leaving Hillsborough without telling her. He said he had gone up to her room; but all was still; and he was a working-man, and the sleep of a working-woman was sacred to him—(he would have awakened a fine lady without ceremony). He assured her he had left a note for her in his box, thanking and blessing her for all her goodness. He said that he hoped he might yet live to prove by acts, and not by idle words, how deeply he felt all she had done and suffered for him.

Jael received these excuses in hard silence. "That is enough about me," said she, coldly. "If you are grateful to me, show it by taking my advice. Leave vengeance to Him who has said that vengeance is His."

The man's whole manner changed directly, and he said doggedly :

"Well, I will be His instrument."

"He will choose His own."

"I'll lend my humble co-operation."

"Oh, do not argue with him," said Grace, piteously. "When did a man ever yield to our arguments? Dearest, I can't argue: but I am full of misery, and full of fears. You see my love; you forgive my folly. Have pity on me ; think of my condition: do not doom me to live in terror by night and day : have I not enough to endure, my own darling? There, promise me you will do nothing rash to-night, and that you will come to me the first thing to-morrow. Why, you have not seen your mother yet; she is at Raby Hall."

"My dear mother!" said he : "it would be a poor return for all your love if I couldn't put off looking for that scum till I have taken you in my arms."

And so Grace got a reprieve.

They parted in deep sorrow, but almost as lovingly as ever, and Little went at once to Raby Hall, and Grace, exhausted by so many emotions, lay helpless on a couch in her own room all the rest of the day.

For some time she lay in utter prostration, and only the tears that trickl d at intervals down her pale cheeks showed that she was conscious of her miserable situation.

Jael begged and coaxed her to take some nourishment : but she shook her head with disgust at the very idea.

For all that, at nine o'clock, her faithful friend almost forced a few spoonfuls of tea down her throat, feeding her like a child : and, when she had taken it, she tried to thank her, but choked in the middle, and, flinging her arm round Jael's neck, burst into a passion of weeping, and incoherent cries of love, and pity, and despair. "Oh, my darling! so great! so noble! so brave! so gentle! And I have destroyed us both! he forgave me as soon as he saw me! So terrible, so gentle! What will be the next calamity? Ah, Jael! save him from that rash act, and I shall never complain; for he was dead, and is alive again."

"We will find some way to do that between us—you, and I, and his mother."

"Ah, yes : she will be on my side in that. But she will be hard upon me. She will point out all my faults, my execrable folly. Ah, if I could but live my time over again, I'd pray night and day for selfishness. They teach us girls to pray for this and that virtue, which we have too much of already ; and what we ought to pray for is selfishness. But no! I must think of my father, and think of that hypocrite ; but the one person whose feelings I was too mean, and base, and silly to consult, was myself. I always abhorred this marriage. I feared it, and loathed it ; yet I yielded step by step, for want of a little selfishness : we are slaves without it—mean, pitiful, contemptible slaves. O God, in mercy give me selfishness! Ah me, it is too late now. I am a lost creature; nothing is left me but to die."

Jael got her to bed, and sleep came at last to her exhausted body ; but, even when her eyes were closed, tears found their way through the lids, and wetted her pillow.

So can great hearts and loving natures suffer. Can they enjoy in proportion ?

Let us hope so. But I have my doubts.

Henry Little kept his word, and came early next morning. He looked hopeful and excited : he said he had thought the matter over, and was quite content to let that scoundrel live, and even to dismiss all thought of him, if Grace really loved him.

"If I love you !" said Grace. "Oh, Henry, why did I ask you to do nothing rash, but that I love you? Why did I attempt his life myself? because you said in your letter— It was not to revenge myself, but to save you from more calamity. Cruel, cruel! Do I love him ?"

"I know you love me, Grace : but do you love me enough ? Will you give up the world for me, and let us be happy together, the only way we can? My darling Grace, I have made our fortune ; all the world lies before us ; I left England alone, for you ; now leave it with me, and let us roam the world together."

"Henry!—what!—when I can not be your wife !"

"You can be my wife ; my wife in reality, as you are his in name and nothing else. It is idle to talk as if we were in some ordinary situation. There are plenty of countries that would disown such a marriage as yours, a mere ceremony obtained by fraud, and cancelled by a stroke with a dagger and instant separation. Oh, my darling, don't sacrifice both our lives to a scruple that is out of place here. Don't hesitate; don't delay. I have a carriage waiting outside; end all our misery by one act of courage, and trust yourself to me; did I ever fail you?"

"For shame, Henry! for shame!"

"It is the only way to happiness. You were quite right; if I kill that wretch we shall be parted in another way, always parted; now we can be together for life. Remember, dearest, how I begged you in this very room to go to the United States with me: you refused: well, have you never been sorry you refused? Now I once more implore you to be wise and brave, and love me as I love you. What is the world to us? You are all the world to me."

"Answer him, Jael; oh, answer him!"

"Nay, these are things every woman must answer for herself."

"And I'll take no answer but yours." Then he threw himself at her feet, and clasping her in his arms, implored her, with all the sighs and tears and eloquence of passion, to have pity on them both, and fly at once with him.

She writhed and struggled faintly, and turned away from him, and fell tenderly towards him, by turns, and, still he held her tight, and grew stronger, more passionate, more persuasive, as she got weaker and almost faint. Her body seemed on the point of sinking, and her mind of yielding.

But all of a sudden she made a desperate effort. "Let me go!" she cried. "So this is your love! With all my faults and follies, I am truer than you. Shame on your love, that would dishonor the creature you love! Let me go, sir, I say, or I shall hate you worse than I do the wretch whose name I bear."

He let her go directly, and then her fiery glance turned to one long lingering look of deep but tender reproach, and she fled sobbing.

He sank into a chair, and buried his face in his hands.

After a while he raised his head, and saw Jael Dence looking gravely at him.

"Oh, speak your mind," said he, bitterly.

"You are like the world. You think only of yourself: that's all I have to say."

"You are very unkind to say so. I think for us both: and she will think with me, in time. I shall come again to-morrow."

He said this with an iron resolution that promised a long and steady struggle, to which Grace, even in this first encounter, had shown herself hardly equal.

Jael went to her room, expecting to find her as much broken down as she was by Henry's first visit; but, instead of that, the young lady was walking rapidly to and fro.

At sight of Jael, she caught her by the hand, and said, "Well!"

"He is coming again to-morrow."

"Is he sorry?"

"Not he."

"Who would have thought he was so wicked?"

This seemed rather exaggerated to Jael; for with all Mrs. Little's teaching she was not quite a lady yet in all respects, though in many things she was always one by nature. "Let it pass," said she.

"'It is a man's part to try,
And a woman's to deny.'"

"And how often shall I have to deny him I love so dearly?"

"As often as he asks you to be his mistress; for, call it what you like, that is all he has to offer you."

Grace hid her face in her hands.

Jael colored. "Excuse my blunt speaking; but sometimes the worst word is the best; fine words are just words with a veil on."

"Will he dare to tempt me again, after what I said?"

"Of course he will: don't you know him? he never gives in. But, suppose he does, you have your answer ready."

"Jael," said Grace, "you are so strong, it blinds you to my weakness. I resist him, day after day! I, who pity him so, and blame myself! Why, his very look, his touch, his voice, overpower me so that my whole frame seems dissolving: feel how I tremble at him, even now. No, no; let those resist who are sure of their strength. Virtue, weakened by love and pity, has but one resource—to fly. Jael Dence, if you are a woman, help me to save the one thing I have got left to save."

"I will," said Jael Dence.

In one hour from that time they had packed a box and a carpet-bag, and were on their way to a railway station. They left Hillsborough.

In three days Jael returned, but Grace Coventry did not come back with her.

The day after that trying scene, Henry Little called, not to urge Grace again, as she presumed he would, but to ask pardon: at the same time we may be sure of this—that, after a day or two spent in obtaining pardon, the temptation would have been renewed, and so on forever. Of this, however, Little was not conscious; he came to ask pardon, and offer a pure and patient love, till such time as Heaven should have pity on them both. He was informed that Mrs. Coventry had quitted Hillsborough, and left a letter for him. It was offered him; he snatched it and read it.

"My own dear Henry,—You have given me something to forgive, and I forgive you without asking, as I hope you will one day forgive me. I have left Hillsborough to avoid a situation that was intolerable and solicitations which I blushed to hear, and for which you would one day have blushed too. This parting is not forever, I hope; but that rests with yourself. Forego your idea of vengeance on that man, whose chastisement you would best alleviate by ending his miserable existence; and learn to love me honorably and patiently, as I love you. Should you obtain this great victory over yourself, you will see me again. Meantime, think of her who loves you to distraction, and whose soul hovers about you unseen. Pray for me, dear one, at midnight, and at eight o'clock every morning; for those are two of the hours I shall pray for you. Do you remember the old church, and how you cried over me? I can write no more: my tears blind me so. Farewell.

"Your unhappy   GRACE."

Little read this piteous letter, and it was a heavy blow to him; a blow that all the tenderness shown in it could not at first soften. She had fled from him; she shunned him. It was not from Coventry she fled; it was from him.

He went home cold and sick at heart, and gave himself up to grief and deep regrets for several days.

But soon his powerful and elastic mind, impatient of impotent sorrow, and burning for some kind of action, seized upon vengeance as the only thing left to do.

At this period he looked on Coventry as a beast in human shape, whom he had a moral right to extinguish; only, as he had not a legal right, it must be done with consummate art. He trusted nobody; spoke to nobody; but set himself quietly to find out where Coventry lived, and what were his habits. He did this with little difficulty. Coventry lodged in a principal street, but always dined at a club, and returned home late, walking through a retired street or two; one of these passed by the mouth of a narrow court that was little used.

Little, disguised as a workman, made a complete reconnaissance of this locality, and soon saw that his enemy was at his mercy.

But, while he debated within himself what measure of vengeance he should take, and what noiseless weapon he should use, an unseen antagonist baffled him. That antagonist was Grace Carden. Still foreboding mischief, she wrote to Mr. Coventry, from a town two hundred miles distant:

"Whatever you are now, you were born a gentleman, and will, I think, respect a request from a lady you have wronged. Mr. Little has returned, and I have left Hillsborough; if he encounters you in his despair, he will do you some mortal injury. This will only make matters worse, and I dread the scandal that will follow, and to hear my sad story in a court of law as a justification for his violence. Oblige me, then, by leaving Hillsborough for a time, as I have done."

On receipt of this, Coventry packed up his portmanteau directly, and, leaving Lally behind to watch the town, and see whether this was a ruse, he went directly to the town whence Grace's letter was dated, and to the very hotel.

This she had foreseen and intended.

He found she had been there, and had left for a neighboring watering-place: he followed her thither, and there she withdrew the clue; she left word she was gone to Stirling; but doubled on him, and soon put hundreds of miles between them. He remained in Scotland, hunting her.

Thus she played the gray plover with him she hated, and kept the beloved hands from crime.

When Little found that Coventry had left Hillsborough, he pretended to himself that he was glad of it. "My darling is right," said he. "I will obey her, and do nothing contrary to law. I will throw him into prison, that is all." With these moderated views, he called upon his friend Ransome, whom of course he had, as yet, carefully avoided, to ask his aid in collecting the materials for an indictment. He felt sure that Coventry had earned penal servitude, if the facts could only be put in evidence. He found Ran-

some in low spirits, and that excellent public servant being informed what he was wanted for, said dryly, "Well, but this will require some ability: don't you think your friend Silly Billy would be more likely to do it effectually than John Ransome?"

"Why, Ransome, are you mad?"

"No, I merely do myself justice. Silly Billy smelt that faulty grindstone; and I can't smell a rat a yard from my nose, it seems. You shall judge for yourself. There have been several burglaries in this town of late, and planned by a master. This put me on my mettle, and I have done all I could, with my small force, and even pried about in person, night after night, and that is not exactly my business, but I felt it my duty. Well, sir, two nights ago, no more, I had the luck to come round a corner right upon a job: Alderman Dick's house, full of valuables, and the windows well guarded; but one of his cellars is only covered with a heavy wooden shutter, bolted within. I found this open, and a board wedged in, to keep it ajar: down I went on my knees, saw a light inside, and heard two words of thieves' latin; that was enough, you know; I whipped out the board, jumped on the heavy shutter, and called for the police."

"Did you expect them to come?"

"Not much. These jobs are timed so as not to secure the attendance of the police. But assistance of another kind came; a gentleman full dressed, in a white tie and gloves, ran up, and asked me what it was. 'Thieves in the cellar,' said I, and shouted police, and gave my whistle. The gentleman jumped on the shutter. 'I can keep that down,' said he. 'I'm sure I saw two policemen in Acorn Street: run quick!' and he showed me his sword-cane, and seemed so hearty in it, and confident, I ran round the corner, and gave my whistle. Two policemen came up; but, in that moment, the swell accomplice had pulled all his pals out of the cellar, and all I saw of the lot, when I came back, was the swell's swallow-tail coat flying like the wind towards a back slum, where I and my bobbies should have been knocked on the head, if we had tried to follow him; but indeed he was too fleet to give us the chance."

"Well," said Henry, "that was provoking: but who can foresee every thing all in a moment? I have been worse duped than that a good many times."

Ransome shook his head. "An old officer of police, like me, not to smell a swell accomplice. I had only to handcuff that man, and set him down with me on the shutter, till, in the dispensation of Providence, a bobby came by."

He added by way of corollary, "You should send to London for a detective."

"Not I," said Henry. "I know you for a sagacious man, and a worthy man, and my friend. I'll have no one to help me in it but you."

"Won't you?" said Ransome. "Then I'll go in. You have done me good, Mr. Little, by sticking to a defeated friend like this. Now for your case; tell me all you know, and how you know it."

Henry complied, and Ransome took his notes. Then he said, he had got some old memoranda by him, that might prove valuable: he would call in two days.

He did call, and showed Henry Coventry's

card, and told him he had picked it up close by his letter-box, on the very night of the explosion. "Mark my words, this will expand into something," said the experienced officer.

Before he left, he told Henry that he had now every reason to believe the swell accomplice was Shifty Dick, the most successful and distinguished criminal in England. "I have just got word from London that he has been working here, and has collared a heavy swag; says he will go into trade: one of his old pals let that out in jail. Trade! then heaven help his customers, that is all."

"You may catch him yet."

"When I catch Jack-a-lantern. He is not so green as to stay a day in Hillsborough, now his face has been close to mine; they all know I never forget a face. No, no; I shall never see him again, till I am telegraphed for, to inspect his mug and his wild-cat eyes in some jail or other. I must try and not think of him; it disturbs my mind, and takes off my attention from my duties."

Ransome adhered to this resolution for more than a month, during which time he followed out every indication with the patience of a beagle; and, at last, he called one day and told Little Hill had forfeited his bail, and gone to Canada at the expense of the trade; but had let out strange things before he left. There was a swell concerned in his attempt with the bow and arrow: there was a swell concerned in the explosion, with some workman, whose name he concealed; he had seen them on the bridge, and had seen the workman receive a bag of gold, and had collared him, and demanded his share; this had been given him, but not until he threatened to call the bobbies. "Now, if we could find Hill, and get him to turn Queen's evidence, this, coupled with what you and I could furnish, would secure your man ten years of penal servitude. I know an able officer at Quebec. Is it worth while going to the expense?"

Little, who had received the whole communication in a sort of despondent, apathetic way, replied that he didn't think it was worth while. "My good friend," said he, "I am miserable. Vengeance, I find, will not fill a yearning heart. And the truth is, that all this time I have been secretly hoping she would return, and that has enabled me to bear up, and chatter about revenge. Who could believe a young creature like that would leave her father and all her friends for good? I made sure she would come back in a week or two. And to think that it is I who have driven her away, and darkened my own life. I thought I had sounded the depths of misery. I was a fool to think so. No, no; life would be endurable if I could only see her face once a day, and hear her voice, though it was not even speaking to me. Oh! oh!"

Now this was the first time Little had broken down before Ransome. Hitherto, he had spoken of Coventry, but not of Grace; he had avoided speaking of her, partly from manly delicacy, partly because he foresaw his fortitude would give way if he mentioned her.

But now the strong man's breast seemed as if it would burst, and his gasping breath, and restless body, betrayed what a price he must have paid for the dogged fortitude he had displayed for several weeks, love-sick all the time.

Ransome was affected: he rose and walked about the room, ashamed to look at a Spartan broken down.

When he had given Little time to recover some little composure, he said, "Mr. Little, you were always too much of a gentleman to gossip about the lady you love; and it was not my business to intrude upon that subject; it was too delicate. But, of course, with what I have picked up here and there, and what you have let drop, without the least intending it, I know pretty well how the land lies. And, sir, a man does not come to my time of life without a sore and heavy heart; if I was to tell you how I came to be a bachelor —but, no; even after ten years I could not answer for myself. All I can say is that, if you should do me the honor to consult me on something that is nearer your heart than revenge, you would have all my sympathy and all my zeal."

"Give me your hand, old fellow," said Little, and broke down again.

But, this time, he shook it off quickly, and, to encourage him, Mr. Ransome said, "To begin, you may take my word Mr. Carden knows, by this time, where his daughter is. Why not sound him on the matter?"

Henry acted on this advice, and called on Mr. Carden.

He was received very coldly by that gentleman.

After some hesitation, he asked Mr. Carden if he had any news of his daughter.

"I have."

The young man's face was irradiated with joy directly.

"Is she well, sir?"

"Yes."

"Is she happier than she was?"

"She is content."

"Has she friends about her? Kind, good people; any persons of her own sex, whom she can love?"

"She is among people she takes for angels, at present. She will find them to be petty, mean, malicious devils. She is in a Protestant convent."

"In a convent? Where?"

"Where? Where neither the fool nor the villain, who have wrecked her happiness between them, and robbed me of her, will ever find her. I expected this visit, sir; the only thing I doubted was which would come first, the villain or the fool. The fool has come first, and being a fool, expects me to tell him where to find his victim, and torture her again. Begone, fool, from the house you have made desolate by your execrable folly in slipping away by night like a thief, or rather like that far more dangerous animal, a fool."

The old man delivered these insults with a purple face, and a loud fury, that in former days would have awakened corresponding rage in the fiery young fellow. But affliction had tempered him, and his insulter's hairs were gray.

He said, quietly, "You are her father. I forgive you these cruel words." Then he took his hat and went away.

Mr. Carden followed him to the passage, and cried after him, "The villain will meet a worse reception than the fool. I promise you that much."

Little went home despondent, and found a long

letter from his mother, telling him he must dine and sleep at Raby Hall that day.

She gave him such potent reasons, and showed him so plainly his refusal would infuriate his uncle, and make her miserable, that he had no choice. He packed up his dress suit, and drove to Raby Hall, with a heavy heart and bitter reluctance.

O cæca mens hominum.

CHAPTER XLI.

It was the great anniversary. On that day Sir Richard Raby had lost for the Stuarts all the head he possessed. His faithful descendant seized the present opportunity to celebrate the event with more pomp than ever. A month before the fatal day he came in from Hillsborough with sixty yards of violet-colored velvet, the richest that could be got from Lyons: he put this down on a table, and told his sister that was for her and Jael to wear on the coming anniversary. "Don't tell me there's not enough," said he; "for I inquired how much it would take to carpet two small rooms, and bought it; now what will carpet two little libraries will clothe two large ladies; and you are neither of you shrimps."

While he was thus doing the cynical, nobody heeded him; quick and skillful fingers were undoing the parcel, and the ladies' cheeks flushed and their eyes glistened, and their fingers felt the stuff inside and out: in which occupation Raby left them, saying, "Full dress, mind! We Rabys are not beheaded every day."

Mrs. Little undertook to cut both dresses, and Jael was to help sew them.

But, when they came to be tried on, Jael was dismayed. "Why, I shall be half naked," said she. "Oh, Mrs. Little, I couldn't: I should sink with shame."

Mrs. Little pooh-poohed that, and an amusing dialogue followed between these two women, both of them equally modest, but one hardened, and perhaps a little blinded, by custom.

Neither could convince the other, but Mrs. Little overpowered Jae by saying, "I shall wear mine low, and you will mortally offend my brother if you don't."

Then Jael succumbed, but looked forward to the day with a simple terror one would hardly have expected from the general strength of her character.

Little arrived, and saw his mother for a minute or two before dinner. She seemed happy and excited, and said, "Cheer up, darling; we will find a way to make you happy. Mark my words, a new era in your life dates from to-day: I mean to open your eyes to-night. There, don't question me, but give me one kiss, and let us go and make ourselves splendid for poor Sir Richard."

When Little came down stairs he found his uncle and a distinguished-looking young gentleman standing before the fire: both were in full dress. Raby had the Stuart orders on his breast and looked a prince. He introduced Little to Mr. Richard Raby with high formality; but, before they had time to make acquaintance, two ladies glided into the room, and literally dazzled the young men, especially Dissolute Dick, who knew neither of them.

Mrs. Little, with her oval face, black brow and hair, and stately but supple form, was a picture of matronly beauty and grace; her rich brunette skin, still glossy and firm, showed no signs of age, but under her glorious eyes were the marks of trouble; and though her face was still striking and lovely, yet it revealed what her person concealed, that she was no longer young. That night she looked about eight-and-thirty.

The other lady was blonde, and had a face less perfect in contour, but beautiful in its way, and exquisite in color and peach-like bloom: but the marvel was her form; her comely head, dignified on this occasion with a coronet of pearls, perched on a throat long yet white and massive, and smooth as alabaster; and that majestic throat sat enthroned on a snowy bust and shoulders of magnificent breadth, depth, grandeur, and beauty. Altogether it approached the gigantic; but so lovely was the swell of the broad white bosom, and so exquisite the white and polished skin of the mighty shoulders adorned with two deep dimples, that the awe this grand physique excited was mingled with profound admiration.

Raby and Henry Little both started at the sudden grandeur and brilliance of the woman they thought they knew, but in reality had never seen; and Raby, dazzled himself, presented her, quite respectfully, to Dissolute Dick.

"This is Miss Dence, a lady descended, like the rest of us, from poor Sir Richard; Miss Dence; Mr. Richard Raby."

Jael blushed more deeply than ladies with white and antique busts are in the habit of doing, and it was curious to see the rosy tint come on her white neck, and then die quietly away again. Yet she courtesied with grace and composure. (Mrs. Little had trained her at all points; and grace comes pretty readily, where nature has given perfect symmetry.)

Dinner was announced, and Raby placed the Dissolute between his sister and the magnificent Beauty dead Sir Richard had developed. He even gave a reason for this arrangement.

"All you ladies like a Rake: you praise sober fellows like me; but what you prefer is a Rake."

As they were rustling into their places, Mrs. Little said to Dick, with a delicious air of indifference, "Are you a rake, Mr. Raby?"

"I am any thing you like," replied the shameless fellow.

All the old plate was out, and blazing in the light of candles innumerable.

There was one vacant chair.

Dick asked if there was any body expected.

"Not much," said Raby dryly. "That is Sir Richard's chair, on these occasions. However, he may be sitting in it now, for aught I know. I sincerely hope he is."

"If I thought that, I'd soon leave mine," said Jael, in a tremulous whisper.

"Then stay where you are, Sir Richard," said the Rake, making an affected motion with his handkerchief, as if to keep the good Knight down.

In short, this personage, being young, audacious, witty, and animated by the vicinity of the most beautiful creature he had ever seen, soon deprived the anniversary of that solemn character Mr. Raby desired to give it. Yet his volubility, his gayety, and his chaff were combined with a certain gentlemanlike tact and dexterity; and he made Raby laugh in spite of himself, and often made the ladies smile. But Henry Little sat opposite, and wondered at them all, and his sad heart became very bitter.

very soon took the form of downright love-making. In fact he staid an hour after his carriage was announced, and being a young man of great resolution, and accustomed to please himself, he fell over head and ears in love with Miss Dence, and showed it then and thereafter.

TWO LADIES GLIDED INTO THE ROOM, AND LITERALLY DAZZLED THE YOUNG MEN.

When they joined the ladies in the drawing-room, Henry made an effort to speak to Jael Dence. He was most anxious to know whether she had heard from Grace Carden. But Jael did not meet him very promptly, and while he was faltering out his inquiries, up came Richard Raby and resumed his attentions to her—attentions that

It did not disturb her composure. She had often been made love to, and could parry as well as Dick could fence.

She behaved with admirable good sense; treated it all as a polite jest, but not a disagreeable one.

Mrs. Little lost patience with them both. She

drew Henry aside, and asked him why he allowed Mr. Richard Raby to monopolize her.

"How can I help it ?" said Henry. "He is in love with her ; and no wonder : see how beautiful she is, and her skin like white satin. She is ever so much bigger than I thought. But her heart is bigger than all. Who'd think she had ever condescended to grind saws with me ?"

"Who indeed ? And with those superb arms ?"

"Why, that it, mother ; they are up to any thing : it was one of those superb arms she flung round a blackguard's neck for me, and threw him like a sack, or I should not be here. Poor girl ! Do you think that chatterbox would make her happy ?"

"Heaven forbid ! He is not worthy of her. No man is worthy of her, except the one I mean her to have, and that is yourself."

"Me, mother ! are you mad ?"

"No : you are mad, if you reject her. Where can you hope to find her equal ? In what does she fail ? In face? why it is comeliness, goodness, and modesty personified. In person? why she is the only perfect figure I ever saw. Such an arm, hand, foot, neck, and bust I never saw all in the same woman. Is it sense? why she is wise beyond her years, and beyond her sex. Think of her great self-denial : she always loved you, yet aided you, and advised you to get that mad young thing you preferred to her—men are so blind in choosing women ! Then think of her saving your life ; and then how nearly she lost her own, through her love for you. Oh, Henry, if you cling to a married woman, and still turn away from that angelic creature there, and disappoint your poor mother again, whose life has been one long disappointment, I shall begin to fear you were born without a heart."

CHAPTER XLII.

"BETTER for me if I had ; then I could chop and change from one to another as you would have me. No, mother ; I dare say if I had never seen Grace I should have loved Jael. As it is, I have a great affection and respect for her, but that is all."

"And those would ripen into love if once you were married."

"They might. If it came to her flinging that great arm round my neck in kindness she once saved my life with by brute force, I suppose a man's heart could not resist her. But it will never come to that while my darling lives. She is my lover, and Jael my sister and my dear friend. God bless her, and may she be as happy as she deserves. I wish I could get a word with her, but that seems out of the question to-night. I shall slip away to bed and my own sad thoughts."

With this he retired unobserved.

In the morning he asked Jael if she would speak to him alone.

"Why not ?" said she calmly.

They took a walk in the shrubbery.

"I tried hard to get a word with you yesterday, but you were so taken up with that puppy."

"He is very good company."

"I have seen the time when I was as good ; but it is not so easy to chatter with a broken heart."

"That is true. Please come to the point, and tell me what you want of me now."

This was said in such a curious tone, that Henry felt quite discouraged.

He hesitated a moment and then said, "What is the matter with you ? You are a changed girl to me. There's something about you so cold and severe ; it makes me fear I have worn out my friend as well as lost my love ; if it is so, tell me, and I will not intrude my sorrow any more on you."

There was a noble and manly sadness in the way he said this, and Jael seemed touched a little by it.

"Mr. Henry," said she, "I'll be frank with you. I can't forgive you leaving the factory that night without saying a word to me ; and if you consider what I had done before you used me so, and what I suffered in consequence of your using me so—not that you will ever know all I suffered, at least I hope not—no, I have tried to forgive you ; for, if you are a sinner, you are a sufferer—but it is no use, I can't. I never shall forgive you to my dying day."

Henry Little hung his head dejectedly. "That is bad news," he faltered. "I told you why I did not bid you good-bye except by letter : it was out of kindness. I have begged your pardon for it all the same. I thought you were an angel : but I see you are only a woman ; you think the time to hit a man is when he is down. Well, I can but submit. Good-bye. Stay one moment, let me take your hand, you won't refuse me that." She did not deign a word ; he took her hand and held it. "This is the hand and arm that worked with me like a good mate : this is the hand and arm that overpowered a blackguard and saved me : this is the hand and arm that saved my Grace from a prison and public shame. I must give them both one kiss, if they knock me down for it. There—there—good-bye, dear Jael, good-bye ! I seem to be letting go the last thing I have to cling to in the deep waters of trouble."

Melted by this sad thought, he held his best friend's hand till a warm tear dropped on it. That softened her ; the hand to which he owed so much closed on his and detained him.

"Stay where you are. I have told you my mind, but I shall act just as I used to do. I'm not proud of this spite I have taken against you, don't you fancy that. There—there, don't let us fret about what can't be helped ; but just you tell me what I can do for you."

Young Little felt rather humiliated at assistance being offered on these terms. He did not disguise his mortification.

"Well," said he, rather sullenly, "beggars must not be choosers. Of course I wanted you to tell me where I am likely to find her."

"I don't know."

"But you left Hillsborough with her ?"

"Yes, and went to York. But there I left her, and she told me she should travel hundreds of miles from York. I have no notion where she is."

Little sighed. "She could not trust even you."

"The fewer one trusts with a secret the better."

"Will she never return ? Will she give up her father as well as me ? Did she fix no time ? Did she give you no hint ?"

"No, not that I remember. She said that depended on you."

"On me?"

"Yes."

Here was an enigma.

They puzzled over it a long time. At last Jael said, "She wrote a letter to you before she left: did she say nothing in that? Have you got the letter?"

"Have I got it?—the last letter my darling ever wrote to me! Do you think it ever leaves me night or day?"

He undid one of his studs, put his hand inside, and drew the letter out warm from his breast. He kissed it and gave it to Jael. She read it carefully and looked surprised. "Why, you are making your own difficulties. You have only got to do what you are told. Promise not to fall foul of that Coventry, and not to tempt her again, and you will hear of her. You have her own word for it."

"But how am I to let her know I promise?"

"I don't know; how does every body let every body know things nowadays? They advertise."

"Of course they do—in the second column of 'The Times.'"

"You know best." Then, after a moment's reflection, "Wherever she is, she takes in the Hillsborough papers to see if there's any thing about you in them."

"Oh, do you think so?"

"Think so? I am sure of it. I put myself in her place."

"Then I will advertise in 'The Times' and the Hillsborough papers."

He went into the library, and wrote several advertisements. This is the one Jael preferred:

"H. L. to G. C. I see you are right. There shall be no vengeance except what the law may give me, nor will I ever renew that request which offended you so justly. I will be patient."

He had added an entreaty that she would communicate with him, but this Jael made him strike out. She thought that might make Grace suspect his sincerity. "Time enough to put that in a month hence, if you don't hear from her."

This was all I think worth recording in the interview between Jael and Henry, except that at parting he thanked her warmly, and said, "May I give you one piece of advice in return? Mr. Richard Raby has fallen in love with you, and no wonder. If my heart was not full of Grace I should have fallen in love with you myself, you are so good and so beautiful; but he bears a bad character. You are wise in other people's affairs, pray don't be foolish in your own."

"Thank you," said Jael, a little dryly. "I shall think twice before I give my affections to any young man."

Henry had a word with his mother before he went, and begged her not to prepare disappointment for herself by trying to bring Jael and him together. "Besides, she has taken a spite against me. To be sure it is not very deep; for she gave me good advice, and I advised her not to throw herself away on Dissolute Dick."

Mrs. Little smiled knowingly and looked very much pleased, but she said nothing more just then. Henry Little returned to Hillsborough, and put his advertisement in "The Times" and the Hillsborough journals.

Two days afterwards Ransome called on him, with the "Hillsborough Liberal." "Is this yours?" said Ransome.

"Yes. I have reason to think she will write to me, if she sees it."

"Would you mind giving me your reason?"

Little gave it, but with so much reticence, that no other man in Hillsborough but Ransome would have understood.

"Hum!" said he, "I think I can do something with this."

A period of expectation succeeded, hopeful at first, and full of excitement; but weeks rolled on without a word from the fugitive, and Little's heart sickened with hope deferred. He often wished to consult Jael Dence again; he had a superstitious belief in her sagacity. But the recollection of her cold manner deterred him. At last, however, impatience and the sense of desolation conquered, and he rode over to Raby Hall.

He found his uncle and his mother in the dining-room. Mr. Raby was walking about looking vexed, and even irritable.

The cause soon transpired. Dissolute Dick was at that moment in the drawing-room, making hot love to Jael Dence. He had wooed her ever since that fatal evening when she burst on society full-blown. Raby, too proud and generous to forbid his addresses, had nevertheless been always bitterly averse to them, and was now in a downright rage: for Mrs. Little had just told him she felt sure he was actually proposing.

"Confound him!" said Henry, "and I wanted so to speak to her."

Raby gave him a most singular look, that struck him as odd at the time, and recurred to him afterwards.

At last steps were heard overhead, and Dissolute Dick came down stairs.

Mrs. Little slipped out, and soon after put her head into the dining-room to the gentlemen, and whispered to them "Yes." Then she retired to talk it all over with Jael.

At that monosyllable Mr. Raby was very much discomposed.

"There goes a friend out of this house; more fools we. You have lost her by your confounded folly. What is the use spooning all your days after another man's wife? I wouldn't have had this happen for ten thousand pounds. Dissolute Dick! he will break her heart in a twelvemonth."

"Then why, in heaven's name, didn't you marry her yourself?"

"Me! at my age? No; why didn't you marry her? You know she fancies you. The moment you found Grace married, you ought to have secured this girl, and lived with me; the house is big enough for you all."

"It is not so big as your heart, sir," said Henry. "But pray don't speak to me of love or marriage either."

"Why should I? The milk is spilt; it is no use crying now. Let us go and dress for dinner. Curse the world—it is one disappointment."

Little himself was vexed, but he determined to put a good face on it, and to be very kind to his good friend Jael.

She did not appear at dinner, and when the servants had retired, he said, "Come now, let us make the best of it. Mother, if you don't mind, I will settle five thousand pounds upon her and her children. He is a spendthrift, I hear, and as poor as Job."

Mrs. Little stared at her son. "Why, she has refused him!"

Loud exclamations of surprise and satisfaction. "A fine fright you have given us. You said 'Yes.'"

"Well, that meant he had proposed. You know, Guy, I had told you he would: I saw it in his eye. So I observed, in a moment, he *had*, and I said 'Yes.'"

"Then why doesn't she come down to dinner?"

"He has upset her. It is the old story: he cried to her, and told her he had been wild, and misconducted himself, all because he had never met a woman he could really love and respect; and then he begged her, and implored her, and said his fate depended on her."

"But she was not caught with that chaff; so why does she not come and receive the congratulations of the company on her escape?"

"Because she is far too delicate;" then, turning to her son, "and, perhaps, because she can't help comparing the manly warmth and loving appreciation of Mr. Richard Raby, with the cold indifference and ingratitude of others."

"Oh," said Henry, coloring, "if that is her feeling, she will accept him next time."

"Next time!" roared Raby. "There shall be no next time. I have given the scamp fair play, quite against my own judgment. He has got his answer now, and I won't have the girl tormented with him any more. I trust that to you, Edith."

Mrs. Little promised him Dick and Jael should not meet again, in Raby Hall at least.

That evening she drew her son apart and made an earnest appeal to him.

"So much for her spite against you, Henry. You told her to decline Richard Raby, and so she declined him. Spite, indeed! The gentle pique of a lovely, good girl, who knows her value, though she is too modest to show it openly. Well, Henry, you have lost her a husband, and she has given you one more proof of affection. Don't build the mountain of ingratitude any higher: do pray take the cure that offers, and make your mother happy, as well as yourself, my son." In this strain she continued, and used all her art, her influence, her affection, till at last, with a weary, heart-broken sigh, he yielded as far as this: he said that, if it could once be made clear to him there was no hope of his ever marrying Grace Carden, he would wed Jael Dence at once.

Then he ordered his trap, and drove sullenly home, while Mrs. Little, full of delight, communicated her triumph to Jael Dence, and told her about the five thousand pounds, and was as enthusiastic in praise of Henry to Jael, as she had been of Jael to Henry.

Meantime he drove back to Hillsborough, more unhappy than ever, and bitter against himself for yielding, even so far, to gratitude and maternal influence.

It was late when he reached home. He let himself in with a latch-key, and went into his room for a moment.

A letter lay on the table, with no stamp on it: he took it up. It contained but one line; that line made his heart leap:

"News of G. C.   RANSOME."

CHAPTER XLIII.

LATE as it was, Little went to the Town-hall directly. But there, to his bitter disappointment, he learned that Mr. Ransome had been called to Manchester by telegram. Little had nothing to do but to wait, and eat his heart with impatience. However, next day, towards afternoon, Ransome called on him at the works, in considerable excitement, and told him a new firm had rented large business premises in Manchester, obtained goods, insured them in the "Gosshawk," and then the premises had caught fire and the goods been burnt to ashes; suspicions had been excited; Mr. Carden had gone to the spot, and telegraphed for him. He had met a London detective there, and, between them, they had soon discovered that full cases had come in by day, but full sacks gone out by night: the ashes also revealed no trace of certain goods the firm had insured. "And now comes the clue to it all. Amongst the few things that survived the fire was a photograph—of whom do you think? Shifty Dick. The dog had kept his word, and gone into trade."

"Confound him!" said Little; "he is always crossing my path, that fellow. You seem quite to forget that all this time I am in agonies of suspense. What do I care about Shifty Dick? He is nothing to me."

"Of course not. I am full of the fellow; a little more, and he'll make a monomaniac of me. Mr. Carden offers £200 for his capture; and we got an inkling he was coming this way again. There, there, I won't mention his name to you again. Let us talk of what *will* interest you. Well, sir, have you observed that you are followed and watched?"

"No."

"I am glad of it; then it has been done skillfully. You have been closely watched this month past by my orders."

This made young Little feel queer. Suppose he had attempted any thing unlawful, his good friend here would have collared him.

"You'll wonder that a good citizen like you should be put under surveillance; but I thought it likely your advertisement would either make the lady write to you, or else draw her back to the town. She didn't write, so I had you watched, to see if any body took a sly peep at you. Well, this went on for weeks, and nothing turned up. But the other night a young woman walked several times by your house, and went away with a sigh. She had a sort of Protestant nun's dress on, and a thick veil. Now you know Mr. Carden told you she was gone into a convent. I am almost sure it is the lady."

Little thanked him with all his soul, and then inquired eagerly where the nun lived.

"Ah, my man didn't know that. Unfortunately, he was on duty in the street, and had no authority to follow any body. However, if you can keep yourself calm, and obey orders—"

"I will do any thing you tell me."

"Well, then, this evening, as soon as it is quite dark, you do what I have seen you do in happier times. Light your reading-lamp, and sit reading close to the window; only you must not pull down the blind. Lower the venetians, but don't turn them so as to hide your face from the outside. You must promise me faithfully not to move under any circumstances, or you would be sure to spoil all."

Little gave the promise, and performed it to the letter. He lighted his lamp, and tried to read book after book; but, of course, he was too agitated to fix his attention on them. He got all Grace's letters, and read them; and it was only by a stern effort he kept still at all.

The night wore on, and heart-sickness was beginning to succeed to feverish impatience, when there was a loud knock at the door. Little ran to it himself, and found a sergeant of police, who told him in a low voice he brought a message from the chief-constable.

"I was to tell you it is all right; he is following the party himself. He will call on you at twelve to-morrow morning."

"Not before that?" said Little. However, he gave the sergeant a sovereign for good news, and then, taking his hat, walked twenty miles out of Hillsborough, and back, for he knew it was useless his going to bed, or trying to settle to any thing.

He got back at ten o'clock, washed, breakfasted, and dozed on two chairs, till Ransome came, with a carpet-bag in his hand.

"Tell me all about it: don't omit any thing." This was Little's greeting.

"Well, sir, she passed the house about nine o'clock, walking quickly; and took just one glance in at your window, but did not stop. She came back in half an hour, and stood on the opposite side of the way, and then passed on. I hid in a court, where she couldn't see me. By-and-by she comes back, on your side the way this time, gliding like a cat, and she crouched and curled round the angle of the house, and took a good look at you. Then she went slowly away, and I passed her. She was crying bitterly, poor girl! I never lost sight of her, and she led me a dance, I can tell you. I'll take you to the place; but you had better let me disguise you; for I can see she is very timid, and would fly away in a moment if she knew she was detected."

Little acquiesced, and Ransome disguised him in a beard, and a loose set of clothes, and a billy-cock hat, and said that would do, as long as he kept at a prudent distance from the lady's eye. They then took a cab and drove out of Hillsborough. When they had proceeded about two miles up the valley, Ransome stopped the cab, and directed the driver to wait for them.

He then walked on, and soon came to a row of houses, in two blocks of four houses each.

The last house of the first block had a bill in the window, "To be let furnished."

He then knocked at the door, and a woman in charge of the house opened it.

"I am the chief-constable of Hillsborough; and this is my friend Mr. Park; he is looking out for a furnished house. Can he see this one?"

The woman said, "Certainly, gentlemen," and showed them over the house.

Ransome opened the second-story window, and looked out on the back garden.

"Ah," said he, "these houses have nice long gardens in the rear, where one can walk and be private."

He then nudged Henry, and asked the woman who lived in the first house of the next block— "the house that garden belongs to?"

"Why, the bill was in the window the other day; but it is just took. She is a kind of a nun, I suppose: keeps no servant; only a girl comes in and does for her, and goes home at night. . I saw her yesterday, walking in the garden there. She seems rather young to be all alone like that; but perhaps there's some more of 'em coming. They sort o' cattle mostly goes in bands."

Henry asked what was the rent of the house. The woman did not know, but told him the proprietor lived a few doors off. "I shall take this house," said Little. "I think you are right," observed Ransome: "it will just answer your purpose." They went together, and took the house directly; and Henry, by advice of Ransome, engaged a woman to come into the house in the morning, and go away at dusk. Ransome also advised him to make arrangements for watching Grace's garden unseen. "That will be a great comfort to you," said he: "I know by experience. Above all things," said this sagacious officer, "don't you let her know she is discovered. Remember this: when she wants you to know she is here, she'll be sure to let you know. At present she is here on the sly: so if you thwart her, she'll be off again, as sure as fate."

Little was forced to see the truth of this, and promised to restrain himself, hard as the task was. He took the house; and used to let himself into it with a latch-key at about ten o'clock every night.

There he used to stay and watch till past noon; and nearly every day he was rewarded by seeing the Protestant nun walk in her garden.

He was restless and miserable till she came out: when she appeared his heart bounded and thrilled; and when once he had feasted his eyes upon her, he would go about the vulgar affairs of life pretty contentedly.

By advice of Ransome, he used to sit in his other house from seven till nine, and read at the window, to afford his beloved a joy similar to that he stole himself.

And such is the power of true love that these furtive glances soothed two lives. Little's spirits revived, and some color came back to Grace's cheek.

One night there was a house broken into in the row.

Instantly Little took the alarm on Grace's account, and bought powder and bullets, and a double-barrelled rifle, and a revolver; and now at the slightest sound he would be out of bed in a moment, ready to defend her, if necessary.

Thus they both kept their hearts above water, and Grace visited the sick, and employed her days in charity; and then, for a reward, crept, with soft foot, to Henry's window, and devoured him with her eyes, and fed on that look for hours afterwards.

When this had gone on for nearly a month, Lally, who had orders to keep his eye on Mr. Little, happened to come by and see Grace looking in at him.

He watched her at a distance, but had not the intelligence to follow her home. He had no idea it was Grace Carden.

However, in his next letter to his master, who was then in London, he told him Little always read at night by the window, and, one night, a kind of nun had come and taken a very long look at him, and gone away crying. "I suspect," said Lally, "she has played the fool with him some time or other, before she was a nun."

He was not a little surprised when his master telegraphed in reply that he would be down by the first train; but the fact is, that Coventry had already called on Mr. Carden, and been told that his wife was in a convent, and he would never see her again. I must add that Mr. Carden received him as roughly as he had Little, but the interview terminated differently. Coventry, with his winning tongue, and penitence and plausibility, softened the indignant father, and then, appealing to his good sense, extorted from him the admission that his daughter's only chance of happiness lay in forgiving him, and allowing him to atone his faults by a long life of humble devotion. But when Coventry, presuming on this, implored him to reveal where she was, the old man stood stanch, and said that was told him under a solemn assurance of secrecy, and nothing should induce him to deceive his daughter. "I will not lose her love and confidence for any of you," said he.

So now Coventry put that word "convent" and this word "nun" together, and came to Hillsborough full of suspicions.

He took lodgings nearly opposite Little's house, and watched in a dark room so persistently, that, at last, he saw the nun appear, saw her stealthy, cat-like approaches, her affected retreat, her cunning advance, her long lingering look.

A close observer of women, he saw in every movement of her supple body that she was animated by love.

He raged and sickened with jealousy, and when, at last, she retired, he followed her, with hell in his heart, and never lost sight of her till she entered her house in the valley.

If there had been a house to let in the terrace, he would certainly have taken it; but Little had anticipated him.

He took a very humble lodging in the neighborhood; and by dint of watching, he at last saw the nun speaking to a poor woman with her veil up. It revealed to him nothing but what he knew already. It was the woman he loved, and she hated him; the woman who had married him under a delusion, and stabbed him on his bridal day. He loved her all the more passionately for that.

Until he received Lally's note, he had been content to wait patiently until his rival should lose hope, and carry himself and his affections elsewhere; he felt sure that must be the end of it.

But now jealousy stung wild, passion became too strong for reason, and he resolved to play a bold and lawless game to possess his lawful wife. Should it fail, what could they do to him? A man may take his own by force. Not only his passions, but the circumstances tempted him. She was actually living alone, in a thinly-peopled district, and close to a road. It was only to cover her head and stifle her cries, and fly with her to some place prepared beforehand, where she would be brought to submission by kindness of manner combined with firmness of purpose.

Coventry possessed every qualification to carry out such a scheme as this. He was not very courageous; yet he was not a coward: and no great courage was required. Cunning, forethought, and unscrupulousness were the principal things, and these he had to perfection.

He provided a place to keep her; it was a shooting-box of his own, on a heathery hill, that nobody visited except for shooting, and the season for shooting was past.

He armed himself with false certificates of lunacy, to show on an emergency, and also a copy of his marriage certificate: he knew how unwilling strangers are to interfere between man and wife.

The only great difficulty was to get resolute men to help him in this act.

He sounded Cole; but that worthy objected to it, as being out of his line.

Coventry talked him over, and offered a sum that made him tremble with cupidity. He assented, on one condition—that he should not be expected to break into the house, nor do any act that could be "construed burglarious." He actually used that phrase, which I should hardly have expected from him.

Coventry assented to this condition. He undertook to get into the house, and open the door to Cole and his myrmidons: he stipulated, however, that Cole should make him a short iron ladder with four sharp prongs. By means of this he could enter Grace's house at a certain unguarded part, and then run down and unbar the front door. He had thoroughly reconnoitred the premises, and was sure of success.

First one day was appointed for the enterprise, then another, and, at last, it was their luck to settle on a certain night, of which I will only say at present, that it was a night Hillsborough and its suburbs will not soon forget.

Midnight was the hour agreed on.

Now at nine o'clock of this very night the chief-constable of Hillsborough was drinking tea with Little scarcely twenty yards from the scene of the proposed abduction. Not that either he or Little had the least notion of the conspiracy. The fact is, Hillsborough had lately been deluged with false coin, neatly executed, and passed with great dexterity. The police had received many complaints, but had been unable to trace it. Lately, however, an old bachelor, living in this suburban valley, had complained to the police that his neighbors kept such enormous fires all night, as to make his wall red-hot and blister his paint. This, and one or two other indications, made Ransome suspect the existence of a furnace, and he had got a search-warrant in his pocket, on which, however, he did not think it safe to act till he had watched the suspected house late at night, and made certain observations for himself. So he had invited himself to tea with his friend Little—for he was sure of a hearty welcome at any hour—and, over their tea, he now told him his suspicions, and invited him to come and take a look at the suspected house with him.

Little consented. But there was no hurry; the later they went to the house in question the better. So they talked of other matters, and the conversation soon fell on that which was far more interesting to Little than the capture of all the coiners in creation.

He asked Ransome how long he was to go on like this, contenting himself with the mere sight of her.

"Why," said Ransome, "even that has made another man of you. Your eye is twice as bright as it was a month ago, and your color is coming back. That is a wise proverb, 'Let well alone.' I hear she visits the sick, and some of them swear by her. I think I'd give her time to take root here; and then she will not be so ready to fly off in a tangent."

Little objected that it was more than flesh and blood could bear.

"Well, then," said Ransome, "promise me just one thing: that, if you speak to her, it shall be in Hillsborough, and not down here."

Little saw the wisdom of this, and consented, but said he was resolved to catch her at his own window the next time she came.

He was about to give his reasons, but they were interrupted by a man and horse clattering up to the door.

"That will be for me," said Ransome. "I thought I should not get leave to drink my tea in peace."

He was right; a mounted policeman brought him a note from the mayor, telling him word had come into the town that there was something wrong with Ouseley dam. He was to take the mayor's horse, and ride up at once to the reservoir, and, if there was any danger, to warn the valley.

"This looks serious," said Ransome. "I must wish you good-bye."

"Take a piece of advice with you. I hear that dam is too full; if so, don't listen to advice from any body, but open the sluices of the waste-pipes and relieve the pressure; but if you find a flaw in the embankment, don't trifle, blow up the waste-weir at once with gunpowder. I wish I had a horse, I'd go with you. By the way, if there is the least danger of that dam bursting, of course you will give me warning in time, and I'll get her out of the house at once."

"What, do you think the water would get as far as this, to do any harm? It is six miles."

"It might. Look at the form of the ground; it is a regular trough from that dam to Hillsborough. My opinion is, it would sweep every thing before it, and flood Hillsborough itself —the lower town. I shall not go to bed, old fellow, till you come back and tell me it is all right."

With this understanding Ransome galloped off. On his way he passed by the house where he suspected coining. The shutters were closed, but his experienced eye detected a bright light behind one of them, and a peculiar smoke from the chimney.

Adding this to his other evidence, he now felt sure the inmates were coiners, and he felt annoyed. "Fine I look," said he, "walking tamely past criminals at work, and going to a mayor's-nest six miles off."

However, he touched the horse with his heel, and cantered forward on his errand.

John Ransome rode up to the Ouseley Reservoir, and down again, in less than an hour and a half; and every incident of those two rides is imprinted on his memory for life.

He first crossed the water at Poma bridge. The village of that name lay on his right, towards Hillsborough, and all the lights were out except in the two public houses. One of these, "The Reindeer," was near the bridge, and from it a ruddy glare shot across the road, and some boon companions were singing, in very good harmony, a trite Scotch chorus:

"We are no that fou, we are no that fou,
    But just a drappie in our ee;
The cock may craw, the day may daw,
    But still we'll taste the barley bree."

Ransome could hear the very words; he listened, laughed, and then rode up the valley till he got opposite a crinoline-wire factory called the "Kildare Wheel." Here he observed a single candle burning; a watcher, no doubt.

The next place he saw was also on the other side the stream; Dolman's farm-house, the prettiest residence in the valley. It was built of stone, and beautifully situated on a promontory between two streams. It had a lawn in front, which went down to the very edge of the water, and was much admired for its close turf and flowers. The farm buildings lay behind the house.

There was no light whatever in Dolman's; but they were early people. The house and lawn slept peacefully in the night: the windows were now shining, now dark, for small fleecy clouds kept drifting at short intervals across the crescent moon.

Ransome pushed on across the open ground, and for a mile or two saw few signs of life, except here and there a flickering light in some water-wheel; for now one picturesque dam and wheel succeeded another as rapidly as Nature permitted; and indeed the size of these dams, now shining in the fitful moonlight, seemed remarkable, compared with the mere thread of water which fed them, and connected them together for miles like pearls on a silver string.

Ransome pushed rapidly on, up hill and down dale, till he reached the high hill, at whose foot lay the hamlet of Damflask, distant two miles from Ouseley Reservoir.

He looked down and saw a few lights in this hamlet, some stationary, but two moving.

"Hum," thought Ransome, "they don't seem to be quite so easy in their minds up here."

He dashed into the place, and drew up at a house where several persons were collected.

As he came up, a singular group issued forth; a man with a pig-whip, driving four children—the eldest not above seven years old—and carrying an infant in his arms. The little imps were clad in shoes, night-gowns, night-caps, and a blanket apiece, and were shivering and whining at being turned out of bed into the night air.

Ransome asked the man what was the matter.

One of the by-standers laughed, and said, satirically, Ouseley dam was to burst that night, so all the pigs and children were making for the hill.

The man himself, whose name was Joseph Galton, explained more fully.

"Sir," said he, "my wife is groaning, and I am bound to obey her. She had a dream last night she was in a flood, and had to cross a plank or summut. I quieted her till supper; but then landlord came round and warned us all of a crack or summut up at dam. And so now I am taking this little lot up to my brother's. It's the foolishest job I ever done: but needs must when the devil drives, and it is better so than to have my old gal sour her milk, and pine her suckling, and maybe fret herself to death into the bargain."

Ransome seized on the information, and rode

on directly to the village inn. He called the landlord out, and asked him what he had been telling the villagers. Was there any thing seriously amiss up at the reservoir?

"Nay, I hope not," said the man; "but we got a bit of a fright this afternoon. A young man rode through, going down to Hillsborough, and stopped here to have his girth mended; he had broke it coming down our hill. While he was taking a glass he let out his errand: they had found a crack in the embankment, and sent him down to Hillsborough to tell Mr. Tucker, the engineer. Bless your heart, we should never have known aught about it if his girth hadn't broke." He added, as a reason for thinking it was not serious, that Mr. Tucker had himself inspected the dam just before tea-time, and hadn't even seen the crack. It was a laboring man who had discovered it through crossing the embankment lower down than usual. "But you see, sir," said he, in conclusion, "we lie very low here, and right in the track; and so we mustn't make light of a warning. And, of course, many of the workmen stop here and have their say; and, to tell you the truth, one or two of them have always misliked the foundation that embankment is built on: too many old landslips to be seen about. But, after all, I suppose they can empty the dam, if need be; and, of course, they will, if there is any danger. I expect Mr. Tucker up every minute."

Ransome thanked him for his information and pushed on to Lower Hatfield: there he found lights in the houses and the inhabitants astir; but he passed through the village in silence, and came to the great corn-mill, a massive stone structure with granite pillars, the pride of the place. The building was full of lights, and the cranes were all at work hoisting the sacks of flour from the lower floors to the top story. The faces of the men reflected in the flaring gas, and the black cranes with their gaunt arms, and the dark bodies rising by the snake-like cords, formed a curious picture in the fluctuating moonlight, and an interesting one too: for it showed the miller did not feel his flour quite safe.

The next place Ransome came to was Fox Farm.

Farmer Emden was standing at the door of his house, and, in reply to Ransome, told him he had just come down from the reservoir. He had seen the crack and believed it to be a mere frost-crack. He apprehended no danger, and had sent his people to bed; however, he should sit up for an hour or two just to hear what Tucker the engineer had to say about it; he had been sent for.

Ransome left him, and a smart canter brought him in sight of what seemed a long black hill, with great glow-worms dotted here and there.

That hill was the embankment, and the glow-worms were the lanterns of workmen examining the outer side of the embankment and prying into every part.

The enormous size and double slope of the bank, its apparent similarity in form and thickness to those natural barriers with which nature hems in lakes of large dimensions, acted on Ransome's senses, and set him wondering at the timidity and credulity of the people in Hatfield and Damflask. This sentiment was uppermost in his mind when he rode up to the south side of the embankment.

He gave his horse to a boy, and got upon the embankment and looked north.

The first glance at the water somewhat shook that impression of absolute security the outer side of the barrier had given him.

In nature a lake lies at the knees of the re-straining hills, or else has a sufficient outlet.

But here was a lake nearly full to the brim on one side of the barrier and an open descent on the other.

He had encountered a little wind coming up, but not much; here, however, the place being entirely exposed, the wind was powerful and blew right down the valley, ruffling the artificial lake.

Altogether it was a solemn scene, and, even at first glance, one that could not be surveyed, after all those comments and reports, without some awe and anxiety. The surface of the lake shone like a mirror, and waves of some size dashed against the embankment with a louder roar than one would have thought possible, and tossed some spray clean over all; while, overhead, clouds, less fleecy now, and more dark and sullen, drifted so swiftly across the crescent moon that she seemed flying across the sky.

Having now realized that the embankment, huge as it was, was not so high by several hundred feet as nature builds in parallel cases, and that, besides the natural pressure of the whole water, the upper surface of the lake was being driven by the wind against the upper or thin part of the embankment, Ransome turned and went down the embankment to look at the crack and hear opinions.

There were several workmen, an intelligent farmer called Ives, and Mr. Mountain, one of the contractors who had built the dam, all examining the crack.

Mr. Mountain was remarking that the crack was perfectly dry, a plain proof there was no danger.

"Ay, but," said Ives, "it has got larger since tea-time; see, I can get my hand in now."

"Can you account for that?" asked Ransome of the contractor.

Mountain said it was caused by the embankment settling. "Every thing settles down a little—houses and embankments and all. There's no danger, Mr. Ransome, believe me."

"Well, sir," said Ransome, "I am not a man of science, but I have got eyes, and I see the water is very high, and driving against your weak part. Ah!" Then he remembered Little's advice. "Would you mind opening the sluice-pipes?"

"Not in the least, but I think it is the engineer's business to give an order of that kind."

"But he is not here, and professional etiquette must give way where property and lives, perhaps, are at stake. To tell you the truth, Mr. Mountain, I have got the advice of an abler man than Mr. Tucker. His word to me was, 'If the water is as high as they say, don't waste time, but open the sluices at once and relieve the dam.'"

The workmen, who had said scarcely a word till then, raised an assenting murmur at the voice of common sense.

Mountain admitted it could do no harm, and gave an order accordingly; screws were applied and the valves of the double set of sluice-pipes were forced open, but with infinite difficulty, owing to the tremendous pressure of the water.

This operation showed all concerned what a giant they were dealing with : while the sluices were being lifted, the noise and tremor of the pipes were beyond experience and conception. When, after vast efforts, they were at last got open, the ground trembled violently, and the water, as it rushed out of the pipes, roared like discharges of artillery. So hard is it to resist the mere effect of the senses, that nearly every body ran back appalled, although the effect of all this roaring could only be to relieve the pressure : and, in fact, now that those sluices were opened, the dam was safe, provided it could last a day or two.

Lights were seen approaching, and Mr. Tucker, the resident engineer, drove up ; he had Mr. Carter, one of the contractors, in the gig with him.

He came on the embankment, and signified a cold approval of the sluices being opened.

Then Ransome sounded him about blowing up the waste-weir.

Tucker did not reply, but put some questions to a workman or two. Their answers showed that they considered the enlargement of the crack a fatal sign.

Upon this Mr. Tucker ordered them all to stand clear of the suspected part.

"Now, then," said he, "I built this embankment, and I'll tell you whether it is going to burst or not."

Then he took a lantern, and was going to inspect the crack himself ; but Mr. Carter, respecting his courage and coolness, would accompany him. They went to the crack, examined it carefully with their lanterns, and then crossed over to the waste-weir : no water was running into it in the ordinary way, which showed the dam was not full to its utmost capacity.

They returned, and consulted with Mountain. Ransome put in his word, and once more remembering Little's advice, begged them to blow up the waste-weir.

Tucker thought that was a stronger measure than the occasion required ; there was no immediate danger ; and the sluice-pipes would lower the water considerably in twenty-four hours.

Farmer Ives put in his word. "I can't learn from any of you that an enlarging crack in a new embankment is a common thing. I shall go home, but my boots won't come off this night."

Encouraged by this, Mr. Mountain, the contractor, spoke out.

"Mr. Tucker," said he, "don't deceive yourself ; the sluice-pipes are too slow ; if we don't relieve the dam, there'll be a blow-up in half an hour ; mark my words."

"Well," said Mr. Tucker, "no precaution has been neglected in building this dam ; provision has been made even for blowing up the waste-weir ; a hole has been built in the masonry, and there's dry powder and a fuse kept at the valve-house. I'll blow up the waste-weir, though I think it needless. I am convinced that crack is above the level of the water in the reservoir."

This observation struck Ransome, and he asked if it could not be ascertained by measurement.

"Of course it can," said Tucker, "and I'll measure it as I come back."

He then started for the weir, and Carter accompanied him.

They crossed the embankment, and got to the weir.

Ives went home, and the workmen withdrew to the side, not knowing exactly what might be the effect of the explosion.

By-and-by Ransome looked up, and observed a thin sheet of water beginning to stream over the centre of the embankment, and trickle down : the quantity was nothing ; but it alarmed him. Having no special knowledge on these matters, he was driven to comparisons ; and it flashed across him that, when he was a boy, and used to make little mud-dams in April, they would resist the tiny stream until it trickled over them, and from that moment their fate was sealed. Nature, he had observed, operates alike in small things and great, and that sheet of water, though thin as a wafer, alarmed him.

He thought it was better to give a false warning than withhold a true one : he ran to his horse, jumped on him, and spurred away.

His horse was fast and powerful, and carried him in three minutes back to Emden's farm. The farmer had gone to bed. Ransome knocked him up, and told him he feared the dam was going ; then galloped on to Hatfield Mill. Here he found the miller and his family all gathered outside, ready for a start ; one workman had run down from the reservoir.

"The embankment is not safe."

"So I hear. I'll take care of my flour and my folk. The mill will take care of herself." And he pointed with pride to the solid structure and granite pillars.

Ransome galloped on, shouting as he went.

The shout was taken up ahead, and he heard a voice crying in the night, "It's COMING ! It's COMING !" This weird cry, which, perhaps, his own galloping and shouting had excited, seemed like an independent warning, and thrilled him to the bone. He galloped through Hatfield, shouting "Save yourselves ! Save yourselves !" and the people poured out, and ran for high ground, shrieking wildly ; looking back, he saw the hill dotted with what he took for sheep at first, but it was the folk in their night-clothes.

He galloped on to Damflask, still shouting as he went.

At the edge of the hamlet, he found a cottage with no light in it ; he dismounted and thundered at the door. "Escape for your lives ! for your lives !"

A man called Hillsbro' Harry opened the window.

"The embankment is going. Fly for your lives !"

"Nay," said the man, coolly, "Ouseley dam will burst noane this week," and turned to go to bed again.

He found Joseph Galton and another man carrying Mrs. Galton and her new-born child away in a blanket. This poor woman, who had sent her five children away on the faith of a dream, was now objecting, in a faint voice, to be saved herself from evident danger. "Oh dear, dear ! you might as well let me go down with the flood as kill me with taking me away."

Such was the sapient discourse of Mrs. Galton, who, half an hour ago, had been supernaturally wise and prudent. Go to, wise mother and silly woman : men will love thee none the less for the inequalities of thine intellect ; and honest Joe will save thy life, and heed thy twaddle no more than the bleating of a lamb.

Ransome had not left the Galtons many yards

behind him, when there was a sharp explosion heard up in the hills.

Ransome pulled up and said aloud, "It will be all right now, thank goodness! they have blown up the weir."

The words were scarcely out of his mouth when he heard a loud sullen roar, speedily followed by a tremendous hiss, and a rumbling thunder, that shook the very earth where he stood, two miles distant.

This is what had taken place since he left the reservoir, but ten minutes ago:

Mr. Tucker and Mr. Carter laid the gunpowder and the train, and lighted the latter, and came back across the middle of the embankment.

Being quite safe here from the effect of the explosion, Mr. Tucker was desirous to establish by measurement that the water in the reservoir had not risen so high as the crack in the embankment.

With this view he took out a measure, and, at some risk of being swept into eternity, began coolly to measure the crack downwards.

At this very time water was trickling over; and that alarmed Carter, and he told Tucker they were trifling with their own lives.

"Oh," said Tucker, "that is only the spray from the waves."

They actually measured the crack, stooping over it with their lanterns.

When they had done that, Carter raised his head, and suddenly clutched Tucker by the arm and pointed upward. The water was pouring over the top, still in a thin sheet, but then that sheet was gradually widening. The water came down to their feet, and some of it disappeared in the crack; and the crack itself looked a little larger than when last inspected. Tucker said, gravely, "I don't like that: let me examine the valve-house at once." He got down to the valve-house, but before he could ascertain what quantity of water was escaping, Carter called to him, "Come out, for God's sake, or you are lost!"

He came running out, and saw an opening thirty feet wide and nearly a foot deep, and a powerful stream rushing over it.

The moment Tucker saw that, he cried, "It's all up, the embankment must go!" And, the feeling of the architect overpowering the instincts of the man, he stood aghast. But Carter laid hold of him, and dragged him away.

Then he came to himself, and they ran across the embankment.

As they started, the powder, which had hung fire unaccountably, went off, and blew up the waste-weir: but they scarcely heard it; for, as they ran, the rent above kept enlarging and deepening at a fearful rate, and the furious stream kept rushing past their flying heels, and threatened to sweep them sideways to destruction.

They were safe at last; but even as they stood panting, the rent in the top of the embankment spread—deepened—yawned terrifically—and the pent-up lake plunged through, and sweeping away at once the centre of the embankment, rushed, roaring and hissing, down the valley, an avalanche of water, whirling great trees up by the roots, and sweeping huge rocks away, and driving them, like corks, for miles.

At that appalling sound, that hissing thunder, the like of which he had never heard before, and hopes never to hear again, Ransome spurred away at all his speed, and warned the rest of the village with loud inarticulate cries: he could not wait to speak, nor was it necessary.

At the top of the hill he turned a moment, and looked up the valley; soon he saw a lofty white wall running down on Hatfield Mill: it struck the mill, and left nothing visible but the roof, surrounded by white foam.

Another moment, and he distinctly saw the mill swim a yard or two, then disappear and leave no trace, and on came the white wall, hissing and thundering.

Ransome uttered a cry of horror, and galloped madly forward, to save what lives he might.

Whenever he passed a house he shrieked his warning, but he never drew rein.

As he galloped along his mind worked. He observed the valley widen in places, and he hoped the flying lake would spread, and so lose some of that tremendous volume and force before which he had seen Hatfield stone mill go down.

With this hope he galloped on, and reached Poma Bridge, five miles and a half from the reservoir.

Here, to his dismay, he heard the hissing thunder sound as near to him as it was when he halted on the hill above Damflask: but he could see nothing, owing to a turn in the valley.

At the bridge itself he found a man standing without his hat, staring wildly up the valley.

He yelled to this man, "Dam is burst. Warn the village—for their lives—run on to Hillsborough—when you are winded, send another on. You'll all be paid at the Town Hall."

Then he dashed across the bridge.

As he crossed it, he caught sight of the flying lake once more: he had gone over more ground, but he had gone no farther. He saw the white wall strike Dolman's farm; there was a light in one window now. He saw the farm-house, with its one light, swim bodily, then melt and disappear, with all the poor souls in it.

He galloped on: his hat flew off: he came under the coiners' house, and yelled a warning. A window was opened, and a man looked out; the light was behind him, and, even in that terrible moment, he recognized—Shifty Dick.

"The flood! the flood! Fly! Get on high ground, for your lives!"

He galloped furiously, and made for Little's house.

CHAPTER XLIV.

LITTLE took a book, and tried to while away the time till Ransome's return; but he could not command his attention. The conversation about Grace had excited a topic which excluded every other.

He opened his window, a French casement, and looked out upon the night.

Then he observed that Grace, too, was keeping vigil; for a faint light shot from her window and sparkled on the branches of the plane-tree in her little front garden.

"And that," thought Henry, sadly, "is all I can see of her. Close to her, yet far off—farther than ever now."

A deep sadness fell on him, sadness and doubt.

Suppose he were to lay a trap for her to-morrow, and catch her at her own door! What good would it do? He put himself in her place. That process showed him at once she would come no more. He should destroy her little bit of patient, quiet happiness, the one daily sunbeam of her desolate life.

By-and-by, feeling rather drowsy, he lay down in his clothes to wait for Ransome's return. He put out his light.

From his bed he could see Grace's light kiss the plane-tree.

He lay and fixed his eyes on it, and thought of all that had passed between them: and, by-and-by, love and grief made his eyes misty, and that pale light seemed to dance and flicker before him.

About midnight, he was nearly dozing off, when his ear caught a muttering outside; he listened, and thought he heard some instrument grating below.

He rose very softly, and crept to the window, and looked keenly through his casement.

He saw nothing at first; but presently a dark object emerged from behind the plane-tree I have mentioned, and began to go slowly, but surely, up it.

Little feared it was a burglar about to attack that house which held his darling.

He stepped softly to his rifle, and loaded both barrels. It was a breech-loader. Then he crawled softly to the window, and peered out, rifle in hand.

The man had climbed the tree, and was looking earnestly in at one of the windows in Grace's house. His attention was so fixed that he never saw the gleaming eye which now watched him.

Presently the drifting clouds left the moon clear a minute, and Henry Little recognized the face of Frederick Coventry.

He looked at him and began to tremble.

Why did he tremble? Because — after the first rush of surprise — rage, hate, and bloody thoughts crossed his mind. Here was his enemy, the barrier to his happiness, come, of his own accord, to court his death. Why not take him for a burglar, and shoot him dead? Such an act might be blamed, but it could not be punished severely.

The temptation was so great, that the rifle shook in his hands, and a cold perspiration poured down his back.

He prayed to God in agony to relieve him from this temptation; he felt that it was more than he could bear.

He looked up. Coventry was drawing up a short iron ladder from below. He then got hold of it, and fixed it on the sill of Grace's window.

Little burst his own window open. "You villain!" he cried, and levelled his rifle at him.

Coventry uttered a yell of dismay. Grace opened her window, and looked out, with a face full of terror.

At sight of her, Coventry cried to her in abject terror, "Mercy! mercy! Don't let him shoot me!"

Grace looked round, and saw Henry aiming at Coventry.

She screamed, and Little lowered the rifle directly.

Coventry crouched directly in the fork of the tree.

Grace looked bewildered from one to the other; but it was to Henry she spoke, and asked him in trembling tones what it "all meant."

But, ere either could make a reply, a dire sound was heard of hissing thunder: so appalling that the three actors in this strange scene were all frozen and rooted where they stood.

Then came a fierce galloping, and Ransome, with his black hair and beard flying, and his face like a ghost, reined up, and shouted wildly, "Dam burst! Coming down here! Fly for your lives! Fly!"

He turned, and galloped up the hill.

Cole and his mate emerged, and followed him, howling; but before the other poor creatures, half paralyzed, could do any thing, the hissing thunder was upon them. What seemed a mountain of snow came rolling, and burst on them with terrific violence, whirling great trees and fragments of houses past with incredible velocity.

At the first blow, the house that stood nearest to the flying lake was shattered, and went to pieces soon after: all the houses quivered as the water rushed round them two stories high.

Little never expected to live another minute; yet, in that awful moment, his love cried firm. He screamed to Grace, "The houses must go!—the tree!—the tree!—get to the tree!"

But Grace, so weak at times, was more than mortal strong at that dread hour.

"What! live with him," she cried, "when I can die with you!"

She folded her arms, and her pale face was radiant—no hope, no fear.

Now came a higher wave, and the water reached above the window-sills of the bedroom floor and swept away the ladder; yet, driven forward like a cannon-bullet, did not yet pour into the bedrooms from the main stream; but by degrees the furious flood broke, melted, and swept away the intervening houses, and then hacked off the gable-end of Grace's house, as if Leviathan had bitten a piece out. Through that aperture the flood came straight in, levelled the partitions at a blow, rushed into the upper rooms with fearful roar, and then, rushing out again to rejoin the greater body of water, blew the front wall clean away, and swept Grace out into the raging current.

The water pouring out of the house carried her, at first, towards the tree, and Little cried wildly to Coventry to save her. He awoke from his stupor of horror, and made an attempt to clutch her; but then the main force of the mighty water drove her away from him towards the house; her helpless body was whirled round and round three times by the struggling eddies, and then hurried away like a feather by the overwhelming torrent.

CHAPTER XLV.

THE mighty reflux, which after a short struggle, overpowered the rush of water from the windows, and carried Grace Carden's helpless body away from the tree, drove her of course back towards the houses, and she was whirled passed Little's window with fearful velocity, just as he was going to leap into the flood, and perish in an insane attempt to save her. With a loud cry he seized her by her long floating hair, and tried to draw her in at the window; but the mighty water pulled her from him fiercely, and all but dragged him in after her; he was only saved by clutching the side of the wall with his left hand: the flood was like some vast solid body drawing against him; and terror began to seize on his heart. He ground his teeth; he set his knee against the horizontal projection of the window; and that freed his left hand; he suddenly seized her arm with it, and, clutching it violently, ground his teeth together, and, throwing himself backward with a jerk, tore her out of the water by an effort almost superhuman. Such was the force exerted by the torrent on one side, and the desperate lover on the other, that not her shoes only, but her stockings, though gartered, were torn off her in that fierce struggle.

He had her in his arms, and cried aloud, and sobbed over her, and kissed her wet cheeks, her lank hair, and her wet clothes, in a wild rapture. He went on kissing and sobbing over her so wildly and so long, that Coventry, who had at first exulted with him at her rescue, began to rage with jealousy.

"Please remember she is my wife," he shrieked: "don't take advantage of her condition, villain!"

"Your wife, you scoundrel! You stole her from me once; now come and take her from me again. Why didn't you save her? She was near to you. You let her die: she lives by me, and for me, and I for her." With this he kissed her again, and held her to his bosom. "D'ye see that?—liar! coward! villain!"

Even across that tremendous body of rushing death, from which neither was really safe, both rivals' eyes gleamed hate at each other.

The wild beasts that a flood drives together on to some little eminence, lay down their natures, and the panther crouches and whimpers beside the antelope; but these were men, and could entertain the fiercest of human passions in the very jaws of death.

To be sure, it was but for a moment; a new danger soon brought them both to their senses: an elm-tree whirling past grazed Coventry's plane-tree: it was but a graze, yet it nearly shook him off into the flood, and he yelled with fear: almost at the same moment a higher wave swept into Little's room, and the rising water set everything awash, and burst over him as he kneeled with Grace. He got up, drenched and half-blinded with the turbid water, and, taking Grace in his arms, waded waist-high to his bed, and laid her down on it.

It was a moment of despair. Death had entered that chamber in a new, unforeseen, and inevitable form. The ceiling was low, the water was rising steadily; the bedstead floated; his chest of drawers floated, though his rifle and pistols lay on it, and the top drawers were full of the tools he always had about him: in a few minutes the rising water must inevitably jam Grace and him against the ceiling, and drown them like rats in a hole.

Fearful as the situation was, a sickening horror was added to it by the horrible smell of the water; it had a foul and appalling odor, a compound of earthiness and putrescence; it smelt like a newly-opened grave; it paralyzed like a serpent's breath.

Stout as young Little's heart was, it fainted now when he saw his bedstead, and his drawers, and his chairs, all slowly rising towards the ceiling, lifted by that cold, putrescent, liquid death.

But all men, and even animals, possess greater powers of mind, as well as of body, than they ever exert, unless compelled by dire necessity: and it would have been strange indeed if a heart so stanch, and a brain so inventive, as Little's, had let his darling die like a rat drowned in a hole, without some new and masterly attempt first made to save her.

To that moment of horror and paralysis succeeded an activity of mind and body almost incredible. He waded to the drawers, took his rifle, and fired both barrels at one place in the ceiling, bursting a hole, and cutting a narrow joist almost in two. Then he opened a drawer, got an axe and a saw out, and tried to wade to the bed; but the water now took him off his feet, and he had to swim to it instead; he got on it, and with his axe and his saw he contrived to paddle the floating bed under the hole in the ceiling, and then with a few swift and powerful blows of his axe soon enlarged that aperture sufficiently; but at that moment the water carried the bedstead away from the place.

He set to work with his saw and axe, and paddled back again.

Grace, by this time, was up on her knees, and in a voice, the sudden firmness of which surprised and delighted him, asked if she could help.

"Yes," said he, "you can. On with my coat."

It lay on the bed. She helped him on with it, and then he put his axe and saw into the pockets, and told her to take hold of his skirt.

He drew himself up through the aperture, and Grace, holding his skirts with her hands and the bed with her feet, climbed adroitly on to the head of the bed—a French bed made of mahogany—and Henry drew her through the aperture.

They were now on the false ceiling, and nearly jammed against the roof; Little soon hacked a great hole in that just above the parapet, and they crawled out upon the gutter.

They were now nearly as high as Coventry on his tree; but their house was rocking, and his tree was firm.

In the next house were heard the despairing shrieks of poor creatures who saw no way of evading their fate; yet the way was as open to them as to this brave pair.

"Oh, my angel," said Grace, "save them. Then, if you die, you go to God."

"All right," said Henry. "Come on."

They darted down the gutter to the next house. Little hacked a hole in the slates, and then in the wood-work, and was about to jump in, when the house he had just left tumbled all to pieces like a house of sugar, and the *débris* went floating by, including the bedstead that had helped to save them.

"O God!" cried Little, "this house will go next; run on to the last one."

"No, Henry, I would rather die with you than live alone. Don't be frightened for me, my angel. Save lives, and trust to Jesus."

"All right," said Little; but his voice trembled now.

He jumped in, hacked a hole in the ceiling, and yelled to the inmates to give him their hands.

There was a loud cry of male and female voices.

"My child first," cried a woman, and threw up an infant, which Little caught and handed to Grace. She held it, wailing, to her breast.

Little dragged five more souls up. Grace helped them out, and they ran along the gutter to the last house without saying "Thank you."

The house was rocking. Little and Grace went on to the next, and he smashed the roof in, and then the ceiling, and Grace and he were getting the people out, when the house they had just left melted away, all but a chimney-stack, which adhered in jagged dilapidation to the house they were now upon.

They were now upon the last. Little hacked furiously through the roof and ceiling, and got the people out; and now twenty-seven souls crouched in the gutter, or hung about the roof of this one house; some praying, but most of them whining and wailing.

"What is the use howling?" groaned Little.

He then drew his Grace to his panting bosom, and his face was full of mortal agony.

She consoled him. "Never mind, my angel. God has seen you. He is good to us, and lets us die together."

At this moment the house gave a rock, and there was a fresh burst of wailing.

This, connected with his own fears, enraged Henry.

"Be quiet," said he, sternly. "Why can't you die decently, like your betters?"

Then he bent his head in noble silence over his beloved, and devoured her features as those he might never see again.

At this moment was heard a sound like the report of a gun; a large tree, whirled down by the flood, struck the plane-tree just below the fork, and cut it in two as promptly as a scythe would go through a carrot.

It drove the upper part along, and, going with it, kept it perpendicular for some time; the white face and glaring eyes of Frederick Coventry sailed past those despairing lovers; he made a wild clutch at them, then sank in the boiling current, and was hurried away.

This appalling incident silenced all who saw it, for a moment. Then they began to wail louder than ever.

But Little started to his feet, and cried "Hurrah!"

There was a general groan.

"Hold your tongues," he roared. "I've got good news for you. The water was over the top windows; now it is an inch lower. The reservoir must be empty by now. The water will go down as fast as it rose. Keep quiet for two minutes, and you will see."

Then no more was heard but the whimpering of the women, and, every now and then, the voice of Little; he hung over the parapet, and reported every half-minute the decline of the water; it subsided with strange rapidity, as he had foreseen.

In three minutes after he had noticed the first decline, he took Grace down through the roof, on the second floor.

When Grace and Henry got there, they started with dismay: the danger was not over: the front wall was blown clean out by the water; all but a jagged piece shaped like a crescent, and it seemed a miracle that the roof, thus weakened and crowded with human beings, had not fallen in.

"We must get out of this," said Little. "It all hangs together by a thread."

He called the others down from the roof, and tried to get down by the staircase, but it was broken into sections and floating about.

Then he cut into the floor near the wall, and, to his infinite surprise, found the first floor within four feet of him. The flood had lifted it bodily more than six feet.

He dropped on to it, and made Grace let herself down to him, he holding her round the waist, and landing her light as a feather.

Henry then hacked through the door, which was jammed tight; and, the water subsiding, presently the wrecks of the staircase left off floating, and stuck in the mud and water: by this means they managed to get down, and found themselves in a layer of mud, and stones, and *débris*, alive and dead, such as no imagination had hitherto conceived.

Dreading, however, to remain in a house so disembowelled within, and so shattered without, that it seemed to survive by mere cohesion of mortar, he begged Grace to put her arm round his neck, and then lifted her and carried her out into the night.

"Take me home to papa, my angel," said she.

He said he would; and tried to find his way to the road which he knew led up the hill to Woodbine Villa. But all landmarks were gone; houses, trees, hedges, all swept away; roads covered three feet thick with rocks, and stones, and bricks, and carcasses. The pleasant valley was one horrid quagmire, in which he could take few steps, burdened as he was, without sticking, or stumbling against some sure sign of destruction and death: within the compass of fifty yards he found a steam-boiler and its appurtenances (they must have weighed some tons, yet they had been driven more than a mile), and a dead cow, and the body of a wagon turned upside down: [the wheels of this same wagon were afterwards found fifteen miles from the body].

He began to stagger and pant.

"Let me walk, my angel," said Grace. "I'm not a baby."

She held his hand tight, and tried to walk with him step by step. Her white feet shone in the pale moonlight.

They made for rising ground, and were rewarded by finding the *débris* less massive.

"The flood must have been narrow hereabouts," said Henry. "We shall soon be clear of it, I hope."

Soon after this, they came under a short but sturdy oak that had survived; and, entangled in its close and crooked branches, was something white. They came nearer; it was a dead body: some poor man or woman hurried from sleep to eternity.

They shuddered and crawled on, still making for higher ground, but sore perplexed.

Presently they heard a sort of sigh. They went towards it, and found a poor horse stuck at an angle; his efforts to escape being marred by a heavy stone to which he was haltered.

Henry patted him, and encouraged him, and sawed through his halter; then he struggled up, but Henry held him, and put Grace on him. She sat across him and held on by the mane.

The horse, being left to himself, turned back a little, and crossed the quagmire till he got into a bridle-road, and this landed them high and dry on the turnpike.

Here they stopped, and, by one impulse, embraced each other, and thanked God for their wonderful escape.

But soon Henry's exultation took a turn that shocked Grace's religious sentiments, which recent acquaintance had strengthened.

"Yes," he cried, "now I believe that God really does interpose in earthly things; I believe every thing; yesterday I believed nothing. The one villain is swept away, and we two are miraculously saved. Now we can marry to-morrow—no, to-day, for it is past midnight. Oh, how good He is, especially for killing that scoundrel out of our way. Without his death, what was life worth to me? But now—oh, Heavens! is it all a dream? Hurrah! hurrah! hurrah!"

"Oh, Henry, my love!" said Grace imploringly; "pray, pray do not offend Him by rejoicing at such a moment over the death, perhaps the everlasting death, of a poor, sinful fellow-creature."

"All right, dearest. Only don't let us descend to hypocrisy. I thank Heaven he is dead, and so do you."

"Pray, don't *say* so."

"Well, I won't: let him go. Death settles all accounts. Did you see me stretch out my hand to save him?"

"I did, my angel, and it was like you: you are the noblest and the greatest creature that ever was, or ever will be."

"The silliest, you mean. I wondered at myself next minute. Fancy me being such an idiot as to hold out a hand to save him, and so wither both our lives—yours and mine; but I suppose it is against nature not to hold out a hand. Well, no harm came of it, thank Heaven!"

"Let us talk of yourselves," said Grace, lovingly. "My darling, let no harsh thought mar the joy of this hour. You have saved my life again. Well, then, it is doubly yours. Here, looking on that death we have just escaped, I devote myself to you. You don't know how I love you; but you shall. I adore you."

"I love you better still."

"You do not: you can't. It is the one thing I can beat you at, and I will."

"Try. When will you be mine?"

"I am yours. But if you mean when will I marry you, why, whenever you please. We have suffered too cruelly, and loved too dearly, for me to put you off a single day for affectations and vanities. When you please, my own."

At this Henry kissed her little white feet with rapture, and kept kissing them, at intervals, all the rest of the way: and the horrors of the night ended, to these two, in unutterable rapture, as they paced slowly along to Woodbine Villa with hearts full of wonder, gratitude, and joy.

Here they found lights burning, and learned from a servant that Mr. Carden was gone down to the scene of the flood in great agitation.

Henry told Grace not to worry herself, for that he would find him and relieve his fears.

He then made Grace promise to go to bed at once, and to lie within blankets. She didn't like that idea, but consented. "It is my duty to obey you now in every thing," said she.

Henry left her, and ran down to the Town Hall.

He was in that glorious state of bliss in which noble minds long to do good actions; and the obvious thing to do was to go and comfort the living survivors of the terrible disaster he had so narrowly escaped.

He found but one policeman there; the rest, and Ransome at their head, were doing their best, all but two, drowned on their beat in the very town of Hillsborough.

CHAPTER XLVI.

ROUND a great fire in the Town Hall were huddled a number of half-naked creatures, who had been driven out of their dilapidated homes; some of them had seen children or relatives perish in the flood they had themselves so narrowly escaped, and were bemoaning them with chattering teeth.

Little spoke them a word of comfort, promised them all clothes as soon as the shops should open, and hurried off to the lower part of the town in search of Ransom.

He soon found the line the flood had taken. Between Poma Bridge and Hillsborough it had wasted itself considerably in a broad valley, but still it had gone clean through Hillsborough twelve feet high, demolishing and drowning. Its terrible progress was marked by a layer of mud a foot thick, dotted with rocks, trees, wrecks of houses, machinery, furniture, barrels, mattresses, carcasses of animals, and dead bodies, most of them stark naked, the raging flood having torn their clothes off their backs.

Four corpses and two dead horses were lying in a lake of mud about the very door of the railway station; three of them were females in absolute nudity. The fourth was a male, with one stocking on. This proved to be Hillsbro' Harry, warned in vain up at Damflask. When he actually heard the flood come hissing, he had decided, on the whole, to dress, and had got the length of that one stocking, when the flying lake cut short his vegetation.

Not far from this, Little found Ransome, working like a horse, with the tear in his eye.

He uttered a shout of delight and surprise, and, taking Little by both shoulders, gazed earnestly at him, and said, "Can this be a living man I see?"

"Yes, I am alive," said Little, "but I had to work for it: feel my clothes."

"Why, they are dryer than mine."

"Aye; yet I have been in water to the throat; the heat of my body and my great exertions dried them. I'll tell you all another day; now show me how to do a bit of good; for it is not one nor two thousand pounds I'll stick at, this night."

"Come on."

Strange sights they saw that night. They found a dead body curled round the top frame of a lamp-post, and, in the suburbs, another jammed between a beam and the wall of a house.

They found some houses with the front wall carried clean away, and, on the second floor, such of the inmates as had survived huddled together in their night-clothes, unable to get down. These, Ransome and his men speedily relieved from their situation.

And now came in word that the whole village of Poma Bridge had been destroyed.

Little, with Ransome and his men, hurried on at these sad tidings as fast as the mud and ruins would allow, and on the way one of the policemen trod on something soft. It was the body of a woman, imbedded in the mud.

A little further they saw, at some distance, two cottages in a row, both gutted and emptied. An old man was alone in one, seated on the ground-floor in the deep mud.

They went to him, and asked what they could do for him.

" Do? Why, let me die," he said.

They tried to encourage him; but he answered them in words that showed how deeply old Shylock's speech is founded in nature:

" Let the water take me—it has taken all I had."

When they asked after his neighbors, he said he believed they were all drowned. Unluckily for *him*, he had been out when the flood came.

Little clambered into the other cottage, and found a little boy and girl placidly asleep in a cupboard up stairs.

Little yelled with delight, and kissed them, and cuddled them, as if they had been his own, so sweet was it to see their pretty innocent faces, spared by death. The boy kissed him in return, and told him the room had been full of water, and dada and mamma had gone out at the window, and they themselves had floated in the bed so high he had put his little sister on the top shelf, and got on it himself, and then they had both felt very sleepy.

" You are a dear good boy, and I take you into custody," said Ransome, in a broken voice.

Judge if this pair were petted, up at the Town Hall.

At Poma Bridge the devastation was horrible. The flood had bombarded a row of fifty houses, and demolished them so utterly that only one arch of one cellar remained ; the very foundations were torn up, and huge holes of incredible breadth and depth bored by the furious eddies.

Where were the inhabitants?

Ransome stood and looked, and shook like a man in an ague.

" Little," said he, " this is awful. Nobody in Hillsborough dreams the extent of this calamity. *I dread the dawn of day.* There must be scores of dead bodies hidden in this thick mud, or perhaps swept through Hillsborough into the very sea."

A little farther, and they came to the " Reindeer," where he had heard the boon-companions singing—over their graves ; for that night, long before the " cock did craw, or the day daw," their mouths were full of water and mud, and not the " barley bree."

To know their fate needed but a glance at the miserable, shattered, gutted fragment of the inn that stood. There was a chimney, a triangular piece of roof, a quarter of the inside of one second-floor room, with all the boards gone and half the joists gone, and the others either hanging down perpendicular or sticking up at an angle of forty-five. Even on the side farthest from the flood the water had hacked and ploughed away the wall so deeply, that the miserable wreck had a jagged waist, no bigger in proportion than a wasp's.

Not far from this amazing ruin was a little two-storied house, whose four rooms looked exactly as four rooms are represented in section on the stage, the front wall having been blown clean away, and the furniture and inmates swept out ; the very fender and fire-irons had been carried away ; a bird-cage, a clock, and a grate were left hanging to the three walls.

As a part of this village stood on high ground, the survivors were within reach of relief ; and Little gave a policeman orders to buy clothes at the shop, and have them charged to him.

This done, he begged Ransome to cross the water, and relieve the poor wretches who had escaped so narrowly with him. Ransome consented at once ; but then came a difficulty—the bridge, like every bridge that the flying lake had struck, was swept away. However, the stream was narrow, and, as they were already muddy to the knee, they found a place where the miscellaneous ruin made stepping-stones, and by passing first on to a piece of masonry, and from that to a broken water-wheel, and then on to a rock, they got across.

They passed the coiner's house. It stood on rather high ground, and had got off cheap. The water had merely carried away the doors and windows, and washed every movable out of it.

Ransome sighed. " Poor Shifty!" said he ; " you'll never play us another trick. What an end for a man of your abilities!"

And now the day began to dawn, and that was fortunate, for otherwise they could hardly have found the house they were going to.

On the way to it they came on two dead bodies, an old man of eighty and a child scarce a week old. One fate had united these extremes of human life, the ripe sheaf and the spring bud. It transpired afterwards that they had been drowned in different parishes. Death, that brought these together, disunited hundreds. Poor Dolman's body was found scarce a mile from his house, but his wife's eleven miles on the other side of Hillsborough ; and this wide separation of those who died in one place by one death, was constant, and a pitiable feature of the tragedy.

At last they got to the house, and Little shuddered at the sight of it ; here not only was the whole front wall taken out, but a part of the back wall ; the jagged chimneys of the next house still clung to this miserable shell, whose upper floors were slanting sieves, and on its lower was a deep layer of mud, with the carcass of a huge sow lying on it, washed in there all the way from Hatfield village.

The people had all run away from the house, and no wonder, for it seemed incredible that it could stand a single moment longer ; never had ruin come so close to demolition and then stopped.

There was nothing to be done here, and Ransome went back to Hillsborough, keeping this side the water.

Daybreak realized his worst fears: between Poma Bridge and the first suburb of Hillsborough the place was like a battle-field ; not that many had been drowned on the spot, but that, drowned all up the valley by the flood at its highest, they had been brought down and deposited in the thick layer of mud left by the abating waters.

Some were cruelly gashed and mangled by the hard objects with which they had come in contact.

Others wore a peaceful expression and had color in their cheeks. One drew tears from both these valiant men. It was a lovely little girl, with her little hands before her face to keep out the sight of death.

Here and there, a hand or a ghastly face appearing above the mud showed how many must be hidden altogether, and Ransome hurried home to get more assistance to disinter the dead.

Just before the suburb of Allerton the ground is a dead flat, and here the flying lake had covered a space a mile broad, doing frightful damage to property but not much to life, because wherever it expanded it shallowed in proportion.

In part of this flat a gentleman had a beautiful garden and pleasure-grounds over night: they were now under water, and their appearance was incredible; the flood expanding here and then contracting, had grounded large objects and left small ones floating. In one part of the garden it had landed a large wheat-rick, which now stood as if it belonged there, though it had been built five miles off.

In another part was an inverted summer-house and a huge water-wheel, both of them great travellers that night.

In the large fish-pond, now much fuller than usual, floated a wheel-barrow, a hair mattress, an old wooden cradle, and an enormous box or chest.

Little went splashing through the water to examine the cradle : he was richly rewarded. He found a little child in it awake but perfectly happy, and enjoying the fluttering birds above and the buoyant bed below, whose treacherous nature was unknown to him. This incident the genius of my friend Mr. Millais is about to render immortal.

Little's shout of delight brought Ransome splashing over directly.

They took up the cradle and contents to carry it home, when all of a sudden Ransome's eye detected a finger protruding through a hole in the box.

"Hallo!" said he. "Why, there's a body inside that box!"

"Good heavens!" said Little, "he may be alive."

With that he made a rush and went in over head and ears.

"Confound it !" said he as soon as he got his breath. But, being in for it now, he swam to the box, and, getting behind it, shoved it before him to Ransome's feet.

Ransome tried to open it, but it shut with a spring. However, there were air-holes, and still this finger sticking out of one—for a signal, no doubt.

"Are ye alive or dead?" shouted Ransome to the box.

"Let me out and you'll see," replied the box; and the sound seemed to issue from the bowels of the earth.

Little had his hatchet in his pocket and set to work to try and open it. The occupant assisted him with advice how to proceed, all of which sounded subterranean.

"Hold your jaw," said Little. "Do you think you can teach me?"

By a considerable exertion of strength as well as skill, he at last got the box open, and discovered the occupant seated pale and chattering, with knees tucked up.

The two men lent him a hand to help him up ; Ransome gave a slight start, and then expressed the warmest satisfaction.

"Thank Heaven !" said he. "Shake hands, old fellow. I'm downright glad. I've been groaning over you ; but I might have known you'd find some way to slip out of trouble. Mr. Little, this is Shifty himself. Please put your arm under his ; he is as strong as iron, and as slippery as an eel."

The Shifty, hearing this account given of himself, instantly collapsed, and made himself weak as water, and tottered from one of his guards to the other in turn.

"I was all that once, Mr. Ransome," said he, in a voice that became suddenly as feeble as his body, "but this fearful night has changed me. Miraculously preserved from destruction, I have renounced my errors, and vowed to lead a new life. Conduct me at once to a clergyman, that I may confess and repent, and disown my past life with horror ; then swear me in a special constable, and let me have the honor of acting under your orders, and of co-operating with you, sir " (to Little), "in your Christian and charitable acts. Let me go about with you, gentlemen, and relieve the sufferings of others, as you have relieved mine."

"There !" said Ransome, proudly ; "there's a man for you. He knows every move of the game—can patter like an archbishop." So saying, he handcuffed the Shifty with such enthusiasm that the convert swore a horrible oath at him.

Ransome apologized, and beckoning a constable, handed him the Shifty.

"Take him to the Town Hall, and give him every comfort. He is Number One."

This man's escape was not so strange as it appeared. The flood never bombarded his house —he was only on the hem of it. It rose and filled his house, whereupon he bored three holes in his great chest, and got in. He washed about the room till the abating flood contracted, and then it sucked him and his box out of the window. He got frightened, and let the lid down, and so drifted about till at last he floated into the hands of justice.

Little and Ransome carried the child away, and it was conveyed to the hospital and a healthy nurse assigned it.

Ransome prevailed on Little to go home, change his wet clothes and lie down for an hour or two. He consented, but first gave Ransome an order to lay out a thousand pounds, at his expense, in relief of the sufferers.

Then he went home, sent a message to Raby Hall that he was all right, took off his clothes, rolled exhausted into bed, and slept till the afternoon.

At four o'clock he rose, got into a hansom, and drove up to Woodbine Villa, the happiest man in England.

He inquired for Miss Carden. The man said he believed she was not up, but would inquire.

"Do," said Little. "Tell her who it is. I'll wait in the dining-room."

He walked into the dining-room before the man could object, and there he found a sick gentleman, with Dr. Amboyne and a surgeon examining him. The patient lay on a sofa, extremely pale, and groaning with pain.

One glance sufficed. It was Frederick Coventry.

CHAPTER XLVII.

"WHAT! you alive?" said Little, staring.

"Alive, and that is all," said Coventry. "Pray excuse me for not dying to please you."

Ere Little could reply, Mr. Carden, who had heard of his arrival, looked in from the library, and beckoned him in.

When they were alone, he began by giving the young man his hand, and then thanked him warmly for his daughter. "You have shown yourself a hero in courage. Now go one step farther; be a hero in fortitude and self-denial; that unhappy man in the next room is her husband; like you, he risked his life to save her. He tells me he heard the dam was going to burst, and came instantly with a ladder, to rescue her. He was less fortunate than you, and failed to rescue her; less fortunate than you, again, it has received a mortal injury in that attempt. It was I who found him; I went down, distracted with anxiety, to look for my daughter; I found this poor creature jammed tight between the tree he was upon and a quantity of heavy timber that had accumulated and rested against a bank. We released him with great difficulty. It was a long time before he could speak; and then, his first inquiry was after *her*. Show some pity for an erring man, Mr. Little; some consideration for my daughter's reputation. Let him die in peace; his spine is broken; he can't live many days."

Little heard all this, and looked down on the ground for some time in silence. At last he said firmly, "Mr. Carden, I would not be inhuman to a dying man; but you were always his friend, and never mine. Let me see *her*, and I'll tell her what you say, and take her advice."

"You shall see her, of course; but not just now. She is in bed, attended by a Sister of Charity, whom she telegraphed for."

"Can I see that lady?"

"Certainly."

Sister Gratiosa was sent for, and, in reply to Little's anxious inquiries, told him that Sister Amata had been very much shaken by the terrible events of the night, and absolute repose was necessary to her. In further conversation she told him she was aware of Sister Amata's unhappy story, and had approved her retirement from Hillsborough, under all the circumstances; but that now, after much prayer to God for enlightenment, she could not but think it was the Sister's duty, as a Christian woman, to stay at home and nurse the afflicted man whose name she bore, and above all devote herself to his spiritual welfare.

"Oh, that is your notion, is it?" said Henry. "Then you are no friend of mine."

"I am no enemy of yours, nor of any man, I hope. May I ask you one question, without offense?"

"Certainly."

"Have you prayed to God to guide you in this difficulty?"

"No."

"Then seek his throne without delay; and, until you have done so, do not rashly condemn my views of this matter, since I have sought for wisdom where alone it is to be found."

Henry chafed under this; but he commanded his temper, though with difficulty, and said, "Will you take a line to her from me?"

The Sister hesitated. "I don't know whether I ought," said she.

"Oh, then the old game of intercepting letters is to be played."

"Not by me: after prayer I shall be able to say Yes or No to your request. At present, being at a distance from my Superior, I must needs hesitate."

"Right and wrong must have made very little impression on your mind, if you don't know whether you ought to take a letter to a woman, from a man who has just saved her life, or not."

The lady colored highly, courtesied, and retired without a word.

Little knew enough of human nature to see that the Sister would not pray against feminine spite: he had now a dangerous enemy in the house, and foresaw that Grace would be steadily worked on through her religious sentiments.

He went away, sick with disappointment, jealousy, and misgivings, hired a carriage, and drove at once to Raby Hall.

CHAPTER XLVIII.

MRS. LITTLE saw her son arrive, met him in the hall, and embraced him, with a great cry of maternal joy, that did her heart good for a moment.

He had to tell her all; and, during the recital, she often clasped him to her bosom.

When he had told her all, she said: "Much as I love you, darling, I am ready to part with you for your good: there is a cure for all your griefs: there is a better woman in this house than ever Grace Carden was or will be. Be a man; shake off these miserable trammels; leave that vacillating girl to nurse her villain, and marry the one I have chosen for you."

Henry shook his head. "What! when a few months perhaps will free my Grace from her incumbrance? Mother, you are giving me bad advice, for once."

"Unwelcome advice, dear, not bad. Will you consult Dr. Amboyne? he sleeps here to-night. He often comes here now, you know." Then the widow colored just a little.

"Oh yes, I know; and I approve."

Doctor Amboyne came to dinner. In the course of the evening he mentioned his patient Coventry, and said he would never walk again, his spine was too seriously injured.

"How soon will he die? that is what I want to know," said Henry, with that excessive candor which the polite reader has long ago discovered in him, and been shocked.

"Oh, he may live for years. But what a life! An inert mass below the waist, and, above it, a sick heart, and a brain as sensitive as ever to realize the horrid calamity. Even I, who know and abhor the man's crimes, shudder at the punishment Heaven inflicts on him."

There was dead silence round the table, and Little was observed to turn pale.

He was gloomy and silent all the evening.

Next morning, directly after breakfast, his mother got him, and implored him not to waste his youth any longer.

"The man will never die," said she: "he will wear you out. You have great energy and courage; but you have not a woman's humble patience, to go on, year after year, waiting for an event you can not hasten by a single moment. Do you not see it is hopeless? End your misery by one brave plunge. Speak to dear Jael."

"I can't—I can't!"

"Then let me."

"Will it make you happy?"

"Very happy. Nothing else can."

"Will it make her happy?"

"As happy as a queen."

"She deserves a better fate."

"She asks no better. There, unless you stop me, I shall speak to her."

"Well, well," said Henry, very wearily.

Mrs. Little went to the door.

"Wait a moment," said he. "How about Uncle Raby? He has been a good friend to me. I have offended him once, and it was the worst job I ever did. I won't offend him again."

"How can you offend him by marrying Jael?"

"What, have you forgotten how angry he was when Mr. Richard Raby proposed to her? There, I'll go and speak to him."

"Well, do."

He was no sooner gone than Mrs. Little stepped into Jael's room, and told her how matters stood.

Jael looked dismayed, and begged her on no account to proceed: "For," said she, "if Mr. Henry was to ask me, I should say No. He would always be hankering after Miss Carden: and, pray don't be angry with me, but I think I'm worth a man's whole heart; for I could love one very dearly, if he loved me."

Mrs. Little was deeply mortified. "This I did *not* expect," said she. "Well, if you are all determined to be miserable—*be*."

Henry hunted up Mr. Raby, and asked him bluntly whether he would like him to marry Jael Dence.

Raby made no reply for some time, and his features worked strangely.

"Has she consented to be your wife?"

"I have never asked her. But I will, if you wish it."

"Wish it?"

"Why, sir, if you don't wish it, please forbid it, and let us say no more at all about it."

"Excuse me," said Raby, with his grandest air: "a gentleman may dislike a thing, yet not condescend to forbid it."

"That is true, sir; and an ex-workman may appreciate his delicacy, and give the thing up at once. I will die a bachelor."

"Henry, my boy, give me your hand—I'll tell you the truth. I love her myself. She is a pattern of all I admire in woman."

"Uncle, I suspected this, to tell the truth. Well, if you love her—marry her."

"What, without her consent?"

"Oh, she will consent. Order her to marry you; she will never disobey the Lord of the Manor."

"That is what I fear: and it is base to take advantage of her in that way."

"You are right, sir," said Henry, and ran off directly.

He found Jael, and said, "Jael, dear, couldn't you like Uncle Raby? he loves you dearly."

He then appealed to her heart, and spoke of his uncle's nobleness in fearing to obtain an unfair advantage over her.

To his surprise, Jael blushed deeply, and her face softened angelically, and presently a tear ran down it.

"Hallo!" said Henry. "That is the game, is it? You stay here."

He ran back to Mr. Raby, and said: "I've made a discovery. She loves you, sir. I'll take my oath of it. You go and ask her."

"I will," said Raby; and he went to Jael, like a man, and said, "Jael, he has found me out; I love you dearly. I'm old, but I'm not cold. Do you think you could be happy as my wife, with all the young fellows admiring you?"

"Sir," said Jael, "I wouldn't give your little finger for all the young men in Christendom. Once I thought a little too much of Mr. Henry, but that was over long ago. And since you saved my life, and cried over me in this very room, you have been in my head, and in my heart; but I wouldn't show it; for I had vowed I never would let any man know my heart till he showed me his."

In short, this pair were soon afterwards seen walking arm in arm, radiant with happiness.

That sight was too much for Henry Little. The excitement of doing a kind thing, and making two benefactors happy, had borne him up till now; but the reaction came: the contrast of their happiness with his misery was too poignant. He had not even courage to bid them good-bye, but fled back to Hillsborough, in anguish of spirit and deep despair.

When he got home, there was a note from Grace Carden.

"MY OWN DEAREST HENRY,—I find that you have called, and been denied me; and that Mr. Coventry has been admitted into the house.

"I have therefore left Woodbine Villa, and taken lodgings opposite. Sister Gratiosa has convinced me I ought to labor for the eternal welfare of the guilty, unhappy man whose name it is my misfortune to bear. I will try to do so: but nobody shall either compel, nor persuade, me to be cruel to my dear Henry, to whom I owe my life once more, and who is all the world to me. I shall now be employed nearly all the day, but I reserve two hours, from three till five, when you will always find me at home. Our course is clear. We must pray for patience.

"Yours to eternity, GRACE."

After reading this letter, and pondering it well, Henry Little's fortitude revived, and, as he could not speak his mind to Grace at that moment, he wrote to her, after some hours of reflection, as follows:

"MY OWN DEAREST GRACE, —I approve, I bless you. Our case is hard, but not desperate.

We have been worse off than we are now. I agree with you that our course is clear; what we have got to do, as I understand it, is to outlive a crippled scoundrel. Well, love and a clear conscience will surely enable us to outlive a villain whose spine is injured, and whose conscience must gnaw him, and who has no creature's love to nourish him. Yours in this world, and, I hope, in the next, HENRY."

Sister Gratiosa, to oblige Grace, staid at Woodbine Villa. She was always present at any interview of Coventry and Grace.

Little softened her by giving her money whenever she mentioned a case of distress. She had but this one pleasure in life, a pure one, and her poverty had always curbed it hard. She began to pity this poor sinner, who was ready to pour his income into her lap for Christian purposes.

And so the days rolled on. Raby took into his head to repair the old church, and be married in it. This crotchet postponed his happiness for some months.

But the days and weeks rolled on.

Raby became Sheriff of the county.

Coventry got a little better, and moved to the next villa.

Then Grace returned at once to Woodbine Villa; but she still paid charitable visits with Sister Gratiosa to the wreck whose name she bore.

She was patient.

But Little, the man of action, began to faint. He decided to return to the United States for a year or two, and distract his mind.

When he communicated this resolve, Grace sighed.

"The last visit there was disastrous," said she. "But," recovering herself, "we can not be deceived again, nor doubt each other's constancy again." So she sighed, but consented.

Coventry heard of it, and chuckled inwardly. He felt sure that in time he should wear out his rival's patience.

A week or two more, and Little named the very day for sailing.

The Assizes came on. The Sheriff met the Judges with great pomp, and certain observances which had gone out. This pleased the Chief Justice: he had felt a little nervous; Raby's predecessor had met him in a carriage and pair and no outriders, and he had felt it his duty to fine the said Sheriff £100 for so disrespecting the Crown in his person.

So now, alluding to this, he said "Mr. Sheriff, I am glad to find you hold by old customs, and do not grudge outward observances to the Queen's justices."

"My lord," said the Sheriff, "I can hardly show enough respect to justice and learning, when they visit us in the name of my sovereign."

"That is very well said, Mr. Sheriff," said my lord.

The Sheriff bowed.

The Chief Justice was so pleased with his appearance, and his respectful yet dignified manner, that he conversed with him repeatedly during the pauses of the trials.

Little was cording his boxes for America when Ransome burst in on him, and said, "Come into court; come into court. Shifty Dick will be up directly."

Little objected that he was busy; but Ransome looked so mortified that he consented, and was just in time to see Richard Martin, alias Lord Daventree, alias Tom Paine, alias Sir Henry Gulstone, alias the Quaker, alias Shifty Dick, etc., etc., appear at the bar.

The indictment was large, and charged the prisoner with various frauds of a felonious character, including his two frauds on the Gosshawk.

Counsel made a brief exposition of the facts, and then went into the evidence. But here the strict, or, as some think, pedantic rules of English evidence, befriended the prisoner, and the Judge objected to certain testimony on which the prosecution had mainly relied. As for the evidence of coining, the flood had swept all that away.

Ransome, who was eager for a conviction, began to look blue.

But presently a policeman, who had been watching the prisoner, came and whispered in his ear.

Up started Ransome, wrote the Crown solicitor a line, begging him to keep the case on its legs any how for half an hour, and giving his reason. He then dashed off in a cab.

The case proceeded, under discouraging remarks from the Judge, most of them addressed to the evidence; but he also hinted that the indictment was rather loosely drawn.

At last the Attorney-General, who led, began to consult with his junior whether they could hope for a conviction.

But now there was a commotion; then heads were put together, and, to the inexpressible surprise of young Little and of the Sheriff, Grace Coventry was put into the witness-box.

At the sight of her the learned Judge, who was, like most really great lawyers, a keen admirer of beautiful women, woke up and became interested.

After the usual preliminaries, counsel requested her to look at that man, and say whether she knew him.

Grace looked, and recognized him. "Yes," said she, "it is Mr. Beresford: he is a clergyman."

Whereupon there was a loud laugh.

Counsel. "What makes you think he is a clergyman?"

Witness. "I have seen him officiate. It was he who married me to Mr.—" Here she caught sight of Henry, and stopped, blushing.

"What is that?" said the Judge, keenly. "Did you say that man performed the marriage ceremony over you?"

"Yes, my lord."

"When and where was that?"

She gave the time and place.

"I should like to see the register of that parish."

"Let me save you the trouble," said the prisoner. "Your lordship's time has been wasted enough with falsehoods: I will not waste it further by denying the truth. The fact is, my lord, I was always a great church-goer (a laugh), and I was disgusted with the way in which the clergy deliver the Liturgy, and with their hollow discourses, that don't go home to men's bosoms. Vanity whispered, 'You could do better.' I applied for the curacy of St. Peter's. I obtained it. I gave universal satisfaction; and no wonder;

my heart was in the work; I trembled at the responsibility I had undertaken. Yes, my lord, I united that young lady in holy matrimony to one Frederick Coventry. I had no sooner done it, than I began to realize that a clergyman is something more than a reader and a preacher. Remorse seized me. My penitence, once awakened, was sincere. I retired from the sacred office I had usurped—with much levity, I own, but, as heaven is my witness, with no guilty intent."

The Judge, to Grace. "Did you ever see the prisoner on any other occasion?"

Grace. "Only once. He called on me after my marriage. He left the town soon after."

The Judge then turned to Grace, and said, with considerable feeling, "It would be unkind to disguise the truth from you. You must petition Parliament to sanction this marriage by a distinct enactment; it is the invariable course, and Parliament has never refused to make these marriages binding. Until then, pray understand that you are Miss Carden and not Mrs. Coventry."

The witness clasped her hands above her head, uttered a loud scream of joy, and was removed all but insensible from the box.

The Judge looked amazed. The Sheriff whispered, "Her husband is a greater scoundrel than this prisoner."

Soon after this the Judge withdrew to luncheon, and took the Sheriff along with him. "Mr. Sheriff," said he, "you said something to me in court I hardly understood."

Then Raby gave the Judge a brief outline of the whole story, and, in a voice full of emotion, asked his advice.

The Judge smiled at this bit of simplicity; but his heart had been touched, and he had taken a fancy to Raby. "Mr. Sheriff," said he, "etiquette forbids me to advise you—"

"I am sorry for that, my lord."

"But humanity suggests— Tell me, now, does this Coventry hold to her? Will he petition Parliament?"

"It is very possible, my lord."

"Humph! Get a special license, and marry Grace Carden to Henry Little, and have the marriage consummated. Don't lose a day, nor an hour. I will not detain you, Mr. Sheriff."

Raby took the hint, and soon found Henry, and told him the advice he had got. He set him to work to get the license, and, being resolved to stand no nonsense, he drove to Grace, and invited her to Raby Hall. "I am to be married this week," said he, "and you must be at the wedding."

Grace thought he would be hurt if she refused, so she colored a little, but consented.

She packed up, with many a deep sigh, things fit for a wedding, and Raby drove her home. He saw her to her room, and then had a conversation with Mrs. Little, the result of which was that Henry's mother received her with well-feigned cordiality.

Next day Henry came to dinner, and, after dinner, the lovers were left alone. This, too, had been arranged beforehand.

Henry told her he was going to ask her a great favor; would she consider all they had suffered, and, laying aside childish delays, be married to him in the old church to-morrow, along with Mr. Raby and Jael Dence?

Oh, then she trembled, and blushed, and hesitated; and faltered out, "What! all in a moment like that? what would your mother think of me?"

Henry ran for his mother, and brought her into the room.

"Mother," said he, "Grace wants to know what you will think of her, if she should lay aside humbug and marry me to-morrow."

Mrs. Little replied, "I shall say, here is a dear child, who has seen what misery may spring from delay, and so now she will not coquette with her own happiness, nor trifle with yours."

"No, no," said Grace: "only tell me you will forgive my folly, and love me as your child."

Mrs. Little caught her in her arms, and, in that attitude, Grace gave her hand to Henry, and whispered "Yes."

Next day, at eleven o'clock, the two couples went to the old church, and walked up the aisle to the altar. Grace looked all around. Raby had effaced every trace of Henry's sacrilege from the building; but not from the heart of her whose life he had saved on that very spot.

She stood at the altar, weeping at the recollections the place revived, but they were tears of joy. The parson of the parish, a white-haired old man, the model of a pastor, married the two couples according to the law of England.

Raby took his wife home, *more majorum.* Little whirled his prize off to Scotland, and human felicity has seldom equalled his and his bride's.

Yet, in the rapture of conjugal bliss, she did not forget duty and filial affection. She wrote a long and tender letter to her father, telling him how it all happened, and hoping that she should soon be settled, and then he would come and live with her and her adored husband.

Mr. Carden was delighted with this letter, which, indeed, was one gush of love and happiness. He told Coventry what had taken place, and counselled patience.

Coventry broke out into curses. He made wonderful efforts for a man in his condition; he got lawyers to prepare a petition to Parliament; he had the register inspected, and found that the Shifty had married two poor couples; he bribed them to join in his petition, and inserted in it that, in consideration of this marriage, he had settled a certain farm and buildings on his wife for her separate use, and on her heirs forever.

The petition was read in Parliament, and no objection taken. It was considered a matter of course.

But, a few days afterwards, one of the lawyers in the House, primed by a person whose name I am not free to mention, recurred to the subject, and said that, as regarded one of these couples, too partial a statement had been laid before the house; he was credibly informed that the parties had separated immediately after the ceremony, and that the bride had since been married, according to law, to a gentleman who possessed her affections, and had lived with him ever since the said marriage.

On this another lawyer got up, and said that "if that was so, the petition must be abandoned. Parliament was humane, and would protect an illegal marriage *per se,* but not an illegal marriage competing with a legal one. That would be to tamper with the law of England, and, indeed, with morality; would compel a woman to adultery in her own despite."

This proved a knock-down blow; and the petition was dropped, as respected Frederick Coventry and Grace Little.

Coventry's farm was returned to him, and the settlement cancelled.

Little sent Ransome to him with certain memoranda, and warned him to keep quiet, or he would be indicted for felony.

He groaned, and submitted.

He lives still, to expiate his crimes.

While I write these lines, there still stands at Poma Bridge one disembowelled house, to mark that terrible flood : and, even so, this human survivor lives a wreck. "Below the waist an inert mass; above it, a raging, impotent, despairing criminal." He often prays for death. Since he can pray for any thing, let us hope he will one day pray for penitence, and life everlasting.

Little built a house in the suburbs leading to Raby Hall. There is a forge in the yard, in which the inventor perfects his inventions with his own hand. He is a wealthy man, and will be wealthier, for he lives prudently and is never idle.

Mr. Carden lives with him. Little is too happy with Grace to bear malice against her father.

Grace is lovelier than ever, and blissfully happy in the husband she adores, and two lovely children.

Guy Raby no longer calls life one disappointment; he has a loving and prudent wife, and loves her as she deserves; his olive branches are rising fast around him; and as sometimes happens to a Benedict of his age, who has lived soberly, he looks younger, feels younger, talks younger, behaves younger, than he did ten years before he married. He is quite unconscious that he has departed from his favorite theories, in wedding a yeoman's daughter. On the contrary, he believes he has acted on a system, and crossed the breed so judiciously as to attain greater physical perfection by means of a herculean dam, yet retain that *avitam fidem*, or traditional loyalty, which (to use his own words) " is born both in Rabys and Dences, as surely as a high-bred setter comes into the world with a nose for game."

Mrs. Little has rewarded Doctor Amboyne's patience and constancy. They have no children of their own, so they claim all the young Littles and Rabys, present and to come; and the Doctor has bound both the young women by a solemn vow to teach them, at an early age, the art of putting themselves into his place, her place, their place. He has convinced these young mothers that the " great transmigratory art," although it comes of itself only to a few superior minds, can be taught to vast numbers; and he declares that, were it to be taught as generally as reading and writing, that teaching alone would quadruple the intelligence of mankind, and go far to double its virtue.

But time flies, and space contracts : the words and the deeds of Amboyne are they not written in the Amboyniana ?

One foggy night, the house of a non-Union fender-grinder was blown up with gunpowder, and not the workman only—the mildest and most inoffensive man I ever talked with—but certain harmless women and innocent children, who had done nothing to offend the Union, were all but destroyed. The same barbarous act had been committed more than once before, and with more bloody results, but had led to no large consequences—*carebat quia vate sacro ;* but this time there happened to be a *vates* in the place, to wit, an honest, intrepid journalist, with a mind in advance of his age. He came, he looked, he spoke to the poor shaken creatures—one of them shaken for life, and doomed now to start from sleep at every little sound till she sleeps forever—and the blood in his brave heart boiled. The felony was publicly reprobated, and with horror, by the Union, which had, nevertheless, hired the assassins ; but this well-worn lie did not impose on the *vates,* or chronicler ahead of his time. He went round to all the manufacturers, and asked them to speak out. They durst not for their lives ; but closed all doors, and then, with bated breath, and all the mien of slaves well trodden down, hinted where information might be had. Thereupon the *vates* aforesaid—Holdfast yclept—went from scent to scent, till he dropped on a discontented grinder, with fish-like eyes, who had been in "many a night job." This man agreed to split, on two conditions : he was to receive a sum of money, and to be sent into another hemisphere, since his life would not be worth a straw, if he told the truth about the Trades in this one. His terms were accepted, and then he made some tremendous revelations ; and, with these in his possession, Holdfast wrote leader upon leader, to prove that the Unions must have been guilty of every Trade outrage that had taken place for years in the district ; but adroitly concealing that he had positive information.

Grotait replied incautiously, and got worsted before the public. The ablest men, if not writers, are unwise to fence with writers.

Holdfast received phonetic letters threatening his life; he acknowledged them in his journal, and invited the writers to call.

He loaded a revolver and went on writing the leaders with a finger on the trigger. *California!* Oh dear no, the very centre of England.

Ransome co-operated with him and collected further evidence, and then Holdfast communicated privately with a portion of the London press, and begged them to assist him to obtain a Royal Commission of inquiry, in which case he pledged himself to prove that a whole string of murders and outrages had been ordered and paid for by the very Unions which had publicly repudiated them in eloquent terms, and been believed.

The London press took this up ; two or three members of the House of Commons, wild, eccentric men, who would not betray their country to secure their re-election to some dirty borough, sided with outraged law ; and by these united efforts a Commission was obtained. The Commission sat, and, being conducted with rare skill and determination, squeezed out of an incredible mass of perjury some terrible truths, whose discovery drew eloquent leaders from the journals ; these filled simple men, who love their country, with the hope that the Government of this nation would shake off its lethargy, and take stringent measures to defend the liberty of the subject against so cruel and cowardly a conspiracy, and to deprive the workmen, in their differences with the masters, of an unfair and sanguinary weapon, which the masters could use, but never have *as yet;* and, by using which, the workmen do themselves no lasting good, and, indeed, have driven whole trades and much capital out of the oppressed districts, to their own great loss.

That hope, though not extinct, is fainter now than it was. Matters seem going all the other way. An honest, independent man, who did honor to the Senate, has lost his seat solely for not conniving at these Trade outrages, which the hypocrites, who have voted him out, pretend to denounce. Foul play is still rampant and triumphant. Its victims were sympathized with for one short day, when they bared their wounds to the Royal Commissioners; but that sympathy has deserted them: they are now hidden in holes and corners from their oppressors, and have to go by false names, and are kept out of work; for *odisse quem læseris* is the fundamental maxim of their oppressors. Not so the assassins; they flourish. I have seen with these eyes one savage murderer employed at high wages, while a man he all but destroyed is refused work on all hands, and was separated by dire poverty from another scarred victim, his wife, till I brought them together. Again, I have seen a wholesale murderer employed on the very machine he had been concerned in blowing up, employed on it at the wages of three innoxious curates. And I find this is the rule, not the exception. "No punishment but for already punished innocence; no safety but for triumphant crime."

The *Executive* is fast asleep in the matter—or it would long ago have planted the Manchester district with a hundred thousand special constables—and the globule of *legislation* now prescribed to Parliament, though excellent in certain respects, is null in others, would, if passed into law, rather encourage the intimidation of one man by twenty, and make him starve his family to save his skin—cruel alternative—and would not seriously check the darker and more bloody outrages, nor prevent their spreading from their present populous centres all over the land. Seeing these things, I have drawn my pen against cowardly assassination and sordid tyranny; I have taken a few undeniable truths, out of many, and have labored to make my readers realize those appalling facts of the day, which most men know, but not one in a thousand comprehends, and not one in a hundred thousand *realizes*, until Fiction—which, whatever you may have been told to the contrary, is the highest, widest, noblest, and greatest of all the arts—comes to his aid, studies, penetrates, digests, the hard facts of chronicles and blue-books, and makes their dry bones live.

THE END.

FRANKLIN SQUARE, NEW YORK, *June*, 1870.

HARPER & BROTHERS'
LIST OF NEW BOOKS.

☞ HARPER & BROTHERS *will send any of the following books by mail, postage prepaid, to any part of the United States, on receipt of the price.*

HARPER'S CATALOGUE, *with* CLASSIFIED INDEX OF CONTENTS, *sent by mail on receipt of Six Cents in postage stamps, or it may be obtained gratuitously on application to the Publishers personally.*

The Life of Count Bismarck,

Private and Political. With Descriptive Notices of his Ancestry. By Dr. GEORGE HESEKIEL. Translated and Edited, with an Introduction, Explanatory Notes, and Appendices, by KENNETH R. H. MACKENZIE, F. S. A., F.A.S.L. With upward of 100 Illustrations. 8vo, Cloth, $3 00.

A very complete account of the personal and political character of Bismarck, and a considerable contribution to contemporary history.—*Morning Post.*

The volume presents us with a clear and harmonious view of the character of the Prussian statesman, * * * and we very heartily recommend it to the English reader.—*Edinburgh Evening Courant.*

The book photographs the man.—*Scotsman.*

The history of a man's life before he dies is a book of rare occurrence, and one which will seldom bear publication. It is one evidence of the value of a man that his character will stand so severe a test.—*Observer* (London).

Cocker's Christianity and Greek Philosophy.

Christianity and Greek Philosophy; or, the Relation between Spontaneous and Reflective Thought in Greece and the Positive Teaching of Christ and his Apostles. By B. F. COCKER, D.D., Professor of Moral and Mental Philosophy in Michigan University. Crown 8vo, Cloth, $2 75.

"This work comprises a profound discussion of the leading philosophical and religious problems of the day, with special reference to the theories of Comte, Sir William Hamilton, Herbert Spencer, and other great thinkers of a recent period, together with a copious exposition of the ancient Greek systems, and the social condition of Athens. It is a work of rare erudition. The writer has mastered his subject and the learning which pertains to it. He is familiar with the prominent systems, and well understands their scope and bearings. He has a remarkable talent for concise, methodical, and exact statements on abstruse subjects. At the same time, his learning does not oppress him—does not interfere with his own mental action. He is a firm and independent thinker. His work forms a valuable guide to the history of ancient and modern speculation, while it is full of important original suggestions. Its publication really forms an epoch in the history of American philosophical literature, and elevates its author to a high rank among the philosophical writers of the age. Every philosophical student in the country will find it a treasure."

Memoir of Dr. Scudder, Thirty-six Years Missionary to India.

Memoir of the Rev. John Scudder, M.D., Thirty-six Years Missionary in India. By the Rev. J. B. WATERBURY, D.D. Portrait. 12mo, Cloth, $1 75.

When Dr. SCUDDER and his accomplished wife went out to India, the work of the Christian missionary was one of experiment, toil, privation, and danger. It involved long banishment from home and country, and many harrassing hardships from which missionaries to that country are now exempt. Dr. WATERBURY tells the story with earnest simplicity, and, without any straining after effect, draws a most interesting and effective picture of the man, his life, and his manner of work. The memoir is enriched with many passages from the letters and journals of Dr. SCUDDER and his wife, which add greatly to its value and interest.

Yonge's English-Greek Lexicon.

An English-Greek Lexicon. By C. D. YONGE. With many New Articles, an Appendix of Proper Names, and Pillon's Greek Synonyms. To which is prefixed an Essay on the Order of Words in Attic Greek Prose, by Charles Short, LL.D., Professor of Latin in Columbia College, N. Y. Edited by HENRY DRISLER, LL.D., Professor of Greek in Columbia College, Editor of "Liddell and Scott's Greek-English Lexicon," &c. 8vo, Sheep extra, $7 00.

Dixon's Free Russia.

Free Russia. By W. HEPWORTH DIXON, Author of "New America," "Her Majesty's Tower," &c. With Two Illustrations. Crown 8vo, Cloth. *(Just Ready.)*

CONTENTS.

Up North.—The Frozen Sea.—The Dvina.—Archangel. — Religious Life. — Pilgrims.— Father John.—The Vladika.—A Pilgrim Boat.—The Holy Isles.—The Local Saints.—A Monastic Household.—A Pilgrim's Day.—Prayer and Labor.—Black Clergy.—Sacrifice.—Miracles.—The Great Miracle.—A Convent Spectre.—Story of a Grand Duke.—Dungeons.—Nicolas Ilyin.—Adrian Pushkin.—Dissent.—New Sects.—The Popular Church.—Old Believers.—Cemetery of the Transfiguration. — Ragoski.—Dissenting Politics.—Conciliation. — Roads. — A Peasant Poet.—Forest Scenes.—Patriarchal Life.—Village Republics.—Communism.—Towns.—Kief.—Panslavonia.—Exile. — The Siberians.—St. George.—Novgorod the Great.—Serfage.—A Tartar Court.—St. Philip.—Serfs.—Emancipation.— Freedom.—Tsek and Artel.—Masters and Men.—The Bible.—Parish Priests. — A Conservative Revolution.—Secret Police.—Provincial Rulers. —Open Courts.—Islam.—The Volga.—Eastern Steppe.—Don Kozaks.—Under Arms.—Alexander.

This is a more important and remarkable work upon the great Muscovite Empire than any foreign traveler has ever even attempted, much less accomplished. Thanks to the writer of this splendid volume, "Free Russia" is brought clearly, boldly, vividly, comprehensively, and yet minutely, within the ken of every intelligent reading Englishman. The book is in many parts as enthralling as a romance, besides being full of life and character.—*Sun* (London).

We claim for Mr. Dixon the merit of having treated his subject in a fresh and original manner. He has done his best to see with his own eyes the vast country which he describes, and he has visited some parts of the land with which few even among its natives are familiar, and he has had the advantage of being brought into personal contact with a number of those Russians whose opinions are of most weight. The consequence is that he has been able to lay before general readers such a picture of Russia and the Russian people as can not fail to interest them.—*Athenæum* (London).

Mr. Dixon's book will be certain not only to interest, but to please its readers, and it deserves to do so. It contains a great deal that is worthy of attention, and is likely to produce a very useful effect. The ignorance of the English people with respect to Russia has long been so dense that we can not avoid being grateful to a writer who has taken the trouble to make personal acquaintance with that seldom-visited land, and to bring before the eyes of his countrymen a picture of its scenery and its people which is so novel and interesting that it can scarcely fail to arrest their attention.—*Saturday Review* (London).

In this picturesque and fascinating work, Mr. Dixon carries his readers over a wide range of country, from the Arctic Sea to the southern slopes of the Ural range, from the Straits of Yenikale to the Gulf of Riga, and by the force of brisk, nervous, and picturesque language, makes them realize the scenery, manners, politics, poetry, of every mile of ground over which he conducts them.—*The Morning Post* (London).

The Free Russia Mr. Dixon paints with a sure and powerful hand is, he tells us in his Preface, "the new empire born of the Crimean War, hoping to be pacific, meaning to be free." His book is no book of travels in the ordinary sense, although much travel has gone to make it. It describes the people rather than the country: it analyzes society instead of photographing scenery. Mr. Dixon has succeeded in producing a book which is at once highly valuable and eminently readable. The information he conveys is very great, his judgments are evidently the result of much reflection, and his style is singularly forcible and picturesque.—*The Standard* (London).

Mr. Dixon's "Free Russia" is another valuable addition to the books of travel which he has given us. It reveals to our view the great mysterious people of Eastern Europe.—*The Daily Telegraph* (London).

We are bound to award to Mr. Dixon the highest praise for the skill with which he has constructed a book at once full of interest and information. "Free Russia" differs widely from an ordinary book of travels; for, in place of being a mere itinerary, it is a masterly analysis of Russian society in its more salient points. References to the physical aspect of the country are incidental, but they are so masterly that they produce a more vivid conception of that portion of the huge empire within his sphere of observation than the most labored efforts of a less skillful hand. Altogether, the work seems all that is necessary to enable the reader to form correct ideas of the working of those great forces which are destined to shape the future of a civilized and regenerated Russia. — *The Observer* (London).

"Free Russia" is one of the most remarkable books that has ever been written in our times, of the value of which it is impossible to speak in terms too highly commendatory.—*The Messenger* (London).

We heartily commend this work to all who wish either for instruction or relaxation. — *Examiner and London Review.*

Sulphur-Cure for Vines and Fruit-Trees.

Hand-Book of the Sulphur-Cure, as applicable to the Vine Disease in America, and Diseases of Apple and other Fruit Trees. By WILLIAM J. FLAGG, Author of "Three Seasons in European Vineyards." 12mo, Paper, 50 cents.

A longer and stronger plea than was contained in Mr. Flagg's earlier work for the adoption by suffering vine-growers in America of the remedy in which he has great confidence, induced by what he saw abroad, and rendered doubly strong by observation and experiment made at home during the last season, "of pestilence far more fatal than ever known before." It is written with the same clearness and enthusiasm which makes every thing from the same pen such easy reading, and those who begin the perusal are likely to go through at a single sitting, and leave off, if not convinced, at least with full faith that Mr. Flagg believes every thing he says. And well he may, for he tells us that during the "sickly season of 1869" he sulphur-treated his own vineyard of twelve-year-old catawbas, located in that doomed district, the Ohio Valley, and for which for the four preceding years had been ravaged by the pest of mildew, and that his success was complete. He cites other instances, the results of which make him doubly earnest in asking for a new hearing and a better heeding. We hope and trust it will find its way into the hands of every person at all interested in the growing of vines. * * * There are also interspersed various valuable suggestions regarding the general management of vines and vineyards, estimates of varieties, etc., etc., worth in themselves more than the cost of the entire work.—*World.*

Mr. Flagg has united to a long experience in the cultivation of the vine in this country an extended examination of the methods of grape culture practiced in the vast vineyards of Europe, and by study and observation has prepared himself to write intelligently, even learnedly, upon his present subject. The vine-disease is owing to a fungus upon the stem and leaves of the plant. A history of its origin and progress is given in this little work, with minute directions for the use of sulphur—the specific remedy for the disease.—*Evening Post.*

Winchell's Sketches of Creation.

Sketches of Creation : a Popular View of some of the Grand Conclusions of the Sciences in reference to the History of Matter and of Life. Together with a Statement of the Intimations of Science respecting the Primordial Condition and the Ultimate Destiny of the Earth and the Solar System. By ALEXANDER WINCHELL, LL.D., Professor of Geology, Zoology, and Botany in the University of Michigan, and Director of the State Geological Survey. With Illustrations. 12mo, Cloth, $2 00.

Professor Winchell presents a popular view of some of the important discoveries and conclusions of modern science, and has succeeded in making a book of much interest. There are very many persons who desire some knowledge of the origin, construction, and development of the earth and of its relations to the other bodies in the solar system, yet have neither the time nor the patience to master the details of the subject. Those details so burden ordinary geological treatises that this class of inquirers is repelled from their study. They will find this summary of the matter better adapted to their purpose than almost any thing else that has appeared.—*Brooklyn Eagle.*

Rarely have we found a work of this character combine so many popular elements as this. It faithfully demonstrates the object the author has sought to accomplish, namely, to supply a general view of the sciences without the labor of tracing numerous scientific treatises by persons of culture, and to supply a comprehensive survey to the student of the outlines of science and the most prominent landmarks. * * * Few works combine so extensive a range of information with so great a popular interest. There is a charm about the work, too, that will hold the attention of the reader closely.—*Pittsburgh Gazette.*

Entertaining and instructive, for the author has studied his subject and is familiar with its details.—*Worcester Spy.*

Bears the marks of much reliable research as well as original thought.—*Philadelphia Post.*

A popular account of the facts and conclusions of geology in an easy, readable style, suited for all classes. While faithful to science, it is reverential to religion and the Bible, so that the Christian meets with no sneers at theology or miracles, but with a devout recognition of God as the author of the system of nature. * * * One charm of the work is that it treats largely of American localities and phenomena, thus instructing the people concerning their own country.—*Advance.*

We would search our libraries in vain for such a popular view of some of the grand conclusions of the sciences regarding the history of matter and of life as is presented in these pages. Rarely, if ever, have the physical sciences been presented in so attractive a light. Even the schoolboy will be absorbed, while the professor can not fail being struck with the author's grasp of subject and breadth of generalization.—*New Orleans Picayune.*

We scarcely think that there is any one who will find this book uninteresting. Its scope is so large, its knowledge so varied, its explanations of popular mysteries so gratifying, and, finally, its terrors so distant, that it will be a novel enjoyment for large numbers of readers, and a pleasant way of recalling old associations of former studies for others.—*Chicago Times.*

Shows large knowledge, and is written with an eloquence that glows from the first page to the last. His pen pictures are so striking that there seems little need of illustrations; but these are so numerous and interesting that they make the book additionally attractive.—*Boston Correspondent of Cincinnati Chronicle.*

Orton's Andes and the Amazon.

The Andes and the Amazon ; or, Across the Continent of South America. By JAMES ORTON, M.A., Professor of Natural History in Vassar College, Poughkeepsie, N. Y., and Corresponding Member of the Academy of Natural Sciences, Philadelphia. With a New Map of Equatorial America and numerous Illustrations. Crown 8vo, Cloth, $2 00.

In July, 1867, a scientific expedition, consisting of Col. Staunton, of Ingham University, Leroy, N.Y.; F. S. Williams, Esq., of Albany; P. V. Myers and A. Bushnell, of Williams College, and Prof. James Orton, of Vassar College, left New York City to explore the Equatorial regions of South America. This exploring expedition was made under the auspices of the Smithsonian Institution. The explorers went by way of Panama to Paita, in Northern Peru, and then to Quito by way of Guayaquil. After exploring the elevated Andean Valley in which it is situated, they went over the Western Cordilleras and through the primeval forest, on foot, to Napo, and then down the Rio Napo to Pebas, on the great river. From Pebas they went to the Atlantic coast by steamer. The expedition reached Guayaquil July 19, 1867, making its journey across the continent to Para. In the volume before us we have Prof. Orton's record of the observations, adventures, and scientific researches of this party during their journey across the Andes and through the Valley of the Amazon. He has done his work well, and the book contains a more accurate and complete account of the regions through which they traveled than can be found in any other single volume.—*Worcester Spy.*

A more charming book of travel than that of Professor Orton on the Equatorial regions of South America has not appeared for years, in England or America. A man of thorough scientific attainments, he is yet not so wholly absorbed in his observations of natural phenomena as to lose sight of those phases of social life under an effete civilization which the reader most desires to have presented to him; nor does any aspect of beauty in the passing cloud or the glittering mountain peak escape him.—*N. Y. Evening Post.*

Free from exaggeration as we feel that it is, eminently truthful touching the character of both country and inhabitants—the fruit of careful study of men, manners, means, and resources—the book is a valuable contribution to our descriptive and topographical literature. Lucid, yet condensed, it is much in little concerning a region that is wonderfully rich in natural advantages, and that is destined ere many years to play an important part in the world's commerce.—*Rural New-Yorker.*

A remarkably vivid description of the physical aspect, the resources, and the inhabitants of a vast country which is destined to become an important field for commercial enterprise, if not national greatness. Prof. Orton is no superficial observer. He is an accomplished scientist, and the results of his observations are valuable contributions to the fund of important knowledge. The book demands a thorough reading from scholars and business men.—*Watchman and Reflector.*

A graphic description of the appearance of the country in its diversity of surface, the richness of the soil, its capabilities, the scenery, and the geological formation of the Andean rocks. The inhabitants are well described—their appearance, manners, habits, religion, etc.—making it altogether one of the most valuable and interesting books of travel.—*Methodist.*

The descriptions are thoroughly picturesque, and transplant the mind of the reader to these far-off regions. Mr. Orton has the rare gift of investing even statistics with poetic drapery, and combines the eye of the artist with the shrewd observation of a natural philosopher.—*Brooklyn Union.*

Tennyson's Poetical Works.

Poetical Works of Alfred Tennyson, Poet Laureate. With numerous Illustrations and Three Characteristic Portraits. New Edition, containing many Poems not hitherto included in his collected works, and with the Idyls of the King arranged in the order indicated by the Author. 8vo, Paper, 50 cents; Cloth, $1 00. *(Fortieth Thousand.)*

The print is clear and excellent; the paper is good; the volume has illustrations from Doré, Millais, and other great artists. Really, the edition is a sort of prodigy in its way.—*Independent.*

Those who want a perfect and complete edition of the works of the great English Poet Laureate should purchase the Harper edition.—*Troy Budget.*

A marvel of cheapness.—*The Christian Era.*

The whole get-up and style of this edition are admirable, and we are sure it will be a welcome addition to every book-case, large or small. But the marvelous thing about it is the price, which is only *one dollar* for the handsome cloth binding.—*Tribune* (Wilmington, Del.)

A marvelous instance of blended beauty and cheapness.—*Charleston Courier.*

Tom Brown's School Days.

By An Old Boy. New Edition. Beautifully Illustrated by Arthur Hughes and Sidney Prior Hall. 8vo, Paper, 50 cents.

Boys will be boys. Under whatever sky—we need not repeat Horace—the race remains substantially the same: has the same joys and griefs, the same ambitions and pitfalls. The picture that was truly limned for the Groves or Academe is true for our own age, and will always be true; nor can it ever be foreign to any one's interest. Mr. Hughes has placed and named his hero. The surroundings are local, but not peculiar, save in trifling details. He sketches a lad at home, follows him to Rugby, and then tells his experiences there. The boy is a boy—not immaculate perfection in any way, but hearty, impulsive, and well-principled. He fights like a good fellow when imposed on. His whole soul goes into football. He is earnest for his party, and has a contemptuous opinion of all rivals. His appetite for study is not supernatural at first, and he can not master the 47th proposition by intuition. No natural inclination drives him to spend unnecessary time at chapel, and he does not pocket all the honors at the close. His record will be all the more valuable because it is not pitched to a juvenile impossibility. It is hearty, manly, and dramatic; educational, and soundly religious. Moreover, it is so graphic that boys will read it all, without "skipping the preachments." Old boys have read it with interest, and will do so again, and should by no means fail to let the younger drink from their own Castaly.—*Philadelphia North American.*

A book upon which praise would be a mere waste of words.—*Tribune* (N. Y.).

"Tom Brown's School Days at Rugby" merits a welcome second to none which a grateful public can give. The familiar and delightful story is here set off with numerous capital illustrations, which in themselves almost tell the tale of the book. I can not conceive how such a volume, even in paper covers, can be afforded for fifty cents, but so it is; and I devoutly trust that fifty thousand youngsters of all ages, with fifty thousand half dollars, may rise up and call artist and publishers blessed.—*Correspondence of Chicago Journal.*

Nothing need be said of the merits of this, acknowledged on all hands to be one of the very best boy's books ever written. "Tom Brown" does not reach the point of ideal excellence. He is not a faultless boy; but his boy-faults, by the way they are corrected, help him in getting on. The more of such reading can be furnished the better. There will never be too much of it.—*Examiner and Chronicle.*

Finely printed, and contains excellent illustrations of various scenes around Rugby or described in the book. "Tom Brown" is a book which will always be popular with boys, and it deserves to be.—*World.*

Can be read a dozen times, and each time with tears and laughter as genuine and impulsive as at the first.—*Rochester Democrat.*

Some of the drawings are very spirited and schoollike.—*Christian Union.*

The illustrations are admirably done.—*New England Farmer.*

Draper's American Civil War.

History of the American Civil War. By John William Draper, M.D., LL.D., Professor of Chemistry and Physiology in the University of New York; Author of "A Treatise on Human Physiology," "A History of the Intellectual Development of Europe," &c. In Three Volumes. 8vo, Cloth, $3 50 per Vol.

That able writer and profound thinker, Professor Draper, in his interesting and instructive works, condenses all history into a theory for which he has written these words, that have added such honor to his name and added so much glory and just renown to American literature.—*Speech of Vice-President Schuyler Colfax, Providence, June 28th, 1869.*

No other book on American history is so calculated to teach important lessons, and lead to sharp observations, wise reflections, as this. * * * Whatever the solution of the precise causes, physical or metaphysical, that built up antagonistic ideas and antagonistic systems in the North and the South, Dr. Draper's appreciation of the essence of those distinctions—of the political complications they drew on, of the passions and convictions they engendered, and of the characters they called out into prominence—can not be too highly praised. He has a fine, sympathetic imagination, which enables him to throw himself into the situation and feelings of either party in the great controversy. He sums up, with rare fairness, the honest complaints brought by the one against the other, and comprehends why they were felt to be honest. He helps to make the belligerent sections understand, and so both pity and respect, one another.—*Christian Examiner.*

The leading political questions involved in the national legislation for nearly half a century are amply discussed, and their influence on recent events is elucidated with clearness and impartiality. A certain dramatic aspect is given to the successive steps which preceded the Rebellion, from the movement of nullification to the conflict in Kansas. The novelty of the work consists not so much in the exhibition of facts before unknown as in the effective grouping of familiar events so as to form a grand historical unity.—*N. Y. Tribune.*

Philosophical breadth of view and perfect impartiality in presenting facts are among the qualifications which should be demanded of him who presumes to write history; and these are certainly possessed in a high degree by Dr. Draper.—*Citizen.*

The plan is carried out with the same ability displayed by the author in his "History of the Intellectual Development of Europe" and his "Thoughts on the Future Civil Policy of America," which have won for him a high place in literature. The facts stated and the reasonings employed are greatly instructive, and show how operative are natural causes in shaping national character and destiny.—*Advance.*

Smiles's Self·Help.

Self-Help; with Illustrations of Character, Conduct, and Perseverance. By SAMUEL SMILES, Author of "The Huguenots" and "Life of the Stephensons." New Edition, Revised and Enlarged. 12mo, Cloth, $1 00.

This is a revised edition of a book which has already been received with considerable favor. It has been reprinted in various forms, translations have appeared in Dutch and French, and others are about to appear in German and Danish. The book has proved attractive to readers in different countries by reason of the variety of anecdotal illustrations of life and character which it contains, and the interest which all more or less feel in the labors, the trials, the struggles, and the achievements of others. The object of the book chiefly is, to re-inculcate these old-fashioned but wholesome lessons—which, perhaps, can not be too often urged—that youth must work in order to enjoy; that nothing creditable can be accomplished without application and diligence; that the student must not be daunted by difficulties, but conquer them by patience and perseverance; and that, above all, he must seek elevation of character, without which capacity is worthless and worldly success is naught.

The writings of Samuel Smiles are a valuable aid in the education of boys. His style seems to have been constructed entirely for their tastes; his topics are admirably selected, and his mode of communicating excellent lessons of enterprise, truth, and self-reliance

might be called insidious and ensnaring if these words did not convey an idea which is only applicable to lessons of an opposite character and tendency taught in the same attractive style. The popularity of this book, "Self-Help," abroad has made it a powerful instrument of good, and many an English boy has risen from its perusal determined that his life will be moulded after that of some of those set before him in this volume. It was written for the youth of another country, but its wealth of instruction has been recognized by its translation into more than one European language, and it is not too much to predict for it a popularity among American boys, who are admirers of pluck and push.—*World* (N. Y.).

Its purpose is to show how it is possible to gain honorable and brilliant success without adventitious aid, and to surmount the difficulties of "iron fortune" by patient and faithful endeavor. That purpose is accomplished by means of striking illustrative facts drawn from the lives of representative and successful men. Mr. Smiles is scarcely equaled in the style which fits itself most happily to practical biographical writing.—*Brooklyn Eagle.*

An arsenal of encouragements, from actual life, for young folks who find the path of self-improvement full of difficulties.—*Advance.*

M'Clintock and Strong's Cyclopædia.

Cyclopædia of Biblical, Theological, and Ecclesiastical Literature. By Rev. JOHN M'CLINTOCK, D.D., and JAMES STRONG, S.T.D. With Maps and numerous Illustrations. To be completed in about Six Volumes, Royal 8vo, of about One Thousand Pages each. Vols. I., II., and III., comprising the Letters A to G, are now ready. The remaining Volumes are in progress. Price, per Volume, Cloth, $5 00; Sheep, $6 00; Half Morocco, $8 00. *Vol. III. just ready. (Sold by Subscription.)*

It will interest a large portion of the reading public to know that the lamented death of the Rev. Dr. M'CLINTOCK will occasion no delay in the PUBLICATION of the remaining volumes of the "*Cyclopædia of Biblical, Theological, and Ecclesiastical Literature,*" prepared under the supervision of the deceased, with the able co-operation of Dr. STRONG. The main body of this important contribution to religious literature was prepared before the first page was put in type; and the several articles now require only to be revised, to add the results of fresh researches and discoveries in scholarship, as the several volumes go to press. In this labor Dr. STRONG has the assistance of many able and accomplished scholars, belonging to different denominations, and nothing will be left undone to secure the utmost thoroughness and accuracy on every page of the work. The third volume, now ready for publication, exhausts the letter *G*; and about three volumes more will be required to complete the alphabet. The whole work, thus comprised within six or seven convenient volumes, will form the most important and compact library of reference in the English language for the student of the Bible, in accuracy of scholarship, comprehensiveness of plan, and fullness of detail and illustration, far surpassing every former work of the kind ever attempted in Europe or America.

This Cyclopædia excels all similar undertakings which have preceded it in fullness, in clearness, in compactness, in pictorial illustrations, and in liberal-

ity of tone. To these excellences we should add its almost absolute accuracy of printing, which is as noticeable in the Hebrew and Greek type as it is in the English. All the articles contributed have been subjected to the most careful editorial supervision, and thus each has been confined to its legitimate limits of space in accordance with the relative value of the subject treated. * * * It is the only work of the kind ever undertaken in this country, and when completed will undoubtedly be the most complete Cyclopædia in existence for the use of biblical and theological students.—*N. Y. Evening Post.*

* * * My impression is that the work will meet a want that is felt more and more every day by clergymen and others. The multiplication of works relating to the Scriptures, the Church, and Theological Science generally, calls for an encyclopædia that shall contain the substance of them all, thereby saving the student both time and expense. The editors of these volumes have performed the difficult task in an admirable manner. They have included in their catalogue the most important topics, and have presented the materials in a very compact form, and in an attractive style. Not the least of the excellences in a work covering so much ground, and relating to so many disputed points, is seen in the candor and fairness of the editorial supervision. I hope that this Cyclopædia will have a wide circulation, believing that it will promote the best interests of sacred learning and religion.—Rev. W. G. T. SHEDD, D.D., *New York.*

March's Anglo·Saxon Grammar.

A Comparative Grammar of the Anglo-Saxon Language; in which its Forms are Illustrated by those of the Sanskrit, Greek, Latin, Gothic, Old Saxon, Old Friesic, Old Norse, and Old High-German. By FRANCIS A. MARCH, Professor of the English Language and Comparative Philology in Lafayette College, Author of "Method of Philological Study of the English Language," "A Parser and Analyzer for Beginners," &c. 8vo, Cloth, $2 50.

The Bazar Book of Decorum.

The Bazar Book of Decorum. The Care of the Person, Manners, Etiquette, and Ceremonials. 16mo, Toned Paper, Cloth, Beveled Edges, $1 00.

The great value of this book to American readers will be found in the fact that it is not merely a useful and trustworthy guide in matters of fashionable etiquette, but also in those that make up the daily round of social and domestic life. The subject is treated with a large liberality of view that takes in many of the practical questions arising in every grade of society, in regard to dress, food, exercise, daily habits of the mind and body, etc. The book is divided into three parts, and treats, 1st, of the Care of the Person; 2d, of Manners; 3d, of Etiquette and Ceremonials. Under each head is given a large amount of information upon points often unconsciously disregarded by Americans. The author tells exactly what people want to know in respect to giving breakfasts and dinners, giving and receiving calls, evening parties, visits of ceremony, addressing notes, letters, invitations, etc., and meets an acknowledged want in a very practical as well as entertaining manner.

A series of sensible, well-written, and pleasant essays on the care of the person, manners, etiquette, and ceremonials. The title *Bazar Book* is taken from the fact that some of the essays which make up this volume appeared originally in the columns of *Harper's Bazar.* This in itself is a sufficient recommendation—*Harper's Bazar* being probably the only journal of fashion in the world which has good sense and enlightened reason for its guides. The "Bazar Book of Decorum" deserves every commendation.—*Independent.*

Journal of the Prince of Wales's Visit to the East.

Journal of a Visit to Egypt, Constantinople, the Crimea, Greece, &c., in the Suite of the Prince and Princess of Wales. By the Hon. Mrs. WILLIAM GREY. 12mo, Cloth, $1 50.

It is rare that one has the privilege of traveling with royalty, and witnessing how kings and princes conduct themselves when relieved from the restraints of court etiquette. This privilege is accorded to the general reader in this book, which would be exceedingly entertaining irrespective of the peculiar circumstances which called it forth. The Hon. Mrs. Grey was a *compagnon de voyage* of the Princess of Wales in her recent Eastern tour, and kept a daily journal of their experiences for her family friends at home. She writes with a colloquial frankness, and with an innocence of any possibility of future publication, which give to her pages a peculiar charm. The volume affords at once the most charming insight into the interior life of royalty, and a very graphic picture of the Orient—a book which, without the least affectation of fine writing, possesses a good deal which is of unusual excellence by reason of its very simplicity.

All her remarks show good sense and an independent spirit, and indicate the author to be a woman of reflection as well as culture.—*Boston Traveller.*

The style of the book is fresh, naive, and lively, and one can not read it without feeling that the author is a very agreeable and estimable person, with fresh feelings, sharp and busy eyes, and capacity to derive much enjoyment from such a tour.—*Worcester Spy.*

Macgregor's Rob Roy on the Jordan.

The Rob Roy on the Jordan, Nile, Red Sea, and Gennesareth, &c. A Canoe Cruise in Palestine and Egypt, and the Waters of Damascus. By J. MACGREGOR, M.A. With Maps and Illustrations. Crown 8vo, Cloth. *(In Press.)*

Mr. Macgregor voyages and writes in such earnest that he carries us along with him from first to last.—*Saturday Review.*

Life and Letters of Mary Russell Mitford.

The Life of Mary Russell Mitford, Authoress of "Our Village, &c." Told by Herself in Letters to Her Friends. With Anecdotes and Sketches of her most celebrated Contemporaries. Edited by Rev. A. G. K. L'ESTRANGE. 2 vols., 12mo, Cloth, $3 50.

The interest of these volumes is twofold—personal and literary. Miss Mitford's life, as mournful as it was beautiful, is more deserving of remembrance than any of her writings. It exhibits a spirit of self-sacrifice, of filial devotion—and shall we add, of filial delusion?—which is to most of us almost past understanding. The letters, which commence with the century and terminate in 1855, abound with delightful literary gossip and personal reminiscences. The style is admirable: simple, unaffected, idiomatic. The bits of rural description remind us of "Our Village," and the remarks on men and books are generous and discriminating. Such a book allures us on from page to page with a curious fascination: every moment the eye is attracted by a familiar name, or by a criticism which compels attention by some pleasant thought or amusing anecdote; and it may be safely said that there is not one tedious chapter in the volumes.—*London Spectator.*

Very interesting and entertaining volumes. Nothing is more striking in these letters than their vivacity and cheerfulness. They show a life full of energy, sympathy, kindness, observation; a mind of extraordinary versatility, in harmony with its times, and keeping its powers and its interest in books and men vigorous to the last. These letters illustrate art and literature of the day for fifty years, and one chief interest of them is the portraits, characters, and traits of distinguished people who came in their author's way.—*Saturday Review.*

The Polar World:

A Popular Description of Man and Nature in the Arctic and Antarctic Regions of the Globe. By Dr. G. HARTWIG, Author of "The Sea and its Living Wonders," "The Harmonies of Nature," &c. With Additional Chapters and 163 Illustrations. 8vo, Cloth, Beveled Edges, $3 75.

By WILKIE COLLINS.

Man and Wife.

A Novel. With Illustrations. *(In Press.)*

The Moonstone.

A Novel. With Illustrations. 8vo, Paper, $1 50 ; Cloth, $2 00.

Armadale.

A Novel. With Illustrations. 8vo, Paper, $1 60 ; Cloth, $2 00.

No Name.

A Novel. Illustrated by JOHN McLENAN. 8vo, Paper, $1 50 ; Cloth, $2 00.

The Woman in White.

A Novel. Illustrated by JOHN McLENAN. 8vo, Paper, $1 50 ; Cloth, $2 00.

The Queen of Hearts.

A Novel. 12mo, Cloth, $1 50.

Antonina; or, The Fall of Rome.

A Romance of the Fifth Century. 8vo, Paper, 50 cents.

No amount of mechanical ingenuity would, however, account by itself for the popularity of Mr. Wilkie Collins's works. He has several other important qualifications. He writes an admirable style ; he is thoroughly in earnest in his desire to please ; his humor, though distinctly fashioned on a model Mr. Dickens invented and popularized, is better sustained and less fantastic and affected than any thing which Mr. Dickens has of late years produced.—*London Review.*

We can not close this notice without a word of eulogy on Mr. Collins's style. It is simple and so manly ; every word tells its own story ; every phrase is perfect in itself.—*London Reader.*

Of all the living writers of English fiction no one better understands the art of story-telling than Wilkie Collins. He has a faculty of coloring the mystery of a plot, exciting terror, pity, curiosity, and other passions, such as belong to few if any of his *confreres*, however much they may excel him in other respects. His style too, is singularly appropriate—less forced and artificial than the average modern novelists.—*Boston Transcript.*

PUBLISHED BY HARPER & BROTHERS, NEW YORK.

☞ *Sent by mail, postage prepaid, to any part of the United States, on receipt of the price.*

BY F. W. ROBINSON.

TRUE TO HERSELF. A Novel. 8vo, Paper, 50 cents.

STERN NECESSITY. A Novel. 8vo, Paper, 50 cents.

FOR HER SAKE. A Novel. Illustrated. 8vo, Paper, 75 cents.

His novels are always attractive, and seize hold of the reader's attention.—*Independent.*
A powerfully-written novel.—*Lutheran Observer.*

CARRY'S CONFESSION. A Novel. 8vo, Paper, 75 cents.

The story is cleverly told, and is very original. It can scarcely fail to be read with thoughtful interest. It is very far above the average run of novels, and deserves to find a longer life than is accorded to ephemeral works of fiction.—*Athenæum.*

CHRISTIE'S FAITH. A Novel. 12mo, Cloth, $1 75.

The interest of this story is so enthralling that it holds the reader enchained during its progress, and the purpose of the story is so admirable that the best among us may justly consider the time well bestowed that is occupied by its perusal.—*London Sun.*

MATTIE: A STRAY. A Novel. 8vo, Paper, 75 cents.

An admirable novel. It is a picture of life so true and vivid as to rivet the attention from first to last.—*London Reader.*

NO MAN'S FRIEND. A Novel. 8vo, Paper, 75 cents.

A good novel. It is original; it is lively; it is interesting; its real merits are considerable. The plottings and counter-plottings, with the localities in which they occur, and the varying circumstances attending them, make up the general interest. All this part is bright, interesting, and original—the originality chiefly consisting in the undisguised worldliness attributed to all the parties concerned, and the skill with which these materials are worked up into an agreeable narrative.—*Athenæum.*

POOR HUMANITY. A Novel. 8vo, Paper, 50 cents.

A novel of intense interest.—*New York Leader.*
There is a reality about the personations which is one of the best evidences of real talent.—*New York Times.*

PUBLISHED BY HARPER & BROTHERS, NEW YORK.

☞ HARPER & BROTHERS *will send any of the above works by mail, postage prepaid, to any part of the United States, on receipt of the price.*